MW00905067

IMPERIAL GERMAN ARMY 1914-18

Organisation, Structure, Orders of Battle

Hermann Cron

Translated by C.F. Colton, MA

Helion & Company

Dedicated to the memory of the German Army in the First World War

Helion & Company Limited
26 Willow Road
Solihull
West Midlands
B91 1UE
England
Tel. 0121 705 3393
Fax 0121 711 4075
Email: publishing@helion.co.uk
Website: http://www.helion.co.uk

Originally published as *Geschichte des Deutschen Heeres im Weltkriege 1914-1918* in Berlin, Germany, 1937
This English edition published by Helion & Company, 2002

Designed and typeset by Helion & Company Limited, Solihull, West Midlands
Dustjacket designed by Bookcraft Limited, Stroud, Gloucestershire
Printed by The Cromwell Press, Trowbridge, Wiltshire

ISBN 1 874622 70 1

British Library Cataloguing-in-Publication Data.
A catalogue record for this book is available from the British Library.

For details of other military history titles published by Helion & Company contact the above address, or visit our website: http://www.helion.co.uk.

We always welcome receiving book proposals from prospective authors.

Contents

Part I
The Supreme Command of the Military Leadership and Administration during the war

Part II
Changes in Army Organisation

Part III
The Higher Command Authorities and their development

Part IV
The History of the Field Army in its individual service arms

Part V
The Lines of Communication

Part VI
The Administrations of the Occupied Territories

Part VII
Authorities and units in Germany

Appendices

Publishers' Note

Despite the vast amount of literature produced in the English language about the First World War, or 'Great War', a detailed work describing the organisation and structure of the German Army has failed to appear. It is hoped that the translation and publication of this book will fill that notable gap. It was originally planned that supplementary order-of-battle material would be added to this volume. However, such an extensive amount of data has been uncovered that it has been decided to issue this separately in additional volumes at a later date. The publishers would be very pleased to receive corrections and additions to this book from interested readers, so that these can be incorporated into future volumes.

Dates: all dates are rendered as day/month/year, hence 1.6.16 = 1 June 1916.

A list of abbreviations and German military terms used in the text can be found in Appendix VI, Abbreviations and Glossary.

Foreword

At the time of the First World War, the German Army is the most interesting historical phenomenon from a military history point of view. It came into being as the result of a massive increase and reorganisation of its peacetime formations. During the war it made astonishing progress in terms of organisation and of weapons technology. However, it did not return to its peacetime state, but disappeared almost at a stroke. Such a dramatic ending might suggest that it is not worth tracing the development of this army. That view would be fundamentally wrong. The very fact that the German army was able to assert itself, often victoriously, for a full four years, in all theatres of war, would alone necessitate our knowing how it was organised and developed, in order that we understand the actions of the war. It is all the more important, since it was in that very World War that the transition was made from the usual form of nineteenth-century warfare, to the battle of matériel. This book should not only contribute to honouring the memory of the army and its organisers, but also extend the basis on which future questions of organisation can be judged.

Herewith, I offer my thanks to the Army Research Institute for Military History for the information which they kindly provided. Considering the countless organisational changes brought about by the requirements of war, I am conscious that my work cannot be without errors, and would crave the reader's indulgence for these.

Hermann Cron

PART I

THE SUPREME COMMAND OF
THE MILITARY LEADERSHIP
AND ADMINISTRATION
DURING THE WAR

A.

THE SUPREME ARMY COMMAND

1. The Kaiser and the Great Headquarters

In accordance with Article 63 of the Constitution of the German Reich of 16 April 1871, the entire land forces of the Reich formed one unitary army. In war and peace it was under the command of the Kaiser. Despite this, separate Prussian, Bavarian and Saxon active lists were maintained. In the Prussian active list the "XIII (Royal Württemberg) Army Corps" appeared separately from the Prussian corps. All this would have to be understood as a consequence of the historical development of the Second Reich and its formation. This came about through the voluntary amalgamation of the German princes, whose sovereignty was to be protected wherever possible. In particular, in order to preserve Bavaria's acceptance of the Reich, Bismarck had made concessions in military matters, to this the second-largest German state. He was trusting in the educational influences of the period. The future proved his assessment to have been correct, since even Bavaria assimilated itself more and more within the overall framework. This is demonstrated, for example, by the introduction of a second, German cockade[1] for the whole army. Certainly the provision of Article 63 of the Reich Constitution, that "the regiments etc will be continuously numbered throughout the entire German Army", did not come to be implemented by Bavaria, which continued to give its own numbers to its units even during the First World War. This principle was only given up, during the course of the war, in the case of a number of new formations.[2]

Despite such superficial differences, at mobilisation Germany's entire Army forces stood ready in complete internal unity. It showed that the idea of unity had entered the very marrow of the German people. This was particularly evident in the position of the Prussian War Ministry with regard to the Bavarian, Saxon, and Württemberg War Ministries that existed alongside it.

> The Federal States of Bavaria, Saxony and Württemberg had their representatives in the (Prussian) War Ministry, who maintained the connection between their own ministries and that in Berlin. The same splendid unanimous collaboration was shown here as it was in the field.[3]

---

1   A.K.O. of 22.3.1897.
2   Even the Bavarian method of naming units was different from the other contingents. While the latter for example wrote Inf. R. (Infantry Regt) 21 or Felda. R. (Field Artillery Regt) 3, Bavaria designated its active units for example as 21 Inf. R. or 3 Felda. R By contrast, since mobilisation it used the customary form for reserve formations, etc, thus, for example, bayer. Res. I.R. 1 (Bavarian Reserve Inf. Regt. 1)
3   Von Wrisberg, page 490.

In practice then, the Prussian War Ministry had undisputed leadership. Its instructions were followed by the other three War Ministries without any obvious problems.

Thus all the conditions were fulfilled for the joint use of the armed forces of the Reich, with the Kaiser as Supreme Commander.[4] Kaiser Wilhelm II had a predilection for taking command at peacetime troop exercises and manoeuvres. This had raised concern in many quarters that in wartime he would essentially be his own Chief of Staff. Such fears proved to be completely unfounded. As early as the general provisions for mobilisation, the Chief of the General Staff of the Field Army was given authority to issue operational orders in the name of the Kaiser. This was to be the case throughout the war. Therefore supreme command remained indubitably in the hands of the Kaiser. He was the embodiment of the Supreme Army Command. Meanwhile, the actual command was in the hands of, and was the sole responsibility of the Chief of the General Staff of the Field Army. He issued his orders in the name of the Kaiser, as "Supreme Army Command", and only then had to seek the Kaiser's agreement in making crucial decisions. In any case, the Chief's regular lectures were there, in advance, to prevent the Kaiser getting out of touch with the thinking of his General Staff.

Decisions by the Kaiser concerning the conduct of the war were, therefore, only rarely expressly given. They had to be made if a high-ranking commander came into sharp disagreement with the Chief of the General Staff, or in the case of differences of opinion between the allies. But it was usual for the Kaiser, as long as the current Chief of the General Staff enjoyed his confidence, to accede to the latter's views.

In the field, the personnel who surrounded the Kaiser were designated as the "Great Headquarters of His Majesty the Kaiser and King". From 3 August 1914 it became mobile. Its members were the Senior General-Adjutant (Aide-de-Camp to the Kaiser) and Chief of the Military Cabinet, General of Infantry Freiherr von Lyncker, with a staff of:

- three General-Adjutants and four Flügel-Adjutants (Aides-de-Camp), of whom one General-Adjutant was at the same time First Commandant of the Gr.H.Q. (Great Headquarters)

- the Chief of the Naval Cabinet together with 2 high-ranking officials

- the War Minister with his mobile staff

- a representative of the Secretary of State of the Reich Department of the Navy

- the Chief of the General Staff of the Field Army with his officials

- the heads of the Supreme Service Arms Authorities

- the Chief of the Admiral Staff of the Navy

- two personal physicians to His Majesty

- the Bavarian, Saxon and Württemberg military plenipotentiaries

4   In accordance with Article 53 of the Reich Constitution of 16.4.1871, the Navy was similarly a single unit under the supreme command of the Kaiser; the same was the case with the colonial troops.

Those not included, however, were non-military officials, the Reich Chancellor, the Chief of the Privy Council and representatives of the Foreign Office.

The other military authorities, not noted here, were under the command of the Second Commandant of the Great Headquarters, concerning whom more details will be given in the section "The Quartermaster General".

In contrast to the 1870/71 Great Headquarters there was no 'host' of German princes. The presence of the three plenipotentiaries for Bavaria, Saxony and Württemberg was based on the fact that the German Reich was a Federal State. Above all, it proved to be useful concerning personnel questions and in the preparation of requirements for the home front. In addition, through these plenipotentiaries the respective 'monarchs' enjoyed the advantage of direct reports on the events of the war.

Naturally, as soon as hopes for a quick end to the war had proved deceptive, the Reich Chancellor could no longer remain for any length of time at the Great Headquarters. By contrast, the War Minister remained for two full years at the Great Headquarters. However, when Hindenburg took over the Supreme Army Command, the War Minister was ordered back to Berlin. Wrisberg comments on this:

> The facts showed that it was not good to tie down the War Minister to one place. It was often more urgent that he should be for longer periods at the Great Headquarters than in Berlin, where the 'machine' ran on as usual. On the other hand, it was necessary for him to be present at his ministry when there was a danger that developments on the home front could have a damaging effect upon the course of the war.[5]

Soon, corresponding with the character of the federal war, an Austrian K.u.K. Plenipotentiary General joined the Great Headquarters. With the entry into the war of Bulgaria and Turkey, Military Plenipotentiaries for these states also appeared. In the same way the Supreme Army Command had its corresponding representations in the allied army commands.

In the Austrian K.u.K. Headquarters, up to 22 January 1915, there was Generalleutnant Freiherr von Freytag-Loringhoven, who was then a Colonel. From 22 March 1915 there was Generalmajor von Cramon, who from 8 January 1917 bore the title German Plenipotentiary General. In addition, Generalmajor von Seeckt was himself employed in the Austrian K.u.K. Army as Chief of the General Staff of the Army Group, and from 30 July 1916 of the Army Front. Archduke Carl (later Joseph) was there during the period from 1 July 1916 to 1 December 1917.

In Turkey, before the war, there was already a German military mission that remained there during the war under the command of General Liman von Sanders. Germany also provided the Chief of the General Staff of the Turkish Supreme Army Command. From Turkey's entry into the war until 1 December 1917, this post was held by Generalmajor Bronsart von Schellendorf, followed by Generalmajor von Seeckt. In addition, on 28 November 1914, the Kaiser attached Generalfeldmarschall Freiherr von der Goltz to the person of the Sultan. Goltz had a high reputation as the reorganiser of the Army in Turkey. On 19 April 1916

5   Von Wrisberg, page 475.

Goltz died while Supreme Commander in Iraq. From 21 September 1916, General von Lossow acted as Military Plenipotentiary in Constantinople.

In Sofia, the military attaché Lieutenant-Colonel von Massow was appointed as Military Plenipotentiary on 17 September 1916. For the sake of completeness it should be mentioned that from 31 May 1918, after the peace treaty of Brest-Litovsk, there was also a German Military Plenipotentiary in Moscow.

Falkenhayn had failed to resolve the question, raised during the war, of a common war command of the Four Power Pact. This was decided affirmatively after Hindenburg took up the post of Chief of the General Staff of the Field Army. On 6 September 1916, an appropriate treaty was brought into force by the signatures of the Chiefs of the General Staff of the Four Powers.

However, in practice this common command was of limited extent. Ludendorff wrote:

> Mutual agreements were demanded. However, the agreements reached still gave to the German Supreme Army Command a certain authority that proved to be useful... A result of setting up the common war command was also that the allied Supreme Army Commands would turn to us when there were questions in dispute between them. The Bulgarian Supreme Army Command was very unwilling to deal on Balkan questions with the Turkish and Austro-Hungarian Army Commands. They too preferred to deal with us than with the Bulgarian Supreme Army Command.[6]

The seat of the Great Headquarters was located as follows:

2 - 16 August 1914 in Berlin

17 - 30 August 1914 in Koblenz

30 August - 24 September 1914 in Luxemburg

25 September 1914 - 19 September 1916 in Charleville-Mezières

20 September 1916 - 10 February 1917 in Pless

11 - 16 February 1917 Chief with Ops Section in Berlin

17 February 1917 - 7 March 1918 in Kreuznach

8 March - 13 November 1918 in Spa

It should be noted that the Chief of the General Staff of the Field Army with the Operations Section, and for the most part also the Kaiser, from 9 May 1915-15 February 1916, and from 16 August 1916 were in Pless. The Chief of the General Staff with the Operations Section, from 18 March-7 September 1918, were in Avesnes.

After the Kaiser's abdication the Supreme Army Command first moved its seat to Wilhelmshöhe in Kassel, where it remained until 11 February 1919, and then to Kolberg. It was to be dissolved there on 3 July 1919.

6   Ludendorff, page 202f.

2. The Chief of the General Staff of the Field Army

a. Chief and First Quartermaster-General

Generaloberst von Moltke had occupied the post of Chief of the General Staff of the Army since 1906. On mobilisation he became, according to plan, Chief of the General Staff of the Field Army. His nervous collapse in the heavy days of the Battle of the Marne caused the Kaiser on 14 September 1914 to replace him with the War Minister Generalleutnant von Falkenhayn. For political reasons, until 3 November 1914 Falkenhayn only acted as deputy. Even after his official appointment he kept his old office of War Minister for some time. On 20 January 1915[7] he was relieved of his office as Minister of State and Minister of War and, remaining in his post as Chief of the General Staff of the Field Army, was promoted to General of Infantry.

In view of the ominous overall situation at the time of the Rumanian declaration of war, and of the general opinion of the German people, the Kaiser made another change. On 29 August 1916 he called on Generalfeldmarschall von Hindenburg, who enjoyed the trust of the people and the Army. The man who had until then been his Chief of General Staff, General Ludendorff, was called to head the General Staff of the Field Army. In doing so, the Kaiser was at one and the same time acknowledging anew how justified Hindenburg had been in saying, in December 1914:

> Report that General Ludendorff and I are inseparably bound together for the duration of this campaign, because we complement each other, and neither of us can do alone what we can do together.[8]

Therefore Ludendorff was given the post of "First Quartermaster-General"[9] which had been specially created for him, while at the same time being promoted to General of Infantry. From that time the Kaiser, as Supreme Warlord, had as his commanders Hindenburg and Ludendorff. They were the men who actually carried out the tasks of the Chief of the General Staff. In any event, this is how the Army and people understood it.

Ludendorff himself described his relationship with Hindenburg as follows:[10]

> The commander has responsibility. He bears it before the world and, what is even harder, before his own Army and his own Fatherland. As Chief and First Quartermaster-General I was fully and equally responsible and was always conscious of the fact... Both our strategic and our tactical views completely coincided, a harmonious and trusting collaboration automatically resulted from this. After discussion with my colleagues, I put my thoughts for the situation and conduct of all operations sharply and concisely to the Generalfeldmarschall and made him a quite definite suggestion. I was happy to say that the

---

7   A.K.O. of 20.1.1915.

8   Graf von Hutten-Czapsli, Vol II, page 175.

9   By order of the War Ministry of 5.9.1916 M.I No 20465. 16.A.1 this post was established.

10   Ludendorff, page 10.

Generalfeldmarschall always - from Tannenberg until my departure in October 1918 - agreed with my thinking and approved my draft orders.

After Ludendorff's resignation on 26 October 1918, Colonel Heye for several days took his place, which was then taken over on 29 October by Generalleutnant Groener.

Overall there were, under the command of the Chief of the General Staff of the Field Army, three groups of authorities and persons: the General Staff Sections, the Quartermaster-General, and individual senior munitions authorities. To these were added as a fourth group some other external authorities.

b. The General Staff Departments

Like every large authority, the General Staff of the Field Army also possessed a Central Section for the reception and direction of documentation to appropriate places, and for personnel. This necessitated a lively traffic with the Military Cabinet, for administration. This section was first under the command of Lieutenant-Colonel or Colonel von Fabeck, who on 26 March 1916 was replaced by Lieutenant-Colonel or Colonel Tieschowitz von Tieschowa.

Closest to the Chief of the General Staff was the Operations Section, which at the same time was the office for his personal correspondence. The Operations Section had to maintain in readiness all those provisions that formed the basis of operational measures with regard to the German Army. Thus they supervised the order of battle and organisation of the entire Army, as well as keeping check on the training, arming and combat readiness of all units. Its Chief was responsible for advising the Chief of the General Staff, for processing his operational plans and for carrying out his orders. The Section's area of operations grew with the strong increase of units in general and of individual arms of the service in particular, such as machine-gun units, heavy artillery, Minenwerfer, air forces and signals formations. Chief of the Operations Section was firstly Generalmajor Tappen.[11] From 31 August 1916 Lieutenant-Colonel Wetzell[12] was chief, praised by Ludendorff for having been "an excellent and dear helper" to him.[13] Finally, from 25 September 1918 there was Colonel Heye.

The extension of the fronts, and the deployment of German troops in distant theatres of war, made it desirable that the Operations Section should be relieved of the responsibility for the Macedonian and the Turkish fronts. For this reason, on 15 August 1916 the branch Operations Section B was formed, which was responsible for dealing with those fronts.

Shortly afterwards the new Hindenburg Army Command took the reins. Recognising the prime importance of the supply of munitions, one of their first measures was to organise the increase in munitions production, and to see how the delivery of munitions could best be regulated. To this end, on 23 September 1916 it dissolved the post of Chief of Field Munitions, took over its duties of replacement of munitions and equipment as Munitions Section in the Operations Sec-

11   Until 4.9.1914 Lieutenant-Colonel, up to 25.6.1915 Colonel.
12   Until 17.12.1917 Major.
13   Ludendorff, page 12.

tion, and then merged this section with a war economy section to form Operations Section II. For this section it found, in Colonel Baue, a chief to whose aptitude Ludendorff testifies[14] in saying that he "made a decisive contribution to the development of the artillery, and that he was of great use to him also in questions of the war economy and in many tactical questions". He also said, "It was his responsibility to represent to those at home the war equipment requirements of the Army and, in discussion with management and workers, to obtain a clear picture of industry's production capacity".

The Intelligence Section, from 20 May 1917 renamed as the Foreign Armies Section, followed the military developments in all countries outside Germany. In particular the Section followed the conduct of the war by enemy states, over whose organisation and division of forces it kept the closest watch. The knowledge gained was described as "the basis" for German decisions.

The department responsible for conveying intelligence concerning the enemy was named Section III B. Its executors were intelligence officers with all armies, and at specific points on the home front. They could be voluntary or paid agents in neutral or enemy countries abroad, and were with the Secret Field Police in the occupied territories. Frontier police posts, and postal censorship, provided rich material concerning military, maritime and political matters, and also the war economy. At the same time, they were the means of misleading and combating enemy espionage. In so far as the posts of the intelligence service and counter-espionage were located in home areas, they dealt with Section III B of the Deputy General Staff, which in this respect was under the command of Section III B at the Great Headquarters. The press service of Section III B, intended to influence public opinion, will be discussed in more detail below, in discussing the War Press Department. The "Vaterländische Unterricht" (patriotic education) introduced at the end of July 1917 was also directed by Section III B, whose Chief, during the entire war, was Major, then Lieutenant-Colonel Nicolai.

The essential function of the Political Section, from 10 February 1916 called the Military-Political Section, is shown in the latter designation. It followed the political affairs, both of the allies, and of neutral and enemy powers. It also dealt with legal questions and kept the military attachés informed. Of its significance, Ludendorff says:[15]

> It was an important task of the General Staff of the Field Army to follow the military policy of the enemy, and of neutral countries abroad, and to carry out liaison with the Reich Chancellor concerning the questions which this process raised. It was the same with developments in the occupied territories, in so far as they were under the control of the Supreme Army Command.[16] The frontiers that the war would give us were of decisive significance for the military security of the Fatherland. All questions connected with them were an important area of the Supreme Army Command's work. The Political Section was the military secretariat in all questions of peace.

14 Ludendorff, page 13.
15 Ludendorff, page 13.
16 The Governors-General of Belgium and Warsaw were under the direct command of the *Kaiser* and mostly received their instructions through the Reich Chancellor.

c. The Quartermaster-General and posts subordinate to him

The office of the Quartermaster-General served to relieve the Chief of the General Staff of the Field Army of all questions that did not directly relate to operations. His area of responsibility originally covered everything that went on in the Army's rear. Thus the whole of the supply lines of communication and railway services, military post, administration of justice, field medical and veterinary services were his responsibility. He was also assisted by a Chief of General Staff whose departmental areas of responsibility can be briefly designated as "Army matters", "Occupied Territories", "Army Judge Advocate General" and "Veterinary Service".[17] After the first officer in this post, Generalleutnant von Stein, became Commanding General on 14 September 1914, the person of the Quartermaster-General changed many times, until on 16 November 1916 Generalleutnant Hahndorff was appointed.

Of the posts subordinate to the Quartermaster-General, the first to be mentioned should be the Intendant-General of the Field Army. He was there for the provision of Army catering, and also formed the head of the Intendances for the Field and Lines of Communication. With the transition to trench warfare, the supervision of food for the population in the occupied territories was added to his responsibilities. To relieve the situation at home, land cultivation in the occupied zone had to be ensured. The agricultural machinery necessary for this had to be provided, and the surplus harvest utilised for the Field Army. Later the industrial exploitation of the occupied territories came to be important. Therefore, on 5 September 1916, another special Economic Section was created for the Intendant-General for the West.

However, this Section proved to be too much work for the Intendant-General. This meant that as early as 1 January 1917 it was made autonomous. With expanded responsibilities and a change of name to Representative of the Quartermaster-General for the Western Theatre of War - officially abbreviated to B.d.G.West – it was placed under the direct command of the Quartermaster-General.[18] The B.d.G.West was now the responsible authority for administration, management and exploitation of the occupied territories in the West.[19] Also under his command were the General Office for Exchange, and the Art Specialist for the Care of Memorials. Battalions of prisoners of war and of civilian workers, the Electro-technical Plants West, a series of workshops for the repair of artillery and train equipment were also part of the responsibility. All this, together with the service for captured material and its collection, was included up to the time when it was placed under the command of its own representative.[20] It is remarkable how the Germans, condemned as barbarians, in spite of the hunger blockade carried out against them, in

---

17   Military spiritual care was not represented. This was led according to the instructions of the Protestant and Catholic Field Provosts of the Army, who both remained in Germany, through the Senior Army Chaplains who were with the Army High Commands.

18   War Ministry of 27.12.1916 M.I. No32 623. A.1.

19   Apart from the General Government of Belgium which formed its own administration.

20   Quartermaster-General of 31.5.1917. No I. A. 22 012.

contravention of human rights, looked after the populations of enemy territory, and even took care to maintain their works of art.

Originally the Chief of the Field Munitions Service, the Chief of Field Telegraphy and the Chief of the Field Railway Service were under the command of the Quartermaster-General. To these posts were added, in March or July 1915, the Chief of the Field Aviation Service and the Inspector of Anti-Balloon Cannon. Since, however, these offices later all came under the command of the Chief of the General Staff of the Field Army, they will not be discussed here, but because of their context will be discussed in the section "Supreme Service Arms Authorities".

The Chief of the Field Medical Service, General Staff Medical Officer of the Army, Professor Dr von Schierning, led the medical service in all areas of war as the supreme head of medical personnel. He controlled the medical service, the care and transport of wounded, the distribution of hospital trains and hospital ships, and determined which military hospitals at home should receive transports. The voluntary nursing service was also under his command, since the Imperial Commissioner and Mlitary Inspector of this organisation was tied to his instructions.

The Head Field Postmaster determined and supervised the activities of the postal service in all theatres of war. To support him, the Field Post Inspectorates East and West were set up.

The Second Commandant of the Great Headquarters was essentially responsible for the security and supply of the Headquarters, and for the discipline of its subordinate personnel. He was in charge of the Infantry and Cavalry Staff Guard, a Landsturm battalion, a field police command, military police, and a mobile wireless station and telephone section. He had three anti-balloon guns that were later replaced by two anti-aircraft batteries. There was a searchlight platoon, which was later extended to form an anti-aircraft searchlight section. The Field Intendance of the G.H.Q, together with field treasury, vehicle park, field postal service, Central Department for Postal Censorship West, along with the GHQ postal censorship office, a canteen and reading room were all part of his responsibility.

The Secret Field Police were similarly under the immediate command of the Quartermaster-General, but worked in close connection with Section III B of the Chief of the General Staff of the Field Army.

In the course of the campaign, in addition to the B.d.G.West, who for the sake of context, had to be discussed above in connection with the Intendant-General, a large number of further posts came under the command of the Quartermaster-General.

First there was attached the Commander of Troops in Luxemburg,[21] a post which had existed from February 1915.

Towards the end of 1916 the newly created Chief of the Field Mechanical Transport Service[22] was added. Originally there had been no such post. But the great increase in mechanical transport formations, and their extended use, caused the Hindenburg Army Command to create a centralised organisation. The Chief of the Field Mechanical Transport Service, following the instructions or having gained the agreement of the Quartermaster-General, was in charge. He was in charge of the commanders of mechanised transport troops at the Army High Com-

21 War Ministry of 6.2.1915 M.I. 1837. 15. A.1.
22 War Ministry of 15.12.1916 No 16. 12. 16. A. 7. V.

mands and of the staff officers of his arm of the service assigned to the Army Groups in the West. From 17 May 1918 his staff included the Commander of the Kampfwagen (Fighting Vehicle) Sections.[23]

At about the same time as the already appointed B.d.G.West the Representative of the Quartermaster-General for the Eastern Theatre of War - B.d.G. Ost - became active, with headquarters in Warsaw. He represented the claims of the Quartermaster-General on the administrative area of the Supreme Commander East and claims on the Warsaw General Government with regard to the exploitation of the land. But after only one year, after the armistice in the East had come into force, his post was withdrawn again.

The Military Mining Administration Valenciennes was placed under the command of the Quartermaster-General in September 1917.[24] A single Military Administration merged the Mining Administrations of Valenciennes and Mons that until then had been separate, and had been part of the Metz Government.

Under the Quartermaster-General's area of responsibility there came the German Representation in Occupied Italy. After the 14th Army had left, it had been set up in February 1918 in Udine, to represent German interests in 'the spoils of war' which had been captured with the Austrians.[25]

From Autumn 1916, shortage of horses, and disease among horses, also necessitated close supervision of the available horses. Therefore the Commander of the 13th Cavalry Brigade with his staff was, on 13 December 1916, assigned to the Quartermaster-General. He already commanded the Military Veterinary Service, with a view to checking the available horses on the Western and Eastern fronts. In February 1918, B.d.G. Pferde was appointed Representative of the Quartermaster-General for Equine Affairs.[26] His main responsibility was, generally, to save horses and to deploy them in places of increased need.

In 1918 the treaties with the allies, concerning a common procedure for resuming trade connections with the individual parts of the former Russian Empire, necessitated the closest collaboration between the General Staff and the central authorities involved. For this reason, the Quartermaster-General dispatched a representative under the designation Representative of the Quartermaster-General in Berlin.[27] At the same time, under his command were placed the posts for imports and exports.

The service for captured material and its collection had, as already mentioned, been organised at the end of May 1918.[28] In spite of this, the success, regarding the very significant material captured in the 1918 Spring offensive, remained very much less than could justifiably be expected. To bring about changes in this area, on 1 June 1918 a Representative of the Quartermaster-General for the Captured Material and Salvage Service was appointed.[29] He succeeded, by supervision and

23 War Ministry 17.5.1918 No 742. 18. G. A. 7. V. He was first designated as Commander of the Assault Armoured Mechanical Transport Sections and redesignated by War Ministry of 2.9.1918 No 1587. 18. G. A. 7.V.
24 A.K.O. of 10.1.1917.
25 Set up 15 February 1918.
26 War Ministry of 21.2.1918 No 939. 18. G. A. M.
27 Quartermaster-General of 2.6.1918. II No 28 281.
28 Quartermaster-General of 31.5.1917. No I.a. 22 012.

education, in convincing the defaulting departments of the importance of even this unprepossessing activity.

The organisation of munitions columns and trains during the course of the war had, for practical reasons, become long established. This required particular measures to meet the increased need for these formations at the 'hot-spots' of the fighting. Thus here, too, a centralisation of weapons technology proved to be necessary. Therefore, in July 1918 there was formed, under the command of the Quartermaster-General, the post of the General of Munitions Columns and Trains in the Great Headquarters.[30] He would make suggestions for the use of his units. Also he would control and supervise their technical services both in the war area and at home. Lastly, he would organise the replacement of draught horses and field equipment.

d. Supreme Arm-of-Service Authorities

According to old custom, foot artillery and pioneers were counted as special arms of the service because their technical training was supervised by inspectors. They were outside the corps unit, while on the other hand their tactical use took place completely within the framework of the general troop command. Thus it was only a necessary continuation of the practice followed in peacetime, if the most senior technical heads, the Inspectors-General, went into the field with the Great Headquarters.

The General of Foot Artillery in the Great Headquarters[31] was, first and foremost, intended to advise the Chief of the General Staff of the Field Army concerning all technical affairs and all questions concerning the use of heavy artillery. In addition, he exercised the decisive influence on training at home that was based on war experience. The later created offices of Inspector of the Artillery Survey Service[32] and the Staff Officer for Heavy Flat-Trajectory Fire[33] were assigned to him. Originally he was not able to directly affect the Generals of Foot Artillery in the Army High Commands. However, in order to unify the artillery, the Supreme Army Command placed the staffs of the "Generals of Artillery" in the place of the field artillery brigade commanders, and of the Generals of Foot Artillery.

The General of Foot Artillery in the Great Headquarters received the title "General of Artillery No 1".[34] In this he henceforth remained, simply *primus inter pares*. But only one month later the Supreme Army Command appointed him Inspector-General of Artillery Firing Schools (General of Artillery No1)[35] and transferred to him the command of gunnery training, for all field and foot artillery, both in the field and at home. On his shoulders henceforth rested the responsibility for the technical gunnery training for all the German artillery and for its education in

29 Established through War Ministry of 4.8.1918. No 3012. 7. 8. 18. A. M.
30 War Ministry of 10.8.1918. No 9924. 7. 18. A. 4.
31 "General of Foot Artillery (Inspector-General of Foot Artillery)".
32 War Ministry of 30.8.1916 No 1579. 16. A. 5.
33 War Ministry of 2.12.1916 No 5320. 11. 16. A. 5. II., from September 1917 designated as "for Super Heavy Flat-Trajectory Fire".
34 War Ministry of 16.2.1917 No 445. A. 4.
35 War Ministry of 28.3.17 No 677. 17. A. 5.

informed collaboration between the field artillery and foot artillery formations. The holder of the post from the beginning of the war until 15 October 1917 was the Inspector-General of Foot Artillery, General of Artillery von Lauter, then Generalleutnant Ziethen.

The General of the Engineer and Pioneer Corps in the Great Headquarters[36] exercised a great influence as the senior service chief of the pioneer arm of the service. He quickly increased and produced new special services during the war. Through the Chief of the General Staff of the Field Army, whom he advised, he took care of the technical and organisational development of the pioneer service. The heads of the special services, which were developing in the field from the pioneer arm, remained under his command. Also under his command were the Inspectors of Minenwerfer Equipment who came into existence from the end of 1915. The Inspector of Gas Regiments[37] was created one year later, and the Inspector of Pioneer Close-combat Weapons,[38] was set up in May 1918, and was under the same control. In August 1918 he received the title General of Pioneers with the Chief of the General Staff of the Field Army.[39] The holder of the post from the beginning of the war until 2 July 1916 was General of Infantry von Clear. However, from 25 August 1914 to 30 June 1915 he was absent as Commanding General, and was deputised for by his Chief of Staff. From 3 July 1916 the post was unoccupied and was again take up by the Chief of Staff, until on 28 August 1918 Generalmajor Marschall von Bieberstein was appointed.

The Chief of the Field Munitions Service, Generalleutnant Sieger, was originally under the command of the Quartermaster-General. In conjunction with the Chief of Field Railways, his duties consisted of bringing up the munitions provided by the War Ministry, together with replacement equipment. Significantly, all of these had to be on time, as and when required. This was done on the basis of the requirement reports of the Army High Commands and the Lines of Communication Inspectorate. On the other hand, he had to inform the War Ministry in advance, of the forecast requirements. Recognition of the equally crucial significance of the munitions question caused the Chief of the General Staff of the Field Army, on 10 May 1915, to place the Chief of Field Munitions under his personal command. Thereby he would facilitate the latter's closer collaboration with the Operations Section. The Hindenburg Army Command went further in this direction. On 23 September 1916 they dissolved the post of Chief of Field Munitions, in order, as mentioned above, that the High Command would itself take over responsibility in the Operations Section for the provision of munitions and equipment.

During the first three years of the war, the Chief of Field Telegraphy, was under the responsibility of the Quartermaster-General. His area of activity included all the signals units and signals equipment of the Field Army. It was, at first, a relatively small involvement because of the Army's scanty equipment in this connection. But it was precisely in the field of communications that the war brought a

36 "Gen v. I. U Pi-Korps (Inspector-General of the Engineer and Pioneer Corps and Fortifications)"
37 War Ministry of 10.12.1916 No 1962. 16. G. A. 6., later called Commander of Gas Troops.
38 War Ministry of 10.5.1918 No 2264. 4. 18. A. 6. II.
39 War Ministry of 21.8.1918 No 648. 8. 18. A. 6. II.

quite unexpected further development, so that when the Hindenburg Army Command took over, it found a whole host of signals formations and equipment. There too, it took steps to carry out a comprehensive reorganisation.

At this point, it is interesting that for each of the western, eastern and south-eastern theatres of war a respective General of Telegraph Troops was created, under the command of the Chief of Field Telegraphy, This was done in order to relieve the latter's workload.[40] However, when even this division of the responsibility was still unsatisfactory, the Supreme Army Command undertook another reorganisation of the Signals Service. They placed the hitherto designated Chief of Field Telegraphy under the immediate command of the Chief of the General Staff, but with the more comprehensive title of Chief of the Signals Service, thus giving him the authority of a Commanding General.[41] Under the command of the Chief of the Signals Service were henceforth all the signals formations in the field and at home. With the approval of the Chief of the General Staff of the Field Army, he controlled organisation, use, training, appointments, replacements, supply, technical requirements and the entire German wireless-telegraph traffic. Holders of the post of Chief of Field Telegraphy, or Chief of the Signals Service, were, in succession, Generalmajor Balck, then from 7 December 1914 Colonel von Wolff, and from 9 April 1917 Colonel or Generalmajor Hesse.

The Chief of the Field Railway Service, Generalmajor Groener, was similarly under the command of the Quartermaster-General. Only after Falkenhayn was relieved was he placed, by Hindenburg, under the direct command of the Chief of the General Staff of the Field Army.[42] Although from the beginning he had an extensive area of responsibility, the railways were of prime importance. On him depended the entire railway service in the war area. Similarly the use of canals, in the field and at home, needed the corresponding formations. Replacement works and also new constructions, were set under way by Groener. On the staff of the Supreme Commander East he was represented by the Chief of Field Railways East, who was also under his command. At all the Army High Commands and Lines of Communications Inspectorates he had his railway representatives. Later he also had his Plenipotentiary General Staff Officers with the allied Powers in Constantinople,[43] Sofia,[44] and Vienna.[45] From mid-1916 he also worked with the Army Groups.[46] At this time Groener decentralised the command of the ever-growing military and war economy transports, while at the same time creating Rail Transport Sections for the great areas West, East, and South-East[47] which were based in the Great Headquarters in Kovno[48] and in Pless. Chief of the Field Railway Service

40 War Ministry of 14.12.1916 No 192. A. 7. V.
41 War Ministry of 12.9.1917 No 415. 17. A. Nch.
42 Chief of the General Staff of the Field Army of 30.9.1916. M.J. No 6124 Z.
43 War Ministry of 13.11.1915 No 23 278. 15. A. 1.
44 War Ministry of 28.12.1915 No 26 124. 15. A. 1.
45 War Ministry of 28.12.1915 No 26 124. 15. A. 1.
46 12.6-15.10.16 at Linsingen, from 9.8.16-13.1.18 with Archduke Carl or Joseph, from 27.8.16 with Crown Prince Rupprecht, 17.10.16-4.4.18 with Böhm-Ermolli, from 28.11.16 with Crown Prince Wilhelm, from 30.11.16 with Mackensen, from 2.3.17 with Duke Albrecht, from 10.7.18 in Charlow.
47 War Ministry of 3.5.1916 No 7165. 16. A. 1.

until 31 October 1916, Generalmajor Groener[49] was followed by Colonel Freiherr von Oldershausen.

Huge numbers of special maps, marked with the positions of fortifications and showing the results of reconnaissance, were required in trench warfare. The survey and cartographic service gained greatly in importance. Precisely in this branch of the service it was a matter of making general use of local experience and making compilations for outline and operational maps. But a central base was necessary for this. Such a base was created, by the Chief of the General Staff of the Field Army in July 1915, in appointing Major Boelcke as Chief of the War Survey Service.[50] Under the latter's command were all the survey formations in the field. He controlled the making and the production of maps. From the end of 1915 gradually, and as need dictated, staff officers of the Survey Service were assigned to the Army Commands in the West and the Army Groups in the East.

At the beginning of the war, in comparisons of air forces, Germany only had superiority in Army airships. However, numbers did not come to fruition as a result of the great vulnerability of the airships. In aviators, both in number and technique, the Germans were inferior to the French. They were equal in the use of tethered balloons, while anti-aircraft defence was still little developed. Naturally they worked feverishly to fill the gaps in air armament. Therefore, in March 1915, the post of Chief of the Field Aviation Service was set up with the Quartermaster-General.[51] This post represented the supreme command, in the wartime area of aviation, airship crews and the meteorological service, which was of great importance for them.

The army airships, since they were only rarely useful for land warfare, remained outside this organisation. At that time anti-aircraft defence was only seen as purely part of the artillery, for which on 1 July 1915 the post of a special Inspector of Anti-Balloon Cannon was created in the Quartermaster-General's command.[52] Since there was also for the home front an excellent organiser of the air and airship service, the further development of the air forces quickly followed. The French had not remained idle. Similarly their advances were a forward impetus to the British air force which at first could not be matched, as the great Battle of the Somme showed, in 1916.

The recognition gained in 1916, that it was necessary to unify all the air forces under one central command was translated into action by the Hindenburg Supreme Army Command. It obtained an A.K.O. of 8 October 1916, by which Generalleutnant von Hoeppner was appointed as Commanding General of the Air Forces (Kogenluft).[53] The worthy Lieutenant-Colonel Thomsen,[54] until then Chief of the Field Air Service, was appointed his Chief of General Staff. The Kogenluft was under the direct command of the Chief of the General Staff of the Field Army

48   Replacing the previous Chief of Field Railways East.
49   Up to 4.9.1914 Lieutenant-Colonel, up to 25.6.15 Colonel.
50   War Ministry of 19.7.1915 No 668. 15. A. 3., separating the Artillery Survey Service.
51   War Ministry of 11.3.1915 No 1104. 3. 15. A. 7.V.
52   Established through War Ministry of 10.7.1915 No 2433. 15. G. A. 4; "Balloon" was changed to "Aircraft" through War Ministry of 31.5.1916 No 1428. 16. A. 4.
53   Established through War Ministry of 2.12.1916 No 1104. 11. 16. A. 7. L.
54   Until 21.3.1916 Major; from 18.8.1918 Colonel.

and was in charge of all the formations of airmen, airship crews, anti-aircraft defence and the meteorological service, both in the field and at home. The post of Inspector of Anti-Aircraft Cannon became unnecessary.

The allocation of responsibilities in the staff of the Kogenluft is extremely informative, because it gives an overview of the great scope of his area of authority. A General Staff Section dealt with deployment, use, orders of battle and service orders for the aviator, anti-aircraft and airship formations. Their collaboration with other arms of the service and the preparation of large-scale combat actions were planned in detail. Special sections for aviators, anti-aircraft and airship personnel were assigned. They also gave support to the General Staff Section, to technology, training, replacement and personnel. Sections for home air defence, the meteorological service and the aerial photography service were added.

An Intelligence Section closely followed the development and activity of the enemy air forces, took care of necessary propaganda, and had a special censorship department for air affairs in Berlin. A Feuerschutz Section took care of the protection of airfields and industrial concerns, but especially of the explosive and munitions plants. A Medical Section was also set up on account of the particular requirements of the air service. Administrative staff, judiciary and intendance were also available with every General Command. Worthy of particular mention are the representatives for Bavarian affairs, the liaison officer for the Chief of the Naval Air Service and that of the Austrian K.u.K. Air Force on the Staff of the Kogenluft. Later the Inspector of Photographic Equipment was also included on the staff.

As immediately subordinate posts the Kogenluft had the Commanders of Aviation,[55] the Commanders of Airship Personnel,[56] und the Commanders of Anti-Aircraft Cannon[57] with each Army High Command.

e. External Departments

In addition to the Military Plenipotentiaries with the Allies, introduced in the section "The Kaiser and the Great Headquarters", some other external offices must be mentioned which were under the direct command of the Chief of the General Staff of the Field Army.

As already mentioned in the section "The General Staff Departments", the 'influencing' of the Press devolved upon Section III B. The complementary Head Office for Censorship, in Berlin, was to ensure the regular implementation of censorship which lay in the hands of the Deputy Commanding Generals. But soon it became evident that the goal to which they aspired in the area of the Press was not being achieved. Therefore, in October 1915, at the instigation of the Supreme Army Command, the War Ministry set up the War Press Office[58] in Berlin and placed it under the direct command of the Chief of the General Staff of the Field Army. The new office absorbed the Head Office for Censorship and received the following tasks:

55 War Ministry on 29.11.16 No 1145. A. 7. L.
56 War Ministry of 23.9.17 No 46. 8. 17. A. 7. L.; previously Staff Officers of Airship Personnel.
57 War Ministry of 7.1.17 No 20. A. 4.
58 A.V.Bl. 1915, No 772, War Ministry of 14.10.1915 No 5576. 15. Z. 1.

- Making easier collaboration possible between the home authorities and the Supreme Army Command in the area of the Press.

- Distribution of information to the authorities and the Press.

- Regular implementation of Press supervision.

The guidelines issued by the central authorities for the implementation of censorship were passed from the War Press Office to the Offices for Censorship. This was a process in which the instructions of the Supreme Army Command were naturally of prime importance. It dealt directly with all authorities without following the prescribed channels. Its internal division produced an information office, a foreign affairs office and a head office for censorship.

Since the War Press Office was an administrative organ of the Supreme Army Command and received its main guidelines principally from Section III B, its Chief, Lieutenant-Colonel Nicolai, largely drew the fury of the Press barons. They had been 'spoilt' in peace and now were very much restricted in war. About this, General Ludendorff makes the very apposite comment, that the military censorship of the Press was, unfortunately, a necessary evil in wartime, and by its very nature was able to satisfy no-one.[59]

Incidentally, about a month before the collapse, the Head Office for Censorship was again taken out of the War Press Office and was placed under the command of the Home Supreme Commander, that is, the War Minister.[60]

In the political area, too, the Chief of the General Staff made honest efforts to play into the hand of the Reich leadership when he took it upon himself to warn them of written material with which he could not agree. As soon as it was recognised what serious damage enemy propaganda was doing to the German cause, without it being effectively countered on the German side, the Supreme Army Command considered it necessary to establish a closer connection with the Foreign Office. To this end, on 1 July 1916, it set up the Military Department of the Foreign Office, which was under its own command but formed part of the Foreign Office. This department worked very closely with the Foreign Office, Section III B of the Deputy General Staff, the War Press Office, the War Ministry, the Admiral Staff and the Reich Naval Department. Its duties consisted in exposing false enemy propaganda and carrying out active propaganda at home and abroad.

On 30 January 1917 it set up a "Pictorial and Photo-Department" which in April 1917 was established as the Pictorial and Film Department.[61] At the instigation of this department, in December 1917 Universum-Film A.G. was founded. It covered the entire German film industry under the decisive influence of the Reich and represented through the Pictorial and Film Department. It proved to be an excellent information tool. In January 1918, because of its economic activity, the Pictorial and Film Department came administratively under the control of the War Office.[62] However, its activities remained tied to the Military Department of the Foreign Office.

59   Ludendorff, page 13.
60   A.V.Bl. 1918, No 1103, War Ministry of 16.10.1918 No 492. 10. 18. Z. 3.
61   A.V.Bl. 1917, no 367, War Ministry on 11.4.1917 No 522. 4. 17. A. 3.
62   A.V.Bl. 1918, No 124, War Ministry of 28.1.1918 No 1047. 1. 18. Z. 3.

In addition to the Pictorial and Film Department the Military Department had a Propaganda Section, a Press Section, and a Graphic Section for information by means of images, posters, and caricature. They had quarters for the neutral Press, an Art and Passport Section together with auxiliary offices. These were in Vienna, Sofia, Bern, the Hague, Stockholm, Christiania, Copenhagen, Kiev, Kharkhov, Minsk, Omsk, and Tiflis. Liaison offices, for reporting purposes, were located with the Army High Commands.

Because of its growing importance, on 9 July 1918 the Military Department was changed into the Foreign Department of the Supreme Army Command. In this, nothing changed regarding its activities.

In a certain sense, the external departments of the Supreme Army Command can be ascribed to the Representative General of the Supreme Army Command for Supervision of Training behind the Western Front.[63] At the beginning of January 1918, he received the task of reviewing and promoting the state of training, and of providing a report. His activity ended in August.

f. The Training Regulations of the Supreme Army Command

For the training of the Army during the war, in the period up to the Battle of Verdun in 1916, little happened on the part of the Supreme Army Command under Falkenhayn. The Official History writes of Falkenhayn in this connection:

> He trusted in the inner goodness of the German Army. It was certainly inferior in numbers to its enemies, but hitherto[64] had proved equal to every test of its capability. It certainly remains disconcerting that he himself abstained from exercising any influence on the tactical training of the troops. They were facing largely new and unaccustomed tasks of attack.[65] He might even have simply issued standardised combat regulations. It is characteristic that during the long months of fighting for Verdun, from the Supreme Army Command only one single short instruction of this kind was issued. It came on 14 April. It concerned the way to combat machine-gun nests. Even in all purely technical questions the Chief of the General Staff sometimes was noticeably reticent.

Nevertheless, during the battle of Verdun, General von Falkenhayn must have recognised the necessity for issuing service instructions that took account of the experiences of the war. In actual fact, in conjunction with the War Ministry, he laid the foundations for a collection of service instructions. These were issued under the collective title "Instructions for trench warfare for all arms of the service" and were to be published by the War Ministry. During his period in office there appeared "Mine Warfare",[66] "Means of Illumination",[67] "Construction of Defences",[68] and "Close-combat Weapons".[69]

63   War Ministry of 10.1.1918 No 82. 18. G. A. M.
64   End of 1915.
65   Attack on the fortress of Verdun.
66   War Ministry of 19.4.1916.
67   War Ministry of 31.5.1916.
68   War Ministry of 20.6.1916.

The Hindenburg Army Command, whose organisational activities were shown in the section "Supreme Service Arms Authorities", also took a detailed and systematic approach to troop training. It dispensed with the collaboration of the War Ministry and issued its own instructions. In this, a decisive factor was that the year 1917 was to bring about a shortening of the front in the West. Therefore the Army of the West had to move on to the defensive. Under this standpoint came the service instruction "Basic Principles for the Conduct of Defensive Fighting in Trench warfare".[70] Concerning the nature of this instruction Ludendorff wrote:

> In sharp contrast to the previous method of defence, which was compressed into rigid, easily recognisable lines, now a wide defence, organised in depth, was created, which in loose forms could be kept mobile. The position should naturally be in our hands when the fighting has finished, but the infantryman now no longer had to say to himself that 'here I stand and fall', because he had the right to make a limited withdrawal in all directions in the face of strong enemy fire. The line that had been lost could be regained in a counter-attack.
>
> The group definitely became the unit in the combat organisation of the infantry. The position of NCOs as group leaders thus gained considerably in importance. Tactics became increasingly individually based. All the lessons for the use of artillery and aircraft, as well as for the collaboration of service arms, which had been taught up to that time by the Battle of the Somme, were put to good use in the new instructions. The requirements set out in it could only satisfy troops who, even if they no longer had first-class training, were filled with a feeling of selfless sacrifice and real discipline as men.

Together with "Defensive Fighting", from Autumn 1916 to Spring 1917 the General Staff created more successive service instructions. "General Instructions concerning the Construction of Defences",[71] "Use and Activities of Artillery Aircraft in Trench warfare",[72] "The Minenwerfer",[73] "Combined Use of Infantry with Aircraft and Captive Balloons",[74] "Details concerning Construction of Defences",[75] and "Close-combat Weapons"[76], were all issued. All these superseded the corresponding instructions issued by Falkenhayn and mentioned above. The essential points for artillery training are contained in "Defensive Fighting". The "Training Instructions for Infantry Troops in War", set up by A.O.K. 1, was obligatory for the entire Army. To reinforce the new instructions, courses were set up for senior troop leaders and General Staff officers, while the existing courses for young officers and NCOs were continued with vigour.

During the course of 1917, as the next printed instruction, there then followed the "Special Booklet to the Collected Booklet of the Instructions for Trench warfare, collected on the basis of experience in the defence against the English-French offensive in Spring 1917".[77] This title alone illustrates the tireless concern of the Supreme Army Command that new experiences of war should be disseminated as quickly as possible throughout the Army. Then it was joined by "Signal Orders",[78] and "Means of Communication".[79] This instruction also contained the basic principles for the war of movement - "General Instructions Concerning the Construction of Defences"[80] superseded the instruction of 1916. "The Infantry Aircraft and the Infantry Balloon",[81] "Use and Deployment of Low-Flying Aircraft",[82] "Instruc-

69   War Ministry of 7.8.1916.

tions Concerning the Deployment of Pursuit Flights,"[83] "Super Heavy Low-Trajectory Fire"[84] and "Means of Communication and Their Use".[85] All of these superseded the older instructions on this subject.

In Autumn 1917 the Supreme Army Command applied itself afresh to carefully developing its programme for 1918, including the area of training. The attempt was to be made to decide the course of the war on the Western Front by attacking. Therefore an instruction entitled "The Attack in Trench warfare" was produced.[86] This instruction is extraordinarily interesting and informative, because it brings out sharply the experience of large-scale fighting, on the attack, by all arms of the service. It makes the Infantry Group, now armed with light machine-guns, the principal unit carrying the attack. It assigns the role of infantry support weapons to heavy machine-guns, light Minenwerfer, flame-throwers and individual batteries. A limited period of overpowering fire from artillery and Minenwerfer was to prepare the attack. Then the infantry and their support weapons, supported by special sections of low-flying aircraft and tanks where available, would carry forward. The rolling fire of the artillery would creep forward ahead of their advance. Even how to act in the case of a 'possible development' of a war of movement, and also in the case of enemy counter-attacks, was explained.

As in the winter of 1916/17 leadership courses were now once more set up. But the attack divisions were carefully trained right up to March 1918.

Before the great attack in France, further service instructions appeared, namely "The Artillery Aircraft and the Artillery Balloon",[87] "Order of Traffic for Means of Communication"[88] and "Use of Battle Flights".[89]

70 Published by the Chief of the General Staff of the Field Army on 1.12.1916, supplemented on 1.3 and 1.9.1917.
71 Still published by the War Ministry on 13.11.1916.
72 Published by the Chief of the General Staff of the Field Army on 1.11.1916, supplemented on 10.2.1917.
73 Published as above on 15.11.1916.
74 Published as above on 1.1.1917.
75 Published as above on 15.12.1916.
76 Published as above on 1.1.1917.
77 Published by the Chief of the General Staff of the Field Army on 10.6.1917.
78 Published as above on 15.6.1917.
79 Published as above on 15.7.1917.
80 Published as above on 15.8.1917.
81 Published as above on 1.9.1917.
82 Published as above on 15.10.1917.
83 Published as above on 25.10.1917.
84 Published as above in November 1917 (no date given)
85 Published as above on 15.12.1917, superseding the instruction of 15.7.1917.
86 Published as above on 1.1.1918.
87 Published by the Chief of the General Staff of the Field Army on 10.1.1918.
88 Published as above on 22.1.1918.
89 Published as above on 20.2.1918.

After the Great Battle in France appeared "The Minenwerfer",[90] "Deployment and Use of Flak Troops",[91] with, once more, "Instructions Concerning the Construction of Defences".[92]

3. Decorations and Honours

The Iron Cross was instituted at the beginning of the War of Liberation and renewed for the 1870/71 War for German Unity. It was also to be awarded in the war that broke out in 1914. This war was to be fought for Germany's very existence. The Iron Cross was to honour, in a worthy form, services to the Fatherland, and to be accessible to every German without restriction. Thus, on 5 August 1914, there appeared the text of a document concerning the renewal of the Iron Cross.[93]

If First Class, the Iron Cross was to be worn on the chest. If Second Class it was to be on a black ribbon with white edging. It was to be awarded as "reward for exceptional services rendered in the theatre of war". In addition, it was allowed to be awarded to "such persons as render exceptional service at home for the benefit of the German Armed Forces and their Allies". However, to differentiate it from that won in the field, it would only be on a white ribbon with black edging. Unfortunately, in March 1915, an alteration in the provisions for the home front was made which specified that the Iron Cross for services at home should also be awarded, "by reason of special military services, on a black ribbon with white edging".[94] The devaluation implied by this, for the beautiful decoration for frontline soldiers was not noticed.

Out of the wish to particularly distinguish those who, with one or several wounds had shed their blood for the Fatherland there arose the institution of the Wound Badge,[95] which, according to the number of wounds (1-2, 3-4, and 5 times and over), was awarded in black, silver, and gold.

Alongside the introduction of the Voluntary Service Law went the institution of the Meritorious Service Cross for War Aid on 5 December 1916. This naturally held little interest for the Army, but was of immediate benefit to it.

The 'Orders' that the individual Federal States instituted for natives of their states are not taken up here, since they were not available to all. No less were the decorative orders for individuals, even when it was a matter of the Blücher Cross for Hindenburg, the Great Cross to the Iron Cross for Ludendorff, or the Oak Leaf Cluster to the Iron Cross of 1870. On the other hand those honours must be mentioned with which the Kaiser at the same time decorated whole units or authorities.

In the foreground of these honours stands the Great General Staff, to whom the Supreme Warlord paid a lasting tribute in simple words, in his Order of 19 June 1918: "I determine that the Great General Staff, in honour of its duties and merits, be raised to the equivalent rank of a Central Authority".[96]

90   Published as above on 5.5.1918.
91   Published as above on 16.5.1918.
92   Published as above "General Instructions" on 10.8.1918, "Details" on 26.8.1918.
93   A.V.Bl. 1914, Special Issue on 6.8.1914, No 2.
94   A.V.Bl. 1915, No 224, A.K.O. of 16.3.1915.
95   A.V.Bl. 1918, No 270, A.K.O. of 3.3.1918.

The names of officers and princes who had particularly proved themselves in war were often taken up in the names given to units, thus above all honouring and pledging the unit. The following formations are involved:

- Infantry Regiment Generalfeldmarschall von Hindenburg (2nd Masurian) No 147[97]

- Infantry Regiment Generalfeldmarschall von Mackensen (3rd West Prussian) No 129[98]

- 'Fighter Flight Boelcke' in memory of the undefeated Captain Boelcke, killed on 28 October 1916[99]

- Dragoon Regiment Generalfeldmarschall Prinz Leopold of Bavaria (Westphalian) No 7[100]

- Infantry Regiment Emperor Karl of Austria and King of Hungary (4th Upper Silesian) No 63[101]

- 'Fighter Group Freiherr von Richtofen No 1' in memory of Rittmeister von Richtofen, killed on 21 April 1918[102]

- Füsilier Regiment General Ludendorff (Lower Rhine) No 39 - awarded 26 October 1918

An honour, quite unusual for a Landwehr unit, was received by Landwehr Infantry Regiment No 2 through A.K.O. of 29 July 1917, as follows:

> In special recognition of the bravery of the regiment in the face of the enemy, the Kaiser declares himself Chief of the Regiment, awarding it the name 'Landwehr Infantry Regiment King Wilhelm II', with his name to be worn on shoulder straps and epaulettes.[103]

96   A.V.Bl. 1918, No 732, A.K.O. of 19.6.1918.
97   A.V.Bl. 1915, No 652, A.K.O. of 27.8.1915.
98   A.V.Bl 1916, No 829, War Ministry of 28.11.16, No 1715. 10. 16. A. 1.
99   A.V.Bl. 1916, No 877, War Ministry of 10.12.1916, No 2585. 11. 16. A. 7. L.
100 A.V.Bl. 1917, No 920, War Ministry of 23.9.1917, No 969, 9. 17. A. 1.
101 A.V.Bl 1917, No 1080, K.A.O. of 3.11.1917.
102 A.V.Bl. 1918, No 534, War Ministry of 14.5.1918, No 10 525. 18. A. 7. L.
103 A.V.Bl 1917, No 800, A.K.O. of 29.7.17, War Ministry of 18.8.17.

B.

WAR MINISTRY

1. The War Minister

On mobilisation, the War Minister went to the Great Headquarters with his mobile staff. In Berlin, General von Wandel as Deputy War Minister managed the Ministry in accordance with his instructions. After Hindenburg had become Chief of the General Staff of the Field Army, the War Minister was assigned Berlin as his base. Therefore, after this, the War Minister appeared only for immediate lectures at the Great Headquarters. With a view to context, however, the War Ministry must be dealt with as an entity on its own. This will be done here, since only in conjuction with the Chief of the General Staff did the War Ministry express the full scope of the Kaiser's powers as Supreme Warlord.

Soon after the return to Berlin, the Deputy Commanding Generals, as was already the case in Bavaria, were placed under the command of the War Minister.[1] The announcement read:

> On the basis of the Order of 31 July 1914, concerning the state of war, the responsible authority for supervision of and complaints against the Military Commanders, is a Supreme Commander in Berlin. The War Minister was appointed to this post by A.K.O. of 8 December 1916.

As an indication of the 'shattered' position of the Kaiser, at the end of October 1918 the Military Cabinet was placed under the command of the War Minister.[2] Therefore, from then on, officer promotions required the counter-signature of the War Minister.

Generalleutnant von Falkenhayn, appointed as War Minister on 7 July 1913, retained the office of War Minister until 20 January 1915, this, even after he had become Chief of the General Staff of the Field Army. There followed him as War Minister Generalleutnant Wild von Hohenborn,[3] who on 29 October 1916 was replaced by General of Artillery[4] von Stein.[5] The latter held the office until 9 October 1918. The last War Minister of the war was Generalleutnant Scheüch.[6]

---

1   A.V.Bl. 1916, No 872, War Ministry of 10.12.1916, No 565. 12. 16. A. 1.
2   A.V.Bl. 1918, No 1167, A.K.O. of 28.10.1918.
3   Previously, from 27.11.14-20.1.1915, Quartermaster-General.
4   Until 31.10.1916 still Generalleutnant.
5   A.V.Bl. 1916, No 763, War Ministry of 2.11.1916 No 2093. 10. 16. K. M. 1.
6   A.V.Bl. 1918, No 581, A.K.O. of 9.10.1918.

2. The War Ministry of August 1914

At the beginning of the war the Administration Department was dissolved. Its previous Director joined the Quartermaster-General's department as Intendant-General of the Field Army. The administration sections became partly autonomous, partly under the control of other departments. In conjunction with some other changes, the following divisions of the War Ministry resulted by August 1914:

- Central Department (Z.D.) comprising: Ministerial Section (Z.1), Financial Section (Z.2) and Central Office for Certification (N.B.) - this for certification of war casualties

- Army Section (A.1) comprising: Reserves Section (C.1)

- General War Department (A.D.) comprising: Infantry Section (A.2), Cavalry Section (A.3), Field Artillery Section (A.4), Foot Artillery Section (A.5), Engineers and Pioneers Section (A.6), Traffic Section (A.7.V), Aviation Section (A.7.L) and Factories Section (B.5) - the latter for the State industrial plants

- War Rationing Section (B.1)

- Peace Rationing Section (B.2)

- Accommodation Department (U.D.) comprising: Accommodation Section East (U.1), Accommodation Section West (U.2), Training Ground Section (U.3), Construction Section (U.4), Clothing Section (B.3) and - Treasury Section (B.4)

- Supply and Justice Department (C.D.) comprising: Pensions Section (C.2), Supply Section (C.3) and Justice Section (C.4)

- Remount Inspectorate (R.I.)

- Medical Section (M.A.)

3. Expansion of the War Ministry up to Autumn 1916

On 8 August 1914, a case was presented by industrialists to the War Ministry that if the war continued for any length of time, there would be shortages in certain metals, chemicals and textiles.[7] Even before he left for the field on 13 August 1914 the War Minister ordered the immediate setting-up of the War Raw Materials Section (K.R.A.) in the War Ministry. This section took on the management of war raw materials. As executive authorities, the K.R.A. relied on the War Raw Materials Companies that had been set up at its instigation and which the K.R.A. closely supervised. At first, only metals, wool and chemicals were managed, but later all the other raw materials important for war armaments were added.

The War Raw Materials Section was established in December 1914 together with two other new authorities, the Central Office for Materials Captured in War (Z.K.) and the War Accommodation Section (U.K).[8] The Z.K. had become neces-

---

7   With copper, for example, German industry faced the cessation of the some 85 percent imported from America. Demeter, page 6.

sary as a result of the enormous amount of captured material and the connected setting-up of special collection points for it. The U.K., however, was to deal with the
use of prisoners of war, the affairs of freed German prisoners of war and questions
concerning war graves. For the rest, accommodation for prisoners of war remained
the responsibility of the Accommodation Sections U.1 to U.3.

On 1 March 1915, an increasing volume of work in the areas of food, clothing
and money led to the Administration Departments (B.D.), which had been dissolved on mobilisation, being set up again. This was followed by its unification
with the B Sections under their control.[9]

The efforts to import raw materials from neutral countries abroad, were con-
fronted by the necessity of keeping the value of German currency from falling. But
raw materials needed for the war effort were not allowed to be exported from the
Reich. For this reason the Reich Chancellor had put in place a Reich Commissar
for Approvals of Imports and Exports. The interests of the Army were represented
to him, from May 1915, by the Section for Imports and Exports (A.8).[10]

At about the same time a Department for Deferrals from Military Service
(A.Z.S) came into existence. Later, this became the War Reserves Department.

The treatment of German prisoners of war by enemy forces was contrary to international law necessitated the setting-up of a military Investigation Department
for Breaches of the Conventions of War. It found abundant evidence to work on.
Therefore, in September 1915, there was established, in the Accommodation Department, a Section for the Protection of Prisoners of War Abroad and for Breaches
in International Law (U.5).[11]

The increase in casualties increased the work involved in arranging pensions.
The Pensions Section that had existed hitherto, in Autumn 1915, could no longer
cope with the volume of work. To assist, a special branch retirement section
(C.2.R) was formed, while the Pensions Section retained its name but with the designation "(C.2.P)" and dealt only with pensions.[12]

The examination of questions concerning a possible use of gas for war purposes had been entrusted to Geheimrat Prof. Dr Haber. From his office there first
arose the Central Department for Chemistry (Z.Ch), which on 15 November
1916 was extended to form the Chemical Section (A.10).[13]

In April 1916, the Section for National Nutrition (B.6) was set up,[14] to ensure
the provision of food for the Army within the national provision of nutrition in
Germany. Questions connected with the provision of food for prisoners of war
were dealt with, from September 1916, by a special Section for the Nutrition of
Prisoners (U.6).[15]

8   A.V.Bl. 1914, No 454, War Ministry of 21.12.1914, No 1188. 12. 14. K. M.
9   A.V.Bl. 1915, War Ministry of 24.2.1915, No 1478. 2. 15. Z. 1.
10 A.V.Bl. 1915, No 366, War Ministry of 6.5.1915 No 972. 4. 15. Z. 1.
11 A.V.Bl. 1915, No 705, War Ministry of 16.9.1915 No 668. 9. 15. Z. 1.
12 A.V.Bl. 1915, No 753, War Ministry of 6.10.1915 No 532. 9. 15. Z. 1.
13 Cron, *Organisation*, page 175.
14 Von Wrisberg, page 479.
15 A.V.Bl. 1916, No 627, War Ministry of 23.9.1916 No 1274. 9. 16. Z. 1.

In July 1916 a division of the previous Section C.3 was made so that a Welfare Section for Officers and Officials (C.3.F) and a Section for the Care of Dependants (C.3.V) were formed.

4. The Hindenburg Programme and the War Ministry from November 1916

Shortly after Falkenhayn's Army Command was superseded by that of Hindenburg, the Chief of the General Staff of the Field Army informed the War Minister of the requirements by which the conditions for a successful further prosecution of the war could be created. He demanded that the production of arms and munitions should be at least doubled and that drafting for military service should be quickly implemented.

The requirements of the Supreme Army Command, designated in short as the "Hindenburg Programme", led to a comprehensive reorganisation in the War Ministry itself.

In order to unify procurement, the Master of Ordnance, Generalmajor Coupette,[16] assumed an autonomous post. He was actually under the control of the War Ministry, but was on 16 September 1916 given command of a Department for the Procurement of Arms and Munitions. To this department was transferred responsibility for procurement of all war materials and munitions, with the exception of material for the Pioneers and for aircraft. Later the Ordnance Department joined this Department for the Procurement of Arms and Munitions. It was an organisation created expressly for war, and designated as Wumba. The Master of Ordnance himself became the Head of Wumba.

But before this final form was found, the War Department of the War Ministry was set up as the central department for the entire war economy. By A.K.O. of 1 November 1916[17] the Kaiser ordered as follows:

> To manage all affairs concerning procurement, use, and nutrition of workers connected with the conduct of the war, as well as the procurement of raw materials, arms and munitions, a War Department will be set up in the War Ministry. This department will also have responsibility for reserves and replacements. The Employment Department, the Ordnance Department together with the Department for the Procurement of Arms and Munitions, the War Raw Materials Section and the Factories Section, as well as the departments of the War Ministry dealing with reserves and replacements, the Section for National Nutrition and the Section for Imports and Exports will all be under the command of the War Department.

To head the War Department, came Generalleutnant Groener. He was replaced, on 16 August 1917, by Generalmajor Scheüch, who in turn, was relieved on 9 October 1918 by Generalmajor Hoffmann. The Ordnance Department was transferred, on 16 November 1916, into the Department for the Procurement of

16 Cron, *Kriegseisenwirtschaft* (War Iron Economy), page 17f and von Wrisberg, pages 478 and 482.
17 War Ministry of 3.11.1916 No 240 . 11. 16. Z. 1., A.K.O. of 1.11.1916.

Arms and Munitions. After this, on 20 November 1916, the War Ministry published its new divisional structure as follows:[18]

- Central Department (Z.D.) comprising: Ministerial Section (Z.1), Finance Section (Z.2), Intelligence Section (Z.3), Section for Supply Statistics with Performance Monitoring and Patent Office (Z.4), Central Office for Certification (N.B.)

- General War Department (A.D.) comprising: Army Section (A.1), Section for the Supply of Officers and NCOs (C.1.a), Infantry Section (A.2), Cavalry Section (A.3), Field Artillery Section (A.4), Foot Artillery Section (A.5), Engineer and Pioneer Section (A.6), Traffic Section (A.7.V), Aviation Section (A.7.L), Chemical Section (A.10)

- Army Administration Department (B.D.) comprising: War Rationing Section (B.1), Peace Rationing Section (B.2), Clothing Section (B.3), Treasury Section (B.4), Central Department for Material Captured in War (Z.K.); affiliated Central Department for Reich Raw Materials

- Accommodation Department (U.D.) comprising: Accommodation Section East (U.1), Accommodation Section West (U.2), Training Ground Section (U.3), Section for the Protection of Prisoners of War Abroad and for Breaches in International Law (U.5), Section for the Nutrition of Prisoners (U.6), War Accommodation Section (U.K.)

- Supply and Justice Department (C.D.) comprising: Pensions Section (C.2.P), Retirement Section (C.2.R), Welfare Section for Officers and Officials (C.3.F), Section for the Care of Dependants (C.3.V), Justice Section (C.4)

- Remount Inspectorate (R.I.)

- Medical Section (M.A.) comprising: Central Department for Probate Affairs (Z.N.)

- War Department (K.) comprising: Recruitment and Labour Office (E.D.) comprising: War Recruitment Office (C.1.b), War Labour Office (A.Z.S.).

- Department for the Procurement of Arms and Munitions (Wumba) comprising: previous Ordnance Department, Factories Section (B.5)

- War Raw Materials Section (K.R.A.)

- Section for Imports and Exports (A.8)

- Section for National Nutrition (B.6)

After the announcement of the new procurement programme, industry with great enthusiasm plunged immediately into implementing the tasks it had been set. In doing so a severe shortage of specialist workers became evident. These workers now had to be drafted back again, out of the Army. But then, as a consequence of the badly worn-out railway stock, a serious transport crisis set in. This meant that in December 1916, even the procurement of steel for guns had to be made second in priority to that of steel for the railway infrastructure and rolling stock. Thus there arose the strange situation that despite an increase in steel production an actual fall in production occurred. It was only

18   A.V.Bl. 1916 No 809, War Ministry of 20.11.1916 No 1020. 11. 16. Z. 1.

to be overcome in the Spring of 1917, after the closest control of procurement had been achieved by means of priority listing.[19]

Criticism is always easy. However, in this case, criticism happened only after all the processes of the economy had been carefully taken into account. Nevertheless, one cannot refrain from mentioning Wrisberg's comments, concerning the placing of the War Recruitment Office under the control of the War Department. He wrote that "in questions of recruitment the creation of the War Department actually became disastrous, since this part of its task was intended first and foremost to raise the levels of production of war matériel. That had to be at the expense of recruitment."[20]

The Supreme Army Command intended that, in the interests of the fighting Army, there would a general obligation for labour service. It meant the freeing for call-up of every man at home, capable of military service. That would be made possible by those incapable of military service, and by women, offering their labour. But this intention could not be fully implemented. The Voluntary Service Law[21] that finally came into force on 5 December 1916, limited itself in its first paragraph, by expressly referring to "male Germans from the end of their 17th up to the end of their 60th year". It also failed to put those eligible for voluntary service on soldiers' pay, so that a stark difference arose between the poor pay of the man under arms and the liberal payment of those undertaking only voluntary service. But great numbers of women, not included in the scope of the law, despite this tried to replace the male labour forces. Voluntary service also came under the management of the War Department.[22]

5. The War Ministry during 1917 and 1918

As a result of the increase in the medical service, the Medical Section had grown greatly in size. Finally they were compelled to undertake a division of work. This took place in May 1917, and involved the formation of a Medical Department with the three sections Medical Personnel (S.1), Medical Affairs (S.2) and Medical Care (S.3).[23] Attached to this remained the Central Office for Probate Affairs. Associated with it was a Central Store for Medical Records.

The Army Section soon similarly proved to be overloaded. On 1 June 1917 it was split into two sections, one of which, keeping the name and the designation "A.1" retained responsibility for peacetime organisation and policy. The other, under the designation Mobilisation Section (A.M.) had, as its area of work, affairs concerning mobilisation and demobilisation, espionage, foreign armies, economic mobilisation, protection of frontiers, coasts, railways and air, postal and telegraph services.[24]

19 Cron, *Kriegseisenwirtschaft*, pages 27-40.
20 Von Wrisberg, page 483.
21 "Law concerning voluntary service to the Fatherland of 5 December 1916".
22 Para 3 of the law.
23 A.V.Bl. 1917, No 435, War Ministry of 7.5.1917, No 519. 4. 17. Z. 1.
24 A.V.Bl. 1917, No 541, War Ministry of 5.6.1917 No 261. 6. 17. Z. 1.

A consequence of the growth of the railway formations was that the business of the railway and shipping services, until now looked after by the Cavalry Section, was detached on 1 July 1917 and transferred to the new Railway Section (A.E.).[25]

The signals service, until now handled as a department in the Traffic Section (A.7.V), similarly became autonomous at about this time. The new Section for Means of Communication (A.D.N.) was formed, which however soon replaced its designation "A.D.N." by "A.Nch."[26]

For the purpose of collecting reports and documents relating to the history of the war, as well as dealing with the claims for conquest money and library services, in January 1918, the Military Historical Section (Z.5) came into existence.[27]

The Allies' claims on Germany had increased continuously. In order to keep them under supervision, they had to be unified in May 1918 into a special department known as the Section for Foreign Armies (A.11).[28]

As a result, the General War Department from then on included 14 sections, which could not be effectively managed from one place. Thus it was decided on 1 August 1918 to split it up, Sections A.4, A.5, A.6, A.7.V and A.10 being taken out and coming under a new department, the Troops Department (T.D.).[29]

As early as June 1918, on account of the large numbers of prisoners of war returning from Russia, a Section for the Welfare of Returning Prisoners of War (U.7) was set up. It received its budget in August 1918.[30]

The Section for National Nutrition (B.6) was on 29 March 1917 placed at the disposal of the Chief of Military Staff of the War Rationing Office and was dissolved on 30 September 1917.[31]

6. The War Ministry at the end of the War

- Central Department (Z.D.) comprising: Ministerial Section (Z.1), Finance Section (Z.2), Intelligence Section (Z.3), Section for Supply Statistics with Performance Monitoring and Patent Office (Z.4), Military Historical Section (Z.5), Central Office for Certification (N.B.); affiliated: Federal States' Mediation Office for Army Supplies

- General and War Department (A.D.) comprising: Army Section (A.1), Mobilisation Section (A.M.), Section for the Supply of Officers and NCOs (C.1.a), Infantry Section (A.2), Cavalry Section (A.3), Railway Section (A.E.), Section for Means of Communication (A.Nch.), Aviation Section (A.7.L), Section for Allied Armies (A.11)

25 A.V.Bl. 1917, No 605, War Ministry on 24.6.17, No 2529. 6. 17. A. 3.

26 A.V.Bl. 1917 No 541, War Ministry of 5.6.1917 No 261. 6. 17. Z. 1.

27 A.V.Bl. 1918, No 211, War Ministry of 18.2.1918, No 546. 1. 18. Z. 1.

28 A.V.Bl. 1918, No 556, War Ministry of 20.5.1918, No 60. 5. 18. Z. 1.

29 A.V.Bl. 1918, No 839, War Ministry of 12.8.1918, No 259. 8. 18. Z. 1.

30 A.V.Bl. 1918, No 900, War Ministry of 26.8.1918 No 50. 6. 18. Z. 1.

31 War Ministry of 29.3.1917, No 2733. 3. 17. K. And of 20.9.1917 No 870. 9. 17. Z. 1.
    - The War Rationing Office remained from 29.5.1916 under the supervision of the Reich Chancellor.

- Troops Department (T.D.) comprising: Field Artillery Section (A.4), Foot Artillery Section (A.5), Engineer and Pioneer Section (A.6), Traffic Section (A.7.V), Chemical Section (A.10)

- Army Administration Department (B.D.) comprising: War Rationing Section (B.1), Peace Rationing Section (B.2), Clothing Section (B.3), Treasury Section (B.4), Pay Section (B.4.a), Central Department for Material Captured in War (Z.K.); affiliated: Central Department for Reich Raw Materials

- Accommodation Department (U.D.) comprising: Accommodation Section East (U.1), Accommodation Section West (U.2), Training Ground Section (U.3), Construction Section (U.4), Section for the Protection of Prisoners of War and Breaches in International Law (U.5), Section for the Nutrition of Prisoners (U.6), War Accommodation Section (U.K.), Section for the Welfare of Returning Prisoners of War (U.7)

- Supply and Justice Department (C.D.) comprising: Pensions Section (C.2.P), Retirement Section (C.2.R), Section for the Welfare of Officers and Officials (C.3.F), Section for the Care of Dependants (C.3.V), Justice Section (C.4)

- Remount Inspectorate (R.I.)

- Medical Department (S.D.) comprising: Organisation of the Medical Corps (S.D.1), Medical Personnel Section (S.1), Medical Section (S.2), Medical Care Section (S.3); affiliated: Central Department for Probate Affairs (Z.N.) and Main Medical Records Store

- War Department comprising: Recruitment and Labour Department (E.D.) with War Recruitment Office (C.1.b) and War Labour Office (A.Z.S.)

- Department for the Procurement of Arms and Munitions (Wumba)

- War Raw Materials Section (K.R.A.)

- Section for Imports and Exports (A.8)

7. General changes in Clothing, Armament and Pay ordered by the War Ministry

On mobilisation, the Field Army had exchanged the colourful peacetime uniform for the field-grey uniform. But the first fighting already taught the lesson that complete suitability for use in the field had not yet been achieved and some conspicuous features had to be discarded. Therefore a hasty order of 19 August 1914, ordered that officers' sashes and the red numbers on helmet covers should immediately disappear. Medals and medal ribbons should be taken off while fighting and the waist belts of officers should be covered in field-grey or replaced by leather straps.[32]

Nevertheless, for the leadership, it was not desirable to dispense with what was a perfectly practical designation of units on helmet covers. Therefore the War Min-

---

32   A.V.Bl. 1914, No 227, War Ministry of 19.8.1914, No 1310. 8. 14. B. 3.

istry had ordered, as early as 15 August 1914, that all arms of the service, with the single exception of the Guard Corps, had to wear green numbers on their helmet covers.[33] This regulation proved to be practicable and remained in force until October 1916. But then the shortage of material for insignia meant that even the green numbers disappeared from the helmet covers.[34]

At the same time as the order of 15 August 1914 mentioned above, a change in the field-grey uniform was introduced. The material for the field-grey jacket was no longer to be produced in the previous shade, but in the somewhat darker shade of the material for the field-grey trousers. On the other hand the material for long trousers as well as for riding breeches was to be supplied in grey. Since the old stocks of course had to be used up, it was permissible to wear the old jacket with new trousers, and vice versa.

The coloured stripe on the field service cap also acted as a betrayer. It was therefore first decided to replace it by a field-grey band.[35] This field service cap band, however, proved to be really unsuitable as a stopgap. Finally, in mid-1917, it was dispensed with and from then a braid stripe in the colour of the field-grey or field-green basic material was introduced which was the same for all arms of the service.[36]

From July 1915, in place of the officers' sword (sabre) which was a hindrance in the field, all officers and those NCOs of fighting units who wore officers' side-arms up to the rank of regimental commander had to put on the short, fixable bayonet.[37] In April 1916, this measure was extended to cover mounted troops and the drivers of special units, as well as mounted troops of senior staffs.[38]

As mentioned above, the dark field-grey for field jackets, introduced on 15 August 1914, had already been thoroughly tested in peacetime. The war made field-grey standard, and made the coloured uniforms of peacetime no longer in keeping with the times. Therefore, after thorough discussions with the regulatory authorities, the Kaiser decided to charge the War Ministry with the task of carrying out a fundamental change in uniform. The Order concerning the Introduction of New Uniform of 21 September 1915[39] continued with the basic grey colour of the trousers instituted by the order of 15 August 1914. This was in place of the previous coloured basic material introduced for all arms of the service, the field-grey similarly ordered on 15 August 1914. The peacetime tunic became a field-grey tunic with the usual coloured braid, since no-one wanted to take away from the peacetime soldier his smart appearance. However, for use in the field, in place of the previous field tunic, a plain field service jacket of standard cut was to be used for all arms of the service.

In the same shade as the tunics, greatcoats also had, for peacetime wear, collars in the colour of the basic material. Leather equipment, boots and gaiters were to be

33 A.V.Bl. 1914, No 228, War Ministry of 15.8.1914, No 992. 8. 14. B. 3.
34 A.V.Bl. 1916, No 735, War Ministry of 27.10.1916 No 2403. 9. 16. B. 3.
35 A.V.Bl. 1915, No 245, Order of 29.3.1915.
36 A.V.Bl. 1917, No 699, War Ministry of 20.7.1917, No 1191. 6. 17. B. 3.
37 War Ministry of 19.7.1915, No 1659. 6. 15. A. 2.
38 War Ministry of 26.4.1916, No 1756. 3. 16. A. 2.
39 A.V.Bl. 1915, No 735, A.O.K. (Army High Command) of 21.9.1915, War Ministry of 27.9.1915 No 1924. 9. 15. B. 3.

generally black. Completely discontinued were the officers' waist belts, epaulettes, epaulette holders,[40] the greatcoat and the temporary hussar tunics of the officers. On the other hand the officers' sash remained for peacetime wear. Sword and sabre were generally to be carried by officers on a belt worn outside the tunic,[41] i.e. on a field service belt of dark-brown leather to be worn in place of the waist belt. The previous grey officers' 'Litewka' (loose tunic) remained under the name 'kleiner Rock', but would be of the field-grey basic material. Helmets and lancer-caps, to be worn generally with chinstraps, were provided with a removable spike or removable cover. As field equipment was generally introduced for officers, they too were issued with haversack, water bottle and drinking cup.

In mid 1916, after much effort, a steel helmet was finally introduced which gave protection against infantry fire, pieces of shrapnel and small shell splinters. It was only gradually brought into use in the field. It appeared at first in the 'hot-spots' of the fighting in the West, where it was most urgently needed. The officers of units equipped with steel helmets, were also provided with them by the Army administration,[42] but on a loan basis only.

The falling purchasing power of the Mark made it necessary to raise the pay of NCOs and other ranks with effect from 21 December 1917.[43] So, for example, the pay of other ranks, in units on active service, rose from 15.90M per month to 21M per month. In addition, from 1 August 1918, there was introduced for NCOs and other ranks a monthly bonus of 9M for units on active service and 6M for units on home service.[44] For officers on active service on 31 July 1918 war tax allowances were granted.[45] Generally, for all officers, military officials and NCOs, on 4 September 1918, a single extraordinary allowance was approved.[46]

40 Uhlans continued to wear shoulder straps.
41 Only with the Hussars were there still belts worn outside the tunic; with the Uhlans the body-belt was discontinued.
42 A.V.Bl. 1917, No 102, War Ministry of 28.1.1917, No 2005. 1. 17. B. 3.
43 A.V.Bl. 1917, No 1186, War Ministry of 6.12.1917, No 181. 12. 17. B. 4.
44 A.V.Bl. 1918, No 809, A.K.O. of 1.8.1918.
45 A.V.Bl. No 924, War Ministry of 31.7.1918, No 838. 7. 18. B. 4. a.
46 A.V.Bl. 1918, No 924, War Ministry of 4.9.1918 No 540. 8. 18. B. 4. a.

PART II

CHANGES IN
ARMY ORGANISATION

A.

GENERAL

To follow the Army's organisation in all its units and formations, during the war, is outside the scope of this work. To do that would require such a comprehensive order of battle, changing almost daily, that it would fill a book the size of a bible. But also such an order of battle would only have any purpose in connection with the history of the war. For military history it suffices to know that the Armies were not units which remained the same, once and for all. From the beginning, there were changes. These were according to the war situation, either reinforced or reduced by changes in their strength. This fate later came even to the Army Corps and Reserve Corps, as will be shown. The ongoing principal unit of the Army was the Division. That alone certainly does not take account of planned changes in its organisation, nor in changes of a temporary tactical nature.

Here it is not a matter of details, but of large-scale interrelationships. It must be shown how the Supreme Army Command worked with its Armies as 'pieces' on the great chessboard of the war, and how the places of the Armies shifted in relation to each other.

B.

IN THE ARMY OF THE WEST

The Supreme Army Command itself had its base in the West. It managed the movements of the Army of the West, consisting of seven Armies, located consecutively by number from the right wing. Management was by means of direct instructions to the individual High Commands. As means of communication they were served by wireless, telegraph and motor vehicles. But before even entering upon large-scale operations, it carried out a standardisation of the movements of the Armies on the left wing, by placing Army High Command (A.O.K.) 7 under the command of A.O.K. 6. This relationship existed during the period 10 August-7 September 1914. A similar system soon evolved on the right wing of the Army. Therefore, in the period 18-27 August 1914, A.O.K. 1 was bound to the instructions of A.O.K. 2. Whether placing one Army commander under a Supreme Commander of a neighbouring Army, he having the same rank, was advantageous, cannot be examined here. It is, however, a fact of the history of the war.

At the time of the Battle of the Marne, after the retreat, changes were made in the relative disposition of the armies. From the 7 September 1914, the 7th and the 6th Armies were moved to the right wing. They left behind Army detachments Gaede and Falkenhausen[1] that were of lesser strength. In the effort to take the enemy's left flank, corps from other Armies were withdrawn and Army High Commands 2 and 4 were used differently. When this so-called 'race to the sea' was ended and the Channel coast was reached, the Army was reorganised on 10 October 1914. At that point the Armies stood southwards from the right wing, abutting the sea, in the sequence 4th, 6th, 2nd, 1st, 7th, 3rd and 5th Army. In addition, there were Army detachments Strantz, Falkenhausen and Gaede, the latter with its left wing on the Swiss frontier. Thereafter, with this arrangement, the 10 High Commands were receiving their orders directly from the Supreme Army Command.[2]

In several large combat actions this route for transmission of orders proved to be unsuitable. Therefore, on 25 November 1914, the Supreme Army Command went over to splitting the Army of the West into three large groups. The particular Army commander with the greatest service seniority was, at the same time, created Supreme Commander of his Group. Thus the following picture emerged:

- Right wing group with 4th, 6th, and 3rd Armies under A.O.K. 6

- Central group with 1st, 7th, and 3rd Armies under A.O.K. 7

- Left wing group with 5th Armies and Army detachments Stranz, Falkenhausen and Gaede under A.O.K. 5.

---

1   These Army detachments were simply Armies of lesser strength.
2   The forces originally held back in Schleswig-Holstein as "the Army of the North" had in the meantime been brought up.

At the end of January 1915, this threefold organisation was replaced by the following organisation into four Groups:

- I Group with 4th and 6th Armies under A.O.K. 6

- II Group with 2nd and 1st Armies under A.O.K. 2

- III Group with 7th and 3rd Armies under A.O.K. 7

- IV Group with 5th Army, Army Detachment Stranz, Combat Sector Metz,[3] Army detachments Falkenhausen and Gaede under A.O.K. 5.

The Supreme Army Command again departed from this organisation of Groups on 7 March 1915. They turned anew to the principle of direct transmission of orders to the High Commands. However, they kept Army Detachment Strantz and Combat Sector Metz under the command of A.O.K. 5, and Army Detachment Gaede under the Falkenhausen High Command.

As a permanent operational intermediate authority, on 1 August 1915, the Supreme Army Command created the Army Group German Crown Prince. Its High Command was that of A.O.K. 5 and included, in addition to this Army, the three Army detachments and Combat Sector Metz. At the time of the autumn battles in Champagne, the 3rd Army also was temporarily (26 September-7 December 1915), under the command of the Army Group.

Since, during the course of the trench warfare, a High Command of the Army centre had proved to be dispensable, the 1st Army was disbanded on 17 September 1915 and divided among the neighbouring Armies.[4] But during the Battle of the Somme, the 2nd Army, which bore the brunt of the fighting, grew to such an extent that the Supreme Army Command, on 19 July 1916, divided it into two still very strong Armies, and alongside A.O.K. 2 set up a new A.O.K. 1. The overall command of the battle, for both Armies, it gave to the Supreme Commander of the 2nd Army, as Army Group Gallwitz.

Army Group Gallwitz was only a stopgap. As early as 29 August 1916 it was replaced by the Army Group Command Crown Prince of Bavaria, bringing in the 6th and 7th Armies. At the same time the 3rd Army rejoined Army Group German Crown Prince. With this, the operational transmission of orders by the Supreme Army Command was simplified into three Commands:

- 4th Army

- Army Group Crown Prince of Bavaria (6th, 1st, 2nd, and 7th Armies)

- Army Group German Crown Prince (3rd and 5th Armies, Strantz, Metz, A,[5] and Gaede)

The Army Group Command Crown Prince of Bavaria was no longer linked to an A.O.K., but to a superior established unit.[6] On the other hand, the German Crown Prince retained A.O.K. 5 until 27 November 1916, when his Army Group Command was also on the establishment.[7]

---

3   From 16.12.1914 this was under the direct command of A.O.K. 5.

4   A.O.K. 1 went to the East and took over command of the 12th Army as A.O.K. 12.

5   Army Detachment Falkenhausen was on 15.4.16 renamed as Army Detachment A.

6   Established by War Ministry on 6.9.1916 M.I. No 30 286. 16. A. 1.

1 March 1917 saw the inclusion of the final still directly commanded 4th Army into Army Group Crown Prince of Bavaria. Up to this time the 4th Army was the last directly commanded army. But its previous Supreme Commander, Duke Albrecht, henceforth received command of the three Army detachments as an Army Group.[8] Shortly afterwards, in the course of shortening the front, on 12 April 1917, A.O.K. 1 left the Army Group on the right wing, and joined the centre Group, on the 16th of that month.

The organisation of the Army of the West was thus, from mid-April 1917, as follows:

- Army Group Crown Prince of Bavaria: 4th, 6th, and 2nd Armies
- Army Group German Crown Prince: 7th, 1st, 3rd, and 5th Armies
- Army Group Duke Albrecht: Army detachments C, A, and B.[9]

For the decisive turn in the course of the war, attempted by attack in 1918, three new Armies were formed and sent to the Western Front. The 18th Army arrived on 27 December 1917, the 17th Army on 1 February and the 19th Army on 4 February 1918. In the same way, before Verdun, on 1 February 1918, the three High Commands there were amalgamated into an Army Group Gallwitz (=A.O.K. 5). Thus, from 4 February 1918, the Army of the West stood ready under the following organisation:

- Army Group Crown Prince of Bavaria: 4th, 6th, 17th, 2nd Armies
- H. Group German Crown Prince: 18th, 7th, 1st, 3rd Armies
- Army Group Gallwitz: 5th Army, Army Detachment C
- Army Group Duke Albrecht: 19th Army, Army Detachments A and B

Army High Command 9, brought from Rumania, on 5 July 1918, found its place in the Army Group German Crown Prince between the 18th and 7th Army. A fifth, Army Group Boehn,[10] formed up on 12 August 1918 between those of the Bavarian and the German Crown Princes. From this date the Army of the West was formed as follows:

- Army Group Crown Prince of Bavaria with 4th, 6th, and 17th Armies
- Army Group Boehn with 2nd, 18th, and 9th Armies
- Army Group German Crown Prince with 7th, 1st, and 3rd Armies
- Army Group Gallwitz[11] with 5th Army and Army Detachment C

---

7   Established by War Ministry of 27.11.1916, M.I. No 30 286. 16. A. 1.
8   Established by War Ministry of 2.3.1917, M.I. No 8169. 17, A. 1.
9   Army Detachment Stranz was renamed Army Detachment C on 2.2.1917, Army Detachment Gaede had on 4.9.1916 already been renamed Army Detachment B; Combat Sector Metz was from 3.1.1917 no longer a discrete unit.
10   Established by War Ministry of 12.8.1918, No 8649. 18. G. A. M.
11   Army Group Command Gallwitz was only established by War Ministry of 1.10.1918 No 10 563. 18. G. A. M.

- Army Group Duke Albrecht with 19th Army, Army Detachment A and B.

However, further changes were soon necessary. The 9th Army had to be dissolved on 9 September 1918. Army Group Boehn became dispensable, with the necessity to shorten the front. Thus, from the afternoon of 8 October 1918, the organisation of the Army of the West, as at 4 December 1918, was reintroduced. That did not change until the armistice.

C.

IN THE ARMY OF THE EAST

Conditions on the Eastern Front were more complicated than in the West. There the character of the Federal war became particularly evident and soon led to the originally separate German and Austro-Hungarian fighting forces, becoming mixed together. At first the 8th Army operated in East Prussia, in Poland. Under its command, but fighting at a great distance from it, was the Landwehr Corps. On 4 September 1914 it came under the command of the Austro-Hungarian 1st Army, located on the left wing of the Austro-Hungarian Army.[1]

The failed offensive of the federal partners caused a new German Army, the 9th, to be set up at Breslau. This was in order to renew the attack on the left wing of the Austrian K.u.K. Army. Hindenburg now gave up command of the 8th Army that he had led to the victories of Tannenberg and the Masurian Lakes. He took over the considerably reinforced 9th Army. However, the Supreme Army Command also expressly reserved for him the general command of the 8th Army. The two Armies were only linked with each other by the loose connection of protecting frontiers that were commanded by the Governors of the frontier fortifications and the Deputy Commanding Generals of the corps areas bordering Russia.

When Hindenburg then brought back the 9th Army from Silesia to Gnesen-Thorn to begin a new operation, the Supreme Army Command appointed him Supreme Commander East.[2] General of Cavalry von Mackensen took command of the 9th Army. With the creation of the post of Supreme Commander East, the Supreme Army Command had now formally relinquished a direct influence on the operations in the East. In the meantime, its indirect influence continued undiminished. Even the Supreme Commander East required the approval of the Supreme Army Command before he undertook any extensive new operation. He was also dependent on them if he needed reinforcements from the Army of the West or if he in turn had to give up troops for the latter.

Hindenburg now formed Army Group Graudenz from frontier guard fortifications and reserve units.[3] It was positioned between the 8th and the 9th Armies on his northern wing. He re-formed the Landwehr corps on the left wing of Army Group Graudenz and the latter into Army Detachment Woyrsch. On 14 November 1914, this came under the Austrian K.u.K. Army Command. After some more Austro-Hungarian units had been placed under its command, it was designated Army Woyrsch.

The serious situation on the Carpathian Front in January 1915 caused the Supreme Army Command to form an Army of the South and to place it at the disposal of the Austrian K.u.K. Army Command.[4] At about the same time, it placed

---

1   On 24.9.1914 it then joined the German 9th Army.
2   A.K.O. of 1.11.1914.
3   On 15.11.1914, from 9.2.1915 Army Group Gallwitz.
4   On 23.1.1915 the Army of the South moved in to the Carpathian Front.

another second new Army, the 10th Army, at the disposal of the Supreme Commander East. That was done in order finally to throw the Russians out of East Prussia.[5] From the beginning of February 1915, with these changes, the Army organisation in the East presented the following picture:[6]

- Supreme Commander East with 10th Army, 8th Army, Army Group Gallwitz[7] and 9th Army
- Austro- Hungarian Army Command with Army Woyrsch, Eastern Hungarian 1st, 4th, 3rd, and 2nd Armies
- Army of the South, Austro-Hungarian Army Group Pflanzer-Baltin

In Galicia, in order to disguise the Spring offensive of 1915, the Supreme Commander East formed Army Detachment Lauenstein and sent it, on 26 April 1915, into Courland. But the newly-formed 11th Army intended for Galicia found its place from 27 April 1915 between the Austro-Hungarian 4th and 3rd Armies with the proviso that A.O.K. 11, as Army Group Mackensen, assumed joint command of the Austro-Hungarian 4th Army. In the North, Army Detachment Lauenstein drew upon itself considerably superior forces, so that the Supreme Commander East was compelled to send A.O.K. 8 there. From Army Detachment Lauenstein, and other reinforcements, they were to form the Army of the Njemen, whose name was taken up by A.O.K. 8. The 8th Army itself was from that time commanded by General Command XX Army Corps. But, in its victorious advance, Army Group Mackensen formed an Army of the Bug[8] beside the 11th Army.

Here something must be said of the transmission of orders to the German units deployed on the Austro-Hungarian front. Tactically, they were bound to the orders of the higher Austrian K.u.K. headquarters. But for a decisive operation, such as the deployment of Army Group Mackensen, the Supreme Army Command agreed the plan and any changes to it, with the Austrian K.u.K. High Command, from which the Army Group then received its orders. On the other hand, the Supreme Commander East had no influence over the German units on the Austro-Hungarian front. By the 12 July 1915 the Eastern Front looked as follows:

- Supreme Commander East with Army of the Njemen, 10th Army, 8th Army, Army Group Gallwitz, 9th Army
- Austro-Hungarian Army Command with Army Woyrsch, Army Group Mackensen (Austro-Hungarian 4th Army, 11th Army, Army of the Bug, Austro-Hungarian 1st Army), Austro-Hungarian 2nd Army, Army of the South, Austro-Hungarian 7th Army

5 August 1915 brought a decisive change for the Supreme Commander East. The Supreme Army Command decided to take command itself of the operations in the East. It did leave the Supreme Commander East his previous area of admin-

5   The 10th Army stood ready from 28.1.1915.
6   The Eastern Front is fundamentally called from the North, that is, from the left wing.
7   Until 8.2.1915 still called Graudenz.
8   On 12.7.1915.

istrative responsibility, but for operations demoted him to Supreme Commander of an Army Group. It took away from him the 9th Army and amalgamated it with Army Detachment Moyrsch that the Austro-Hungarian Army Command had to give up to the Army Group Prince Leopold of Bavaria. At the same time, Army Group Gallwitz was redesignated 12th Army. On 25 August 1915 Army Group Mackensen, with the 11th Army and the Army of the Bug, came under the command of the Supreme Army Command. From 1 September 1915 the Eastern Front was formed as follows:

- Army Group Hindenburg with Army of the Njemen, 10th, 8th, and 12th Armies
- Army Group Leopold with 9th Army and Army Detachment Woyrsch
- Army Group Mackensen with 11th Army and Army of the Bug
- Austro-Hungarian Army Command with Austro-Hungarian 4th, 1st, and 2nd Armies, Army of the South, Austro-Hungarian 7th Army

Soon new changes were made. After the offensive had ended on 29 September 1915, the 8th Army was dissolved. The southern wing of the Army of the Njemen was, on 28 October 1915, made autonomous as Army Detachment Scholtz. The Army of the Njemen was itself renamed, on 30 December 1915, as the 8th Army.[9] But, on 19 September 1915, Generalfeldmarschall Mackensen left for Hungary in order to lead the attack on Serbia. The 11th Army had been dissolved 10 days earlier, in order with its main parts to fight in the Balkans under the previous A.O.K. 12[10], now renamed A.O.K. 11. The place of the previous Army Group Mackensen on the Eastern Front was taken by Army Group Linsingen (=A.O.K. Bug). From 1 January 1916, the Eastern Front was in the following form:

- Army Group Hindenburg with 8th Army, Army Detachment Scholtz, 10th and 12th Army
- Army Group Leopold with 9th Army and Army Detachment Woyrsch
- Army Group Linsingen with Army of the Bug and Austro-Hungarian 4th Army
- Austro-Hungarian Army Command with Austro-Hungarian 1st and 2nd Armies, Army of the South and Austro-Hungarian 7th Army

This organisation lasted a relatively long time. It was not even disturbed by the Russian attacks in March 1916. By contrast, the Russian offensive in June created new conditions to which the Army Command on the Eastern Front also had to adjust.

Ludendorff[11] writes about this:

In the difficult and tense days which we experienced in Kovno from the beginning of June, we stood in the closest connection with the Supreme Army Command. We had repeatedly pointed to the necessity for a single Supreme

9   I.e. the High Command reassumed its original designation.
10   A.O.K. 12 was replaced by A.O.K. 1 from the West, which took the number 12.
11   Ludendorff, page 178f.

Command on the Eastern Front... As early as the end of June the Generalfeldmarshall and I were ordered to Pless to explain our views concerning the situation in the East... Our journey to Pless brought no success for the regularisation of the Supreme Command. Resistance was still too great... On 27 July we were again ordered to Pless. The news of the fall of Brody, which arrived that day, caused the Austrian K.u.K. High Command partly to depart from its previous point of view. It gave approval for Generalfeldmarschall von Hindenburg to take over Supreme Command as far as south of Brody.

Thus, from 30 July 1916, there was in the East again a single command of the German front by the Supreme Commander East. His area of command, from now on, stretched from the sea in the North to the district west of Brody. This area of command was also called Army Front Hindenburg to differentiate from the Army Front Archduke Carl that adjoined it to the South. Supreme command of the previous Army Group Hindenburg was taken over by A.O.K. 10 under the name Army Group Eichhorn. When, after a few weeks, Hindenburg was appointed Chief of the General Staff of the Field Army on 29 August 1916, he was succeeded as Supreme Commander East by Prince Leopold of Bavaria[12]. His previous Army Group, from then on, appears as Army Group Woyrsch. Meanwhile the 9th Army was transported to Hungary, from 19 September 1916, to be sent into action there against Rumania. To match this, on 28 August in Northern Bulgaria, a new Army Group Mackensen had already come into existence. Taking into account all these changes, the Eastern Front on 19 September 1916 appeared as follows:

- Army Front of Supreme Commander East
- Army Group Eichhorn with 8th Army, Army Detachment Scholtz, 10th Army
- Army Group Woyrsch with 12th Army, Army Detachment Woyrsch, Army Detachment Gronau
- Army Group Linsingen with Army of the Bug, Austro-Hungarian 4th Army
- Austro-Hungarian 2nd Army with Army Group Eben
- Army Front Archduke Carl
- Army of the South, Austro-Hungarian 3rd Army, Austro-Hungarian 7th Army
- Austro-Hungarian 1st Army, 9th Army, Army Group Mackensen with Army of the Danube and 3rd Bulgarian Army

As early as 4 October 1916 the Army organisation changed again. The German Army Front was extended to the Carpathians, while from the Austro-Hungarian 2nd Army, the Army of the South, and the Austro-Hungarian 3rd Army, the Austro-Hungarian Army Group Böhm-Ermolli was formed and put under the command of the Supreme Commander East. The 12th Army was dissolved and replaced on 10 October 1916 by Army Detachment Scheffer. After Archduke Carl ascended the throne, his Army Front was, from 1 December 1916, called

12   People also referred to it as the Army Front Prince Leopold of Bavaria.

Archduke Joseph. The 9th Army finally came on 1 December 1916 under Army Group Mackensen, while the Army of the Danube came on 5 January 1917 as a General Command under the 9th Army. From 5 January 1917 the following organisation emerged:

- Army Front of Supreme Commander East
- Army Group Eichhorn with 8th Army, Army Detachment D,[13] 10th Army
- Army Group Woyrsch with Army Detachment Scheffer, Army Detachment Woyrsch, Army Detachment Gronau
- Army Group Linsingen with Army of the Bug, Austro-Hungarian 4th Army
- Austro-Hungarian Army Group Böhm-Ermolli with Austro-Hungarian 2nd Army, Army of the South, Austro-Hungarian 3rd Army
- Army Front Archduke Joseph
- Austro-Hungarian 7th Army, Austro-Hungarian 1st Army, Army Group Mackensen with 9th Army and 3rd Bulgarian Army

For a long time there was no essential change to this organisation. The Austro-Hungarian 3rd Army, on the right wing of the German front, on 15 July 1917, came under the command of the Austro-Hungarian Army Front. After the armistice came into force in the Eastern theatre of war, Army Group Woyrsch was the first to be dissolved on 15 December 1917.

During the armistice, and particularly after the Peace of Brest-Litovsk was concluded, the Eastern Front could be further dismantled. The Army Group Command Böhm-Ermolli and the German Army of the South were dissolved on 3 February 1918. The Army Front Archduke Joseph together with all the Austro-Hungarian Armies up to the 2nd disappeared by the beginning of April 1918. The Austro-Hungarian 2nd Army from 16 April 1918 carried the name Austro-Hungarian Army of the East. Army Group Eichhorn was dissolved on 28 March 1918. Its commander, on 3 April 1918, also took command of the previous Army Group Linsingen. From 16 April 1918 the picture of the Eastern Front was simplified as follows:

- Supreme Commander East with 8th Army, 10th Army and Army Group Eichhorn-Kiev (from 1 May: 'Eichhorn', from 13 August: 'Kiev', without Army units)
- Austro-Hungarian Army of the East
- Army Group Mackensen with 9th Army and 3rd Bulgarian Army

After the conclusion of peace with Rumania, Army Group Mackensen was, from 1 July 1918, named Army of Occupation in Rumania. The High Command of the 9th Army had already left on 18 June 1918 to be used on the Western Front. The 3rd Bulgarian Army ceased to exist with the Bulgarian special armistice on 30 September 1918.

13   Until 9.1.1917 still called Army Detachment Scholtz.

Some mention should be made of the expedition of 3 April-29 July 1918 that was to liberate Finland. It was carried out by the Baltic Division that had been specially formed for the purpose. It was under the direct command of the Supreme Army Command.

D.

ON THE ITALIAN FRONT

A German Front against Italy first came into existence, to a certain extent unofficially, in 1915. Italy had on 24 May 1915 declared war on Austria-Hungary. But the German government, in taking its position relating to this event, limited itself to the simple announcement that the Italians would also have to reckon with meeting German forces. On its part, it had no reason to declare war on Italy, and Italy too did not consider the initiative to declare war to be advisable. So it came to the strange state of affairs that the Alpine Corps, formed for the purpose, was, during the period 28 May-12 October 1915, fighting on the Austrian defensive front in the Tyrol. Meanwhile, a state of peace still officially existed between Germany and Italy.

Only at the time of the Rumanian declaration of war did Italy also, on 28 August 1916, declare war on Germany. This time the German answer was somewhat longer delayed, only then to break with shattering force on the Italian Army.

In 1917 the war against Italy was commanded by the Austrian K.u.K. South-Western Front Command of Archduke Eugen, under whose command from 23 August 1917 were the Army Group Tyrol and the Army Group Boroevic (with the 1st and 2nd Armies of the Isonzo). In mid-September a German army, the 14th, began forming up behind the Austrian front. The 14th Army, as an autonomous Group, then pushed between the two Austrian K.u.K. Army Groups, but, after the planned offensive had brilliantly succeeded, left again for France. The Army High Command was transported away on 22 January 1918 and soon afterwards appeared on the Western Front as A.O.K. 17.

E.

ON THE BALKANS FRONT

After Italy had declared war on Austria-Hungary, frontier defence on the Serbian border was provided by the Austro-Hungarian General Command Bosnia and by the Austro-Hungarian Army Group Tersztyanszky. But as soon as Germany had decided, along with Austro-Hungary and Bulgaria, to conquer Serbia and Generalfeldmarschall von Mackensen had been designated as the overall commander, 30 September 1915 saw the following order of battle come into existence on the Balkan Front.[1] Army Group Mackensen: Austro-Hungarian 3rd Army, Austro-Hungarian Army Group Fülöpp, 11 Army.

As the attack proceeded, on 14 October 1915 the 1st and 2nd Bulgarian Armies joined the 11th Army on the left. With the conclusion of the conquest of Serbia on 30 November 1915, an, at first, peaceful assembly of troops stood by ranged along the Serbian-Bulgarian-Greek border. Since the Entente had begun there were strong landings of troops in Saloniki. Now comprehensive help was given from the 11th Army to the Bulgarians, principally in heavy artillery, machine-gun and technical troops, for which Bulgarian divisions joined the 11th Army. From then on, the 11th Army and the 1st and 2nd Bulgarian Armies constituted mixed units of real brothers in arms. Under these circumstances, the High Commands of the 11th and the 1st Bulgarian Armies could, on 9 December 1915, for operational reasons, simply exchange with each other. The Bulgarian Supreme Army Command however, as a result of special agreements with the German Supreme Army Command, received overall command in Macedonia. On 20 January 1916, the Bulgarian 1st Army came under Mackensen, while the Austro-Hungarian 3rd Army from the end of December 1915 formed a special Austrian front.

In this way, from the 20 January 1916, the Balkan Front changed as follows:

- Austro-Hungarian 3rd Army (from 15 March 1916 General Command Albania).
- Bulgarian Army Command with Army Group Mackensen (with Bulgarian 1st Army and 11th Army), Bulgarian 2nd Army.[2]

Since Generalfeldmarschall von Mackensen from 30 July 1916 had to take precautions for the threatening war with Rumania on the Bulgarian border, his Army Group was dissolved that day. All the Armies came under the direct command of the Bulgarian Supreme Army Command, after the High Commands of the 11th and the Bulgarian 1st Armies had again exchanged with each other in view

1　From West to East = from right to left.
2　The Bulgarian 3rd Army is not considered here; it carried out coastal defence on the Black Sea and frontier defence against Rumania.

of the war situation. On 12 October 1916 a German Army Group Command had again been arrived at. On that same day, the following organisation was produced:

- Austro-Hungarian General Command Albania

- Bulgarian Supreme Army Command with Army Group Below (11th Army, Bulgarian 1st Army, Bulgarian 2nd Army)

With this, the conduct of the fighting in Macedonia lay exclusively in German hands. This division of forces remained until the end of the war. Army Group Below, since its Supreme Commander had been called to the Western Front on 21 April 1917 to take over command of the 6th Army, received with his successor the designation Army Group Scholtz.

From 30 September 1918, as a result of the Bulgarian special armistice, Army Group Command Scholtz still had command of the German forces. The Command covered the 11th Army and the formations that had been deployed with the two Bulgarian armies. It therefore became dispensable. On 10 October 1918, as High Command Scholtz, it came under the Army of Occupation in Rumania, in which from June 1918, there had no longer been an Army High Command.

F.

IN ASIA

When it entered the war, Turkey already had a valuable support in the German Military Mission. Its members, with the approval of the Supreme Army Command, were used in a whole series of Turkish senior command and General Staff posts. Thus the Chief of Mission, General of Cavalry Liman von Sanders, led the victorious defence at Gallipoli. Later in increasing amounts, after the railway through Serbia was freed, German aid in the form of war matériel and instruction units arrived.

Actual German troop units went to Turkey for the first time, in Spring 1916, as Expedition Pascha[1] and took part in the expedition against the Suez Canal.[2]

A second, large-scale German aid scheme was undertaken, from mid-1917, by Expedition Pascha II. With the strength of a brigade, it was formed from troops from all arms of service, designated in Turkey as the Asia Corps, and was gradually dispatched. At that time it was a matter of retaking Baghdad, which on 11 March 1917 had fallen into British hands.

After German-Turkish agreement, the supreme command of this operation was entrusted to General of Infantry von Falkenhayn. At the end of June he began the journey out with his staff as Army Group Command F. On 20 July 1917 he was appointed, in Constantinople, Supreme Commander of Army Group Yildirim. Before this Army Group could be assembled, the situation of the Turks on the Sinai front had taken a sinister turn. The Army Group Command was therefore deployed not in Iraq, but on the endangered Sinai front. There, it had at its disposal the 7th and 8th Turkish Armies. The slow rate of the arming of troops, traffic conditions in Asia Minor and Palestine, as well as all kinds of incidents, hindered progress Thus the individual units of the German Asia Corps[3] arrived with long intervals between them.

By contrast, the 1918 expedition in the Caucasus represented a purely German operation.[4] It was supposed to safeguard the Baku oil production for war purposes, but as a result of the threatening collapse of Bulgaria had to be prematurely broken off.

1   M.G. Coys. 601 - 608, Foot Artillery Btn. 60, Balloon Defence Gun Platoons 133-136, Minenwerfer Btls. 350-352, Aviation Detachment 300, Telephone Detachment 103 and Wireless Command 105.
2   4.7-12.8.1916.
3   Staff 201 Inf. Brig., Inf. Btns. 701-703 together with, respectively, 1 M.G. Coy., 1 Cavalry Platoon, 1 Infantry Gun Platoon, 1 Pioneer Btn. and 1 Minenwerfer unit, Field Artillery Btn. 701, Aviation Det. 301-304, Pioneer Coy. 205, Signals Btn. Pascha II; from 1.5.1918 also Reserve Jäger Btn. 11, from 15.5.1918 also Jäger Regt 146.
4   From 8.6.1918 - 5.2.1919: 1st Bavarian Reserve Jäger Btn. (Extended to Bav. Reserve Jäger Rgt), 25th Bav. Inf. (Jäger) Rgt, Assault Btn. 10, II Btn Reserve Field Artillery Rgt 65, Aviation Det. 28, AFV M.G. Sec. 176, Signals Sec. 1750, at times also 7th Bav. Cavalry Brig.

PART III

THE HIGHER
COMMAND AUTHORITIES
AND THEIR DEVELOPMENT

A.

SENIOR COMMAND AUTHORITIES NEWLY-CREATED DURING THE WAR

1. The Supreme Commander East

The creation of the post of Supreme Commander East on 1 November 1914 has already been described in Part II C. The post combined the direction of operations with the administration of occupied territory. This double task was also expressed in the division of responsibilities in the High Command. This had three main groups - General Staff, Administrative Staff and Senior Quartermaster. The Senior Quartermaster was assigned a Chief of Administration, who carried out the administration of the country in accordance with the general guidelines of the Senior Quartermaster. These were approved by the Chief of General Staff O.B. Ost (High Command East). His duties resembled those of the Representative of the Quartermaster-General for the West.[1] This comment must suffice, since the administration of the Supreme Commander East can only be explained in conjunction with the Government-General and Military Administrations.

Of interest here is the military side only of the Senior Quartermaster's area of responsibility, expressed through the posts of Intendant, Chief of the Field Medical Service together with General Delegates of Voluntary Aid, Construction Directorate, Field Post and Secret Field Police. With Hindenburg, from the Staff of the originally autonomous 8th Army, operating alone in the East, had also come, via A.O.K. 9 to the Staff of the Supreme Commander East, the Chief of Field Railways East, the Chief of the Field Munitions Service East and the Chief of Field Telegraphy.

The extension of the posts under the Chief of the General Staff of the Field Army was also reflected in High Command East. It was joined by an Intelligence Officer of the Supreme Army Command on 7 November 1914, a Chief Veterinary Officer[2] on 1 April 1915, a Staff Officer of Air Defence Cannon[3] on 1 October 1915, a Military Police Inspectorate[4] on 30 January 1916, a Field Postal Inspectorate East[5] on 7 February 1916, an Inspector of the Artillery Survey Service on 23 September 1916,[6] a Staff Officer of Motorised Vehicle Troops on 15 December 1916,[7] a Staff Officer from, respectively, the Field and the Foot Artillery on 16 February 1917,[8] as well as a Staff Officer of Pioneers on 24 January 1917.[9] Several of

1 Cf I.A.2.c.
2 War Ministry of 25.3.15 No 1018. 3. 15. A. 3.
3 War Ministry of 16.10.1915 No 3783. 15. G. A. 4.
4 War Ministry of 19.1.1916 No 1075. 16. A. 1. M.I.

the posts which had existed from the beginning expanded the field of their activities quite extraordinarily and were thus correspondingly renamed. Thus, in place of the simple Intelligence Officer of the Supreme Army Command there came on 19 January 1916 a Press Section.[10] To this, a few months later, was affiliated an Audit Office in the interests of providing good reading material for the soldiers' libraries.[11]

The reorganisation of the Field Railway Service changed the post of the Chief of the Field Railway Service East on 13 May 1916 into a Railway Transport Section East.[12] But the Chief of Field Telegraphy East took, with his expanded field of operations, in December 1916, the name General of Telegraph Troops No. 2. His later change of name to General of Signals Troops No.2 took place in the course of the second great reorganisation of his arm of the service.

The limitation of the military powers of the Supreme Commander East came on 5 August 1915. After a year, his combat front had rapidly expanded from the sea in the North to Brody in the South, to be followed soon afterwards as far as the Carpathians. This has already been discussed in Part II C.

Supreme Commander East was Generalfeldmarschall von Hindenburg,[13] who was succeeded as Supreme Commander on 29 August 1916 by Generalfeldmarschall Prince Leopold of Bavaria. Acting as Chief of General Staff was Generalleutnant Ludendorff.[14] From 29 August 1916, there was Colonel Hoffmann, who on 29 October 1917 became Generalmajor Hoffmann.

On 1 November 1914 the Headquarters of the Supreme Commander East were in Czenstochau. From 4 November 1914 it was in Posen, from 4 February 1915 in Insterburg, from 22 February 1915 in Lötzen, from 20 October 1915 in Kovno and from 1 August 1916 in Brest-Litovsk. From there on 2 January 1919 it returned to Königsberg in Prussia, where it was eventually dissolved.

2. Army Group High Commands

a. General

The direction of an army of millions, over a relatively narrow area, was the great problem facing the Supreme Army Command in the Western theatre of war.[15] According to the opinion of one of the most competent experts and participants in a

5   War Ministry of 21.1.1916 M.I. 249. 16. A. 1.
6   War Ministry of 30.8.1916 No 1579. 16. A. 5.
7   War Ministry of 15.12.1916 No 16. 12. 16. A. 5.
8   War Ministry of 16.2.1917 No 445. 2. 17. A. 4.
9   War Ministry of 24.1.17 No 105. 17. A. 6.
10   Established by War Ministry of 24.3.1916, M.I. 5645. A. 1.
11   War Ministry of 25.7.1916 M.I. 15 127. 16. A. 1.
12   War Ministry of 13.5.1916, M.I. 7165. 16. A. 1.
13   Until 26.11.1914 still Generaloberst.
14   Until 26.11.1914 still Generalmajor.
15   The Army of the West consisted of some 1,800,000 men.

decisive position, that of General of Infantry von Kuhl,[16] the problem was not solved.

> Direction was lacking from the highest level. From Koblenz and Luxemburg it was impossible to control the reins. Communication was completely insufficient, an exchange of ideas not possible. Long written orders were overtaken even as they arrived. The Army High Commands were often left to their own devices and were forced to rely on mutual understanding. With what result, is shown by how events turned out. They acted as well as they could see from their standpoint, but not always in harmony with their neighbours and within the framework of the large-scale operational situation.[17]

The temporary measure of putting the Army on the right and left wing under the joint operational command of the Supreme Commander of the adjoining neighbouring Army has already been discussed.[18] But according to Kuhl this only led to friction, because "an Army which is itself involved in fighting finds it difficult to put itself completely in the place of the Army fighting beside it and at the same time take a balanced view of the overall situation. At the time we did not yet know the arrangement of the Army Groups".[19]

After trench warfare set in with its special conditions which made things simpler for the Supreme Command, the Chief of the General Staff of the Field Army at first had no reason to give up the transmission of direct commands to the Armies. But after he had recognised the high value of having reserves that could be rapidly moved, he decided to set up specific reserves for several Armies. To this end, in November 1914, he divided the Army of the West into several groups of a temporary nature. Meanwhile, he placed the High Commands of each group under the joint command of the oldest group commander.[20]

But according to the judgement of the Chief of General Staff this system in itself did not prove viable and was therefore soon abandoned again.[21] Later, in spite of this, much use was made of temporary Army Groups, even after the first established Army Group Command Mackensen had been created.

Between the Army Groups themselves, with regard to their combat value, there were quite considerable differences. While in the West, without exception, they represented the striking force of a various number of Armies, this was not always the case in other theatres of war. Thus Army Group Prince Leopold of Bavaria, and its successor Army Group Woyrsch, could just as well have been designated as Armies. As well as personal reasons, the deciding factor may have been the wide spaces of the East. Even Army Group Mackensen against Rumania was, up to the time it incorporated the 9th Army. In fact, it was really only a camouflage, in pursuit of which General Command 52 under its command was also given the ambitious name "Army of the Danube". However, the Army Group Commands Below and Scholtz in Macedonia, together with, to a greater degree,

16   In August/September 1914 Chief of General Staff of the 1st Army.
17   Von Kuhl, page 261f.
18   In Part II B.
19   Von Kuhl, page 27.
20   Cf Part II B.
21   Von Falkenhayn, page 32.

Army Group Command F in Palestine, are best viewed as German posts of supreme command for the Bulgarians and Turks. Thus the other German support was limited to numerically small but technically very valuable and indispensable forces.[22]

When an Army Group Command was linked to the High Command of an Army it required no special Staff. On the other hand, the established Army Group Command was also in this connection left to itself. Its establishment was specially determined in each individual case. But as a model for the later establishments we may look at the provision of the Staff of Army Group Mackensen, which contains the following posts:[23]

Supreme Commander, Chief of General Staff (Div. Cdr), Senior Quartermaster (Brig. Cdr), 1 Staff Officer of the General Staff (Rgt Cdr), 5 General Staff Officers (2 of these Intelligence Officers), 1 Auxiliary Signals Officer, 2 Adjutants, 7 Orderly Officers, 1 Field Registrar, 78 NCOs and other ranks as clerks, printers and train (service corps) troops, 72 vehicle drivers and escorts for 9 staff baggage wagons, 2 field printing units, 24 motor cars and 12 lorries, Headquarters Commandant with Supply Officer, leaders of the baggage section of the train and commandants of the vehicle park, staff guard and supply column, Intendance, Medical Officer, field post, military police command, Couriers, Secret Field Police.

Concerning this statement of establishment it must however be pointed out that the Army Group Command as a general rule possessed no Senior Quartermaster, since as operational command post between the Supreme Army Command and the Armies it was not called on to become involved in administration. The above example represents an exceptional case, the special circumstances of an Army Group mixed with Allies and extending over foreign lines of communication. Army Group Command Prince Albrecht of Württemberg also had an Senior Quartermaster, because a large part of its command area was on home soil. Dealing with the Governor and the authorities of Alsace-Lorraine required special care and political considerations.

But generally an Senior Quartermaster was only assigned to an Army Group when, at times of very large accumulations of troops, special measures to delimit areas for supply and rapid mutual aid were required.

b. Army Group Hindenburg

An Army Group Hindenburg existed, in the period from 5 August 1915 until 30 July 1916, as a shortened front of the Supreme Commander East. It must be mentioned separately from the other Army Groups because it represents the only instance in which the Army Group Command was neither specifically established nor linked with the High Command of an Army. Rather, it was commanded by the Supreme Commander East. His duties during this period were much more extensive, because he had to administer the district Upper East, in which there were also parts of the lines of communication of the neighbouring Army Group Prince Leopold of Bavaria.[24]

---

22 From September 1916, the German 11th Army in Macedonia no longer possessed any completely German division.

23 War Ministry of 14.10.1915 M.I. 20 540. 15. A. 1.

c. Temporary Army Groups

Apart from the first attempts in France in 1914, and in the Winter of 1914/15, in which the term 'Army Group' had not yet been used, as 'temporary' Army Groups there existed the following:

Army Group Mackensen, from 22 April-8 September 1915, was linked to the High Command of the 11th Army. It was led by Generalfeldmarschall von Mackensen[25], up to the time of the Gorlice-Tarnow breakthrough. The victorious offensive moved through Galicia to Rawa Ruska and, turning northwards into Poland, as far as Biala. As advisor, there stood at the side of the Generalfeldmarschall his Chief of General Staff, Generalmajor von Seeckt.[26] When the 11th Army was dissolved, on 8 September 1915, A.O.K. 11 moved to Hungary to change there into the established Army Group Command Mackensen and to lead the campaign against Serbia. The places in which the headquarters of the 11th Army had been located were Neu Sandec, Jaslo (9 May), Yaroslav (27 May), Rawa Ruska (30 June), Lublin (8 August) and Biala (28 August).

Army Group Linsingen, linked with the High Command of the Army of the Bug, formed the continuation of the above. It came into existence on 8 September 1915 when the Supreme Commander of the Army of the Bug was charged with taking over command of Army Group Mackensen. Only from 20 September 1915 was it designated Army Group 'Linsingen'. General of Infantry von Linsingen ended the offensive in Poland. In 1916 he brought Brusilov's assault to a standstill and in March 1918 led his Army Group deep into Russia as far as Kiev. The Army of the Bug itself, after Linsingen had taken command of the Army Group, only appeared in its lines of communication. Meanwhile the Army itself was split into a number of Army Groups over which the Army Group Command had command. The HQ was located in Jablon. From 15 June 1916 it was in Kowel, from 25 October 1916 in Cholm, and from 21 March 1918 in Kiev. On 31 March 1918 A.O.K. Bug and with it Army Group Linsingen were dissolved. The troops were taken over by the established Army Group Command Eichhorn that had been transferred from Vilna to Kiev.

Army Group Prince Leopold of Bavaria, linked with the High Command of the 9th Army, came into existence after the capture of Warsaw. The Chief of the General Staff of the Field Army, on 5 August 1915, separated the 9th Army that was on the southern wing of the Supreme Commander East and unified it into a new Army Group with Army Detachment Woyrsch. This latter was fighting on the northern wing of the Austro-Hungarian Army. The HQ moved, as the offensive continued, via Siedlce (15 August), Siematycze (23 August), Bialowiez (7 September) to Slonim (22 September 1915), where it remained. When on 29 August 1916 Generalfeldmarschall Prince Leopold of Bavaria was nominated to succeed Hindenburg as Supreme Commander East, his Army had already been dissolved at a month's notice. He handed over the Army Group to the Supreme Commander of Army Detachment Woyrsch.

---

24 Ludendorff, page 119.
25 Until 21.6.1915 still Generaloberst.
26 Until 25.6.1915 still Colonel.

Army Group Eichhorn (Vilna), linked with A.O.K. 10, took the place of the previous Army Group Hindenburg when the Supreme Commander East was entrusted with the command of the expanded German front on 30 July 1916. Generaloberst, from 18 January 1917 Generalfeldmarschall von Eichhorn retained his previous HQ in Vilna. When the War Ministry on 5 March 1918 established Army Group Command Eichhorn[27] and in doing so separated it from Army High Command 10. This was already being done with a view to another use. Because Army Group Eichhorn (Vilna) was shortly afterwards, i.e. on 31 March 1918, dissolved without receiving a similar command post as successor. On the other hand, a winding-up took place at Army High Command 8 during the month of April under the name 'Army Group Riga'. Army Group Command Eichhorn itself went to Kiev in order to take over the area of the previous Army Group Linsingen.

Army Group Gallwitz came into existence during the Battle of the Somme. By dividing the 2nd Army, which was heavily struggling there, new 1st and 2nd Armies were created. The Supreme Command of the latter, together with the joint command of both Armies, was given to General of Artillery von Gallwitz who had been brought from Verdun. This Army Group only existed for a short time, from 19 July-28 August 1916. On the latter date it was taken over into the newly formed established Army Group of Generalfeldmarschall Crown Prince Rupprecht of Bavaria. The HQ had been at St Quentin.

d. Established Army Group Commands

Army Group German Crown Prince. The first permanent Army Group Command in the West was initiated in the Army Group German Crown Prince. It was created on 1 August 1915 as the left wing of the Army by reinforcement of Army High Command 5. But the unhealthy nature of the connection of these two High Command posts showed itself immediately in the battle for Verdun. So it was that the Army Group divided the 5th Army and formed an Attack Group West and Attack Group East. To the command of these, the Supreme Army Command ordered the Supreme Commander of the 11th Army, General of Artillery von Gallwitz, and General of Infantry von Lochow, who had been released from his Corps. After this had been done, to a certain extent as a preparatory measure, the new Army Command decided to complete the separation of the Army Group Commands from the Army High Command. At the end of November 1916 it consolidated the Army Group Command as an autonomous command authority.[28] This remained unchanged until the end of the war, even though in Spring 1917 and again in March 1918 it was moved sharply to the right. From 27 January 1917, the Supreme Commander was Generalleutnant, General of Infantry, Crown Prince Wilhelm. His Chief of General Staff was Generalleutnant Freiherr von Lüttwitz (Walter), who on 30 January 1916 was replaced by Colonel Graf von der Schulenburg (Friedrich).[29] The HQ was in Stenay. From 6 March 1917 it was in Mézières, from 5 November 1918 in Maulsort near Givet, and from 10 January

---

27   War Ministry of 5.3.1918 No 2572. 18. G. A. M.
28   War Ministry of 27.11.1916 M.I. 30 286 .16. A. 1.
29   From 12.6.18 Generalmajor.

1918 in Vielsalm. During the march back to Germany the Army Group bore the designation "B".

Army Group Command Mackensen was set up against Serbia. As already mentioned, in connection with the first Army Group Mackensen, it had been formed by transformation of Army High Command 11 and was in existence from 18 September 1915.[30] The newly assembled 11th Army within the Army Group received a new High Command in the previous A.O.K. 12.[31] Generalfeldmarschall von Mackensen conquered Serbia, advanced as far as the Greek border, and then took up defensive positions in Macedonia against the armed forces landed by the Entente in Saloniki. His HQ was first in Temesvar. From 30 January 1915 it was in Semendria, from 13 November in Kragujevac, from 19 December in Nisch and from 8 February 1916 in Ueskueb. The Chief of General Staff, Generalmajor von Seeckt, left the Army Group in mid-June 1916 to take up the same post with the Supreme Commander of the Austrian K.u.K. Army Group Archduke Karl. Soon afterwards, on 30 July 1916, the Feldmarschall himself went with his Staff to Bulgaria to organise Bulgarian counter-measures in the face of the threatening attitude of Rumania. With this, Army Group Mackensen in Macedonia came to an end. From then on the Armies were under the direct command of the Bulgarian Supreme Army Command.

After Rumania's declaration of war on Austria-Hungary on 27 August 1916, Army Group Command Mackensen, to which a new Chief of General Staff, Generalmajor Tappen, was assigned, united the 3rd Bulgarian Army and German auxiliary troops. At first it was a new, still really weak, Army Group. Despite this, the Generalfeldmarschall succeeded in holding the Danube line and victoriously establishing himself in the Rumanian Dobrudscha. As the advance of the 9th Army launched from Transylvania took effect, he forced a crossing of the Danube. He then advanced with the Army of the Danube on Bucharest, 'joining hands' in the fighting on the Arges with the 9th Army which had been placed under his command from 1 January 1916. On 7 December 1916 the Chief of General Staff changed when Colonel Hell[32] was called to replace Generalmajor Tappen who had been appointed a Divisional Commander.

The further operations, mainly comprising trench warfare, forced Rumania to an armistice in December 1917 and to conclude peace at the beginning of July 1918. There was then no further justification for the existence of the Army Group. After a Military Administration Rumania had been affiliated to it by A.K.D. of 12 January 1917. Both Army Group and Military Administration were dissolved on 1 July 1918 by the creation of the High Command of the Army of Occupation in Rumania. Since this only represented a renaming of the Army Group Command, and the Feldmarschall remained with the Army of Occupation, it was given the abbreviated designation 'O.K. Mackensen'. The HQ moved from Tirnovo on 12 January 1916 to Bucharest, where it remained until 10 January 1918. Then, as a result of the collapse of the Bulgarian front, and Rumania's fresh declaration of war, they had to retreat to Hermannstadt.

30 Established by War Ministry of 16.10.1915, M.I. 21 321. 15. A. 1.
31 While the 12th Army was newly taken by the High Command of the dissolved 1st Army.
32 From 20.5.17 Generalmajor.

Army Group Woyrsch was the successor of the temporary Army Group of Prince Leopold of Bavaria. The Supreme Commander of Army Detachment Woyrsch and from then on also the Supreme Commander of the Army Group named after him, was Generaloberst von Woyrsch. He had previously held the established post of Commanding General of the Landwehr Corps, for which he had, from 13 December 1914, put in place a deputy. From then on three command posts, each senior to the other, were combined in his person! Therefore the Supreme Army Command ordered the establishment of Army Group Command Woyrsch,[33] but determined that the Generaloberst should at the same time command the Army Detachment. In doing so, the unique and exceptional situation was created that an established senior command post was linked with a subordinate non-established one. Acting as Chief of General Staff was Colonel Heye. He had been at the Generaloberst's side since the beginning of the war and remained with the Army Group until Autumn 1917. The HQ was permanently in Slonim. After the armistice in the East, Army Group Woyrsch could be dispensed with. The Supreme Army Command therefore dissolved it, and used its High Command to set up that of the 18th Army.

Army Group Command Crown Prince Rupprecht of Bavaria. On 28 August 1916, during the battle of the Somme, the temporary Army Group Gallwitz incorporated within it the two adjoining Armies. It was established immediately.[34] As Chief of General Staff, Generalleutnant von Kuhl stood at the side of Generalfeldmarschall Crown Prince Rupprecht. The HQ moved from Cambrai to Mons (15 March 1917), to Tournai (24 April 1918), to Mons again (2 September 1918), and finally to Brussels (17 October 1918). These movements reflect the withdrawal of the Front in Spring 1917 and the attack and retreat in 1918. During the march back to Germany, the Army Group bore the designation 'A'.

Army Group Command Below. In Macedonia, after the transfer of Army Group Command Mackensen to the future front against Rumania, the Armies were, from the end of July 1916, under the direct command of the Bulgarian Army Command. But the Supreme Army Command soon gained the impression that a firmer grip had to be taken on the Bulgarian Armies.[35] It therefore agreed to form with Bulgaria a special Army Group under overall German command. Nevertheless, for its part it would still be dependent upon the Bulgarian Supreme Army Command. This Army Group Command Below came into existence out of the previous Army High Command 8, on 11 October 1916.[36] Supreme Commander was General of Infantry von Below (Otto), Chief of General Staff Generalleutnant von Böckmann. The HQ was in Ueskueb. General von Below was called away again, on 21 April 1917, to take over supreme command of the 6th Army in the West.

Army Group Command Scholtz. From then on, the name of the High Command was changed to Army Group Command Scholtz, just as it was taken over on 23 April 1917, by General of Artillery von Scholtz. He was the previous commander of the Army Detachment named after him.[37] The previous Chief of Gen-

33 War Ministry of 20.9.1916, M.I. 21 337. 16. A. 1.
34 War Ministry of 6.9.1916, M.I. 19 896. 16. A. 1.
35 Ludendorff, page 219.
36 War Ministry of 11.10.1916, M.I. 24 310. 16. A. 1. The A.O.K. with the 8th Army was replaced by the A.O.K. of the dissolved 12th Army.

eral Staff remained until he was appointed to be Commanding General, and was replaced, on 15 August 1917, by Lieutenant-Colonel Graf von Schwerin.[38] The German Supreme Commander succeeded in getting the Bulgarian Armies, which were supported by only a few German troops, to hold out until the middle of September 1918. But not even all the Bulgarian divisions could cope any longer with the general attacks of the Entente which were then launched and carried through with enormous technical superiority. The defensive front fragmented and collapsed. At the same time, there were Bulgarian divisions that still fought very well during the retreat. The Army Group retreated from Ueskueb on 24 September 1918 via Leskovac and Nisch (27 September) back to Jagodina (28 September). There it was met with the news that the Bulgarians had ceased fighting as a result of the armistice concluded with the Entente. With this the Army Group was shattered. The High Command therefore on 6 October 1918 placed the command of the German troops from the 1st and 2nd Bulgarian Armies into the hands of A.O.K. 11. As 'High Command Scholtz' they were at the disposal of the High Command of the Army of Occupation in Rumania via Belgrade (8 October), thence to Bucharest (10 October), where the organisation of the Danube defence was assigned to it.

Army Group Command of Generalfeldmarschall Duke Albrecht of Württemberg. The southern wing of the Army of the West in Lorraine and in Alsace with its 3 Army Groups, generally designated as a quiet front, was taken over, on 7 March 1917, by the Army Group Command of Generalfeldmarschall Duke Albrecht of Württemberg[39], with its HQ in Strasburg in Alsace. This Army Group was often used for 'refreshment' of battle-weary divisions and for introducing divisions coming from the East into the combat methods of the Western Front. During the march back to Germany it was given the designation 'D'.

Army Group Command F. A really thankless task fell to the lot of General of Infantry von Falkenhayn, appointed on 27 June 1917 as Supreme Commander of Army Group Command F.[40] He was to lead an Army Group to be assembled from Turkish troops to retake Baghdad. A reconnaissance trip he had already begun at the beginning of May first acquainted him with the difficulties involved in bringing up German support.[41] He says about this:

> The Anatolian railway line that led over the mountains of Asia Minor ended at the nearer foot of the mighty Taurus massif. From there, to the front in Armenia, traffic had to complete its journey on the 700-800km land route that ran through wild and desolate mountain districts. Communications with the fronts in the south-east was indeed eased because individual sections of railway could be used. Thus one railway worked in the Adana plain from the eastern foot of the Taurus to the western slopes of the Amanus. Another bridged the stretch between Aleppo and Jerusalem. A third was under construction from the eastern foot of the Amanus to Aleppo and from there in the direction of the Euphrates.

37   Chief of the General Staff of the Field Army of 22.4.1917. B. 53 439. op.
38   From 22.3.1918 Colonel.
39   War Ministry of 2.3.1917, M.I. 8169. 17. A. 1.
40   War Ministry of 2.7.1917 1046. 6. 17. A. 1. T.
41   German Asia Corps; cf Part II F.

But all these stretches of track suffered the gravest shortages in rolling stock, in materials for construction and heating. There were shortages of workers and also of usable construction material and operational personnel. What the German engineers and German railway troops achieved to overcome these conditions is certainly the greatest achievement which has ever been accomplished in such an area. The construction of the line over the high mountains of the Taurus through the obstacle of the mountains of the Amanus, of the viaduct north-west of Aleppo, of the bridge over the Euphrates, are all great technical achievements of the highest quality.

Army Group Yildirim. The war situation forced General von Falkenhayn, appointed Supreme Commander of Army Group Yildirim,[42] to dispense with the campaign in Iraq and to take in hand the command of the Turkish armies in Palestine. He began actual work in Aleppo on 11 September 1917 and on 5 November 1917 transferred his HQ to Jerusalem. But the unfavourable developments in the fighting in southern Palestine, as early as 14 December, caused the High Command to be withdrawn to Nazareth, where it remained until 20 August 1918. Since General von Falkenhayn and his Chief of General Staff, Colonel von Dommes, could not get used to Oriental unreliability, it was for them a relief from unbearable conditions when, on 1 March 1918, they were able to hand over their duties to General of Cavalry Liman von Sanders, and to Colonel Kiazim Bey. Sanders was the head of the German military mission, and victor of Gallipoli, and he was also familiar with the Turkish way of thinking. Liman von Sanders held the Turkish armies in their positions in central Palestine for another six months. This lasted until the battle that flared up on 19 September 1918 and that shattered the Turkish troops, to the point of dissolution. The retreat of the Army Group is marked by HQs in Damascus (22 September), Baalbek (27 September), Aleppo (6 October), and Adana (23 October). On 30 October 1918 the German Staff left the Turkish army. Liman von Sanders handed over supreme command to Mustapha Kemal Pasha.

Army Group Gallwitz. Even the last year of the war led to the creation of some more new Army Groups. The reinforcement of the Western Front by three Armies, which was necessary in view of the great offensive in France, necessitated in turn a new division of forces. Therefore, on 1 February 1918, Army Group Gallwitz was formed round Verdun. The High Command was at first linked to that of the 5th Army. But as soon as the large-scale fighting had begun in Champagne and on the Maas, steps were taken to establish it.[43] The post of Supreme Commander was held by General of Artillery von Gallwitz. The post of the Chief of General Staff was taken in succession by a Lieutenant-Colonel von Pawelsz, then from 18 April 1918 by Lieutenant-Colonel Keller, and from 5 January 1918 by Generalleutnant von Sauberzweig. The march back to Germany put the Army Group under the designation 'B', whereby General von Gallwitz commanded both Army Groups C and D until 5 December 1918.

---

42   Nildirim = flash of lightning: considering the slowness of all operations on Turkish areas, this was really ironic.
43   War Ministry of 1.10.1918, No 10 563. 18. G. A. M.

Army Group Command Eichhorn established on 5 March 1918,[44] took over on 3 April 1918 the dissolved Army Group Linsingen under the name Army Group Eichhorn-Kiev.[45] The addition 'Kiev' was discontinued on 30 April. But after Generalfeldmarschall von Eichhorn had fallen victim to a Bolshevik assassination attack, on 13 August 1918 it was renamed Army Group Kiev. The Supreme Commander was Generaloberst Graf von Kirchbach. The Chief of General Staff, who had had this post under Eichorn, was Colonel Frotscher. The HQ was in Kiev until 20 January 1919, then in Brest-Litovsk, from where it was moved on 3 February 1919 to Stettin.

Army Group Boehn[46] was the last to appear on 12 August 1918 during the large-scale fighting on the Somme. Its Supreme Commander, Generaloberst von Boehn, set up his HQ in Le Cateau, but on 20 September moved to Avesnes. His Chief of General Staff was Generalmajor von Lossberg, of whom Ludendorff says:[47] "This outstanding officer and combat organiser often helped the Fatherland and the Army." The necessity to withdraw the front of the Army of the West caused Army Group Boehn to disappear again on 8 January 1918.

44   War Ministry of 5.3.1918, No 2572. 18. G. A. M.
45   War Ministry of 3.4.1918, No 3755. 18. G. A. M.
46   War Ministry of 12.8.1918, No 8649. 18. G. A. M.
47   Ludendorff, page 16.

B.

COMMAND AUTHORITIES FROM ARMY HIGH COMMAND TO DIVISION LEVEL

1. General

While the senior command authorities between the Supreme Army Command and the Army High Commands only grew out of the demands of the war, the subordinate command posts existed partly from peacetime, partly as planned since mobilisation. Therefore their command staffs were also put together according to certain similar basic principles. At the side of the Supreme Commander of an Army and the Commanding General of an Army, or Reserve Corps, stood a Chief of General Staff. He had to give advice and to share responsibility. In the Division, which only possessed one General Staff Officer, that task fell to him. To carry it out required, besides strength of character, an extraordinary tactical sense and knowledge of men. The Chief of a General Staff had first to have proved his worth in all his service posts before he was called to this position. In it he had to single-handedly direct everyday activities and issue orders, except those of the most basic kind. This was done in his own name with the addition "On behalf of the Army High Command" or "General Command". If he failed, he was held to account in the same way as his Supreme Commander or Commanding General, but the glory of success attached itself to the Commander whose adviser he was.

Within the Staff under the command of the Chief of General Staff, or the General Staff Officer of the Division, the division of responsibilities was, in the main, the same for all senior command authorities and comprised: General Staff (I.), Adjutantur (Administrative Staff) (II.), Court martial and legal affairs (III.), Intendance and finance service (IV.a.), Medical service (IV.b.), Veterinary service (IV.c.), Military chaplaincy service (IV.d.), Commandant of the Headquarters (or Divisional Staff Quarters) and Orderly Officers, of whom at least one must also be a translator.

During the war nothing changed in this division of responsibilities, apart from the fact that when several adjutants were available usually only one was occupied in the General Staff Section. However, over the course of time many special services were also added.

The Army High Command in particular also had a Senior Quartermaster. At one and the same time he was a representative of the Chief of the General Staff and, in a lesser degree, had the same duties as the Quartermaster-General in the Great Headquarters. He was responsible for the rationing and all the supplies of the Army, and, after discussion with the Chief of the General Staff, he set the guidelines for the Army's Inspector of Lines of Communication.

2. Army High Commands and Coastal Defence High Command

While the Army Group Commands represented an express intermediate command authority, the Army High Command retained the double nature of the Supreme Army Command. Namely, this was the combination of tactical-strategic activities with comprehensive administrative duties. For these latter duties it possessed a Senior Quartermaster. Therefore the area of responsibility assigned to an Army was divided into responsibility for operations and responsibility for lines of communication. The first comprised the actual combat zone and that part of the area behind the lines that in general could no longer be reached by enemy artillery. Certainly, the increase and improvement in air forces soon exposed not only the lines of communication but also parts of the home area to occasional air attacks.

Apart from the posts already mentioned, the Staff of an Army Command had one Staff Officer respectively of the Foot Artillery, of Pioneers, and of Telegraph Troops, a representative of the railway service and a Director of Field Postal Services. For siege purposes, a General of Foot Artillery and a General of Engineers and Pioneers were also usually assigned. During the course of the war trench warfare and a more prominent use of technical weapons, however, were the cause of a considerable increase in the Staff of an Army Command.

Firstly, it proved necessary to set up a Munitions Section that would monitor the Army's munitions situation and keep the Supreme Army Command informed. Secondly, it had to provide intelligence for Section III.B. of the Chief of the General Staff of the Field Army. An Intelligence Officer was attached, under whose command was another officer with special responsibility for the prevention of espionage. Thirdly, in October 1914, there were also added an Arms Collection Officer, who in July 1918 was raised to the rank of Staff Officer for Captured Material and Salvage Services.

In March 1915, was added the Commander of Motorised Vehicle Troops, under whose command hitherto had been the Lines of Communication Inspectorate. Also added was a Staff Officer for Aviation, who in November 1916 became Commander of Aviation (Koflak). In July 1915, was added a Staff Officer for Anti-Aircraft Cannon, replaced from January 1917 by a Commander of Anti-Aircraft Cannon (Koflak). In September 1915, there was added a Survey Section, after the increase of which, during 1917, a Staff Officer for the Survey Service was added. In August 1917, a Staff Officer for the Machine Gun Service (Stomag) was added. In October 1916, a Staff Officer for the Train[1] (Stotrain), was added. In December 1916, a Commander of Munitions Columns and Trains (Akomut) was added to command the columns and trains, previously under the command of the General Command, which from this time on were Army units. A Commander of Telephone Troops, and one of Wireless Troops, were both replaced in September 1917, by a Commander of Signals Troops (Akonach). In January 1917, a Commander, respectively, of Railway Troops (Kodeis) and Electric Power Detachments was added. In February 1917, a General of Artillery, in place of the previous Gen-

---

1   Translator's note: 'Train', which should remain untranslated, corresponds to the British Army Service Corps.

eral of Foot Artillery, was added, together with a second Staff Officer for Artillery. In August 1917, a Staff Officer of Gas Troops (Stogas) and an Education Officer for Patriotic Education were added. In September 1917, a Commander of Airship Troops (Koluft) and the Construction Directorate previously under the Lines of Communication were added. Finally in January 1918, there was added an Inspector of Horses.

With the Armies of August 1914, the assignment of responsibilities to so-called Army Troops was different. That was according to the expected first combat actions and operational goals. Only the 2nd to the 6th Armies were provided with siege artillery. The 1st to 6th Armies were provided with (siege) Pioneer Regiments. The best provided was the 2nd Army with 14 heavy batteries and 2 pioneer regiments, then the 5th and the 6th Armies each with 8 heavy batteries and 2 pioneer regiments. At the same time, with all the Armies, there belonged to the Army Troops one Aviation, one Airship and one Army Telegraph Detachment, as well as a Wireless Command with 2 heavy wireless stations.

Different from the rest was the High Command of the 8th Army. Operating alone in the East, it had at its disposal a cavalry division. In the West, the cavalry divisions belonged to the Cavalry Corps[2] and were directly under the command of the Supreme Army Command. Also to be pointed out are the three airships[3] of the 8th Army and the placing of a Reserve Division under the direct command of High Command 8.

The provision of the Armies with Mixed Landwehr Brigades for lines of communications work maintained its numbers between 1 and 5. A gathering together of such brigades under a 'Senior Landwehr Commander' (later Landwehr Division) took place with the 5th and the Northern Army, which had at their disposal 5 or 4 brigades.

In the meantime, measures that had been prepared for the war of movement, and had proved effective, could no longer remain in force. As the war fundamentally changed its character, it became tied to continuous trench systems. The significance of technical weapons, supported by new discoveries, increased to a quite unexpected degree.

After trench warfare began, the Army High Commands needed forces that could be made available extremely quickly. These were needed to defend against sudden attacks breaking out close at hand, as well as for their own offensive operations. For this it was not sufficient to hold back individual divisions as Army reserves. It was also necessary to have in place the overpowering force of technical means for decisive deployment. But now the unique character of trench warfare, which had degenerated into regular combat activity, flared up with particular intensity into a battle. That meant that the General Commands deployed had to change from time to time, but the Divisions had to change within ever-shorter periods. In this way, the Army High Commands became the places that represented the stable point within the changing of their units. Thus, in conjunction with consideration of the capability of the railways, the formations that were not expressly required to move from one Army to another had to stay within Army areas.

2   In the order of battle designated as Senior Cavalry Commander Nos 1-4.
3   In all other instances the airships were under the command of the Supreme Army Command.

From this there resulted the constantly growing strength of the so-called Army Troops, i.e. those which in the order of battle were not under the command of a General Command or a Division, but under the direct command of the High Command. The division of these Army Troops was carried out, like that of the General Commands and Divisions, by the Supreme Army Command. But the Army Troops by no means remained in the Armies' reserve, but were temporarily placed at the disposal of the combat groups. Also, a High Command did not continue to have the same number of Army Troops, but, according to how the war situation changed, the Supreme Army Command provided them to an Army sometimes in lesser, sometimes in greater strength.

Apart from specific divisions as Army reserve, individual formations of all arms of the service came to be considered for use as Army Troops, particularly the foot artillery and the air forces. Then included were the Assault (Storm) Battalions, Machine Gun Marksman Detachments, Minenwerfer Detachments, Gas Troops and Flamethrowers, to mention the main ones.

The Army Commands[4] were as follows:

A.O.K. 1, set up in Stettin, used in the West. On the advance to the Marne Generaloberst von Kluck was in command with Generalmajor von Kuhl as his Chief of Staff. The HQ was, from 30 September 1914, Folembray, where the Army was dissolved on 17 September 1915, while the A.O.K. went off to the East with No. 12.

A new *A.O.K. 1* was set up, on 19 July 1916, during the Battle of the Somme under General of Infantry von Below (Fritz) with Colonel von Lossberg as Chief of Staff. The HQ was Bourlon, from 12 April 1917 to 8 January 1918 Rethel, and on the march back, finally Neuwied (24 January 1918).

A.O.K. 2, set up in Hanover, used in the West. On the advance to the Marne Generaloberst von Bülow was in command with Generalleutnant von Lauenstein as Chief of Staff. The HQ was from 10 January 1914 to 20 March 1917 in St Quentin, then until 27 March 1918 in Le Cateau. During the battle on the Somme the then Supreme Commander with his Chief of Staff went to the 1st Army, while A.O.K. 2 was taken over by General of Artillery von Gallwitz. During the 1918 offensive, General of Cavalry von der Marwitz was in command. The 2nd Army was dissolved on 13 January 1918 in Gembloux.

A.O.K. 3, set up in Dresden, used in the West. During the advance to the Marne Generaloberst Freiherr von Haufen was in command with Generalmajor von Hoeppner as Chief of Staff. From 12 September 1914 to the end of the war Generaloberst[5] on Einem was Supreme Commander, who during the Autumn battle in Champagne had Colonel von Lossberg as Chief of Staff. The HQ was for a long time in Béthinville (12 September 1914-2 January 1915), Bouziers (3 January 1915-15 January 1917) and Maison Rouge (from 16 January 1917-12 January 1918). On the march back to Germany the A.O.K. reached Wetzlar on 30 January 1918.

A.O.K. 4, set up in Berlin, used in the West. Until the beginning of 1917 it was commanded by Generaloberst Duke Albrecht of Württemberg, initially with Generalleutnant Freiherr von Lüttwitz as Chief of Staff. From 25 February 1917

4   Cf 'Supreme Commanders and their Chiefs of General Staff' in Appendix V.
5   Until 26.1.15 still General of Cavalry.

General of Infantry Sixt von Arnim was Supreme Commander with Generalmajor von Lossberg as Chief of Staff (the latter from 12 June 1917-6 August 1918). The HQ was from 20 January 1914 in Thielt where, interrupted by periods spent in Courtrai and Roubaix, it remained until 21 January 1918, to end the march back to Germany on 28 January 1918 in Münster.

A.O.K. 5, set up in Koblenz, used in the West. First Generalleutnant Crown Prince Wilhelm was in command with Generalleutnant Schmidt von Knobelsdorf as Chief of Staff. From 17 January 1916-22 September 1918 General of Artillery von Gallwitz had supreme command, after him General of Cavalry von der Marwitz. The HQ was from 13 September 1914 in Stenay, then from 4 January 1916 in Montmédy, from where it began the march back home on 2 January 1918 that ended on 30 January 1918 in Bad Nauheim.

A.O.K. 6, set up in Munich, used in the West first in Lorraine, from the second half of September 1914 in northern France. Until 28 August 1918 Generaloberst Crown Prince Rupprecht of Bavaria was in command; during the Spring battle at Arras in 1917 General of Infantry von Below (Otto) took over command until 12 June 1917 with Colonel von Lossberg as Chief of Staff. The HQ was from 8 January 1914 in Lille, from 29 February 1916 in Douai, from 15 March 1917 in Tournai and from 15 April 1918 again in Lille, from where on 1 January 1918 it began its withdrawal, which ended on 29 January 1918 in Iserlohn.

A.O.K. 7, set up in Karlsruhe, used in the West up to 7 September 1914 as left wing of the Army, then in the centre of the Army. Until 28 August 1916 Generaloberst von Heeringen was in command; from the great Aisne-Champagne defensive battle in 1917 Generaloberst von Boehn[6] had command with Colonel Reinhardt as Chief of Staff. The HQ was from 13 September 1914 in Laon, from 14 March 1917 in Marle, to return on 2 June 1918 to Laon and then to change many times. At the end of November 1918 it reached Marburg.

A.O.K. 8, set up in Posen, used in the East. First Generaloberst von Prittwitz und Gaffron was in command, after him from 23 August-18 September 1914 Generaloberst von Hindenburg with Generalmajor Ludendorff as Chief of Staff, and from 7 January 1914 General of Infantry von Below (Otto) with Generalmajor von Böckmann as Chief of Staff. On 26 May 1915, A.O.K. 8 took over command of the German troops in Courland as the Army of the Niemen, while the 8th Army received a deputy High Command in General of Artillery von Schotz (XX A.K. (Army Corps)) and on 29 September 1915 was dissolved. The HQ was for a long time only in Lyck (18 February-12 August 1915).

A new *8th Army* came into existence on 30 January 1915 by renaming the Army of the Niemen, while the old A.O.K. 8 reassumed its original designation.[7] But as early as 4 January 1916 it was transferred to Macedonia as Army Group Command Below. Meanwhile the previous A.O.K. 12 took over command of the 8th Army. The HQ was in Schaulen, from 1 April 1916 in Mitau and from 15 September 1917-31 January 1918 in Riga, from where it arrived from its retreat on 12 January 19 in Königsberg in Prussia.

A.O.K. 9, set up on 19 September 1914 in Breslau,[8] first used against Russia. During the campaign in southern Poland Generaloberst von Hindenburg was in

6   Until 21.3.18 still General of Infantry.
7   Chief of the General Staff of the Field Army of 28.12.15 No 20 690 op.

command with Generalmajor Ludendorff as Chief of Staff, then in northern Poland from 2 January 1914 Generaloberst von Mackensen[9] and from 17 April 1915
Generalfeldmarschall Prince Leopold of Bavaria. The HQ was from 2 January-21
July 1915 in Lodz, from 22 September 1915 in Slonim, where, after the Army was
dissolved, it stayed on until 29 August 1916 as an Army Group Command.

A new *9th Army* was formed on 19 September 1916 in Hungary under the old
A.O.K. 9. Until the end of April 1917 they were under the command of General of
Infantry von Falkenhayn, with Colonel Hesse as Chief of Staff. It threw the Ruma-
nians out of Transylvania and penetrated deep into Rumania itself. From 11 January 1917 it had its HQ in Rimnicul Sarat, where it stayed until it was transported to
the West on 19 June 1918.

The *9th Army* in France went into action on 5 July 1918 and was commanded
by General of Infantry von Eben, from 6 August 1918 by General of Infantry von
Carlowitz. The HQ was Crépy, from 27 August 1918 Marle. On 18 September
1918 the Army was dissolved, while A.O.K. 9 was used to establish Army Group
Command Gallwitz (Verdun).

A.O.K. 10, set up on 26 January 1915 in Cologne,[10] used in the East. It was
commanded by Generaloberst von Eichhorn, at first with Colonel Hell as Chief of
Staff. General of Infantry von Falkenhayn followed as Supreme Commander on 5
March 1918. The HQ was from 6 March-8 August 1915 in Marggrabowa, from
29 September 1915-12 June 1918 in Vilna, then in Minsk, from where it began its
march back home on 6 January 1918.

A.O.K. 11, set up on 9 March 1915 in Kassel.[11] It appeared according to its
original destination in Maubeuge on 16 March 1915, but was then transported to
Galicia and arrived on 22 April 1915 in Neu Sandec. The victorious route of the
Army under Generaloberst von Mackensen[12] with Colonel von Seeckt[13] as Chief of
Staff led to Rawa Ruska and then northwards through Poland as far as Biala. There
the Army was dissolved and its High Command changed into that of Army Group
Mackensen.[14]

On 30 September 1915 a new *11th Army* stood ready on the Serbian border
under the previous A.O.K. of the 12th Army. During the Serbian campaign General of Artillery von Gallwitz was in supreme command with Colonel Marquard as
Chief of Staff. The HQ was for a long time in Beles (from 31 January 1916) and
Prilep (from 5 January 1916-21 September 1918), to begin then the withdrawal
via Jagodina to Szolnok in Hungary, from where on 7 January 1918 it was transported to Allenstein.

A.O.K. 12, in the East. Army Group Gallwitz, whose commander had on 18
March 1915 been awarded the rank of Supreme Commander of an Army, received
on 7 August 1915 the designation 12th Army.[15] It was commanded by General of

8   War Ministry of 20.9.14 M.I. 5809. 14. A. 1.
9   Until 16.12.14 still General of Cavalry.
10   War Ministry of 24.1.15, M.I. 1603. 15. A. 1.
11   War Ministry of 3.3.1915, M.I. 4191. 15. A. 1.
12   From 22.6.15 Generalfeldmarschall.
13   From 26.6.15 Generalmajor.
14   War Ministry of 14.10.15 M.I. 20 540. 15. A. 1.

Artillery von Gallwitz with Colonel Marquard as Chief of Staff. In Grodno on 22 September 1915 the High Command received instructions to take over command of the new 11th Army against Serbia. At the same time as new A.O.K. 12 there arrived, under General of Infantry von Fabeck, the A.O.K. of the 1st Army that had been dissolved in the West. The later dissolution of the 12th Army, whose HQ from 29 September 1915 was Lida, took place on 9 January 1916, while its High Command took over command of the 8th Army.

A.O.K. 14 was set up on 16 September 1917, in Krainburg, against Italy.[16] Its Supreme Commander was General of Infantry von Below (Otto) with Generalleutnant Krafft von Dellmensingen as Chief of Staff. The HQ was located from 10 January 1917 in Vittorio. The Army was dissolved there on 22 January 1918, and its High Command renamed as No. 17.

A.O.K. 17 was formed on 1 February 1918 against France out of the earlier A.O.K. 14. On 12 January 1918 General of Infantry von Mudra succeeded Supreme Commander General of Infantry von Below (Otto). The HQ in St Amend was changed on 6 April to Douai, on 1 May to Denain and on 18 October to Mons and on the march back home reached Zülpich on 19 January 1918.

A.O.K. 18 was formed on 27 December 1917 against France using the dissolved Army Group Command Woyrsch.[17] Supreme Commander was General of Infantry von Hutier, until 20 June 1918 with Generalmajor von Sauberzweig as Chief of Staff. The HQ was located, with some interruptions, until 12 January 1918 in Leschelle (from 9 May–27 August in Auroir) and on the march back to Germany reached Biedenkopf on 2 January 1918.

A.O.K. 19 was formed by renaming the A.O.K. of the dissolved Army of the South on the Western Front. It was commanded by Generaloberst Graf von Bothmer, with Colonel Ritter von Hemmer as Chief of Staff. Its HQ was in St Avold, from where on 15 November it began the march back home which it ended on 24 January 1918 in Maulbronn.

A.O.K. South was formed on 11 January 1915 in Breslau by transformation of General Command II A.K. (Army Corps) for the Hungarian Carpathian front. Its commander was General of Infantry von Linsingen with Generalmajor von Stolzmann as Chief of Staff. The HQ was in Munkacz, from 5 June 1915 in Stryj. There, on 8 July 1915, the A.O.K. was transferred to the newly formed Army of the Bug, while General Command II Bavarian A.K. succeeded as A.O.K. South.[18] From then on, General of Infantry Graf von Bothmer was in command with Lieutenant-Colonel Hemmer as Chief of Staff. The HQ was from 4 September 1915 in Brzezany, from 15 January 1916 in Chodorow, from 4 August 1917 in Czortkow, where on 25 January 1918 the Army was dissolved.

A.O.K. Army of the Niemen was formed on 26 May 1915 from A.O.K. 8 to command the troops in Courland.[19] The HQ was from 27 August 1915 in Schaulen, where on 30 January 1915 the Army was renamed 8th Army.[20] For the

15   War Ministry of 9.8.15, M.I. 16 146. 15. A. 1.
16   War Ministry of 9.9.17, No 4000. 17. G. A. M.
17   War Ministry of 13.12.1917, No 8023. 17. G. A. M.
18   Telegram from the Chief of General Staff of the Field Army of 6.7.15.
19   War Ministry of 30.5.15, M.I. 10 966. 15. A. 1.

Supreme Commander General of Infantry von Below (Otto) and his Chief of Staff Generalmajor von Böckmann this meant a return to their earlier designation.

A.O.K. Army of the Bug was formed on 8 July 1915 by renaming the previous A.O.K. South[21] with HQ in Lemberg. After the commander, General of Infantry von Linsingen, had been appointed on 20 September 1915 to simultaneous command of the Army Group named after him, the Army of the Bug was split into Army Groups that were under the direct command of the Army Group Command. The dissolution of the last of these on 23 January 1918 meant also the end of A.O.K. Army of the Bug.

Generaloberst Freiherr von Falkenhausen was Commander of Coastal Defence High Command. The intensification of the war raised the possibility that there might also be an attack against the German coast, or the European part of Denmark. Generaloberst Freiherr von Falkenhausen, until then commander of the Army Detachment of the same name, was appointed, by A.K.O. of 14 April 1916, as Supreme Commander of Coastal Defence, with his base in Hamburg.[22] It had a Chief of General Staff and, until 5 March 1918, also a Senior Quartermaster. A General of Foot Artillery was assigned until 30 June 1917, a General of Pioneers until 24 January 1917.

The task of the High Command consisted in preparing all measures to maintain the coastal defences in a state of combat readiness and to immediately assemble a defensive army if required. To achieve this, under his command were placed the Deputy General Commands of the Corps areas bordering the sea. Their collaboration in coastal defence was allowed for, as well as the frontier defence against Denmark. Included were all troops designated for coastal defence, and in addition all the coastal fortifications of the land forces within the borders of the Reich and the North Sea islands, except Wangeroog.

A programme of collaboration with the Navy was prepared. Accordingly, the High Command had at its disposal formations of Corps areas I, XVII, II, IX, and X, together with, from September 1916, including Holland, VII and VIII. Temporarily, specialist higher units were also held in readiness. They were such as the Altona and Stettin Divisions, from 1 July-10 January 1916[23], and later the 251st-253rd Infantry Divisions, on home service from 10 January 1917-25 February 1918.[24] During the start of this second period, the formation of Combat Group Commands had been prepared. That was by order of the Supreme Army Command. At the High Command's disposal there were also General Command 65, as Army Group North, from 21 January-21 February 1917 and General Command XXXIX R.K. (Reserve Corps) as Army Group Westphalia.

As a result of cuts in establishment, on 18 September 1918 the post of Supreme Commander was discontinued. On 1 November the High Command was declared as being 'off' active service and on 24 January 1918 it was dissolved.

20 Chief of the General Staff of the Field Army of 28.12.15, No 20 690 op.
21 Chief of the General Staff of the Field Army of 10.7.15 No 3833 r.
22 War Ministry of 24.4.16, M.I. 8278. 16. A. 1.
23 Afterwards 202 and 203 I.D. (Infantry Division) with the Field Army.
24 Afterwards dissolved.

3. Army Detachments and Army Groups

The concepts of Army Detachment and Army Group were not sharply differentiated from each other and often overlapped. Fundamentally one can distinguish between them if one holds to the definition that lies in their names. The Army Detachment represented 'something detached from the Army', so was not under the command of an A.O.K. but itself formed a small army. Therefore, eventually it was also provided with a High Command, as was the case with Army Detachments A–D. The general orders of the Supreme Army Command, and the orders of the War Ministry, applied to the Army Detachments, in the same way as to the Army High Commands. The Army Group, on the other hand, meant a group within an Army, and thus under its command. The classic example of this is the continuing process, from Autumn 1915, of splitting the Army of the Bug into several Army Groups. For the most part the Army Groups were only formed as a temporary measure for particular tactical aims, when a second Group, and in some circumstances a third, would be placed at the disposal of one Army Command.[25]

The Army Detachments were as follows:

Army Detachment A as northern part of the front in Alsace-Lorraine. It was set up on 17 September 1914 from the parts of the 6th Army which had remained behind in Lorraine under the Staff of the dissolved Ersatz Corps (General of Infantry Freiherr von Falkenhausen) as Army Detachment Falkenhausen, and on 15 April 1916 established as Army Detachment A.

Army Detachment B as Vosges front. After the 7th Army had repulsed the French invasion at Mülhausen, it marched via Zabern to the 6th Army and left in Upper Alsace only three Landwehr brigades under the active Deputy General Command XIV A.K. This detachment of troops was on 19 September 1914 named after its commander, General of Infantry Gaede, as Army Group Gaede, on 25 January 1914 changed into Army Detachment Gaede[26] and established on 30 January 1914. On 4 September 1916 the Army Detachment was given the designation B.

Army Detachment C, to a certain extent the left wing of the 5th Army made into an autonomous unit. It was formed on 18 September 1914 under General Command V A.K. as Army Detachment Strantz.[27] General of Infantry von Strantz remained at the same time Commanding General of V A.K., but was deputised for in this post by a Divisional commander. Thus it remained until 2 February 1917, on which date the Army Detachment was established with the designation C. The HQ was, from 15 June 1915-12 September 1918, in Chateau Moncel at Jarny.

Army Detachment D before Dünaburg. It was formed on 8 January 1915 from the southern wing of the Army of the Niemen as Army Detachment Scholtz.[28] It was under the Commanding General of XX A.K., General of Artillery von Scholtz,

---

25 The 'Army Group' should not be confused with the 'Group', of which more will be said under the section concerning the General Commands.

26 Chief of the General Staff of the Field Army of 27.11.14, No 10 259. op.

27 Chief of the General Staff of the Field Army telegram of 15.9.14 and Order of 25.11.14, No 417.

28 O.B. East of 8.10.15, No I b. 13 333.

and established on 13 January 1917 as Army Detachment D.[29] The HQ was in Uzjany, from 28 February 1918 in Dünaburg. It was dissolved on 2 January 1918 as the new General Command XX A.K. was created.

Army Detachment Woyrsch in the East. It was created on 3 January 1914 by the appointment of the Commanding General of the Landwehr Corps, Generaloberst von Woyrsch, as Supreme Commander of Army Detachment Woyrsch. Thus his established command remained the Landwehr Corps, for which he put in place a deputy. In the period from 14 January 1914-4 August 1915 the Army Detachment was under the command of the Austro-Hungarian Army Command. Generaloberst von Woyrsch also had another Austro-Hungarian Army at his disposal, so that at that time they also spoke of an Army Woyrsch. On 20 September 1916 High Command Woyrsch was established as an Army Group Command[30] and dissolved on 15 January 1917.

Army Detachment Lauenstein in Courland, from 22 April-25 May 1915, was under the direct command of Supreme Commander East. Synonymous with General Command XXXIX R.K. (Reserve Corps).

Army Detachment Gronau (= Genkdo (General Command) XXXXI R.K.) from 18 September 1916-27 March 1918, in the east, under H. Group (Army Group) Woyrsch or Linsingen.

Army Detachment Scheffer (= Genkdo XVII R.K.)[31] from 9 January 1916-17 September 1917, as successor to the dissolved 12th Army on the Beresina under H. Group Woyrsch.

Only once was an Army Detachment under the command of an Army High Command. That was the case with *Army Detachment Mackensen* (= Genkdo XVII A.K.) during the battle for Warsaw and the subsequent re-grouping from 8 October 1914 to 2 January 1915. It is true that in this case it involved A.O.K. 9 whose Supreme Commander was at the same time exercising Supreme Command in the East.

The Army Groups, in contrast to the Army Detachments, generally formed particular parts within an Army. Meanwhile there were designated as Army Groups certain command units to which this characteristic does not apply.

There was *Army Group Gallwitz*, which came into existence through the Commanding General of the previous Guard Reserve Corps taking over command on 9 February 1915 of Army Group Graudenz (frontier defence). Its commander, General of Artillery von Gallwitz, was under the direct command of the O.B. East and on 18 March 1915 was even awarded the rank of Supreme Commander of an Army.

From the history of the Army High Commands it is known that, from 7 August 1915, Gallwitz commanded his Army Group as the 12th Army, and that in Autumn 1915 he was called to command the 11th Army to conquer Serbia. But, in Spring 1916, he appears within the 5th Army as commander of Maas Group West-Verdun, to the command of which he was ordered away from his 11th Army from 29 March-16 July 1916. A unique case was an Army commander as subordinate

29   War Ministry of 13.1.17, M.I. 897. 17. A. 1.
30   War Ministry of 20.9.16, M.I. 21 337. 16. A. 1.
31   War Ministry of 11.10.16, M.I. 24 310. 16. A. 1.

commander under the High Command of another Army, even if the command of the latter was joined with an Army Group Command.

It can be seen from this example how the frequent changes in command and General Staff posts were conditioned by the wish to assign particularly suitable personalities to the tasks which were important at the time.

Maas Group East-Verdun also has a distinctive characteristic. It existed within the 5th Army from 16 April-27 September 1916 and like the West Group it also had its own High Command held by the General Command of the III A.K., which was straight away represented by a "Second General Command" in the Corps belonging to another Army.

The two *Army Groups Beseler*, before Antwerp from 27 September 1914 to 10 January 1915, and before Novogeorgievsk from 21 July to 24 August 1915, were commanded by the Commanding General of the III R.K., General of Infantry von Beseler. They were under the direct command of the O.H.L. (Supreme Army Command) or the Supreme Commander East.

The remaining Army Groups that belonged to an Army, and were commanded by one of the Commanding Generals of that Army, represent the norm, but are devoid of military-historical interest. Only those of them will be mentioned which are generally well known because they existed for a long time. These were:

Army Group Gronau (=Genkdo XXXXI R.K.) with the Army of the Bug from 20 September 1915-18 September 1916, then raised to the status of an Army Detachment.

Army Group Marwitz (=Genkdo VI A.K.) with the Army of the Bug and the Austro-Hungarian 4th Army from 15 June 1916-22 August 1917, from 9 January 1916 mostly designated as Sector Luga.

Army Group Litzmann (= Genkdo XXXX R.K.) with Austro-Hungarian Armies and the Army of the Bug from 28 July 1916-28 January 1918, from 10 January 1917 also called Sector Slonim.

Army Group Eben (= Genkdo I A.K.) from 6 August 1916-25 February 1918 with the Austro-Hungarian 2nd Army, from 1 January 1916 mostly designated as Sector Zloczow.

4. General Commands

At the beginning of the war the Army Corps was composed of two infantry divisions, and the Reserve Corps of two reserve divisions. A central position, as it were, was taken by the Guard Reserve Corps that joined an infantry with a reserve division. It was equipped just like an active corps, compared with which it only lacked the Aviation Detachment. Thus the troops of the active corps outside the divisional unit consisted of a battalion of heavy field howitzers, an Aviation Detachment, a Telephone Detachment, the Corps Pontoon Train, a searchlight battalion, 2 munitions column sections, 1 Foot Artillery munitions column section, and 2 Train battalions. Those formations as a whole were designated Corps troops. Of those, the Reserve Corps[32] had merely the telephone detachment, together with 4 sections of munitions columns and Trains, the internal equipment of which was, however,

---

32 Apart from the Guard Reserve Corps which, as mentioned, was almost the same as an active corps.

less. The Landwehr Corps had as Corps troops only 1 munitions column section and some supply columns. The IX Reserve Corps, originally held back on the home front as "Army of the North" had at its disposal as Corps troops, one 10cm cannon battalion,[33] an airship detachment, a pioneer regiment,[34] a telephone detachment, together with 2 sections each of munitions columns and Trains.

To meet the requirements of the war the less comprehensively equipped corps had to be brought as quickly as possible to the status of the active corps. This happened by internal extension. Incidentally, the Supreme Army Command made repeated efforts to return to their original corps divisions and formations. Because of the vicissitudes of war those had temporarily left that command. Also, with the first great new formations during the war, autonomous corps units were created each with 2 divisions. Thus there came into existence, in October 1914, the XXII-XXVII Reserve Corps, and in December 1914, the XXXVIII-XXXXI Reserve Corps. Later this procedure was repeated once more, when in July 1915 the XVII Reserve Corps was formed, but this merely represented the formal establishment of a state of affairs that had existed as a temporary measure since November 1914.

Soon it was recognised that it was difficult to maintain the traditional Corps unit in trench warfare. Viewed from a purely schematic point of view, in places where on one day two divisions were sufficient, the next day twice or three times that strength would become necessary. But there was also another consideration. The particular conditions of trench warfare had to make it desirable to keep the General Command for as long as possible in its sector. Everyone had become accustomed to the peculiarities of which it knew exactly. Meanwhile the divisions, being subjected to a greater degree to the law of wear and tear, necessarily had to be dissolved more frequently, and the change between 'hot-spots' of the fighting and quieter positions became a vital necessity. But with this the breaking-up of the Corps unit became the rule.

At the same time, the division of the Corps into two proved to be impracticable. It forced the Commanding General to create for himself a reserve, by taking forces from his two divisions, thus breaking up their units. This undesirable state of affairs was countered by the device of creating no new General Commands for the divisions that were set up later. Thus, seen from a purely schematic point of view, being in the position to give a third division to each of the existing Corps. In any event, the ratio of available General Commands to the number of divisions, which at the beginning of the war was 41 to 92, rose by the end of 1915 from 52 to 161.[35] But apart from the fact that a schematic allocation of the new divisions was quite out of the question, even in a Corps divided into three it would not have been possible to prevent the corps unit being broken up. With the intensification of the fighting the wear and tear on divisions became more rapid.

Thus the Hindenburg Army Command, at the end of 1916, had no other choice but to change its approach, making the General Commands into definite Combat Group Commands. As circumstances dictated, they were assigned a greater or less number of changing divisions. So then the General Commands, where the fighting was at its most intense, had up to 6 divisions under their com-

---

33   II Btn. 2nd Guard Foot Artillery Regt with 4 batteries.
34   No 31 with 2 battalions, each with 2 companies.
35   Apart from 1 temporary division.

mand! This resulted in the Commanding General having a far greater influence on the combat action than he had had previously. With the discontinuation of the Corps unit, often, but definitely not fundamentally, instead of General Command, the term 'Group', joined with the name of the Commanding General, or particular locality, was used.

Whenever during the further course of the war a new Group command became necessary, a 'General Command for special purposes' (Genkdo z.b.V) was created.

The increase of the General Commands during the war, taking account also of those set up on a temporary basis, was as follows:

Date	Corps	Total
2 August 1914	Guard Corps I – XXI. A.K XII I – III Bavarian A.K. Guard Reserve Corps I, III-X, XIV XVIII Reserve Corps I Bavarian R.K. Landwehr (Ldw) Corps	40
18 August 1914	Ersatz Corps	41
1 September 1914	Corps Eberhardt (from 1 January 1914: XV R.K.)	42
18 September 1914	Dissolution of Ersatz Corps (see Army Detachment A)	41
October 1914	XXII-XXVII R.K. Corps Zastrow (from 21 July 1915: XVII R.K)	48
20 November 1914	Naval Corps	49
January 1915	XXXVIII-XXXXI R.K. II Bavarian R.K.	54
10 January 1915	Change of Genkdo II A.K. into A.O.K. South	53
9 February 1915	Change of Genkdo Guard Res. Corps into H.Gr Gallwitz	52
7 July 1915	Change of Genkdo II Bavarian R.K. into A.O.K. South; but replaced by Corps Marschall (from 18 April 1916: Guard Res. Corps)	52
3 August 1915	Group Mitau (from 20 January 1916 Genkdo z.b.V. 60)	53
18 September 1915	Dissolution of XX A.K. (see Army Detachment D)	52
6 June 1916	Corps Bernhardi (from 1 January 1916: Genkdo z.b.V. 55)	53

September 1916	Genkdo z.b.V. 51-54	57
November 1916	Genkdo z.b.V. 56-59 and 61	62
January 1917	Genkdo z.b.V. 62-65	66
9 May 1917	Genkdo z.b.V. 66	67
17 September 1917	Genkdo z.b.V. 67, but dissolution of XVII R.K.	67
March 1918	Genkdo z.b.V. 68, but dissolution of Genkdo z.b.V. 56	67
12 August 1918	Dissolution of XXIII R.K.	66
October 1918	Re-formation of XX A.K. but dissolution of Genkdo 62	66

Therefore at the end of the war there were 66 General Commands in existence, as against 40 at mobilisation.

Two General Commands for a long time had different names. Those were the IV Reserve Corps which was officially renamed Carpathian Corps, while it was from 24 July 1916-22 January 1917 part of the Austro-Hungarian 7th Army. The XXXVIII R.K., which from 1 April 1915-22 January 1917 was commanded in the Eastern theatre of war as the Beskiden Corps.[36]

Of the temporary named corps, Corps Zastrow, Marschall and Bernhardi, together with Group Mitau, are already included in the above table as predecessors of the XVII R.K., the new Guard Reserve Corps, General Command 55 or General Command 60. Corps Oven existed for only 3 days, from 24-27 August 1914, under the command of the Governor of Fortress Metz. Corps Posen, however, was a unit composed of Landwehr and Landsturm, which was under the command of the Governor of Fortress Posen from 15 January 1914 until 13 June 1915 and was immediately dissolved.

Other units which appeared under the designation 'Corps' were in reality nothing but temporarily reinforced divisions; of these only Corps Thorn should be mentioned, which was also called Corps Dickhuth and in the period from 7 February-20 August 1915 formed the predecessor of the 87th Infantry Division.

The naming of the General Commands after their commanders does not belong to the general history of the Army. On the other hand it must be shown which General Commands were hidden under the names of the Groups designated by place names, particularly since the orders for these Groups almost never referred to the corresponding General Commands:

Aisne, from 17 April-25 June 1917 Guard Corps, 27 June-31 July 1917 XVIII R.K., 26 September-10 January 1918 I R.K.

Argonne, from 18 October-8 January 1916 and from 28 April 1917-15 March 1918 XVI A.K., 15 March-5 January 1918 Genkdo 58.

---

36 It must also be emphasised here that the Alpine Corps was, in spite of its name, a division.

Arras, from 3 April-11 June 1917 IX R.K., 12 June 1917-15 March 1918 XIV R.K.

Aubers, from 19 April-9 May 1917 III Bavarian A.K., 10 May-14 June 1917 I Bavarian R.K., 14 June 1917-8 April 1918 XIX A.K.

Beaumont, from 17 October-11 January 1918 IX R.K.

Bensdorf, from 19 February-25 June 1918 XII R.K., 26 July-5 January 1918 XV A.K.

Brimont, from 10 April-30 January 1917 X R.K., 30 January 1917-29 May 1918 XV A.K.

Busigny, from 23 November 1916-7 January 1917 XXIII R.K., 7 January 1917-20 March 1918 XIV A.K.

Cambrai, from 12 April 1916-6 January 1917 IX A.K., 24 February-20 March 1918 XXXIX R.K.

Caudry, from 12 April 1917-20 March 1918 XIII A.K.

Combres, from 14 March 1917-11 January 1918 V A.K.

Crépy, from 10 April-27 May 1917 XXIII R.K., 27 May-29 August 1917 Genkdo 54, 29 August 1917-27 April 1918 VIII R.K., 27 April-5 June 1918 Genkdo 54.

Czortkow, (Sector), from 13 August 1916-22 January 1917 XXV R.K.

Dixmude, from 11 May-23 August 1917 XIV A.K., 23 August-5 September 1917 Guard Corps, 5 September 1916-13 January 1917 Guard Res. Corps (G.R.K.), 13 October 1916-14 January 1917 XVIII A.K., 14 January 1917-5 April 1918 X R.K.

Dormoise, from 28 April 1917-6 April 1918 XXVI R.K., 6 April-16 May 1918 Genkdo 57.

Ebene, from 17 September 1917-11 January 1918 XIII A.K.

Flanders, from 7 April 1917-11 January 1918 X R.K.

Gorz, from 31 January 1917-17 May 1918 XXXVIII R.K., 18 May 1917-11 January 1918 Genkdo 57.

Hardaumont (Sector), from 18 October 1915-4 January 1916 XII A.K., 4 January 1916-9 March 1917 XIV A.K.

Heiligblasien, from 23 October 1916-10 January 1917 Governor Strasburg, 10-30 January 1917 and 22 January 1917-22 April 1918 XXI A.K., 26 September 1917-19 January 1918 VII A.K.

Herlingen, from 26 September 1917-11 January 1918 XIX A.K.

Houthulst, from 14-21 January 1917 XVIII A.K., 28 September 1917-15 January 1918 G.R.K.

Jablonow (Sector), from 23 October 1916-22 January 1917 XXV R.K., from 23 January 1917-16 January 1918 XXVII R.K.

Kanal, from 12 April-23 May 1917 VI R.K. (with 2nd Army).

Kowel (Sector), from 2 January 1916-17 February 1918 Genkdo 55, 17 February-17 March 1918 XXII R.K.

Lech, from 23 May-25 July 1918 II Bavarian A.K. (with 17th Army).

Lewarde, from 25 January 1917-17 March 1918 XVIII A.K.

Lida (Sector), from 17 September 1916-31 January 1917 Genkdo 67.

Liesse, from 10 April-11 May 1917 Genkdo 54, 11 May 1917-21 January 1918 XXXIX R.K., 2 January-20 March 1918 XXV R.K.

Lille, from 18 April 1917-14 April 1918 II Bav. A.K.

Lipa (Sector), from 7 January 1916-17 February 1918 XXII R.K.

Loos, from 3 April 1917-8 April 1918 IV A.K.

Luga (Sector), from 9 January 1916-22 August 1917 VI A.K.

Maas Group East (from 18 October-30 January 1916 as a continuation of Attack Group East under a special Supreme Commander-Commanding General III A.K.), from 2 July-21 January 1917 V R.K., 21 January 1917 to 6 January 1918 XI A.K., 7 January-12 June 1918 Genkdo 63, 12 June-4 January 1918 V R.K.

Maas Group West, from 18 October 1915-30 January 1916 and 2 July 1917-24 April 1918 VII A.K., 1 May 1917-3 January 1918 XXI A.K.

Mihiel, from 12 March-25 June 1918 I Bavarian A.K., 26 June 1917-9 January 1918 XII R.K.

Mörchingen, from 20 April 1917-31 January 1918 XV R.K., 4 February 1917-11 January 1918 Genkdo 66.

North with 4th Army, from 7 January 1917-27 September 1918 Naval Corps.

North with 1st Army, from 7 January 1916-19 January 1917 I Bavarian R.K., 19 January -15 February 1917 XIV R.K.

Nowogrodek, from 6 September 1916-9 May 1917 Staff of Governor of Grodno as predecessor of Genkdo 68.

Oise, from 12 April 1917-15 March 1918 XVII A.K.

Ornes, from 2 September 1916-21 January 1917 XI A.K., 22 January 1917-11 June 1918 V R.K., 18 August 1917-3 January 1918 Austro-Hungarian XVIII Corps.

Prosnes, from 16-25 April 1917 XIV A.K., 25 April 1917-9 February 1918 III A.K., 10 February-30 May 1918 XXIV R.K.

Py, from 5 January 1916-12 January 1918 XII A.K., 12 October 1917-4 January 1918 XXV R.K.

Quéant, from 19 April-22 May 1917 XIV R.K., 22 May-31 August 1917 G.R.K.

Quentin, from 12 April 1916-8 January 1917 XVIII A.K., 10 January 1917-5 April 1918 IX A.K.

Rheims, from 16 April 1917-30 May 1918 VII R.K.

Rohatyn (Sector), from 1 July-10 August 1917 XXV R.K.

Saarburg, from 29 May 1917-11 January 1918 Genkdo 59.

Schwarzer Berg, from 27 April-27 September 1918 G.R.K. (with 4th Army).

Sierenz, from 10 June-26 August 1917 VIII R.K., 27 August-5 September 1917 X A.K., 10 August 1917-5 January 1918 XXV R.K., 15 October 1917-11 January 1918 XII A.K.

Sissonne, from 9-18 April 1917 XV R.K., 19 April 1917-23 May 1918 Genkdo 65.

Slonim (Sector), from 15 January 1917-28 January 1918 XXXX R.K., 29 January to 1 April 1918 Landwehr (Ldw) Corps.

Souchez, from 3 April-27 May 1917 VIII R.K., 27 May 1917-6 February 1918 VI R.K., 6 February-8 April 1918 XXXX R.K.

Staden, from 13 January 1917-3 April 1918 G.R.K.

Stanislau, from 24 July-6 August 1917 additional designation for Army Group Litzmann (XXXX R.K.) with Austro-Hungarian 3rd Army.

South (the Army of the Niemen), from 26 May-7 July 1915 XXXIX R.K, 8 to 26 July 1915 Senior Cavalry Commander (H.K.K.) 1.

Turna (Sector), from 30 August 1917-13 February 1918 XII R.K.

Vailly, from 10 April-29 August 1917 XI A.K., 29 August 1917-27 April 1918 Genkdo 54, 27 April-19 June 1918 VIII R.K.

Vaux (Sector), 18 January 1916-26 June 1917 XVIII R.K., 26 June 1917 to 7 January 1918 Genkdo 63.

Vervins, from 25 April-6 May 1917 and 3 January-23 February 1918 XXXIX R.K.

Vimy, from 3 April-10 May 1917 I Bav. R.K., 10 May-13 June 1917 III Bav. A.K., 14 June 1917-17 March 1918 I Bav. R.K.

Weiler (from 22 April-26 September 1918 *Weiler-Heiligblasien*), from 2 February 1917-7 January 1918 XV R.K.

Wytschaete, from 7 January-13 June 1917 XIX A.K., 13 June 1916-23 January 1917 IX R.K., 24 November 1916-4 January 1917 XIV A.K., 4 January 1917-7 January 1918 IX R.K., 8 January-27 July 1918 XVIII R.K.

Ypres, from 3 February-1 April 1917 IX R.K., 2 April-14 June 1917 XII R.K., 15 June-9 September 1917 III Bav. A.K., 10 September 1917-14 January 1918 G.K.

Zloczow, from 1 January 1916-25 February 1918 I A.K.

The internal structure of a General Command under its Chief of General Staff presented at the beginning of the war the following picture:

- General Staff Section with I.a. for operations and tactics, I.b. for affairs behind the lines, I.c. for intelligence services, I.d. as assistance for I.a

- Adjutantur (administrative staff) with II.a as adjutants for particulars, II.b as 2 adjutants as personal assistants to the Commanding General, II.c as 2 adjutants for reinforcements and equine affairs

- Section III for field judicial affairs

- Section IV.a as Corps Intendant for supply services with Field Intendance, with finance section and field supply depot

- Section IV.b as Corps Medical Officer with a surgical advisor assigned to him

- Section IV.c as Corps Veterinary Officer

- Commandant of Headquarters with cavalry and infantry staff guard, field police, field post office, 2 orderly officers

- Assigned: Commander of munitions columns, Commander of Trains, Commander of the pioneer battalion and Commander of the Telephone Detachment

The total of the personnel on the establishment in a General Command, besides the field administration authorities, came to: 66 officers and officials, 245 NCOs, other ranks and subordinate officials.

The General Command was first completed by an intelligence officer of the O.H.L. (Supreme Army Command) for the secret intelligence service, a munitions expert, an intelligence officer,[37] an adviser on hygiene and a staff pharmacist.

Then, on 1 May 1915, the administrative separation of the munitions columns and Trains was brought to an end, as the General Command received for both these service posts a 'Komut' (Commander of Munitions Columns and Trains). Incidentally, from the beginning the columns and Trains were never separated but always used in conjunction, while being divided into a combat échelon, a I and II échelon.

Therefore three divisional train échelons were also placed at the disposal of the new Komut. However, these four posts only existed until 23 December 1916,[38] because on that date the munitions columns and trains were removed from the General Command and made into Army troops. When the General Command was then assigned, in February 1918, a new Group divisional train échelon, this only served to support the Army's Commander of Munitions Columns and Trains.

From October 1915, the General Command had a topographical officer, whose post was extended in Spring 1917 into a Group Topographical Section. Incidentally, the designation of service posts as 'Group' posts clearly expresses the change of the General Command into a Combat Group Command.

The posts of Group Telephone Commander and Group Wireless Commander, set up in December 1916, were combined in September 1917 into a Group Signals Commander (Grukonach). As representatives of the air force, there appeared in December 1917 the Group Commander of Aviation (Grufl) with an affiliated photographic post. However, that was later placed under the command of a special Group Photographic Officer, together with, in January 1917, a Group Commander of Anti-Aircraft Cannon (Flakgruko).

As artillery advisers, in February 1917 a Staff Officer, from the field artillery and foot artillery respectively, joined the General Command. Three months later a Staff Officer of Pioneers for technical questions relating to the pioneers and supply

---

37   Translator's note: for reconnaissance, observation, hostile activity &c.
38   War Ministry of 23.12.1916 No 32 970. 16. A. 1.

of stores was added. He was to replace the Commander of the Pioneer Battalion previously assigned to the General Command, who had been removed as a consequence of each division being provided with a Pioneer Battalion Staff.

Posts for a Group Salvage Officer, to supervise the divisional salvage and collection services, and an advisory Machine Gun Officer were set up in mid-1917. With the addition of a Captain of Motorised Vehicle Troops in August 1918, the formation of the General Command structure was completed.

5. Senior Cavalry Commanders

Germany had, as planned, formed 4 cavalry corps for the Army of the West, while the East had at first to be satisfied with one single cavalry division. In contrast to the Army Corps, the Cavalry Corps possessed neither a General Command, nor Corps troops, but only 2 or 3 Divisions. As a result, its commander was also not designated as Commanding General, but as Senior Cavalry Commander (H.K.K.). This expressed the intention that he should be a command authority concerned only with tactics and strategy. This capacity was also particularly clearly expressed by the fact that a Chief of General Staff was assigned to his staff that in itself, was small. With regard to administration and supply the cavalry divisions were autonomous.

The development of the Cavalry Corps was naturally entirely dependent upon the possibilities for using it. They were faced with great tasks in places where wide-open spaces allowed them to develop to the full their particular characteristics. They lost any justification for their existence as soon as trench warfare created uninterrupted fronts closely facing each other.

As early as 9 September 1914 the necessity in the East of countering the Russian masses of cavalry with sufficient German cavalry caused H.K.K. 3 (Army Cavalry Corps 3), to be transported to the East. That was before the front of the 6th Army could have found any significant use for them. With no proper employment they were transported to the East. Soon afterwards the entire Western Front had sunk into trench warfare, so that on 6 November H.K.K. 1 was dispatched to take part in the campaign in northern Poland and H.K.K. 4 was transferred to the East on 14 November. The Supreme Army Command, however, at the end of November 1914, withdrew H.K.K. 2 back to Belgium. There, on 23 January 1914, it was dissolved. That happened shortly after having prepared the same fate for H.K.K. 4, for which, in the meantime, there were no longer any possibilities of its use in the East.

So, at the end of 1914, only H.K.K.s 1 and 3 remained. How little scope was offered for their use, as proper cavalry, is clear from the changing designations under which they were used in the armies of the East. They were either proper cavalry units or mixed troop units. Thus H.K.K. 3 was from 24 September 1913-2 January 1914 designated as Corps Frommel. From 2 January 1914-14 May 1915 it was Cavalry Corps Frommel, from 8 January-1 August 1915 as Army Group Frommel. From 6 August-7 September 1915 it was known as Cavalry Corps Frommel and from 8 September 1914-18 January 1915 as Corps Frommel. In a similar way, H.K.K. 1 changed between Cavalry Corps Richtofen, Corps Richtofen and Group Richtofen.

With the offensive in Courland there developed, between the 10th Army and the Army of the Niemen, a wide open space which grew even larger as the 10th Army advanced. This caused the Army of the Niemen to set up at first, on 3 June 1915, beside H.K.K. 1, which was under its command, a second temporary Cavalry Corps Schmettow. Its commander, Generalleutnant Graf von Schmettow (Egon), was established as H.K.K. 5 on 18 August 1915.[39] On the same day the War Ministry sanctioned the setting up of H.K.K. 6 with the 10th Army. Its cavalry divisions penetrated deep into enemy territory during the battle at Vilna. But with the conclusion of the offensive all four Senior Cavalry Commanders were assigned sectors of the front, and thus took over the activity of any other General Command. Hand in hand with this proceeded the inevitable organisation of their Staffs, according to the establishment of those authorities.

This fact also explains why, for the Rumanian campaign, not one of the existing Senior Cavalry Commanders were brought in. However, in Hungary a temporary Cavalry Corps Schmettow was formed under the command of Generalleutnant Graf von Schmettow (Eberhard). It continued to be used as cavalry up to January 1917.

After the Supreme Army Command had decided to dispense with the Corps unit in its old form and to use the General Commands as Combat Group Commands. In places where it appeared to be necessary to deploy a new Group, it formed "General Commands for special purposes" (Genkdo z.b.V). But the Senior Cavalry Commanders were actually already deployed in this way. It seemed logical, instead of their original designation which had long been no longer appropriate, to give them this new designation. This happened on 20 November 1916 by renaming H.K.K.s 1, 3, 5, and 6 as General Commands for Special Use Nos 56-59. The temporary Cavalry Corps Schmettow, however, was established on 11 January 1917 as Genkdo z.b.V. 65.[40]

6. Infantry Divisions (with Jäger, Reserve, Landwehr, Ersatz, and Naval Divisions together with Senior Construction Staffs)

The organisation of a Divisional Staff can be inferred from the general explanations concerning the division of responsibilities in the Staffs of the higher command authorities. On the establishment of an Infantry Division Command, as well as field administrative authorities, there were the Divisional Commander, 1 Staff Officer of the General Staff, 2 adjutants, 1 orderly officer, 1 commander of transport, 1 commandant of the divisional staff quarters, 1 divisional intendant with 5 intendance and 7 supply depot officials, 2 field judiciary officials, Divisional Medi-

---

39 War Ministry of 18.8.15, M.I. 16 868. 15. A. 1.

40 War Ministry of 20.11.16, M.I. 28 660. 16. A. 1.

41 Translator's note: The word 'Ersatz', when used alone, means 'draft' or 'reinforcement'. When prefixed to the title of a unit, e.g. 'Ersatz-Battalion', it either means 'depot' or 'supplementary unit formed by a depot'. It thus seems best to leave the word untranslated.

cal Officer with assistant, 2 chaplains, 5 field postal officials together with 80 NCOs, other ranks and subordinate officials.

The Staffs of the Reserve Divisions also did not deviate fundamentally from this norm. By contrast, Landwehr and Ersatz Division Staffs that were only formed during the first weeks of the war; at first, in these divisions, had only 'Senior Landwehr (or Ersatz) Commanders' with simplified Staffs.

The General Staff Officer had not only to deal single-handedly with all the General Staff work but, moreover, was also responsible for the whole Staff. It very soon became apparent that it was necessary to relieve him of some responsibilities by appointing a second General Staff Officer. In addition, the number of orderly officers had to be increased, from one to three, in order to provide assistance.[42] A Staff Veterinary Officer and an Intelligence Officer from the Supreme Army Command also joined the divisional Staff. As other assignments, there appeared in July 1915, a Divisional Topograhical Section, from January 1917 the Commander of the Divisional Pioneer Battalion, from September 1917 the Divisional Signals Commander together with Anti-Gas, Training and Salvage Officers, and from February 1918 a divisional train échelon.

After mobilisation was completed the troops of the Infantry Division normally consisted of 12 infantry battalions,[43] 4 machine-gun companies,[44] 3-4 squadrons,[45] 12 field artillery batteries,[46] 1-2 pioneer companies, the divisional pontoon train and 2 medical companies. In addition, in one division of the Corps there was normally added 1 Jäger battalion, with machine-gun company, cycle company, and Jäger motorised vehicle column.[47]

There were only a few departures from this format. The 29th Infantry Division with the Baden XIV Infantry Corps was notable because it was the only division to comprise three infantry brigades (=18 battalions). The Alsatian 31st Infantry Division was also above the normal strength, in that one of its two infantry brigades had three regiments. On the other hand, the 4th Bavarian Infantry Division appears as qualitatively weaker, because as well as its one infantry brigade, its second brigade was only a reserve infantry brigade.

The Reserve Division differed in its composition from the Infantry Division in that not all reserve infantry regiments were equipped with machine-gun companies. Also, there were individual reserve infantry regiments with only two battalions. Principally, however, there was a significantly smaller provision of artillery. Instead of a brigade there was only a reserve field artillery regiment with 6 batteries. The Reserve Cavalry Regiment always numbered only 3 squadrons. Incidentally, the Reserve Divisions without exception only had 1 medical company.

---

42 These were respectively assigned duties as I.a for War Diary and Signals, I.b for Columns and Press Service, and I.c for Replacements and Casualties.

43 i.e. 2 infantry brigades, each with 2 infantry regiments, each with 3 battalions, each with 4 companies.

44 One per infantry regiment.

45 Half-regiment with 3 squadrons or regiment with 4 squadrons.

46 i.e. a field artillery brigade with 2 regiments, each with 2 sections, each with 3 batteries.

47 During the advance the Jäger battalions were almost all ordered to accompany the cavalry divisions.

However, in the Reserve Divisions themselves there were notable deviations from this normal composition. Thus the 1st Guard Reserve Division, with one machine-gun company to each infantry regiment, a field artillery brigade with 12 batteries and with a reinforcement of 2 reserve Jäger battalions, definitely had the character of an active division.

Increased artillery provision was also displayed by the 23rd and 24th Reserve Divisions of the Saxon XII Reserve Corps. Their field artillery regiments possessed three battalions instead of the usual 2, so that these reserve divisions each commanded 9 batteries.

Seven reserve divisions enjoyed a qualitative improvement in infantry, as the 10th, 11th, 14th and 17th Reserve Divisions had received an active brigade in addition to a reserve infantry brigade, and the 25th, 26th and 36th Reserve Divisions each possessed 1 active infantry regiment. By contrast, the 9th and 15th Reserve Divisions, with only 10 or 9 battalions respectively, remained below the normal infantry strength.

A notably good level of provision with machine guns raises the 1st Reserve Division in this connection even above the active divisions. Three of its regiments had marched out with 2 machine gun companies each, so that this division numbered, in total, 7 of them. The 3rd Reserve Division, under the immediate command of the Army High Command, had its own munitions columns and trains.

The Ersatz Division was originally organised in three mixed Ersatz Brigades, whose troops in total reached the strength of 13-15 battalions, 6 M.G. (machine gun) Ersatz battalions, 3 cavalry Ersatz sections, 12 batteries and 2 pioneer companies.

The senior Landwehr commander in the Landwehr Corps finally had at his disposal 12 battalions, without any machine gun formations, 3 or 7 squadrons, 2 field artillery batteries and 1 pioneer company, 1 Landwehr Division pontoon train together with 1 telephone detachment.

Since, in peacetime, Germany had by no means made full use of its universal conscription, there were available, apart from many volunteers flocking to the colours, many men who were untrained but fit for military service. Therefore the War Ministry was, as early as August 1914, in a position to begin the formation of the 45th-54th together with the Bavarian 6th Reserve Division, and to send them to the Field Army. At the end of the year these were followed into the field by the 75th-82nd and the 8th Bavarian Reserve Division. With this, the resources at home were temporarily exhausted. Despite this, however, the need for more divisions continued undiminished.

The Chief of the General Staff of the Field Army commented on this situation:[48]

Temporarily, as a result of the shortage of NCOs and armaments, there was no longer any question of forming new units. Moreover the need, in view of the likely duration of the war which from this point on could be predicted with certainty, to deal sparingly with replacement of men, argued against this. The greatest successes at the front were hopeless if the position at home became untenable due to shortage of labour... The moral and technical superiority of the

48   Falkenhayn, page 36f.

German soldier over the enemy, which was daily becoming more evident, offered a way out. This showed itself to be so great that, on the instigation of the Director of the General War Department, a Colonel von Wrisberg, it was possible to contemplate reducing, by about a quarter, the strength of the combat units, in the divisions, without damaging their performance. The measure was against that of the enemy units in their strength to date. By this means it became possible to form further troop units of trained, armed, properly led troops from those who had been taken from the old units. This method, after the necessary materiel in terms of artillery, machine guns and other war equipment could be procured, worked very successfully.

Added to this were the bitter experiences, not mentioned here, of using Reserve Divisions 43–54. They were at first thrown into the battle as almost pure recruit formations, the great impetus of whose patriotic fervour was not able to counterbalance the lack of training, technical material, and war experience.

From then on, for all these reasons, the Supreme Army Command produced the necessary new divisions mainly by taking troops from already existing divisions. In that process it naturally remained bound to the replacement of personnel and material from Germany that resulted from war casualties. Hand in hand with this there proceeded the extension of the reserve regiments with the technical formations which they still lacked. The war presented the reserve regiments with the same demands as the active divisions. Consequently, new divisions were therefore also fundamentally designated as infantry divisions. Only Bavaria sent one more reserve division[49] into the field, and the one Ersatz Division which had also been created[50] only owed its designation to the fact that it had already been in existence for a long time as a temporary division. In parallel, there proceeded the formation of Landwehr and Landsturm formations that for the most part were fully equipped in technical terms.

The combat troops of the first instalment of reserve divisions, mentioned above, (Nos 43-54 and Bavarian 6) comprised each two reserve infantry brigades, 1 reserve cavalry troop, 1 field artillery regiment with 3 battalions and 1 to 2 pioneer companies. In comparison with most of the reserve divisions, these new divisions, very weak in cavalry, at mobilisation possessed the same complement of infantry. But they had only one additional field artillery battalion, which, however, did not involve any increase in the number of guns, since the new batteries were formed of only 4 guns instead of 6.

The second instalment of reserve divisions (Nos 75-82 and Bavarian 8), in contrast to the first, commanded only 1 brigade of infantry, but with three regiments, and in artillery one field artillery brigade of 2 regiments, each with 2 battalions, each with 3 four-gun batteries.

The later divisions, no longer set up as discrete corps units, were fundamentally equipped with munitions columns and trains.

The infantry divisions of the 'fifties' series (50, 52, 54, 56, and 58), formed in March 1915, displayed the infantry brigade divided into three and one field artil-

49 9th Bavarian Reserve Division from September 1916.
50 5th Ersatz Division, on the establishment June 1916, temporarily designated as Division Basedow since June 1915.

lery brigade. Thus, compared with the active divisions, they had 1 infantry regiment fewer and, as a result of the new basis of the four-gun battery, had only 48 as against 72 field guns. But in addition to this they each had 1 foot artillery battalion with 2 batteries. Two of these divisions were mixed with reserve infantry regiments; thus with the 54th Infantry Division there were two, with the 58th Infantry Division one reserve infantry regiment.

The infantry divisions numbered in the series 101-123[51], also came into existence at the same time in 1915, thus maintaining the infantry brigade divided into three. But they could only each be equipped with one field artillery regiment with 2 battalions and one foot artillery regiment. In these divisions a thorough mix of active and reserve infantry regiments was already beginning to take place. Even the 107th Infantry Division only had reserve infantry regiments.

The equipment of the infantry with machine guns can only be briefly touched on here. By the end of 1915, every infantry regiment and every autonomous battalion at the front had its own machine gun company.

Apart from some divisions created by belated establishment of units that already existed on a temporary basis, the infantry divisions set up later were composed of the infantry brigade divided into three. In each Division, each battalion soon possessed its own machine gun company, 1 squadron, 1 field artillery regiment with 2 battalions, which was increased as soon as possible to 3 battalions, and 1-2 pioneer companies. From the beginning younger divisions already had from the beginning a Minenwerfer company,[52] an artillery commander (Arko),[53] a Pioneer Battalion Staff,[54] and a divisional signals commander.

Gradually all divisions, even the Landwehr and Ersatz divisions, were brought into line with this structure, whether this was by removing from them formations which exceeded the norm or supplementing them with formations they had previously lacked. Assignment of heavy artillery in accordance with orders of battle, as had often happened previously, no longer took place. Heavy artillery was assigned only as each set of circumstances dictated.

In the interest of forming more units, the Hindenburg OHL (Hindenburg Army Command) ordered that, as soon as the equipment of their companies with 3 machine guns each had been carried out, the combat strength of the infantry and Jäger battalions should be lowered to 650 men. That was against the 919 in the existing instructions regarding combat strength. The distinctions between classes of recruits became ever more blurred during the course of the war. In 1918 in the West the only distinction made was between divisions capable of attack, divisions capable of defence in large-scale battles, and those only suitable for trench warfare. The divisions in the East for 1918 can, it is true, not be included in these observations. They had to give up all their younger troops, as well as a large part of their technical formations for the decisive battle in the West.

The divisions in the West at the time of the beginning of the great battle in France were structured as follows:[55]

51   i.e. 101, 103, 105, 107-109, 113, 115, 117, 121 and 123 I.Ds.
52   From Autumn 1916.
53   From the beginning of 1917.
54   From Autumn 1917.

- Infantry Brigade Command with 3 regiments, each with 3 battalions (each with 4 companies, 1 M.G.K. (machine gun company) with 12 M.G., 6 Minenwerfer) together with an assigned machine gun marksman detachment (27 MGs)

- Artillery Commander with 1 artillery regiment with 3 battalions (each with 3 batteries, 6 MGs and light munitions column), together with 1 foot artillery battalion with 2 heavy field howitzer batteries, 1 10cm gun battery, 6 MGs and 3 light munitions columns)

- Pioneer Battalion Staff with 2 pioneer companies and 1 Minenwerfer company)

- Divisional Signals Commander with signals detachment

- Medical company, 2 field hospitals, veterinary hospital, field recruit depot; divisional motorised vehicle column; divisional train échelon with 3 munitions columns, field bakery column and field butchery column

There are still a number of divisions to consider which fell outside the general framework. In the mountains of Macedonia the troops who, according to the order of battle, belonged to the 101st Infantry Division, had to be deployed in locations of the front which were at some distance from each other, for which the previous command structures proved unsatisfactory. Therefore the units of this division were on 12 July 1917 declared to be autonomous, while the Divisional Staff was given the designation 'Div. Kdo z.b.V No 101'. Similar circumstances had already caused Divisional Commands 301 and 302 to be formed in the Vulcan Mountains or in Macedonia, and in September 1917 led to the formation of Division Kdo 303 in Rumania.[56]

On the part of the Navy, on 29 August 1914, assistance had already been lent to the Field Army in the form of a Naval Division. It comprised a naval brigade and a naval artillery brigade[57] as well as a naval field battery, while the units that were lacking were made up from the Land Army. From the end of November 1914, 2 Naval Divisions were in existence, and in June 1917 a third was added. Of these three divisions, the 1st Naval Division continued to keep its division into 2 brigades. It was supplemented by a naval field artillery regiment and a naval pioneer battalion. The 2nd Naval Division took on the brigade divided into three, and similarly developed a naval pioneer battalion. The 3rd Naval Division, however, comprised with its 3 naval infantry regiments the infantry element of the Navy from home. Therefore, supplemented in its other service arms from the Land Army, it was used like any infantry division.

Finally there were also three Jäger Divisions, of which the Alpine Corps, set up on 21 May 1915, was the oldest.[58] At first, it possessed 2 Jäger brigades. One was composed of the Bavarian Leib Infantry Regiment and 1st Jäger Regiment. The

---

55 Details for individual units can be seen in Part IV under the appropriate arms of the service.

56 Div. Kdo 301 was withdrawn to the Western theatre of war and there, on 1.6.18, renamed as 301 I.D.; Div. Kdo 302 was dissolved during the withdrawal from Macedonia; Div. Kdo 303 also bore the designation Landsturm Division 303.

57 Used as infantry!

other consisted of 2 Jäger regiments, 10 mountain MG detachments, 1 squadron, 3 field artillery battalions each with 2 batteries, 1 mountain artillery battalion with 3 batteries, 2 foot artillery batteries, 2 pioneer companies and 4 mountain Minenwerfer detachments.

The 200th Infantry Division, formed on 6 August 1916, joined a Jäger brigade of 3 Jäger regiments, with other formations on the model of the Alpine Corps.

The structure of the German Jäger Division, set up on 14 January 1917, first as a reinforced brigade, did not have the mountain formations of the previous two divisions. What is notable in this division is that command of the infantry lay with the Staff of an Infantry Ersatz Brigade, and that the three Jäger regiments each consisted of a cavalry regimental staff and 3 Jäger battalions.

After the characteristic features of the individual divisional types have been illustrated, details are shown of the divisions available at the beginning of the war, the increase in their numbers up to the end of 1917, and the dissolution of divisions that took place before the end of the war.

On 2 August 1914 there were mobile or newly-formed:

- 1st-3rd Guard Infantry Divisions
- 1st-42nd and Bavarian 1st-6th Infantry Divisions
- 1st, 3rd, 5th-7th, 9th-19th, 21st-26th, 28th, 30th, 33rd, 35th, 36th and Bavarian 1st and 5th Reserve Divisions   (1,2. Gde Res Divs).
- 1st-4th Landwehr Divisions[59]
- Guard Divisions 4th, 8th, 10th, and 19th Ersatz Division together with Bavarian Ersatz Division.

Therefore, on 2 August 1914 there were available: 51 infantry, 31 reserve, 4 Landwehr and 6 Ersatz divisions; total: 92 divisions.

During the course of 1914 were added:

- in August: Landwehr Division Wening, which on 20 September 1914 became 1st Bavarian Landwehr Division, and the Naval Division, which only existed up to 28 January 1914
- in September: 1st and 2nd Naval Divisions
- in October: Division Rekowski, which on 8 January 1914 became 39th Reserve Division, together with 43rd-54th and Bavarian 6th Reserve Divisions
- end of December: 75th-82nd and Bavarian 8th Reserve Division

The increase during 1914 thus amounted to: 23 reserve, 1 Landwehr and 2 naval divisions. To this were added the following temporary divisions: Ldw. Div. Bredow (from 5 September), Ldw. Div. Einem (from 12 October), Ldw. Div. Waldow (from 22 October), Ldw. Div. Königsberg (from 27 October), Div. Breugel (from 3 November), the two divisions of the temporary Corps Posen (from 15 November), Div. Westernhagen (from 15 November), Div. Wernitz (from 19

58   The Alpine Corps was intended to support the Austrians in the Tyrol, although Italy had declared war on 23.5.15 only on Austria-Hungary.
59   At that time still designated as Senior Landwehr Commander Nos 1-4.

November), and Div. Menges (from 29 November), in total therefore 10 temporary divisions.

Accordingly, on 1 January 1915 there were available: 51 infantry, 54 reserve, 5 Landwehr, 6 Ersatz, 2 naval and 10 temporary divisions; in total 128 divisions.

In 1915 were formed:

- In January: 5th Ldw. Div. (L.D. Waldow ceasing), 7th, 8th and 9th together with Bav 6th Ldw. Div.

- In February: 10th Ldw. Div., 11th Ldw. Div. (L.D. Einem ceasing), Corps Dickhuth (division)

- In March: 50th, 52nd, 54th, 56th, 58th, 111th, 113th, 119th, 121st, 123rd Divs, together with Bav. 10th and 11th Infantry Divisions, 15th Ldw. Div.

- In April: 115th and 117th Inf. Div., 12th Ldw. Div.

- In May: 4th Guard Inf. Div., 101st, 103rd, 105th and 108th Inf. Divs, Alpine Corps, [60] 13th Ldw. Div.

- In June: 83rd and 84th Inf. Div. (Div. Wernitz ceasing), 87th Inf. Div. (Corps Dickhuth ceasing), 88th Inf. Div. (Div. Menges ceasing) and 89th Inf. Div. (Div. Westernhagen ceasing)

- In July: 14th Ldw. Div.

- In August: 86th Inf. Div. (Div. Wernitz ceasing), 87th Inf. Div. (Corps Dickhuth ceasing), 88th Inf. Div. (Div. Menges ceasing) and 89th Inf. Div. (Div. Westernhagen ceasing)

- In September: 85th Ldw. Div. (Div. Breugel ceasing)

- In October: 16th Ldw. Div. (L.D. Königsberg ceasing)

- In November: 109th Inf. Div. and 17th Ldw. Div.

- In December: 18th Ldw. Div. (Ldw. Div. Bredow ceasing)

Altogether, therefore, for 1915 there was an addition of 27 infantry, 1 Jäger and 15 Landwehr divisions together with 1 temporary division. Against this all 10 temporary infantry divisions from 1914 ceased to exist. Consequently on 1 January 1916 there were available: 78 infantry, 1 Jäger, 54 reserve, 20 Landwehr, 6 Ersatz, 2 naval and 1 temporary division; in total 162 divisions.

In 1916 the following new units were formed:

- In June: 92nd Inf. Div. (at first temporary Div. Rusche), 183rd, 185th, 187th, 192nd, and 201st Infantry Divisions, 47th Ldw. Div. and 5th Ers. Div. (The latter on Div. Basedow ceasing)

- In July: 91st Inf. Div. (at first temporary Division Clausius), 204th Inf. Div. and Bav. 12th Infantry Division

- In August: 195th, 197th-200th, and 206th-208th Inf. Div. Together with Bav. 14th Infantry Division (of this, the 200th I.D. as Jäger division)

60   The Alpine Corps is to be counted as a Jäger division.

- In September: 211th-218th, 221st-223rd and 301st Infantry Divisions, Bav. 9th Reserve Division, 19th, 20th, and 25th Landwehr Divisions together with the temporary Command North of Group Nowogrodek

- In October: 93rd, 202nd, 203rd, and 224th Infantry Divisions

- In November: 205th, 225th, and 226th Infantry Divisions

- In December: 302nd Infantry Division and Bav. 2nd Landwehr Division

Thus the increase in 1916 totalled: 37 infantry, 1 Jäger, 1 reserve, 5 Landwehr and 1 Ersatz division, together with one temporary division. Against this, the temporary division from 1915 had ceased to exist. Therefore on 1 January 1917 there were available: 115 infantry, 2 Jäger, 55 reserve, 25 Landwehr, 7 Ersatz and 2 naval divisions, together with 1 temporary division; in total 207 divisions.

In 1917 the following new units were formed:

- In January: 5th Guard Infantry Division, 219th, 220th and 255th Infantry Divisions, together with Bavarian 16th Infantry Division, 26th Landwehr Division[61]

- In February: 227th Infantry Division, 21st and 45th Landwehr Divisions

- In March: 231st-242nd Infantry Division and Bavarian 15th Infantry Division, 46th Landwehr Division

- In April: 228th and 243rd Infantry Divisions (the latter against the cessation of 8th Ersatz Division), 22nd, 23rd, 38th, and 44th Landwehr Divisions

- In May: 94th Infantry Division (against the cessation of Command North of Group Nowogrodek), 95th and 96th Infantry Divisions

- In June: 3rd Naval Division

- In September: 303rd Infantry Division and 48th Landwehr Division

- In November: German Jäger Division

In total, therefore, 1917 brought an increase of 25 infantry, 1 Jäger, 9 Landwehr and 1 naval divisions, while 1 Ersatz and 1 temporary division disappeared. Consequently, on 1 January 1918 there were available: 140 infantry, 3 Jäger, 55 reserve, 34 Landwehr, 6 Ersatz and 3 naval divisions; in total 241 divisions.

In 1918 no more new units were formed. On the contrary, because of the recruitment situation and the lack of moral fibre in the troops, steps had to be taken to dissolve entire divisions. The following reductions thus resulted:

- In January by 1 division (Div. Kdo z.b.V. 101, previously 101 I.D.)

- In June by 1 division (9th Bav. Res. Div.)

---

61   Divisions nos 251-253, set up in January 1917 and dissolved in February 1918, are not taken account of here, since they were divisions on home service.

- In August by 9 divisions (109th, 211th, 235th and Bav. 10th Inf. Divs, 6th, 33rd, 46th, 47th Res. Divs together with 10th Ldw. Div.)

- In September by 12 divisions (108th, 183rd, 222nd, 223rd, 225th and 233rd and Bav. 14th Inf. Divs, 43rd, 53rd, 54th, 77th and 78th Res. Divs)

- In October by 5 divisions (197th, 201st and 302nd Inf. Divs, 25th Res. Div and Bav. Ers. Div.)

- Finally at the beginning of November by one more division (202 I.D.)

Thus a total reduction amounting to 29 divisions took place, so that at the end of the war only 212 divisions still existed.

The Staff of the dissolved 6th Reserve Division were to be further used in Macedonia. In the period from 23 September 1917 to 4 January 1918, on the retreat, it formed 'Division Dietrich'. From 11-18 January 1918 it gathered troops under its command at divisional strength; after this, however, it could only be described as the Command of a mixed brigade.

Some of the Staffs of the dissolved divisions found further use as Chief Construction Staffs.[62] As such they were under the direct command of an Army High Command and took over responsibility for directing the consolidation and extension of positions to the rear. Such construction works had been tackled as early as Spring 1917. They included work such as the creation of the Hermann-Stellung (Hermann Line) behind the 6th Army, the Hunding-Stellung behind the 7th Army, the Brunhild-Stellung behind the 3rd Army and the Kriemhild-Stellung behind the 5th Army, line positions which played a part during the fighting withdrawal in Autumn 1918. From then on the released Divisional Staffs were assigned the direction of these works or the creation of further positions to the rear. A Divisional Command deployed in this way as a Chief Construction Staff retained its previous designation, but had smaller strength than before. There remained assigned to it the Artillery Commander, the Staff Officer of Pioneers, the Machine Gun Officer and the Signals Officer. It was assigned a construction section, as construction troops a number of labour battalions were transferred to it.

7. Cavalry Divisions

In peacetime only one cavalry division had existed with the Guard Corps. The other 10 cavalry divisions mobilised on 2 August 1914 were new formations which were formed by each drawing together three active brigades. Their Staffs were weaker than those of the Infantry Division. Being assigned to no definite Corps unit[63] and therefore administratively autonomous, from the beginning they had two General Staff Officers. Apart from at the beginning, the activity of these divisions as proper cavalry was only possible in the offensive in Courland and on Vilna in 1915. They were needed for a short time in Rumania and in the 1918 support of

---

62　Staffs of the 108, 109, 183, 197, 222, 223 and 225 I.D., and Staffs of the 43 and 47 R.D.

63　The Senior Cavalry Commanders which commanded them were only tactical posts and did not possess the administrative apparatus of the General Commands.

the Ukraine. For the rest of the time the cavalry divisions were mostly used as infantry.

The increasing shortage of horses led in October 1916, for the first time, to the 4th, 5th and 9th Cavalry Divisions being converted into dismounted units and afterwards to the 3rd Cavalry Division being dissolved. In November 1917 the War Ministry, with the curt order "the 6th and 7th Cavalry Divisions will dismount", removed their mounts from these divisions too, and converted their regiments to infantry under the designation Cavalry 'Schützen' Regiments.[64] The same fate was suffered in March 1918 by the Guard Cavalry Division, so that, after the corresponding name had also been introduced for the Divisional Command, there were from May 1918 three Cavalry 'Schützen' Divisions. In the meantime, however, in the first months of 1918 the 5th, 8th, and 9th Cavalry Divisions had been dissolved.

Consequently, from May 1918 only the Bavarian 1st, 2nd and 4th Cavalry Divisions still kept their old names. Meanwhile, even the activity of the latter division, as already indicated, was mostly that of Cavalry 'Schützen', Moreover, from mid 1918, the 4th Cavalry Division was, in its structure, a pure Landwehr division. Thus, towards the end of the war there were 3 cavalry divisions in the East, 3 cavalry 'Schützen' divisions in the West, as well as, in the West, 1 cavalry division Staff with Landwehr troops.

The history of the individual cavalry divisions ran as follows:

Guard Cavalry Division on the Western Front until 4 January 1914, then until 30 June 1915 frontier guard duties against Holland, then in Russia, from 16 March-9 April 1918 re-formation and training on the Zossen troop training ground, afterwards as Guard Cavalry 'Schützen' Division[65] on the Western Front.

Bavarian Cavalry Division on the Western Front until 24 January 1914, then occupation duties in Belgium until 19 January 1915, then training, from 2 April 1915 in Russia, from 16 January 1917 in Rumania, from 1 April 1918 in the Ukraine. It is notable that during the period from 25 November 1917-21 March 1918 this division was without cavalry and from 20 April 1918 onwards, beside other formations, only had 2 cavalry brigades.

1st Cavalry Division for a long time on the Eastern Front (from 6 January 1915-22 August 1917 coastal defence duties in northern Courland), finally in the Ukraine (until 29 January 1919). From 16 January 1918 it numbered only 1 brigade with 3 regiments.

2nd Cavalry Division until 12 January 1914 on the Western Front, then in Russia, from 25 November 1915-31 January 1916 in Rumania, afterwards again in the West, in fact from 26 February-10 September 1917 as frontier guard on the Dutch border, then again in Russia, finally in the Ukraine, but here only 2 cavalry brigades strong.

3rd Cavalry Division until 4 January 1914 on the Western Front, then occupation duties in Belgium, from 6 April 1915 in Russia. Dissolved there on 1 September 1916, on 9 September 1916 re-formed in Hungary and after that in Transylvania. Finally dissolved on 2 January 1916.

---

64   War Ministry of 14.11.1917 No 1210 10. 17. A. 3. G. Translator's note: 'Schützen' regiment is not translated, but corresponds approximately to British 'Rifles'.
65   War Ministry of 8.5.1918 No 4547. G. A. M.

4th Cavalry Division on the Western Front until 5 January 1914, then until 31 March 1918 in Russia and after that again in the West. From October 1916 dismounted. Apart from the other formations, from 6 April 1918 the 4th Cavalry Division consisted mainly of cavalry 'Schützen' regiments, but from 15 June 1918 consisted of the Staff of the 39th Cavalry Brigade with 3 Landwehr Regiments and 3 assigned Cavalry "Schützen" Regiments, of which up to 14 September 1918 all but one disappeared. From that time onwards the 4th Cavalry Division could be counted as a Landwehr division.

5th Cavalry Division on the Western Front until 27 January 1914, then on the Eastern Front, from 14 July-1 September 1915 designated as Cavalry Corps Hendebreck, from October 1916 dismounted, dissolved on 27 February 1918.

6th Cavalry Division in the Western theatre of war until 29 January 1914, afterwards in Russia, dissolved there on 14 January 1916, on 20 January 1916 re-formed in Hungary and then until 10 February 1917 in Rumania. After that again in France and on 5 May 1918 re-grouped to form the 6th Cavalry 'Schützen' Division.[66]

7th Cavalry Division on the Western Front until 27 January 1915, then until 10 January 1916 occupation duties in Belgium, after that in Transylvania and Rumania until 22 January 1917, then again in the West and on 14 May 1918 re-grouped to form the 7th Cavalry 'Schützen' Division.[67]

8th Cavalry Division on the Western Front until 30 August 1914, then in the East, from 1917 dismounted, and dissolved on 9 April 1918.

9th Cavalry Division on the Western Front until 31 January 1914, after that in Russia, from October 1916 dismounted, and dissolved on 3 March 1918.

Apart from these units on the establishment, mention need only be made of *Cavalry Division North*. It was assembled on 1 September 1917 under the command of the commander of the 8th Cavalry Division who had been ordered away from that division. It was in existence during the battle for Riga and the subsequent operations (1 September 1916-22 January 1917). Other names of cavalry divisions that appear are without exception only cover names for temporarily autonomous, reinforced cavalry brigades, such as 'Cavalry Division A' for the reinforced 45th Cavalry Brigade from 19 November 1916 to 1 February 1917.

---

66 War Ministry of 6.5.18 No 18, g. A. M.
67 War Ministry of 27.5.18 No 5476. 18. G. A. M.

PART IV

THE HISTORY OF THE FIELD ARMY IN ITS INDIVIDUAL SERVICE ARMS

A.

THE INFANTRY

1. The Brigade

The Infantry Brigade, even that of the Reserve, Landwehr, etc., comprised two regiments. Its Staff, in peacetime, were employed in supervising the regiments under its command. As a senior recruiting authority, in wartime, it was restricted to directing combat operations. It was disliked in the regiments insofar as the assembly of a brigade reserve always involved the breaking up of a regimental unit. Therefore, in trench warfare, individual battalions of divisions that had been held in reserve, or Landwehr and Landsturm formations, were often assigned for a limited period. With the transition to the division of only 3 infantry regiments, for the fourth regiment one of the two brigade Staffs had to be dispensed with. The remaining Staff became the command authority for 3 regiments. Based on the model of the divisional artillery commander, the infantry brigade commander, from then on, was in many cases often designated as Infanterieführer (infantry leader or commander).

The brigade Staffs, thus released, were either dissolved or used to form new divisional Staffs. They had to equip new brigades and in rare cases even a new regiment. At this point it is sufficient to indicate that often brigade Staffs were renamed. As a result it became considerably more difficult to keep track of them. Thus, in the 1st Bavarian Reserve Division, from 2 August 1914-5 April 1915, there were the 1st and 2nd Bavarian Reserve Infantry Brigades. On 6 April 1915 the 1st Bavarian Reserve Infantry Brigade was discontinued. It was to be used in the formation of the Bavarian 11th Infantry Division. The former 2nd was renamed as 1st Bavarian Reserve Infantry Brigade

This new 1st Bavarian Reserve Infantry Brigade existed until 1 August 1916 when it was replaced by a Brigade Samhaber, that originally had been called 11th Bavarian Reserve Infantry Brigade. It now took on its third designation, as 1st Bavarian Reserve Infantry Brigade. It even happened that numbers were swapped around between mixed Landwehr brigades. Thus on 1 April 1915 the (Württemberg) 51st Landwehr Brigade became the (Prussian) 55th Landwehr Brigade, while the former (Prussian) 55th Landwehr Brigade was renamed as the (Württemberg) 51st Landwehr Brigade. Later, temporary brigades that were put on the establishment received a number, in place of the commander's name.

The appearance of autonomous brigades was not unusual. They could be divided into three distinct groups: those that continued to be autonomous, those that were originally autonomous, and those that were temporarily autonomous. The latter were, for a longer or shorter period, outside the divisional unit from which they had originated, but then returned to it. They are of no interest for the history of the Army. It is different in the case of the first two groups named above. In many instances their brigades took on the position of divisions.

Of brigades that continued to be autonomous there were:

29th Landwehr Brigade, from the beginning of the war. It grew, through troops being assigned to it, to such a strength, that in the period from 1 June 1914-20 January 1915 it was designated as a division or rather Troop Detachment Wyneken.[1] From 19 January 1917 it comprised, according to the order of battle, 2 Ldw. Inf. Regiments, 1 squadron, 1 field artillery regiment, 1 pioneer company and 1 Minenwerfer company.

31st Landwehr Brigade, from the beginning of the war. Until 12 February 1917 it formed Advanced Sector IV, then Advanced Sector III of the combat sector of the fortress of Metz. Besides assignments from the fortress, in 1918 it possessed 2 Ldw. Inf. Regiments, 1 squadron, 1 artillery commander, 1 field artillery regiment, 2 pioneer companies and 1 divisional signals commander.

61st Landwehr Brigade, formed on mobilisation as the (Württemberg) 52nd Landwehr Brigade. It was used from 22 August 1913-1 January 1914 as Detachment, or rather Division Ferling.[2] On 1 January 1914 it changed into a Prussian brigade[3] and on 28 March 1915 was renamed as 61st Landwehr Brigade. It continued to be reinforced by formations from other arms of the service.

84th Landwehr Brigade, formed as acting 84th Inf. Brig., from 13 September 1914 it was used as a mobile unit, Brigade Neuber. On 1 January 1914 it was put on the establishment as 84th Landwehr Brigade. It was first designated as Donon Brigade, from 15 April 1915 as Sector Plaine and from 16 April 1918 as Sector Mailly. It continued to be reinforced by troops from all arms of the service.

2nd Infantry Cycle Brigade, from 1 August 1916. Formed by the assembly of at first 3, from 22 May 1917, 5 and more cycle battalions. From 8 January 1918 it numbered two cycle regiments each with 3 battalions, a field artillery regiment and a divisional signals commander.

Of the brigades that were only autonomous at the beginning, the following should be mentioned:[4]

1st Bavarian Landwehr Brigade, from 2 August 1914-3 April 1915, afterwards part of the 6th Bav. Ldw. Division. From 26 August-30 September 1914 it formed Ldw. Div. Eichhorn.

1st Reserve Ersatz Brigade, from 19 September 1914-28 September 1916, then part of the 221st Inf. Division. From 19 August-28 September 1916 it formed the Argonne Division.

11th Landwehr Brigade, from 2 August 1914-18 February 1917, then part of the 21st Ldw. Division.

21st Landwehr Brigade, from 2 August 1914-17 February 1915, afterwards in Corps Dickhuth.[5] From 10-21 September 1914 it formed Frontier Guard Division Gabriel and from 13-28 January 1914 Division Wrochem.

1   Generalleutnant Wyneken, commander from 19.3.15 to 3.11.17.
2   Generalleutnant Ferling, commander.
3   In its place the (Prussian) 57 Ldw. Brigade which was part of the (Württemberg) 7 Ldw. Division was on 1.4.15 renamed as the (Württemberg) 52 Ldw. Brig.
4   For the other brigades which were autonomous at the beginning-210 I.Brig., 3 Bav and 60 Res. Inf. Brig., 2, 6, 9, 10, 13, 14, 25, 26, 27, 37, 38, 41, 42, 43, 44, 45, 49, 60 and 70 Ldw. Brig., 2 and 5 Bav. L.Brig., 55 Ers. Brig., 1 L.E. Brig., 2 R.E. Brig and 1 Landsturm Brig.-see list of brigades in Appendix III.

47th Landwehr Brigade, from 2 August 1914-7 June 1916, then part of 47th Ldw. Division. From 10 May 1915, as a reinforced brigade, it formed the predecessor of that division.

51st Landwehr Brigade. Formed on 2 August 1914 as a Württemberg formation, it fought under the designation Detachment Frech. It changed on 1 April 1915 into the (Prussian) 55th Ldw. Brigade and on 17 April 1915 joined the 12th Ldw. Division.

55th Landwehr Brigade. Formed on 2 August 1914 as a Prussian formation and used as Brigade Mathy. On 27 January 1915 it joined the 7th Ldw. Division, where on 1 April 1915 it was renamed as the (Württemberg) 51st Ldw. Brigade.

56th Landwehr Brigade. Its Staff had been set up on 2 August 1914 as the Command of the Upper Rhine fortifications. From 13 August 1914 it formed Brigade Bodungen. This brigade was put on the establishment on 1 January 1914 as the 56th Landwehr Brigade and on 25 January 1915 joined the 8th Landwehr Division.

61st Reserve Infantry Brigade. Formed on 28 August 1914 as Brigade Ipfelkofer, put on the establishment on 8 January 1914 as 61st Res. Inf. Brig. On 17 May 1915 it joined the 13th Ldw. Division.

183rd, 185th, 187th and 192nd Infantry Brigades. Coming into existence in mid-1915, these formed the predecessors of the Inf. Divisions of the same number. In July 1916 they were finally renamed accordingly.

In this list there is a whole series of 'Landwehr Brigades'. This designation already indicates that they, in contrast to the 'Landwehr Infantry Brigades', represented troop units in which there were other Landwehr formations besides infantry. Therefore these divisions were at the beginning also designated as 'mixed Landwehr Brigades'.

2. Infantry Regiment - also Reserve, Landwehr, Ersatz, and Landsturm Infantry Regiments; Field Recruit Depots

The infantry regiment of 2 August 1914 consisted of the regimental Staff, 3 battalions and a machine gun company. The latter was lacking in about a third of the Reserve Infantry Divisions,[6] and in all the Landwehr Infantry Regiments. By contrast, the brigade Ersatz battalions of the Ersatz divisions, at the beginning not formed into regiments, possessed individual machine gun detachments, which together made up about half the total number of battalions.

Some reserve regiments and one Landwehr infantry regiment had at first only 2 battalions.[7] By contrast, Reserve Infantry Regiment 130, with 4 battalions, the Infantry Training Regiment and also Res. Inf. Regiments 1, 3, and 18, each with 2 machine gun companies, exceeded their strength.

5   Later 87 Inf. Div.
6   Without MGK (machine gun company) were: R.I.R. 17, 26, 28, 32, 36, 40, 65, 71, 76, 81, 84, 87, 90, 102, 118, 133, together with Bav. 7, 12, and 13.
7   The following had only 2 battalions: R.I.R. 17, 23, 30, 51, 55, 57, 60, 69, and 94, together with Bav. 11 and L.I.R. 4.

Since the operation of machine guns during the war was not restricted to the infantry regiment, its development is to be dealt with separately. It will only be considered here to the extent necessary to give the correct picture of the combat strength of an infantry regiment.

A regimental Staff comprised 4 officers (commander, adjutant, medical officer, train transport commander), 49 NCOs and other ranks (including 37 regimental musicians), 16 horses, 1 entrenching tool wagon and 1 baggage wagon.

The establishment of an infantry battalion comprised the battalion commander, 4 company commanders, 18 lieutenants (including adjutant and supply officer), the battalion medical officer and assistant medical officer, the paymaster, 1,054 NCOs and men - including 30 Train troops - 58 horses and 19 vehicles. Of the latter, the 4 ammunition wagons, the medical wagon and the 4 field kitchens were in the first line transport, the rest, i.e. 5 baggage wagons and 5 supply wagons, were in the train transport.

This establishment was also essentially the same for the Reserve, Landwehr and mobile Ersatz battalions. However, it is true it should be noted that, at the beginning, many of them lacked the field kitchens, a shortfall which was, however, made up as quickly as the lack of a machine gun company, mentioned above.

In general, the battalion strength, even if the casualties from time to time caused considerable reductions in strength, could be maintained intact up to the end of 1916. Thereafter there took place the reduction of the battalions equipped with 3 light machine guns to a combat strength of 650 men, as mentioned above in discussing the divisions. Finally, however, the difficulties in recruitment compelled the Supreme Army Command to issue the order of 18 August 1918. Those divisions whose average battalion combat strength[8] amounted to fewer than 650 men would have to divide their battalions into only 3 companies. This measure had to be implemented in most of the divisions of the Army of the West.

During the course of the war, as far as organisation and armament were concerned, the infantry (Reserve, Landwehr, Ersatz) regiments were further developed to a quite considerable extent. Naturally, such changes were fundamentally first carried out in the Western theatre of war, where they continually faced an enemy more than amply equipped with technical means. In the East it was still often necessary to 'shift for oneself'. From time to time they would even exchange better for something less good, in order to strengthen the Army of the West. In view of these circumstances, and because the innovations could not become effective at the same time for all regiments, the developments in organisation and weapons will be illustrated in the example of a regiment of a division in the West, that also once fought in the East Galician campaign 1915.

For this regiment, developments were as follows:

11 December 1914	Equipped for the first time with hand grenades
4 January 1915	Equipment with individual telescopic sights
1 February 1915	Equipped with rifle grenades

8   A distinction was made between 'supply strength', which comprised all those who belonged to the battalion, and 'combat strength', i.e. those men used with weapons in the fighting line, thus excluding clerks, transport troops, the sick, etc.

9 March 1915	Exchange of 98 Rifle for captured Russian rifles
25 April 1915	Introduction of protective shield for machine guns
29 April 1915	Equipment with battalion entrenching tool wagons
5 June 1915	Rearmament with 88/05 Rifle
15 August 1915	Introduction of the short bayonet in place of the officer's sword
14 December 1915	Equipped with gas masks
1 January 1916	Equipped with 98 Rifle
1 February 1916	Divisional field recruit depot set up
5 August 1916	Increase of strength of MGK to 15 machine guns
15 August 1916	Equipped with steel helmets
26 September 1916	Machine gun company (MGK) set up in each battalion by splitting up the former MGK. (Each MGK at first with 6 heavy machine guns, whose number increased to 12 by the Autumn). Enlargement of the regimental Staff by the addition of a Staff Machine Gun Officer
15 February 1917	Assignment of 24 Granatwerfer[9] (they were deployed by the regiment into 3 detachments each with 2 batteries each with 4 Granatwerfer). Discontinuation of rifle grenades
28 February 1917	Equipped with 12 light Minenwerfer (for each battalion 1 detachment of 4 Minenwerfer)
18 April 1917	Assignment of 4 light machine guns for training
24 April 1917	Equipped with 3 telescopic sights per company
6 May 1917	Each company equipped with 2 light machine guns
28 August 1917	Granatwerfer detachments dissolved, 2 Granatwerfer assigned to each company.
1 September 1917	Increase in the number of light machine guns to 4 per company
20 December 1917	Formation of a regimental signals section
1 February 1918	Increase in the number of light machine guns to 6 per company; two field wagons to carry these 6 LMGs, plus ammunition
15 March 1918	Division of the regimental signals section into 4 signals detachments, of which one joined the regimental Staff and the others, respectively, joined the Staff of each battalion

9   Translator's note: Granatwerfer or the earlier Granatenwerfer is a 'stick' bomb-thrower, but the term is usually not translated.

| 4 September 1918 | Discontinuation of the battalion Minenwerfer detachments: regimental Minenwerfer Company set up |
| 21 October 1918 | Formation of the battalions into 3 companies |

After these changes, the appearance of the regiment was as follows: Regimental Staff with Machine Gun Officer and Signals Detachment, 3 battalion Staffs, each with a signals detachment, 9 companies each with 6 light machine guns and 2 Granatwerfer, 3 machine gun companies each with 12 heavy machine guns, a Minenwerfer company (3 medium and 9 light Minenwerfer).

The increase in the numbers of infantry regiments can be seen from the list of mobile troops in Appendix IV. Here, it suffices to know that those regiments that to begin with had only 2 battalions, were all supplemented up to 3 battalions during the course of the war. Provision of other equipment was regularised, in which process, in fact, the divisions in the East in 1918 must be disregarded, since basically they only had to carry out policing duties.

If one wishes to compare the number of regiments at the beginning of the war with the highest number they reached later, the latter can only be ascertained from the position in Spring 1918. Later, because of the difficult recruitment situation, 58 regiments were dissolved before the end of the war.[10] With this proviso, it can be seen that the total number of mobile regiments (excluding Jägers and Landsturm) had risen from 406[11] to 700.[12] In actual fact it is true that far more regiments were formed during the course of the war than is shown by the difference between these two figures. In the meantime, such regiments merged into regiments that were set up later. Thus the Posen Occupation Infantry Regiments merged into Infantry Regiments 329-336. The Landwehr Ersatz Infantry Regiments merged into Infantry Regiments 351-354 and into five Landwehr Infantry Regiments. Lastly, some of the Ersatz Infantry Regiments merged into the 6th and 7th Guard Infantry Regiments, as well as into Infantry Regiments 376-378. That was tangible evidence that the original clear distinction accorded to active status, Reserve, Landwehr etc. had become completely blurred.

The brigade Ersatz battalions formed at the beginning of the war were assembled into Ersatz infantry regiments. In the same way, the 'field battalions' set up in Germany, and intended as IV battalions, also disappeared through the creation of the regiments for the 75th-82nd Reserve Divisions. The IV battalions set up by some regiments as a result of the good recruitment situation had just as short a life. In 1918 the only autonomous infantry battalions were the special formations for Turkey, with the numbers 701-703. However, these were something quite differ-

10 Prematurely dissolved: I.R. 193, 332, 334, 342, 361, 364, 372, 377, 378, 389, 390, 397, 418, 419, 427, 432, 454, 455, 456; R.I.R. 11, 20, 24, 32, 34, 67, 75, 81, 116, 130, 215, 216, 218, 220, 233, 243, 246-248, 257-260,; Bav. R.I.R. 4-6, 8, 11, 13-15, 18, 21; L.I.R. 9 and 110; Ers. I.R. 29; Bav. Ers.I.R. 3; Res. Ers.R 1.

11 Mobile according to plan regulation: 218 I.Regts, 113 R.I. Regts; 75 L.I. Regts = 406 regts. If one adds on the Brigade Ersatz battalions as 29 regiments, this totals 435 regiments.

12 364 I. Regts,197 R.I. Regts, 125 L.I.Regts, 10 E.I. Regts, 4 R.E.I. Regts = 700 regiments (apart from 16 Jäger and 27 mobile Landsturm regiments).

ent from the other battalions, and each represented in itself a detachment of mixed troops.

Of the 334 Landsturm battalions set up according to plan regulation, 142 were mobile as early as the end of August 1914. To protect the extended borders in the East, Landsturm had been brought up from the start. Later the Landsturm took the place of the Landwehr in lines of communications areas. They were also used in relatively quiet areas of the Western Front and, in extended form, on the Eastern Front. Therefore, from 1915 onwards, individual battalions were brought together into mobile Landsturm Infantry Regiments. However, 2 changed into Infantry Regiments, and one into a Landwehr Infantry Regiment,[13] so that finally 27 mobile Landsturm Infantry Regiments were available. In addition to this, Landsturm battalions were also merged into infantry regiments.[14]

The designations of Landsturm battalions changed many times during the war, so that it is not always easy to keep track of any given battalion. At the beginning, they were designated according to the place in which they were formed, such as 'Ldst. Inf. Batt. Braunsberg 1'. With the growing number of battalions the system was changed to a numerical system and designated the same battalion as '1 Ldst. Inf. Batt. Braunsberg (XX 10)'.

At the beginning, the training of recruits was at the beginning confined to the home front, as was usual. Of course the shortage of training staff with war experience made itself felt as soon as the reinforcements were deployed at the front. For this reason, as early as 1914, individual Corps began to make use of the conditions of trench warfare in order to give recruits training in field conditions, behind the front, before they were enlisted into active units. The setting-up of such Field Recruit Depots for this purpose was immediately generally recommended by the War Ministry,[15] with the provision that there should be at least four weeks of initial training in Germany. As the results proved to be favourable, the field recruit depots were soon included in the order of battle for each division. They were under the direct command of the division, and so were named after it. Dependent upon the recruitment situation, each infantry regiment could reckon on reinforcements to the level of 1-2 companies, being available from the depot.

The Supreme Army Command placed a decisive value on a thorough and simultaneous training scheme, as preparation for the great offensive battles of 1918. As will be recalled from the history of the Chief of the General Staff of the Field Army,[16] this led to a general being charged with the responsibility for supervising training behind the Western Front. Since he had to confine himself to tours of inspection of the divisions as combat units, he had set up the post of a special Inspector of Field Recruit Depots.[17] His task was to make the principles of the offensive battle also the guiding principles for training on a smaller scale.

13   Ldst I.R. 1 and 2 into I.R. 329 and 330, Ldst. I.R. 109 into Ldw. I.R. 111.
14   I.R. 331-336, 342, 346, 432-434.
15   War Ministry of 8.12.1914, No 9853, 14. A. 1.
16   Part I, A.2. e.
17   Established by War Ministry of 25.3.1918, No 3365. 18. G. A. M.

3. The Jäger Battalion and the Jäger Regiment

Originally, the peacetime Jäger battalions were intended to be drawn from those men eligible for military service who worked on forestry work. Later, people from other professions joined them. However, the conditions for acceptance were more stringent than those for the rest of the infantry, so that the Jäger battalions always represented an élite. Their tactical use, however, generally corresponded to that of the infantry. Only rarely during the course of the war were opportunities offered for exploiting the special advantages of the Jäger. This was first the case at the beginning of the war, when the active Jäger battalions had been brought up to accompany the Independent Cavalry. For that task they had been specially fitted, by each being equipped with a cycle company and a motorised vehicle column for troop transport. After that, it was action in mountain fighting into which it was preferred to send Jäger. The mountains of the Tirol, the Carpathians and the Italian Alps caused the battalions to be assembled into Jäger divisions.[18] Meanwhile, in Macedonia Jäger regiments were in operation.

The strength of a Jäger battalion's establishment, with its 4 companies, was the same as that of the infantry battalion. The one difference was that the Jägers brought with them double the number of ammunition wagons, that is, eight. In addition, they were specially equipped with a machine gun company, on the model of that of the infantry regiment.[19] They had a Jäger cycle company, comprising 3 officers and 124 NCOs and other ranks, together with a Jäger motorised vehicle column of 10 vehicles, each with a driver and escort. So that, as far as firepower and mobility were concerned, a Jäger battalion appeared considerably superior to the infantry battalion.

For the 1st and 2nd Bavarian Jäger Battalions, equipment with machine guns had not been able to be implemented in peacetime. Thus, at first, they went into the field without a machine gun company. The Reserve Jäger Battalions to begin with possessed neither machine-guns, cycle company, nor motorised vehicle column. It was only in equipment with machine guns that they later caught up. Landwehr, mobile Ersatz and Landsturm formations were not formed for Jägers.

The 18 Jäger battalions[20], ready on mobilisation, were only increased during the war by the addition of Jäger Battalion 27.[21] It served to train the voluntary Finns and to which, for this purpose, an artillery and a pioneer section had also been assigned. However, it only existed from 1 May 1916 to 14 February 1918. At the beginning of the war, the 18 Reserve Jäger Battalions were increased by the assignment, to the 43rd-54th Reserve Divisions, of Jäger Reserve Battalions 15-26.

During the course of 1915, the active Jäger battalions each received a second cycle company. But in August 1916 the establishment of all the Jäger battalions saw an increase to two machine gun companies together with a Minenwerfer company with 8 light Minenwerfer.[22] While these MG and Mwf (Minenwerfer) forma-

---

18   Alpine Corps, 200th Inf. Div., and German Jäger Division.
19   For establishment, see Machine Gun Formations.
20   Including Guard Schützen Battalion.
21   A Jäger battalion set up in Germany at the end of 1916-No 31-remained on home service.

tions remained for the duration with the Jäger battalions. But out of the 36 cycle companies, 21 left during the course of 1917, to form cycle battalions which had nothing more to do with the Jäger.

By being assembled into regiments, whose formation went back to May 1915, the Jäger battalions themselves lost a large part of their autonomy. Jäger Battalion 3 was in July 1916 changed into Assault (Sturm) Battalion 3.[23]

At first, use of the Jäger in the regimental unit took place in conjunction with the formation of the Alpine Corps. It was formed out of Jäger Regiments 1-3 and the Bavarian Infantry Body Regiment. If this opportunity took only 6 battalions of Jäger, that was because Jäger Regiment 3 consisted of ski battalions. Later, in the period from July to October 1916, Jäger Regiments 4-10 joined together and as the last instalment Jäger Regiments 11-14 in May 1918. To this were added two more new formations, which did not quite fit within this framework. Thus the Bavarian Infantry Regiment 29 was, by the addition of 11 January 1917 ('Jäger Regiment') changed into a Jäger formation,[24] after it had shortly before received three Jäger battalions instead of infantry. Despite its unique designation it was a 'proper' Jäger regiment, something that cannot be said of the Bavarian Reserve Jäger Regiment 15, set up in the Caucasus on 9 October 1918. This latter possessed only 1 Jäger battalion and alongside this merely another 'Railway Protection Battalion' temporarily put together from freed prisoners of war.

4. Special Formations

a. Mountain and Ski Formations

The mountain formations were distinguished from the rest of the infantry by the suitability of their clothing for mountain conditions, and by their being equipped with special means of transport. In place of jackboots there were climbing boots and puttees, and a rucksack replaced the pack. For the transport of supplies from the valley up the mountain, columns of pack animals were also provided.

In peacetime, the Jäger battalions and the 82nd Infantry Brigade had already gathered some experience of mountain warfare through regular exercises in Colmar in Alsace. During the war it was first the Vosges which were considered, for which, however, no special mountain troops could be made available Despite heavy fighting to start with, the Vosges front soon became a 'sideshow' in the West, to which, therefore, no one wanted to assign particularly high-grade special troops. Nevertheless, in the Winter of 1914/15, it became apparent that there it was not possible to dispense with skiers without damaging consequences.

As a result of this need, there came into existence in December 1914 the Bavarian Ski Battalion 1[25] and the Württemberg Ski Company.[26] In the second half of the winter, preparations were made to set up three further ski battalions, so that in May 1915, when the Alpine Corps began to be formed, there were already four of

22   War Ministry of 25.8.1916, No 1273. 16. A. 2. Or of 8.7.1916 M.I. 14 180. 16. A. 1.

23   War Ministry of 8.7.16, M.I. 14 180. 16. A. 1.

24   Bav. War Ministry of 11.1.1917, No 3833.

25   Bav. War Ministry of 14.11.14, No 52 348.

26   Württemberg War Ministry of 25.11.14, No 3485. K. 14. A.

them. These four battalions were now brought together as Jäger Regiment 3. Out of this and Jäger Regiment 2, the 2nd Jäger Brigade of the Alpine Corps was formed.[27]

The Württemberg Ski Company that had remained behind on the Vosges front, was first, on 31 March 1915, renamed as the Württemberg Mountain Company. On 1 January 1915, it was enlarged into the Württemberg Mountain Battalion with 6 companies.[28] It remained as such on the Vosges front as late as October 1916, then took part in the fighting in the Rumanian mountains. It was to be used later like any other infantry battalion, especially after it had been changed, on 3 May 1918, into the Württemberg Mountain Regiment on the Western Front.[29]

b. Cycle Formations

Not only the ski and mountain formations were connected to the Jäger arm of the service, but also the cycle units. As will be recalled from the discussion of the Jäger battalions, the ski and mountain formations, insofar as they were of active status, possessed, to begin with, one, later two cycle companies. By the end of 1915, the total number of cycle companies ran to 36.

Alongside these were also developed cycle formations from the infantry. Thus, the Reserve Divisions formed at the end of 1914 each received a Reserve Cycle Company.[30] It was no longer possible to provide them with cavalry, to the same extent as at mobilisation. The same thing happened in the infantry divisions of the numerical group 52-58,[31] as well as in a number of other divisions. In part they had set up autonomous temporary cycle units. In this way, up to the beginning of 1916, in the infantry there were formed 30 cycle companies and 11 reserve cycle companies.

At the beginning of August 1916 began a process of bringing together the individual companies into battalions. Thus, firstly, Cycle Battalions 1-3 were formed,[32] then on 9 September 1916 Nos 4 and 5, on 1 July 1917 No 6 together with, in October or November 1918, Nos 8 and 7. Each battalion possessed 6 cycle companies and 1 machine gun company, in which 21 Jäger cycle companies, 18 cycle companies and 8 reserve cycle companies were used.

The inclusion of the first 6 battalions in the 2nd Infantry Cycle Brigade and the formation of the brigade, from October 1918, into 2 cycle regiments has already been mentioned under the history of the brigades.

c. Assault (Sturm) Battalions

Since the battles for fortifications in earlier wars, specially assembled assault troops had already been known for a fairly long time. If the enemy fortifications had not

27 Jäger R. 3 retained its 4 battalions until 22.10.18; on that date Ski Battalion 2 was dissolved.
28 War Ministry of 13.9.15, No 676. 9. 15. A. 2.
29 Württ. War Ministry of 3.5.18, No 6329. K. 18. A. 1.
30 War Ministry of 16.12.14, M.I. 11 204. 14. A. 1.
31 War Ministry of 1.3.15, M.I. 3844. 15. A. 1.
32 Established by War Ministry of 29.7.1916, No 1153. 16. G. A. 2.

been able to resist the armour-piercing effect of the German heavy artillery, it would have thus made formal siege unnecessary. Trench warfare, not only before Verdun, but also in many other places on the front created, for the infantry, conditions similar to fortifications. Experience taught that well-prepared attacks foundered in the fire from positions in the rear, or from flanking positions.

Therefore the Supreme Army Command decided to test a method of attack in which the first line of attack went forward covered by armoured shields. But, at the same time it had to have such firepower as to be able successfully to combat the enemy's rear lines and flanking positions. That would also include the field guns. Prompted by these thoughts, a trial unit was set up at the Wahn artillery range, under Major Calsow, from Pioneer Battalion 18. It consisted of 2 pioneer companies with protective shields, and 1 detachment of 20 3.7cm cannons with overhead shields.[33] This trial unit was first sent into action on the Loretto front. However, because of their conspicuous and clumsy armoured shields, they drew particularly intense enemy artillery fire, so that they lost half their complement, and many guns.

After this failure the Supreme Army Command placed the remains of Assault Section Calsow at the disposal of Army Detachment Gaede.[34] On its part, the Army Detachment charged Captain Rohr of the Guard 'Schützen' battalion, with the task of reorganising the unit. Rohr dispensed with the protective shields, trained the companies on the basis of actual war experience, and practised collaboration with machine guns and artillery. As the Assault Battalion of Army Detachment Gaede, Rohr's troops proved themselves brilliantly in the re-taking of the Hartmannsweiler Kopf on 22/23 December 1915. At the beginning of 1916, Assault Battalion Rohr joined the 5th Army. Its activity there gave the impetus for more assault battalions to be formed.

At first the Jäger battalions were selected for this purpose, but later it was decided to form new units from specially suited men. On 8 July 1916, only Jäger Battalion 3 was changed as a complete unit into an assault battalion.[35] Meanwhile, the newly formed battalions were first introduced to the establishment from December of that year.[36] They were to consist of 2-3 assault companies, 1 machine gun company and 1 Minenwerfer company together with a flamethrower detachment. So there were then, besides the specially-equipped Battalion Rohr, as a pioneer formation, another Jäger battalion designated as an assault battalion, as well as 8 assault battalions belonging to the infantry. They were assigned numbers regardless of which arm of the service they belonged to. In that process the Jäger battalion kept its number 3, but Assault Battalion Rohr was assigned the number 5. On 7 February 1917 the War Ministry accorded the latter the designation 'Assault Battalion No 5 (Rohr)' in honour of its commander. This honour will prove to be well founded in the activities of the battalion during 1916, which will be discussed later.[37]

The various points of origin of the assault battalions, which were given the same name, was the cause, in February 1917, of a special order regarding uniform. In particular, it meant that the assault and MG companies of Battalion 3 had to wear Jäger uni-

33 War Ministry of 2.3.1915, No 415. G. A. 6.
34 War Ministry of 8.5.1915, No 982, 15. G. A. 6.
35 War Ministry of 8.7.1916, M.I. 14 180. 16. A. 1.
36 War Ministry of 4.12.1916, No 3038, 16. A. 1. g.
37 See Part IV E 9.

form, Battalion 5 pioneer uniform, and the other battalions' infantry uniform. On the other hand the Minenwerfer companies had to wear pioneer uniform with the insignia 'M.W.' The artillery section in Battalion 5 had to wear the uniform of the field artillery, with No 5 and a 'shell'. Apart from in the 3rd and 5th Battalions, the other ranks were designated as 'grenadier'.[38]

At the beginning of 1918, there were in existence Assault Battalions 1-12 and 14-17 and also Assault Companies 13 and 18. Assault Company 13 was taken over in March by Assault Battalion 12. Assault Company 18 was taken over in August 1918 by Assault Battalion 18. On the other hand, Assault Battalion 9 had to be dissolved in May, Assault Battalion 17 was dissolved in August, and Assault Battalion 12 in October 1918. Meanwhile, each of the Assault Battalions 1, 2, 4, 6-8 and 16, lost 1 to 2 companies.

d. Automatic Rifle Battalions

The automatic rifle is the only weapon that Germany brought in from abroad during the First World War. It represented a rifle whose magazine held 25 cartridges, so that the rapidity of fire was superior to that of the infantry. This was particularly advantageous in defending against assault. The automatic rifle, produced in Denmark, could, however, not be reproduced. On the other hand, however, since it could never replace a machine gun, its trial in use did not last long.

In Autumn 1915, two automatic rifle battalions were set up[39] whose companies each carried 30 automatic rifles. It is notable that, on 10 March 1916, the War Ministry ordered that these new battalions should be renamed as Battalions IV and V Infantry Regiment 117, but then, only a month later, rescinded this order. Since that time the designation 'Automatic Rifle Battalions 1 and 2' persisted with great stubbornness, even when the battalions had long since no longer had automatic rifles. Since, in war, things tend rapidly to become obsolete, as early as Spring 1917, it proved necessary to replace the automatic rifles by machine guns.

From that time on, the automatic rifle battalions were machine gun units. A year later they were changed into machine gun marksman detachments,[40] without their designation as automatic rifle battalions being affected.

---

38   A.V.Bl. 1917, No 543, of 7.6.1917.
39   War Ministry of 10.8.1915, No 3427. 7. 15. A. 2.
40   War Ministry of 22.4.18, No 34. 4. 18. A. 2.

B.

MACHINE GUN FORMATIONS

1. Development under the Falkenhayn Army Command

The equipment of the Army with machine guns had been implemented shortly before the War. Each of the standing infantry regiments and Jäger battalions, with the exception of the 1st and 2nd Bavarian Jäger Battalions, had its machine gun company. In addition, there were fortress MG detachments. On the other hand, the planned equipment of the reserve infantry regiments that were to be formed, had not yet been carried out.

Thus, at the outbreak of war, in the Field Army, there were 219 infantry regiment MGKs (machine gun companies),[1] 16 MGKs in the Jäger battalions,[2] 88 Reserve MGKs in the Reserve infantry regiments,[3] 11 MG detachments in the cavalry divisions and 43 Ersatz MG detachments in the Ersatz divisions.

The establishment of a MG company comprised 2 officers, 95 NCOs and other ranks, 45 horses, 6 MGs drawn by two horses, 1 reserve MG, 3 ammunition wagons, 1 field kitchen, together with, respectively, 1 store wagon, 1 fodder wagon and 1 baggage wagon.

Differing from this, the establishment of a MG detachment had, for the same number of officers, 115 NCOs and other ranks, 87 horses - including 27 riding horses - and 15 vehicles, including 6 MGs each drawn by 4 horses, 1 reserve MG and 3 small arms ammunition wagons.

It was self-evident that efforts would be made to make as valuable a weapon as the machine gun as widely available as possible. At first it was a matter of equipping those infantry regiments which had no machine guns to the same standard as the active infantry regiments. In addition to this there was the matter of equipping the 26 divisions which had been newly formed in 1914.

At first, to meet these requirements, there were available 5 Reserve MG detachments, 105 fortress MG detachments and 155 fortress MG detachments. It is true that the fortress formations would only be free as soon as there was no longer any threat to the fortress. Therefore it proved necessary to form many new units. In this connection consideration was given to reinforcing the infantry regiments above the machine gun strength which had hitherto been the norm.

For this latter purpose, the Supreme Army Command demanded individual MG detachments. The War Ministry set up, in the first 12 months of the war, Field MG Detachments 1-530 and Bavarian MG Detachments 1-38. They subsequently sent into the field, between August 1915 and September 1916, MG Sup-

---

1   The Inf. Training Regt possessed 2 MGKs.
2   Bav. Jäger Batts 1 and 2 had no MGK.
3   25 Res. Inf. Regts had not yet been provided with machine guns.

plementary Sections 531-878 and Bavarian MG Supplementary Sections 1-6. By this measure, most divisions saw a reinforcement of their infantry regiments to the tune of 2 machine gun detachments. In addition to this, the number of machine guns per company was also gradually increased, from 6 to 12, and over.

From then on, the Supreme Army Command was able to carry out its long-cherished plan and make the MG company an element in its own right on the establishment of every battalion. It ordered that"in the future every active, Reserve, Landwehr, Ersatz and Landsturm infantry regiment - but excluding the Landwehr, Landsturm and garrison troops used in lines of communications areas and in the areas of the General Governments of Belgium and Warsaw - shall receive for each of its battalions a MG company of 6 MGs. Every Jäger battalion, assault battalion and every autonomous battalion being used in the front line shall receive 2 MG companies".[4] Where existing companies had more than 6 machine guns, these were given up to form the new MG companies. The autonomous field and supplementary MG sections were dissolved.

This process of reorganisation included a very significant development that confirmed the tendency, resulting from long combat experience, for the infantry and the machine gun to grow together. It inseparably linked the basic combat unit of the infantry - the battalion - with a MG company. However, for the purpose of technical supervision a MG Officer joined the Staff of every infantry regiment and autonomous battalion.

In the course of providing the High Commands with so-called Army Troops, the Supreme Army Command conceived the idea to provide the Armies with a reserve of particularly capable machine gun formations that could be deployed at decisive points. To this end, it ordered, at the beginning of 1916, the formation of MG Marksman Sections from battle-tested and combat-experienced troops.[5] Two hundred such sections were formed during the period between mid-February and mid-May 1916. After laying the foundation in this way, the Supreme Army Command gathered together every 3 sections into a MG marksman detachment, by which process the sections were transformed into companies.[6] The Supreme Army Command reserved to itself the disposition of the detachments with individual Armies. This did not prevent these detachments often being assigned for months on end to particular divisions.

While the Supreme Army Command was moving towards its goal of linking the tried and tested machine gun with the infantry battalion, it recognised at the same time that there were some combat situations in which the machine gun, because of its weight, could not be on the spot as quickly as required. For this reason, it decided to implement the trial construction of a lighter model that was to be assigned to the infantry marksmen themselves. As a result, from then on, in parallel with 'machine gun 08' (which was designated 'heavy'), the 'light machine gun 08/15' was produced. It differed from the heavy machine gun principally in having no weighty sledge. To operate the new weapon, in July 1916, Light MG Detachments 1-111 were set up.[7] Since there were already 170 divisions with some 1530 battal-

4   War Ministry of 25.8.1916, No 1273. 16. A. 2.
5   War Ministry of 17.1.1916, No 1291. 16. A. 2.
6   War Ministry of 25.8.1916, No 1273. 8. 16. A. 2.
7   War Ministry of 25.7.1916, No 2199. 7. 16. A. 2.

ions, these detachments could only represent the first trial stage of a new development. It would no longer be granted to the Falkenhayn Army Command to carry that through.

When the Alpine Corps was sent into action in May 1916 to reinforce the Austrians in the Tirol, the Supreme Army Command gave it 10 MG detachments specially equipped for mountain warfare. The guns and ammunition were loaded on to pack animals. On the basis of experience gained in the Tirol, soon afterwards they had such sections also formed for other parts of the front. In this way, there came into existence, Mountain MG Detachments 201-251,[8] to which more were added later.

To summarise, it must be stressed that, on the part of the Falkenhayn Supreme Army Command, a decisive impetus was given to the development of machine gun units by tripling their number in the infantry. It created for the Army High Commands a MG Reserve of exceptional combat capability. Thus it initiated the introduction of a lighter machine gun alongside the heavy machine gun, and brought into existence the special formations for mountain warfare.

2. Developments under the Hindenburg Command

When the Hindenburg Army Command took up its duties, the organisation, as regarded the heavy machine gun, was as good as completed. But since the Army Command was convinced of the decisive role of technical weapons, it was intent upon increasing the number of guns in the heavy MG formations. It ordered, after the increase in production it had prompted was begun, that the number of guns in the machine gun companies and MG marksman sections should be doubled.[9] This meant that in the companies in question[10] the number of guns was increased to 9, later to 12.

Like its predecessor, the Hindenburg Army Command was also convinced of the importance of the light machine gun, but, going a step further, immediately linked the necessary trials directly with the infantry companies. It ordered, in December 1916, that every infantry and Jäger company should be equipped with 3 light machine guns each.[11] To transport these guns and their ammunition, a field wagon joined each company.

Only five months later the final arrangement was made as the 111 autonomous light MG units that were formed in the Falkenhayn era were dissolved. A MG unit was then formally put on the establishment of every infantry and Jäger company.[12] In this way, keeping pace with production in Germany, the number of light machine guns was increased from 3 to 6. Just as the heavy machine gun was linked to the battalion, so from now on the light machine gun became a component of the company.

8   War Ministry of 21.8.1915, No 2002. 8. 15. A. 2.
9   War Ministry of 17.9.1917, No 2340. 9. 17. A. 2.
10   The MG marksman section was organised into 3 companies.
11   War Ministry of 12.12.1916, No 1273. 12. 16. A. 2.
12   War Ministry of 4.6.1917, No 477. 17. A. 2.

With particular consideration being given to the planned offensive for 1918, the Supreme Army Command made efforts to bring about a real amalgamation of the infantry with the light machine gun. They had to drum into the infantry the difference in the use of both service arms. The fact, however, that this aim had by no means been reached at the end of 1917 is testified by Ludendorff himself as he explains:[13]

> In the infantry company the light machine gun had to become accepted as a normal part of the unit. It was still viewed as a weapon ancillary to the infantry. The fact that the light MG is itself part of the infantry and the infantry carry the gun had not yet penetrated into the marrow of the infantry, never mind the Army. The light MG, because of its firepower, was and had to become the main component of the infantry's firepower in combat. That should not mean that the gun carrier would not have to shoot - on the contrary, the greatest value was placed on the fact that he should. Light machine gun and gun carrier formed groups of infantry marksmen who, if need or danger arose, if the fighting was a matter of life and death, had to hold together... To the heavy machine gun with its greater ranges and better performance fell the task of keeping the enemy under fire and thus making it easier for the groups of marksmen to work their way closer to the enemy from positions to the rear. Self-evidently, it had to link itself with the action of the infantry. In this way, although it was itself part of the infantry, it had become a sort of ancillary weapon.

It remains to be mentioned that, in August 1918, the cycle companies also each received 3 light machine guns with specially designed cycles for transportation.[14]

Towards the end of the war, the Supreme Army Command also extended its efforts for organisational amalgamation to the mountain MG sections. It brought together 18 of these formations into Mountain MG Sections 260-265,[15] in which process each old section formed a company in one of the 6 new sections. Considering also the other formations designated as MG sections, it is thus necessary to distinguish, by unit strength, between two types: (a) MG Marksman Sections and Mountain MG Sections Nos 260-265, which all comprised 3 companies, and (b) Reserve MG Sections, MG Sections of the cavalry divisions and Mountain MG Sections - apart from Nos 260 to 265 - which corresponded to one MG company.

The machine gun found a special use for surprise advances in conjunction with armoured vehicles. After some trials, on 16 November 1916 Armoured Vehicle MG Section 1 was formed.[16] It was able suddenly to emerge at close quarters and thus quickly break down infantry resistance. But it was limited to the roads and offered a good target for artillery. It had good successes in the Ukraine and in the Caucasus, where it was principally a matter of guerrilla warfare. In 1917 and 1918 another 10 individual units were formed, each with 2 armoured road vehicles. To those were added wireless equipment, together with masts which could be wound up to a height of 7 metres.

---

13 Ludendorff, page 460f.
14 War Ministry of 20.8.1918, No 524. 8. 18. A. 2. V.
15 War Ministry of 30.10.1918, No 3195. 9. 18. A. 2. IV.
16 War Ministry of 16.11.1916, No 3413. 10. 16. A. 2.

The Hindenburg Army Command was the first to introduce a systematic programme of instruction for machine gun personnel. As a school for the MG élite it set up, in October 1916, the MG Marksman Command West in Rozoy,[17] which was later transferred to Tongern. On the other hand, general training remained in the hands of the Army High Commands, in which, in November 1917, machine gun schools were established.[18] At about the same time every Army received a MG repair shop, to enable damaged materiel to be more quickly repaired.

As well as with the infantry, and with the arms of the service related to the infantry, during the war the machine gun also appears in conjunction with other arms of the service. At the beginning certainly it was only found as an accompaniment to the cavalry divisions in the form of one MG section to each. Of these 11 sections, in the end, only 4 remained,[19] while the rest changed into MG companies. By contrast, from October 1916, a comprehensive issue of machine guns to the cavalry took place, as every dismounted Cavalry Schützen Regiment and every Cavalry Schützen Regiment each formed one MG marksman squadron with 6 machine guns drawn by two horses.[20] Meanwhile, the cavalry regiments that had remained mounted were each equipped with a MG squadron with 6 machine guns drawn by 6 horses.[21] In addition 3 light machine guns were assigned to the dismounted and Schützen squadrons. It was only in August 1918 that the mounted cavalry was similarly equipped with the light machine gun.[22] Pack animals served to transport the machine guns and ammunition.

Only a brief mention will be made here of the equipment of the aviation service with the machine gun.[23] In the West, during the course of 1917, it proved necessary to also assign machine guns to the artillery for anti-aircraft defence and for close quarters defence in the event of an enemy breakthrough. Therefore, the Supreme Army Command, in the Winter of 1917, ordered that every field artillery and foot artillery battery on the Western Front should be equipped with a MG detachment of 2 guns.[24]

For the same purpose, in August 1917, 2 machine guns were put on the establishment of every column in the Army of the West.[25]

The machine gun also found a use protecting installations and railway stations close behind the combat front in France. For this purpose, in August 1917, 25 Anti-Aircraft MG Battalions, each with 3 companies, each with 12 guns, were created, in addition to which there were also in existence 103 individual detachments.[26]

17 War Ministry of 31.10.1916, No 2851. 10.16. A. 2.
18 War Ministry of 12.11.1917, No 1875. 8. 17. A. 2.
19 Guard MG Section 1, MG Sections 2 and 3, Bav. MG Section 1.
20 War Ministry of 9.10.1916, M.I. 23 351. 16. A. 1.
21 War Ministry of 17.3.1917, No 336. 17. G. A. 2.
22 War Ministry of 20.8.1918, No 524. 8. 18. A. 2. IV.
23 Cf IV. F. 2. c.
24 November 1917.
25 War Ministry of 23.8.1918, No 173. 7. 18. A. 2. VI.
26 War Ministry of 1.8.1917, No 1343. 7. 17. A. 2. Cf also "Anti-Aircraft Defence" (Part IV F2e).

Finally, it should be mentioned that machine guns were also part of the equipment of the fighting vehicle sections.[27]

If the development of the machine gun service is reviewed as a whole, it can be seen that it developed from a purely infantry weapon to a very valued aid also for the cavalry, the light and heavy artillery, the air forces, fighting vehicles and columns. Its focus, of course, remained with the infantry. It was also in the infantry that its use was most widely expanded.

If within the infantry, at the beginning of the war, 323 MG companies with 6 guns and 43 mobile MG Ersatz detachments (=14 MGKs) had gone into the field, towards the end of the war the number of these companies had increased to around 2500. That is more than seven times their number at the beginning. If it is also reckoned that the number of guns in individual companies rose from 6 to 12, and if the 6 light MGs for every infantry and Jäger company are added, this indicates an eighteenfold increase in the mechanical firepower of the infantry during the war![28]

27 Cf also 'Armoured Fighting Vehicle Units' (Part IV H).
28 This calculation produces the same result if it is applied to the individual infantry company. At the beginning the infantry regiment possessed a MGK with 6 guns, so that ½ a MG was apportioned to the individual company. At the end every battalion had its MGK with 12 guns and every infantry company its 6 light MGs, so that 9 guns were apportioned to the company. This of course does not take account of the fact that the majority of infantry battalions on the Western Front had, towards the end of the war, to be contracted from 4 to 3 companies.

C.

CAVALRY

1. The Cavalry Brigade Staffs

For the cavalry, mobilisation meant a split into Army and Divisional Cavalry. In the cavalry that was divided by regiment or half-regiment among the divisions, the brigade ceased to exist. Therefore, of the peacetime brigades, 22 had to be dissolved,[1] of which only the Staff of the 39th Cavalry Brigade was re-formed.

Of the 34 mobile brigade Staffs, at the time when three divisions were changed into Cavalry Schützen Divisions, nine were formed into Cavalry Schützen Commands, keeping their original numbers,[2] and taking over the functions of the infantry regiment commander.

From Autumn 1916 onwards, sixteen brigade Staffs became autonomous, and in 1918 mostly formed mixed units in Russia and the Ukraine. The 2nd Guard Cavalry Brigade was in Finland, with 2 dismounted cavalry regiments, the Staffs of the 3rd Guard Cavalry Brigade, and the 8th and 19th Cavalry Brigades served as communication Staffs behind the Western Front.

On 8 February 1916, the commander of the 13th Cavalry Brigade, with his Staff, joined the Warsaw General Government as Cavalry Inspector. At the end of that year he was ordered to the Staff of the Quartermaster-General where, as mentioned in discussion of this office, he was employed as 'B.d.G. Pferde' (Representative of the Quartermaster-General for Equine Affairs). The 40th Cavalry Brigade was dissolved in the Spring of 1918, and the 18th ended up as part of the XXXXI Reserve Corps.

Thus, at the end, by way of proper cavalry brigades, there were only 5 with the mounted cavalry divisions, 4 autonomous brigades in the East and one in the Caucasus.[3] Despite the fact that the history of the cavalry brigades in the First World War does not represent an upward development, but rather a downward one, nevertheless some temporary formations of this kind were formed.

The ad hoc Guard Cavalry Brigade operated in the East from 5 January 1915 until 12 January 1916. The Transylvanian Cavalry Brigade, formed for the Rumanian campaign out of the remains of the dissolved 3rd Cavalry Division, on 1 June 1917, joined the established Bavarian 7th Cavalry Brigade was formed. Apart from

---

1   Dissolved on mobilisation were the 4rd Guard Cav. Brig., Cav. Brigs. 4, 6, 7, 10, 15, 20, 21, 24, 27, 29, 31, 34, 35, 37, 39, 43 and 44 together with the Bav. Cav. Brigs. 2, 3, and 6.

2   Cav. Schü. Kdos 3, 5, 11, 14, 28, 30, 38, 41 and 45; in Spring 1918.

3   The 2nd Cav. Brig with the 1st Cav. Div., the 22nd and 25th Cav. Brigs with the 2nd Cav. Div., the 1st and 5th Bav. Cav. Brigs with the Bav. Cav. Div.; the Leib Hussar Brigade, 4th Bav., 17th and 23rd Cav. Brigs in the East, the 7th Bav. Cav. Brig in the Caucasus.

these, there only appears the 4th Landwehr Cavalry Brigade, established at the end of September 1914 within the 4th Landwehr Division. The justification was that this division was the only division in the German Army that had mobilised with two cavalry brigades.[4] The other cavalry brigades that appeared temporarily during the war under the names of their commanders, are nothing more than reinforced cavalry regiments. Thus, for example, Cavalry Brigade Berring[5] was under the control of the Staff of Jäger zu Pferde Regiment 10. Cavalry Brigade Charisius was under the control of the Staff of Reserve Dragoon Regiment 1. Cavalry Brigade Koss was under the Staff of Uhlan Regiment 1, and Cavalry Brigade Kaufmann was under the Staff of Uhlan Regiment 6.

2. The Cavalry Regiment

At mobilisation, 110 active, 33 Reserve, 2 Landwehr and 1 Ersatz cavalry regiments, together with 38 Landwehr squadrons and 19 cavalry Ersatz detachments, were assigned to the Field Army. Since one squadron per regiment remained in Germany, the regiments each numbered 4 squadrons. The only exceptions were 6 regiments that were brought up to a strength of 6 squadrons and split into 2 half-regiments. They joined the two divisions of their Army Corps. The Reserve and Landwehr cavalry regiments had been formed with 3 squadrons.

The establishment of a 4-squadron regiment consisted of 36 officers, 688 NCOs and other ranks, 709 riding horses, 60 draught horses, 2 bridge wagons, 1 telephone wagon, 1 medical wagon together with 5 each of baggage wagons, supply wagons and fodder wagons. In the establishment of the 6-squadron regiment these figures were respectively, 51, 1017, 1057, 76, 2, 1, 0 and 7 each. In the 3-squadron Reserve cavalry regiment they were 27, 511, 532, 36, 0, 0, 0 and 4 each.

The provision of the Army with cavalry was tailored to the requirements of the war of movement at the beginning. According to the Army cavalry, they were organised into 4 cavalry corps and one individual division, and provided strategic reconnaissance. The cavalry from the infantry division provided the more narrowly delimited tactical reconnaissance. Therefore, when trench warfare along uninterrupted fronts set in, there was no longer any proper use for the cavalry. If it was not wished simply to hold them back on police service behind the front, or as reserves for a later offensive, then they had to be used as infantry. At first, this only happened on a modest scale. But when, as the supply of horses became more scarce, the necessity to provide draught horses for new artillery formations became a burning question, the Supreme Army Command had to take the difficult step of dispensing with superfluous cavalry. The way this was done in the cavalry divisions has already been indicated.[6]

For the divisional cavalry a measure was conceived that was put into force through the War Ministry at the beginning of August 1916. According to this measure, a new allocation of cavalry was to be introduced in the Army of the West. Ev-

4   The Staff of the 4th Ldw. Cav. Brig was changed on 1.10.1916 into the Staff of the 215th Inf. Brig.
5   Brig. Berring was also called 43rd Cav. Brig., but this was only of temporary local significance, since the peacetime 43rd Cav. Brig was not re-formed.
6   Compare 'Cavalry Divisions' (Part III B 7).

ery division and autonomous brigade was to command only one squadron. Since this arrangement also immediately came into force in the East, the Landwehr and Ersatz formations together with the individual squadrons and Reserve Cavalry Detachments set up during the war for new divisions, ceased to exist.

During the reorganisation, the Chief of the General Staff of the Field Army was changed. The Hindenburg Supreme Command approved this development which they found in the process of being implemented. Now they also reduced the establishment of the regiments in the cavalry divisions so that the regiment formed into 4 squadrons numbered only 675 horses instead of 769.[7]

The horses released by this measure offered a welcome opportunity to refresh the cavalry divisions' stock of horses by exchange. After this had taken place, the horses could be used for new batteries that were to be set up, or for batteries that were to be made mobile.

For the cavalry regiments, allotted in individual squadrons among the divisions, the regimental unit ceased to exist for all practical purposes. Nevertheless, the regimental Staffs in question were not dissolved, but were for the most part left in place in the divisions in which they found themselves, for special use.[8] All the same, 16 regimental commanders, retaining their designation, found new employment as horse inspectors[9] with responsibility for tours of inspection and balancing of the stock of horses within certain districts. Two regimental Staffs, however, were changed into infantry regimental Staffs,[10] and three were changed into the Staffs of Jäger Regiments 11, 12, and 13.[11]

But the Supreme Army Command did not stop with the reduction of the divisional cavalry, but took away the horses from entire regiments and used them as infantry. This was the first time that the designation 'Cavalry Schützen Regiment' appeared. However, it was at first restricted to inactive dismounted regiments, while the remaining dismounted regiments were indeed deployed as infantry, but without being identified by the word 'Schützen' in their names. Only from the end of 1917, after any hope of re-forming mounted regiments had finally disappeared, as a result of the pronounced shortage of horses, were the dismounted cavalry, with a few exceptions, generally identified by the designation Cavalry Schützen Regiment.

In the Cavalry Schützen Regiment, the regimental commander was allotted the role of an infantry battalion commander, and the squadron commander allotted that of a company commander. Meanwhile, such a regiment could not be viewed as full replacement for an infantry regiment, because the establishment of

7   War Ministry of 2.10.1916, M.I. 22 756. 16. A. 1.
8   Thus, for example, in 1918 the Staff of Cuirassier Regt. 8 was in command of a cycle regiment in the 2nd Inf. Cycle Brigade.
9   Staffs of Curassier Regt 6, 2nd Guard Dragoon Regt, Dragoon Rgs 6, 7, 10, 11, Leib Guard Hussar Regt, Hussar Regts 5 and 17, 2nd Guard Uhlan Regt, Uhlan Regts 14 and 20, Mounted Grenadier Regt 3, Jäger zu Pferde Regts 1, 4, and 5 - Chief of the Gen. Staff of Field Army of 10.1.18, No I. C 75 297 op.
10 The Staff of Cav. Regt 86 became the Staff of I.R. 433, the Staff of Res. Uhlan Regt 1 became the Staff of I.R. 434 - October 1916.
11 Staffs of Drag. Regt 4, Uhlan Regt 2 and Bav. Chevauleger Regt 8 - War Ministry of 5.4.1918, No 3469. G. A. M.

the Schützen squadron[12] consisting of 4 officers and 109 NCOs and other ranks remained considerably below the strength of that of the infantry company.

As a consequence of changing three cavalry divisions into cavalry Schützen divisions in Spring 1918, the number of cavalry Schützen, or dismounted cavalry regiments, rose to 51.[13] However, 19 fell victim to being dissolved before the end of the war.

Of the Reserve Cavalry, in so far as it had not been changed into Schützen regiments, the only regiments to retain their names were those whose squadrons had been allotted to the divisions.[14]

The equipment of the cavalry with machine guns has already been considered in the section concerning that weapon. Here it suffices to re-state that the cavalry Schützen regiment was equipped with ancillary weapons in exactly the same way as the infantry battalion, that is, with the MG squadron, 4 light Minenwerfer and within each Schützen squadron with 6 light machine guns.

It is notable that the trial of automatic rifles made with the infantry was also carried over to the cavalry, as in August 1915 one squadron each of three regiments received 6 of these guns.

If one considers the cavalry at the end of the war, there only appear as active 22 of the special and mounted cavalry regiments, ie a fifth of the 110 active cavalry regiments which marched out on mobilisation. In addition to these there still existed 27 active and 5 dismounted Schützen regiments created during the course of the war,[15] together with about 250 individual mounted squadrons, as divisional cavalry.[16] They carried on the names of 61 active and 22 reserve cavalry regiments.

12 War Ministry of 2.10.1916, M.I. 22 756. 16. A. 1.
13 Cav. Schützen Regiments from Autumn 1916: Cav. Regts 84, 85, 87-89, 93, 94, Heavy Res.Reiter Regt 3, Res. Drag. Regts 1, 2, 5 and 7 (Nos 1 and 2 being renamed as Nos 13 and 12), Res. Hussar Regts 1 and 2, Res. Uhlan Regts 3, 4, 5 and Saxon, Bav. Res. Cav. Regt 5, Ldw. Cav. Regts 1, 2 and 90-92 (Nos 1 and 2 from now on Nos 10 and 11). Dismounted Regts according to War Ministry of 30.12.1916, M.I. 32 801. 16. A. 1.: Guard Curassier Regts 1 and 4, Drag. Regt 8, Hussar Regts 8, 11 and 13, 1 and 3 Guard Uhlan Regts, Uhlan Regts 5, 11, and 15, Jäger zu Pferde Regts 2, 6, and 13, Saxon Carabinier Regt.
14 Heavy Regt Reiter 1 and 2; Regt Dragoon Guard, 3, 4, 6, 8 and Württ; Res. Hussars 4-9 and Saxon Regt.; Guard Uhlan, and Uhlan Rgts 1, 2, and 6; Jäger zu Pferde Regt 1; Bav. Cav. Regts. 1 and 6.
15 In 1918 were dissolved Cav. Schü. Regts 84, 87, 88, 89, 93, 94, Heavy Regt Reiter 3, Regt Drag. 12 (2), 13 (1) and 5, Regt Hussars 1 and 2, Regt Uhlans 3, 5, and Saxon, Bavarian Res. Cav. 5, Ldw. Cav. 10 (1), 11(2) and 90.
16 In addition the Cav. Squadron of the Alpine Corps, Cav. Squadrons 4 and 205, Res. Cav. Detachments 44, 45, 47, 50-53 and Bav. 8.

D.

Artillery

1. Senior Artillery Commanders

Even at the beginning of the war, field artillery and foot artillery were strictly separated from each other. There were even those among the field artillery, who held to the line that the heavy field howitzer battalions were too cumbersome for the war of movement. This opinion was proved wrong in the first battles. From that time the sympathy of the infantry, bearing the main brunt of the fighting, who were best qualified to judge, definitely turned to the heavy artillery with its greater effect. However, in the course of trench warfare, the senior commanders of the field artillery and heavy artillery got to know the nature of their sister arm. They were charged with the responsibility for ensuring the collaboration of the light and the heavy guns. The joint need for working together necessarily gave rise to the thought of unifying the senior artillery command structure. But it was only the Hindenburg Army Command that risked taking this decisive step.

In the field artillery, senior command had originally rested with the field artillery brigade commander of the infantry division. At first there were 52. As a consequence of new units being formed and units being combined during the period 1914-1916, this number rose by 18 field artillery commands, 14 reserve artillery commands, 1 Landwehr field artillery command and 4 Ersatz field artillery brigade commands.[1]

Things were different with the foot artillery, since the active corps, at mobilisation, had only one heavy field howitzer battalion each, and the rest had no foot artillery. There were therefore no senior artillery commanders. Rather, such commanders were located, as Generals of Foot Artillery 1-3[2] and Foot Artillery Brigade Commanders 1-9,[3] with the Army High Commands or in the Reserve of the Supreme Army Command. Those Armies that carried stronger siege artillery with them also had a senior commander of foot artillery. Thus the 2nd Army had General of Foot Artillery 3, the 4th and 6th Armies had Foot Artillery Commander 1 or Bavarian 1, while in the 5th Army, General of Foot Artillery 1 was with Foot Artillery Brigade Commander 6, who was under his command. But since a result of

---

1   Added to this were the commands of the 5th Guard Field Artillery Brig., the 10th Bav. Field Art. Brig., the 50th, 52nd, 54th, 56th, 58th-67th, 123rd and 220th Field Art. Brigs (of which Nos 61, 65, and 66 were under the direct command of General Commands), the 23rd, 24th, 26th, 28th, and 75th-82nd Reserve Field Art. Brigs, the 1st and 8th Bav. Reserve Field Art. Brig, the 1st Bav. Landwehr Field Art. Brig, together with the 4th, 8th, 10th and 19th Ersatz Field Art. Brigs.

2   i.e. the three Inspectors General of Foot Artillery (The Inspector General was in the Great Headquarters).

3   The 8 peacetime Foot Artillery Brigade Commanders were joined in August 1914 by a ninth, Bav. No 2.

trench warfare was a quite extraordinary increase in foot artillery, along the whole front, the Supreme Army Command felt compelled to assign to each Army a senior commander for the heavy artillery. They also placed, on readiness, several more for special eventualities.

To this end, in Autumn 1915, bringing together the previous posts, it created 20 new posts with the standardised designation 'Generals of Foot Artillery'.[4] With that measure, responsibilities for the distribution of fire and fire control for all the foot artillery of an Army were unified in the General of Foot Artillery. The massing of heavy artillery round Verdun then led to the realisation that senior artillery commanders would also have to be assigned to the General Commands at the 'hotspots' of the front. Therefore the number of Generals of Foot Artillery was increased to 37.[5]

So the Hindenburg Army Command found, as senior artillery commanders, 89 field artillery brigade commanders, and 37 Generals of Foot Artillery, who during the course of the war had become familiar with both branches of the artillery. Imbued with the importance of artillery as a deciding factor in battle, and with the use of an effective organisation being the indispensable precondition for the effective collaboration of both branches of the artillery, the Supreme Army Command did not hesitate in unifying those command posts into a single artillery command. To this end, in February 1917, it brought about a War Ministry order[6] which, by bringing together the field artillery brigade commands and the posts of General of Foot Artillery, organised a common senior artillery command: (1) Generals of the Artillery Nos 1-13 at the disposal of the Supreme Army Command,[7] and (2) The Artillery Commanders (Arko) as commanders of the light and heavy artillery belonging to, or assigned to, a division.

The 13 Generals of the Artillery, among whom was included, as No 1, the Inspector General of Artillery Schools of Gunnery with the Chief of the General Staff of the Field Army. All came, with one exception, from the foot artillery. Of these posts, No 9 was dissolved again in March 1917. In its place the post of General of Artillery No 14 was set up on 6 July 1917. The last of these posts were created on 14 July 1918 as Nos 15 and 16. The Supreme Army Command deployed the Generals of the Artillery, as individual circumstances dictated, with those Armies whose combat situation necessitated the assembly of strong artillery groups. The main field of activity of these generals was of course in the Western theatre of war.

The General of the Artillery had the rank of a brigade or regimental commander and had 2 adjutants. As soon as he was assigned to an Army High Command, the first and second Staff Officers of Artillery together with the Artillery Signals Section on the establishment of the High Command came under his command. The office of the 1st Stoart (Staff Officer of Artillery) was the place for all tactical, organisational, and training questions, for very heavy low trajectory fire, gas, and high explosive munitions, together with the execution of the 'errors' of the day. The 2nd Stoart was assigned responsibility for supply for all the artillery and also for the fixed and mobile artillery repair shops. Finally, the signals section, in conjunction with the Balloon Report Centres,[8] the Staff Photographic Section[9] and

---

4   War Ministry of 17.9.1915, No 1545. 15. G. A. 5: Generals of Foot Artillery Nos 1-6 and Bav. 1-3, together with the General of Foot Artillery with the General Government of Warsaw, while a General of Foot Artillery had, from 25.11.1914, been

the Artillery Survey Section,[10] created the most accurate picture possible of the distribution of enemy forces. They were responsible too for the issue of artillery maps.

Here consideration must be given to an artillery commander who had first successfully proved his worth in the East in the battle at Lake Narotsch on 29 April 1916. It was achieved by assembling strong artillery through a strictly centralised command structure. Lieutenant-Colonel (from 1918 Colonel) Bruchmüller, held that rank in the peacetime army before the war, and after the reorganisation of the artillery command had held the established post of Artillery Commander 86. In view of the difficulties in directing the rolling fire, i.e. the artillery fire which crept forward with the attack, and as a result of the massive increase in artillery, it was no longer possible to fill all artillery command posts with sufficiently experienced officers.

Early on, Colonel Bruchmüller had recognised the advantage of a centralised direction of fire from the Army High Command. During the year 1917 there was almost no opportunity for the application of the creeping barrage in the West. However, in the East he created the necessary command structure so successfully that in 1918 the Supreme Army Command assigned him as artillery adviser to the Army High Commands on the offensive fronts.[11] Bruchmüller's method proved itself brilliantly. There is a stone under his carved image, on one of the seven Army memorial stones, on Burg Hoheneck, in central Franconia. It proudly announces: "Colonel Bruchmüller, nicknamed 'Durchbruchmüller,'[12] commanded, on 21 March 1918, the artillery of the 18th Army, whose creeping barrage made possible the great breakthrough in the direction of Amiens."

The overpowering German fire, 'for effect', opened up by surprise, the great offensives of 1918. It should not be forgotten that it was only made possible by the careful training provided by the so-called Pulkovski Method. On the basis of scientific calculations, the Method eliminated the 'errors' of the day, and made it possible to dispense almost completely with initial registration fire.

The posts of divisional Artillery Commanders, created at the same time as those of the Generals of the Artillery, were thus provided with field artillery troops in places where field artillery brigades were already in existence. 27 posts were assigned to Generals of Foot Artillery.[13] The rest were newly created and provided

with the General Government of Belgium and one followed with the Coastal Defence High Command on 18.5.1916.
5　War Ministry of 30.6.1916, No 1058. 16. G. A. 5. This number does not include the three generals with the General Governments and the Coastal High Command.
6　War Ministry of 16.2.1917, No 445. 2. 17. G. A. 4.
7　The 'General of the Artillery' is not to be confused with the 'General of Artillery', which latter designates a service rank equivalent to a General of Infantry.
8　cf Part IV. F. 1. b.
9　cf Part IV. F. 2. d.
10　cf Part IV. D. 3.
11　Ziethen, page 62/63.
12　Translator's note: a pun which is untranslatable in English: 'Durchbruch' in German means 'breakthrough'.
13　Generals of Foot Artillery 2, 3, 5, 7-12, 14, 15, 18-20, 23, 24, 26-28, 30-32 and Bav. 1-5.

with commanders of whom some came from the field artillery and some from the foot artillery. Their numbers ran from Guard 1-8, Bavarian 1-23 and Nos 1-255 (leaving out 65 numbers). In that numbering process no distinction was made as to origin, such as Reserve or Landwehr. According to this, therefore, there were 221 Arkos. In rank, the Arko was under the regimental commanders. On his Staff were 1 adjutant, 2 orderly officers and 1 signals officer.

The divisional artillery commander can truly be seen as the decisive command post of the artillery in the battle. Under his command was not only the artillery on the establishment of his division, but also the massive field and heavy artillery reinforcements which were assigned to him, over the superior General Command, by the General of the Artillery with the Army High Command. The Arko had autonomy in implementing the combat tasks assigned to him. On the other hand, the General Command was responsible for the unified collaboration of the artillery of neighbouring divisions and for its mutual reinforcement, especially on the flanks.

The engagement of distant targets was, as will be described further below, the responsibility of the Army High Command.[14]

2. The Troops

a. Field Artillery

a1. In the first two years of the war

On 2 August 1914, the Field Artillery mobilised for the Field Army, 102 regiments, 29 Reserve regiments, 11 horse artillery battalions, 40 Ersatz battalions, 3 Landwehr battalions together with 5 Landwehr and 22 Landsturm batteries. Its units were to be found exclusively in the divisions and autonomous brigades. Neither the Army High Command nor the General Command had field artillery under its direct command.

In the equipment of the individual divisions, however, considerable differences came to light. While the infantry divisions and the 1st Guard Reserve Division each possessed a field artillery brigade (of 2 regiments, each with 2 battalions, each with 3 batteries), the Reserve divisions had each only one field artillery regiment. That was generally composed of 2 battalions, but in the 23rd, 24th and 26th Reserve Divisions of 3 battalions. The two divisions of the Landwehr Corps initially only had 2 batteries each at their disposal. The cavalry divisions each had 1 mounted field artillery battalion of 3 batteries. But each battalion - apart from the Landwehr and mobile Ersatz battalions that were only equipped with 2 batteries - had one light ammunition column, one ammunition wagon for each gun.

The strength of the establishments as the units marched out were as follows:

Staff of a field artillery regiment: 6 officers (commander, adjutant, orderly officer, train transport commander, regimental medical officer, regimental veterinary officer), 16 NCOs and other ranks, 20 horses, 1 baggage wagon

Staff of a field artillery (gun or field howitzer) battalion: 7 officers (commander, adjutant, supply officer, battalion MO, 2 veterinary officers, 1 paymaster), 27 NCOs and other ranks, 29 horses, one observation wagon, one supply wagon and one baggage wagon

Staff of a horse artillery battalion: as above, apart from 1 more MO, 3 NCOs and other ranks and 9 horses

Field artillery battery: 5 officers, 148 NCOs and other ranks, 139 horses, 6 guns (drawn by 6 horses), 11 vehicles

Horse artillery battery: 4 officers, 133 NCOs and other ranks, 180 horses, 4 guns (drawn by 6 horses), 9 vehicles

Light ammunition column: 4 officers, 188 NCOs and other ranks, 196 horses, 27 vehicles

Light ammunition column of the horse artillery battalion: 4 officers, 144 NCOs and other ranks, 204 horses, 25 vehicles - including 7 for the infantry small arms ammunition wagons designated for the cavalry.

The establishment strength of Reserve and Landwehr formations does not significantly differ from the above.

By way of guns, the field artillery had the new pattern 7.7cm field gun 96, and the 10.5cm light field howitzer 98/09. One each of the four battalions of the field artillery brigades was equipped with the latter, together with one battalion each of the 3rd Guard Reserve Field Artillery Regiment and Reserve Field Artillery Regiment 26. Thus the ratio of the field gun to the light field howitzer was 3:1 within the field artillery brigades, but 5:1 within the Field Army as a whole. The light field howitzer was principally designed to engage field fortifications, but also was effective against the other targets reserved for the field gun.

Of interest is the opinion of the Chief of the General Staff of the Field Army concerning these guns. General von Falkenhayn writes:[15]

> Just as the high trajectory fire of all our guns proved its worth, principally that of the light and heavy field howitzer, to which the enemy could bring up nothing approaching its effectiveness, so the men felt uncomfortably conscious of the inferiority, in terms both of range and effectiveness, of our field gun to the French version. To help to overcome this shortfall, steps were taken to develop a new field gun and more effective ammunition. Of course, production had to take some time: the issue of the new gun to units could only begin at the end of 1916.

So, although the new field gun (F.K. 16) could only begin to appear at the beginning of the Hindenburg Supreme Army Command, the credit for this rearmament remains with General von Falkenhayn. Similarly, much of what he had laid the ground for only came to fruition, or could be evaluated in organisational terms under his successor.

In addition there was concern about compensating for the less effective performance of the German field gun, as against the French version, as had become evident in trench warfare. At the beginning, the question of the procurement of

15   Von Falkenhayn, page 39.

ammunition weighed heavily on the shoulders of the Chief of the General Staff of the Field Army. The first battles had already demanded a very much greater expenditure of ammunition than had been forecast. But the imperative holding back on use of ammunition was matched by the fact that the enemy had similarly to limit its expenditure, because they too were faced by a munitions crisis.

However, thanks to the energetic production of munitions at home, as early as 1915 the Supreme Army Command "were relieved of any serious concern in this regard. This happy state of affairs continued until the high summer of 1916. Only the need for munitions during the large-scale battles taking place simultaneously in the Maas area, on the Somme, in Galicia and in Poland in August 1916 - a need that surpassed every expectation - caused the munitions situation temporarily to become shaky again. The production programme that had been imposed, however, delivered such massive supplies of munitions in continually increasing amounts that the munitions shortage which had come about was swiftly overcome."[16]

In peacetime there had been many arguments as to whether, exploiting the special characteristics of the quick-firing gun, it was not more efficient to move from the 6-gun battery, to one of only 4 guns, with a correspondingly greater supply of ammunition. During the war this question resolved itself, since, in view of the matériel available and to be supplied, it was necessary, by force of circumstance, to adopt the 4-gun type. Thus, the 13 Reserve field artillery regiments, for the Reserve divisions formed in October 1914, were each set up with 3 battalions (2 gun battalions and 1 howitzer battalion), each with 3 batteries, each with 4 guns. Thus, in comparison with most of the Reserve field artillery regiments at the time of mobilisation, these regiments, for the same overall number of guns, possessed one more howitzer battalion.

The second draft of Reserve divisions reverted to the field artillery brigade, in that, for the 75th-82nd Reserve Divisions, eight brigades were created, each with 2 regiments, each with 2 battalions, each with 3 batteries, and each with 4 guns. These newly formed units were distinguished by the fact that each regiment consisted of a gun battalion and a howitzer battalion. The active field artillery brigade, at the time of mobilisation, counted among its four battalions, only one with light field howitzers. Therefore, the new Reserve field artillery brigade possessed, for the same number of battalions, two light field howitzer battalions. If the former had among its 72 guns, 18 light field howitzers, so the latter, equipped with 4-gun batteries, displayed 24 light field howitzers out of a total number of 48 guns.

The field gun resources at home had been already fairly well exhausted with the formation of the first new units, and new production of materiel was not yet available. Therefore, as early as December 1914, it was necessary to have recourse to the stock of the Field Army. It was possible to do this because the Field Army had over 900 6-gun batteries,[17] out of which, by applying the principle of the 4-gun battery, some 300 new batteries were to be gained. In this re-formation the batteries required to form new units were taken, as 4-gun batteries, out of the regiments

---

16   Von Falkenhayn, page 38/39.

17   In the Field Army there were 612 batteries in the 102 Field Art. Regts, 183 batteries in the 29 Reserve Field Art. Regts, 33 Horse Artillery batteries, 80 Ersatz batteries, 11 Ldw batteries and 22 Ldst batteries. In total 941 batteries, of which, however, the Horse Artillery batteries were only equipped with 4 guns.

which were giving them up. The remaining batteries within the regiments were supplemented to 4-gun batteries. In March 1915, more field artillery brigades were formed for the infantry divisions in the 'fifties' series, on the pattern of those already discussed.

The Supreme Army Command had taken new steps in the formation of these new units and, to a certain extent, had conducted trials. Thus, from then on it adopted the principle of equipping every division with only one field artillery regiment of 2 gun battalions and one howitzer battalion, in which the battalion consisted of 3 batteries each with 4 guns. In the course of time therefore, the 4-gun battery also came to be implemented in the older regiments that had given up troops. In parallel with this went the process of supplementing, with a howitzer battalion, the Reserve regiments that had consisted of only 2 gun battalions. On the other hand, the field artillery brigade unit was at first left as it had been.

In the East, the batteries temporarily formed in the East from captured guns were indeed later put on the establishment. But after the campaign in Russia had ended they were all dissolved again. The individual battalions formed during the war immediately went into a new regiment or were extended to form one. The good preparation of the field artillery for war failed in the special use that needed to be made of it in the mountains. However, mountain warfare had been practised in peacetime throughout the year in the Vosges. General of Artillery Krafft von Dellmensingen writes about this:[18]

> The German field artillery went to war without any preparation in mountain warfare. The consequences were already evident in the first battles in the Vosges, exacerbated by the fact that on the German side only second and third line troops were fighting there, but on the French side there were well-practised field and mountain troops. Here, already, great difficulties often arose in bringing the guns of the German batteries into position. Things were made still more difficult by the fact that these German field artillery formations had no high-trajectory firing guns (light field howitzers) at all. The frontier corps (XIV and XV) which had in peacetime been based near the Vosges were not present in these battles, but had not yet drawn from their peacetime practices the consequences that the fighting in the Vosges required special precautions for the field artillery. Thus the French, with their mountain and field artillery for a long time had the advantage. Only later in the static trench warfare and after many high-trajectory firing guns had been brought up, could the Germans satisfactorily come to terms with the special conditions of mountain combat.

In the meantime, the Supreme Army Command had ordered the formation of 14 mountain batteries.[19] They were equipped with 7.5cm, later 7.7cm guns. A mountain howitzer detachment with light field howitzers was also set up. From the first three gun batteries it was possible, as early as November 1914, to put together Mountain Artillery Battalion 1.[20] After completing its training, it was first used in the Carpathians. Then, in May 1915, there followed Battalions 2 and 3. In August, No 4 was notable, because the mountain howitzer detachment was assigned to it.

18   In the book *Ehrenbuch der deutschen Feldartillerie,* under Organisation.
19   War Ministry of 12.10.1914, No 79. 10. 14. A. 4.
20   War Ministry of 4.11.1914, No 395. 11. 14. A. 4.

In October of the same year, No 5 consisted of 2 gun batteries and one howitzer battery, and remained the model for the mountain artillery battalions formed later.

The manual of the field artillery contained the regulation that individual batteries had to accompany the infantry attack to the closest possible quarters. This happened several times during the fighting, in the first months of the war, despite the extensive effect of enemy infantry fire. Later in trench warfare, there arose in the Minenwerfer, an aid against close-quarters targets which they could not overcome on their own. On the other hand, it became evident, in the attacks from positions that the Minenwerfer was not capable of following that the infantry assault and immediately intervening to help when it was a case of surmounting obstacles formed by individual nests of resistance or flanking positions and of preventing reverses. For this, again artillery was needed to accompany the infantry, but of course not the heavy field gun that was too heavy for this purpose. So the search was on for an effective lighter gun. At first, in May 1916, a battery of 3.7cm guns was assigned to the troops. From July of the same year, Russian 7.62cm guns were used for repelling an assault. But the 3.7cm guns did not prove to be sufficiently effective, and the Russian guns' barrels soon became worn out.

a2. Under the Hindenburg Army Command

When Hindenburg was appointed Chief of the General Staff of the Field Army, the reorganisation of the artillery, from the 6-gun battery to that of 4 guns, had been completed. Also, the preparation of the new field guns and improved light field howitzers had reached such an advanced stage that, in the Winter of 1916/17, the rearmament which had been put in hand on the training grounds behind the front could begin.

The new guns proved their worth, all the more so because the effect of shot had been increased by new ammunition and improved fuses. For the field gun the range had been increased from 7,800 to 10,700 metres, for the light field howitzer from 7,200 to 9,700 metres. The originally excellent field howitzer thus gained a further advance on the similar enemy guns, and from now on the new field gun proved itself to be equal to the French one.

The artillery regiment of two gun battalions and one howitzer battalion each of 3 batteries, introduced by the Falkenhayn Army Command, was retained. As well as the divisions equipped with such a regiment there were, however, many others with their original artillery brigades of 2 regiments each with 2 battalions. So in these divisions the principle of the 3-battalion divisional field artillery regiment was still to be implemented. But this aim was only of secondary importance to the Supreme Army Command. It saw as its most pressing task the creation of a strong reserve of Army field artillery in order to be equal, or superior, to the mass enemy deployment at the decisive spots in the fighting.

Thus the first step of the Supreme Army Command consisted of removing from each of the artillery brigades one regimental Staff, each with one battalion, and taking it into the Army Reserve.[21] The other battalion of these regiments was left with the divisions until such time as the divisional field artillery regiments had received their third battalions. This was the case until Spring 1917. Immediately,

---

21   Chief of the General Staff of the Field Army of 7.10.1916, No I. C. 36 509 op.

the second battalions of the field artillery regiments, left until then, followed their regiments, for which the third battalions were also being very rapidly procured. By Autumn 1917 the organisation of the unitary field artillery regiment was completed.

In December 1917, of the horse artillery battalions, four were changed into field artillery battalions, since one cavalry division had been dissolved and three cavalry divisions had had their horses taken away.[22] One year later the same thing happened to the four other horse artillery battalions.[23]

One more change in the battery's gun provision was temporarily introduced. In order to increase to a maximum the firepower for the great offensive in 1918, 2 more non-horse-drawn guns were given to every battery on the Western Front. This was an emergency measure, because if it had been possible to provide draught horses, new units would have been set up. In any event, nothing changed regarding the principle of the 4-gun battery.

In order to have available a quickly movable body of troops within the field artillery of the Army Reserve, in May 1918 the Supreme Army Command had six regiments temporarily motorised, ie the guns were loaded for transport on to lorries, the limbers coupled up to them.[24] These regiments were very often sent into action with great success. Their weakness was in bringing the guns up, at the right time, to the lorries that were tied to the roads.

The artillery was being harried by enemy aircraft, and there was the need for better means of defence against surprise attacks from close quarters. That led in November 1917 to all batteries on the Western Front each being equipped with 2 machine guns, to operate which every battery formed an MG detachment. This measure proved to be very advantageous.

The engagement of enemy aircraft by anti-aircraft gun, however, can only be discussed in connection with the air forces, in which the anti-aircraft defence was incorporated in December 1916.

The light munitions columns were originally seen as an inseparable component of the field artillery battalions whose designations they therefore also bore. In actual fact, however, these columns, because of the many movements of the battalions in conjunction with the overloading of the railways, were often separated from their battalion. They were used to help out another battalion whose own column had not been able to follow it. Because of this the distribution of the Light Munitions Columns became confused.

This circumstance, and the need to relieve the railway of all transport that was not absolutely necessary, caused the Supreme Army Command to fundamentally separate the light munitions columns from their units and to put them under the command of the divisional train échelons of the Armies.[25] As Army units the columns were numbered consecutively and were assigned to the battalions as circumstances dictated. Their total number rose to 785.[26] But the great offensive of 21

22 War Ministry of 11.12.1916, No 847. 12. 16. A. 4. (Horse Arty Btns of Field Art. Regts 3, 5, 8, and 10)
23 Horse Artillery btns of Field Art. Regts 1. G., 11, 12 and 35.
24 War Ministry of 15.5.1918, No 2031. 5. 18. A. 4 (Field Art. Regts 93, 201, 266, 280, 502 and 505)
25 War Ministry of 20.1.1917, No 160. 1. 17. A. 4.

March 1918 once again launched a period of the war of movement. In the West the light munitions columns were once again assigned, for the time being, to the field artillery battalions.

In the Rumanian campaign, the Hindenburg Army Command gave particular attention to the special area of mountain artillery. For the mountain artillery battalions in action there it ordered the formation of a pack animal column in the strength of 5 officers, 541 NCOs and other ranks - including 210 men in charge of the pack animals - and 400 pack animals.[27] That gave an extraordinary boost to the usability of the mountain guns. To the existing 6 mountain battalions a seventh was added which is particularly notable in that it included a 10.5cm Krupp mountain howitzer battery in conjunction with two 7.5cm Skoda gun batteries.[28] The use of the mountain artillery did not always correspond to its special characteristics. Eventually, out of the 7 batteries, 2 were in Flanders, 2 in the Vosges, 2 in Macedonia and 1 in Finland.

For anti-tank purposes the OHL ordered the formation of Close-combat Batteries 201-250 with the new pattern Field Gun 96.[29] But since machine guns with armour-piercing shells were very successful at close range against tanks, and field and foot artillery were very successful at longer range, the close-combat batteries were withdrawn again as early as May 1917. Therefore, they were used partly to form new third battalions for field artillery regiments, and partly to form new batteries of 'infantry guns'.

The Hindenburg OHL had already ordered a number of the latter with 7.7cm guns that could be dismantled. These units became mobile by August 1917. IGBs (batteries of 'infantry guns') 28-50, formed out of the earlier close-combat batteries, were unsatisfactory and in November 1917 were dissolved again. That was apart from No 28 that remained with Assault Battalion 5 for instructional purposes. Then the OHL succeeded in acquiring 7.5cm Skoda mountain guns from the Austro-Hungarian Army administration, so that from then on it was possible to form proper IGBs. They appeared at the front in May as IGBs 29-36,[30] from June as IGBs 37-51. They performed really well.

With the smaller number of proper IGBs the system of the infantry escort batteries had to be retained for assistance. The batteries selected for this task were, as fitted their use, equipped with the new pattern Field Gun 96 that was distinguished by its greater mobility.

For the training of the field artillery in tactics and gunnery technology, the Supreme Army Command ordered the setting up of special training grounds behind the front. Thus in December 1916 the training grounds at Sebourg, Maubert-Fontaine and Signy l'Abbaye were set up.[31] In February 1917 the training ground was set up at Thimongies,[32] and in April 1917, those at Grodno and Orany.[33] At

---

26   Nos 101-172 Bav., 176-526 (only 9 columns) and 741-1416 (with interruptions).

27   War Ministry of 4.11.1916, No 27 601. 16. A. 1.

28   War Ministry of 12.5.1917, No 1389. 17. G. A. 4.

29   War Ministry of 26.1.1917, No 300. 17. G. A. 4.

30   War Ministry of 18.5.1918, No 1386. 18. G. A. 4.

31   War Ministry of 1.12.1916, No 3327. 16. A. 4.

32   War Ministry of 20.2.1917, No 545. 17. A. 4.

about the same time, from February 1917, one field artillery recruit depot was formed with every Army and every Army Detachment.[34] In Autumn 1917 there were formed the Army Artillery Gunnery Schools of Bitsch, Mouzon and Mauberge for training in the collaboration of the field artillery with the heavy artillery.[35] Finally, in June 1917 a training ground at Dourlers was set up for the batteries of 'infantry guns'.

Altogether, towards the end of the war, the mobile field artillery comprised 297 regiments. Those were 3 horse artillery battalions,[36] 6 independent battalions and 7 mountain artillery battalions, 15 batteries of the original battalions behind the front, 6 independent batteries and 50 batteries of 'infantry guns', together with 3 IG detachments in Palestine.

Thus, the total number of batteries in the Field Army had grown from 941 at the beginning of the war, to 2,820. The number of the guns increased from 5,580 to 11,280. Calculated on the basis of gun type, the gun batteries had increased from 782 to 1,691, the light field howitzer batteries from 159 to 1,103. Added to this, were the Skoda mountain guns of Mountain Artillery Battalion 7 and the newer batteries of 'infantry guns'. Consequently the total number of batteries had approximately trebled, that of the gun batteries had more than doubled, that of the light field howitzers had increased by something approaching sevenfold. The ratio of the light field howitzer to the field gun within the Field Army had improved from 1:5 to 1:2.

Thus, in detail before the armistice, the field artillery was equipped as follows: 755 batteries with the new Field Gun 16, 751 batteries with the new light Field Howitzer 16, 66 batteries with the new Krupp light field howitzer, 6 batteries with guns on trial, together with 936 batteries with the new pattern Field Gun 96 and 286 batteries with the tried and tested light Field Howitzer 98/09.

With regard to munitions, during the war the universal shell[37] had been dropped again and a return had been made to the earlier divided construction of shrapnel and high explosive shell. For anti-tank purposes, armour-piercing shells had been introduced, for special purposes, at night star shells, and for close-range defence the old case shot had been brought back again. Often - and with great success - the field artillery also worked with gas shells. With regard to gas gunnery it is notable that on 1 October 1916 the Supreme Army Command formed an artillery brigade Staff and a field artillery Staff and foot artillery Staff to supervise this type of gunnery. But in July 1917 they were combined as advisory posts and renamed as Artillery Staffs for Special Use Nos 1-3.[38] To give an idea of how the use of munitions increased, it should be mentioned that the planned new production for the field gun had been set at 200,000 rounds, that for the light field howitzer at 70,000 rounds, whereas, in 1918, the monthly rate of use for the field gun varied between

33 War Ministry of 3.4.1917, No 996. 17. A. 4.

34 War Ministry of 20.2.1917, No 302. 17. A. 4.

35 War Ministry of 2.10.1917, No 1949. 17. A. 5.

36 There remained as horse artillery battalions, those of Field Artillery Regts 1, 15, and Bav.5.

37 Translator's note: Sometimes called the 'combined shell' (i.e. high explosive plus shrapnel).

38 War Ministry of 11.8.1917, No 3123. 7. 17. A. 10.

1,082,000 and 7,842,000 rounds and for the light field howitzer between 531,000 and 3,792,000 rounds!

b. Heavy Artillery
b1. In the first two years of the war

With mobilisation, the regimental unit of the foot artillery almost ceased to exist, in so far as the battalions of the heavy artillery were assigned individually to the Army Corps and the regimental Staffs were used in the Army Commands as needed. With the Field Army there marched out 26 heavy field howitzer battalions in the active corps, and the Guard Reserve Corps, one 10cm gun battalion with the IX Reserve Corps (initially held back as the Army of the North), and, as siege artillery with the Armies, 14 mortar battalions and one 10cm gun Reserve battalion. In total, therefore, there were 140 heavy batteries.[39] In that arrangement, the howitzer and gun battalions each had 4 batteries, the mortar battalions each had 2 batteries; but all the battalions each had 1 light munitions column and 1 foot artillery munitions column battalion.

Those active battalions and the Reserve battalions[40] not brought into the Field Army, formed a part of the planned complement of the fortification and coastal works. At the same time the Reserve battalions were designated as Army Reserve.

By way of very heavy high-trajectory fire artillery, 5 heavy coastal mortar (30.5cm) batteries had been assembled, each with 2 guns - including 2 set up for mechanical transport, for this there were also 2 steam locomotive parks -, in addition 3 short naval gun (42cm) batteries, including 2 for transport by rail, 1 for motorised transport. The latter was only ready in the first days of mobilisation and was equipped with a traction machine park assembled by the firm of Krupp.

In detail, the establishment strengths of the various units were:

The heavy field howitzer battery: 6 officers (battery commander, 3 lieutenants, 1 Train officer, 1 veterinary officer), 224 NCOs and other ranks, 122 horses, 4 guns (drawn by 6 horses) and 14 vehicles

The mortar battery: 6 officers, 249 NCOs and other ranks, 148 horses, 4 gun carriages, 4 travelling carriages,[41] 4 'wheel belt' wagons, 4 ammunition wagons, all drawn by 6 horses, plus 6 other vehicles

The 10cm gun battery: as for heavy field howitzer battery, but with 1 more officer and 26 more men

The light munitions column: 5 officers, 261 NCOs and other ranks, 193 horses, 29 ammunition wagons, etc

The non-horse-drawn coastal mortar battery: 6 officers, 129 NCOs and other ranks, 16 horses and 3 vehicles

---

39 26 heavy field howitzer battalions with 104 batteries, 2 gun battalions with 8 batteries, 14 mortar battalions with 28 batteries.
40 With the exception of one 10cm gun battalion which marched out with the Siege Artillery.
41 Translator's note: for mortars.

The short naval gun battery: as above, but with 105 more NCOs and other ranks

Steam locomotive park: 2 officers, 70 NCOs and other ranks, 25 locomotives, 3 large and 12 small tenders, 3 small cars

The decisive role of the heavy artillery became evident as early as the first battles. That was all the more so when it showed itself to be decidedly superior in terms of high-trajectory fire. Its importance increased still more when, because of the special conditions of trench warfare, high-trajectory and long-range guns were needed almost everywhere. Heavy artillery had to be made available both to the old and to the newly formed Reserve corps. Care had to be taken to reinforce the front by means of long-range guns. However, at first, only 34½ of the 50 active foot artillery battalions had been used to equip the Field Army, while 15½ battalions had been designated for fortification and coastal defence. All the Reserve foot artillery, with the exception of one battalion disposed with the Field Army, stood with 49 battalions at the disposal of the OHL in the fortresses. At the same time, there were disposed as foot artillery reserve, in part still without draught horses and columns.

In the first instance, these Reserve formations were available for use in the Reserve Corps. There was soon no longer any question of a threat to most of the German fortresses. Apart from a few which remained with coastal defence, the active formations along with most of the Landwehr batteries, many Landsturm batteries, and also surplus batteries, could be taken from the fortresses. Recourse was also had to Ersatz batteries. To supplement the insufficient low-trajectory fire, the Navy made available guns from armoured ships that had been put out of service.

These reinforcements could be successful only gradually, but nevertheless in January 1915 the point had been reached at which on average two heavy field howitzer batteries could be assigned to every division.

Corresponding with this was also the provision, on the establishment of each of the infantry divisions of the 'fifties' series, formed in March 1915, of one heavy field howitzer battalion with 2 batteries. Meanwhile it had no longer been possible to assign heavy artillery so lavishly to the next series, the infantry divisions numbered 101-123. They each had to be satisfied with one foot, artillery battery that was taken from existing battalions. These batteries were immediately renamed and received the number of their division. For instance, 'in the interest of clarity', the 1st Battery Foot Artillery Regiment 13 with the 111th Infantry Division became Foot Artillery Battery 111.[42] In actual fact, the disposition of the foot artillery had already become really confused.

The reduction of the number of batteries in the foot artillery battalion, from 4 to 3, released a number of batteries that first, under the compulsion of having to provide assistance simultaneously in many places, were used individually. For this reason the newly formed units were also, at first, formed as autonomous batteries. However, the necessity to bring them together, as soon as possible, into battalions had already been taken into consideration. In order to create a firm backbone to the Armies' artillery defence, from March 1915 a large number of non-horse-drawn battalions were equipped with guns of older design - principally with 9cm guns - or with captured guns. In this process, materiel from the Belgian and French for-

42   War Ministry of 2.8.1915, No 2586. 7. 15. A. 5.

tresses, and from August also from Russian fortifications was used. In this way there came into existence in 1915, Foot Artillery Batteries Nos 201-631 and in 1916 more batteries up to No 796.

The partly horse drawn, partly motorised, effective and much-loved 15cm gun batteries, whose guns were provided by the Navy, were specially numbered as Nos 1-31, and later up to 48.[43] The non-horse-drawn batteries formed the constant element in the constantly changing equipment of the Armies. With heavy artillery, they had every now and again to carry out a change of position. To this end, at the beginning of 1916 the Supreme Army Command ordered the formation of draught horse detachments, first in the Western fortifications, but soon also with the Armies,[44] and also ordered the formation of 7 foot artillery tractor parks.[45] The latter were, as Army troops, renamed, as early as the end of the same year, as Army Foot Artillery Tractor Parks and their number increased to 10,[46] so that almost every Army received such a Park. On the other hand, the Falkenhayn Army Command soon dissolved some of the draught horse detachments in favour of forming new foot artillery battalions. That was a process that the succeeding Army Command continued more vigorously and had completed by Spring 1917.

Meanwhile, the Supreme Army Command did not exhaust itself in bringing into existence hundreds of individual batteries with mainly old and captured equipment, but set everything on creating new foot artillery battalions with mainly modern armament. As early as 1915 it had 29 battalions formed (including 8 of the Landwehr). They were joined in the following year by 104 new battalions (including 21 Landwehr battalions); it is true that some of these only appeared after the change of Supreme Army Command. In order to give the individual batteries a common command of fire 35 battalion Staffs were set up, of which 11 were reformed into regimental Staffs as early as 1916. Changed into such Staffs were the 15 Landwehr foot artillery regimental commands of August 1914, originally designated as on home service.

From the middle of 1915 onwards, to support the infantry in close combat, the foot artillery formed 18 trench gun battalions, with 3.7cm 'revolver guns' from the flanking defences of the fortresses.[47] These guns, however, could only be used in defence, so that as soon as a usable infantry gun had been introduced, they were dispensed with again.[48]

Special mountain equipment was also introduced for the heavy artillery. That was certainly not in the form of a special gun, but in the form of special means of transport. In the Balkans a number of mountain échelons proved their worth for the transport of howitzers and 10cm guns.[49] Each of these échelons consisted of 48 carts that took over the transport of the dismantled guns and ammunition from the

43   First formations by War Ministry of 25.2.15, No 207. 15. G. A. 5.

44   War Ministry of 6.1.1916, No 2501. 12. 15. G. A. 5.

45   War Ministry of 3.2.1916, No 1516. 1. 16. A. 5.

46   War Ministry of 15.12.1916, No 16. 12. 16. A. 7. V; among them No 3 Bavarian..

47   War Ministry of 16.6.1915, No 2410. 6. 15. A.5.; in accordance with War Ministry of 11.3.16, No 352. 16. G.A.5. manned by infantry.

48   War Ministry of 11.2.1918, No 229. 2. 18. A. 5.

49   War Ministry of 2.10.1915, No 1851. 15. G. A. 4.

valley road up into the mountains. According to need, these échelons were newly formed or dissolved again. In the end there were only 14 left.

Initially the Supreme Army Command viewed the heavy artillery as Army troops, insofar as, according to the order of battle, it did not belong to the divisions or Army corps. It was assigned to the General Commands and divisions, but did not move with them. Instead, it came under the command of the relieving command. Even so, the heavy artillery formations were frequently moved in accordance with the war situation.

Particularly noteworthy is the reformation of the mortar battalions of 2 4-gun batteries, into 3 batteries of 2 guns. Also, a newly built 15cm gun was tested as a trial gun.

Artillery Park companies were formed for those battalions designated for fortress warfare. They carried the designation of their battalion, but did not follow it in use in the field. Since they naturally found a wide field of activity in trench warfare, the OHL made them into Army troops towards the middle of 1915. But their removal from the establishment of the battalions with corresponding change of designation only took place at the end of 1917.[50]

By way of munitions columns every active battalion had taken with it into the field 8 (mortar 4) together with 1 light column. As they were used in the field, most of the Reserve battalions had been temporarily equipped with columns. Taking account of the conditions of trench warfare, in July 1915 the OHL took steps towards a comprehensive reorganisation of the columns. It dissolved the columns that had existed up to that point, re-formed them and assigned a column to every horse-drawn battery. The rest were made into Army columns that were numbered consecutively in the Army.[51] The Army columns took over responsibility for supplying ammunition to the non-horse-drawn batteries. As a battery received draught horses that were, for the most part, put in place under the Hindenburg Army Command, an Army column was permanently assigned to it, so that the Army columns gradually disappeared again.

While at the beginning of the war only 148 heavy batteries were with the Field Army, at the end of the Falkenhayn era their number on the Western and Eastern Fronts amounted altogether to about 1,380, including some 290 formed with captured matériel. Falkenhayn had created the 3-battery battalion and had reorganised the columns. The processes of bringing the individual batteries together into battalions, re-arming them with modern equipment and providing them with draught horses were under way. The superiority in high-trajectory fire had existed from the beginning and was maintained. On the other hand there had been no success in catching up with enemy advances in very heavy low-trajectory fire. The munitions situation as a consequence of the enormous expenditure of shells, on the Maas and on the Somme, appeared to be unsatisfactory.

50 War Ministry of 19.12.1917, No 2480. 17. G. A.; redesignated as Artillery Park Companies Nos 1-61 and Bav. 1-6.
51 First by War Ministry of 19.12.1915, No 1007. 15. G. A. 5. Army Foot Artillery Munitions Columns 1-303, together with individual higher numbers, were formed.

b2. Under the Hindenburg Army Command

The third Supreme Army Command took up the case of the heavy artillery with particular interest. Its first measures were directed at rectifying the shortage of munitions, at quickly increasing the number of battalions, and at strengthening the very heavy low-trajectory fire. At this time also the 15cm Gun 16, which had been tested as a trial gun, was introduced.

The Winter Programme managed to provide draught horses for new heavy field howitzer and 10cm battalions by reducing the strength of the munitions columns. It then raised the strength of the Landwehr and Landsturm battalions in general to 6 batteries, and set up 14 more 15cm batteries with naval guns. The 1916/17 Winter programme called for, inter alia, 14 horse-drawn battalions, 13 batteries of heavy field howitzers, 6 batteries of 15cm guns with tractors, 14 non-horse-drawn Landwehr battalions, 4 railway defence batteries with 24cm guns - providing a straight increase of 145 batteries. In Spring 1917, there were added a further ten 15cm gun batteries, twenty-two 24cm gun batteries, and five 21cm batteries, together with ten crane units for changing the positions of the 21 and 24cm guns. By using Navy stock, another fourteen 17cm gun batteries became available by June 1917.

It is particularly noteworthy that, at the end of 1916, the OHL agreed with the War Ministry's suggestion of a fresh reorganisation of the mortar battalions into the 2 or 3-gun battalion, but always with 3 guns per battery.

If, with the restoration of organisational coherence, Foot Artillery Regiments 3, Guard 21-28, Bavarian 4-6 together with Regiments 12 and 19 were set up, the changing combat conditions prevented special regiments being deployed. Instead, apart from directing the OHL Reserves the regimental staffs were employed mainly in commanding larger artillery groups. In the same way the 25 regimental Staffs without troops were formed under Falkenhayn, the number of which was increased by a further 15.[52]

On the other hand, the foot artillery battalion appeared more and more expressly as the tactical unit of the heavy artillery. Indeed, apart from the Landwehr and Landsturm battalions, they were in the form of the 3-battery battalion adopted under Falkenhayn. Based on the experience of the war, in this battalion high-trajectory fire was linked with low-trajectory fire. For this reason, in 1917 the heavy battalions generally had to be re-formed into 2 heavy field howitzer batteries and one 10cm gun battery. Also, often two 21cm mortar batteries were combined with one 15cm gun battery into a battalion. The munitions column for every battery remained, having been introduced under Falkenhayn. From Autumn 1917 onwards every division, with the exception of those in the East, received in the order of battle a heavy battalion of 2 howitzer batteries and one gun battery. This battalion in many cases did not remain with its division, but was ordered away, or replaced by another, as the war situation dictated.

The Landwehr foot artillery battalions for the most part had no draught horses. They often only appeared as the combination of earlier autonomous batteries and changed the number of these from 4 to 9.

52   cf Appendix IV.

Only a few of the many batteries outside the battalion unit remained in existence, among them mainly those armed with very heavy high and low-trajectory guns. Towards the end of the war there were still the following individual batteries: 7 short naval gun batteries,[53] 8 heavy coastal mortar batteries,[54] and four 15cm gun batteries,[55] together with 46 other batteries (mostly very heavy low-trajectory fire).

Fundamentally, the question of the number of guns in the heavy battery was settled in August 1917 by a new regulation concerning battery strength.[56] According to this regulation, the heavy field howitzer battery and the 10cm gun battery were each to have 4 guns. The 21cm mortar battery and the 13cm gun battery were each to have 3 guns. The heavy 15 and 17cm gun battery as well as the 30.5cm mortar battery and the 42cm short gun battery were each to have 2 guns. Here, only the most common types of gun are mentioned, but, at this point, it should be noted that for each gun type there were various models. Thus, for instance, there were four models of the heavy field howitzer. All in all during the war there were 73 models of gun, including 57 captured models. The latter were a stop-gap which was dispensed with as soon as German materiel was available.

As already noted, right at the beginning of the war the German high-trajectory fire was superior to that of the enemy. Efforts were made, by means of improvement of matériel, to maintain this advance if at all possible. That was all the more so when, with regard to increases in gun numbers, it was not possible to keep pace with the enemy forces. Thus the long, heavy, field howitzer 13, and the long 21cm mortar were created by lengthening the barrels by 3 calibres. That increased the range of the howitzer from 8,500 to 9,400 metres, and that of the mortar from 9,400 to 10,200 metres. A newly-constructed 18.5cm howitzer, which gave the same performance as the 21cm mortar, but was more mobile, was put to use in only 3 batteries. The previous 10cm gun was lengthened by 10 calibres and, as the 10cm Gun 17, replaced its predecessor.

By contrast, a new experimental 13cm gun produced in 1918, which was supposed to combine the effectiveness of the 15cm gun with greater mobility, was rejected by the troops. They stuck by the excellent 15cm gun that was in actual fact more effective.

However, the effectiveness of the heavy artillery was not only fundamentally improved with respect to guns, but also in its shells. By screwing on false caps, in the case of high explosive shells it was possible to better overcome air resistance and thereby achieve greater ranges. In 1917 also, it became possible to produce a new time fuse with longer running time so that it could also be used at long range. Quite early on,[57] special registration shells were developed to produce coloured and particularly dense smoke. There were also new 9, 12, and 15cm cast steel shells and a 15cm cast steel shrapnel shell.

In 1918, the heavy artillery was used as follows. Its arm of the service was under the command of the Army High Commands, including some parts designated

53 5 had joined battalions.
54 2 had been drafted into battalions.
55 42 had been absorbed into battalions. There remained as individual batteries Nos 16, 20, 21 and 39. Batteries 11 and 17 were dissolved.
56 War Ministry of 13.8.1917. A. 5.
57 War Ministry of 26.11.1915, No 60. 11. 15. A. 5.

as Supreme Army Command Reserve. It was thus available to the Army only by special permission. Besides this there was one battalion each with every division. The Army High Command assigned its heavy artillery to the General Commands and kept back a reserve, at any rate one, or several, long-range artillery groups. In turn, the General Command distributed artillery among the divisions the artillery assigned to it. The effect it had on the artillery war, consisted, as already mentioned, in the assignation of targets and in orders which guaranteed mutual support by the divisions. Therefore the actual artillery war lay in the hands of the divisional artillery commander, while long-range targets were engaged by the long-range artillery group of the Army.

The long-range artillery groups were supposed to cripple the long-range enemy artillery. They had also to force back enemy balloon and ground observation, to hinder movements to the rear of the enemy front and to effect the destruction of the enemy munitions and equipment stores, railways, bridges, airfields and occupied areas.

As early as November 1916, the Supreme Army Command appointed a Staff Officer for very heavy low-trajectory fire[58] to gather and evaluate experience as long-range fire was of such significance. On the instructions of the Supreme Army Command, this officer advised the command authorities concerning the deployment and activity of the very heavy batteries. He also clarified their technical and ballistic questions. He reported on the status of construction of positions and railways for the very heavy guns. He conducted courses of instruction and promoted training in accordance with the instructions of the Supreme Army Command. His activities were taken over, on 13 August 1918, into the Operations Section of the Chief of the General Staff of the Field Army.[59] In the Army High Command the 1st Staff Officer of Artillery made the preparations for deploying the very heavy low-trajectory batteries. As soon as an enemy attack was imminent, or a German offensive was planned, the Supreme Army Command assigned to the Army High Command in question a Section Staff for a very heavy long-range artillery group. That would be if one were not already available.

Counted in the very heavy low-trajectory artillery were all the long-barrelled guns of 17cm calibre and over made available by the Navy. Those were brought together into 44 batteries. They included the 17cm quick-firing gun with a range of 24,200 metres. The 21cm quick-firing gun had a range of 26,400 metres. The 24cm quick-firing gun had a range of 26,600 metres. The 28cm quick-firing gun had a range of 27,750 metres. The 35.5cm quick-firing gun had a range of 47,500 metres, and the 38cm quick-firing gun had a range of 38,700 metres.

The specially built 'Paris gun', which bombarded Paris between 23.3 and 9 August 1918, achieved a range of some 130 kilometres. It had a calibre of 21cm and, by means of a cartridge loading of 300kg, fired high-explosive shells weighing 150kg at a muzzle velocity of 1600 m/s. The elevation went up to 55 degrees. At a distance of 120km the shells reached a height of 40km so that they covered most of their course in the vacuum of space, and hit their target after 3 minutes in the air.

58 War Ministry of 2.12.1916, No 5320. 11. 16. G. A. 5. (Initially called 'Staff Officer for Heavy Low-Trajectory Fire')
59 War Ministry of 13.8.1918, No 1498. 18. G. A. 5.

The gun, 7 of which were produced, first fired from the district of Laon (128km), then Beaumont (109km), and finally Chateau-Thierry (87km).

As with the field artillery in some regiments, and the heavy artillery, the Supreme Command, in 1918, had Foot Artillery Battalions 142, 167, 168, 169 and 171 equipped with tractors.

In November1916, the need to provide rapid replacement led to the formation of a foot artillery Ersatz battalion in those Armies which had that year undergone the heaviest fighting, that is, the 2nd and 5th Armies, as well as Army Group Below which was in particularly poor condition. Four months later, these battalions plus another battalion were put on the establishment as Foot Artillery Ersatz Battalions 1-5.[60] In December 1917 they were increased by the addition of a sixth battalion. During the decisive year of 1918 they were all in the West.

A foot artillery gunnery school in the war zone was set up in January 1917 in Guise,[61] but was moved to Maubeuge as early as 21 March. At that time, in the same area, there came into existence the Maubeuge Foot Artillery Training Ground, New training grounds were set up at Jurbise, Longnyon, Insmingen and Namur,[62] on which the comprehensive processes of assembling new units and rearming took place. In May 1917 the Hirson training ground was added, and in February 1918 that of Liège. The latter was expressly designated for winding up foot artillery formations which had been withdrawn.[63]

Alongside these, the Army Gunnery Schools were set up at the beginning of October 1917, in Bitsch, Mouzon and Maubeuge[64]. The latter replaced the Maubeuge foot artillery gunnery school and served to provide joint training for the field artillery and heavy artillery in unified collaboration in battle.

In 1918, just as had happened with the field artillery, the heavy batteries also each received two machine guns for anti-aircraft and close-range defence.

In 1915 the eight workshops of the siege artillery that dated from mobilisation[65] in1915, had already been increased to 12 by the Falkenhayn Army Command, with the formation of new Armies. Also taking into consideration the Army Detachments in the West, the Hindenburg Army Command brought their number to 21.[66] In addition to these, it set up, with the General Commands, 50 artillery repair shops,[67] the number of which finally rose to 57. They increased by 7 the 14 mobile workshops with motor traction which they had taken over from the Falkenhayn Army Command. In addition, it introduced 6 new railway-mounted workshops.[68] The repair shops were also placed at the service of the south-eastern allies. They themselves advanced as far as Baghdad and Damascus. This opportu-

60 War Ministry of 9.3.1917, No 482. 17. G. A. 5.
61 War Ministry of 20.1.1917, No 144. 17. G. A. 5.
62 War Ministry of 10.3.1917, No 483. 17. G. A. 5.
63 War Ministry of 18.2.1918, No 295. 18. G. A. 5.
64 War Ministry of 2.10.1917, No 1949. 17. G. A. 5.
65 One with each Army: Nos 1-7 and Bav. 1.
66 Nos 1-17 and Bav. 1-4.
67 War Ministry of 4.6.1917, No 3909. 5. 17. A. 5.
68 War Ministry of 3.6.1917, No 1195. 17. G. A. 5. Mobile repair shops with motor traction Nos 1-4 and 21-27, railway-mounted Nos 15-20.

nity can be taken to also consider the German munitions factory in Constantinople, whose outstanding performance made it possible to bring the fighting at Gallipoli to a victorious conclusion.

In the end, if the external growth of the heavy artillery with the Field Army is considered, the 148 heavy batteries that marched out on mobilisation compared finally with over 1550 batteries, ie a tenfold increase.[69] This increase also corresponded with their deployment in battle. In August 1914, in the three Armies on the right wing of the Army, there were 60 heavy batteries, in the Armies in the breakthrough of 21 March 1918, ie the 17th, 2nd and 8th Armies, however, there were 633 heavy batteries, that is, more than a tenfold increase.

3. The Artillery Survey Service

The successful use of artillery involves reconnaissance of the target, and observation of the impact of shells. As long as the field artillery was firing from open firing positions, with direct observation, this was simple. But since the French artillery basically came into action in covered positions, great difficulties resulted. Those were only less with the foot artillery because firing from covered positions had already penetrated into the very marrow of their bones. Some help was given by far advanced, if possible elevated, observation. But nevertheless in the face of artillery formed under cover they were almost helpless, as was shown in the battle before Nancy-Epinal. Of course the difficulties increased with trench warfare.

At first the only aid available was balloon observation[70] and that provided a really good service. They also used some giant periscopes whose masts consisted of steel tubes telescoped together and were firmly tied down to a vehicle. Raised and extended by means of a winding mechanism, the mast carried the objective lens at its upper end, the ocular lens at its lower end, so that the periscope could be used, from behind cover, up to about 25 metres high. Balloon observation and the later artillery observation by aircraft will be discussed in the section on the air forces.[71] Here however, discussion will be restricted to the means the artillery itself had at its disposal.

In the foot artillery they worked with the plans to which they had become accustomed in preparing for fortress warfare, and for larger artillery groups had set up

69   Towards the end of the war:
    37 Foot Art. Regts (23 with 3, 9 with 4, 5 with 2 battalions) = 115 battalions = 345 batteries
    25 Res. Foot Art. Regts (10 with 3, 8 with 4, 7 with 2 battalions) = 76 battalions = 228 batteries
    169 Foot Artillery battalions (163 with 3, 6 with 6 batteries each) = 525 batteries
    55 Ldw Foot Art. battalions (with 3 to 9, most with 6 batteries) = 340 batteries
    6 Foot Art Ersatz battalions in France, one in Macedonia = 20 batteries
    Foot Art batteries (autonomous) = 46 batteries
    15cm gun batteries (autonomous) = 4 batteries
    Coastal mortar batteries (autonomous) = 8 batteries
    Short naval gun batteries (autonomous) = 7 batteries
70   With each Army there was an airship battalion with several balloon units.
71   See Part IV F 2 b.

artillery survey sections. But at the same time an observation procedure had been developed which led, in September 1915, to the formation of 101 survey sections.[72] To set them up the previous survey sections were used. The new survey sections worked both for the heavy artillery and for the field artillery. In 1916, they increased those to 29 and in 1917 to 177. At the end of 1917 the artillery survey sections changed their name to observation groups,[73] in order to avoid confusion with a second survey method introduced in 1916.

The observation groups served both to establish the position of the enemy guns and to observe their own shots. Initially, the rough method of obtaining a bearing on the enemy gun flashes gradually developed into an almost exact establishment of the position of individual enemy guns. At the same time, the method of shell impact observation was perfected, from the fixing of the explosive cloud on impact, to the so-called time fuse elevation survey gunnery in which neither high ground, woods, nor marshes, could hinder observation. The whole procedure, however, depended upon the availability of the maps produced by the survey sections. Those had to contain some topographical features, the position of which had been determined by trigonometric means.[74]

An observation group comprised 5 to 6 survey posts and an artillery plan post. The latter served to evaluate the survey results, in it there were the commander, 2 lieutenants and 27 NCOs and other ranks. The individual survey post, on the other hand, had a complement of only 11 men.

In parallel with this survey method another was developed, called sound ranging. It was carried out in the same way as the observation procedure, except that instead of the gun flash the sound of the gun muzzle firing was used as the object of measurement. Only during the war had it been observed that shells with a greater initial velocity than that of the sound caused two bangs. There was the usual bang at the muzzle and a second as a result of the compression of the air in front of the head of the shell. So the second reached the ear of the observer first. The time between the two disturbances of the air, called report separation, was by experiment linked to the calibre of the guns. That meant that in sound ranging not only the location of the target but also the calibre of the enemy gun could be determined. In addition, this survey method had the advantage of being able to be used in bad weather, and in the mountains, too. On the other hand, it could not be used in the case of bombardment. After it had been satisfactorily developed, by the end of 1915, 51 sound ranging sections were formed,[75] which within a year increased in number to 129. In the establishment of the sound ranging sections there appeared 2 officers and 14 NCOs and other ranks, as the complement of the artillery plan post and 12 men to man each survey post.

The importance of the survey sections increased even more. They succeeded in extending an artillery sound ranging procedure to the trigonometric determination of topographical features on their own ground. By those means, survey and observation posts as well as battery positions could be exactly determined, within a very short time, by trigonometric means. By this means the survey service, previously

72   War Ministry of 29.9.1915, No 1811. 15. G. A. 5.

73   War Ministry of 8.11.1917, No 1697. 17. G. A. 5.

74   Schwab, page 70.

75   War Ministry of 25.1.1916, No 1582. 1. 16. A. 5.

tied to positions taken by carto-graphical means, gained greater mobility and could be made use of for the war of movement.[76]

An important role in artillery gunnery was played by considering the current effects of the weather. The range tables of the artillery were set for conditions of medium air pressure and wind speed, thus on two factors that only extremely rarely coincided. It was therefore of great importance to forecast, in advance, the weather situation as far as it affected gunnery. This was so successful that, in August 1917, it was possible to introduce 31 artillery reporting sections to carry out meteorological calculations.[77] These sections worked in conjunction with the weather stations,[78] the further extension of which, however, led to the sections being able to be dispensed with from May 1918.[79]

Survey procedures and meteorological calculation had thus achieved a stage at which it was possible to unobtrusively prepare the artillery attack and to carry it out effectively and with surprise. On the other hand, a similarly prepared enemy attack could only be identified by the aerial photographs taken by aircraft. But aircraft also remained indispensable for gunnery observation outside concentrated fire, and in the war of movement.

In May 1918, a third survey method came on the scene. It was based upon the combination of obtaining bearings visually and by sound ranging. For this, 3 direction finder detachments were formed, by amalgamating 3 observation groups and 5 sound ranging sections.[80] Ground survey sections with the numbers 501-503,[81] brought out in August 1918, appeared too late to be able to be developed into a fourth survey procedure.

The survey sections were Army troops, and were placed at the disposal of the groups and divisions for as long as they were present on the Army front. Thus the artillery commander of a combat division in the West had at his disposal an observation group and a sound ranging section.

The importance of the artillery survey service and the large number of individual small formations necessitated close supervision to ensure uniformity of procedure and to safeguard the evaluation of experience. Therefore, in August 1916, an Inspector of the Artillery Survey Service was assigned to the General of Foot Artillery in the Great Headquarters.[82] Shortly afterwards a similar post was set up on the Staff of the Supreme Commander East. The Inspectors served as technical service heads. The Artillery Survey School was set up on 31 October 1916, in Wahn, and made an essential contribution to the further development of the survey service.

76   Schwab, page 20.
77   War Ministry of 26.8.1917. No 1654. 17. G. A. 5.
78   See below: Part IV F 2 f.
79   War Ministry of 25.5.1918, No 4203. 5. 18. A. 5.
80   War Ministry of 15.5.1918, No 1823. 5. 18. A. 5.
81   War Ministry of 12.8.1918, No 1515. 18. G. A. 5.
82   War Ministry of 30.8.1916, No 1579. 16. A. 5.

E.

Pioneers

1. Generals and Regimental Commanders

Every Army of the mobilised Army Commands had a General of Pioneers, as adviser to the Supreme Commander, on all questions concerning the pioneers. That was apart from the General of the Engineers and Pioneer Corps in the Great Headquarters. As new Armies and Army Detachments were formed, the numbers of these generals increased, so that in 1917 it had risen to 21.[1] The Generals of Pioneers, however, did not remain all the time with the same Army Command, but often changed. For instance, Generalmajor von Mertens, from 6 January 1917 Generalleutnant, found himself successively with the 7th, 10th and 8th Armies, then with Army Groups Linsingen and Mackensen, and with the 5th, 2nd, 1st and 17th Armies.

The already many-faceted pioneer arm of the service greatly increased during the war and developed new branches of its activity. Therefore the area of the tasks also grew that fell to a General of Pioneers with the Army High Command. As the development of the pioneer service reached its height, these tasks can be outlined as follows: Technical preparation - to the extent that this involved the pioneers, of all offensive and defensive measures taken by the High Command; Supervision - of the organisation, training, use and deployment of all pioneer formations, and also of field fortification within the Army; Evaluation - of experience; Supply - of all forms of pioneer equipment; Minenwerfer, together with munitions, field fortification materials and Close-combat weapons; Direction - of construction in positions to the rear; Supervision - of the pioneer field recruit depots and the Army's Minenwerfer School. In addition, he controlled the pioneer siege train, the Army and Group pioneer parks, the Army construction materials store and high explosives store, the pioneer collecting station, and the Minenwerfer Park together with repair shops.

On mobilisation 10 pioneer regiments had been formed for siege purposes.[2] In Summer 1915, the enemy fortresses in the area of advance in the West had been taken and those in the East had fallen. Meanwhile, everywhere along the front the need for pioneers was growing. Also the unity of the regimental units could no longer be maintained. Therefore the regimental commanders, some earlier, some later, were separated from their regiment and were placed by their Army High Command at the disposal of the groups to direct larger scale pioneer technical works and operations. By the end of 1915 their number was already no longer sufficient for these purposes. In the period up to October 1916, the Supreme Army Command set up the posts of Staff Officers of Pioneers Nos 51-56, and Bavarian 1.[3] They were

1   Generals of Pioneers 1-20 and 31.
2   Pioneer Regts 18-20, 23-25, 29-31 and Bav. Pioneer Regt.

153

given the authority of regimental commanders and which were called by the troops with the abbreviation 'Stopi'.

In the reorganisation of the pioneers by the Hindenburg Army Command the pioneer regiments were also dissolved as far as their name was concerned. Their commanders then similarly received the designation Staff Officers of Pioneers.[4] Through the increase in the number of posts which took place at the same time, the number of Stopis rose to 23.[5]

Thus, the Stopis (regimental commanders) were placed at the disposal of the General Commands, as individual circumstances required. From January 1917, in the establishment of the General Command itself. The battalion commander of pioneers had been replaced by a 'Staff Officer or Captain of Pioneers'. This, as the 'or' suggests, involved younger officers. But now in the course of 1917 really difficult supply conditions often arose on the main combat fronts. That meant the Supreme Army Command decided to assign to the affected Groups permanent 'Staff Officers of Pioneers with a General Command'.[6] They were given the numbers 150-165 and Bavarian 40-42. These Stopis, like the earlier ones, had the rank of regimental commander. They differed from the latter only in the fact that they were not assigned for a time, but remained with their Group even when the General Command commanding the Group changed. The 'Staff Officer or Captain' on the establishment of the General Command came under the Stopi as long as a Stopi was assigned or as the General Command led a Group provided with a Stopi.

Meanwhile, the fighting in 1918 taught that the differentiation between Stopi, and permanent Stopi, at least as far as the conditions in the Western theatre of war were concerned, was no longer effective. But rather each of the General Commands in the West required a permanent and inseparable adviser on technical questions concerning the pioneers. The Supreme Army Command therefore removed the distinction between the designations 'Stopi' and 'Stopi with a General Command'. Instead they assigned the pioneer regiment commanders with the general service designation 'Stopi' (but without changing their numbers) to the Western General Commands. By that process the Stopi became part of their establishment and took into his Staff the previously established 'Staff Officer or Captain'.[7]

The service instructions for the pioneer regimental commander (Stopi) stipulated[8] that "he is the adviser of the Commanding General on technical questions affecting the pioneers, and forms the pioneer section of the General Command. He controls the supply of pioneer equipment in the Army Corps or Group. He is available as director of all the pioneer works that have not been assigned to the divisions. He makes recommendations concerning deployment and use of the pioneer formations under the direct command of the General Command. He is, however, not the service head of the divisional pioneer formations. For him there is no special

3   For the first time by order of the War Ministry of 12.12.1915, No 1008. 12. 15. A. 6.
4   War Ministry of 24.1.1917, No 105. 17. G. A. 6.
5   Stopis 51-71, 73 and Bav. 1.
6   War Ministry of 11.5.1917, No 474. 17. A. 6.
7   War Ministry of 4.9.1918, No 1482. 18. G. A. 6.
8   Issued by War Ministry of 11.5.1917, confirmed by 4.9.1918.

service route to the troops under the command of the General Command." The last sentence, which at first seems disconcerting, can be explained as a necessary consequence of the first sentence of this service instruction, according to which the pioneer regiment commander was head of section in the General Command.

Finally, as Stopis, there were the service posts numbered 51-71, 73-77, 150-168, 170, Bavarian 1-3 and Bavarian 40-42.

2. Field Pioneers and Miners, together with Close-combat Weapons

a. Until the end of 1916

On mobilisation every peacetime pioneer battalion formed two battalions, each with 3 companies. Thus, for example, from Pioneer Battalion 3 were set up the 'I Battalion of Pioneer Battalion 3', with 1, 2 and 3 Companies together with a searchlight section. The 'II Battalion of Pioneer Battalion 3' was set up with the 4th Company and the 1st and 2nd Reserve Companies. The I Battalion gave to the III Army Corps the 1st company. They gave to the 5th Infantry Division, the 2nd and 3rd companies to the 6th Infantry Division. The II Battalion gave to the III Reserve Corps the 4th company to the 5th Reserve Division, the 1st and 2nd Reserve companies to the 6th Reserve Division. Meanwhile the battalion Staffs joined the respective General Commands. The searchlight section was incorporated within the corps troops of the active corps. The battalion commanders remained heads of their troops, took care of technical supplies relating to the pioneers and most particularly were also expert advisers for their General Command.

The establishment of a pioneer company comprised 6 officers (commander, 2 lieutenants, MO), 264 NCOs and other ranks There were 22 horses, 4 pioneer store wagons, field kitchen, a supply wagon and a baggage wagon.

Nine of the peacetime battalions[9] each formed, from their two field battalions, a pioneer regiment for the siege formations of the Armies, in which process they took the battalion number as regimental number. That was with the exception of the Bavarian Pioneer Regiment. Added to these was Pioneer Regiment 31, formed from one field battalion respectively of the Guard Pioneer Battalion and Pioneer Battalion 28. Nine of these regiments carried a pioneer siege train with it. Pioneer Regiment 31 was only equipped with one in December 1914. The Staff of the pioneer regiments was distinguished by the fact that its complement of officers included, in addition to the commander and 2 adjutants, also one more Staff Officer and two captains for special use. As well as the baggage wagon, they also included another registration wagon and two touring-cars.

Beside these troops, on mobilisation, another two Landwehr pioneer companies, 2 Landsturm pioneer companies and 14 Ersatz pioneer companies marched into the field. While the establishment of these companies did not essentially differ from that of the active companies, the pioneer section of a cavalry division had 2 officers, 46 NCOs and other ranks. They had 31 horses and 6 cavalry pioneer wagons to transport personnel and materiel.

---

9   Nos 18-20, 23-25, 29, 30 and Bav. Pi. Btl.

The other pioneer formations that were mobilised, i.e. searchlights, pioneer siege trains together with park companies and pontoon trains, are given their tribute below.[10]

The equipment of the divisions with pioneers, tailored to meet the requirements of the war of movement, did not meet the requirements of trench warfare. Therefore the Supreme Army Command first had recourse to the companies of the pioneer regiments, but without dissolving their regimental unit. As early as 1914, they brought another 109 pioneer companies into the field, including 27 from the Reserve, 42 from the Landwehr, 27 from the Landsturm, and 13 Ersatz companies. In the following years, too, this increase was continued. In that process, 10 already-existing mobile Ersatz companies and 4 Bavarian Reserve Companies were re-named. The 10 companies' flamethrower units, set up for the III and IV Battalion of the Guard Pioneer Battalion, are not discussed here.

By the end of 1916 the number of 218 pioneer companies[11] originally with the Field Army rose to 592 companies.[12] So the Falkenhayn Army Command had changed nothing in terms of organisation, but had raised the number of pioneer units by more than 2½ times. In the meantime, the number of divisions in the meantime had also risen to over 200 and a whole series of pioneer companies were engaged in special duties. From then on most divisions possessed two pioneer companies. This weighed in the scales even more since meanwhile, the number of infantry regiments in the division had been reduced from 4 to 3. That was a weighty matter.

But the Supreme Army Command had also, from another point of view, seen to it that pioneer technology relieved the infantry. As early as 1915, it set up in the infantry divisions, pioneer training courses for the infantry. That meant the infantrymen trained there could serve as preparatory workers and were trained for the construction of defences. Thus they might not be used as infantry pioneer companies in their own right, which was for some time the case with many divisions. In any event, the infantry became less dependent on the pioneers than they been previously.

By far the most prevalent special use of the pioneers during the Falkenhayn era, apart from the Minenwerfer that will be dealt with separately,[13] was in providing mining services. During trench warfare the battle underground, which had been seen as dispensable in the age of the strongest effects of artillery, revived again. Often the opposing positions approached to within a few metres of each other, so that the artillery was not able to bombard the enemy trenches without detrimentally affecting their own. So on both sides the need had to arise to undermine the enemy position and blow it sky-high.

The works required for this were technically not easy, so that individual pioneer companies were specially trained and made ready to provide this service. Such

10   See Part IV E 3, 10 and 11.
11   Pi. Btls Guard, 1-30 and Bav. 1-4 each with 4 active companies = 140 companies
      Pi. Btls G., 1-27 and Bav. 4 each with 2 Res. Pi. Coys = 58 coys
      Pi. Btl. Bav. 1 and 2 each with 1 Res. Pi. Coy = 2 coys
      In addition: 2 Ldw., 2 Ldst., and 14 Ers. Coys = 18 coys
12   On mobilisation 218 coys, added 1914: 109, 1915: 188, 1916: 77.
13   See Part IV E 4.

companies were taken up into the Army troops and made available to the front as circumstances required. The work began with sinking vertical shafts to the required depth. From there, horizontal workings were driven to a point at which they were under the enemy position, loaded with high explosive, sealed off and detonated at the time of the planned infantry attack. Since the enemy was working in the same way, special listening posts had to be set up to establish that enemy mining activity was taking place and to warn the German miners. If work was going on from both sides, it was a matter of reaching the target first or crushing the enemy workings with a special explosive charge.

The companies of miners were counted in the series of the other pioneer companies, but in their use remained strictly separate from the latter. They were systematically set up in April 1916.[14] Before and after that date only individual units were formed. Under the designation 'Pioneer Miner Companies', their number eventually amounted to 46.[15]

b. From January 1917

Soon after taking up office, the Hindenburg Army Command also set about fundamentally reorganising the pioneers and letting a sharp distinction be made between the divisional and Army troops. This intention found its definitive expression in the order of 6 January 1917[16] that read:

> Every division shall receive at least 2 pioneer companies and a pioneer battalion Staff. Pioneer Regiments 18-20, 23-25, 29-31 and the Bavarian Pioneer Regiment shall be dissolved. The I Battalions of Pioneer Regiments 18-30 and the Bavarian Pioneer Regiment shall remain with 4 companies. The II Battalion Pioneer Regiment 31 will remain with 3 companies as self-contained pioneer battalions with the designation Pioneer Battalion 18 pp. Alongside the Army troops will remain, or will be incorporated, the Pioneer Miner Companies, the Landwehr and Landsturm Pioneer Companies (insofar as they do not, in the order of battle, belong to the divisions), together with the companies designated for special tasks. The gas troops,[17] flamethrowers[18] and pontoon trains[19] will not be affected.

From then on, in the pioneer battalions, the division into I and II Battalions was discontinued. The I Battalions took the simple designation of their peacetime battalion, while the II Battalions received consecutive numbers.[20] By bringing in the renamed previous Reserve and Landwehr pioneer battalion Staffs, as well as a result of new units being formed, in this way the number of 'Pioneer Battalions' rose to 238.

---

14 War Ministry of 7.4.1916, No 608. 16. G. A. 6.
15 Pi. Miner Coys 281, 292-300, 309, 311-314, 318-327, 329, 330, 333, 352, 398-400, 410-415 and Bav. 1-8.
16 Chief of the Gen. Staff of the Field Army of 6.1.1917, No I. C. 43 755. op.
17 See Part IV E 5.
18 See Part IV E 6.
19 See Part IV E 11.
20 War Ministry of 24.1.1917, No 105. 17. G. A. 6.

The addition of a Minenwerfer company and a searchlight section to every pioneer battalion will only be mentioned here; details concerning these units will be given separately later.[21] But for the sake of consistency it must be anticipated and pointed out at this point that in January 1918 the searchlight sections, leaving out the portable searchlight detachments, joined the Army troops. Meanwhile, the Minenwerfer companies, from August of the same year onwards, left the pioneer battalions, and were distributed among the infantry regiments to form their own Minenwerfer companies.

Of the special equipment of the pioneer companies, mention should be made of the light-pistols. An established number of 9 of those were always carried with them. However, they soon appeared in the infantry companies and artillery batteries - 3 of them at first, later 5.[22] From the beginning of trench warfare, hand grenades were first used by the pioneers with great success. After some initial temporary designs, a stick grenade with time fuse came to be introduced, of which every pioneer and infantryman carried 8 with him. Because of its great effect on morale, in attack it proved its worth quite exceptionally in attack. The 'Egg' hand grenades brought into use later did not have the same quality of making a strong impression on the mind. They were very effective and could be carried around in great quantities. They were especially recommended for defence.[23]

From February 1915[24] every pioneer company possessed 6 light Minenwerfer. To these were added in September 1916 two Granatwerfer,[25] which were equipped with Minenwerfer barrels and could fire their bombs a distance of 300 metres. They replaced the Minenwerfer at close range and had the advantage over the latter that they were less easy for the enemy to spot. The rifle grenades used previously had not proved effective, since they lacked the necessary accuracy of fire.[26]

All these combat weapons were grouped together under the designation 'Close-combat weapons'. To transport them every pioneer company received on their establishment 2 Close-combat weapons wagons.[27] In April 1917, on the Staff of the General of Pioneers in the Great Headquarters, the service post of, and Inspector of Pioneer Close-combat Weapons was created, to whom fell responsibility for supervision, improvement and use of this matériel.[28]

At about the same time that the Supreme Army Command had to take the Minenwerfer companies out of the pioneer battalions, it reinforced the pioneer battalions with another very effective combat weapon. In September 1918 it gave orders that the pioneer companies on the Western Front, and first those with the infantry divisions, should each be equipped on their establishment with 3 portable flamethrowers.[29] As the first instalment every company received 2 flamethrowers,

21   See Part IV E 4 and 3.
22   War Ministry of 26.6.1917, No 615. 6. 17. A. 6.
23   War Ministry of 30.12.1916, No 1559. 12. 16. A. 6.
24   War Ministry of 5.2.1915, No 158. 15. G. A. 6.
25   War Ministry of 22.9.1916, No 1433. 8. 16. A. 6.
26   War Ministry of 30.12.1916, No 1559. 12. 16. A. 6.
27   War Ministry of 9.1.1917, No 996. 12. 16. A. 6.
28   War Ministry of 10.5. 1918, No 2264. 4. 18. A. 6.
29   War Ministry of 28.9.1918, No 1672. 18. G. A. 6.

to use which they formed a special unit under the command of an officer. The use of the flamethrower regiment, whose history will be specially detailed later,[30] remained unaffected by this new measure. It retained its special tasks as a combat unit to resolve difficult tasks, as a training school for the Army and as the responsible authority for the further development of its arm of the service.

The setting-up of field recruit depots behind the front met, in the case of the pioneers, with greater difficulties than with the other arms of the service. That was because not every kind of terrain was suitable for the many-faceted pioneer service. In Autumn 1915, General of Infantry von Mudra, the Commanding General of the XVI Army Corps, and earlier Inspector-General of Engineers and Pioneer Corps, had set up for his divisions that were engaged in the difficult fighting in the Argonne,[31] two pioneer field recruit depots. In the following year similar establishments were set up with another two Armies. However, it was only the Hindenburg Army Command that equipped every Army with a pioneer field recruit depot.[32]

In December 1916, for the purpose of training whole pioneer battalions, the Supreme Army Command created the Pioneer Training Ground of the Army Reserve at Jeumont.[33] In May 1917, it incorporated in this Pioneer School, one for further training of pioneer officers and NCOs.[34] The Pioneer School in Kovno, set up at the same time, only existed until the beginning of March 1918.

An overall view shows an increase in the number of pioneer companies with the Field Army, from 218 at mobilisation, to 649 towards the end of the war. That was a threefold increase. Enormous quantities of pioneer equipment, explosives, means of ignition and field fortification materials rolled up from Germany for the pioneers. In order to give an idea of the amount, it should be mentioned here that, in August 1918 alone, 3500 tons per day arrived for the Army of the West.[35]

3. Searchlight units

At the beginning of the war searchlight units had been brought along almost exclusively for illumination of the territory in front of the main battle line. Among them a distinction should be made between those of the pioneers and those of the anti-aircraft defence. Although at first they were all served by pioneers, a consequence of bringing together the air forces under one Commanding General was that the searchlights of the anti-aircraft defence were transferred into the air forces. Here it is possible only to deal with those searchlight formations which continued to belong to the pioneers.

In the Field Army of 1914 there was a searchlight section with each of the General Commands of the active corps and the Guard Reserve Corps as well as in the Great Headquarters. In addition, searchlights were carried by the pioneer siege trains.

30   See Part IV E 6.
31   War Ministry of 14.10.1915, No 442. 10. 15. A. 6.
32   War Ministry of 6.12.1917, No 1013. 17. G. A. 6. - Pi. Field Recruit Depots 1-16 and 18.
33   War Ministry of 6.12.1916, No 427. 12. 16. A. 6. - In August 1918 moved to Huy.
34   War Ministry of 30.5.1917, No 154. 5.'17. A. 6. - In August 1918 moved to Andenne.
35   From 5.8. - 1.9.1918: 9954 railway trucks each with a load of 10 tons.

The searchlight section had an establishment of 2 officers, 39 NCOs and other ranks. They had 28 horses, 2 light searchlights, 2 equipment wagons and a fodder wagon. The searchlight was composed of the light carriage and the mechanised limber. The carriage carried the 60cm parabolic mirror. There were four portable acetylene searchlights on the equipment wagon. While these portable searchlights were distributed in the trenches, the carriage-mounted searchlights went as darkness fell into the searchlight position and disappeared again at daybreak. Thus they escaped any planned bombardment.

As soon as the situation on the Western Front had become frozen, the searchlight sections were no longer suitable, all the less so when in the East, too, the war soon came to a standstill. It was therefore necessary to have recourse to a part of the fortress searchlight units and, for the time being to make do with temporary illumination of the terrain before the lines. However, in 1914 another 12 Reserve searchlight sections were formed. The two, following years brought an increase of 100 or 101, and 1917 an increase of 7 more formations. Thus, after taking away 52 sections that were redesignated, and 50 that transferred to the air force, finally 241 searchlight sections were available.

In the reorganisation of the pioneers in January 1917 the searchlight sections were incorporated into the pioneer battalions. Some months later the portable acetylene searchlights were dispensed with. In exchange, for every searchlight section received incandescent lamp searchlights in such numbers that every pioneer company received 15 together with a battery-charging machine.[36] In addition, from October 1917 a number of autonomous portable searchlight units were formed with the same equipment.[37] From then on, the supply of portable incandescent lamp searchlights had become so great that it was sufficient to meet the local purposes of the divisions. Thus the Supreme Army Command could think of bringing back the mobile searchlights under their control, in order to be able to deploy them in large-scale battles. Therefore, in January 1918, the searchlight sections, leaving behind their portable equipment, were taken into the Army Reserve, while the portable incandescent lamp searchlight sections remained with the pioneer battalions as portable searchlight units. But from then on all units were recognised on the establishment.[38]

4. Minenwerfer units

a. Under the Falkenhayn Army Command

From the time of the fighting between the Russians and the Japanese for Port Arthur, the German General Staff had recognised the high value, in attacking fortifications, of great explosive charges fired at short range. It therefore placed an order with the firms of Krupp and Erhardt for the construction of firing pieces of this kind. They took over from Erhardt's factory the heavy Minenwerfer that Erhardt had produced. Those were weapons that possessed a rifled barrel with recoil, and a calibre of 25cm. They fired, to a distance of almost 420 metres. They had high ex-

36 War Ministry of 21.7.1917, No 1205. 6. 17. A. 6.
37 War Ministry of 24.10.1917, No 1204. 10. 17. A. 6.
38 War Ministry of 22.4.1918, No 654. 18. A. 6.

plosive shells with time and percussion fuses. To meet the possibility that an enemy force might appear with similar weapons, the General Staff also had produced another medium Minenwerfer. It had a range of 800m and, with 17cm calibre, could fire high explosive shells weighing 50kg. Finally, another Minenwerfer was approved. It was the light Minenwerfer which with a barrel recoil and 7.6cm calibre fired fixed ammunition, with shells weighing 4.75kg. It achieved a range of 1050m.

The Minenwerfer were kept strictly secret so that the German Army was the only army that took Minenwerfer with them into the field. Meanwhile, at mobilisation only 70 heavy and 116 medium Minenwerfer were ready, while the lighter models were still in the process of being delivered. The Minenwerfer were located in the pioneer siege trains and were manned by specially trained personnel as circumstances dictated. At that time, there were not yet any special Minenwerfer formations. If the Minenwerfer did not prove their worth in the sieges in the West, because of the massive destructive power of the 30.5cm and 42cm mortars, they proved themselves completely, once they were put into action.

Here, too, trench warfare brought the decisive turning point. As soon as an attack was undertaken from fixed positions it was evident that, because of the mostly short range of the enemy trenches, the artillery had not succeeded in destroying particular targets which were decisive for the success of the attack. Here the Minenwerfer, with its high angle fire and its accurate firing, was of assistance. As a result of this a general demand for Minenwerfer arose. The Supreme Army Command was all the more willing to accede to this demand because, within its own limited range, the Minenwerfer had the same penetrative effect as the artillery. Moreover, it had an extraordinary effect on morale. Its weaknesses were that it took a very long time to dig in, that its rapidity of fire was less, and that there was a greater danger of it being spotted by the enemy. Because of its short range it had to go into position close to the infantry line.

At first the Supreme Army Command brought up the Minenwerfer which had been held back in the fortresses at home, and gave orders for the production of temporary Minenwerfer by the pioneers. In addition, it unified the heavy Minenwerfer already to hand in the pioneer siege trains into the special commands of Minenwerfer Sections 1-7.[39] It further determined that every Army Corps and Reserve Corps should receive 2 heavy Minenwerfer sections each with 2 Minenwerfer, and a medium Minenwerfer section with 6 Minenwerfer.[40] Finally, in January 1915, it assigned 6 light Minenwerfer to every pioneer company[41] and set up a great number of autonomous sections with heavy, medium, or light Minenwerfer.

The great importance attributed to the Minenwerfer as an offensive weapon caused the Supreme Army Command, as early as April 1915, to raise by one more Minenwerfer battalion the Army Reserve of 7 heavy sections which it had been planned to deploy in action.[42] The establishment of this battalion carried in its Staff the commander, 1 captain for special use, 1 scientific adviser, 1 adjutant, 2 meteo-

39 War Ministry of 18.12.1914, No 2526. 14. G. A. 6.; these were mounted on motor vehicles.
40 War Ministry of 5.2.1915, No 158. 15. G. A. 6.
41 War Ministry of 16.1.1915, No 2512. 12. 14. A. 6.
42 War Ministry of 16.4.1915, No 750. 15. G. A. 6.

rologists, 1 MO, 1 veterinary officer and 1 paymaster.[43] The battalion at first consisted of 5 Minenwerfer sections each with 4 medium and 2 light Minenwerfer. On the establishment there were also attached a survey unit and a weather unit. Together with a signals section they had to create the basis for firing gas shells and to produce the firing maps for the Minenwerfer. However, during the course of 1915, firing gas shells proved to be ineffective because there was not sufficient massed strength. It was dependent upon the wind direction and that caused trouble. Therefore it was principally the tried and tested high explosive Minenwerfer shells that were used. As early as 1915, the Supreme Army Command set up three further battalions for the Army Minenwerfer Reserve.

In Autumn 1915, the men of the Minenwerfer units received as a distinguishing insignia to their pioneer uniform the letters 'M.W.' on their epaulettes and underneath the number of their autonomous battalion either in Roman or in Arabic numerals.[44] A year later this insignia, in its usual gilt form on the epaulettes, was also given to the officers.[45]

After a large number of Minenwerfer sections and non-established Minenwerfer detachments had been created at the front,[46] the Supreme Army Command moved towards their plan of bringing together these still loose and confused formations. From September 1915 onwards it brought together the sections and detachments into companies which came directly under the command of the divisions.[47] The divisional Minenwerfer company joined together a detachment with 2 heavy Minenwerfer, one with 4 medium Minenwerfer, and one with 6 light Minenwerfer, for transporting which 6 limbers and 8 ammunition wagons (which also had room to carry the light Minenwerfer) were provided. Every company formed its own Minenwerfer survey unit, for which it received equipment for surveying, observation, signalling and copying.[48] In conjunction with the divisional topographical section[49] the survey unit produced the Minenwerfer firing maps. For the surveying procedures the observation groups of the artillery served as a model.[50]

In conjunction with this new organisation, the Supreme Army Command put in place in the Great Headquarters an Inspector of Minenwerfer[51] who was responsible for supervision of the units and the equipment.

At the end of 1915 the status of the Minenwerfer arm of the service, after all these changes, was as follows: Inspector of Minenwerfer, 4 heavy Minenwerfer battalions and 8 heavy Minenwerfer motorised vehicle sections as Army Reserve, 105 divisional Minenwerfer companies, as well as 6 light Minenwerfer with every pioneer company.

43 War Ministry of 13.7.1915, No 1358. 15. G. A. 6.
44 A.V.Bl. 1915. No 750. War Ministry of 5.10.1915, No 2361. 6. 15. B. 3.
45 A.V.Bl. 1916. No 606. War Ministry of 19.9.1916, No 31. 8. 16. B. 3.
46 86 heavy, 108 medium and 114 light sections, 113 heavy, 169 medium and 206 light detachments.
47 War Ministry of 22.9.1915, No 1743. G. A. 6.
48 Translator's note: i.e. copying by means of printing, hectograph, etc.
49 See Part IV G.
50 See Part IV D 3.
51 War Ministry of 24.12.1915, No 1092. 11. 15. G. A. 6.

In 1916 the number of Minenwerfer companies, with 112 new units being formed, rose to 217, that of the Minenwerfer battalions to 7. At the same time the establishment of the companies was increased to 3 heavy, 6 medium and 12 light Minenwerfer.[52] Among the companies there were, as a special type, the mountain Minenwerfer companies, designated with the numbers 170-175. These were equipped with mules and carts, and where they were from time to time assigned was a decision that the Supreme Army Command reserved for itself. In 1917, these mountain formations were further increased by the addition of Company 176. It is also notable that in 1916 the assault battalions [53] and the Jäger battalions[54] in the West each received a Minenwerfer company of 8 light Minenwerfer.

b. Under the Hindenburg Army Command

The change of Supreme Army Command in Autumn 1916 also brought radical changes for the Minenwerfer. Until this point the light Minenwerfer both in the Minenwerfer companies and the battalions were used in conjunction with medium and light Minenwerfer. Thus the Hindenburg Army Command decided that the latter two, more effective, types of Minenwerfer were to be the only weapons of the Minenwerfer battalions and companies. Meanwhile the light Minenwerfer were to pass from the pioneers to the infantry.[55] On the other hand, the Minenwerfer companies and battalions received a new establishment, the companies to have 4 heavy and 8 medium Minenwerfer, the battalions to have 4 of these companies. The battalions' involvement in gas gunnery was completely discontinued and with it the weather service in the battalion Staff.

This reorganisation represented, as far as the light Minenwerfer were concerned, a definite stop-gap. Originally the Supreme Army Command had thought of equipping the divisions with a second Minenwerfer company. But this intention failed because the pioneers, already loaded down with many other special duties, could no longer provide the necessary replacements. Now, by making the light Minenwerfer an auxiliary weapon of the infantry and giving every infantry battalion 4 Minenwerfer, the Supreme Army Command achieved something like the same success by a different route. It was that the division from now on had at its disposal 48 Minenwerfer as against the previous 21.[56]

In conjunction with the organisational changes, the Supreme Army Command attached a Minenwerfer Officer to every infantry regiment. They set up Army Minenwerfer Schools behind the front,[57] to instruct the infantry regiment and battalion commanders in the use and operation of the Minenwerfer, and to raise the level of training of personnel. Since the area of responsibility of the Inspector of Minenwerfer in the Great Headquarters had become too large, the Supreme

52 War Ministry of 27.4.1916, No 667. 16. G. A. 6.
53 War Ministry of 11.3.1916, No 3268. 16. A. 1.
54 War Ministry of 8.71916. M.J. 14 180. 16. A. 1.
55 War Ministry of 16.11.1916, No 1784. 16. G. A. 6.
56 Previously 1 Mwf. Coy with 3 heavy, 6 medium and 12 light Minenwerfer; from now on 1 Mwf. Coy with 4 heavy and 8 medium Minenwerfer, in addition 9 x 4 = 36 infantry battalion Minenwerfer.
57 War Ministry of 13.10.1916, No 179. 10. 16. A. 6.

Army Command assigned three Inspectorates.[58] In July 1917 they even added four.[59] Also under the command of the Minenwerfer Inspectors, from now on numbered 1-4, were the Minenwerfer repair shops. Some of those had already come into existence singly in 1916,[60] but only in 1917 and 1918 were they generally created for every Army.

Because of the extensive equipping of the infantry with light Minenwerfer, the increase of Minenwerfer for the pioneers, was able to be kept within more modest limits. In 1917 only 39 new Minenwerfer companies were formed, bringing the total number to 256.

On the other hand, a transition was being made to the construction of a Flügelminenwerfer,[61] the effects of which weapons being used by the enemy in the Battle of the Somme, had been impressive. The Flügelmine,[62] thanks to its being guided by fins, had the advantage of not turning over but always hitting the target with the point, and boring into the ground. Thus it had a far greater effect on the surrounding area. The Flügelminenwerfer were produced in two models, and differentiated from each other by the names of their builders, as Iko[63]-Werfer and Albrecht-Werfer.[64] They achieved a range of 3500m.

In 1917, in order to make ready a stronger Minenwerfer Reserve for the large-scale battle and to succeed in breaking through by the mass deployment of medium and heavy Minenwerfer, the Supreme Army Command undertook another considerable increase of the Minenwerfer Reserve. It increased to 13 the number of the 7 Minenwerfer battalions at its disposal and also took charge of another 40 divisional Minenwerfer companies. Then, in 1918, it used these 40 companies to form Minenwerfer Battalions 14-23;[65] at the same time the battalions were also equipped with 3.7cm anti-tank guns.

Particular care was needed in the training of the Minenwerfer company commanders. Since the existing educational institutes could not provide this, in October 1917, the Army Reserve School Valenciennes[66] was set up. Even senior commanders and General Staff Officers took part in the courses.

For the great offensive, in Spring 1918, the Supreme Army Command had issued the instructions, already discussed earlier, concerning the 'Attack in trench warfare'.[67] With regard to the Minenwerfer the instructions read:

> All Minenwerfer of the Minenwerfer battalions and companies are in the offensive a component part of the offensive artillery. They shall be brought together

---

58 War Ministry of 7.1.1917, No 2155. 12. 16. A. 6.

59 War Ministry of 8.7.1917, No 2249. 6. 17. A. 6.

60 Initially by War Ministry of 28.2.1916, No 264. 16. G. A. 6.

61 Translator's note: a type of mortar firing trench mortar bombs with fins.

62 Translator's note: trench mortar bomb with fins.

63 i.e. 'Ingenieur-Komitee' (Engineering Committee).

64 In this way the designation 'Albrecht-Mörser-Kommando' (Albrecht Mortar Command) came about; this was the temporary name for the Park formation of the Albrecht-Werfer, later Pioneer Park Company 38.

65 War Ministry of 25.7.1918, No 365. 7. 18. A. 6 and of 20.8.1918, No 628. 8. 18. A. 6.

66 War Ministry of 26.10.1917, No 691. 10. 17. A. 6.

67 See Part I A 2f.

as a whole or in sectors under Minenwerfer commanders and be integrated as groups in the order of battle of the offensive artillery. Even the light Minenwerfer of the infantry can, to ensure unified preparatory fire, be temporarily incorporated in the offensive artillery.

With this instruction the Minenwerfer's main characteristic as an offensive weapon, and as a substitute for artillery at close ranges, was again clearly spelled out. But placing it under the command of the artillery formed the necessary precondition for unified collaboration of both arms of the service.

Up to that point the battalion commanders had been the most senior officers of the Minenwerfer troops. Then in the large-scale battle, several battalions were to be brought together to ensure a unified effect. Therefore, correspondingly more senior officers were lacking. Therefore, in February 1918, the Supreme Army Command changed the 4 Inspectors into Minenwerfer Staff Officers Nos 1-4 and gave them authority of regimental commanders.[68] At the same time it put in place the Inspectors of Minenwerfer Equipment Nos 1 and 2.[69] They were allocated responsibility for supervision of matériel, while the Minenwerfer Staff Officers, besides their responsibilities as battle commanders, supervised the standardisation of training and the activities of the troops.

In view of the requirements of the decisive year 1918, field recruit depots for the Minenwerfer, too, were set up in the Army of the West. They were numbered 1-6.[70]

As will be recalled, difficulties in recruitment for the pioneers had at the end of 1916 led to the light Minenwerfer being handed over to the infantry. However, those difficulties increased in 1918 to such an extent that the Supreme Army Command in August felt compelled to now dissolve even the divisional Minenwerfer companies.[71] They apportioned their medium Minenwerfer among the 3 Infantry Regiments of the division. At the same time it took the heavy Minenwerfer into the battalions of the Army Reserve. But the infantry regiments now each formed, out of the medium Minenwerfer assigned to them and the light Minenwerfer already available in their battalions, a 13th company, the establishment of which was determined as 3 medium and 9 light Minenwerfer. The Minenwerfer officer on the regimental Staff was discontinued.

The reorganisation was not yet completed when the armistice took place. If one wants to find out how many Minenwerfer companies existed at the end of the war, one must start with the fact that from the high point of 256 divisional Minenwerfer companies, 40 had been used to form the last 10 Minenwerfer battalions. Consequently the distribution of the companies works out as follows: 92 companies of the 23 Minenwerfer battalions, 200 x 3 = 600 Minenwerfer companies of the infantry regiments and 16 old divisional Minenwerfer companies. That is, 108 manned by pioneers and 600 manned by infantry, in total 708 companies.[72]

---

68   War Ministry of 24.2.1918, No 1239. 2. 18. A. 6.
69   The difference in responsibilities from the earlier inspectors, who were called 'Inspectors of Minenwerfer', is expressed in the difference between their names.
70   War Ministry of 19.2.1918, No 292. 18. A. 6.
71   Chief of Gen. Staff of the Field Army of 17.8.1918. No II 9870 geh op.; War Ministry of 17.9.1918, No 1498. 18. G. A. 6.

5. Gas Troops

The German Army had not been prepared for gas warfare. But soon there were grounds to suspect that the French were busy with experiments testing the use of gas for combat purposes. Therefore the OHL charged the War Ministry with testing the possibilities of using gas as a weapon of war. In the War Ministry, Geheimrat Dr Haber undertook this work and recommended the so-called emission of gas clouds procedure. This procedure required that the iron cylinders filled with chlorine gas should be secretly installed in the German positions. They were to be opened when a favourable wind was blowing towards the enemy, so that the gas cloud was rolled by the wind on to the enemy positions. The weakness of using gas in this way was the fact that the attack was dependent upon the wind direction. Thus, German troops were in danger both from direct hits on the installed cylinders and also from the ground wind suddenly changing direction and blowing back towards them.

From mid-January 1915, after the preparatory work had reached a satisfactory stage, the War Ministry ordered the formation of two pioneer companies under Colonel Petersen. Under the direction of Dr Haber's assistants, they were to practise the use of gas in warfare, on the Wahn firing range.[73] For reasons of secrecy this unit was first given the name 'Disinfection Unit'. After completing their training both companies joined the 4th Army as gas warfare troops and were increased to 6 companies. On 29 March 1915, the Supreme Army Command ordered their formation into a regiment of 2 battalions, each with 3 companies.[74] The regimental Staff received reinforcements consisting of a technical Staff and a meteorological Staff, together with a telephone section. Designated from 12 April as Pioneer Regiment 35,[75] it carried out its first gas attack, under favourable conditions, on 22 April 1915 to the north of Ypres, with complete success. Since the enemy Powers had till then achieved nothing with their own experiments with gas, they used this first German gas attack to blacken the name of Germany, before all the world, as the originator of a new and terrible weapon of war.

As early as May 1915, a second gas regiment was formed as Pioneer Regiment 36. In August the establishment for the two regimental Staffs was finally fixed.[76] It amounted to 17 officers and 32 NCOs and other ranks. Among the officers were the commander, 1 Staff Officer for special use, 2 adjutants, 8 officers for the field weather station, an MO, veterinary officer, a lieutenant in the fortress construction service and a paymaster for each regiment. At the same time, a Park company for control of equipment, was incorporated in each regiment with a strength of 3 officers, 89 NCOs and other ranks.

Only in December 1916 did the Hindenburg Supreme Army Command approve the appointment of an Inspector of Gas Regiments with the General of Pio-

---

72   To this were added the light Minenwerfer of some 50 infantry regiments which had not yet been able to form Minenwerfer companies.

73   War Ministry of 14.1.1915, No 90. 15. G. A.6.

74   Chief of the Gen. Staff of the Field Army of 29.3.1915, No 19 241. op.

75   War Ministry of 12.4.1915, No 734. 15. G. A. 6.

76   War Ministry of 5.8.1915, No 1347. 15. G. A. 6.

neers in the Great Headquarters. He had to supervise training and regularly to evaluate experience, experiments and new developments.[77]

During the course of 1917 it became evident that the regimental unit was superfluous for deploying gas troops and that the reconnaissance preliminary to an attack was best controlled directly from the Great Headquarters. Therefore, in August 1917, both regiments were dissolved and their place taken by the autonomous Pioneer Battalions 35-38. The previous Inspector was appointed as Commander of Gas Troops.[78] The two Park companies of the previous regiments, however, joined to form the Park Company of Gas Troops.

At the same time a new attack procedure came to be introduced. Some 50 gas cloud attacks had up to this point been carried out with varying degrees of success. Again and again the absolute dependency on the weather had been found to be very unpleasant. At that stage recourse was taken to the earlier experiments with Minenwerfer and gas bombs, but in doing so the method was changed. Instead of a kilometre-deep gas attack on the enemy front, which could be carried out with favourable winds, then what was required was a surprise gas attack. It had to be timed to the minute, and directed on important targets in one limited locality. Those targets had to be so far from the German front that even with a change in the wind direction, and with good anti-gas protection, there was no obstacle.

For this new combat procedure, every battalion received simple gas mortars with 10cm wide smooth steel barrels and a range of 1600m. The gas bombs were fired off in salvoes by means of electrical fuses. The first time they were used, in the fighting on the Isonzo on 24 October 1917, they brought sweeping success.

Therefore, on 1 February 1918, the Supreme Army Command increased the number of gas battalions by adding Pioneer Battalion 39, and on 22 June 1918, by adding Pioneer Battalions 94-96. Finally there were 8 gas battalions. At the same time, however, the introduction of rifled barrels gave the gas weapons significant increases in range and accuracy.

On 23 September 1916, field companies of expert workers were formed in Valenciennes and Warsaw, to fill the gas cylinders, and later the gas bombs. On 6 February 1917, Field Munitions Establishments 1 and 2 emerged from these. While the field companies in Warsaw had to be dissolved again, as a result of the armistice on the Eastern Front, the establishment in Valenciennes was extended, to form Field Munitions Depot West, with 2 Park companies.[79]

Alongside the use of gas against the enemy, went the measures to protect German troops from injury by enemy gas warfare. As early as 1915, anti-gas protective devices were issued that were soon perfected into gas masks. The reorganisation of the gas troops, on 23 August 1917,[80] also systematised anti-gas protective measures. At that time a Staff Officer of Gas Troops was put in place with every High Command in the West. He was responsible not only for giving technical advice to the High Command and supervising the gas troops of his Army, but also for ensuring that all troops were equipped with anti-gas protective devices and knew how to use them. Similarly, on 23 August 1917, appeared the post directly subordinate to him

77 War Ministry of 10.12.1916, No 1962. 16. G. A. 6.
78 War Ministry of 23.8.1917, No 391. 17. G. A. 6.
79 War Ministry of 23.12.1917, No 1153. 11. 17. A. 10.
80 War Ministry of 23.8.1917, No 391. 17. G. A. 10.

in rank. That was the Gas Officer on the divisional Staff. Under his command was the gas officer in every other battalion, while every other company possessed a non-commissioned gas office within their narrower framework. All these anti-gas protection authorities carried out the responsibilities of the Staff Officer of Gas Troops in the Army High Command.

6. Flamethrower Units

As early as the war in East Asia, the Japanese had used burning fluids against the Russians. In Germany this fact was considered but not imitated. Then, at the end of 1914, Diplom-Ingenieur Reddemann, as commander of a Landwehr pioneer company, in conjunction with Ingenieur Fiedler, produced an apparatus that could be used in war. It sprayed a light, inflammable oil, and ignited it as it emerged by means of an igniter. This discovery was immediately taken up by the Supreme Army Command, since the apparatus required no lengthy trials. It was produced in 2 different sizes. Also it was suitable both for installation in positions, and for being carried on the back, That promised many possibilities for use.

Thus, in January 1915, Section Reddemann comprised 48 selected pioneers and 12 heavy flamethrowers. Once equipped, and after training was completed, it was assigned to the 5th Army. There the section was sent into action as early as 26 February 1915 in the attack on Bois de Malancourt. They reaped a degree of success that exceeded all expectations. With this a decisive affirmative answer was given to the question of further extension of the new weapon.

Then, in March 1915, in the Guard Pioneers Ersatz Battalion, the III Battalion was formed from firemen and suitable volunteers. They came from all arms of the service with the 9th-12th Companies as flamethrower formations. In the same year the 13th and 14th Companies were added. In February 1916, the IV Battalion, with 2 more companies, were added. From these component parts, in April 1916, the Supreme Army Command set up the Guard Reserve Pioneer Regiment,[81] under the command of Major Reddemann.

This flamethrower regiment was brought up to the strength of 3 battalions, each with 4 companies. An experimental company and a training company were attached. In addition, every battalion received a workshop section. Of the 12 combat companies each one carried 3-40 portable flamethrowers, which on marches followed up with all fuel and spare equipment in a wagon column belonging to the company. Meanwhile further supplementary stores were brought up on lorries, which carried in addition another 12 to 15, heavy flamethrowers.

The regiment was under the direct control of the Supreme Army Command, close to which was located the regimental Staff. As circumstances required, battalions or individual companies were placed at the disposal of the Armies. It was only the flamethrower detachments of the assault battalions which always remained detached. With the regimental Staff were the training and experimental companies. The latter had responsibility for the regulation of supplies as well as for carrying out experiments and improvements in the apparatus. Those parts of the regiment not in action also had their quarters here. Thus, the regimental commander was able to base his monthly reports to the Supreme Army Command on the direct comments

---

81   War Ministry of 20.4.1916, No 681. 16. A. 6.

of his troops. The comments were related to the course of the fighting, experience gained, and included their wishes relating to improvement of the combat method and matériel.

The use of flamethrowers in defence was easy, but not so in attack, which it was primarily meant to serve. At first, the surprise attack with heavy flamethrower fire was prepared. That involved installing the flamethrowers, during the night, at a distance of 30-40m from the enemy trenches. That was in order, in conjunction with the infantry advance, to drive the enemy out of their protective trenches with streams of fire. This primitive method of attack did, of course, not lend itself to being used everywhere.

Therefore, from 1916, the preferred method was the more flexible attack with small flamethrowers. Those were based on skilled leadership, unobtrusive creeping up by the flamethrower carriers, and their support by machine gun fire and hand grenades. To this end, each of the three platoons of a flamethrower company formed into 5 flame detachments, 1 MG and 1 Ersatz detachment. Each flame detachment carried two flamethrowers with them, with which each flamethrower was able to give 30 bursts of fire with a range of 20m. Machine gun nests and other strong points were the principal targets considered. In 'rolling-up' enemy trenches the flamethrower was a well-liked and always an effective weapon. Its effect on enemy morale always remained massive. On the other hand, creeping up on the enemy demanded many sacrifices. It is indicative of how much confidence rested on the success of the flamethrower that the number of attacks carried out with it rose. From 32 in 1915, through to 160 and 165 in 1916 and 1917, and to 296 in the last year of the war. Overall, 82% of the attacks succeeded.

At an early stage the new arm of the service found high recognition and honour by the Kaiser. He, by A.K.D. of 28 July 1916, awarded the Guard Reserve Pioneer Regiment the Death's Head insignia. It was to be worn on the left forearm. From that time on, the flamethrower men were pleased to call themselves 'Death's Head Pioneers'.

7. Cavalry Pioneer Sections

In the cavalry divisions each had, according to the order of battle, a pioneer section in the strength of half a cavalry troop. It consisted of 2 officers, 3 pioneer and 1 Train NCOs, 27 pioneers, and 15 train troops. There were 31 horses and 6 cavalry pioneer wagons, each drawn by four horses for supplying personnel and explosives. The sections remained linked to their divisions and shared their fate, so that their numbers fell from an original 11 to 4 sections.[82]

8. Special Formations

During the course of the war, some pioneer companies that fell outside the framework of the general activities of the pioneers, were formed for special tasks. These are specially explained below.

When there was an urgent call for pioneers on the Western Front, the pioneer companies trained at the beginning of the war in landing assault services, were

82 In the 2nd Cav. Div there were in 1918 two pioneer sections.

called up for general pioneer service. In their place the new 'Pioneer Landing Company' was set up.[83] On 22 July 1915, it moved from Harburg to Neufahrwasser, from where it could be brought up, as need required, to mobile use. It took part in the crossings of the Danube in the Serbian and Rumanian campaigns, in taking the Baltic islands and in the expedition to the Aaland islands.

From the end of 1915 there was Pioneer Ferry Company 275,[84] and from Spring 1916, Pioneer Waterworks Company 310.[85] The latter, however, only existed until June 1918.

In February 1918, the Pioneer Drilling Machine Company 421 was formed[86] to serve drilling machines for tunnelling in rocky ground.

In the interest of saving explosives, a move was made to blasting with liquid hydrogen in tunnelling and in the mining war. But this required specially trained personnel for directing and supervising the work. These personnel were brought together in April 1918, as Pioneer Liquid Air Company 422.[87]

In Summer 1918, excavators came into use to increase the rate of construction of trenches in areas to the rear. To man them, the War Ministry established Pioneer Trench Excavator Company 423.[88] But this company could only be used a little, since the excavators used a great deal of fuel of which there was a severe shortage.

9. Assault Battalion 5 ('Rohr')

As already explained in the History of the Infantry, Assault Battalion Rohr was the only assault battalion to remain a pioneer formation.[89] But its origins had to be outlined in connection with the other assault battalions, since they formed the foundation for setting up such battalions in the infantry. But the further development of Battalion Rohr, from the time it joined the 5th Army at the beginning of 1916, took place along quite different lines from the younger assault battalions.

After Battalion Rohr had rendered outstanding services during the first three weeks of the battle for Verdun, it was withdrawn. This was because the fighting during this period had shown that the infantry was not yet up to scratch in using Close-combat weapons, nor in working together with the other arms of the service. Therefore, High Command 5 chose Assault Battalion Rohr as a model unit to train the Army's infantry. A suitable training area was found at Doncourt. As the Supreme Army Command was satisfied with the success of the courses held there, it charged Battalion Rohr with responsibility for giving courses for the other Armies on the Western Front, followed by those on the Eastern Front. But in parallel with this, the battalion was gaining new experience, since it continued to send some of its men to fighting at the front.

83   War Ministry of 21.4.1915, No 728. 15. A. 6.
84   War Ministry of 8.11.1915, No 639. 11. 15. A. 6.
85   War Ministry of 12.4.1916, No 2917. 3. 16. A. 6.
86   War Ministry of 1.2.1918, No 597. 1. 18. A. 6.
87   War Ministry of 16.4.1918, No 588. 18. A. 6.
88   War Ministry of 19.7.1918, No 2129. 5. 18. A. 6.
89   See Part IV A 4c.

During that period the battalion was brought up to 4 companies, and with the park company, formed for assault purposes was incorporated as 5 Company. The place of the unsatisfactory 3.7cm battery was taken by a full 10.5cm mountain howitzer battery. In addition, they were assigned 2 machine gun companies, a Minenwerfer company, with light Minenwerfer, and a flamethrower platoon. Up to Spring 1917, the battery trained over 30 battery crews for infantry gun batteries. They also trained a number of field artillery batteries in the activity of accompanying the infantry.

In 1918, in reinforced form, the battalion was detached and sent to the front. In the last year of the war it was in the large-scale fighting, at first in two half-battalions, then as a single unit. In between times, it trained the Guard Cavalry Schützen Division in the methods of fighting in the West. They also trained in attack procedures the Austro-Hungarian units which had been brought to the Western Front. Made use of, to the utmost, in the defensive fighting in Champagne and on the Maas, it was finally called upon as a reliable unit to guard the Great Headquarters.

10. Pioneer Siege Trains and Pioneer Park Companies

With the exception of Pioneer Regiment 31, the 10 pioneer regiments formed on mobilisation[90] each carried with it a Pioneer Siege Train that bore the number of its regiment. The train for Pioneer Regiment 31 was formed in December 1914.[91] The strength on the establishment of this train was as follows:

Command of the Pioneer Siege Train: 4 officers (commander, adjutant, MO, paymaster), 9 NCOs and other ranks, 9 horses and 1 baggage wagon

Park Company: 3 officers, 205 NCOs and other ranks, 7 horses, 1 baggage wagon and 1 supply wagon

Train Column: 3 officers (including 1 veterinary officer), 84 NCOs and other ranks, 154 horses, 36 pioneer store wagons as well as 1 baggage wagon and 1 fodder wagon

On the pioneer store wagon there was material for constructing positions and assault equipment. As soon as it was deployed in fortress warfare, the pioneer siege train formed several pioneer parks from which the pioneers and the attacking infantry were supplied. In 1915, the War Ministry formed more pioneer siege trains for the 10th, 11th, and 12th Armies, but no more after that.

Trench warfare brought the pioneer siege trains new tasks, as their park companies, from then on, remained deployed to supply the front. However, both before and after, the commander of the pioneer siege train was under the command of the pioneer regiment commander. After the pioneer regiments were dissolved[92] he came under the direct command of the General of Pioneers in the Army Command and remained in this relationship until 4 September 1918. On that day his post, and the train column belonging to it, were dissolved.[93]

90   Pi. Regts 18-20, 23-25, 29-31 and Bav. Pi. Regt.
91   Initially it bore the number 9 (after the Army) and was soon redesignated as 31.
92   Chief of Gen. Staff of the Field Army of 6.1.1917, No I. C. 43 735 op.

The pioneer park companies established themselves permanently as extended works operations. While the Bavarian companies were numbered from 1-17, it was only in September 1917 that the others took the consecutive numbering 39-57. In support, 37 Landsturm pioneer park companies[94] were brought up of which, however, three were dissolved again in 1918.

The pioneer park company did not only represent the distributor between the home front and the troops, but also, to a greater and greater extent, was a producer. Timber was supplied to them from the woods of the war area. Iron, in the form of pig iron, iron bars and structural steel as well as rivets, was supplied to them only from Germany. Any other processing they undertook for themselves. To achieve this the park company set up many works operations such as forges, operations for metalworking, plumbing, iron smelting, yellow metal smelting, tree felling, sawmill, carpentry, assembly plant, factory for illuminating ammunition. Cylinders of wire for entanglements and knife rests[95] they manufactured themselves. For so many operations the company required a considerable number of ancillary workers, some were men on detachment, some were workers from the occupied area. Thus, in the last two years of the war, the 2nd Pioneer Company of Pioneer Siege Train 25 employed 230 men on detachment and 660 Belgian workers, in addition to their own 260 pioneers.

11. Pontoon Trains

At the beginning of the war every Army Corps and every infantry, Reserve, and Landwehr Division was equipped with a pontoon train. Thus, the pontoon trains of 26 corps, 51 divisions, 26 Reserve divisions and 2 Landwehr divisions took to the field with their units. In addition, every active cavalry regiment had 2 pontoon wagons. On the left wing of the Army of the West was the heavy Rhine pontoon train as a special formation. The establishments were as follows:

> *Corps pontoon train:* a) Train: 6 officers, 136 NCOs and other ranks, 235 horses, 26 pontoon wagons, 2 trestle wagons and 10 other wagons; b) Pioneer escort: 2 officers, 64 NCOs and ORs, 2 horses
>
> *Divisional pontoon train:* 2 officers, 59 NCOs and ORs, 98 horses, 15 pontoon wagons and 6 other wagons. The (or a) divisional pioneer company served for bridge building purposes
>
> *Heavy Rhine pontoon train:* a) Train: 10 officers, 305 NCOs and ORs, 542 horses, 118 pontoon and other wagons; b) Pioneer escort: 5 officers, 259 NCOs and ORs, 12 horses, 3 wagons

In January 1915, to these pontoon trains the Supreme Army Command added Army Pontoon Sections 1-9.[96] A further section was set up two years later as Bav. No 10,[97] while on 13 April 1917, the heavy Rhine Pontoon Train was designated

93   War Ministry of 4.9.1918, No 1482. 18. G. A. 6.
94   Initially by War Ministry of 27.4.15, No 2875. 3. 15. A. 6.
95   Translator's note: wire entanglements (German: 'Spanische Reiter').
96   War Ministry of 11.1.1915, No 2. 1. 15. A.6.
97   War Ministry of 5.3.1917, No 649. 1. 17. A. 6.

Army Pontoon Section No 11.[98] The Army Pontoon Section had no train column, and thus only received draught horses as need dictated. The establishment comprised 1 officer, 77 NCOs and ORs as well as 62 pontoon wagons.

The pontoon trains provided very good services during the period of the war of movement. It is true, that during positional fighting, they could not be used as they were actually intended. However, they had to be on hand, in readiness for the longed-for time when freedom of movement was restored. Therefore, as new formations, in 1915 and 1916 a further 35 pontoon trains were created. In March 1917 the Supreme Army Command made all the pontoon trains into Army troops and placed them under the command of the commanders of the Army Command munitions columns and trains.[99] At the same time, the strength of their establishments, in men and horses, was significantly reduced. In the Corps pontoon train they were limited to 6 officers, 101 NCOs and ORs and 160 horses, in the divisional pontoon train to 2 officers, 39 NCOs and 57 other ranks.

The shortage of horses then, in August 1917, caused whole pontoon trains to be dissolved. At that time, 7 Corps pontoon trains and 24 divisional pontoon trains were affected.[100] Further units were dissolved, especially in Spring 1918, so that at the end of the war only about half of the pontoon trains were still available.

98 War Ministry of 13.4.1917, No 1352. 3. 17. A. 6.
99 War Ministry of 27.3.1917, No 516. 17. G. A. 6.
100 War Ministry of 14.8.1917, No 1349. 17. G. A. 6.

F.

Air Forces

1. Command

a. Until October 1916

At the outbreak of war the air forces were still little developed and existed only as individual formations in the Field Army. Apart from the seven usable Zeppelin airships at the disposal of the Supreme Army Command, each Army High Command possessed a field airship section and a field aviation section. Each active General Command had a field aviation section and anti-aircraft defence was limited to some special guns. But scarcely had the fighting begun, than hot competition arose for primacy in the air. Increases in the number of formations, as well as perfection of equipment and armament, began to develop rapidly.

Early on the Supreme Army Command early on recognised the decisive importance of aviation for mastery of the skies. It was also conscious that, with regard to matériel, armament and numbers, the German aviators had to be made able to compete. Therefore, in March 1915, it took the decisive step and called into the Great Headquarters Major Thomsen. He had tactical and organisational as well as technical experience, as Head of the Field Aviation Service.[1] Concerning this, General von Falkenhayn writes:[2]

> The tasks which had been intended for dirigible airships had to be taken over by the aviators. As a consequence of this, and also in view of the fact that the enemy was striving to place special emphasis on the war in the air, a rapid extension of the air service became necessary, which in actual fact amounted to a reorganisation into something very much larger. The then Major Thomsen was given responsibility by the Chief of the General Staff for dealing with this question. In doing so he created an everlasting memorial to himself. He not only understood how to direct aircraft production at home, along the right lines, but also how to keep up the true aviator's spirit among the men, without which all technical skills would have meant nothing at all.

Under the command of the Head of Field Aviation were all the aviation, airship and weather service formations in the Field Army as well as the Inspector of Aviation Troops at home. The Aviation Staff Officers, who from the end of 1914 had been assigned to the High Commands to provide a unified direction to the field aviation formations, from now on became part of the establishment.

1   War Ministry of 11.3.1915, No 1104. 3. 15. A. 7. V.
2   Von Falkenhayn, pages 40/41.

An essential precondition for the success of the plans of the Head of Field Aviation was the sympathetic collaboration of the Inspector of Aviation Troops at home. Concerning the last Inspector, Major Siegert, Arndt writes:[3]

> As a result, his ebullient spirit, and his imagination, which seemed almost utopian, was often misunderstood. But he anticipated developments by many years and was always productive. To Major Siegert, as well as to the steely but sober organiser Major Thomsen, aviation troops owe their massive scale of development. It was unique in the history of the German Army.

Alongside the airmen worked the airship crews. For the most part, they worked as airship sections with the already long-tested tethered balloon, and to a lesser extent as crews for the dirigible airships. The latter did not, in the war on land, fulfil the great hopes that had been placed on them. By contrast, the tethered balloons proved their worth to such an extent that the airship sections were greatly increased. In spite of this the need for bringing together the many loose units was at first not evident. Only during the battle of the Somme was there an increase in field airship formations in Army Group Gallwitz. The fighting there led to the commander bringing up an Airship Staff Officer as an adviser. On 20 September 1916, this Staff Officer was then placed on the establishment[4] for Army Group Crown Prince Rupprecht.[5]

The anti-aircraft defence, initially weak and underdeveloped, was in the sphere of activity of the artillery and month-by-month gained in importance. Soon so many defence formations were coming into existence that the Supreme Army Command gave them a service head in the Great Headquarters, in the form of the Inspector of Anti-Balloon Gun (Bak).[6] Under his command were the Bak Staff Officers. From May they had been provisionally placed with the High Commands in the West. But from then on, were part of their establishment. In October of the same year a Bak Staff Officer joined the Supreme Commander East. Gradually all the Army Group Commands in the East also received a Bak Staff Officer. The words 'Ballon-Abwehr-Kanone' (Anti-Balloon Gun) were replaced, on 31 May 1916, by the more accurate 'Flugabwehr-Kanone' (Anti-Aircraft Gun) and this was generally used in its abbreviated form 'Flak'.

b. Under the Commanding General of the Air Forces

> Despite the efforts of the General Staff, before the war began, we went to war with unsatisfactory weapons for the war in the air. Germany and the German Army owe it to the massive creative force of Colonel Thomsen and of Lieutenant-Colonel Siegert. They effectively worked on the home front. That meant that during the war our air forces developed more and more successfully. The air forces, notably the aviation arm of the service, had attained such strength that it seemed necessary to place them under the command of a special Commanding General. He, for his part, was under the command of the Chief of the

---

3   Arndt, *Die Fliegertruppe im Weltkriege.* Siegert was appointed by A.K.O. of 27.7.1916; previously he was Staff Officer on the Staff of the Head of Field Aviation.

4   War Ministry of 20.9.1916, No 2060. 8. 16. A. 7. L.

5   As an extension of Army Group Gallwitz

6   War Ministry of 10.7.1915, No 2433. 15. G. A. 4.

General Staff. Its head was Colonel Thomsen [until then head of the field aviation service].[7]

With these words Ludendorff points to the great reorganisation of the air forces which was introduced by the A.K.O. of 8 October 1916, concerning the setting up of the General Command of the Air Forces. The reorganisation programme originated from Thomsen and was, in its military part, correspondingly implemented. On the other hand, the Supreme Army Command was not able to succeed in bringing about the creation of a supreme Reich air authority, seen as necessary by Thomsen.

The task of the Commanding General of the Air Forces - Kogenluft - was, as the A.K.O. of 8 October 1916 stated, "to extend in a uniform way, to make ready and to deploy all the air war and anti-aircraft weapons of the Army in the field and at home". Under him were thus joined flying, aeronautics, anti-aircraft defence and weather service.

The officers under the direct command of the Commanding General of the Air Forces were with the Armies. There, the previous Aviation Staff Officers - Stofl - were changed into Aviation Commanders – Kofl. Thus they were in command posts which directed the aviation formations of the Armies according to the instructions of the Army High Commands.[8] They controlled the battle for air supremacy, long-range reconnaissance, aerial photography, bombing attacks. They worked out the intervention of aviation in battle, as well as its collaboration with the artillery, and took care of training, recruitment and supply. They had command over the aircraft park and the petrol depots of their Army.

For the main fighting fronts, where aircraft formations in great numbers had been brought together, the Commanding General of the Air Forces appointed, as need arose, Aviation Group Leaders - Grufl.[9] Within the group area deployment for aerial reconnaissance and aerial warfare, the group leader was responsible for the evaluation of the results of reconnaissance, and for uniformity in aerial photography of the enemy and of the German positions. On the other hand, he had no influence with regard to how they were used, nor on the aircraft formations assigned to the divisions, nor on the use of the artillery command posts.

As already mentioned with the airship crews, as already mentioned, Army Group Crown Prince Rupprecht had, on 20 September 1916, received on their establishment a Staff Officer as an advisory authority. Later, the two other Army Groups were also similarly provided. That of the German Crown Prince in September 1916[10] and that of Duke Albrecht of Württemberg on 1 April 1917.[11] In the meantime, with the airship crews too a tighter organisation proved to be necessary. It was similar to those that already existed for the aviators. Therefore, in their place, in September 1917, the Commanding General of the Air Forces dispensed with the Airship Staff Officers in the Army Groups. In their place he gave to every Army Command in the West, a Commander of Airship Troops.[12] In addition to the

7   Ludendorff, page 305.
8   War Ministry of 29.11.1916, No 1145. 16. A. 7. L.
9   War Ministry of 28.12.1916, No 1425. 16. A. 7. L.
10   War Ministry of 5.10.1916, No 208. 10. 16. A. 7. L.
11   War Ministry of 1.4.1917, No 1917. 3. 17. A. 7. L.

Commander of Airship Troops, also set up on 26 November 1917, the Supreme Commander East joined the new 18th Army only a month later.

The Commander of Airship Troops - Koluft - controlled, in agreement with his Army Command, the deployment and the use of the balloons. He also supervised the Army's airship troops, as well as their technical affairs, balloon protection, air raid warning service and aerial photography from balloons. Also created on 23 September 1917, were the Balloon Report Centres under his command, into which the balloon reports flowed and were examined. Meanwhile, the aircraft warnings and the weather forecast, as well as the results of survey sections, went the opposite way, from the balloon report centres to the balloons.

After anti-aircraft defence, until now separate from the air forces, had been drawn into the area of responsibility of the Commanding General of the Air Forces.[13] The latter took over supreme control of the defence service as a special section in his own Staff. That meant that the post of the Inspector of Flak was discontinued. Later it proved to be practical to relieve the Kogenluft's flak section of the responsibility for supervision of equipment. For that, a special Inspector of Flak Equipment was put in place.[14]

At the same time as the previous Flak Inspectorate was discontinued, the advisory Flak Staff Officers with the High Commands also disappeared. Their place was taken, as with the aviation service, by commanders. For each Army High Command in the West there was a Commander of Anti-Aircraft Gun – Koflak.[15] At the same time, for each of the subordinate General Commands there was an Anti-Aircraft Gun Group Commander - Flakgruko. By contrast, in the East, only the Army Group Command received a Koflak, and the Army High Command received a Flakgruko.

The Koflak deployed the anti-aircraft gun and searchlights in accordance with the instructions of the Army High Command and controlled the aircraft reporting service.[16] He was responsible for training, recruitment, supply of equipment and munitions. The Flakgruko under his command saw to the implementation of his measures in the area of their Groups.

In Turkey, from March 1915, First Lieutenant, later Captain Serno, built up the aviation service. Even for Finland, Germany appointed a head of the air service.[17]

2. The Units

a. Dirigible Airships

Dirigible airships flew in the war, in the service of the Army and the Navy. For the Field Army 12 airships became mobile, of which, however, only 7 Zeppelins

12 War Ministry of 23.9.1917, No 46. 8. 17. A. 7. L.
13 War Ministry of 2.12.1916, No 1104. 11. 16. A. 7. L.
14 War Ministry of 17.10.1917, No 2121. 10. 17. A. 4.
15 War Ministry of 7.1.1917, No 20. 17. A. 4.
16 See Part IV F 2 e4.
17 Kogenluft of 8.4.1918, No 152 777. Fl. I.

proved to be suitable for use in war. To serve the ships on the ground, the airship crews equipped 18 units.

The crew of a Zeppelin airship consisted of a captain, a wireless officer and a flight engineer, 2 steersmen, a wireless operator and, according to the number of motors, 4 to 8 mechanics. For the flights, a General Staff Officer was ordered aboard for reconnaissance purposes.

To an airship troop belonged 3 officers, 146 NCOs and mechanics, 5 horses, 1 touring-car and 2 lorries, the latter for hand tools, equipment and gas.

Since there was not always sufficient trained personnel available, experts employed on contract. They were not liable for military service nor had they prior service when they were taken on. As a result of this, the airship captain and the flight engineer were distinguished by the officer's field cap and an armband.[18] Later, the contract personnel received uniform.[19] The qualified engineer and flight engineer wore the uniform of the Government building contractor without epaulettes, but with a silver 'J' on the corners of the collar. Engineers, technicians and mechanics wore the uniform of the communication troops without epaulettes and braiding, but similarly with a silver 'J'. Steersmen and machinists wore 2 crossed propellers, and onboard wireless operators wore a silver lightning flash on the corners of the collar.

It was the task of the airships to take over strategic long-range reconnaissance. They had to bomb important points behind the enemy front, such as bridges, railway junctions, depots in fortresses, etc. At first they had great success in Belgium and France and also in the East. Soon, however, it became evident that their operating altitude, especially when loaded with bombs, was too low to escape the effect of enemy artillery.

Meanwhile, it had been possible to improve, in total, the 36[20] airships built during the war, in such a way that their operating radius and altitude were considerably increased. Again, great hopes were placed on the Zeppelins. Meanwhile, the enemy too had not remained idle, but had considerably raised the operating altitude of their aircraft. From the beginning of 1916 they gave their aircraft phosphorus incendiary shells for attacking airships. Since it only needed one direct hit on a gas cell to ignite the hydrogen content of the ship, and as there had been no success in producing a little less inflammable gas, the airships against the aircraft were almost defenceless. Therefore, at the beginning of 1917 they had to be withdrawn from Army use.

Later on, the airship continued to be of great importance to the Navy, since at sea it was in less danger than on the fronts on land. From the time the blockade was implemented it was the best, and always successful, means of spotting early raids by the British fleet. As fleet escort they served as the eyes of the fleet.

In Autumn 1917, the well-known airship Z 59 flew out to East Africa from Jamboli with 15,000kg of war matériel for Lettow-Vorbeck. When it was over eastern Egypt, it was called back by wireless telegraph, as it did not belong to the land forces but to the Navy.

---

18   A.V.Bl. 1914, No 384 of 12.11.1914.
19   A.V.Bl. 1915, No 843 of 1.11.1915.
20   Excluding the new airships built for the Navy.

The airship units increased in number from 18 to 25. However, at the beginning of 1917 as the Field Army dispensed with using airships, they became surplus to requirements and the units were dissolved.

b. Field Airship Troops

The weapon of the field airship troops was the tethered balloon from which enemy activities could be observed and photographed, and firing corrections transmitted to the batteries.

On mobilisation, one field airship section joined each Army. One also joined the IX Reserve Corps, at first held in readiness as the Army of the North. The section essentially consisted of the commander, 4 observation officers, 177 NCOs and ORs, 123 horses, 12 gas wagons, 2 equipment wagons, 1 winch wagon and 1 telephone wagon. The special gas column belonging to the section followed up, with 12 gas wagons and 1 equipment wagon.

As early as 1914, 5 further sections were formed, in 1915 as many as 30 more, including the 20 fortress airship troops from Germany.[21] Finally there were another 9 sections.

In order to guarantee replacements of equipment, balloons, winches and gas, in November 1916 field airship parks[22] were set up with the Army Groups. At the beginning of 1918 all the parks that had, in the meantime, increased to 13, joined the Armies and Army Detachments in the West.

The autonomous field airship sections proved themselves, during the course of time, to be unwieldy in meeting the changing battle situations. Rather, what was needed was to bring together by Armies a changing number of balloons for observation directed in a uniform way. To do that, more elastic forms of distribution were necessary, such as those that were created in the reorganisation of March 1917.[23] At that time, the sections were split into continuously numbered field airship Staffs and into self-contained balloon detachments.

This opportunity was also taken to dispense with the special numbering, beginning with 'one', of the Bavarian formations. That was to give them two series of higher numbers in order both to prevent confusion, and to maintain the special rights of the Bavarians. Thus there came into existence the field airship Staffs with the numbers 1-45 and Bavarian 61-68[24] as well as Balloon Detachments Nos 1-112 and Bavarian 201 to 223, a total then of 135 units, the number of which later grew to 182. At the same time, the previous field airship sections 46 and 47 went to the Namur Airship School, and the Naval Observer School. For Turkey the Ottoman Balloon Detachments 2 and 3 were formed.

The field airship Staff from this point on generally came under a General Command. Its commander supervised training, combat readiness, reconnaissance and observation activities. In addition, photography was carried out by the balloon detachments that were assigned to him at the time. In this way, a balloon detachment was tactically under the command of every division on the fighting front. As

21   War Ministry of 20.9.1915, No 1273. 8. 15. A. 7. L.
22   War Ministry of 29.11.1916, No 903. 11. 16. A. 7. L.
23   War Ministry of 3.3.1917, No 590. 2. 17. A. 7. L.
24   Bav. War Ministry of 2.7.1917, No 19 116 A.

before, the enemy was monitored from the balloon and the effects of artillery were observed. Panoramic photographic views were taken, called 'Rundbilder' (panoramas). Since these tasks also belonged to the aviators, the commander of the airships had to keep in constant contact with the Group Leader of Aviation. That was in order to suggest to the General Command how the work should be allocated, between aircraft and balloon, with regard to artillery observation and aerial photography, as jointly advised by the airship commander and the group leader.

If the tethered balloon, because of its principal activity, could also be designated as an artillery balloon, so in its less common service to the infantry it was officially named an 'infantry balloon'. Specifically, that was when a division had to make use of a special balloon to maintain contact with the forward infantry line. For this purpose, signalling equipment and a wireless telegraph ground station were at the disposal of the observer. Meanwhile, he was connected by telephone with the ground station.

As regards the uniform of the airship crews it is to be noted that in November 1917 the 'shako' was discontinued for mobile formations.[25]

c. Aeroplanes

In contrast to the Army airships and airship personnel, until the war, aeroplanes represented an arm of the service that had been less well developed in Germany. Thus initially there was only one reconnaissance flight with each of the Army Command and active Corps for reconnaissance purposes. But the aircraft were not always used properly, their excellent reconnaissance results were, at first, often regarded with mistrust. Only gradually did the real value of the new service arm begin to penetrate through to those in command.

The 33 reconnaissance flights, with the Field Army, were each formed of 6 aircraft. The flight leader had at his disposal, for use in the air, 14 officers, of whom 7 were pilots, 6 were observers and one was for special use. If the need arose, the pilots could be replaced with civilian pilots. The rest of each flight was intended to carry out work on *terra firma*, and consisted of 116 NCOs and ORs with the wagon park which included 5 touring-cars, 1 motorised omnibus and 6 aircraft tugs. There were also workshop wagons, fuel wagons, store wagons, munitions wagons together with baggage wagons.

The aircraft consisted mainly of two-seater Albatros biplanes with 80-100hp engine, speed of 100km/h, medium operating altitude of 1200m and a supply of petrol for about 4 hours in the air. Armament of carbine and quick-firing pistol was, compared to the French armament of a built-in machine gun, decidedly inferior. That fact, however, at first was only rarely evident because at the beginning even with the enemy, aircraft only turned up in relatively small numbers. To transmit information the aviators had flare signals in various colours.

In the lines of communication of each Army there was a lines of communication aircraft park. In addition to 10 lorries for tents, tools, workshops and reserve material, they also kept in readiness for each reconnaissance flight in the Army, 2 pilots, 1 observer and 3 aircraft. There, too, provision was made for replacement with civilian airmen.

25   A.V.Bl. 1917, No 1142; War Ministry of 19.11.1917, No 267. 11. 17. B. 3.

As a result of the short war of movement the aviators were able to secure the confidence of the commanders and the troops in their reconnaissance activities. Thus, the Supreme Army Command also took steps to rapidly increase the number of reconnaissance flights. At first the eight, fortress flights available in Germany but only equipped with 4 aircraft, were increased in number to 17.[26] Their complement was made up to the strength of reconnaissance flights and, still in 1914, brought up into the Field Army. Combined with the formation of 10 new units, at the beginning of 1915 there were already 60 reconnaissance flights were available.

The value of the reconnaissance aircraft rose in a quite unexpected way. The taking of photographs from the aircraft was being perfected to such an extent that from mid-1915 it was possible to get photographs of the ground seen from a vertical perspective. More detail concerning the aerial photography service will be given later.[27]

Reconnaissance activity itself, during the first period of trench warfare, suffered greatly as a result of the insufficient armament of German aircraft compared with the enemy aircrafts' arming with machine guns. Thus, the German airman had to restrict himself to short surprise forays only when out beyond his own front line. In fact he was not able to hold his own against the enemy machines. In addition, it became evident that the German machines, faced with the enemy artillery, did not have the necessary manoeuvrability to attain the great heights that were needed. Reconnaissance flights were used increasingly for providing observations of enemy fire to the German artillery. The shortcomings of German planes, in having insufficient armament and lack of manoeuvrability, was felt and even exacerbated, resulting in unsatisfactory reporting procedures. Therefore, in Germany, with almost feverish enthusiasm, they set about constructing new aircraft with better performance, improved reporting systems and stronger armament. In the process, however, the lack of expert direction and firm guidelines was felt. Only from the moment when the Supreme Army Command in March 1915 appointed Major Thomsen to the post of Head of Field Aviation,[28] created for just this purpose, did the air force receive that amazing impetus which it maintained until the end of the war.

The Head of Field Aviation's programme, approved by the Supreme Army Command, included the large-scale organisation of the air force and the reorganisation of the units. All of that was determined by the construction of new aircraft. The large-scale changes could be immediately implemented.[29] That meant the bringing together of all the aircraft formations of an Army under the Aviation Staff Officer in the Army High Command. It also meant the removal of the Inspectorate of Aviation Troops, and the Inspectorate of Airship Troops from their unnatural connection with the communications service. Instead, they were placed under the direct command of the Head of Field Aviation. Finally, the aircraft parks were taken from the lines of communication and into the Army troops. By those means the provision of supplies to the units would be greatly accelerated.

---

26   War Ministry of 13.9.1914, No 669. 9. 14. A. 7. L.
27   See Part IV F 2d.
28   See Part IV F 1a; War Ministry of 11.3.1915, No 1104. 3. 15. A. 7. V.
29   War Ministry of 2.4.1915, No 1104. 3. 15. A. 7. L.

For the aircraft and units themselves the guidelines consisted of the following requirements. There was the introduction of a new observation aircraft with better performance, and with the observer's seat in front of the pilot's. That was to make it easier for the observer to operate both the machine gun and the photographic apparatus. The equipping of special flights for the artillery observation service with wireless telegraphy would enable quicker and more reliable transmission of information. There would be construction of special combat aircraft to attack and pursue the enemy aircraft. An increase would be made in the numbers and in improvement of the quality of bomber aircraft.

The equipment of the reconnaissance flights, with improved aircraft fitted with machine guns, was implemented in the period up to Spring 1916.At the same time, the number of flights was also increased to 83. Artillery reconnaissance flights required by the Head of Field Aviation, were built and equipped according to his instructions. They were to be formed from August 1915 onward.[30] At that time the first to appear were Artillery Reconnaissance Flights 201-206. Within a year they were increased to 43 flights, each with 4 aircraft.[31]

Similarly, in Summer 1915, the much-longed-for combat aircraft was able to be introduced. It was the so-called Fokker single-seater fighter with built in machine gun. From this point onwards the fighter aircraft were incorporated individually in the reconnaissance flights. Immediately, with incomparable courage, they went over to the attack. Where they appeared, they guaranteed that the reconnaissance and artillery aircraft could successfully carry out their work. Soon the names of the victors of these duels in the air were on everyone's lips. Above all were those of Immelmann and Boelcke. By Spring 1916 the number of single-seater fighters was brought up to 90.

As bombers, large twin-engined aircraft were produced, by which the older bomber aircraft were gradually replaced. Their crew consisted of the pilot, the observer and the air gunners. They were first brought together into bomber squadrons under the cover name 'Carrier Pigeon Section' M and O.[32] After the trials were completed they took the designation OHL Bombing Squadrons Nos 1 and 2.[33] Each of these squadrons was composed of 6 flights each with 6 aircraft. The year 1917 brought the number of squadrons to 7.

As well as the bomber, trials were also being carried out on a still larger variant of this model, called the 'giant' aeroplane, or R-Plane. This possessed 3-4 engines and had an impressive crew. It consisted of the commander, 2 aeroplane pilots, 1 observer, 1 wireless operator, 1 air gunner and 1 onboard engineer. Later, that aircraft type was not developed any further. At this point, in anticipation, its history should be told in full.

Initially in January 1916, R-Plane Flight 500[34] was formed. Then, on 3 August 1916 there followed No 501, and on 28 December 1916, Nos 502 and 503. The flights were used in the East. In Autumn 1917, the 4 flights were brought together into two. From 22 September 1917, they bore the designation R-Plane Flights 500

30   War Ministry of 6.8.1915, No 553. 15. G. A. 7. V.
31   Artillery Reconnaissance Flights Nos 201-240 and Bav. 101-103.
32   M = Metz, O = Ostend.
33   War Ministry of 20.12.1915, No 397. 15. G. A. 7. L.
34   War Ministry of 31.1.1916, No 55. 16. A. 7. L.

and 501, and were brought to the Western Front. There, in July 1918, they were reorganised into R-Plane units under the command of the commander of R-Plane Flight 501.[35] The commander was under the direct command of the Supreme Army Command for special bombing missions.

Before the battle for Verdun, in February 1916, the 5th Army had brought its single-seater fighter aircraft into 2 Groups, one of which Boelcke commanded. Of their importance, for the tactics of the war in the air, one expert says:[36]

> It is to the immortal Boelcke's credit that he recognised the preconditions for the tactics of aerial combat which were now required. On the basis of his outstanding personal achievements, he was chosen as commander of one of these single-seater fighter aircraft groups. From then on he controlled the deployment of his forces according to the situation in the air at any given time. He was the creator of the later fighter flights.

The battle of Verdun led for the first time to the unification of stronger German air forces. Gradually, the number of the units used there, rose to 36 reconnaissance flights and 30 combat aircraft. In that battle a new task arose for the reconnaissance flights. It was that of 'infantry' aircraft. That is to say, if in bombardment all the forms of communication failed and the commanders were left in the dark about what was going on at the most advanced point of the front, then aircraft were sent out. They could determine how things were going at the most forward part of the line. Thus, in order to be able to distinguish friend from foe, in the desert of craters which was the battlefield, the aircraft were forced to fly low, and in that way link up with the infantry. Hence the designation 'infantry' aircraft. At first this use of aircraft only brought moderate results. That was because the infantry were totally unprepared for the possibilities of reaching an understanding with the aircraft. However, in part they were also mistrustful. But after these obstacles had been overcome, the collaboration of the aircraft with the infantry soon settled down successfully.

While at Verdun the aviators had successfully held their own, in the air, so the battle on the Somme, in Summer 1916, at first brought a setback. There was an almost fourfold numerical superiority of the enemy air forces. But the enemy predominance in the air was broken again as soon as the single-seater fighters of Verdun appeared, under the command of Boelcke.

During 1916, alongside the single-seater fighter flights, formed by the 5th Army, there appeared another 14 temporary Fokker combat flights or single-seater combat flights. The four combat flights S 1-3 and Bavarian 36 joined forces as bombers.[37]

In March 1916, a change was introduced in the uniform of the aviation formations. They were awarded an insignia to be worn on the left upper sleeve of the service jacket, the jacket and the greatcoat. It consisted of light grey cloth with a red

35   War Ministry of 6.7.1918, No 10 710. 18. A. 7. L.

36   Arndt, *Die Fliegerwaffe*, page 317.

37   S.1 (previously Cologne, then Trier, then 31) from 19.1.1916, S.2 (previously Freiburg, then 32) from 1.3.1916, S.3 (previously T) from 6.7.1916, Bav. 36 from 15.6.1916.

number in braid designating the formation, in the Army aircraft park with the letters 'Fl. P.'[38]

On the basis of experience in the great battles of Verdun and the Somme, the Head of Field Aviation decided during the winter to reorganise the aviation service. By Spring 1917, he implemented a new distribution of the air forces. The division and the distribution of the formations was made strictly in accordance with the differing tasks for which the aviators were responsible, i.e.:

- for operational reconnaissance one reconnaissance flight with mosaic[39] equipment to each Army High Command,

- for tactical reconnaissance and for long-range artillery purposes one reconnaissance flight with photographic equipment to each General Command,

- for artillery observation one artillery reconnaissance flight and one escort flight to each division,

- combat aircraft as fighter forces, reserved to the Supreme Army Command for deployment as need arises,

- bomber squadrons as before at the disposal of the Supreme Army Command.

The appointment of a Commanding General of the Air Forces, with the previous Head of Field Aviation as his Chief of General Staff, encouraged that ambitious plan.

In November 1916, the available 83 reconnaissance and 43 artillery reconnaissance flights a radical reorganisation.[40] From them were formed Reconnaissance Flights Nos 1-48 and Reconnaissance Flights A201-255. The latter were designated as artillery reconnaissance formations by the prefix 'A'. All the flights each consisted of 6 aircraft. The former reconnaissance flights which were not immediately affected by the reorganisation changed, in 1917, into Reconnaissance Flights A. The number of those, because of the changes, and because of the formation of new units, rose to Number 298.

The Reconnaissance Flights A were under the command of the division for reconnaissance and for observation of artillery and Minenwerfer fire. For this, every aircraft was equipped with a wireless station and lamp signalling apparatus. Its wireless transmissions were received at the aerodrome by the divisional Arko and his subordinate groups. Since, against the repeated wishes of the troops, special flights could not be made available for infantry aircraft service, so the reconnaissance flights A had to take over that service. For that purpose the number of their aircraft was increased from 6 to 9.

The infantry aircraft, called 'Jfl.', monitored the battlefield. Both in attack and in defence they offered the quickest and most reliable transmission to the command post of events and progress, on the most advanced front, at any given time. Since, in the meantime, the infantry had learned to value the importance of this

---

38   A.V.Bl 1916, No 336, War Ministry of 20.3.1916, No 1097. 3. 16. B. 3.
39   Translator's note: a type of aerial photograph.
40   War Ministry of 29.11.1916, No 1145. 16. G. A. 2.

link, they indicated their position to the aircraft by means of ground signal cloths or flares. The aircraft, by dropping messages or ground signals, communicated to the infantry, and also reported, by wireless telegraph, to the Ifl. station of the division.

The new reconnaissance flights 1-48, served for tactical reconnaissance and were equipped with photographic apparatus. But when it became possible to replace the photographic plate, in aerial photographs, with reels of film, special formations were equipped with the 'mosaic apparatus'. The special formations that this required were either attached as units to the existing reconnaissance flights, or placed as self-contained mosaic units, under the direct command of the Army High Commands. After 7 detachments and 11 units had been set up, the War Ministry gave the mosaic photography service a better organisational basis. In March 1918,[41] a number of reconnaissance flights, even A-flights, were amalgamated with the mosaic detachments and units into 'Reconnaissance Flights Lb.' Thus, the new flights originated from already existing flights and retained their original numbers, so that the Reconnaissance Flights Lb appeared as Nos 3, 5, 12, 18, 23, 39, 40, 44-46, 260, 261, 276 and 289. They came under the command of the Army Commands. The reconnaissance flights without a suffix, remained with the General Commands, and the Reconnaissance Flights A remained with the divisions.

The 1 January 1917, brought a transition into new organisations[42] for the single-seater fighter and Fokker fighter flights that had been brought together, in part temporarily, and in part as established units.

27 escort flights were formed to protect the Reconnaissance Flights A that were engaged in artillery observation and active as infantry aircraft with the divisions. Into these were transferred the Fokker combat flights, and 24 flights from the previous combat squadrons of the Supreme Army Command. Although their number was soon brought up to 30, they could only be deployed on the main fighting fronts. There they were assigned for a period to the divisions.

But as 1917 began it was the newly-formed fighter flights each with 14 aircraft which received as their task the actual battle for air supremacy. At that time, by bringing together all the single-seater fighters, at first Fighter Flights 1 to 37 came into existence. No 2 bore the name of Boelcke, in memory of its founder, Captain Boelcke. He had been killed, unbeaten, on 28 October 1916.

As a result of the formation of the escort flights, the number of the Supreme Army Command's bombers had fallen from 162 to 126. Therefore the previous combat squadrons 1-7 had to be dissolved and put together into the new OHL Bomber Squadrons, abbreviated to Bogohl, 1-4. The number of bomber squadrons, all provided with large, twin-engined aircraft, increased in December 1917 by three.[43] In that process the still self-contained Bavarian Combat Flight 36 was included. The last squadron came into existence, as No 8, in March 1918.[44] Of the bomber squadrons, that commanded by Captain Keller (No 1) deserves special mention, since its attacks on Dunkirk forced the British to withdraw their flying base to Calais. Particular success also fell to the 'England' Squadron (No 3) under

41   Kogenluft of 10.3.1918, No 41 272. Fl. II.
42   War Ministry of 1.1.1917, No 1425. 16. A. 7. L.
43   War Ministry of 17.12.1917, No 1010. 17. G. A. 7. L.
44   Bav. War Ministry of 2.3.1918, No 48 149 A.

Captain Brandenburg. From the middle of 1917 the bombing raids basically took place by night.

The programmed increase in the air forces received a new impetus as soon as it was clear that the United States of America would intervene in the war. In August 1917, after thorough consideration, the Supreme Army Command demanded that the War Ministry should, by 1 March 1918, increase the fighter flights to double their current number.[45] Despite the shortage of materials, and the great difficulties in training personnel, the War Ministry managed to meet this urgent demand punctually. Thereby they laid the foundation for air supremacy even in the last year of the war. On the other hand, the increase in the Reconnaissance Flights A, in itself desirable, had to be dispensed with.

In the meantime, however, the battle in Flanders in 1917 set the air force its hardest test. The enemy took to the air with such superiority that, even after bringing up forces which could be managed without elsewhere, the German aircraft faced the enemy in a ratio of 1:3. Yet, even this battle considerably advanced the achievements of the airmen. For the conditions forced the escort flights not only to protect the reconnaissance and artillery aircraft, but also to intervene themselves, in the battle on the ground, by going in to the attack. In that way the escort flights became an important ancillary weapon for the infantry in the battle.

In view of the massed enemy forces, in the battle for air supremacy, in the fighter flights there developed the need to bring together their forces and to fight in larger units. Therefore the fighter squadrons were brought together, in groups of 3-4 flights, where the group commander directed the deployment of his flights from the ground. An exception to this procedure was the existing group of Rittmeister von Richtofen, which consisted of 4 flights. Von Richtofen formed his group as a fighter squadron[46] to be used as a single unit and led it personally. The astounding success of this squadron, under its charismatic leader, is well known. It was established on 28 October 1917 as Fighter Squadron No 1 and received, after its exemplary commander was killed in action, on 21 April 1918, the name 'Fighter Squadron Freiherr von Richtofen No 1.'[47]

Before the Great Battle in France began, the complement of the aircraft formations was as follows:

- 93 reconnaissance flights A - i.e. excluding Nos 260, 261, 276 and 289 which had become rec.flts Lb, and excluding No 220, used for a escort flight

- 37 reconnaissance flights – i.e. without Nos 4, 11, 15, 21, 24, 25 and 47, brought up to form battle flights

- 14 reconnaissance flights Lb - i.e. Nos 3, 5, 12, 18, 23, 39, 40, 44, 45, 46, 260, 261, 276 and 289

- 8 OHL bomber squadrons each with 3 flights - No 3 with 6 flights

- 2 R-Plane flights - the heaviest bombers

- 38 battle flights - previously called escort flights[48]

45   War Ministry of 27.8.1917, No 744. 17. A. 7. L.
46   Chief of the Gen. Staff of the Field Army of 23.6.1917, No I. C. 58 341 op.
47   War Ministry of 14.5.1918, No 10 525. 18. A. 7. L.; A.V.Bl.1918, No 534.

- 3 fighter squadrons - each with 4 fighter flights[49]

- 70 fighter flights

- 9 single-seater fighter flights to defend against enemy raids on home areas

Of all these forces, 16 reconnaissance flights, 2 reconnaissance flights A and 4 fighter flights were outside the Western Theatre of war,[50] the single-seater fighter flights on the western border of the Reich.

Concerning the demands on the battle flights and their importance, Ludendorff says:[51]

> To provide air support for the infantry attack, special battle flights were formed. These, as previous individual aircraft had done, would dive from high in the sky and fly low over the ground. They would attack with machine guns and light bombs the enemy infantry, the artillery and, as occurred more and more, also the enemy reserves, columns and trains as well as columns of march coming up from far away. Originally intended as an ancillary infantry weapon, at the end these battle flights were also given great tactical tasks. In this way the air force gained a new field of activity of the very highest importance. The aircraft were not only instruments of reconnaissance but had to fight in the course of carrying out their duties. They were not only bombers carrying destruction far into the enemy's rear, they, just like the infantry and artillery and all the other arms of the service, also had to intervene in the fighting on the ground. Like the other combat weapons, they too were weapons of destruction in the great land battle. That was their purpose, the battle in the air remained only a means to that end.

In the large-scale battle, the battle flights too, were brought together into larger units called battle flight groups. But these only appeared as such as occasion demanded, so that it was enough to establish three 'Battle Flight Group Leaders' and to hold them in readiness.[52]

Among the fighter aircraft there existed, as already outlined, only Fighter Squadrons Nos 1-3. The other 70 fighter flights remained as single units because there was a shortage of suitable leaders to form squadrons. Thus, as in the battle in Flanders, it was necessary to make do with direction from the ground to inform groups. For this purpose 12 'Fighter Flight Group Leaders' had been appointed.[53]

It was precisely with the airmen, who developed from small beginnings into a strong and many-faceted arm of the service, that good training was a precondition for success. Certainly, as a consequence of this service being voluntary and as a consequence of the special conditions of recruitment, they had selected material by way of personnel. However, there was still a need for a very thorough training until

---

48   Established with this new name by War Ministry of 27.5.1918, No 5126. 18. A. 7. L.

49   Fighter Squadrons 2 and 3 established by War Ministry of 27.5.1918, No 4524. 18. A. 7. L.

50   Under the Kofl 11 in the Balkans: Rec. Flts 20, 22, 30, 34 and 38, Rec. Flts A 230 and 246, Fighter Flights 25 and 38.

51   Ludendorff, page 463.

52   Kogenluft of 8.5.1918, No 42 936. Fl. II.

53   Established by War Ministry of 28.10.1917, No 709. 10. 17. A. 7. L.

the necessary control of the aeroplane, certainty in observation and ability to use the weapons in the air war were gained. Later, it was necessary to learn the techniques of flying and fighting as a unit. Therefore many training establishments came into existence, first in Germany, but soon also in the field. Of the latter there should be mentioned:

- Aviation Observer School Alt Auz from 28 June 1916, afterwards, from 26 March 1917, called Artillery Aircraft School II East

- Artillery Aircraft School I from 27 October 1916

- Single-Seater Fighter School Warsaw from 25 April 1916, then from 8 August 1917 Fighter Flight School 2, after transfer to Valencennes

- Fighter Flight School 1 from 29 November 1916, for training single-seater fighters to fight as a unit

- Aviation Observer Schools West and East from 23 January 1917

- Aviation Gunnery School Asch from 23 April 1917

- Aviation Training Flight Sedan from 17 January 1917 - 10 March 1918, for training General Staff Officers in reconnaissance from aircraft

- Aviation Training Flight Mouzon from 3 June 1918, purpose as above

- Battle Flight School Saultain from 1 September 1918, for training battle-flight airmen how to fly in flights and squadrons and how to attack targets on the ground.

From April 1915, replacement of matériel, originally from the lines of communication aircraft parks, came from the Army Aircraft Parks of which there were 21. In Spring 1918 to re-supply in the area of the northern part of the Western Front, the Aviation Depot North in Maubeuge, and the Aircraft Engine Workshop Brussels, were set up. The requirements for hangars and tents were met by the Aircraft Hangar Works at Schirmeck, Valenciennes and Auz.

Even in the last year of the war the German fliers maintained their high performance in the most unfavourable circumstances. Although, in terms of numbers, finally the fighter aircraft faced a fivefold enemy superiority, their victories in the air, compared with their losses, still maintained a ratio of 3.5:1! But as early as May 1918, the German aircraft were frequently grounded as a result of the rationing of fuel. By October only a third of the necessary fuel could be delivered to them.

With regard to the growth of the air service arm, the number of aircrew gives the best indication. In 1914 there were five hundred men, but in 1918 there were exactly nine times as many. But of the aircrew alone, some 6,830 airmen were killed in action, including 3,021 officers.[54] Because the air force followed and evaluated the air battles in very great detail, it can be established that it achieved 7,425 victories in the air, including 358 in the East.

d. Aerial Photography Service

Taking photographs of terrain from the air was originally a task for the balloon observers. By means of highly perfected apparatus they produced from the balloon

54   Hoeppner, page 174.

panoramic views, called panoramas, which reproduced with mathematical precision the position of the various targets. Thus they created the basis for planning attacks and artillery fire.

Since the aircraft, in contrast to the tethered balloon, were not tied to one place and could also fly out over enemy territory, they soon began to compete with the photographic reconnaissance from balloons. But only after they were protected by single-seater fighters, that is from about Summer 1915, were they able to deliver the proper aircraft photograph, i.e. the vertical photograph of sections of terrain. By fitting together the various photographs it was then possible to produce the aerial photographic map with details of all man-made features. In the course of 1916 the film reel replaced the light-sensitive photographic plate and tremendously facilitated photography of larger areas in the form of mosaics. The previous section has already discussed the mosaic units and detachments which were formed and their absorption into reconnaissance flights Lb.

After Aviation Staff Officers had been assigned to the Army High Commands, and in the East to the Army Group Commands, the aerial photography service, too, became systematised. From then on, with every Aviation Staff Officer, there was a photographic expert who had the photographic reconnaissance from the entire Army area collected and evaluated. He ensured the entry of the reconnaissance results on to maps by the survey section of his Army[55] and monitored the running of the photographic equipment. By that time, special photographic officers were also being thoroughly trained in aerial photography. This training was taken over by the Aviation Testing and Repair Establishment that had existed in Germany since 6 October 1915.

With the change of the Aviation Staff Officers into Commanders of Aviation Troops,[56] the post of the photographic expert, had in the meantime really expanded its area of responsibility. The post also received its necessary re-formation into the Staff Photographic Section,[57] called by the troops 'Stabia'. After a Commander of Airship Troops had been assigned to the Armies in the West,[58] an officer from his Staff joined the Staff Photographic Section to ensure its effective collaboration with the balloon observers.

In the meantime, the Aviation Group Leaders, set up on the main fighting fronts with the General Commands,[59] had considered it necessary to evaluate the photographic reports flowing in within their areas. That was done in order to be able to let the units have the results more quickly. The photographic sections set up for this, at first remained temporary. It was only in April 1918 that they were established as group photographic sections.[60] The opportunity was also taken to provide those Group Commands that had no Grufl with their own permanent group photographic section. Evaluation in the group photographic section was a preliminary. Checking and evaluation for the Army maps took place in the Staff section.

55   See Part IV G.

56   War Ministry of 29.11.1916, No 1145. 16. G. A. 7. L.

57   Kogenluft 18.1.1917, No 184. 17. Lb., established by War Ministry of 5.7.1917, No 1081. 6. 17. A. 7. L.

58   War Ministry of 23.9.1917, No 46. 8. 17. A. 7. L.

59   War Ministry of 28.12.1916, No 1425. 16. A. 7. L.

60   War Ministry of 21.4.1918, No 7663. 4. 18. A. 7. L.

Thus the aerial photography service was concentrated in the Staff photographic section of the Commander of Aviation Troops of an Army. To that system the group photographic sections brought information to the Staff photographic section and also formed the medium by which the Kofl's information was passed to the troops. From the training manual of the Staff photographic officer himself, the following duties should be particularly noted. "Supervision of all the photographic reconnaissance of an Army according to the instructions of the Kofl. Supervision of the tactical evaluation of photographic material, technical treatment of photographs and equipment as instructed. Supply the Army units with equipment and materials, production of the situation maps, the target maps and the aerial photographic maps, and further training of the photographic officers in the air formations of his Army."

e. Anti-Aircraft Weapons and the Aircraft Reporting Service

e1. Anti-Aircraft Guns

At the time the war broke out, anti-aircraft defence was, in Germany, still being developed. At that time there were only 18 special guns, designated as Anti-Balloon Defence Gun, or Bak, to combat targets in the air. Of these, one motorised vehicle Bak was assigned to each of the I, VIII, and XXI Army Corps, and two to the XV A.K. The remaining horse-drawn Baks were set up to protect strategically important points along the Western area of advance. The enterprising spirit of the enemy airmen soon made itself felt, and compelled the Armies to an extended use of 9cm guns and modified captured matériel, because initially more special guns were not available.

Later, when the altitude and speed of the aircraft increased, special guns of medium calibre and large-calibre guns with high muzzle velocity were introduced. The Supreme Army Command recommended 8.8cm and 10cm guns to be transported on wheeled carriages, on motorised vehicles and on pivots. The 15cm gun to be transported on naval or coastal carriages, and the 3.7cm machine gun too, to be appropriately mounted, as were field and 9cm guns.[61]

To avoid fragmentation, as early as 1914, preparations were made to join individual Baks into Bak platoons,[62] and later Bak batteries were also set up. The incorporation of the Bak into the field artillery was given up and anti-aircraft defence was placed in the hands of the troop commanders. In this process the motorised vehicle and machine Bak were placed under the command of the Army Commands. In May 1915, each received a Bak Staff Officer, or Stobak, while the horse-drawn Bak were assigned to the divisions.

From July 1915, the Inspector of Bak in the Great Headquarters formed the head of the Bak service. From then on it was regarded as a special arm of the service.[63] As far as organisation, use, and further development were concerned, it was under his command. He worked in close conjunction with the Stoflug and Stoluft, with whose support he extended the aircraft reporting service. Then the Stobaks,

---

61   Chief of the Gen. Staff of the Field Army of 25.8.1915, No 5974 r.
62   War Ministry of 25.11.1914, No 2763. 14. A. 4.
63   War Ministry of 10.7.1915, No 3433. 15. G. A. 4.

too, were established in the Armies in the West, whereas in the East, at first, only the Supreme Commander East received a Stobak, on 1 October 1915.

From Spring 1915, there existed in Ostend a training command for motorised vehicle Bak. This was now extended, by the Inspector, into a Bak School[64] and also took over the Telemeter School set up in La Fère.[65]

In May 1916, the designation 'Anti-Balloon Defence Gun'" was replaced by the more accurate 'Anti-Aircraft Defence Gun' - Flak.[66] Towards the end of that year there were 173 mobile and 2 fixed flak batteries, 16 motorised vehicle flak batteries, 217 mobile and 122 fixed flak platoons, 14 machine flak platoons and 80 individual motorised vehicle flaks.

Meanwhile, experience in the battle of the Somme had taught that the previous organisation of the flak service was no longer satisfactory. Above all it proved to be necessary to make the link between the combat forces in the air and the ground defence closer. It was necessary to set up within the combat groups (Genkdos) a tighter command structure. Account was taken of these requirements when, initially at the beginning of December 1916, the flak service was included in the area of responsibility of the Commanding General of the Air Forces. Since the Kogenluft took over, into his own Staff, responsibility for the business of the previous Inspector of Flak, the post of the Inspector was discontinued.

From then on the Stoflak were under the direct command of the Kogenluft. With their new designation, 'Flak Commanders' or Koflak, they gained wider influence. Subordinate to them were the posts of Group Flak Commanders - Grukoflak - which from then on were introduced into the Group Commands (Genkdos). By these measures, command and supervision was significantly tightened up. At the same time the Kogenluft expanded the range of duties of anti-aircraft defence. Not only was aerial reconnaissance and artillery registration to be denied to the enemy, but also support had to be given to the German aircraft in aerial combat. Therefore value was placed on the construction of pivot-mounted medium-calibre guns and large-calibre guns on motorised vehicles.

If the new units formed in 1917 and 1918 were added in, the Flak reached a strength of 116 heavy motorised batteries. Each had 2 to 3 guns, 39 light motorised vehicle batteries with 2 guns, 168 horse-drawn batteries, 166 fixed batteries, 3 railway flak batteries, 183 machine flak detachments, 49 horse-drawn flak detachments, 173 fixed flak detachments and 80 individual motorised vehicle flak.

The Flak School Ostend changed, in Spring 1917, into the Flak Gunnery School. At the same time the Flak Motorised Vehicle School Valenciennes was formed.[67] Later, another Flak Experimental Section was created in Lille.[68]

e2. Anti-Aircraft Machine Guns

As well as the guns, the machine gun also found a use, at first temporarily, in anti-aircraft defence. It could not, of course, be viewed as a replacement for guns, but

64   War Ministry of 15.10.1915, No 3766. 15. A. 4.
65   War Ministry of 29.6.1915, No 2357. 15. G. . 4; later in Ghent.
66   War Ministry of 31.5.1916, No 1428. 16. A. 4.
67   War Ministry of 15.4.1917, No 1183. 17. A. 4.
68   War Ministry of 3.8.1918, No 7526. 7. 18. A. 4.

was intended to be effective against low flying aircraft. To this end, from August 1917,[69] Anti-Aircraft Machine Gun Detachments Nos 1-103 were formed to protect the industrial plants in the western area of Germany. In addition Anti-Aircraft MG Sections Nos 801, 803, 901-921 and 925[70] were set up, called, on account of their long name, 'Flamga'. In contrast to the detachments, they remained autonomous, and took over the protection of the quarters, munitions depots and centres of communication directly behind the main fronts in the West. each section consisted of three MG companies each with 12 guns.

e3. Flak Searchlights

Since air traffic and air raids do not depend on daylight, anti-aircraft defence had from the beginning to be linked with searchlights. At first the heavy 90cm fortress searchlights with their complement of pioneers were made available. But once all the air forces had found their common head in the Commanding General of the Air Forces, they also took over the commandeered pioneers together with their searchlights and formed their own Swf (searchlight) formations. From the beginning of 1917 there came into existence in rapid succession 321 Flak Swf. Detachments,[71] which were followed the next year by 69 more. Then Flak Swf Batteries were also formed,[72] which had been achieved by bringing together 3 detachments for each. So that, for the 87 new batteries, 261 detachments disappeared again and only 129 flak Swf detachments remained autonomous. The close link between the anti-aircraft defence and the searchlights caused the flak searchlight formations to regard themselves as part of the flak artillery. They then gave, in recognition, the service designation 'gunner' to their troops.[73]

To complete the theoretical and practical training, the Training Command set up, in October 1916, was only two months later expanded into the Flak Searchlight School.

e4. Aircraft Reporting Service

All flak formations were equipped with listening apparatus, to be able to establish, early on, the approach of enemy aircraft. At night, therefore, for the flak searchlights there arose the possibility of being able to illuminate the enemy aircraft by surprise. The fact that this blinded the pilot made it difficult for him to maintain his direction of flight, prevented him from spying out terrain (which was always possible, even at night), and at the same time made it difficult to drop his bombs on target. Also, so as not to come under defensive fire, he had to seek greater height. For the German flak fire, however, the illumination of the enemy aircraft was the precondition of successful gunnery during the night.

The listening service, carried out uninterrupted day and night, soon expanded into a comprehensive aircraft reporting service. Further to the rear of the front, where there were only individual defensive formations, they helped themselves by

69 War Ministry of 28.8.1917, No 599. 8. 17. A. 4.
70 War Ministry of 1.8.1917, No 1343. 7. 17. A. 2. g.
71 War Ministry of 5.3.1917, No 478. 17. A. 4.
72 War Ministry of 27.2.1918, No 5011. 2. 18. A. 4.
73 A.V.Bl 1917, No 718; War Ministry of 23.7.17, No 4089. 7. 17. A. 4.

forming aircraft lookout stations. Therefore, by noting the direction of the enemy's flight, they could warn the 'objectives' which might be thought to be under threat. The regulations for the aircraft reporting service required:

- Reporting by all front listening stations to the flak central exchanges with the Group Flak Commander

- Reporting on, by the Flakgruko, to the aircraft reporting centres of the Flak Commander with the Army Command. St times of active air traffic, there was also a special aerial defence officer of the air forces. Then the reports passed on to the flak units and flak searchlight units to the rear, and also to the more distant aircraft lookout stations

- Reporting on, by these posts, to all the reporting points lying in the enemy's direction of flight, and reports back to the Koflak, as long as the enemy is over the Army district in question. The Koflak saw to it that the fighter flights and the balloon report centres were informed.

By means of this reporting system, early warnings were to be given not only of air raids in the war zone but also in home front areas. It could also be ensured that the fighter aircraft and air defences were prepared for the approaching enemy aircraft. Of course the observation of the return flight of enemy aircraft had to be carried out with the same care.

A special aerial defence reporting network saw to it that all the authorities in question co-operated without friction. Attached to this network were all the flak and flak searchlight formations, fighter units, aircraft reporting centres, flak centres, balloon report centres and the central exchanges of the neighbouring Armies. If circumstances required wireless telegraphy could also assist.

f. Meteorological Service

The need for systematic weather observation for flying had already been recognised before the war. On 1 April 1913, that led to the organisation of a military meteorological service that was centred in the Military Meteorological Exchange, set up on 6 February 1914 in Berlin.[74] As the war was, fortunately, to be carried into enemy territory - immediately in the West and soon in the East - the necessity arose of setting up this type of exchange, for the various theatres of war. At first there came into existence, in November 1914, the Field Meteorological Exchange Brussels,[75] then in April 1915 that of the Supreme Commander East,[76] which later moved forward to Warsaw. Finally, in October 1915, the Field Meteorological Exchange Temesvar,[77] was established, on 8 September 1916 it moved to Sofia, as well as to Constantinople.

For local meteorological observation, and to exchange results with the exchanges, from September 1914 onwards, 24 fixed field meteorological stations[78] in

74 During the war, on 3.10.1916, it was moved to Niedergörsdorf near Jüterbog (A.V.Bl. 1916, No 817)
75 War Ministry of 3.11.1914, No 1938. 10. 14. A. 7. L.
76 War Ministry of 3.4.1915, No 1784. 3. 15. A. 7. L.
77 War Ministry of 1.10.1915, No 1521. 9. 15. A. 7. L.

the occupied areas and 27 mobile stations with the Armies were formed. They came under the command of the Head of Field Aviation. In addition, in the period from October 1914 to January 1916, there came into existence another four field kite balloon stations.[79] These included one in the East and one in the south-west. The kite balloons, with the aid of a small tethered balloon carrying instruments (kite balloon) measured the temperatures at various altitudes.

Not only for flying did the meteorological service retain its great importance. It soon also became indispensable for the use of poison gas that was dependent upon the ground wind. It was used in connection with the efforts of the artillery to make themselves freer of the registration of 'errors' of the day.

In September 1916, the previous stations were changed into field meteorological stations or field kite balloon stations, while the exchanges were redesignated as Chief Meteorological Observatories.

As soon as the experience which had been gathered indicated that meteorological observation had to be placed in the immediate proximity of the front, the Commanding General of the Air Forces provided the broader foundation necessary for the meteorological service. He set special Front Meteorological Stations, which the War Ministry established on 25 August 1917.[80] After that the meteorological service was divided up as follows:

- a chief meteorological observatory in each theatre of war
- 24 fixed field meteorological stations in the occupied areas (Nos 101 to 116, 130-133)
- 27 Army meteorological stations (Nos 1-27)
- 210 front meteorological stations (Nos 201-415 with interruptions)
- 12 field kite balloon stations

In that way the Army meteorological stations formed, within their districts, the exchanges for the front meteorological stations and the affiliated field kite balloon stations. They also carried out wind measurements like the front stations, while the kite balloon stations retained, as their special area of competence, the measurement of temperature. The meteorological forecast was issued through the Army meteorological station.

In the meteorological formations, meteorologists were employed on contract. They wore the uniform of the Government building contractor without epaulettes, but with a silver 'W', and pilot balloon, on the corners of their collar.[81]

78   War Ministry of 1.9.1914, No 1169. 8. 14. A. 7. L.
79   On 18.10.14, 10.6.15, 12.10.15 and 21.1.16 (Nos 51-54).
80   War Ministry of 25.8.1917, No 598. 17. A. 7. L.
81   A.V.Bl. 1915, No 843 of 1.11.1915.

G.

Survey and Topographical Service

On mobilisation, all officers were issued with the war maps of the area in question. As soon as an Army entered a new sector of operations, the necessary topographical material was issued to it from Germany. In spite of this, it often happened in the war of movement that the troops had already "marched off the map" before they received the continuation map sheets. Having ready the supplies of maps printed in peacetime, the printing of new maps, and sending them on to the Armies in the field formed one of the areas of responsibility of the Deputy General Staff of the Army.

As soon as trench warfare set in, the small-scale maps[1], which had been completely suitable for the requirements of mobile operations, were no longer sufficient. From then the entry on maps of even minor topographical features was required. Thus the production of the necessary large-scale maps had to be carried out at the front.

At first the 11 fortress survey sections formed on mobilisation were brought up to take over the carto-graphical work for the production of the battery boards of the heavy artillery. Then field survey sections for the Army High Commands were brought together from trained and practised personnel.[2] Further units were formed to meet the increasing need, so that soon a special technical organisation of the survey service appeared to be necessary.

For this purpose on 4 July 1915 the Supreme Army Command set up the post of Head of Field Surveying, in the Great Headquarters.[3] The Head of Field Surveying was, as service chief, to direct the work of the survey formations. He had to ensure the replacement of personnel, the testing of instruments and the formation of new units. Also he had to supervise the production of general and operational maps, to procure and supplement the material for making war maps, and generally to be responsible for all questions concerning the field survey service. He redistributed the formations, while at the same time the artillery survey service was separated from the field survey service. In the form of artillery survey sections, there came about organic collaboration with the heavy artillery. However, the fortress survey sections and the field survey detachments, however, were dissolved by the Head of Field Surveying. From them he created survey sections,[4] one of which joined each Army in the West and each Army Group in the East. As a detachment, there only remained one single formation for taking measurements in the mountains.

1   1:100,000 in border areas, 1:80,000 in France and Belgium, 1:126,000 in Russia, 1:300,000 as a general map.
2   War Ministry of 7.12.1914 and of 23.1.1915, No 1206. 1. 15. A. 3.
3   Chief of the Gen. Staff of the Field Army of 4.7.1915, No 3675 r; War Ministry of 19.7.1915, No 668. 7. 15. A. 3.
4   War Ministry of 28.9.1915, No 1348. 9. 15. A. 3.

A survey section contained a geologists' group, a trigonometry unit and a stereo-scopic unit, in addition a printing shop and map office. The geologists' group was re-sponsible for advising the troops as soon as difficulties arose in the construction of fortifications, in mining work, in water supply, drainage and obtaining raw materi-als, as well as in technical and hygienic installations. The trigonometry unit created the very finely measured reference points necessary for the production of the maps of the front. Finally, the stereoscopic unit, in conjunction with the balloon sections, and by using a long-range camera, saw to the work of photographing enemy terrain.

In producing the maps needed in trench warfare it was a matter of spotting, and continually observing, the changes the enemy made to the terrain. New features were entered on the maps and made accessible to the troops. Serving as sources of informa-tion there were the long-range camera photographs, the reports of the troops, balloon reconnaissance, the results of the artillery survey units and above all the aerial photo-graphs taken from aircraft vertically over the terrain. To collect all reports concerning correction of maps, permanent topographical sections were set up with the General Commands, a Group Topographical Sections, with the divisions. In this process the divisional topographical sections completed the entries on the basis of the observa-tions of the artillery survey sections. Meanwhile the Group topographical sections evaluated the topographical implications of reconnaissance information, from air-craft and balloons.

Later, combat conditions necessitated the formation of a second survey section in individual Army areas. When such circumstances arose, the Head of Field Sur-veying assigned to the High Command in question, a Staff Officer of the survey ser-vice. This happened first on 11 December 1915 with the 6th Army, then in Autumn 1916 there followed the Army Groups Eichhorn and Woyrsch, in 1917 Army Group Below and all the Armies in the West. The survey service Staff officer directed in his Army district all geological, trigonometrical, topographical and photographic work as well as the production and supply of maps, he supervised the organisational conditions within the survey sections, the maintenance and supply of equipment.

The more the survey service expanded the more it proved advisable to assemble the topographical photographs according to theatres of war. This was the case princi-pally in France, when the strategic withdrawal in Spring 1917 had considerably shifted the Army areas. But in the Balkans too circumstances were pressing in this di-rection. Therefore in July 1917 the Supreme Army Command appointed Com-mander of Survey Troops No 1 for the West and No 2 for the South- East.[5] Two months later the Survey Service Staff Officer of Army Group Woyrsch was pro-moted to Commander of Survey Troops No 3 for the Eastern theatre of war.[6]

Under the command of the Commander of Survey Troops were the survey ser-vice Staff officers with the Armies and with the Army Groups in the East. He received his instructions from the Head of Field Surveying and put the latter in the picture concerning the wishes of the High Commands. He harmonised the work of the Staff Officers and took care of the balanced distribution of personnel and materials be-tween the Army areas and controlled the joint work in the areas where Armies ad-joined.

5   War Ministry of 13.7.1917, No 159. 7. 17. A. 3.
6   War Ministry of 12.9.1917, No 1135. 9. 17. A. 3.

H.

Armoured Fighting Vehicle Units

The armoured fighting vehicle called the 'tank,' by the enemy Powers, was the only weapon that on the German side could not be properly developed during the war. However, it had already been sent into action by the enemy during an attack in the Somme area on 20 October 1916. The Supreme Army Command did charge the Head of the Field Motorised Vehicle Service "to push forward with tank construction", but at first nothing came of it that was any use in war.

Ludendorff comments regarding this:[1]

> The tank model which the Head of Field Motorised Vehicles presented in Spring 1917 to the Supreme Army Command did not meet the requirements. I asked him particularly to promote tank construction energetically. It is possible that I should have used stronger pressure, it is possible that we then might have had a few more tanks for the decisive battle in 1918; but I don't know what requirements of the Army we would have had to shelve in favour of the tanks. More workers could not be allowed to leave, the authorities at home could not summon up any. Had they been available then we had to draft them as replacements into the Army. In 1918 we never managed a mass deployment of tanks, and it is only *en masse* that the tank is effective.

It must be remembered in this connection that in 1917 production at home was already suffering greatly from the shortage of raw materials and skilled workers, and also from the difficulties in transport. Therefore production was forced by circumstances to restrict itself to meeting only the most urgent needs. But this demanded submarines, railway matériel, aircraft, munitions, guns, and motorised vehicles to move reserves. So for the production of tanks, even disregarding the fact that there was as yet no model which could be used in war, there was very little left over.

Thus, while in 1917, on the German side, tank construction only proceeded slowly, in the tank battle of Cambrai on 20 November 1917 the enemy brought up the tank *en masse* and reaped a victorious breakthrough. Ludendorff, however, with complete justification, ascribed to the fact that this attack had struck a thin position, partly manned by older troops and poorly provided in terms of artillery.[2] In any event, the German counter-attack that began 10 days later snatched back from the enemy any territory they had gained and captured a considerable number of tanks.

Meanwhile, success had also been achieved in producing a German model of tank, the 'A7V Wagen',[3] which could be used in war. So it was possible, by the time

1 Ludendorff, pages 462/463.
2 Ludendorff, page 462.
3 'A7V' signified: Verkehrs-Abteilung des Kriegsministeriums (Traffic Section of the War Ministry).

the great offensive of 1918 began, to put five 'Sturm-Panzerkraftwagen-Abteilungen' (assault armoured vehicle sections) into the field. They consisted partly of A7V Wagens and partly of captured English tanks. The tanks of Sections No 1-3,[4] assembled from German matériel, possessed a similar armament for each of their 5 tanks, each with a 5.7cm rapid-firing gun and 5 machine guns. On the other hand the sections with captured matériel each consisted of 2 tanks carrying guns (male tanks) and 3 tanks carrying machine guns (female tanks). In each of the months of April, May, and August it was managed to set up another section with captured tanks. Thus, overall the number of sections rose to eight. It is obvious that with such small forces successful deployment was not possible, although the German fighting vehicles fought well in the places they were used.

In terms of weapons technology, the direction and training of the fighting vehicles was, from May 1918, in the hands of the Commander of Sturm-Panzerkraftwagen-Abteilungen, who belonged to the Staff of the Head of Motorised Vehicles in the Great Headquarters. The somewhat clumsy designation of the new arm of the service was changed on 22 September 1918 into 'Schwere Kampfwagen-Abteilungen' (Heavy Fighting Vehicle Sections).[5] The adjective 'schwere' (heavy) is explained by the fact that at that time the creation of light, and hence, more mobile, fighting vehicle section was also under way. But they never managed to be used.

4   Formed in accordance with War Ministry of 29.9.1917, No 815. 9. 17. A. 7. V.; mobile from 8.1 or 26.2.1918.
5   War Ministry of 22.9.1918, No 1587. 18. G. A. 7. V.

I.

Signal Troops

1. Until Autumn 1916

For the war of movement the German Field Army was provided with a signals service which was completely appropriate to its purpose. Initially, in the Field Army there were the following signals formations:

- in the Great Headquarters the Chief of Field Telegraphy as director of the whole signals service in the field, a motorised vehicle wireless station and a telephone section

- with every Army Command a Staff Officer of Telegraph Troops as adviser and technical director in the Army area, an Army Telegraph Section, a Wireless Command and 2 heavy wireless stations

- with every General Command a Corps Telephone Section[1]

- with every cavalry division a Signals Section with 1 heavy and 2 light wireless stations[2]

- with the units of all service arms telephone and flag signalling equipment

Worthy of emphasis from the establishments of the individual formations are the telephone section (divided into 5 detachments) with 2 station wagons and 20 construction wagons, the Corps Telephone Section with 4 station wagons and 12 telegraph material wagons. The Army Telegraph Section was divided into a telegraph company, train column, and motorised vehicle telephone detachment, with 1 station wagon, 4 motorised telephone wagons and 14 material wagons. The Heavy Wireless Station had 1 station wagon, 1 wireless mast wagon, and 1 pioneer store wagon. The Light Wireless Station had 1 station wagon and 1 store wagon. The total number of formations amounted to 1 motorised wireless station, 26 telephone sections, 8 wireless commands, 8 Army telephone sections, 29 heavy and 22 light wireless stations, 14 Reserve telephone sections, 2 Ersatz telephone detachments. The number of these formations grew automatically as new Armies and Corps were formed, in which process, however, the heavy wireless stations of the cavalry divisions were withdrawn and used elsewhere.

As a non-military unit every Lines of Communications Inspectorate had at its disposal a civilian Lines of Communications Telegraph Directorate. In the signals service too, trench warfare demanded a strong increase in the number of formations and prompted improvements and specialisation. At first the Supreme Army Command extended its own telegraph and telephone services, as in September

---

1   With the Reserve Corps: Reserve Telephone Section; with the Landwehr Corps only 2 Ersatz telephone units.
2   Two heavy and 2 light stations with the Bav. Cav. Div and the 4th Cav. Div.

1914 incorporated a Telephone Office, a Telegraph Office and a Telephone Construction Unit, from which a year later emerged the Telephone Directorate of the Great Headquarters.[3]

The very favourable experiences in listening-in to enemy wireless traffic provided in November 1914 the impetus for setting up a special listening service,[4] as a Wireless Reception Station was attached to every Army High Command. Since important wireless messages were also transmitted, by the enemy and also in code, a special decoding service developed that flourished to a high degree of perfection. If listening-in to enemy wireless messages was valuable, the enemy transmitting station itself, when it had been located, had at the same time to give away the location of its unit. Success was finally obtained in determining a position in such a way by taking bearings from various points by means of frame aerials and gunnery director.

For detecting this activity, in November 1915 two direction-finder units were formed for every Army.[5] The firing of enemy artillery with observation support from aircraft using wireless telegraphy asserted itself in a very troublesome way. Since on the German side at first combat aircraft were not available, the suggestion was made to jam the enemy wireless traffic, i.e. to bring it into confusion by transmitting German wireless waves. This task was taken over by the aeroplane jamming station introduced with every Army from July 1915.[6]

For transmitting signals in the mountains, in May 1915 four signal units were assigned to the Alpine Corps; these worked with heliographs. The lamp signalling system developed by these units proved its worth so well that the War Ministry introduced it in August of the same year for general Army use.[7] Within a year, in addition to the Mountain Signals Units (the number of which had increased to 8), formed 300 ordinary signals units which were assigned according to the situation of the troops.

The infantry and Reserve divisions had marched to war without telephone and wireless formations. It was, however, precisely with them, as the main fighting units, that the necessity for the most lavish equipment with signalling apparatus made itself felt. Therefore, in August 1915, the Supreme Army Command ordered that, in the order of battle, every division should be equipped with a telephone traffic operations unit and a telephone construction unit. These units were coupled together and passed over to the divisions as divisional telephone detachments.[8] In addition, the Supreme Army Command created a further number of autonomous construction and traffic operations detachments in the Armies at their own immediate disposal.

1916 at first brought a change in the signals formations of the Army Commands. In February the previous Army Telegraph Sections were re-formed into Army Telephone Sections and given consecutive numbers.[9] At the same time, the

3 War Ministry of 4.8.1915, No 22 507. 15. A. 7. V.
4 War Ministry of 20.11.1914, No 2127. 14. A. 7. V.
5 War Ministry of 1.11.1915, No 2432. 10. 15. A. 7. V.
6 War Ministry of 22.7.1915, No 1435. 7. 15. A. 7. V.
7 War Ministry of 24.8.1915, No 1559. 8. 15. A. 7. V.
8 War Ministry of 28.10.1915, No 2371. 10. 15. A. 7. V. and of 29.11.1915, No 2333. 11. 15. A. 7. V.

civilian 'Telegraph Directorates of the Lines of Communications Inspectorate' disappeared and was replaced by military telephone sections. However, later they were not under the command of the Lines of Communications Inspector, but joined the Army troops as second Army Telephone Sections. They were distinguished by a number which was a hundred higher than that of the 'first' section.[10] Each of the two sections comprised a Staff, a Motorised Telephone Construction Detachment and a Telephone Traffic Operations Section. They had a total of 30 officers and almost 900 NCOs and ORs.

In the battle at Verdun the traditional means of signalling failed in the overpowering artillery fire. Thus the most advanced infantry were assigned small wireless stations which really proved their worth. The Supreme Army Command therefore ordered their general introduction. From July 1916, they were formed as 'wireless sections (small stations)' each with 2 stations.[11]

The battle of Verdun was very fruitful for the development of the signals service, because never had the difficulties between fighting front and command posts been so great as they were here. Therefore the carrier pigeons in the charge of the pioneers were brought up. Satisfactory experiments were made with messenger dogs. Signalling troops and light rockets were used. It was in this battle, too, that the concept of the infantry aircraft arose.[12] The listening set stations, introduced as early as the end of 1915 also proved their worth. These, working from the most forward trenches, used the earth lines to listen in to the enemy telephone conversations in the trenches opposite. They were therefore often able to report when the enemy was relieved and to warn of imminent attacks.

When the Falkenhayn Supreme Command stepped down, it left the signals service as follows:

- in the Great Headquarters: Chief of Field Telegraphy, GHQ Telegraph Directorate, 1 motorised vehicle wireless station, 1 telephone section

- with every Army Command: Staff Officer of Telegraph Troops, 2 Army Telephone Sections, 1 Wireless Command, 2 heavy wireless stations, 1 wireless reception station, 2 direction-finder units, 1 aeroplane jamming station, together with telephone construction and telephone traffic operations detachments as OHL Reserve

- with every General Command: 1 telephone section

- with every division: 1 divisional telephone detachment, together with, as the situation required, wireless sections (small stations), signalling troops or mountain signalling troops, and listening set stations

- with every cavalry division: Signals Section with 2 light wireless stations.

9 War Ministry of 6.2.1916, No 2295. 1. 16 A. 7. V.
10 War Ministry of 30.8.1916, No 1189. 8. 16. A. 7. V.
11 War Ministry of 28.7.1916, No 230. 7. 16. A. 7. V.
12 See Part IV F 2c.

2. First Reorganisation under the Hindenburg Army Command

a. Service Chiefs

The Hindenburg Army Command started from the premise that not only was a tighter organisation of the signals service necessary, but that also it would be expedient to separate the two main means of signalling, i.e. telephone and wireless telegraphy. Therefore it first dissolved the post of the Staff Officer of Telegraph Troops with the Army Commands, which was the head of both the telephone and wireless services. They replaced it with Army Telephone Commanders - Akoferns.[13] With that the Commander of the Wireless Command became autonomous. The fact that he was placed on a level with the Akofern was soon afterwards expressed in the similarity in designation of his post. From March 1917, his post became Army Wireless Commander - Akofunk.[14]

Until this point, no senior signals officer had been attached to the General Commands. But now the tighter direction of the signals formations was also to gain ground within the Groups. Thus, in December 1916, every General Command received a Commander of Telephone Troops and a Commander of Wireless Troops. In March 1917, their designation was changed to Group Commander of Telephone Troops - Grukofern - or of Wireless Troops - Grukofunk.

If the service chiefs with the Army Commands were moved downwards in this way, so also between them and their chief with the Supreme Army Command was placed another intermediate post, the General of Telegraph Troops - Gentel. Three such generals were put in place, one each for the Eastern, the Western and the South-Western theatres of war. It is true that for the East it just meant a change of name. The Chief of Field Telegraphy already had under him a representative with the Staff of the Supreme Commander East, who was now called General of Telegraph Troops No 2. For the rest, the insertion of the 'Gentel' resulted in it being easier to carry out movements and balancing of forces within a theatre of war. It also meant the Chief of Field Telegraphy being relieved of some workload.

With the Army Groups in the West the Staff of the Supreme Commander was increased, in April 1917, by one signals expert for dealing with relevant questions. The expert was, from a technical point of view, under the command of the General of Telegraph Troops 1, but was himself not a service chief of the signals formations.

b. Units

The telephone sections with the General Commands and the divisional telephone detachments were both re-formed and renamed in the organisation of 14 December 1916.[15] From then on, to the General Command belonged a Group Telephone Section, and to the division a Divisional Telephone Section. The first had a station detachment, 2 telephone detachments and an equipment column, the second di-

13   War Ministry of 14.12.1916, No 192. 12. 16. A. 7. V.
14   War Ministry of 12.3.1917, No 2867. 2. 17. A. 7. V.
15   War Ministry of 14.12.1916, No 192. 12. 16. A. 7. V.

vided into a station detachment and 3 telephone detachments. Their establishment of personnel amounted in the Group Telephone Section to 11 officers, 285 NCOs and ORs. In the Divisional Telephone Section there were 65 more men. In total, 62 Group Telephone Sections and 250 Divisional Telephone Sections came into existence.

During the fighting in the West in 1917, special telephone formations also had to be created for the three Army Group Commands there. They were formed, in May 1917, as Army Group Telephone Sections Nos 200-202[16] and increased in number, in 1918, by Nos 203 and 204. They corresponded with the number of Army Groups in France.

The previous signal units were more appropriately designated lamp signalling detachments, of which the majority were incorporated in the divisional signals sections. The rest were combined by the Supreme Army Command, in groups of 4, into autonomous lamp signalling detachments. The OHL retained these at its immediate disposal.[17] Thus there came into existence Lamp Signalling Detachments 1-59 and 101-112, as well as No 1750. The use of the lamp signalling stations was, despite their restricted range of 6km, very frequent. By means of Morse code from powerful lamps they linked, for instance, the advanced infantry with the infantry aircraft and the infantry balloon. Mist, smoke, and strong sunlight affected the operation. There was also the frequent possibility of the message being read by the enemy, so that, if at all possible, lamp-signalling messages were sent in code.

The wireless formations of the Army Commands, with the exception of the aeroplane jamming station, were combined by the Supreme Army Command in May 1917 into Army Wireless Sections,[18] each consisting of Staff, 2 heavy wireless stations, 2 direction-finder detachments and 1 wireless receiving station. Their establishment had a strength of 7 officers, 114 NCOs and ORs. Their wireless messages could cross 300km. The Army Wireless Sections bore the numbers 1-23, 26 and 1'722.

The 20 aeroplane jamming stations with the Army Commands got a bad reputation, since they severely disrupted German wireless traffic, as well as the enemy's. They were used in July 1917 to help with the formation of the Group Wireless Stations of the General Commands. These stations, the effective area of which extended to 100km, only 6 weeks later took the name Group Wireless Sections.[19] The establishment of each of these formations, the number of which grew to 63, amounted to 2 officers, 37 NCOs and ORs.

On 24 November 1916, the wireless sections (small stations) which were assigned to the divisions on the main fighting fronts, had already been designated as Small Wireless Sections.[20] On 30 May 1917 they were changed into Divisional Wireless Sections[21] and in the order of battle taken into the divisions. The increase

16 War Ministry of 22.5.1917, No 401. 5. 17. A. 7. V.
17 War Ministry of 10.4.1917, No 467. 4. 17. A. 7. V.
18 War Ministry of 30.5.1917, No 17. 5. 17. A. 7. V.
19 War Ministry of 12.9.1917, No 415. 7. 17. A. 7. V.; Group Wireless Sections 501-563.
20 War Ministry of 24.11.1916, No 2701. 11. 16. A. 7. V.
21 War Ministry of 30.5.1917, No 17. 5. 17. A. 7. V.; Divisional wireless Sections 1-192, as well as No 1724 for Turkey.

in the number of these units from 107 to 192, necessary for this, took place within a year. Each section was composed of the Staff, a wireless station and 2 wireless detachments. Their radius of action extended to 100km.

The divisions used in the mountains were, from October 1916, assigned Mountain Wireless Sections.[22] During the course of 1917 those reached a total number of 10. In contrast to the divisional wireless section, the mountain wireless section possessed two wireless stations together with 50 more personnel.

From the end of 1915 the listening set stations had already been engaged in the listening-in service. Only in January 1918 was the service in the trenches confirmed on the establishment. But at the same time, there became apparent the need to bring them together for the purpose of supervision and of evaluation of intelligence within each Army. As a result of this intention, in February 1917, there came into existence the 22 Listening Set Station (Arendt) Sections.[23]

Up to Spring 1917, telephone and wireless depots were operated in the lines of communication for replacement and repair purposes. From then on, the Supreme Army Command dissolved these depots and created in their place with each Army an Army Telephone Park[24] and an Army Wireless Park.[25] They assigned to the autonomous telephone construction and traffic operations detachments a further number of station detachments.

A special service instruction of August 1917 prepared for the collaboration of the Army and the Fleet. Its practical use took place, in October 1917, in relation to the taking of the Baltic islands.

3. Second Reorganisation under the Hindenburg Army Command

a. Service Chiefs

The organisational division into two of the direction of the signals service with the Army Commands - Akofern and Akofunk - and with the General Commands - Grukofern and Grukofunk - had soon proved to be unfavourable for the collaboration of telephone and wireless telegraphy. Also the connections between the signal service in the field and that at home proved to be too loose. Therefore, in August 1917 the Supreme Army Command again removed the separation of the command posts and gave the signals service, from the top down, new foundations that were formally expressed in the establishment on 12 September 1917.[26] In accordance with this, the relationships of the service chiefs were structured as follows:

The previous Chief of Field Telegraphy in the Great Headquarters was from then on called Chief of the Signals Service and was under the direct command of the Chief of the General Staff of the Field Army. As service chief of the entire sig-

22 War Ministry of 24.10.1916, No 1855. 10. 16. A. 7. V.; Mountain Wireless Sections 1-9 and Bav. 1; No 8 later as No 1725 in Turkey.
23 War Ministry of 26.2.1917, No 307. 2. 17. A. 7. V.
24 War Ministry of 7.3.1917, No 393. 3. 17. A. 7. V.
25 War Ministry of 12.3.1917, No 2867. 2. 17. A. 7. V.
26 War Ministry of 12.9.1917, No 415. 9. 17. G. A. Nch.

nals service in the field and at home he was given all the authority of a Commanding General. As adviser and executive arm of the Supreme Army Command he was in charge of all the affairs of the signals service, and was in command of all German wireless telegraph traffic. In order to get the correct idea of his area of responsibility, it is necessary to know that his Staff dealt with extension and direction of the strategic telephone systems. They covered all theatres of war, the telephone lines to the East and South East, the special telephone systems for anti-aircraft defence, the aircraft reporting service and fortresses, the military, naval, and coastal defence telephone systems at home, cable installations and undersea cables. Via the Telegraph Section Orient in Sofia he was connected with Constantinople, Konia, Aleppo, Damascus, Jerusalem, Mossul, Sivas and Diabeker. Liaison officers of the Inspector-General of Artillery Gunnery Schools and the Commanding General of the Air Forces, together with those of the Bavarian and Saxon War Ministries, were with him.

Like their supreme chief, now also the Generals of Telegraph Troops were redesignated. From now on they were called Signals Generals Nos 1-3 and had the authority of the brigade commanders. Among their service responsibilities were standardising the organisation and handling of the signals service, as well as of the allocation of wavelengths and codes in their theatre of war. They made recommendations for the assembly and distribution of the signals formations for special purposes and supervised technical support, and the technical service, in their area of responsibility. No change was made in the duties of the signals experts with the Staff of the Army Group Commands.

By contrast, from that point on, the Akoferns and Akofunks of the Armies were discontinued. Their duties were transferred to the Army Signals Commander - Akonach -, who was assigned to every Army Command. The Akonach had the authority of a regimental commander. In service terms he was under the command of the Signals General of the Army in question and was the service chief of all signals formations in his Army, in so far as they were not assigned to the General Commands or Divisions. However, in the whole Army area he bore the responsibility for dealing with all signals affairs, for making recommendations concerning deployment, collaboration and special use of the signals formations and for their technical activity and readiness for action and for wireless telegraph discipline. The Akonachs, within the Army as a whole, were numbered from No 1 to No 26.

Following the pattern of the developments in the High Commands, in the General Commands the previously separate service posts of the Grukofern and Grukofunk were merged. The new post was of Group Signals Commander, Grukonach, who in service terms was under the Akonach. The duties of a Grukonach corresponded, within the smaller area of responsibility of the Group, with those of the Akonach. In addition, it should be noted that, at the same time, the Supreme Army Command set up four Grukonachs for its own special use. They bore the numbers 202-204 and 206.

The reorganisation of 12 September 1917 brought something completely new in assigning to the establishment of every division a Divisional Signals Commander - Divkonach. The scale of the signals service methods within a division demanded, after a decision had been taken, to introduce a uniform system of management. By its very nature a particularly tight control was needed within this large combat unit.

The importance of expert and uniform control of all the signals services within the division were again particularly expressed in February 1918. In that, for all the 120 divisional sectors on the Western Front, a permanent signals unit officer was put in place,[27] who, with his precise knowledge of local conditions, was to give support to the Divisional Signals Commanders who came and went with their divisions.

b. Units

The units themselves were only affected by the restructuring of the organisation in so far as carrier pigeons, messenger dogs and aircraft wireless telegraphy were brought in to the signals service. The carrier pigeon service had always belonged to the pioneer service. During the long period of trench warfare, carrier pigeon lofts were also set up on the Western Front and in November 1916 placed on the establishment.[28] From then on, however, the Chief of the Signals Service took over all the carrier pigeon establishments at home and in the field.[29] With this, the pigeon lofts permanently established in every divisional sector came under the Divkonach of the division that was in the sector at any one time. The pigeons showed their usual reliability, and during bombardments often were the only means of getting reports through from the most forward line to the command. Even from balloons and aircraft the pigeons were used as messengers.

As well as the pigeon, the dog also proved its worth as a dispatch runner. For training purposes, messenger dog schools had been set up,[30] which now came into the signals service. The Chief of Signals used these so-called schools to form out of them for every Army, a messenger dog depot[31] with a strength of 1 officer, and 70 NCOs and ORs together with messenger dogs. These depots were attached to the Army Signals Parks. They sent to the divisions messenger dog sections consisting of 5 handlers and some 20 messenger dogs.

The Army Signals Parks just mentioned similarly came into existence on 17 March 1918. In fact, they were formed, by combining the Army Telephone Parks and the Army Wireless Parks. Each one of these 23 parks comprised Staff, telephone depot, wireless depot, telephone and wireless personnel depots, messenger dog depot and equipment column, with a complement of 9 officers and 300 NCOs and ORs.

The transfer of the wireless telegraph stations of the air forces to the Chief of the Signals Service was completed in January 1918.[32] They were placed under the command of the Signals Commander in whose area of responsibility the aircraft formation lay. In this process a distinction was made between different types of station in accordance with the equipment of the aircraft units in question. So, only the aircraft of a part of the 'reconnaissance flights A' were equipped for two-way

---

27   War Ministry of 10.2.1918, No 13. 1. 18. A. Nch.

28   War Ministry of 30.11.1916, No 1990. 16. A. 6.

29   War Ministry of 17.11.1917, No 705. 9. 17. A. Nch.

30   Chief of the Gen. Staff of the Field Army of 20.8.1917, No I c. 61 838 op; 5 in the West, 4 in the East.

31   War Ministry of 17.3.1918, No 374. 18. A. Nch.

32   Chief of the Gen. Staff of the Field Army of 26.1.1918, No I c. 76 154 op.

wireless telegraph traffic, while the remaining artillery reconnaissance flights and all the ordinary reconnaissance flights only had transmitters on board.

In this way there came about, in April 1918, the following order of the War Ministry regarding establishment.[33] One airfield wireless telegraph station and one wireless telegraph station near the firing line for every reconnaissance section A with two-way wireless telegraph traffic. Only one wireless telegraph reception installation for the remaining reconnaissance flights A and the ordinary reconnaissance flights. In accordance with this, there were 53 airfield wireless telegraph stations, 53 wireless telegraph stations near the firing line and 86 wireless telegraph reception installations. Efforts were made to have two-way wireless traffic fitted in all reconnaissance flights A and accordingly to replace the reception installations with 2 stations respectively. In addition, in July 191 the three pursuit squadrons also received airfield wireless telegraph stations with the numbers 601-603,[34] while the other stations took the number of their aircraft formation.

In the artillery all the Staffs were equipped with wireless telegraph reception installations. In 1918 every battery also received an artillery reception installation. Linked to this were the Signals Instruction and Training Commands that were set up from Spring 1918 at all the artillery training grounds. From these, in August 1918, a Signals School was created in each Army.[35] On the other hand, as early as October 1917, the Signals School already in operation since July 1917 was reorganised to form the Army Signals School Namur.[36]

In March 1918, the listening set stations were in March 1918 split up into autonomous listening stations.[37] In doing so, a total number of 292 stations was achieved, so that in addition to the units given to the divisions there would still be a certain reserve in hand. However, the Staffs of the sections that had been dissolved found a use in the evaluation offices that were opened at the same time with the Akonach and Grukonach. Experiments to evaluate the earth lines for sending reports back from the trenches to the rear, in addition to listening-in to the enemy, were carried out by power buzzer stations. In the meantime, they produced no satisfactory results since the conductivity of the ground proved in practice to be too variable. Also, listening-in by the enemy formed a disadvantage that could not be excluded. Therefore the use of earth current telegraphy was again restricted to the listening stations.

The infantry had carried telephone equipment with them since the beginning of the war, had formed telephone detachments to operate it. In February 1918, the process of equipping them was completed and for every regimental Staff of the infantry, the cavalry Schützen, as well as for every battalion a unit signals section had been formed,[38] to which messenger dogs and carrier pigeons were also assigned. But the signals detachments were not only intended to deal with the telephone service. They also looked after all the other signalling that had been introduced in units

33 War Ministry of 8.4.1918, No 731. 18. A. Nch.
34 War Ministry of 8.7.1918, No 366. 6. 18. A. Nch.
35 War Ministry of 7.8.1918, No 1377. 18. G A. Nch.
36 War Ministry of 10.10.1917, No 117, 9. 17. A. Nch.
37 War Ministry of 17.3.1918, No 374. 18. A. Nch.
38 War Ministry of 21.2.1918, No 56. A. Nch.

during the course of the war, i.e. flare pistols, sound signals (signal horns, sirens, bells, gongs) and ground signals (flags, cloths), and also flare signals for firing from Granatenwerfer, and cylindrical drum flares for identifying the most advanced part of the line to aircraft. Even signal shells were used, which the light Minenwerfer or Granatenwerfer would fire to the rear in a fixed direction.

Towards the end of the war, the signals formations, apart from the formations of signals units within the other service arms, reached the following status:

- at the disposal of the OHL: 96 motorised vehicle telephone construction detachments, 30 telephone construction detachments, 97 telephone traffic operations detachments, 20 telephone station detachments, 72 lamp signalling sections, Army Signals School, Army Signals Park

- with the Army Groups: 5 Army Group telephone sections

- with the Army High Commands: 47 Army telephone sections, 23 Army wireless sections, 20 Army Signals Parks together with 17 messenger dog squadrons

- with the General Commands: 71 Group telephone detachments, 63 Group wireless detachments

- with the divisions: 242 divisional telephone sections, 193 divisional wireless sections, 292 listening stations, 617 pigeon lofts

- with the air forces: 82 airfield wireless telegraphy stations, 74 wireless telegraphy stations near the firing line, 95 airfield wireless telegraphy receiver stations

4. Female Signals Corps

The recruitment situation, growing more and more serious, had long since led to the clerical posts at home being filled, if possible, by female staff. In August 1918 the Supreme Army Command turned to a policy of using female forces to permit an extended process of replacing the signals service troops. On 3 October 1918, in carrying out the will of the OHL, the War Ministry issued regulations for implementing this process.[39] According to that process, the 'at first' NCOs and other ranks, in signals posts at home, in the General Governments, in the area of the Supreme Commander East and in the lines of communication were, as far as possible, to be relieved by auxiliary forces of women. These female auxiliary forces with the necessary welfare officials and other non-technical auxiliary and medical personnel formed the 'Female Signals Corps', and the women used in technical operations received the designation 'Nachrichtlerinnen'. However, the armistice was called too soon to allow this newly formed service to come into full effect.

---

39   War Ministry of 3.10.1918, No 444. 8. 18. A. Nch.

J.

Field Railway Authorities and Troops

1. The Organisation of the Field Railway Service

In its everyday business the entire field railway service was directed by the Chief of the Field Railway Service, called Fech. At first he was on the Staff of the Quarter-master-General with the rank of a brigade commander. The Hindenburg Army Command gave him the rank of a Commanding General, as befitted his importance. He was placed under the direct command of the Chief of the General Staff of the Field Army, expressly as the service chief of all railway formations in the field and on the home front.[1] For the Eastern theatre of war the Fech allowed himself, until 3.5.16, to be represented by the Chief of the Field Railway Service East.[2] With every Army and every Lines of Communication Inspectorate the Fech had a subordinate railway representative who was part of the establishment of the Chief of Field Railways. Initially, 2 Military Railway Directorates and 47 mobile Railway Station Commandants' Offices stood ready for deployment.

The Staff of the Fech was at first quite small. He had sections for operations, for organisation and intelligence/signals, for transports, for operations and traffic, for construction and also for waterways. The advance of the German armed forces in France, Russia, in the Balkans, in Asia Minor, in Iraq and in Palestine involved a quite massive expansion of the field railway service. That was also reflected in the Staff of the Fech, which in 1918 comprised 13 working groups (Chief - Personnel - Organisation - Intelligence/Signals - Politics and Economics - Transports - Operations and Traffic - Railway Construction - Water Transport - Medical Service - Demobilisation - War History - Intendance).

The railway representatives had the role of advisers to their Army High Command, or Lines of Communication Inspector, in all affairs involving railway or water transport. In particular the railway representative with the A.O.K. dealt with troop movements, whether he directed small-scale operations himself or whether, in the case of greater changes, he turned to the Fech. Later, he used the intermediate authority of the Railway Transport Section. The railway representative with the Lines of Communication Inspectorate took care of supplies from Germany and from the occupied territory. He was responsible for transport of replacements, military hospital transports and leave trains.

The Military Railway directorate, MED, was under a Military Railway director with the rank of a regimental commander. It had a section respectively for transport, for construction and operations, for machines and workshops, for telegraphy, for traffic with a main finance section and also for intendance. Added later

---

1 Chief of the Gen. Staff of the Field Army of 30.9.1916, No M.J. 6124. Z.
2 War Ministry of 3.5.1916, No 7165. 16. A. 1; he was replaced by Railway Transport Section 2.

were more sections for health services, commissariats and canteens. The Military Railway Directorates were to take over the direction of operations in enemy territory.

As early as August 1914 not only were the two prepared Directorates deployed in Lille and Sedan, but also MED 3, mobilised for Hirson. Then, in August 1915, there followed MEDs 4 and 5 in Warsaw and Vilna. In October 1915 there were MEDs 6 and 7 in Brest-Litovsk and Nisch. In November 1915 there was MED 8 in Schaulen, and exactly one year later MED 9 in Bucharest. In January 1918 came MED 10 in Craiova and finally, in March 1918, MED 11 in Dorpat. Each one of them, to a certain extent, was a memorial to the victorious conclusion of an offensive. Not designated as MEDs, but with similar duties, there operated from October 1916 Military Operations Directorate Dobrudscha, Mebedo. From February 1918, the Military Operations Directorate Ukraine was set up and from July 1918, the Railway Central Office Kiev. Under the command of the Military Railway Directorates were the Railway Station Commanders' Offices, and the technical operations offices of their area. Of these offices there were in total: 59 for operations, 35 for traffic, 6 for workshops and 31 for machines. In addition, there were also 9 Military Railway Workshop Sections and 9 Military Goods Offices.

The mobile railway station commandants' offices served to maintain military discipline at important centres of communications. At first they were designated within the home Corps that formed them. For example, as 1[3] to 5,[4] but from April 1917 were assigned consecutive numbers within the Army. Within the (heavily interrupted) numerical group 1 to 499 together with No 601 and 925-929 there were in total 320 mobile commandants' offices as against 47 on mobilisation.

The line of commands that existed on the home front, to preserve military interests, as against the civilian railway authorities, were used in Belgium and Luxemburg as 'operational line commands'. There, on 2 September 1914, the Line Commands Luxemburg and Liège were set up, and on 1 January 1914 Line Command Brussels. A Line Command Lodz existed only temporarily from 13 January-30 September 1915.

The authorisation of limited public traffic with a view to helping the war economy, caused the Administrative Council of the Belgian railways to be put in place on 24 October 1914. When later, to relieve the Staff of the Chief of Field Railways, a Military General Directorate was formed in Brussels, the administrative council was absorbed into it. In addition, there came into existence the administrative councils in Warsaw on 1 October 1915 and Bucharest on 15 April 1917. On 1 February 1916 and 1 February 1918 they were respectively transferred into the Military General Directorates Warsaw and Bucharest. To the Military General Directorates fell responsibility for the direction of business operations, traffic and administration in the whole of their district. The Military Railway Directorates were placed under the command of the General Directorates. That is, MEDs 1-3 under the General Directorate Brussels, MEDs 4-6, 8 and 11 under the General Directorate Warsaw, MEDs 7, 9 and 10 and Mebedo under the General Directorate Bucharest.

3   War Ministry of 19.4.1917, No 10 416. 17. A. 1.
4   A.V.Bl. 1914, No 253 of 2.9.14.

At the head of the Military General directorate was the Military Railway President with the rank of a brigade commander. His Staff was organised into respective sections for Military Affairs, Personnel and Administration, Finance, Construction, Operations, Traffic and also Machines and Workshops. The civilian president, subordinate to the Military Railway President, could, in his administrative council, only raise and make decisions on non-military questions, in so far as these concerned matters of subordinate importance. Otherwise he required the agreement of the military president.

In the first two years of the war the movement of military transports was directed by the Fech, personally. In the East his deputy directed movements. In Spring 1916,[5] however, the Fech, to relieve himself of work, inserted three Railway Transport Sections - Etra - with Etra 1 for the Western, Etra 2 with Supreme Commander East for the Eastern, and Etra 3 in Pless for the South-Eastern theatres of war. The Fech's deputy in the East was discontinued. From that time on, the direction of military transports, within the three theatres of war, was permanently carried out by the appropriate Etra. If a question of the home front or another theatre of war came up, the Etra established liaison with the appropriate authorities. Thus, the Etra directed the Army movements and the entire system of Army supply as far as the technical aspects of the railway were concerned. Water transport too was its responsibility.

A special Group Balkans of Etra 3 supervised the questions of import and export for Rumania, Bulgaria and Turkey as well as travel through Austria-Hungary. Both were for the purpose of supplying the German troops and assisting the allies, and also, to an increasing degree, for the purpose of importing food supplies and raw materials from those countries into Germany, such as, for example cereals and fodder from Rumania. In this the Danube played an important role as a transport route.

With every Army Command, as well as the railway representative, there was a Commander of Railway Troops, Kodeis. He was the service chief of the railway formations in his Army. Apart from this command he was, as far as technical matters were concerned, dependent upon the MED responsible for his Army district. That meant that, in so far as he was responsible for the direction and supervision of the narrow gauge, field and support railways, as well as for the extension of the standard-gauge railway in his operational district.

From December 1914, gradually five Regimental Commanders of Railway Troops, Rekodeis, were introduced in the most important Military Railway Directorates.[6] The Rekodeis fulfilled the duties as service chief of the Kodeis of those Armies whose districts fell within the area of his MED. He was also responsible for seeing to it that the extension of the Armies' network was extended in a uniform way. For the on-the-spot direction of the construction works, the Rekodeis and Kodeis had under them 34 Staff Officers of Railway Troops, of whom 4 originated from the time of mobilisation. From March 1917[7] another 34 Captains of Railway Troops for Special Use were assigned to these Staff Officers.

---

5   War Ministry of 3.5.1916, No 7165. 16. A. 1.
6   War Ministry of 5.12.1914, No 2218. 14 g. A. 7. V.
7   War Ministry of 10.3.1917, No 2507. 2. 17. A. 7. V.

Finally, note should be taken of the special agencies of the Fech for initial contact between parties and reporting. They formed 3 groups:

Plenipotentiary General Staff Officers with the allies in Constantinople from
12 November 1915, in Lom Palanka from 13 November 1915 to 13 January 1916,
then in Sofia, and also in Vienna from 1 January 1916

Plenipotentiary General Staff Officers with command authorities, ie with the
Coastal Defence High Command from 15 April 1916, with Army Group
Linsingen from 12 June - 15 October 1916, with Army Group (Army Front) Archduke Carl (Joseph) from 9 August 1916 - 13 January 1918, with Army Group
Crown Prince Rupprecht from 27 August 1916, with Army Group Böhm-Ermolle
from 17 October 1916 - 4 April 1918, with Army Group German Crown Prince
from 28 November 1916, with Military Administration Rumania (later with the
Army of Occupation) from 30 November 1916, with Army Group Albrecht from
2 March 1917, with Army High Command 14 from 14 September 1917 - 12 January 1918, for Taurus and Crimea from 10 July 1918 and from the same day for
the Ukraine in Kharkov

Liaison officers with the Austro-Hungarian transport commands from 1914,
also in Odessa, Nikolayev, Cherson and Yekaterinoslav from 10 July 1918 when it
was a matter of making the Ukraine economically useful for Germany

To summarise, then, the following organisation resulted:

- Chief of the Field Railway Service in the Supreme Army Command with
representative agencies with the allies and the Army Groups. Also liaison
officers with the Austro-Hungarian field transport commands; Railway
Transport Section and Military General Directorate for each of the three
theatres of war

- Military Railway Directorates and Regimental Commanders of Railway
Troops in the area of the Military General Directorates

- Railway representative and Commander of Railway Troops with every
Army Command

- Railway representative with every Lines of Communication Inspectorate

2. Railway Troops

During the war, with the railway troops it was in not a question of reorganisation,
but just of extending the increase in formations necessary for the theatres of war
and of introducing some special services. The increases were:

- 67 Railway Construction Companies, in 1914 increased by 12, in 1915
by 19, in 1916 by 16, and in 1917 by 7, giving a final total of 121

- Railway Operations Companies (each one counting among its NCOs 4
stationmasters, 1 dispatch official, 12 locomotive drivers, 7 chief Guard, 7
baggage masters and 3 point-men first class) in 1914 increased by 21 to
36, in 1915 to 71, in 1916 to 100 and in 1917 to 127

- Military Railway Operations Sections (Staffs) by 6 to 14

The 4 Railway Workers Battalions, by means of a reformation of labour battalions were, in December 1916, increased to 9 and were designated Railway Auxiliary Battalions. However, on 4 May 1918, they were split into 36 autonomous Railway Auxiliary Companies. In conjunction with these companies another 71 labour companies were engaged on field railway work. The Depot Workers Companies, increased from 15 to 29, received the name Lines of Communication Auxiliary Companies, corresponding to their use.

The 13 armoured sections formed in the border fortresses, because of the rigidity of the fronts, soon had nothing to do, and were reduced to 7. The armoured section possessed 2 locomotives at the centre of the train. To those were coupled up, from both sides, an infantry wagon, then an artillery wagon, and finally a machine gun wagon.

By way of new formations, there came into existence, in August 1915, Field Railway Operations Companies[8] and Aerial Railway Operations Detachments.[9] The former, at first numbering 6 and, in 1916, increased by 12, in 1917 reached a total number of 28. In addition, from February 1917, another 43 Field Railway Operations Sections[10] were formed. The Aerial Railway Operations Detachments, initially 13 in number, by the end of 1916 already numbered 30. At the end of 1917 there were as many as 92. From March 1916 there were also 5 Aerial Railway Sections.[11]

Of the other auxiliary formations involved in serving the field railway there should be mentioned 7 River Detachments, set up from March 1915, and equipped with diving gear. The 2 Tunnelling Companies in the area of MED 7, were set up from April 1917. The 7 Tree-Felling Companies were set up from March 1916, 3 Railway Works Companies from October 1917, and 18 Well Sinking and Construction Companies from December 1916. In addition, 8 civilian workers companies and 80 prisoners of war companies, among them 6 composed of miners, together with 7 Russian detachments for the railway workshops in the lines of communication. The Guard were Landsturm.

Into Turkey had been sent 12 Railway Special Detachments, 2 Special Drilling Detachments for wells and a Special Fuel Detachment Arabia to procure heating material.

The military railway personnel in the field grew from 20,000 to 108,000 men. To those were added another 70,000 civilian workers. The total length of track operated in Spring 1918, measured 19,658km - of this 7,943 in the Western, 8,076 in the Eastern and 3,639 in the South Eastern theatres of war. The stock of locomotives amounted at that time to 6,627 (3,938 + 1,786 + 903), that of railway wagons 178,046 (127,223 + 30,386 + 19,987).[12]

8   War Ministry of 16.8.15, No 366. 8. 15. A. 7. V.
9   War Ministry of 25.8.1915, No 785. 8. 15. A. 7. V.
10 War Ministry of 28.2.1917, No 274. 2. 17. A. 7. V.
11 War Ministry of 21.3.1916, No 792. 3. 16. A. 7. V.
12 Heubes, page 224.

3. Waterways

The administration of the waterways in the war zone was at first carried out by the Lines of Communications Inspectorates and the Military Governments. Meanwhile, the military water transports proceeded on the orders of the Chief of the Field Railway Service. For the administration and the direction of the operation, since mobilisation, there existed 29 Dock Commandants' Offices that were put in place as required and were later increased. They were mainly active in Belgium and northern France, where extensive waterway networks favoured inland navigation. In the General Government of Belgium, as early as the beginning of 1915, an extensive organisation of the waterways transport service began, as the Port Offices of Brussels, Charleroi, Loos, Liège, Mecheln, Namur and Turhout[13] were set up. Somewhat later in the same year the Port Offices of Huy, Herenthals, Klein Ter and Löwen, under the command of which were the Dock Commandants' Offices of their district.

At the beginning of 1916, the excessive demands on the railways necessitated a more intensive use of the waterways. Therefore, the Quartermaster-General gave orders that inland navigation would be given a uniform management system by the Chief of the Field Railway Service.[14] The latter set up with the Military General Directorate of Railways in Brussels a new section as the Military Canal Directorate[15] Brussels. As its agencies the Canal Operations Offices St Quentin and Lille, to which were added in the same year the same offices in Ghent and Sedan. Each Canal Operations Office had a waterway construction and waterway operations company, as well as several dock offices.

About the middle of 1918 it seemed advisable also to take tighter control of the inland navigation in Alsace-Lorraine. For this purpose the Fech created Canal Directorate No 2 in Strasburg and assigned to it Canal Operations Office 5 together with Waterway Operations Companies 5 and 6.

During the first years of the war, in the Eastern theatre of war there could not be much talk of waterway transport outside the German borders. Only after the fortress of Libau had been taken, was a Waterways Transport Section created, in the General Government Libau, by the Marine Transport Section of the Reich Office, for the Navy. In mid-1916 it joined the Inland Navigation Group of the Railway Section of the Deputy General Staff. It also organised the transport to the Balkans on the Danube, and on 9 March 1918 as the Inland Navigation Group with the Chief of the Field Railway Service came under the direct command of the Fech.[16]

---

13 Gen. Govt. Belgium of 14.2.1915, No I b. 2378.
14 Quartermaster- General of 8.2.1916, No I c. 2582.
15 War Ministry of 4.4.1916, M.J. 2525. 16. A. 1.
16 War Ministry of 9.3.1918, No 787. 2. 18. A. E.; for more detail see Part VII A.

K.

Motorised Vehicle Troops

1. Until March 1915

The German Army marched into the field, partly with military motorised vehicle formations, partly with civilian vehicles and drivers. The latter were a stop-gap, which is explained by the fact that in peacetime there were no touring-cars on the establishments of the senior Staffs and that for the eventuality of war contracts had been drawn up with members of the Imperial Voluntary Automobile Corps.

By contrast, the provision of lorries was militarily organised. Apart from a motorised vehicle park for the particular purposes of the Supreme Army Command there were:

- in the lines of communication of every Army a Commander of Motorised Vehicle Troops with a Lines of Communication Motorised Vehicle Park and a number of Lines of Communication Motorised Vehicle Columns appropriate to the tasks of the particular Army - in the 1st and 2nd Armies 18 each, in the 3rd Army 9, in the 4th and 5th Armies 5 each, in the 6th Army 8 (including 3 designated as Lorry Columns), in the 7th Army 3, in the 8th Army none; in the Landwehr Corps 2

- in the eleven cavalry divisions, one Cavalry Motorised Vehicle Column per division

- in the active Jäger battalions in total 16 motorised vehicle columns for supplying troops

- for super heavy batteries 3 steam locomotive parks and 2 benzole tractor columns

- motorcycles provided the dispatch rider service in senior Staffs and the columns

The advance in the West brought a rich haul of captured motor vehicles. Even if the vehicles were not systematically retrieved, yet as early as September 1914 a Meat Lorry Column had been set up for every Army Corps.[1] Also motor vehicle columns had been formed for transporting away the wounded. From September 1914, Postal Motor Vehicle Parks began to be assembled for the military post of the Armies. To ensure the lines of communication the War Ministry created Motorcyclist Sections.[2] At first, however, it was only possible to speak of a proper organisation of the motorised vehicle service in the General Government of Belgium. There, in only the second month of the war, a motorised vehicle command authority had been set up. However, it is true that it was only established very much later.[3]

---

1   War Ministry of 3.9.1914, No 266. 9. 14. A. 7. V.
2   War Ministry of 23.9.1914, No 182. 9. 14. A. 7. V.

In view of the bad road conditions in the East, in the late Autumn of 1914 the cavalry motorised vehicle column from the West was sent East. Partly using the Jäger motorised vehicle column, they formed new cavalry motorised vehicle columns.

2. The Organisation of the Motorised Vehicle Service from 10 March 1915 and its development up to December 1916

In March 1915 the Quartermaster-General decided to set in order and give a more uniform structure to the motorised vehicle service in the field.[4] His instructions culminated in the following points:

- constant supervision of motor vehicle traffic by motor vehicle supervisory authorities in order to put an end to unauthorised driving

- equipment of the Reserve Corps with Meat Lorry Columns such as the Army Corps had already had since September 1914

- surrender of the Jäger and cavalry motorised vehicle columns to the Lines of Communication, except for those expressly left to the troops

- assembly of all the motor vehicles serving medical needs into the Lines of Communication Medical Motorised Vehicle Section - Et. Sanka[5] - to be set up with every Army and to be under the command of the Lines of Communication Medical Officer

- registration of the motorised vehicle columns provided by the General German Automobile Corps in the L of C (Lines of Communication) Medical Motorised Vehicle Column, where they were in the first instance available to transport Voluntary Aid personnel and 'comforts'[6] transports, but which were, on the orders of the L of C Medical Officer, also to be brought up to transport the wounded

- placing the motorcyclist sections under the sole command of the L of C Inspectors

- establishment of the Postal Motor Vehicle Parks, each with 8 motor vehicles[7]

- placing all touring-cars and lorries which did not belong to the establishment of a particular formation, into the L of C motor vehicle parks

According to these instructions, the Commander of Motorised Vehicle Troops in each Army was, as an agency of the L of C Inspector, under whose command he remained. He was in command of the L of C Motorised Vehicle Columns, the L of C Motorised Vehicle Park with its petrol depots, the Jäger and

3   War Ministry of 1.4.1915, No 6249. 15. A. 7. V.
4   Quartermaster-General of 10.3.1915, No I a. 5737.
5   War Ministry of 23.4.1915, No 1758. 15. A. 7. V.
6   Translator's note: i.e. gifts to soldiers in the field.
7   War Ministry of 30.7.1915, No 1078. 7. 15. A. 7. V.

cavalry motorised vehicle columns surrendered to the lines of communication. The Et. Sanka, the Postal Motor Vehicle Park and the cyclist sections; to the other formations he served as technical service chief.

In Autumn 1917, the Quartermaster-General again dissolved the Meat Lorry Columns which had in the meantime been introduced with all corps. He gave to each of the General Commands its own Corps Motorised Vehicle Column for all transport purposes.[8] Every L of C Inspectorate received for its L of C motorised vehicle columns another L of C Motorised Vehicle Echelon with 3 columns. The General Government of Warsaw, however, was provided with a motorised vehicle service command on the model of Belgium's.

After ten super heavy batteries had been motorised by the end of 1917, attention was turned in 1916 to the great number of non-horse-drawn foot artillery batteries. In order to be able to move even these from place to place, as circumstances demanded, and not to have to have recourse to the draught horses of other units, from February 1916 a Foot Artillery Motor Traction Park was set up for every Army.[9] It consisted of 9 lorries with trailers. But to supply munitions to the non-horse-drawn batteries every Army received a Foot Artillery Munitions Motorised Vehicle Column.[10]

3. The Reorganisation of 15 December 1916 and development up to the end of the war

If the focus of the motorised vehicle service had until then been in the lines of communication, so the Hindenburg Supreme Army Command recognised that the emphasis had gradually shifted into the area of operations. Account had to be taken of this fact by means of a fundamental reorganisation. The motorised vehicle troops were to become Army troops and the Army Command itself had to decide whether the individual formations were to be assigned to the Groups or to the lines of communication.

To keep this reorganisation capable of development, the Supreme Army Command, on 15 December 1916, appointed the Chief of Field Motorised Vehicles in the Great Headquarters with the rank of a brigade commander. He had to take over the supreme direction of the motorised vehicle service in the field and at home.[11] By this order the Motorised Vehicle Inspectorate, at home, came under the command of the Chief of Field Motorised Vehicles, because only in this way could uniformity be preserved in extension, in preparation for action and in replacement of troops and equipment.

To support the implementation of his orders, Staff Officers, for special use, were assigned to the Chief of Field motorised Vehicles. Already, at the beginning of 1917, he was placing such a 'Stokraft' on detachment to the Supreme Commander

8   War Ministry of 7.10.1915, No 1414. 9. 15. A. 7. V.

9   War Ministry of 3.2.1916, No 1516. 1. 16. A. 5.

10 War Ministry of 12.4.1916, No 1995. 3. 16. A. 7. V. First designated as Army Munitions Motorised Vehicle Column; redesignated as Foot Artillery Munitions Motorised Vehicle Column by War Ministry of 28.8.1916, No 1028. 8. 16. A. 7. V.

11 War Ministry of 15.12.1916, No 16. 12. 16. A. 7. V.

East and to the Army Groups of the German and of the Bavarian Crown Princes.[12] In 1918 a Stokraft joined two further Army Groups in the West and in September of that year the 5 Stokrafts were appointed as Regimental Commanders of Motorised Vehicle troops - Rekokraft.[13]

The 23 Commanders of Motorised Vehicle Troops in the lines of communication, with this reorganisation, came directly under the command of the Army High Commands as Commanders of Motorised Vehicle Troops of the Army in question - Akokraft. From then onwards they had the rank of autonomous battalion commanders and carried out the orders of the Chief of Field Motorised Vehicles within their respective Army areas. The Stokrafts sent out to some of the Army Group Commands were not in command of the Akokrafts; that only began when the Stokrafts were appointed as Rekokrafts in September 1918.

In the reorganisation, the previous L of C Motorised Vehicle Echelons joined the Army troops, were provided with continuous numbers[14] and in June 1917 renamed as Army Motorised Vehicle Echelons.[15] At this opportunity the Postal Motorised Vehicle Parks gave up their autonomous character and were taken over into the échelons. They then provided the required lorries to the field post. Within each échelon there were three sections each with 10 light, 10 medium and 30 heavy wagons together with a motorised plough section[16] with 6-10 motorised ploughs. While the motorised plough section by its name suggested that it was to be used for agricultural purposes, the remaining vehicles - with the exception of those commandeered by the postal service - generally served to maintain communications between the operational area and the lines of communication.

The L of C Motorised Vehicle Parks, in the reorganisation joined the Army troops, also took the name Army Motorised Vehicle Parks and were provided with continuous numbers. They supplemented the needs of the motorised vehicle troops for personnel, motor vehicles, parts and fuels, and carried out repair work and took care of the evaluation of building materials. For providing fuel and changing tyres the Parks set up petrol depots, some were fixed, and some were mobile.

Another unit to go from the lines of communication to the Army troops was the L of C Sankas in the form of Medical Motor Vehicle Sections.[17] Meanwhile the Foot Artillery Motor Traction Parks, under the designation Army Foot Artillery Motor Traction Parks, were increased from 7 to 10.

With the dissolution of the existing 58 Corps Motor Vehicle Columns, in December 1916 all divisions also received their own Divisional Motor Vehicle Column. Until then only the 'autonomous' divisions had had them. With this the number of divisional motorised vehicle columns within the numerical group 530-800 rose to 236.[18]

---

12 War Ministry of 9.1.1917, No 651. 1. 17. A. 7. V.
13 War Ministry of 6.9.1918, No 770. 8. 18. A. 7. V.
14 War Ministry of 3.2.1917, No 2610. 1. 17. A. 7. V.
15 War Ministry of 18.6.1917, No 1924. 5. 17. A. 7. V.
16 Motorised plough sections had been first created on 1.3.1916 by the Supreme Commander East.
17 War Ministry of 21.1.1917, No 1698. 1. 17. A. 7. V.
18 War Ministry of 30.12.1916, No 2076. 16. A. 7. V.

The Supreme Army Command did not yet, at the beginning of 1917, possess an Army Reserve of motorised vehicles. But now, in large-scale battles and surprise attacks by the enemy as well as in the face of successful enemy breakthroughs, made itself felt. The need to have at hand a transport reserve not only for the increased munitions requirements but also for quickly bringing up whole troop units was increased. Therefore the Supreme Army Command had recourse to the 9 Jäger, 52 cavalry, 102 L of C and 33 Foot Artillery Munitions Motorised Vehicle Columns, not yet affected by the reorganisation, and brought them together under the designation Army Motorised Vehicle Columns under its own special command.[19] These columns within the numerical group 1-384, increased in number to 318. They also added to them Caterpillar Track Columns 1111-1122 for transporting munitions off the made roads.[20]

There still remains to be mentioned the setting up of a motorised vehicle service command. It was to be on the General Government model in the Military Administration Rumania in January 1917. The take-over into the Army troops happened four months later for the L of C cyclist sections as Cycle Sections 1-20. The setting up of two field recruit depots for the motorised vehicle troops took place in April 1918.

In the last year of the war, the provision of motorised artillery reserves became a burning question. The Supreme Army Command solved it as far as the available means allowed, and assigned a motorised vehicle échelon to each of 6 Field artillery regiments and 5 Foot artillery battalions.[21] These échelons counted as being commandeered and remained technically under the command of the Rekokraft in question at any one time.

In August 1918, the continuing sharp combat activity in the Western theatre of war caused 50 posts of permanent Captains of Motorised Vehicle Troops to be set up for the purpose of supporting the Motorised Vehicle Commanders.[22]

Particularly numerous were the supporting motorised vehicle formations that Germany provided to Turkey during the course of the war. If it was at first a matter of completing the as yet uncompleted railway lines in the Taurus and Amanus Mountains, so later was added the need to supply Army Group F in Palestine. In total, there were in Turkey 1 Army Motorised Vehicle Park, 4 Motorised Vehicle Parks, 1 Medical Motorised Vehicle Park, 1 Motorised Vehicle Echelon, 15 Army Motorised Vehicle Columns, 17 Motorised Vehicle Columns and 1 Motorised Vehicle Section. A service command of German motorised vehicles in Turkey had been set up on 5 November 1916. From 30 January 1918 it was called 'Motorised Vehicle Command with the German Military Mission in Constantinople'.[23] From 23 July 1917 military supervision was carried out by Stokraft 771, who on 17 September 1918 took the designation 'Rekokraft Turkey'. Under his command were the Akokrafts of the 6th Turkish Army (from 5 April 1917), the 7th Turkish Army (from 1 June 1916) and the 8th Turkish Army (from 7 January 1916), who in February 1918 were renamed respectively Akokraft Iraq, Syria, and Palestine.

19   War Ministry of 19.3.1917, No 1311. 3. 17. A. 7. V.
20   War Ministry of 18.9.1917, No 199. 9. 17. A. 7. V.
21   See Part IV. D 2 a1 & 2 and b1 & 2.
22   War Ministry of 14.8.1918, No I. B. 536. 8. 18. A. 7. V.
23   War Ministry of 30.1.1918, No 1338. 1. 18. A. 7. V.

4. Imperial Voluntary Automobile Corps

The members of the Imperial Voluntary Automobile Corps had contractually pledged themselves to provide a service as drivers, with their private cars, for the command posts. For that, an A.K.O. of 10 August 1914[24] awarded them, for as long as the mobilised state lasted, the rank of officers. That was "insofar as they were not in any military service and were contractually used in the Field Army and the Army of Occupation as drivers with their motor cars, or if they were liable for military service and did not have the rank of officers". Therefore, on their club uniforms they wore the lieutenant's epaulettes without insignia, while the mechanics they took with them received non-commissioned officer rank and were distinguished by plain silver braid on the collar. From 30 May 1915 the members of the corps and their mechanics were taken on to the nominal rolls of their service units.[25]

5. Imperial Motor Boat Corps

On 30 September 1914, the Kaiser approved the formation of a Voluntary Motor Boat Corps for the duration of the war.[26] The captains of the boats, members of the Motor Boat Club, pledged themselves together with their steersman and mechanics for the duration of the war. They wore their blue club uniform and were distinguished by a black-white-red armband with a heraldic eagle, to be worn on the upper left arm. In addition the boat captains, if they did not have a more senior military service rank - received officer's rank and put on the lieutenant's epaulettes without insignia.

The Motor Boat Corps was under the command of Vice Admiral Aschenborn (retired), who placed the boats at the disposal of the senior command authorities to protect rivers, canals and lakes. Armed with guns and manned by troops, the boats often became involved in fighting, such as on the Danube and the Narotschsee.

A year after it was formed, the Motor Boat Corps, instead of their club uniform, received grey-brown uniform, in which the steersmen and mechanics were distinguished as holding non-commissioned officer rank by a motor boat insignia in the corner of both collars.[27] In Spring 1916 the Corps came under the War Ministry.[28]

With the beginning of 1917 they were renamed the Imperial Motor Boat Corps,[29] the armband was discontinued and was replaced by an embroidered matt field grey imperial crown on both forearms. Finally, an A.K.O. of 6 September 1918 annexed the Army motor boat service to the motorised vehicle service,[30] whose Chief became service chief of the Motor Boat Corps which from now on was called the Imperial Motor Boat Corps.

24   A.V.Bl. 1914, No 219 of 10.8.14.
25   A.V.Bl. 1915, No 254 of 30.5.15.
26   A.V.Bl. 1914, No 313 of 30.9.14.
27   A.V.Bl. 1915, No 681 of 30.8.15.
28   A.V.Bl. 1916, No 167 of 8.3.16.
29   A.V.Bl. 1917, No 23 of 30.12.16.
30   A.V.Bl. 1918, No 949 of 6.9.18.

L.

Munitions Columns and Trains

1. At the beginning of the war

In peacetime 'the Train' formed a service arm in itself. On mobilisation it was dissolved to man the many planned train columns. But the train squadrons, marching out as self-contained formations, were distributed in the area of the advance among the initially temporary depot supply columns. Together with the infantry munitions columns, and the artillery munitions columns set up by the field artillery, the train formations came under the common concept of 'munitions columns and trains'. Of these there were:

- with each Army Corps: 2 munitions column sections (4 infantry and 9 artillery munitions columns), 1 foot artillery munitions column section (8 columns), together with 2 train sections (12 field hospitals, 6 supply columns, 7 vehicle park columns, 2 horse depots, 2 field bakery columns)

- with each Reserve Corps: 2 Reserve munitions columns and 2 Reserve train sections with smaller strength than with the Army Corps

- with every L of C: 4-8 L of C munitions columns, 5-14 L of C vehicle park columns and 8-15 train squadrons to take over the depot supply columns[1]

- with the Corps there marched out in total: 80 munitions column sections[2] with 149 infantry munitions columns[3] and 296 artillery munitions columns,[4] 40 foot artillery munitions column sections[5] with 264 foot artillery munitions columns, 81 train sections[6] with 397 field hospitals,[7] 182 supply columns,[8] 266 vehicle park columns,[9] 54 horse depots[10] and 81 field bakery columns.[11]

---

1 The lines of communication have been dealt with here for the sake of completeness; but these formations must be dealt with in more detail within the particular framework of the Lines of Communication (Part V B).
2 Including 29 Reserve and 1 Landwehr
3 Including 47 Reserve and 2 Landwehr.
4 Including 71 Reserve and 2 Landwehr.
5 Including those of the siege artillery.
6 Including 27 Reserve.
7 Including 77 Reserve.
8 Including 24 Reserve.
9 Including 80 Reserve, 4 Landwehr.
10 Including 4 Reserve.
11 Including 27 Reserve, 2 Landwehr.

The Reserve Corps, formed later, were therefore correspondingly equipped with munitions columns and trains, as were the newly-formed individual divisions, outside the corps unit. The gaps in this connection, in the Reserve and Landwehr units, were soon filled.

The division, of the munitions columns and trains, into 2 munitions column sections and 2 train sections with each Corps was purely administrative. In the Corps order of battle there was a mix of the munitions columns and trains, but there was a split into a II, and a II 'échelon of munitions columns and trains'. If a battle was in prospect, they were even divided into three, since a special 'combat échelon' moved up as far as the nearest fighting troops. The field bakery columns received special orders, since on account of baking they could only move forward in jumps. But when at all possible they moved right up to the advanced guard.

2. From 1915

a. Service Chiefs

The fact that the munitions columns and trains with the Corps were administratively split into 4 sections, and tactically into two or three échelons, in the long term proved not to be practical. The Supreme Army Command therefore, on 1 May 1915, dissolved the 4 section Staffs of the Corps and assigned to each General Command a 'Commander of Munitions Columns and Trains' (Komut). Also included were three divisional train échelons under his command.[12] The Komut bore the designation of his General Command. The divisional train échelons, which eventually grew in number to 277, were numbered through the whole Army and, with the usual interruptions, were commanded as Nos 1-3 Guard, Nos 1-555 and Nos 1-28 Bavarian. That system remained in place until the Hindenburg Supreme Army Command fundamentally changed the whole organisation of the munitions columns and trains.

The reorganisation of December 1916[13] drew its conclusions from the conditions of trench warfare. It removed the munitions columns and trains from the General Commands and placed them under the command of the more locally fixed Armies. In this process the Komuts of the General Commands were discontinued, while each Army High Command was joined by a 'Commander of Munitions Columns and Trains of the Army' (Akomut). The Akomuts, designated as Nos 1-30 and Bavarian 1-3, had the rank of regimental commanders. They controlled the divisional train échelons, the latter having only been affected by the new distribution insofar that instead of the Komut they were now under the command of the Akomut, who assigned a divisional train échelon to each of the divisions within the Army area.

But the experience of war, in 1917, taught that on the main fighting fronts an intermediate authority needed to be inserted, as a divisional train échelon with the General Command. Since there were already enough divisional train échelons, in February 1918 only 21 of these needed to be changed into Group Train Echelons.[14]

12 War Ministry of 1.5.1915, M.J. 7994. 15. A. 1.
13 War Ministry of 23.12.1916, No 32 970. 16. A. 1.
14 War Ministry of 24.2.1918, No 4662. 2. 18. A. 4.

They were given the numerical groups 31-48 and Bavarian 4-6, which followed on from the numbers of the Akomuts.

In August 1918, the Supreme Army Command put in place the General of Munitions Columns and Trains in the Great Headquarters.[15] He supervised the technical service of the munitions columns and trains, both in the war zone and at home, and saw to it that the Armies were supplied with draught horses and stores.

b. Munitions Columns

As already mentioned, the infantry and the artillery munitions columns had been formed and incorporated within the Corps troops by the field artillery, whereas the foot artillery munitions columns had been formed by the foot artillery. With the unit itself were the Light Munitions Columns of each field artillery battalion and each foot artillery battalion.

From Autumn 1916 onwards, the efforts to simplify the columns service led to all the infantry munitions columns, and all artillery munitions columns, being changed *en bloc,* into 'New Type Munitions Columns'.[16] That was irrespective of whether they had been designated for infantry or field artillery munitions, or whether they were of active, Reserve or Landwehr status. After the new organisation was implemented the prefix, 'New Type', was discontinued. From then on it was called simply 'munitions column' in conjunction with a continuous number within the Army.[17]

Since at the beginning of 1917 the Light Munitions Columns of the field artillery were separated from their sections and taken over into the Army troops, so those 507 munitions columns were joined by a second group of another 785 Light Munitions Columns of the field artillery. They were similarly consecutively numbered within the Army.

A third group was formed by the foot artillery munitions columns already assembled, in July 1917, as Army troops, from the foot artillery munitions column sections and the Light Foot Artillery Munitions Columns. However, apart from 11, they were gradually taken away again to join newly formed horse-drawn foot artillery batteries, as battery columns.

Finally, as a result of this there were, with the Army troops, 507 munitions columns for infantry and field artillery jointly, 785 Light Munitions Columns of the field artillery[18] and 11 Army munitions columns. Among the units, on the other hand, one munitions column remained as a permanent component of every foot artillery battery. Other than those, only individual munitions vehicles were on the establishment of the troop units. Those were units such as 1 small arms ammunition wagon, with each infantry company, and 2 with Jäger companies. They in-

---

15 War Ministry of 10.8.1918, No 9924. 7. 18. A. 4.

16 War Ministry of 22.9.1916, No 2526. 16. A. 4., and of 7.11.1916, No 2948. 16. A. 4.

17 War Ministry of 30.3.1918, No 171. 3. 18. A. 4. - Munitions Columns Nos 1-364, 367-374, 376-395, 406, 409, 435-437, 448, 466-502, 504-508, 517, 601-608 and Bav. 1-58.

18 For the 1918 offensive some of the Light Munitions Columns of the field artillery rejoined the field artillery battalions.

cluded a small arms ammunition wagon with every machine gun detachment, an ammunition wagon with every gun of the field artillery and the foot artillery.

In October 1917, the difficulties in providing replacements in the artillery led to only the light munitions columns of the field artillery, the battery columns of the foot artillery and the remaining 11 Army foot artillery munitions columns retaining their artillery replacements. Meanwhile, the other munitions columns from then on were manned with Train troops.

c. Trains

Out of the medical trains, the field hospitals were a component of the Corps troops and were numbered within each Army Corps, from 1 to 12. The same situation was retained in the case of the field hospitals of the later autonomous infantry divisions. By contrast, the Reserve field hospitals of the Reserve Corps and individual Reserve Divisions were consecutively numbered, through the whole Army. For practical reasons, the latter principle was also employed, from December 1916, on the field hospitals.

At that time, taking account of the conditions of trench warfare, the field and Reserve hospitals were removed from the Corps troops. Instead, two hospitals joined every division,[19] while the rest were taken over into the Army Reserves. They were to be thrown in at the places where the need was greatest. The total number of field hospitals rose to 592, including 113 Reserve, and 26 Landwehr field hospitals.

The composition of a field hospital should be noted. There were 6 medical officers, 1 senior pharmacist, 9 medical NCOs, 14 military hospital orderlies, 1 ambulance, 2 medical wagons and 4 stores wagons.

The supply trains were split into supply and supply park columns. The former consisted of 27 supply wagons, each drawn by four horses, the latter of 48 supply park wagons, each drawn by two horses. Originally designated after their Corps, in January 1917, after being taken over into the Army troops, they were consecutively numbered throughout the Army as supply or supply park columns.[20] In this way there were counted 180 supply and 444 supply park columns.[21]

Pack animal columns, for supplies in the mountains, were first formed by Army Detachment Gaede in Spring 1915, and later also came into existence with 12 individual divisions.[22] They were established, in May 1918, as Pack Animal Columns Nos 1-19[23] and treated as Army troops.

In the case of the horse depots, their transfer from Corps to Army troops took place on 1 February 1917.[24] Finally, there were 5 Army Horse Depots, 10 Cavalry Horse Depots and 48 Horse Depots.

19 War Ministry of 23.12.1916, No 32 970. 16. A. 1.
20 War Ministry of 29.1.1917, No 249. 17. A. 4., and of 28.2.1917, No 540. 17. A. 4.
21 There existed temporarily many auxiliary columns which were never established and just as suddenly disappeared again; like the 'Panje Columns' in Russia.
22 With the 22nd, 56th, 103rd, 123rd and 192nd I.D.s, the 11th and 15th Bav. I.D.s, the 13th, 14th and 19th Res. Divs, 2nd Ldw Div and 19th Ers. Div.
23 War Ministry of 28.5.1918, No 1459. 18 g. A. 4.
24 War Ministry of 1.2.1917, No 2681. 17. A. 1.

Veterinary hospitals and collecting stations were creations of the war. They were set up, in Spring 1915, with the Corps, the cavalry divisions and the autonomous divisions.[25] But the collecting stations were later changed into veterinary hospitals. However, on their redistribution, on 1 February 1917, the latter received consecutive numbers. From then on, of the 288 veterinary hospitals, one was on the establishment of every division, 6 were specially established as mange hospitals, and 28 as Group Veterinary Hospitals with the Army troops.

The field bakery columns, each with 12 baker's ovens, and 12 store wagons each drawn by four horses, were originally designated within each Corps as No 1 and No 2. In the Reserve Corps they were called Reserve Bakery Columns. In Spring 1917 they were all standardised into field bakery columns with consecutive numbers and taken over into the Army troops.[26] Their total number finally amounted to 184.

During the advance, provision of meat was effected through requisition or from the lines of communication. In trench warfare, requisition was taken in hand by the Corps and Divisions themselves. The butcheries, formed in this way, were established on 10 May 1917, by the Supreme Army Command, as field butchery sections with the Army troops.[27] They were in such numbers that every division, during its stay in the Army district in question, had a section at its disposal. There were, overall, 239 field butchery sections within the numerical group 1-281. To these were added the butchery sections which had previously been attached to the L of C bakery columns. In April 1918 they were changed into the autonomous Field Bakery Sections 301 to 349.

The fact that the pontoon trains were placed under the command of the Commander of Munitions Columns and Trains with each Army is only briefly mentioned here, since it has already been discussed.[28]

In August 1918 the extraordinary sharpening of the war, waged on the Western Front, led to even the columns there each being equipped with 2 machine guns, to defend themselves against enemy aircraft. In the same month a Train Field Recruit Depot became part of every Army Group in the West, and a Field Train School was set up in Ghent.[29]

25   War Ministry of 2.5.1915, No 1032. 4. 15. A. 3.
26   War Ministry of 3.4.1917, No 896. 17. A. 4.
27   War Ministry of 10.5.1917, No 1231. 17. A. 4.
28   See Part IV E 11.
29   War Ministry of 6.8.1918, No 9925. 7. 18. A. 4.

M.

The Medical Service in the Field

The medical service formed a facility that had branches through all the formations in the Field Army. Therefore it must be considered in total. After mobilisation there were:

- in the Great Headquarters: the Chief of the Field Medical Service
- at the disposal of the OHL: 11 hospital and 7 auxiliary hospital sections
- in every Army High Command: the Army medical officer
- in every L of C Inspectorate: the L of C medical officer with hygienic adviser, ambulance section, L of C medical depot and several military hospital sections (one for each Corps)
- in every General Command: the Corps medical officer
- in the Corps troops: 12 field hospitals (in Res. Corps only 4-6)
- in every Division: the divisional medical officer and 1 or 2 medical companies
- in the units: medical officers, hospital orderlies and auxiliary stretcher bearers

In the hands of the Chief of the Field Medical Service rested the direction of the entire medical service and the voluntary aid service. Their military inspector was attached to the Chief of the Service. During the war, as little changed in his post as it did in that of the Army medical officer who was responsible for the entire Army area, including the lines of communication. Under his command were the Corps medical officers and the L of C medical officer. Both the Army MO and the Corps MO respectively had at their disposal an Advisory Surgeon and a Hygienic Adviser who had already been assigned to them in 1914. The divisional MO was responsible for the direction of the medical service within the division, and the regimental or unit MOs received instructions directly from him.

The comprehensive reorganisation by the Hindenburg Army Command also affected the original distribution of the medical formations. From December 1916 a medical company and 2 field hospitals belonged, in the order of battle, to every division. Meanwhile, the second medical companies, available in many divisions, and the field hospitals not needed to equip the division, were taken over into the Army troops.

In April 1915, the motorised vehicles, captured in the first months of the war and incorporated in the medical service, had been established as Lines of Communication Medical Motor Vehicle Sections.[1] With the reorganisation of the motorised vehicle service they joined the Army troops and were from that time called Medical Motor Vehicle Sections - Sanka.[2] If the L of C Sanka already had 25 mo-

---

1   War Ministry of 23.4.1915, No 1758. 4. 15. A. 7. V.

tor vehicles for every Corps, under the command of the Army, so the Sanka comprised a reserve of 10 motor ambulances, and 5 lorries with ambulance trailers, as well as a supply of 10 motor ambulances each, for every division of the Army. The main duty of the Sanka consisted of transporting the wounded, and in supplying medical stores throughout the Army area. It was also involved in taking X-Ray pictures and in disinfection duties.

The clearing hospitals, appearing with the field hospitals, were not autonomous formations. They were set up, as circumstances required, by the L of C's military hospital sections, each of which included personnel for 3 hospitals. The difference between the two types of hospital was a consequence of the system of dealing with the wounded.

The medical company opened the main dressing station of the division. From there, or directly from the unit dressing stations, those wounded who were capable of walking were marched to the Slight Wounds Collection Station. Those not capable of walking were transported to a field hospital. Those slightly wounded then came into a section for mild cases, in the area of the lines of communication, which the L of C MO set up. Those severely wounded were separated into those capable of being transported and those not capable of being transported. Meanwhile the latter were treated in the field hospital. Those capable of being transported were sent off, by means of the ambulance section, in hospital trains to the Reserve hospitals in Germany.

If operations were moving forwards, then the field hospitals with their personnel and material were relieved by clearing hospitals of the clearing hospital section that cared for the wounded until they were well enough to travel. In trench warfare, the main dressing stations often took over the care of those not capable of being transported. The field hospitals were not relieved. Instead, clearing hospitals, often like peacetime hospitals, were set up further to the rear. In periods of 'quiet' trench warfare the wounded could therefore be cared for, until they were well, in the theatre of war itself. For that purpose sanatoria and convalescent homes were set up in the L of C area.

Finally, as a result of the increases in the medical formations that were necessitated by the growth of the Army, there were 314 medical companies. There were 592 field hospitals, including 113 of the Reserve and 26 of the Landwehr. There existed 72 field hospital directors. All this included clearing hospital sections, 22 ambulance sections, 62 hospital trains,[3] 100 trains for mild cases,[4] 85 auxiliary hospital trains,[5] 23 L of C medical depots.

An idea emerges of the range of the medical service, quite apart from the care of those Army members who had fallen ill, when one recalls that the German Army during the war registered 4,215,662 wounds.[6] That is a number approaching the

2   War Ministry of 21.1.1917, No 1698. A. 7. V.
3   This number includes the auxiliary hospital trains, increased in number to 32, since they later were also designated as hospital trains.
4   Set up by order of the Chief of Field Medical Service of 24.11.1914, No 6620. 14.
5   Equipped and maintained by private individuals or by local authority districts.
6   *Heeres-Sanitätsbericht* (Army Medical Report) III, page 9. In the statistics based on official casualty lists 'wounds' and not 'wounded' are counted, since many participants in the war were wounded not just once but several times.

size of the supply strength of the entire Army on mobilisation (Field Army: 2,578,646 and Army of Occupation 1,863,566 = total 4,442,212). Of every 100 wounded, 94 had their lives saved.[7]

7   *Heeres-Sanitätsbericht* III, page 66.

N.

The Field Police

The Field Police formed the military police in the war zone. It was composed, in proportions of one-third from each, of senior policemen from the peacetime provincial police, of NCOs, and of lance-corporals of the cavalry appointed as field police. This composition was also reflected in the Field Police Service that was organised in patrols. Each consisted of a senior police officer, an NCO and a lance-corporal. Apart from 6 senior police officers in the Great Headquarters, the field police was attached to the General Commands and L of C Inspectorates. In the former were units each consisting of 60 field police officers. In the L of C Inspectorates they varied in strength, but both unit and section were commanded by a Rittmeister (captain), to whom a Wachtmeister (sergeant-major) was assigned for routine duties. The number of sections rose during the course of the war from 33 to 115, at which point it should be noted that Section 112 with Army Group German Crown Prince was established as Field Police Squadron 112.[1]

More senior field police units were formed only in the East, where the field police brigade was in the General Government of Warsaw, and in the Field Police Inspectorate of the Supreme Commander East. The origins of the former went back to March 1915,[2] the latter to January 1916.[3]

During the second half of 1918, a breakdown in discipline had broken out to a considerable extent in the rear of the Army of the West. Consequently, at the beginning of October that resulted in a special reinforcement of the military police by a 'Field Police Corps for Special Use'.[4] It was formed out of 5 cavalry squadrons and on 5 November 1918 took the name Police Regiment 9.[5]

1   War Ministry of 9.9.1917, No 6177. 17. A. M.
2   1.3.1915 according to OB Ost of 12.2.1915, No II b. 1530.
3   War Ministry of 19.1.1916, No 1075. 16. A. 1.
4   War Ministry of 4.10.1918, No 10 757. 18 g. A. M.
5   War Ministry of 5.11.1918, No 12 643. 18 g. A. M.

O.

Labour Units

The change of fortresses from peacetime to a wartime footing required many earthworks and other works. Those had to be carried out by planned formations of men liable for service in the Landwehr. But since the war was soon to be played out almost exclusively on enemy soil, and developed into trench warfare, the labour units also had to be used in the war zone outside the home area. Thus they were even used for work in the so-called second line of the most advanced combat position and often suffered casualties. In Spring 1917, the War Ministry took account of their increasing importance in having them brought together in a parallel military organisation of labour battalions.[1] 217 such battalions were formed. They were counted as Army troops and were, as circumstances required, placed at the disposal of the lines of communication, and the Front, right up to the most advanced line.

A certain improvement in the status of the labour battalion soldier, popularly called 'Schipper' (shovellers), took place when in Autumn 1915 the labour units received field grey service jackets, trousers and caps, in place of the peacetime uniform, which in the war zone was felt to be of inferior status.[2]

1   War Ministry of 13.2.1915, No 1927. 15. A. 1., and of 10.4.1915, No 5870. 15. A. 1.
2   A.V.Bl. 1915, No 835; War Ministry of 31.10.1915, No 1981. 10. 15. B. 3.

P.

Technical and Administrative special formations

1. Works Departments

The Works Departments originally formed a part of the Lines of Communication Inspectorates. Within that they were increased in number from 8 to 19. In addition, there was a Works Department with the General Government Belgium, with the Supreme Commander East, with the Military Administration Rumania, and with the Senior L of C Inspectorate Yildirim. From the beginning of trench warfare, the activities of the work departments involved them in both the lines of communication and the operational area. On 21 September 1917 the Quartermaster-General placed the departments under the direct command of the Senior Quartermasters.

The chief of a works department had the rank of a Staff Officer. On his Staff he had an adjutant and two senior officials, one of whom belonged to the hydraulic engineering side and one to the road construction side. Labour units were provided, in the first instance, by the road construction companies of which there were 76 in number. But, following that, civilian prisoners, civilian workers, prisoners of war and those liable for auxiliary service were also considered. The Works Department saw to the supply of all construction material, tools, road-building equipment, field tramway materials and steamrollers. It carried out the construction of roads, structural engineering and the construction of accommodation of all kinds in the operations area, and in the lines of communication area.

2. Electric Power Detachments

Electric power installations were needed in the war zone for the purpose of providing lighting, for charging wire entanglements and for workshops. In Spring 1917 the temporary units, formed to serve the installations, were given a parallel organisation by the Supreme Army Command.[1] The available parts were brought together into 41 companies and another 76 individual detachments were set up. These companies and detachments came, as circumstances required, under the Staffs of the Electric Power Detachments that were formed at the same time with every Army. The Detachment Commander was under the direct command of the Senior Quartermaster of his Army. In addition to his companies and detachments he was also in command of the Army Electric Power Depot. He was responsible for the installation and running of all electric power installations, switching stations

---

1   War Ministry of 16.3.1917, No 7516. 17. A. 1.

and exchanges in the whole of his Army area, as well as for the supply of electrical machinery and installation material.

3. Salvage Formations (Salvage and Collection Services)

The innate German sense of order made it obvious that in 'tidying up the battle-field' not only were the dead buried, but also the large quantities of weapons, am-munition and items of equipment which were lying around were collected up and taken back. Considerations of the shortage of raw material, however, soon forced a systematic organisation and operation of this collection activity. Thus, in line with an instruction of the Quartermaster-General of 31 May 1917 the service was ex-tended to cover all weapons and weapons parts lying around on the battlefield and in billets. Munitions and munitions parts, items of military clothing and equip-ment as well as items right down to the smallest scrap of cloth or leather, pack re-ceptacles, Army property, raw materials and trade goods of all kinds were collected.

At the beginning of the war the troops collected captured items, weapons and cartridge cases and sent them back in their supply vehicles that returned, empty, to the depots. To promote this salvage activity, as early as October 1914, the post of a Salvage Officer was set up with every Army High Command.[2] Then every L of C Inspectorate received an L of C Salvage Company. Meanwhile, in the General Government Belgium, a Salvage Command was formed with the General of Foot Artillery.

But even if the service heads were frequently required to give robust encour-agement to the salvage service, the troops could summon up no enthusiasm for this activity. Therefore the Supreme Army Command felt obliged to exercise strong pressure. In July 1917, they made the salvage service the responsibility of Army High Commands in the West, the Supreme Commander East, Army Command Scholtz in the Balkans, and Army Command Mackensen in Rumania.[3] The previ-ous salvage officer with the Army Command became, with this order, an expert consultant to the Senior Quartermaster. Under his command was the salvage com-pany that had until then belonged to the lines of communication. The number of salvage companies in an Army varied and depended upon circumstances. In all there were 39, not counting the temporary formations of this kind.

The Salvage Officer, as consultant expert to the Senior Quartermaster, allo-cated and monitored the salvage formations. At the same time he administered the Army Dispatch Office. This office was to repair what was repairable, but to direct what was unusable back to Germany. To carry out these duties it was divided into an Infantry Section, with weapons store and repair workshop, an Artillery Section, a section for items of equipment, a section for anti-gas material, a bottle sorting sta-tion, a dispatch section, and finally, a raw materials section that worked in collabo-ration with the representative of the War Ministry.[4]

2   War Ministry of 24.10.1914, No 7486. 14. A. 1.
3   War Ministry of 29.7.1917, No 4469. 6. 17. Z. K. 1.
4   See in Part IV Q 4.

Similarly, from mid 1917, for the Groups there were permanent Group Salvage Officers who were assigned to the General Commands in question. Meanwhile the Divisional Salvage Officer belonged to the establishment of the division, and supervised the regimental, battalion and section salvage officers active in the units.

A further revival of salvage activity was to be introduced by the Representative of the Quartermaster-General for Salvage and Collection Services - BdG Beute - appointed on 1 June 1918.[5] His duties consisted of exercising personal influence on the Army Commands. As the war drew to its end and salvage activity became pointless, the post of BdG Beute was dissolved shortly before the armistice took effect.[6]

It remains to mention that with the establishment of the BdG Beute the salvage officers of the Army High Commands were designated Staff Officers for the Salvage and Collection Service. Their activity was concentrated on the area of operations, while for the lines of communication an L of C Salvage Officer was assigned to every L of C Inspectorate.

4. The Representatives of the War Ministry for Extraction of Raw Materials from the Occupied Areas in the West, and their agencies

Early on in the war, in the occupied areas, many agencies were engaged in obtaining raw materials. The growing shortage of raw materials forced the process of impounding to be extended, even to the austerity metals already used. For example, the brass in door and window fitments was commandeered. The heavily-industrialised area of the Western theatre of war appeared to be a particularly productive field for raw materials. On an instruction of 12 September 1916 from the Quartermaster-General[7] the responsibility for the removal of austerity metals from the industrial and commercial facilities of the operational and lines of communications areas was passed to the War Ministry Inspectors in Valenciennes, Sedan and Ghent. They had been established as BdKMs 1-3. In the first half of 1917, BdKMs 4 and 5, in Longwy and Maubeuge respectively, were added.

Each BdKM had at his disposal carefully selected personnel comprising 4 engineers with officer rank, 17 NCOs as dispatch and technical directors, as well as 28 other ranks. In addition he had under his command a similarly selected Metal Salvage Unit consisting of 1 officer and 170 NCOs and other ranks. From July 1917 there was a search and loading group consisting of men on detachment from the Field Railways.[8]

The BdKM, within the parameters assigned to him by the War Ministry, had to systematically seize raw materials and send them back to Germany. It was a process in which the Army High Commands were expected to lend him any support

---

5   Established by War Ministry of 4.8.1918, No 3012. 7. 18. A. M.
6   War Ministry of 7.11.1918, No 9251. 18 g. A. M.
7   Quartermaster-General of 12.9.1916, II c. 26 026.
8   BdG West of 16.7.1917, No VII a VI c 45 523.

he required. The removal of the austerity metals - ie all metals apart from iron - was the responsibility of the BdKM alone and was not to be carried out by works or salvage companies. Other items to be seized by the BdKM were ores, iron, steel, scrap metal, graphite, electrical machinery and machines for working metal and wood.[9]

5. Prisoner of War and Prisoner Formations

The 100,000 prisoners of war, in their own interest, had to be kept occupied. The shortage of labour on the one hand, and the treatment of German prisoners of war by the enemy Powers on the other hand, were the cause of using some of the prisoners of war for labouring work. They were sent to the areas of the General Governments, Military Administrations and lines of communication for road building, for railway and agricultural work. Apart from those employed in the railway service[10] there came into existence, in the war zone, 151 prisoner of war labour battalions, (from September 1915), 57 French detachments (from March 1916), 26 English detachments (from May 1916), 38 Rumanian detachments (from October 1916), 22 Italian detachments and 2 Portuguese detachments (from June 1918).

The work-shy elements in the occupied areas of the West were, from mid-October 1916, brought together into 34 civilian worker battalions and 10 civilian worker columns.

From 3 October 1917, in the area of the Field Army alone, 78 military prisoner companies had to be formed. That was a visible sign of the plummeting morale in the Army. Guards for all these formations were provided by the Landsturm infantry.

9   BdG West of 23.3.1917, VI c 12 641.
10   See Part IV K 2.

PART V

THE LINES OF COMMUNICATION

A.

The Lines of
Communication Inspectorates

The Lines of Communication formed the conveyor of the Army and took away everything that had to be got rid of by the Army. Put another way, the L of C Inspectorate were the middlemen between home and Army. They were also responsible for acquiring aids for the war zone. Its importance for the prosecution of the war is clearly shown by the fact that its most senior command was with the Quartermaster-General, on the Staff of the Chief of the General Staff of the Field Army.

At the head of the L of C Inspectorate of every Army stood the L of C Inspector who received his instructions from the Senior Quartermaster in the Army High Command. For his part, he received the general views of the Quartermaster-General. This tried and trusted organisation remained the same throughout the entire war. Even the appointment of the Representative of the Quartermaster-General for the Administration of the Occupied Areas in the West[1] did not change the organisation. That was because this representative was appointed merely to relieve the workload of the Quartermaster-General and was with him in the Great Headquarters. The Army Group Commands later inserted, between the Supreme Army Command and the Army High Commands, as purely operational and tactical commands, had no lines of communications agencies. They were instructed to refrain from intervening in any way in the supply of the Armies and the administration of the occupied areas.[2] In any event, it was only seldom and only in exceptional circumstances that they had a Senior Quartermaster.

In the direction of the enemy, the lines of communication area bordered on to the area of operations, or to the rear onto a General Government[3] or directly on to home territory. When an advance was under way the borders of the individual L of C Inspectorates were constantly changing. In trench warfare they were more stable.

The L of C Inspector had the rank of a divisional commander. His Staff, under the direction of a Chief of General Staff, consisted of 1 General Staff Officer, 1 adjutant, 1 MO and 1 pioneer officer, 3 veterinary officers, 1 paymaster, the chief of the field police units and the railways representative. As field administration authorities they were attached to the administrations of the L of C Intendant, the L of C MO with hygienic adviser, the L of C Judge Advocate General and the Army Postal Director as well as the civil administration under a senior official. Later there were also added chaplaincy services, anti-gas protection, graves administration, voluntary aid and the development of the civil administration into general provin-

1 See Part I. A. 2 c; the BdG Ost only existed temporarily.
2 Quartermaster-General of 27.7.1917, No I. 29 413.
3 See Part VI. A.

237

cial administration, agricultural and industrial section together with forestry administration.

The L of C Intendant was under the command of both the L of C Inspector and the Army Intendant. Within his service remit were intendance, depot, bakeries, pay department, Army clothing depot and the economic committee set up from 18 February 1915. The Army clothing depot was not located immediately close to him but in the collecting station at home where it was linked with repair workshops; however, later most of the Armies brought their clothing depot up closer.

The importance of the L of C Inspectorates justifies following them individually with significant dates:

L of C Inspectorate 1 from mobilisation with the 1st Army, dissolved with the latter on 17 September 1915 and used to supplement L of C Insp. 11.

(New) L of C Inspectorate 1 from 15 September 1916 with the 1st Army, newly-formed on 19 July 1916. Formed out of parts of the dissolved L of C Insp.12.

L of C Inspectorate, 1, 2, 3 ,4, 5, 6 and 7 were from the beginning of the war to the end with the Armies of the same number.

L of C Inspectorate 8 from mobilisation with the 8th Army, on 29 June 1915 took over a part of L of C Insp. 10 and on 10 July 1915 changed into L of C Insp.8/10.

L of C Inspectorate 8/10 existed from 10 July to 5 October 1915 for the 8th and the 10th Armies. It formed the continuation of L of C Insp. 8 and on 5 January 1915 changed into the new L of C Insp. 10.

(New) L of C Inspectorate 8 on 30 December 1915 formed from the L of C Insp of the Army of the Njemen, as this Army was renamed 8th Army. Since the L of C Insp. Njemen for its part formed the continuation of the old L of C Insp. 10, so finally the new L of C Insp. 8 was formed from the old L of C Insp. 10 and the new L of C Insp. 10 out of the old L of C Insp. 8.

L of C Inspectorate 9 was formed on 15 September 1914 for the 9th Army. After giving up some units to L of C Insp. 15, it carried on the L of C function for the 9th and 12th Armies jointly. When the (old) 9th Army was dissolved, it changed on 20 August 1916 into the new L of C Insp. 12.

(New) L of C Inspectorate 9. It came into existence on 26 June 1918 by a process of renaming L of C Insp. 15 that had been transferred with the 9th Army from Rumania to France. It was dissolved on 29 September 1918.

L of C Inspectorate 10 set up on 24 January 1915 for the 10th Army. On 29 June 1915 it joined the Army of the Njemen under the designation L of C Insp of the Army of the Njemen, and on 30 December 1915 was changed into the (new) L of C Insp. 8.

(New) L of C Inspectorate 10. It was formed for the 10th Army on 5 October 1915 out of L of C Insp. 8/10 and was dissolved on 25 August 1918. Its administration transferred to the Military Government of Lithuania.[4]

L of C Inspectorate 11 was set up on 16 April 1915 for the 11th Army and was with that Army first in Galicia and Russia, from 9 September 1915 in the Balkans where it was reinforced by parts of the dissolved L of C Insp. 1.

4   Quartermaster-General of 24.7.1918, No II. 2433 geh.

L of C Inspectorate 12. The ancillary L of C Gallwitz of L of C Insp. 8 was on 29 June 1915 extended to form the L of C Inspectorate of Army Group Gallwitz. When on 7 August 1915 the Army Group was raised to the status of the 12th Army, the L of C Inspectorate was designated as L of C Inspectorate 12. After giving up some units to L of C Insp. 1 and 15, on 9 August 1916 it was taken over into L of C Insp. 9, which for its part was redesignated on 20 August 1916 as the (new) L of C Insp. 12.

(New) L of C Inspectorate 12, formed on 20 August 1916 out of L of C Insp. 9 and with the 12th Army until 9 October 1916. On that date the 12th Army was dissolved and L of C Insp. 12 joined Army Detachment Scheffer. It remained with that Army Detachment until the latter was dissolved on 17 September 1917; then it was divided into L of C Commands 12 and 14.

L of C Command 12, formed on 17 September 1917 out of parts of the new L of C Insp. 12, served the Lida Sector of the 10th Army - later called Southern Sector of 10th Army - and was attached to L of C Insp. 10. The L of C Command 12 was dissolved on 6 August 1918.

L of C Command 13 existed from 26 May - 7 July 1915 only in preparation in Breslau and was then used to form the L of C Insp of the Army of the Bug.

L of C Command 14 and L of C Inspectorate 14. On 17 September 1917 the (new) L of C Insp. 12 gave up part of its complement as L of C Command 14 of the 14th Army which was to take part in the Italian campaign. The L of C Command was on 28 January 1917 extended to form L of C Inspectorate 14. But the latter only existed until 28 January 1917 and on that date was again returned to the status of L of C Command 14. On 15 January 1918 the L of C Command was dissolved; parts still remained as the 'German Administration in Occupied Italy' under the commander there. The remaining parts joined L of C Insp.17.

L of C Inspectorate 15. It was formed on 1 September 1916 from units given up by the old L of C Inspectorates 9 and 12 for the Rumanian campaign of the 9th Army. With the Army it was transported out of Rumania on 20 June 1918 and on 26 June 1918 in France was designated L of C Insp. 9.

L of C Command 16. Set up on 10 November 1917 for the German troops with the Austro-Hungarian 11th Army in Upper Italy, on 30 January 1917 attached to L of C Insp. 14. The Command was on 14 January 1918 transported out of Upper Italy to Strasburg in Alsace and there was extended into an Inspectorate.

L of C Inspectorate 16 set up on 21 January 1918 from L of C Command 16 and parts of the L of C Insp of the Army of the South for Army Detachment A.

L of C Inspectorate 17 formed on 22 January 1918 for the 17th Army from parts of L of C Command 14 and L of C Command 20.

L of C Inspectorate 18 formed on 19 January 1917 for the 18th Army out of the dissolved L of C Inspectorate Woyrsch.

L of C Inspectorate 19 formed on 21 January 1918 for the 19th Army from the previous L of C Insp. A and parts of the L of C Insp.South.

L of C Command 20 formed on 22 July 1916 for the Carpathian Corps and put under the command of the L of C of the Austro-Hungarian 7th Army, from 25 April 1917 directly under Army Front Archduke Joseph. Dissolved on 17 January 1918 for the purpose of setting up L of C Insp.17.

L of C Command 21 existed from 28 June - 12 November 1916 as a branch authority of L of C Army of the Bug for the German troops with the Austro-Hungarian 2nd Army and Army Group Litzmann.

L of C Command 22 existed from 17 December 1916 - 12 May 1918 as a branch of L of C Insp. 15 for the German troops with the Austro-Hungarian 1st Army. Afterwards parts of the Command together with the mobile L of C Command 147 formed the rear Transport Office Lemberg.

L of C Command 28 and L of C Inspectorate 28. Army Detachment B (originally Gaede) which stood almost entirely on German soil in Upper Alsace, only on 19 February 1917 received an L of C administration in the form of L of C Command 28, which on 28 October 1918 was raised in status to L of C Inspectorate 28.

L of C Inspectorate A. On 14 September 1914 the L of C Insp for Army Detachment Falkenhausen was set up. With the later renaming of the Army Detachment the L of C Inspectorate took the designation L of C Insp.A. On 21 January 1918 it transferred from Army Detachment A to 19th Army and from then on was called L of C Insp. 19, while L of C Insp. 16 came to Army Detachment A.

L of C of the Alpine Corps. It existed while the Alpine Corps was being used on the Austrian front in the Tirol from 31 May - 24 September 1915 and left behind an L of C Inspectorate which was still active for the period the Alpine Corps was used in the Balkans.

L of C Inspectorate of the Army of the Bug assembled on 12 July 1915 from L of C Command 13 and the 'Ancillary L of C of the 11th Army for the Beskiden Corps'. From 18 September 1915 it served for the whole of Army Group Linsingen (from 31 March 1918 H.Gr. Eichhorn-Kiev, from 30 April 1918 Group Eichhorn, from 13 August 1918 H.Gr. Kiev).

L of C Inspectorate C. It was set up on 1 October 1914 as the L of C Insp of Army Detachment Strantz and on 2 February 1917 was changed, with the renaming of the Army Detachment, into L of C Insp.C.

L of C Administration Dobrudscha was formed on 24 October 1916 to look after the Bulgarian and Turkish interests in the old Bulgarian Dobrudscha.

L of C Inspectorate of the Army of the Niemen coming into existence on 29 June 1915 out of the old L of C Insp. 10 and on 30 December 1915, at the same time as the Army of the Niemen was renamed, it was renamed L of C Insp. 8.

Ancillary L of C Plevna existed only from 20 September-31 December 1916 under L of C Insp. 11.

L of C Inspectorate South was formed on 11 January 1915 for the Army of the South. Dissolved on 20 January 1918 and used in the formation of L of C Inspectorates 16 and 19.

L of C Inspectorate Syria came into existence on 21 March 1918 for Army Group F as the successor of the dissolved Senior L of C Inspectorate Yildirim with its base in Damascus.

L of C Inspectorate Woyrsch was set up on 3 January 1914 for the Army Detachment and later Army Group Woyrsch. When the Army Group was dissolved on 15 December 1917, the L of C Inspectorate gave its administration section to L of C Insp. Bug and went with what was left to the West to be used there as L of C Insp. 18.

Senior L of C Inspectorate Yildirim with its base in Aleppo, from 1917 looked after the requirements of the German formations in the Turkish lines of communication in Syria and Mesopotamia and represented a continuation of the activities of the German Plenipotentiary General with the Iraq Group in Baghdad. It was dissolved on 21 March 1918 and left behind L of C Insp. Syria for Army Group F.

B.

Lines of Communication Formations

Responsibility for bringing up and administration of munitions and equipment was in the hands of the Commander of Lines of Communication Munitions Administration. He was under the direct command of the L of C Inspector. In March 1917 this administration received the designation L of C Munitions and Equipment Administration.[1]

As with the Army Corps, for the L of C munitions columns and trains there was, at first a special command for each, the Commander of the L of C Munitions Columns and the Commander of the L of C Trains. These posts were discontinued on 30 March 1917[2] and were replaced by the Commander of L of C Munitions Columns and Trains, who had at their disposal several divisional train échelons. The autonomy of the Commander of L of C Munitions Columns and Trains was later significantly limited. From 11 July1918 difficulties in getting replacements made it necessary to place him under the command of the Akomut with regard to the balanced allocation of personnel, horses and materiel.

The increase in numbers of the L of C columns since mobilisation was as follows: L of C Munitions Columns from 57 to 90, L of C supply parks from 88 to 331, L of C depot supply columns from 142 to 292, L of C bakery columns from 9 to 27,[3] L of C auxiliary bakery columns from 31 to 48, L of C horse depots from 14 to 47. To these were added the other formations which only came into existence during the course of the war, namely 74 veterinary hospitals,[4] 47 L of C auxiliary companies,[5] 18 blood test centres,[6] 8 L of C auxiliary battalions,[7]and 21 L of C oxen supply parks.[8] The Animal Diseases Institutes East and West[9] were counted in the Lines of Communication.

The area of responsibility of the L of C medical officer does not need to be discussed here, since it has been outlined in the more comprehensive description of the medical services in the field.[10]

The efforts of the Supreme Army Command to exploit the aids of the occupied areas and to allow repair work to be carried out in the war zone itself led to the

---

1   War Ministry of 13.3.1917, No 5548. 17. A. 1.
2   War Ministry of 30.3.1917, No 924. 17. A. 1.
3   The Butchery Sections attached to them became part of the Army troops in April 1918. See Part IV, M 2c.
4   From 18.2.1915.
5   From 28.2.1915.
6   From 10.4.1915.
7   From 23.4.1915.
8   From 24.4.1918.
9   East from 3.6.1917, West from 28.9.1917.
10 See Part IV N.

creation of many industrial Army works with all kinds of works formations to serve them. From the multiplicity of these formations, from April 1916 onwards, the War Ministry formed 344 Works Companies.[11] In the area of the Supreme Commander East, in November 1917, 33 of these companies were divided into 52 works groups,[12] of which Nos 1-33 joined the Military Administration Lithuania, Nos 34-44 the Military Administration Bialystok-Grodno, and Nos 45-52 the Military Administration Courland.

Originally belonging to the Lines of Communication, the following later joined the Army troops: the L of C Aviation Park on 2 April 1915, the L of C Telegraph Directorate (as Army Telephone Section) on 30 August 1916, the Commander of Motorised Vehicle Troops (as Akokraft) and the L of C Motorised Vehicle Park on 15 January 1916, the L of C Motorised Vehicle Columns on 19 March 1917, and the Works Directorate on 21 September 1917.

The whole L of C area of an Army was militarily divided into L of C commandants' offices. Each of them had its particular base and its strictly defined area of responsibility. As regarded traffic to and from the operations area, and also as regarded administration and exploitation of the country, the L of C Command represented a miniature L of C Inspectorate. Their number rose from 165 to 354. They had a Staff Officer as commandant, on whose Staff there were an adjutant and a judge advocate general. Later, there was often a medical officer and chaplain.

Originally, in order to secure the Lines of Communication, the L of C Inspector had at his disposal mixed Landwehr brigades. Each consisted of 6 Landwehr battalions, 1 Landwehr squadron and 1 Landsturm battery. There were 3 of each with the 1st and 8th Armies, 2 each with the 2nd and 3rd Armies and one brigade with the other Armies. But since some of these brigades were drafted to the front in August 1914, and all of them by December 1914, they were replaced in the L of C by Landsturm.

11 War Ministry of 22.4.1916, No 7460. A. 1.
12 War Ministry of 27.11.1917, No 6914. 11. 17. A. M.

C.

The Supply Service

Since the Line of Communication represented the 'middleman' between the front and Germany, the Supply Service should be considered in conjunction with it.

The munitions trains from Germany ran first to the munitions station of the OHL Reserve, or to the Army Groups Munitions Station, or to one of the sidings stations inserted between those and the L of C munitions depots. From there, they were taken to the L of C munitions depot and unloaded. Depending on the conditions, they were transported by means of the L of C munitions columns to the Corps munitions columns or, alternatively, directly by the latter.

The supplying of equipment was carried out, by train, by the War Ministry through its responsible agencies. Depending on the type of materiel, it went either to the main equipment depot, or to the gun forwarding office of any given Army. From these points, materiel was supplied directly to the various equipment depots, to the workshop of the siege artillery, and to the artillery repair workshops.

The supply trains from Germany unloaded in one of the two L of C main supply depots of their Army. From these, supply columns went to the L of C supply depot and to the supply depot of the troop units.

Clothing and equipment went from the war clothing departments of the Corps districts at home, via the forwarding office, to the Army clothing depots and from these by land transport to the Army's clothing issue station.

The re-supply of the L of C medical depot of an Army was carried out with the involvement of several authorities in Germany. Medical equipment went through the main medical depot in Berlin. Medicines and dressings went via the re-supply depots of the home Corps. Salvaged stock went through the main medical depot Belgium. Veterinary material went via the Military Veterinary Academy in Berlin. Train equipment went through the home train depots, and finally, works materials and rations through the intendances at home. In the L of C main medical depot the clearing hospitals of the L of C area and the medical storehouses of the Groups received goods in part directly, in part via a medical branch depot. The medical storehouses formed the points of issue for the field hospitals and medical companies of a Group.

The requirements of the troops went through official channels. But the exchange of guns, barrels, and gun carriages all reported through official channels, was carried out directly at the Group collection station. The requirements for equipment for the pioneers, for field fortification and signals, however, went through the official service channels to the General of Pioneers in the Army Command, or to the Army Signals Commander.

PART VI

THE ADMINISTRATION OF THE OCCUPIED TERRITORIES

A.

General Governments

1. General Government Belgium

O n the basis of the organisation of the Lines of Communication, by A.K.O. of 26 August 1914, a General Government was set up in Belgium under Generalfeldmarschall von der Goltz. However, von der Goltz desired to be more actively involved in the war. Therefore, in view of his great popularity in Turkey, as early as 27 November 1914, the Supreme Army Command assigned him to the person of the Ottoman Emperor. Generaloberst Freiherr von Bissing was called to take his place. When Bissing died on 18 April 1917, Generaloberst Freiherr von Falkenhausen followed him as Governor-General.

The Governor-General was directly responsible to the Kaiser:

> Without doubt it would have been more correct, from the very beginning, to set up the organisation quite differently and to place the General Government in all respects, under the command of the Supreme Army Command. Later in the war that happened in Rumania, where there was also room for a General Government. Nevertheless, only a military administration was set up. Many sources of confusion and friction could then have been avoided.[1]

The General Government at first comprised the nine Belgian provinces, with the exception of parts of Western Flanders. It included the parts of France that protruded into Belgian territory around Maubeuge and Givet. But after the front had finally become stable in Autumn 1914, Western and Eastern Flanders, the Tournai district and the French territory of Maubeuge had to revert back to the Lines of Communication. In connection with the withdrawal into the Siegfried Line the Government lost areas around Mons and Arel.

Finally, in October 1918, a consequence of the retreat was that the border between General Government and Lines of Communication ran close to the west of Brussels. In Eastern and Western Flanders, the governments were dissolved again in Autumn 1914. However, the civilian administrations continued to exist in those parts of the country that reverted from the General Government back to the Lines of Communication.

There were Military Governors based in the Belgian provinces of Antwerp, Brabant, Hennegau, Limburg, Liège, Luxemburg and Namur. The governors of the fortresses of Antwerp, Liège and Namur and the capital, Brussels, later proved not to be needed in addition to the military governors of the provinces. Those disappeared, first in Brussels, where in March 1915 capital and province were combined into the 'Military Government Brussels and Brabant'. Liège remained a fortress only until 30 June 1916.[2]

---

1   Winterfeldt, page 6.

The task of the Governor-General was twofold. He had a military responsibility of securing German rule, and a civil one of administration of the country. For the first, he had at his side the Chief of General Staff, for the second the Head of Civil Administration. The Governors in the provinces were responsible to the Governor-General alone. However, the provincial presidents of the civil administration were responsible both to the Head of Civil Administration and to the Military Governor of their province.

The military sections, together with intendance and representatives of the technical service arms, were in the Staff of the General Government, about the same as in every Army Command. To be noted here is only the Staff Officer of Pioneers No 164. In addition to his responsibility for pioneer affairs, he was also an Army contractor on a large scale. Under his command were 20 military forestry departments, 12 military sawmills and 3 military timber works for obtaining and evaluating timber. There were also 4 military steelworks, 8 military rolling mills, 4 military wireworks, 2 military metal and pressing works and forges, 3 military foundries and forges, one military screw factory, 6 military cement factories, 3 military cooperages, 2 glassworks, a cement pipe factory, 5 materiel procurement departments, a pioneer park, 2 electricians' units and 2 military carpenters' workshops!

The civil administration of the Governor-General was reflected in his sections. They were the Head of Administration, Finance, Trade and Commerce, Politics and Banking. To those were added the Chairmen of the Central Harvest Commission and the Food Commission. Also added were the Inspectors from the Reich Colonial Office and the German Reich Audit Office as well as the Director of the Civil Chancellery.

On 1 July 1917, a division of administration was made on the basis of Flemish and Walloon provinces. To the head of administration for Flanders, belonged the provinces of Antwerp, Brabant and Limburg. To the area of responsibility of the head of administration for Wallonia were added the provinces of Hennegau, Namur, Liège and Luxemburg.

2. General Government Warsaw

As early as 16 March 1915, for the parts of Poland lying in the territory of the Supreme Commander East, a civil administration for Russian Poland had been set up with its seat in Posen.[3] However, on 24 August 1915, after Warsaw had been taken, an Imperial Order was issued. It placed the part of Poland that was in the German sphere of influence, as a General Government under the command of the previous General of the III Reserve Corps, General of Infantry von Beseler.[4] The General Government covered the Polish districts on the Silesian border and the province to the north of the West-East flowing Piliza. The remaining parts of Poland fell into the administrative area of the Austrians.

2   Chief of the Gen. Staff of the Field Army of 17.6.1916, No 29 411 op.
3   War Ministry of 16.3.1915, No 745. 3. 15. A. 1.
4   The establishment of the Govt Staff was effected by War Ministry of 20.10.1915, M.J. 21 305. 15. A. 1.

The Staff of the Governor-General, with its attached posts, corresponded to that of an Army High Command. Authorities that are particularly worthy of note are the Inspectors of the Education Service of the Polish Wehrmacht, of the Horse Purchasing Service and the Sperrkommando[5] as well as the Command of the Polish Legion. Military Governors were put in place in Czenstochau, Grodzisk, Kalisch, Lodz, Lomza, Lukov, Mlawa, Plock, Siedlce, Wloclawek, and in Warsaw. Under the command of the Military Governor of Warsaw, were also the Commandant of Fortress Modlin,[6] and the Gendarmerie Brigade of the General Government.

The Head of Administration, along with the General Government, controlled a central administration, and sections for Finance, for Justice, for Commerce and Works, for Religious Affairs, for Forestry, for Press Affairs, for Mining, for Geology and for Publishing. Subordinate to the central administration, were the two city and provincial districts, Warsaw and Lodz, as well as the other 28 provincial districts.

5   For guarding the borders.
6   German name for Nowogeorgiewsk.

B.

Military Administrations

1. The Territory of the Supreme Commander East

The General Government Warsaw generally lay to the south of East Prussia. However, from Autumn 1915, the territory of the Supreme Commander East reached to the east of East Prussia and the northern half of Poland. It covered the great lines of communication area on the far side of the East Prussian homeland and the General Government. In order to give the Lines of Communication Administration there a uniform structure, the Quartermaster-General relinquished its command and put it in the hands of the Supreme Commander East. He accordingly governed, by means of a military administration, the Russian territory outside Poland, from Bialystok in the south to the sea in the north. The responsible post for this administrative task was the Oberquartiermeister on the Staff of the Supreme Commander East. The first was Colonel von Eisenhart-Rothe, who became Generalmajor from 18 August 1916. From 2 January 1917 onwards it was Lieutenant-Colonel, and from 18 April 1917, Colonel von Brandenstein.

In Autumn 1915 there came into existence the administrative areas Courland, Lithuania (Kowno), Suwalki, Vilna, Grodno and Bialystok. Suwalki did not remain autonomous for long and on 1 May 1916 was combined with Vilna into the administrative district Vilna-Suwalki. But on 11 October 1916, Vilna-Suwalki was taken over into the Military Administration Lithuania with its seat in Kowno. On the same date, there took place the amalgamation of Grodno and Bialystok into the administration Grodno-Bialystok with its seat in Bialystok. Finally, on 1 February 1918, the Administration Lithuania also took over Grodno-Bialystok, while the Administration Courland soon extended to cover Livland and Estonia. Thus the administrative territory of the Supreme Commander East from then on was organised into the Administration Courland as its northern, and Lithuania as its southern part. Lithuania directed the subordinate sectors, North with Vilna, and South with Bialystok. From 1 August 1918 onwards the Lithuania administration took the name Military Government Lithuania.

The main administration of the Supreme Commander East comprised Sections V-XI of his Staff. Section V was for Policy and Internal Affairs, Section VI for Finance, Sect VII for Agriculture, Forestry, and Cultivation, Sect VII for Church, Schools Service, Arts and Science, Sect IX for Legal Affairs, Sect X for Post and Telegraph Administration, and lastly Sect XI for Trade and Commerce. The Police Inspectorate was also under the control of the main administration.

In the administrative districts the Administrative Order, issued by the Supreme Commander East on 7 June 1916, was implemented. In accordance with this Order, the Heads of Administration were responsible both to the Head of the Main Administration, and to the L of C Inspectors in whose area the administration fell. Under the heads of administration operated the town leaders, in the larger towns, and the provincial leaders, by whom the mayors and the managing committees were supervised. In addition, at the disposal of the heads of administration were economic officers for running the provincial economy, agencies for obtaining raw materials, and gendarmes for running the police. As well as the L of C courts, there were district courts for the population, with the area courts in the larger towns being superior to them. The High Court in Kowno formed the highest authority.

Since the big forestry complexes did not match the division of districts, they were divided into special Inspectorates under the direct control of the Main Administration. 8 of these Inspectorates were in Courland and 23 in Lithuania. Added to these were the Military Forestry Administration Bialowies in Bialystok with a main administration, and 11 Forestry Departments.

2. Military Administration Rumania

On 23 November 1916, when the 9th Army had already taken the western Walachei, and Army Group Mackensen was crossing the Danube in the direction of Bucharest, a Military Administration for occupied Rumania was formed. On 28 November 1916, General of Infantry Tülff von Tschepe und Weidenbach was appointed as Governor-General. An A.K.D. of 12 January 1917 then determined that occupied Rumania, with the exception of Dobrudscha that had previously belonged to Bulgaria,[1] should form, as a military administration, a single unified administrative territory under the High Command of Army Group Mackensen. After peace was concluded with Rumania, on 7 May 1918, both the Army Group Command and the Military Administration were dissolved on 1 July 1918. In place of them both came the High Command of the Army of Occupation in Rumania, under Generalfeldmarschall von Mackensen.

Before entering the war Rumania had sold extensive quantities of cereals and fodder to Germany and Austria-Hungary. Therefore, after the occupation of Rumania, both states had great interest in Rumanian production. Bulgaria and Turkey also raised their own claims. The alliance was therefore also reflected in the new Military Administration, in that Plenipotentiary Generals from, respectively, Austria-Hungary, Bulgaria and Turkey were on the Staff of the Military Governor. The special requirements of Austria-Hungary were also emphasised in the Staff of the Military Administration itself. The latter, placed under the direction of a Chief of the General Staff, was divided into General Staff, Oberquartiermeister Staff, Economic Staff, Supply Officer for the Civilian Population, Police Section, Central Police Department and Command of Fortress Bucharest. In that structure the Economic Staff was directed by an Austro-Hungarian General to whom a German Chief of General Staff was assigned. They therefore possessed both a German and an Austro-Hungarian Central Section. To be noted as characteristic of the individual sections of the Economic Staff, are those for Nutrition and Feedstuffs, for War Raw Materials, Mineral Oils, Timber Utilisation, Electrical Engineering, Machines, Fisheries, Mines and War Industrial Plants.

The province was divided into 14 District Commands. They controlled 2-4 L of C Commands. Three of these District Commands were staffed by Austro Hungarian authorities.

---

1 Dobrudscha itself was administered by the German L of C Administration Dobrudscha as trustee for the Bulgarian and Turkish claims.

PART VII

AUTHORITIES AND UNITS IN GERMANY

A.

The Deputy General Staff of the Army and the home front agencies of the Chief of the Field Railway Service

1. The Deputy General Staff of the Army

The Chief of the General Staff of the Field Army was represented, on the home front, by the Chief of the Deputy General Staff of the Army, who was under his command. The posts set up during the course of time, by the Chief of the General Staff of the Field Army, to be at his own disposal. The Military Office of the Foreign Office, the Policy Section and the Intelligence Officer in Berlin, were administratively affiliated to the Central Section of the Deputy General Staff of the Army.

The II Section of the Deputy General Staff of the Army retained its tasks relating to the Army in Germany. In addition they took over the tasks of supplying the Field Army with war maps, printing the printed instructions of the OHL, dealing with couriers, checking consignment notes, the affairs of war technology and the economic information service.

The Section Foreign Armies only remained in existence for a little over a year. As its tasks had to be carried out by the General Staff of the Field Army, it was dissolved on 25 October 1915. Its section chief took over, as his section, the War Records Checking Office, which had been attached to it since 23 January 1915. The Checking Office collected and checked the operational records sent back from the Field Army, saw to it that they were complete, and assembled the war experience contained in the records.

Section II.B of the Deputy General Staff of the Army received its instructions directly from the chief of the section of the same name in the Supreme Army Command. It was directed to supplement the intelligence service in the field with that on the home front. It was responsible for counter-espionage in postal, telegram, telephone and trading traffic. It monitored war reporting, pictures and films and was the central office for border controls and passport affairs.

The tasks of the Section Foreign Fortresses and the Office for Examination of Captured War Material, written and printed, are fully evident from their names.

The Survey Department had finally been dissolved on mobilisation. It had left behind, under the II Section, a Section for Distribution and one for Administration of Maps. However, in September 1917 it was set up again to prepare peacetime organisation.[1]

---

1   War Ministry of 24.9.1917, No 551. 9. 17. A. 3.

The Railway Section of the Deputy General Staff of the Army, not mentioned until now, occupied a definite special position and is therefore dealt with below in another context.

2. The home front agencies of the Chief of the Field Railway Service

On the instructions of the Fech, the Railway Section of the Deputy General Staff of the Army was in charge of ensuring the integrated use of the railways at home, for war purposes. Meanwhile the Line Commands[2] informed the civil railway authorities of military requirements, and supervised their implementation.

In addition to its Central Group and Transport Group, at the period of its greatest development, the Railway Section also had a Shipping Group and a section for transport connected with the war economy.

The Shipping Group had been set up on 1 June 1916 to direct the provision of supplies by water to the Eastern theatre of war. It had to exploit to the full the waterways at home, for transports connected with the war economy.[3] To this end, it had at its disposal the Shipping Ancillary Groups in Kovno, Windau, Libau and, from November 1916, in Semendria.

The section for transports connected with the war economy, usually called Kriweis, was formed on 13 January 1917 in the Railway Section.[4] In view of the increasing difficulties of the transport situation, it was to eliminate any uneconomic features in railway goods traffic. In other words they had to determine the shortest transport routes for raw materials, half-finished and finished products. They had to work towards achieving the fullest use of the waterways on behalf of the military service posts and war industry, and to take over responsibility for all transports running for the armaments industry, and lastly to supervise the circulation and control of rolling stock.

Two months later, on 31 March 1917, the Chief of the Field Railway Service sent the "Commissioner of the Field Railway Chief in the war management directorate of the Prussian Ministry of Public Works". His lengthy service designation was shortened to Kommeis. The Commissioner had to act as the Chief's permanent representative to all military railway, military, and civil authorities on the home front.[5] The Kommeis had to look after the military and economic interests in the management of the war. They had to give the necessary instructions to the military railway authorities to enable them to carry out the measures that had been decided, and to support the authorities in their work of improving the communications situation.

In carrying out these tasks the Kommeis had to intervene, both in the area of responsibility of the Kriweis and also in that of the Shipping Group in the Deputy

2   The existing Line Commands were joined on 8.8.1917 by L.2 in Kattowitz and Q.2 in Essen, while L in Breslau and Q in Eberfeld were from then on designated as L.1 and Q.1 respectively.
3   War Ministry of 20.5.1916, No 413. 5. 16. A. 3.
4   Established by War Ministry of 16.3.1917, No 2020. 3. 17. A. 3.
5   War Ministry of 31.3.1917, No 1287. 3. 17. A. 3.

General Staff. Therefore, with the appointment of the Kommeis, both these sections were removed from the Railway Section of the Deputy General Staff of the Army and placed under the command of the Kommeis. At about the same time, Shipping Groups East (in Berlin), West (in Duisburg) and Danube (in Vienna) were formed[6] as subordinate agencies of the Shipping Group, now called the Shipping Section.

From April 1917, after these changes, there existed, in parallel, on the home front, the Railway Section of the Deputy General Staff of the Army and the Kommeis, with the Kriweis and the Shipping Section under his command.

This division of responsibilities continued to exist until the beginning of March 1917, but was then dissolved and replaced by another organisation. On 9 March 1918, the Chief of the Field Railway Service took the Shipping Section under his own direct command. He dissolved the Railway Section of the Deputy General Staff of the Army, and the post of Kommeis, and transferred the responsibilities of both to the Kriweis, which was now under his direct command.[7] As a result of this the Kriweis became the only home front agency of the Chief of Field Railways for all questions relating to the military railway service.

6   War Ministry of 24.3.1917, No 1466. 3. 17. A. 3.
7   War Ministry of 9.3.1918, No 787. 2. 18. A. E.

B.

The War Department of the War Ministry, the War Department posts and War Economy Departments

1. The War Department

The War Ministry itself has already been acknowledged.[1] It still remains to describe the area of responsibility of the War Department, created on 1 November 1916.[2] The head of the War Department consisted of its actual Staff for dealing with general questions. The technical Staff was required for general technical matters, and questions relating to the closing down or amalgamation of works. The central office existed for supervision of explosives and munitions factories, as well as the Scientific Commission for research and description of the entire war economy and for dealing with practical questions concerning the economy.

The War Recruitment and Labour Department was subordinate to the War Department. But they had Staff, Economic Staff, Representatives of the War Ministries of Bavaria, Saxony and Württemberg, a Legal Section and Women's Group. Under it was the War Recruitment Office (C.1.b) for recruitment of manpower for the Army and the War Labour Office (A.Z.S.) for the procurement of labour forces for the war industry.

In addition there was under the War Department, the Department for the Procurement of Arms and Munitions (Wumba). The origin of it, from the Ordnance Department, has already been described in Part I B 4. The Ordnance Department had, in peacetime, controlled the Inspectorate of the Technical Institutes of the Infantry (with Infantry Construction Office, 3 weapons factories and munitions factory). They had controlled the Inspectorate of the Technical Institutes of the Artillery (with Artillery Construction Office, 4 artillery workshops, gun foundry, 2 shell factories, 2 artificer laboratories and 3 gunpowder factories), the Artillery Depot Inspectorate (with 4 depot inspectorates), the Train Depot Inspectorate (with 2 train depot inspectorates) and the Military Experimental Department. However, as mobilisation began, the artillery and train depots had come under the command of the Deputy Commanding Generals, or the Fortress Governments, under whom they remained until September 1916. After the Wumba, as a wartime organisation, had absorbed the Ordnance Department and several organisational changes had been effected, it was organised as follows:

Central Section (W.Z.), Inspectorate of the Technical Institutes of the Infantry (W.1), Inspectorate of the Technical Institutes of the Artillery (W.A.), Depot

1 See Part I B.
2 War Ministry of 3.11.1916, No 240. 11. 16. Z. 1, A.K.O. of 1.11.16.

Inspectorate (W.D. with sections for Munitions, Weapons and Stores, Adminis-tration, Demobilisation, Construction), Administration Inspectorate (W.V.), Chief Engineer (W.R. with Staff, Main Technical Office, Section for Armaments Industry Construction, Section for Machinery and Machine Tools, Section for Electrical Machinery and Plants, Section for Imports and Exports, Section for Ar-tillery Traction Machines, Manufacture and Production Office).

The War Raw Materials Section of the War Department dealt with:

- all measures to achieve new possibilities in production, the management of goods seized at home and in the occupied territories, the mobilisation of goods already in use and the control of imports

- the limitation of civilian requirements, the distribution of raw materials to the various consumer groups, possibilities for making savings or re-placements

- the control of maximum prices for raw materials and half-finished prod-ucts, price agreements.

The War Raw Materials Section managed coals and their derivatives, mineral oil products (apart from petroleum), production and distribution of electrical power, the raw materials for iron production, iron and steel including rolled iron and foundry steel, graphite, the base metals including metals for refining steel, the raw materials of the chemical industry - insofar as these were not required for the production of gunpowder and explosives -, skins, leather, cork, tannic acids, rub-ber, asbestos, charcoal, wood for making paper, wood cellulose, cement, the raw materials for the textile industry as well as paper.

The War Raw Materials Companies, formed on the orders of the War Raw Materials Section, were mostly limited companies which were not allowed to work for profit, but whose capital was guaranteed by the Reich and whose management it supervised through KRA commissioners. Soon, however, the companies felt compelled to claim high bank loans on the security of the Reich, as a result of which the influence of the State on the companies naturally multiplied.

"At that moment", wrote Wiedenfeld,[3] "the back of the war companies was broken, and from that time we have to designate them as agencies of the official war economy. The Raw Materials Commissioners always sit in the companies' board-rooms and no step of any importance may be taken by the companies without the State commissioner concerned having approved it. We can even go so far as to say that the State commissioner combines the roles of a managing director and chair-man of a planning committee. So strongly are the areas of responsibility tailored to fit him."

The principle of business management by the War Ministry commissioner as-signed to every war company is drastically evident in the fact that, for example, the commissioner of iron companies had already been appointed some weeks before the iron industry was amalgamated into Eisenzentrale G.m.b.H. Even in the later loose forms of war raw materials organisations the War Raw Materials Commis-sioner of the War Ministry played the leading role.

3   Wiedenfeld, pages 8/9.

The Section for Imports and Exports, subordinate to the War Department, represented Army interests in approving export applications as well as in the negotiations concerning export compensations and import quotas.

2. War Department offices

The War Department offices were set up by the War Ministry order of 18 November 1916.[4] They formed the agencies of the War Department with the Deputy General Commands and were at first attached to the latter, but on 9 February 1917 were placed under their command.[5] They were designated according to the service base of their Deputy General Command, which was also theirs. The following exceptions should be noted.

The War Department office in the Marches covered the command area of the High Command in the Marches, i.e. Guard and III Corps. Two War Department offices, Düsseldorf and Münster, were under the command of Deputy General Command VII A.K. The War Department office Düsseldorf was responsible for all factories and enterprises in the industrial districts of Rheinland-Westphalia and Aachen. The War Department office Metz was responsible for the fortress of that name, while the remaining areas of Corps district XVI were looked after by the War Department office Saarbrücken (XXI).

At first the War Department offices were to operate simply as intelligence organisations of the War Department, and to provide liaison between the War Department and the works and organisations in their district engaged in the war economy. But from February 1917 they were given a more practical role and the following areas of work:

- as agencies of the War Department to the voluntary service in the Fatherland, women's labour and women's welfare, questions of communication and encouragement of production for the procurement of arms, munitions and matériel

- as agencies of the Deputy General Command the provision of labour forces for State-run and private war businesses, control and supply of raw materials, nutrition of the population engaged in work for the war economy as well as questions of export and import

Attached to every War Department office was the Machine Equalisation Office set up by the Institute of German Engineers. From 1917 it was called District Technical Services Office - Tebedienst.

With shortages in all areas, further tasks accrued to the War Department offices. These included the amalgamation and shutting down of works, provision of welfare, monitoring consumption of coals, gas and electricity, procurement of timber, certification of work, salvage and auxiliary service, control of construction, procurement of work clothing and fertiliser, and metal mobilisation.

War Department ancillary offices came into existence in those Corps districts where the War Department office itself needed to be relieved of some workload,

4   War Ministry of 18.11.1916, M. 3. (O.R.). 302. 11. 16. K.
5   War Ministry of 28.2.1917, No St. M. 3 a. 4940. 2. 17. K.

i.e. in Diedenhofen, Mannheim, Ludwigshafen, Mülhausen in Alsace, Siegen and Kattowitz.

The War Department offices set up outside Germany in Vienna, Brussels and Warsaw, were simply intelligence organisations of the War Department.

3. War Economy Departments

On the occasion of the War Department offices being placed under the command of the Deputy General Commands, War Economy Departments were set up on 8 January 1917, as agencies of the War Department for agricultural questions. They represented civil administrations under military direction. They were not linked to the Corps districts but to the political division into provinces, from the provincial capitals of which they took their names. But when the seat of a General Command was not in the provincial capital, a War Economy Department ancillary office was set up, with the General Command concerned, as a link between the latter and the responsible War Economy Department.

The chairman of the War Economy Department of a Province was appointed by the War Department. He had to be an officer familiar with agriculture. The other department members were 2 senior administrative officials, 1 representative of the Railways Directorate, 1 veterinary and 2 farmers. They were appointed by the Provincial President. The duties of a war economy office consisted of drafting in managers and workers, and deferring their military service. They had to procure work horses, machinery and means of production, and also look after the total cultivation of the fields and the bringing in of the harvest.

C.

The Deputy General Commands

At home, the mobile and active General Commands had left behind their deputising authorities. The Deputy Commanding Generals had the same rights
and duties as his active predecessor. In the meantime, there was placed on him the
responsibility for keeping the peace. That came strongly into the foreground on the
basis of the siege law. He had also to maintain order and keep up morale. In this
connection, however, on 8 December 1916 he was placed under the command of
the war minister appointed as Supreme Military Commander on the home front.[1]
The military side of his activities lay in procuring, training and dispatching recruits
for the Field Army and in implementing the orders of the Supreme Army Command and the orders of the War Ministry. The service bases and districts of the
Deputy General Commands remained the same as in peacetime.[2] The exception
was that the deputy for the XVI Corps was moved from Metz to Saarbrücken and
came under the command of the Deputy Commanding General of the XXI A.K.
The General Command there was thus designated XVI/XXI.

Initially the Rhine formed the rearmost border of the war zone in the West, so
that Deputy Commanding Generals XIV and XV were responsible to Army High
Command 7 and those of the XVI/XXI Corps to A.O.K. 5. The Deputy Commanding General of the XIV Corps was even brought to the front on 13 August
1914, where he, with an Army Detachment which was immediately named after
him,[3] took over the watch on the High Vosges and at the Burgundian Gate. It was
only on 30 December 1914 that his successor as Commanding General was appointed. From 1 September 1914 onwards only Alsace-Lorraine (with the exception of northern Alsace and eastern Lorraine) was counted as being within the war
zone.

In the East the operations of the 8th Army were at first played out on East
Prussian soil. For a long time West Prussia, Posen and Silesia also had to be regarded as under threat. It meant that the Corps districts I, XX, XVII, V and VI
were counted as being in the war zone. From August 1914 onwards, there were sent
to the Front, Ersatz units and Landsturm formations. From 1 January 1915 onwards, the war zone in eastern Germany was limited to the immediate border areas
and the province of East Prussia. With the advance of the Army of the East, on 1
October 1915, it shrank to the north-eastern tip of East Prussia which only returned again to the homeland on 13 April 1916.

1   See Part I B 1.
2   Berlin (Gd and III), Stettin (I), Magdeburg (IV), Posen (V), Breslau (VI), Münster
    (VII), Koblenz (VIII), Altona (IX), Hanover (X), Kassel (XI), Stuttgart (XIII),
    Karlsruhe (XIV), Strassburg in Alsace (XV), Danzig (XVII), Frankfurt am Main
    (XVIII), Leipzig (XIX), Allenstein (XX), Saarbrücken (XVI/XXI), Munich (I
    Bavarian), Nuremberg (III Bavarian).
3   Army Detachment Gaede.

The subdivision of the 25 home front Corps districts into divisions disappeared with mobilisation, as the Divisional Staffs left no deputies behind. Instead the deputy infantry brigades and the Landwehr Inspectors came under the direct command of the Deputy General Command, and were given divisional jurisdiction. In the Deputy Guard Corps there was an exception. Instead of the deputy infantry brigade, an inspector of the Guard Infantry, on home service, was provided. However his place was soon taken by 4 similar inspectors. For this reason the Deputy Guard Corps and the XVIII also possessed no Landwehr Inspector. But in September 1915 the Deputy XVIII A.K. received two inspectors for its Landwehr formations.

The duties of the War Department offices, outlined above, had previously been carried out by the Deputy General Commands, although to a lesser extent. After they had been set up in November 1916, the War Department offices were at first attached to the Deputy General Commands, but soon placed under their command.[4] Of the other areas of responsibility of the Deputy General Commands, particular mention should be made of those that were occasioned by the war. Those were frontier, coastal and anti-aircraft defence, censorship of the press, prisoners of war, approval for travel abroad and into occupied territory. Others were counter-espionage and counter-sabotage, intelligence service, anti-gas protection, war graves, petitions for exemption from military service, military training for youth, patriotic education, supervision of motor vehicle traffic, and observation of the conditions of production and consumption of goods.

By A.K.O. of 21 May 1918,[5] supplies, support and welfare affairs were taken away from the Deputy General Commands. From then on those affairs formed the area of responsibility of the Supply Office which was set up at the seat of each General Command. However they were under the direct control of the War Ministry. At the same time the Supply Office of the Guard Corps also took over the relevant affairs of the Intendances of the Military Communications Service, the Military Institutes and the Air Forces.[6]

Also deserving of particular mention are the Landsturm Inspectorates. The number of Landsturm battalions set up in the individual Corps districts varied greatly. Therefore Landsturm Inspectorates were not put in place with all Corps. In contrast, however, some Corps districts showed two Landsturm Inspectors. As for example the XX Corps, which, in accordance with its plans, deployed part of its Landsturm, under the second Inspector, in frontier defence to block the sea narrows at Rudczanny. The VII Corps even possessed 3 Landsturm Inspectors.

In conclusion, those organisations under the command of the Deputy Commanding General should be described. They consisted of deputy infantry brigades, a Landwehr Inspector, a Landsturm Inspector, a Commander of machine gun Ersatz troops,[7] an Inspector of Ersatz squadrons,[8] and an Inspector of field artillery Ersatz sections.[9] Lastly there were the Ersatz units of the other service arms, fire control posts of the anti-balloon cannons,[10] the Line Command, fortresses, troop

4   See Part VII B 2.
5   A.V.Bl 1918, No 578.
6   See Part VII K 3.
7   See Part VII F; from December 1916.
8   See Part VII G.

training grounds, firing ranges, garrison commands, the Corps medical department and Corps district delegate of the Voluntary Aid, together with the Inspector of Prisoner of War Camps.[11]

9   See Part VII H 1.
10   See Part VII K 2c; from April to December 1916.
11   A.V.Bl. 1915, No 17; War Ministry of 14.1.1915, No 256. 1. 15. U. 3.

D.

Fortress Governments and Commands

The Fortresses were under the command of the Commanding Generals in whose district they lay. That was unless the war zone area of responsibility included them, and thus brought them under the command of an Army High Command. They were armed and declared mobile in the border provinces. On mobilisation, the fortresses could soon, as the Army advanced, be considered to be again on home service. On the other hand, the fortress of Metz, with two external sectors located on the rigid positional front, remained permanently mobile. That too was the case with the coastal and island fortifications. The fortress of Strassburg was initially in the operational zone, but later in the zone of the lines of communication.

A siege of German fortresses did not take place during the war. Even the small fortress of Boyen played its part only within the context of the battle for the field position Lötzen-Angerapp. On the other hand, the border fortresses both in the West and in the East could give up their combat-ready troops to the Field Army. All fortresses could give up an abundant supply of personnel and matériel to the front.

Command of a great fortress was held by a Governor. Small fortresses were commanded by a Commandant. The Governor was assisted by a Chief of General Staff, with his General Staff and administrative staff. Attached to the Government staff were the commandant as commander of the core fortress with fortress police chief and fortress fire brigade. In addition, they had the General of Foot Artillery with the artillery Staff Officer. The General of the Engineers and Pioneer Corps had engineer officers and pioneers. The officer of the signals service, and the communications officer, had their communications formations. They had responsibility for the fortress railway, telephone and telegraph network. The machine gun officer, the Government Court, the Government Intendance with fortress supply depot, the Government medical officer with Government field hospital, the Government veterinary officer, the fortress construction depot, the fortress police section and the fortress chaplaincy were all included.

The duties of these posts are indicated by their names. Only in connection with the signals officer must special mention be made. He controlled the activities of the scouts, carrier pigeons, observation posts and airship troops. The necessary maps and plans were prepared by the map section.

The order of battle of a fortress generally showed a division into sector complements, such as the core fortress complement, main reserve, foot artillery and pioneer reserves, communications and labour formations.

While the main reserves of the main border fortresses each possessed one Reserve Division, even some of the foot artillery reserves showed active formations. The main reserve, accompanied by the foot artillery were intended to fight to delay the fortress being surrounded, in order then to lead the defence on the main battle front. There the main mass of the foot artillery and pioneers could then also be deployed. The sector commanders were in command of the complement of their sectors' permanent fortification works, of the complement of the intermediate fortresses and of a sector reserve.

The captured enemy fortresses were manned by complements on the model of the home front fortresses, in case it was decided to use them as supporting points for possible reverses. Otherwise the fortifications were destroyed.

E.

Infantry and Jäger

As they marched out, the 218 active infantry regiments[1] had each left behind one Ersatz battalion of 4 companies, with 2 recruit depots. The 18 active Jäger battalions[2] had each left one Ersatz section with 2 companies, and a reserve depot. Added to these were the Ersatz battalions of the 113 Reserve and 75 Landwehr Infantry Regiments. In total, therefore, 406 infantry Ersatz battalions and 18 Jäger Ersatz sections.

21 stationary Landwehr infantry regiments and 334 stationary Landsturm infantry regiments at first remained at home. But many Landsturm battalions were brought up into the field as early as August 1914.

The training of the Ersatz battalions, except in the case of the Guard Corps, was supervised by the deputy infantry brigade commanders who themselves were under the direct command of the Deputy General Command. In the Guard Corps, training was carried out by the 'Inspector of the stationary Guard Infantry'. Later four such Inspectorates were set up. The only difference between the organisation of the Guard Corps and that of the other Corps was one of nomenclature.

As a result of the many reorganisations for the Field Army, a disparity soon arose between the formations demanding replacements and the Ersatz battalions whose number had been reduced through giving up entire Ersatz troop units for use as mobile troops. Thus the planned basis for providing replacements was shifted to the Field Army. For this reason the War Ministry ordered, at the end of January 1915, that all Ersatz units in the active infantry regiments and Jäger battalions should be doubled in number.[3] But the second Ersatz battalions set up as a result of this order could not be retained until the end of the war since the shortage of manpower which had developed undermined any justification for their existence.

The number of Landsturm Infantry battalions in August 1914 varied greatly between 6, with the XV Corps, and 23 with the VII Corps. It was only later that the Guard Corps formed Landsturm units. Overall, 834 Landsturm Infantry battalions were formed, of which 492 were mobile. Some of the Landsturm were used permanently or from time to time as mobile troops, in the occupied territories, the lines of communication and also at the front. In that way, for instance, Infantry Regiments 432, 433 and 434, formed in the field, were entirely composed of Landsturm battalions.[4] Since the Upper Alsatian Landsturm was initially allocated to different Corps districts, strange names arose such as 'Upper Alsatian Landsturm Infantry Battalion No 58 (Mülhausen) Ulm', and 'Bavarian Upper Alsatian Landsturm Infantry Battalion Bamberg (II. Bavarian 18)'.

1   Including the Infantry Training Regiment.
2   Including Guard Schützen Battalion.
3   War Ministry of 28.1.1915, M.G. 961. 15. A. 1.
4   I.R. 432 with VI. 13 and 26 and IX.2; I.R. 433 with XVIII.14 and 15 and XX.6; I.R. 434 with IV.1 and VII. 65 and 66.

The Landsturm Infantry battalions served to protect certain borders. The X 2 protected the coastal defence of Oldenburg, X 37 protected Borkum, X 41 was at Nordeney, XII 14 at Freiberg in Saxony, XII 15 at Zittau and the 'stationary Landsturm Infantry Regiment Lörrach' with Landsturm Infantry battalions XIV 19, 34 and 35 for guarding the border between Baden and Switzerland.[5] The stationary Landsturm Infantry Regiments 601, 602, 606 and 611-614 were set up in the Corps districts VII-X when it was being planned to declare unrestricted submarine warfare and there was concern about the attitude of the neutral countries.[6]

As well as the stationary Landsturm, there were soon created in individual Corps districts, special formations for guard duties, such as the Works Companies Posen 1-10 on 8 November 1914, and on 9 November 1914 the Garrison Guard Companies of the Königstein fortress. Such formations were later brought together to form garrison battalions, of which there were three with III Corps, two with V Corps, four with VI Corps,[7] one with XIII Corps, two with XVII Corps,[8] two battalions with XX Corps and one battalion with I Bavarian Corps. The XV Corps, on 11 June 1915, formed the Garrison Regiment Strassburg with 6 companies. The Guard Corps brought together its three garrison battalions, on 23 June 1917, to form Garrison Regiment Berlin. With the other Corps the Landsturm was used for the same purposes, without special designations.

As soon as it was realised that the war would go on for some time, concern about the new generation of leaders again came to the fore. Therefore, in July 1915, the War Ministry ordered that the Inspectorate of Infantry Schools, that had been dissolved on mobilisation, should be set up again.[9]

---

5   Brought together on 1.8.1915.
6   See also Part III B 2 in the Coastal Defence High Command.
7   Initially 7.
8   Initially 5.
9   War Ministry of 22.7.1915, No 2045. 6. 15. C. 1.

F.

Machine gun troops

Alongside the active infantry regiments, 219 MGKs[1] had marched out. With the active Jäger battalions 16,[2] and with the Reserve infantry regiments 88.[3] For these 323 MGKs in every Corps district, two MG Ersatz companies were set up. Meanwhile for the 11 MG sections of the cavalry divisions in II Bavarian, III and XIX Corps districts, special Ersatz sections had been brought into being.

The setting up of special mountain MG formations in the Field Army was reflected at home, in the formation, firstly, of the Bavarian Ersatz Mountain MG Section. From 6 September 1915 onwards, they were followed by the formation of Ersatz Mountain MG Sections 1-5 with the X, IV, V, VI and X Army Corps. Ersatz sections were not set up for the MG marksman sections, since they were recruited from selected personnel of the other MG units. By contrast, for the MG squadrons, special MG Ersatz squadrons were created, on 27 July 1915, in the MG training course in Döberitz, and on 28 January 1917 with the XIX A.K. The automatic rifle battalions also received an Ersatz formation, in the form of the Ersatz company for automatic rifle troops of the XVIII A.K., formed on 18 November 1915. In the meantime the latter disappeared again as soon as the automatic battalions were re-armed with machine guns.

The Inspectorate of the MG service had been dissolved on mobilisation, but was set up anew in November 1915.[4] The extraordinary increase in the number of MG formations in the field was also reflected in the swelling of the ranks of the Ersatz sections. In Autumn 1916 that increase caused the Supreme Army Command to appoint a commander of the Ersatz MG units for each of the 25 home front Corps districts.[5]

For training the officers, NCOs and the No. 1s[6] there served the MG training courses that were held from 1 September 1914 onwards, in Döberitz. These were later increased in number by the provision of parallel courses in Zossen and Hammelburg. Training in combat conditions, on the troop training grounds of the individual Corps, took place from the beginning of 1916 by means of special training commands. These commands were established in June 1917 as Infantry MG Training Commands.[7]

---

1   Infantry Training Regt with 2 MGKs.
2   The 1st and 2nd Bav. Jäg. Btn possessed no MGKs.
3   Only part of the R.I.Rs possessed a MGK.
4   War Ministry of 14.11.1915, No 541. 11.15. A. 2.
5   Established by War Ministry of 19.12.1916, No 1180. 11. 16. A. 2 and Bav. War Ministry of 14.1.17, No 3069; in the deputy Guard Corps from 21.10.16-19.12.16 this post was called 'Inspector of the Ersatz MGK of the Guard Corps'.
6   Translator's note: the men who aimed and fired the machine guns.
7   War Ministry of 4.6.1917, No 477. 17. A. 2.

G.

Cavalry

From the cavalry, 33 brigade Staffs had joined the cavalry divisions without leaving behind deputising authorities. The remaining brigade Staffs, who had given up their regiments to the infantry divisions, were dissolved.[1]

Of the 110 active cavalry regiments, 101 Ersatz squadrons and 9 Ersatz depots remained behind.[2] The latter of those, however, were extended into Ersatz squadrons as early as 1914. If every Corps district had on average 4 Ersatz squadrons, so in Guard I-XIV, XVII-XX Corps and Bavarian I Corps 1, more Reserve Ersatz squadrons were added to meet the requirements of the 33 Reserve cavalry regiments. These, however, at the end of 1916, were again discontinued as a consequence of the reduction in cavalry. The Landwehr and mobile Ersatz formations of the Field Army's cavalry did not have their own sources of recruitment.

The General Inspectorate of Cavalry and the Cavalry Inspectorates ceased to exist on mobilisation. Instead, in each Corps district an Inspector of Ersatz Squadrons took over control of training and the supply of horses. Only the VI, VII and VIII Corps each had 2 Inspectors.

Great variations were shown in the Landsturm squadrons of the individual Corps districts. The Guard Corps, XV, XVI and XXI Corps had formed no Landsturm cavalry. The XVII and the Bavarian I and II Corps had only mobile units. In the other Corps, the number of Landsturm squadrons varied between 1 and 10, but only about a third of these remained on home service.

1   Dissolved: 4th Guard Cav.Brig, 4th, 6th, 7th, 10th, 15th, 20th, 21st, 24th, 27th, 29th, 31st, 32nd, 34th, 35th, 37th, 39th, 43rd and 44th Cav.Brigs, 2nd, 3rd, and 6th Bav. Cav.Brigs (9th Cav. Brig created again on 28.9.1914 in the field).
2   6 Prussian Cav.Regts had marched out with all - i.e. 6 - squadrons, 3 Bav. Cav. Regts possessed only 4 squadrons in peacetime.

H.

Artillery

1. Field Artillery

Neither for cavalry nor for field artillery were deputy brigade Staffs set up. The Inspectorates of Field Artillery also disappeared on mobilisation.

The place of the 102 active field artillery regiments that had marched out[1] was taken by 100 Ersatz battalions. Each had 2 batteries, and the Ersatz battalion of the Field Artillery Gunnery School had 3 batteries.[2] The supervision of training within each Corps district was the responsibility of the Inspector of Field Artillery Ersatz Battalions.

A special Inspector supervised the Field Artillery Ersatz Unit Jüterbog, formed on 1 November 1914 in Jüterbog with 2 field artillery Ersatz regiments. This unit changed on 3 May 1916 into the Field Artillery Ersatz Brigade Jüterbog.[3] Its previous Inspector was appointed as Inspector of Field Artillery Gunnery Schools. In this capacity there were under his command, in addition to the Jüterbog Brigade, the Ersatz Field Artillery Regiment Zossen, as well as the Field Artillery Gunnery Schools in Rembertow (General Government Warsaw) and in Beverloo (General Government Belgium).

For the mountain artillery, from December 1914 there came into being three mountain artillery Ersatz battalions. Two Inspectors of Field Artillery Equipment were in operation from mid-1916.[4]

In May 1917 Bavaria put in place an Inspector of Artillery.[5] He was also responsible for supervising the Bavarian Mountain Artillery Gunnery School Sonthofen, set up on 1 September 1917, and for the Artillery Gunnery School Grafenwöhr that was created on 19 July 1918.

2. Foot Artillery

In a similar way to its parallel service arm, the Foot Artillery Gunnery School had formed an active regiment, the 2nd Guard Foot Artillery Regiment. For each of the 25 foot artillery regiments that thence active, an Ersatz battalion with 6 batteries (in Bavaria 4 batteries) together with recruit depot and draught horse battalion was set up. The Artillery Testing Commission, however, which had mobilised 5 heavy 30.5cm coastal mortar and 3 short 42cm naval cannon batteries, formed for these formations which had hitherto been kept secret an Ersatz battalion of 2 batteries.

The 16 active foot artillery brigades had not yet been handed over to the Field Army.[6] They were still engaged in coastal defence and in the border fortresses.[7]

---

1   Including the 5th and 6th Guard Field Artillery Regiments formed from the Field Artillery Gunnery School.
2   As recruitment source for the 5th and 6th Field Art Regts.

271

Even for the first month of the war, they could only with great reservations be counted as part of the Army of Occupation, as they could have been ordered away at any moment.

There was a similar situation with the Reserve foot artillery, consisting of 22½ regiments and 2 individual battalions in strength. They had already been designated by the Supreme Army Command as available troops. Only the 10 Reserve foot artillery battalions, formed without draught horses, at first remained at home.

24 Landwehr and 22 Landsturm foot artillery battalions together with 48 Landwehr foot artillery battalions, that were surplus to establishment, were formed to man fortresses. However, of these the Landwehr formations later joined the Field Army.

The strong increase in heavy artillery at the front led to an increase in the batteries in the Ersatz battalions. In conjunction with them, the formation of Foot Artillery Regiments Nos 21-28, led to the formation of a further 8 Ersatz battalions. However, No 27 was soon changed into a Landwehr battalion and joined the Field Army.

The supervision of training was carried out by the Deputy General Inspectorate of Foot Artillery. Meanwhile, the Foot Artillery Inspectorates had been dissolved and the foot artillery brigade Staffs had left no deputies behind. As a consequence of the raised level of recruitment, the General Inspector felt it necessary in October 1915 to order the setting up of 4 Inspectorates of the foot artillery Ersatz troops.[8] Later, in March 1918, it even proved necessary to set up another two Inspectorates.[9] The seats of Inspectorates 1-6 were Posen, Magdeburg, Metz, Strassburg, Bromberg and Cologne. In May 1917, Bavaria appointed a joint Inspector for the field and foot artillery.[10]

Foot artillery garrison batteries came into being, from the end of 1915, in various numbers in all Corps districts. In addition, coastal garrison batteries were formed in Pillau, Swinemünde, on Sassnitz and Borkum. In some Corps districts

3   War Ministry of 3.5.1916, No 1103. 16. A. 4.
4   War Ministry of 10.7.1916, No 235. 5. 16. A. 4 and of 11.8.1916, No 5568. 7. 16. A. 4
5   Bav. War Ministry of 24.4.1917, No 5950. 2. A; see also the following battalion on the foot artillery.
6   Of the 25 regiments (=49 battalions with 4 and 1 battalion with 2 batteries) 27 battalions each with 4 batteries were placed with the XXV Army Corps, the Guard Reserve Corps and IX Reserve Corps, 14 battalions each with 2 batteries (mortar) were placed in the siege artillery. The mortar battalions had been created by splitting up the relevant peacetime formations. Thus there remained still available 15 battalions each with 4 batteries and 1 battalion with 2 batteries.
7   Foot artillery Regts 8, 16 and Bav. 2 together with I Battalion Foot Art. Regt 12 in Metz, Foot Art Regt 2 in Swinemünde and on the North Sea islands, Foot Art Regt 17 in Neufahrwasser and Pillau, II Battalion Foot Art Regt 11 in Thorn, II Battalion Foot Art Regt 13 and I Battalion Foot Art Regt 14 in the Upper Rhine fortifications, II Battalion Foot Art Regt 15 in Kulm, II Battalion Foot Art Regt 1 in Königsberg.
8   War Ministry of 2.10.1915, No 2942. 9. 15. A. 5.
9   War Ministry of 19.3.1918, No 564. 18. Geh. A. 5.
10 See Part VII H 1.

the batteries developed into garrison battalions. Thus on 27 June 1916 the Foot Artillery Garrison Battalion Jüterbog, on 13 January 1917 the Foot Artillery Garrison Battalion Thorn and Wahn, and on 20 September 1918 the Foot Artillery Garrison Battalion Strassburg came together.

The Foot Artillery Gunnery Schools Wahn, Jüterbog and Thorn were set up anew on 1 July 1916.[11] As training units there were, for Wahn, at first the Ersatz Battalion Foot Artillery Regiment 18, transferred from Metz. For Jüterbog there was the Ersatz Battalion 2 Guard Foot Artillery Regiment, and the Foot Artillery Garrison Battalion Jüterbog. For Thorn there was the Ersatz Battalion Foot Artillery Regiment 11.

The General Inspectorate of Foot Artillery was dissolved on 1 March 1917 and changed into the Inspectorate of Foot Artillery Gunnery Schools. They were under the direct command of the Inspector-General of Artillery Gunnery Schools in the Great Headquarters.[12]

11 War Ministry of 26.6.1916, No 3628. 5. 16. A. 5.
12 In accordance with War Ministry of 16.2.1917, No 445. 17. A. 5.

I.

Pioneers and their variants

1. Pioneers, Engineer Committee and searchlight formations

On mobilisation the 35 active pioneer battalions had each been reinforced by 2 Reserve pioneer companies. Each left one Ersatz battalion of 3 companies, together with a recruit depot, at home. For purposes of fortification, 44 Landwehr and 40 Landsturm pioneer companies as well as 8 fortress Landwehr pioneer sections were formed. At first they remained on the home front, but later changed into field formations. The mobile pioneer Ersatz companies were from the beginning with the Field Army.

The training of recruits was directed by the 6 Pioneer Inspectorates that had existed since peacetime. Among them were one Bavarian and one Saxon Inspectorate. The 4 Prussian Inspectorates were joined, on 29 October 1917, by a fifth in Cologne. From then on, under the 1st Pioneer Inspectorate, were Ersatz Pioneer Battalions 1 and 2 Guard, 3, 5, 6, and 28, together with the Searchlight Ersatz Battalion. Under the 2nd Pioneer Inspectorate were Ersatz Battalions 8, 11, 13, 21, 25 and 30. Under the 3rd Pioneer Inspectorate were Ersatz Battalions 14, 15, 16, 19, 20 and 27. Under the 4th Pioneer Inspectorate were Ersatz Battalions 1, 2, 17, 18, 23, 26 and 29. Under the 5th Pioneer Inspectorate were Ersatz Battalions 4, 7, 9, 10, 24 and 36. Over the Prussian Inspectorates was, as in peacetime, the General Inspectorate of the Engineer and Pioneer Corps and the Fortresses.

The Engineer Committee under the direct command of the Inspector-General also continued its work.[1] It was a testing agency for technical innovations and improvement as well as an agency for the procurement of pioneer weapons and equipment. When the Department for the Procurement of Arms and Munitions was set up in Autumn 1916, responsibility for the whole of Army procurement was passed to this department. However, by 28 November 1916, the Engineer Committee had been inserted again as the agency for ordering special vehicles, construction materials and equipment for trench warfare.[2] In January 1917 it was again also given responsibility for procurement of Minenwerfer ammunition as well as close-combat weapons, explosives and fuses. At the same time the newly formed Pioneer Procurement Office was placed under its control.[3]

In view of the enormous need for materials in trench warfare, and to complement the pioneer parks with the Field Army, as early as 1914 it proved to be necessary to set up collection centres in Germany. They came into existence as the Pioneer

---

1 Until 20.2.1916 designated as 'deputy'; thereafter without this prefix.
2 War Ministry of 28.11.1916, No 2397. 10. 16. A. 6.
3 War Ministry of 24.1.1917, No 1753. 12. 16. A. 6.

Army Parks Berlin (later Danzig),[4] Mainz and Cologne. As soon as the war with Russia could be regarded as ended, demobilisation camps were set up at home for the pioneer equipment. Construction materials had become available in the East.[5] At about the same time the War Ministry set up the Inspectorate of Army Pioneer Parks in Berlin.[6] It was their responsibility to provide integrated direction for the Army Parks and demobilisation camps. On 10 June 1918 this Inspectorate changed its name into the Pioneer Park Inspectorate Berlin and was charged with the direction of the Pioneer Park Directorates East (Berlin) and West (Mainz).[7] Among them were divided the Army parks and demobilisation camps. In Bavaria there existed the Bavarian Park Battalion in Mühldorf.

The mobile Pioneer Testing Company became stationary on 6 June 1918, and on 1 October 1918, in Jänickendorf, was extended into the Pioneer Testing Battalion.[8] As such, the battalion had 2 testing companies and one construction company, as well as the close-combat weapons testing establishment. There was a pioneer training ground at Markendorf.

For the replacement of searchlight personnel, a Searchlight Ersatz Section was formed in Spandau as early as 16 October 1914.[9] On 19 July 1915 Bavaria formed the Searchlight Ersatz Section Munich and attached it to the Bavarian 1st Pioneer Ersatz Battalion. The Prussian section expanded on 16 July 1916 into the Searchlight Ersatz Battalion.[10] Even after the flak searchlights were separated from the pioneers, they still provided replacements for the flak searchlight formations until 31 May 1917.

2. Minenwerfer troops and Close-combat Weapons Park troops

The great importance of the Minenwerfer, even in the first months of the war, had led to the formation of a considerable number of Minenwerfer formations in the field. Therefore special Ersatz formations soon had to be created at home. The first Minenwerfer Ersatz section came into being in February 1915.[11] But after only 14 days it was expanded into Minenwerfer Ersatz Battalion 1, with an attached Minenwerfer School.[12] The Minenwerfer Inspection Command, set up on 11 October 1914 in Unterlüss, was extended in 1915 to form the Minenwerfer School Unterlüss. Meanwhile, a Minenwerfer School also came into existence in Arys. By way of Minenwerfer Ersatz battalions, 1915 brought in No 2, like No 1 on the Mwf firing range Markendorf, 1916 brought in No 3 on the troop training ground Heuberg, No 4 in Bilbach near Bad Orb, No 5 in Unterlüss, No 6 in Arys, No 7 in

4   War Ministry of 4.11.1914, No 1252. 10. 14. A. 6.; move to Danzig 26.1.17.
5   War Ministry of 3.1.1918, No 2093. 12. 17. G A. 6.
6   War Ministry of 3.2.1918, No 2255. 1. 18. A. 6.
7   In accordance with War Ministry of 21.7.1918, No 973. 7. 18. A. 6.
8   War Ministry of 2.10.1918, No 1253. 8. 18. A. 6.
9   War Ministry of 16.10.1914, No 500. 10. 14. A. 6.
10 War Ministry of 16.7.1916, No 1960. 6. 16. A. 6.
11 War Ministry of 25.2.1915, No 188. 15. A. 6.
12 War Ministry of 9.3.1915, No 499. 15.A. 6.

Neuhammer, and Bavarian No 1 in Munich, 1917 brought No 8 in Königsbrück (Saxony), No 9 in Feldstetten (Württemberg), and Bavarian No 2 in Grafenwöhr.

Minenwerfer Ersatz Battalion 1, however, along with its attached Minenwerfer School, was on 5 June 1916 extended to form Minenwerfer Ersatz Regiment Markendorf.[13]

Towards the end of 1915, the Deputy General Inspectorate of the Engineer and Pioneer Corps proposed to provide special service supervision for the home front Minenwerfer troops. Accordingly, on 15 January 1916 an Inspector of Minenwerfer Ersatz Troops was appointed.[14] Bavaria followed suit and on 14 April 1917 created the post of the Bavarian Inspector of Minenwerfer Ersatz Troops.

A special park unit for close-combat weapons was created on 7 August 1917 under the direction of the Inspector of Minenwerfer Park Troops.[15] This park unit was not a single compact body. In fact its individual parts were far more under the command of the Pioneer Inspectorates in whose areas they lay. They were Garrison Pioneer Battalion 406, Close-Combat Weapons Park Battalions 407, 408 and 409, Minenwerfer Park Companies 1-3, 416 and 417, Minenwerfer Garrison Companies 418-420, as well as inspection personnel and training command.

3. Gas troops and anti-gas protection

At the beginning of 1915, the gas troops in the field were branched off from the pioneers. In the course of time they were increased in number to 8 battalions. From May 1915 their replacements came from 'Ersatz Battalion of Pioneer Regiments 35 and 36'.[16] In September 1915 it was renamed as Pioneer Ersatz Battalion 36.[17]

The restocking of gas munitions took place in the field munitions establishments. But from April 1915 also in the home front Gas Munitions Establishments at Adlershof and Breloh.

For the use of anti-gas protection devices, in 1915 anti-gas protection courses were started in Berlin, Greppin and Leverkusen, to which officers were sent by the Field Army. The combination of these three training sections brought into being, on 7 October 1916, the Army Gas School Berlin. At this time, the question of anti-gas protection for the home front itself, especially in the Western border provinces, was increasing in importance. To implement these measures, in November 1916, the Inspector of the Anti-Gas Protection Service for Home Territory was created.[18] Under his command were placed the Army Gas School, the Gas Establishment Breloh and the Anti-Gas Protection Store, whose stocks had until this point been administered by the main medical depot.

13 War Ministry of 5.9.1916, No 1392. 16. A. 6.
14 In accordance with War Ministry of 24.12.1915, No 1092. 11. 15. A.6.
15 War Ministry of 7.8.1917, No 1033. 17 g. A. 6.
16 War Ministry of 5.5.1915, No 931. 15 g. A. 6.
17 War Ministry of 23.9.1915, No 1785. 15 g. A. 6.
18 War Ministry of 13.11.1916, No 1261. 10. 16 g. Z. Ch.

4. Flamethrower troops

The Guard Reserve Pioneer Regiment, restructured in the field as a flamethrower formation, drew its recruits preferably from volunteers, from all units. At first they received the necessary special training in a recruit depot attached to the regiment. For other replacements the Flamethrower Regiment continued to have recourse to the Guard Pioneer Ersatz Battalion.

J.

Air Forces

1. Under the Inspectorate of the Military Air and Motorised Vehicle Service

In peacetime the Air Forces had at first been under the command of the Inspectorate of the Military Air and Motorised Vehicle Service. Only on 1 October 1913 had two new service posts, the Inspectorate of Airship Troops and the Inspectorate of Aviation Troops, been inserted as intermediaries between this Inspectorate and the units. At first this relationship continued to exist even after mobilisation.

Replacements for the 6 airship detachments that had become mobile[1] were provided by 5 airship Ersatz sections each with 3 companies and the Bavarian airship ersatz section with 3 companies. These sections belonged to the Corps districts Guard (1 and 2 Detachments) I, VIII, XIV and Bavarian I.

On the home front the place of the 5 aviation detachments was taken by 5 aviation Ersatz sections, one each in the Corps districts Guard, V, VIII, XV and Bavarian I.

The experiences of the first months of the war caused the Chief of the General Staff to create, in March 1915, a common command for the air forces in the field. This took the form of the Chief of Field Aviation in the Great Headquarters. Under his direct command were the home Inspectorates of Airship and of Aviation Troops.[2] As a consequence of this, on 1 April 1915, the air forces at home were taken out of the area of responsibility of the previous Inspectorate of the Military Air and Motorised Vehicle Service. Bavaria too adhered to this procedure and formed the Bavarian Inspectorate of the Military Air Service.

2. From April 1915

a. Airship troops and Meteorological stations

Under the command of the Inspectorate of Airship Troops - Iluft - were the airship Ersatz sections and the meteorological stations at home. In connection with the setting up of a General Command of the Air Forces, the 12 December 1916 became an important day for the development of the home front organisation.[3]

On that day, to relieve the Iluft's workload, a Commander of Airship Troops Ersatz Sections was put in place. A Field Airship Troops School Command was set up, a Command of Airship Troops, Airship Fields and Military Gas Establish-

---

1   Including the Bavarian Air and Motorised Vehicle Battalion.
2   See Part IV F 1a.
3   War Ministry of 12.12.1916, No 2599. 11. 16. A. 7. L.

278

ments was formed, and an Airship Experimental Establishment was founded. All new formations were under the direct command of the Iluft.

The 5 Prussian sections controlled by the Commander of Airship Troops Ersatz Sections increased on 16 February 1918 by the addition of a sixth section for Saxony. In due course, on 5 April 1918, Bavaria strengthened its airship troops Ersatz section by the addition of a training section.

The Command of Airship Troops, Airship Fields and Military Gas Establishments controlled the 23 Army airship fields and 10 gas establishments. But as early as 3 September 1917, it had to be dissolved once more after every hope of continuing to use the airships in land warfare had disappeared. However, on 23 March 1918, the Iluft brought together again the military gas establishments and put them under a special command.

In the same way, on 22 March 1917[4] the Field Airship Troops School changed its name to the Airship Troops Observer School Namur. The experimental and technical section under its command from then on came under the Balloon Command. At the same time the previous Command of the Airship Troops Experimental Establishment had changed into the latter. Under the Balloon Command, apart from the new experimental section, were the Airship Central Procurement and Inspection Office. They were split into the Airship Raw Materials Section and the Procurement, Inspection and Stores Section for airship equipment, i.e. three Airship Armament Sections and the Airship Freight Section.

The main meteorological station in Germany, with its 42 meteorological stations and 4 kite balloon meteorological stations, was also placed under the Iluft. The Bavarian Inspector controlled 6 meteorological stations, 1 kite balloon meteorological station and 1 mountain kite balloon meteorological station. The main meteorological station on 27 March 1918 took the designation Home Meteorological Stations Command. On 12 November 1918 Bavaria created the Main Meteorological Station Munich, and on 1 October 1918 gave it the name Bavarian Army Main Meteorological Station. Up to 9 September 1917 the meteorological stations bore the designation of the locality in which they were based, after that they received the numbers 141-192 and Bavarian 1-6.

As early as 1917 an Ersatz company for the aeroplane barrage sections had been set up.[5] This company, with the Aeroplane Barrage Ersatz Command, came on 22 March 1918 under the command of the Iluft.

b. Aviation Troops

At first the aviation Ersatz sections were directly supervised by the Inspectorate of Aviation Troops. Of the 4 Prussian sections, No 1 was in Adlershof (from February 1916 in Altenburg), No 2 in Döberitz (from August 1915 in Schneidemühl), No 3 in Darmstadt (from February 1915 in Gotha) and No 4 in Posen. The Bavarian Ersatz section was in Schleissheim. With the great increase in the air arm in the field, the number of Ersatz sections at home also rose. In 1914 No 5 was created in Hanover and No 6 in Grossenhain. In 1915 were formed No 7 in Cologne (from 1 March 1917 in Brunswick), No 8 in Graudenz, No 9 in Darmstadt, No 10 in

4   War Ministry of 22.3.1918, No 1759. 18. A. 7. L.
5   War Ministry of 20.3.1917, No 1215. 2. 17. A. 7. L.

Böblingen and No 11 in Brieg, then in 1917 No 12 in Kottbus, No 13 in Bromberg and No 14 in Halle.

To meet the Bavarian requirements, as well as the already-existing section, Bavarian Aviation Ersatz Section 2 was formed in Fürth. The R-Plane sections were served from 20 April 1916 by a special R-Plane Section in Döberitz. In 1917 it was moved to Cologne.

From March 1915 Military Flying Schools were attached to all sections. These were later designated as Nos 1-14 and Bavarian 1 and 2.[6]

In 1916 it proved necessary to relieve the workload of the Idflieg with some urgency. In addition to supervising training, they were responsible not only for recruitment of personnel and replacement of material, but also for aircraft construction. Therefore on 6 May 1916 the Commander of Aviation Ersatz Sections was appointed, subordinate to the Inspector.[7] Within the area of responsibility of this commander also came the Squadron School Freiburg[8] - later Paderborn[9] - and the 6 Motor Schools set up from July 1917.[10]

In November 1916 the Idflieg created observer schools in Grossenhain and later Thorn, Königsberg, Warsaw and Schwerin. As a common command on 6 January 1917 they were given the Commander of Aircraft Observer Schools.[11] At the same time another school was created in Cologne and the Artillery Observer School Jüterbog, which had been in operation since 15 August 1915, changed its name to the Aircraft Observer School Bavaria. In October 1916 it had set up the Bavarian Aircraft Marksman School Lechfeld, and also brought into being an Aircraft Observer School in Schleissheim.

In order to achieve an accelerated rate of training of pilots in single-seater fighters, at the beginning of 1917 the two Single-Seater Fighter Schools Paderborn and Grossenhayn were opened.[12]

For the supervision of aircraft and engine construction as well as for the inspection and arming of machines, on 6 October 1915 Idflieg set up the Aviation Troops Testing and Aircraft Repair Establishment in Adlershof.[13] On 1 January 1917 this establishment took the name Aircraft Ordnance, set up a store in Aachen and one in Liegnitz and created the Aircraft Engine Works Brussels.

After the flak had been transferred to the air forces, on 23 April 1917 the Idflieg organised the Commander of Aircraft Weapons Sections for inspecting and testing the machine guns and flak, as well as for their provision with armament.[14] The command controlled an experimental section for aircraft weapons, an armaments section, the aircraft weapons stores Aachen and Mannheim, and also the Aircraft Gunnery School Asch in Belgium.

6   Idflieg of 1.9.1915, No IV b 3629. Kr.
7   War Ministry of 6.5.1916, No 475. 4. 16. A. 7. L.
8   War Ministry of 18.8.1916, No 2043. 7. 16. A. 7. L.
9   Moved to Paderborn on 21.4.17.
10   War Ministry of 7.7.1917, No 1307. 6. 17. A. 7. L.
11   War Ministry of 6.1.1917, No 1211. 12. 16. A. 7. L.
12   War Ministry of 10.1.1917, No 2323. 12. 16. A. 7. L.
13   War Ministry of 6.10.1915, No 1072. 9. 15. A. 7. L.
14   War Ministry of 23.4.1917, No 251. 17 g. A. 7. L.

The wireless telegraphy placed at the service of the aircraft in the field was taken into account at home. The personnel had to be trained and also the wireless telegraphy equipment had to be procured, tested and installed. For this purpose on 11 January 1917 the Idflieg put in place the Command of Aviation Wireless Telegraphy Sections.[15] Under this command were the Commander of the five Aviation Wireless Telegraphy Training Sections - including one for officers - also the Aviation Wireless Telegraphy Experimental Section and the Commander of the Wireless Telegraphy Equipment Section. It was organised into sections for procurement, inspection and consignment, workshops and equipment stores. On 1 February 1918 the word 'Telegraphy' in the designation of the Commander of Aviation Wireless Telegraphy Training Sections was dropped.

At the same time as the organisation of the wireless telegraphy for the aircraft, the Command of the Aerial Bombing Section was formed.[16] Under that command was the Aerial Bombing Training Section and the Bomb Experimental Section. Both were in Frankfurt an der Oder, together with the Command of the Bomb Armament Sections and Bomb Stores East and West, as well as the Bomb Procurement Section Döberitz.

In the field of photographic services on 11 February 1916 the Idflieg set up a photographic section for the procurement of photographic equipment.[17] In April 1917 it was joined for training purposes, by the Aviation and Airship Photographic Command.[18] Both authorities merged on 7 January 1918 to form the Photographic Service Inspectorate.[19] Itself under the command of the Idflieg, the new inspectorate controlled the training, experimental and aerial survey sections, the photographic ordnance department, the photographic technical section and the section for photographic reporting, as well as the Flight Section Karlshorst. The main duties of the Photographic Inspectorate were to provide the Army and the Navy with photographic materials, to train photographic officers, to further develop the photographic and photographic survey service, as well as to provide pictures and films for propaganda purposes.

c. Home Air Defence

c1. Until mid-December 1916

In preparing for mobilisation, account was already being taken of possible air raids on Germany. Therefore, according to plan, some of the available anti-balloon cannons - Bak - were put in place to secure the advance to strategically important points, for example the Rhine bridges. This air defence was then specially extended, in view of the importance of the Western industrial district, a process in which machine guns were also used. Responsibility for air defence was in the hands of the Deputy General Commands, according to which, in June 1915 in the area of

---

15   On 11.1.1917, in accordance with War Ministry 1031. 11. 16. A. 7. L.
16   On 11.1.1917, in accordance with War Ministry 2233. 11. 16. A. 7. L.
17   War Ministry of 11.2.1916, No 1631. 1. 16. A. 3.
18   War Ministry of 26.4.1917, No 1918. 3. 17. A. 7. L.
19   War Ministry of 7.1.1918, No 2101. 12. 17. A. 7. L.

the XIV A.K., the defence was brought together in the artillery centres of Karlsruhe and Mannheim.

In August 1915, in order to advise the General Commands in the use of the Bak, the War Ministry appointed an Inspector of Bak,[20] who in addition was to supervise training and equipment. The Inspector brought the defence into groups and in April 1916 gave to each of the 20 groups a fire control post.[21]

For providing replacements for the Bak formations with the Army and on the home front, in September 1915 a Bak Ersatz battery was formed in Frankfurt am Main,[22] from which on 1 November 1915 Bak Ersatz Section 1 was developed.

In mid-1915, after it had been decided in the Field Army to deploy fighter aircraft to win air supremacy, from August onwards, individual single-seater fighter sections were also made ready for the offensive defence of home territory. Hand in hand with this went the setting up of a home front aircraft reporting service,[23] which worked in close conjunction with the corresponding services in the war zone, but was under the direction of the Deputy General Command.

c2. Under the Commander of Air Defence

With the formation of the General Command of the Air Forces anti-aircraft defence was also incorporated into the air force. In no other arm of the service was communication between the front and Germany so necessary as in anti-aircraft defence which by means of the aircraft reporting service stretched out its feelers right into the operational area. Therefore on 8 December 1916 the Kogenluft assigned to a Commander of Home Air Defence - Koluftheim -[24] command over all the relevant formations on the home front. For his part he was under the direct command of the Kogenluft. With this move the General Commands were relieved of responsibility in this area. The post, of the Inspector of Bak in the home territory, was discontinued.

The Koluftheim increased the existing fire control posts to 38. In April 1917 they were given the designation Flak Groups,[25] command of each of which within the Corps districts was taken over by a Staff Officer of Flak Troops - Stoflak.[26] The Stoflaks had their bases in Essen (VII), Cologne (VIII), Hamburg (IX), Emden (X), Stuttgart (XIII), Freiburg (XIV), Frankfurt am Main (XVIII), Saarbrücken (XXI), Munich (I Bavarian) and also Diedenhofen.

The machine guns of the anti-aircraft defence on the home front and in the rear areas of the war zone were brought together in August 1917 into 103 detachments.[27] They were put in groups, under the command of the Stoflaks. Thus Group 5, with MG Detachments 39-46, came under the Stoflak Saarbrücken, and Group 6, with MG Detachments 47-60, under the Stoflak Diedenhofen.

20   War Ministry of 13.8.1915, No 2739. 15 g A. 4.
21   War Ministry of 13.4.1916, No 3736. 3. 16. A. 4.
22   War Ministry of 4.9.1915, No 3184. 15. A. 4.
23   See Part IV F 2 e4.
24   War Ministry of 8.12.1916, No 3408. 16. A. 4.
25   Established by War Ministry of 29.5.1917, No 2195. 5. 17. A. 4.
26   Kogenluft of 9.1.1917, No H. 939.
27   War Ministry of 28.8.1917, No 599. 8. 17 g. A. 4.

The already existing Flak Ersatz Section Frankfurt am Main was joined in December 1916 by a second in Freiburg-im-Breisgau.[28] Both sections were placed under the command of the Commander of Flak Ersatz Sections. In March 1917 they were formed into a regiment and took the designation Commander of the Flak Ersatz Regiment.[29]

The home front single-seater fighter sections were from Autumn 1916 called fighter flights and were gradually increased in number from 6 to 9. To provide them with an integrated command, in October 1916 the Koluftheim put in place the Aviation Staff Officer in Frankfurt-am-Main[30] whose designation was changed, in February 1918, into Home Territory Aviation Commander.[31] Four months later he was given command of the 18 Airfield Wireless Telegraph Stations, in the numerical group 101-140, to complete the link between his flights and the command posts on the ground.[32]

By way of recognition of the achievements of the always combat-ready single-seater fighter flights, on 3 October 1918 the Supreme Army Command placed them in the class of fighter flights. They were given the designation Fighter Flights 82-90, but gave their Kofl the name Commander of Fighter Flights Home Territory.[33]

A singular new defensive weapon against air raids on factory plants came into existence at the beginning of 1917 in the so-called aeroplane barrage sections. A system of small, unmanned, static balloons capable of rising to 2,500m was organised around the targets to be protected. Many thin wires hung down from the balloons and spread out in the wind, creating a danger zone for the enemy aircraft that had to avoid or fly over it. In this way accurate bombing, especially by night, was made very difficult for them. The aeroplane barrage sections, initially 5 in number, later 9, were divided throughout the border area.

In addition there was another barrage section in the operational area itself with the 5th Army. Command and supervision was the responsibility of the Staff Officer of Airships Home Territory. Established on 20 March 1917.[34] It was under the command of the Koluftheim but he had his base in Metz, in the operational area. The Ersatz company of the aeroplane barrage sections, set up at the same time, came under the Inspector of Airship Troops.

Under the command of the latter, as already explained, were also the home front meteorological stations. But the great importance which was assigned to the weather forecast for air raids on the western home territory and thus for defence readiness, caused a special 'Home Air Defence Meteorological Station' to be assigned to the home air defence in the Taunus observatory.[35]

28   War Ministry of 9.12.1916, No 3141. 16. A. 4.
29   War Ministry of 9.3.1917, No 4174. 2. 17. A. 4.
30   War Ministry of 7.10.1916, No 2039. 9. 16. A. 7. L.
31   War Ministry of 22.2.1918, No 2931. 18. A. 7. L.
32   War Ministry of 14.6.1918, No 1084. 4. 18. A. Nch.
33   War Ministry of 3.10.1918, No 2082. 18. A. Nch.
34   War Ministry of 20.3.1917, No 1215. 2. 17. A. 7. L.
35   War Ministry of 12.2.1917, No 2088. 17. A. 7. L.

The aircraft reporting service was reorganised by the Koluftheim who had taken over from the Deputy General Commands, on his appointment. He divided the western border area into the aircraft reporting areas North, West, and South. In each of those a Staff Officer of the aircraft reporting service formed an aircraft reporting section with the aircraft lookout stations under his command. Of these, the Fluma North had its centre in Hamburg, the Fluma West in Cologne and the Fluma South in Karlsruhe.[36] In March 1917 these sections were joined by a fourth in Saarbrücken as Fluma South-West. But when Bavaria set up the Fluma Munich in December 1917, the four older sections were also named after their service bases. In the last year of the war the reporting network in the West was further concentrated as, on 4 May 1918, Fluma Trier and, on 29 October 1918, Fluma Düsseldorf were inserted.

After flying in war had developed to a certain extent, the delineation between home and operational territories became blurred. Therefore those formations which had played an active part in defending against an air raid on a target in home territory were recognised as having taken part in the fighting for the day in question. The flight leaders and pilots of the single-seater fighter flights were regarded as mobile.[37] The increasing frequency of enemy air raids in the districts of Stoflaks Diedenhofen, Saarbrücken, Cologne, Mannheim, Karlsruhe and Stuttgart, from mid-1917, caused the flak formations, anti-aircraft machine guns, aircraft lookout stations and aeroplane barrage sections to be in a continual state of combat readiness. Thus, in October 1917 they were declared as fully mobile in those districts.

The flak searchlight formations had, before the Kogenluft was appointed, belonged to the pioneers. After they had been incorporated into the air forces, by the Hindenburg Army Command, the Kogenluft set up for their training, a training command for flak searchlight troops in Frankfurt-am-Main and an experimental command for direction-finding apparatus in Cologne. The pioneers continued to be the source of replacements. Only on 1 June 1917 did the flak searchlights receive their own Ersatz formation. On this date there came into being the Command of the Flak Searchlight Ersatz Troops in Hanover[38] with a flak searchlight Ersatz section. The Flak Searchlight School Hanover brought together from the training and experimental commands mentioned above, the Flak Searchlight Testing and Experimental Section, together with the Flak Searchlight Target Section.

3. The Intendance of the Air Forces

On 6 March 1916 an A.K.O. was issued[39] according to which the administrative, clothing, equipment, construction and financial affairs of the airship and aviation troops were to be taken away from the Intendance of the Military Communications Service. They were to be passed to an Intendance of the Air Forces which was set up on a trial basis. Later a special pay department of the air forces was also set up.[40] These services became established on 20 November 1916.[41] The airship and aviation forces were united on this date under the collective designation Air Forces.

36 War Ministry of 8.12.1916, No 3408. 16. A. 4.
37 War Ministry of 5.9.1916, No 941. 16 g. A. 7. L.
38 War Ministry of 22.5.1917, No 1426. 17. A. 4.

In the order of succession of the service arms the air forces received their special place, between the pioneers and the communications troops.

39   A.V.Bl 1916, No 166.
40   A.V.Bl. 1916, No 621; War Ministry of 18.9.1916, No 1108. 9. 16. B. 4.
41   A.V.Bl. 1916, No 810; War Ministry of 20.11.1916, No 1751. 10. 16. A. 1.

K.

Signals Troops

In place of the Inspectorates of Telegraph Troops, dissolved on mobilisation, came the Inspectorate of Ersatz Companies of the Telegraph Troops. The 10 peacetime telegraph battalions had each left behind an Ersatz company that was provided with a recruit depot. Such Ersatz companies existed with the Deputy General Commands (1 and 5 Companies), the III, VIII, X, XII, XIV, XVI/XXI and I Bavarian Corps (1 and 2 Bavarian Companies).

Differences in training soon showed that a separation of the telephone and wireless troops was desirable. This happened on 6 May 1915, as 10 telephone and 5 wireless companies were formed out of the previous Ersatz companies.[1] At the same time the Inspectorate of the Telegraph Troops Ersatz Companies took the designation Inspectorate of Telegraph Troops.

Set up in June 1915, the Large (high power) Wireless Field Station Königswusterhausen, on 16 July 1915, was incorporated into the wireless Ersatz section.[2] It carried out daily a seven-hour wireless traffic with Constantinople. In this way it relieved of a quite considerable workload the Large Wireless Field Station Nauen that already existed at the beginning of the war. A third large wireless station was opened in Autumn 1915, in Eilvese. The responsibility for controlling wireless telegraph traffic was taken over by the Wireless Telegraph Control Department Berlin.[3]

On 8 June 1915 a special Signals Ersatz Section was set up for the signals troops.[4] In the first reorganisation of the signals service by the Hindenburg Army Command the Inspectorate of Telegraph Troops disappeared. On 14 December 1916 its place was taken by the separate Inspectorates of Telephone Troops and of Wireless Troops.[5] At the same time the telephone Ersatz sections received an Inspector of the Telephone Ersatz Sections and soon increased in number to 20. For training purposes, on 4 November 1916 a Wireless School was created, and nine days later an Interpreters School, and on 14 December 1916 a Telephone School. Out of the Wireless Telegraph Control Department Berlin was formed the Wireless Telephone Section Home Front. Meanwhile Bavaria set up, on 26 January 1917, the Bavarian Wireless Telegraph Control Command.

The second reorganisation of the signals service was first expressed in a new organisation at home. As early as 21 May 1917 the Inspector of Telephone Troops was changed into the Inspector of Signals Troops. As such he was the most senior representative on the home front of the Chief of Field Telegraphy.[6] At the same time the Inspectorate of Telephone Ersatz Sections was replaced by two Inspector-

1 War Ministry of 6.5.1915, No 3056. 4. 15. A. 7. V.
2 War Ministry of 16.7.1915, No 2306. 6. 15. A. 7. V.
3 War Ministry of 10.10.1916, No 3382. 9. 16. A. 7. V.
4 War Ministry of 8.6.1915, No 108. 6. 15. A. 7. V.
5 War Ministry of 14.12.1916, No 192. 12. 16. A. 7. V.

ates of Signals Ersatz Troops, at the head of which were, for No 1, the previous Inspector of Telephone Ersatz Sections, and, for No 2, the previous Inspector of Wireless Troops. According to this organisation there were, under the command of the Inspector of Signals troops:

- Inspector of Signals Ersatz Section No 1 with the signals Ersatz sections in the eastern half of the Reich
- Inspector of Signals Sections No 2 with the signals Ersatz sections in the western half of the Reich
- Signals Troops Training Institute, formed by uniting the Telephone, Wireless and Interpreters Schools
- Wireless Telegraph Section Home Front with the Large Wireless Stations Nauen, Königswusterhausen and Eilvese
- Military Telegraph Section Home Front with the Telegraph Operations Sections Berlin, Frankfurt am Main and Königsberg in Prussia
- Inspectorate of the technical sections of the signals troops, which in the last days of the war was redesignated Means of Communication Inspection Commission

Each Signals Ersatz Section was organised into telephone operators, wireless operators and wireless telegraph station. Their number increased to 22 (Guard and Nos 1-21), which in October 1918 were divided into seven Inspectorates, while the three Bavarian Ersatz sections were under one Bavarian Inspector.

In November 1917, after the whole of the German wireless telegraph communications had passed to the responsibility of the Chief of the Signals Service, the latter charged the Inspector of Signals Troops with responsibility for directing wireless telegraph communications at home. To this end, on 31 December 1917 the Inspector raised the Wireless Telegraph Section Home Front to the status of Wireless Telephone Command Home Front and provided it with extensive plenipotentiary powers. Accordingly, the Wireless Telegraph Command was responsible for:

- control of wireless telegraph communications between ground stations and aircraft
- control of wireless telegraphy for home air defence, the connection of wireless telegraphy at home to that of the Field Army
- control of the activities of the large wireless field stations

For every signals Ersatz section, messenger-dog reporting centres were set up on 12 March 1918. Carrier pigeon lofts were set up three months later.

The introduction of the Female Signals Corps, ordered on 3 October 1918,[7] had required previous training at home. Therefore every Deputy General Command set up a Signals School which had 3 officers as teachers and 12 NCOs as teaching assistants.

6   War Ministry of 21.5.1917, No 138. 5. 7. 17. A. 7. V.
7   War Ministry of 3.10.1918, No 444. 8. 18. A. Nch; cf Part IV J 4.

L.

Railway Troops

On mobilisation the four Prussian railway regiments[1] had each left behind a railway Ersatz battalion which was organised into 2 construction companies, 2 operations companies and an auxiliary company, together with 2 recruit depots. It was only on 8 December 1914 that an Ersatz battalion came into being for the Bavarian railway battalion in Munich.

Since peacetime the Inspectorate of Railway Troops had remained in existence in Berlin. It was responsible for all railway troops and depots at home. In accordance with the instructions of the Field Railways Chief, the Inspector directed all service operations. He undertook the formation of new units, the carrying out of trials, the production of the necessary statistics. He also continued the business of providing railway personnel and matériel to assist the allies, and saw to it that the recruit depots were kept topped up. Also under his direct command was the operations section of the Military Railway Jüterbog, which was divided into operations company, traffic office, traffic control and consignment note inspection department.

Between the Inspector and the railway Ersatz battalions was the Inspectorate of Railway Troops Ersatz Battalions, but this was discontinued as early as 28 February 1915. Later the lack of an intermediate authority for supervising training became evident and led on 6 April 1917 to it being set up again, from now on under the name Inspectorate of Railway Ersatz Battalions. Under this also came the Boat Ersatz Battalion, set up on 5 March 1917.[2]

The depot administrations had continued to exist of both the railway Brigades that had been dissolved on mobilisation, and of the 4 railway Regiments. For these administrations, on 15 September 1916, the Inspector of Railway Troops created a tighter organisation.[3] At the head he placed the Commander of Railway Ersatz Park. At the same time the depot administration of the 1st Brigade was changed into the Railway Ersatz Park, that of the 2nd Brigade was changed into the Ancillary Ersatz Park 2, in Hanau. At the same time an Ancillary Ersatz Park 1 was newly set up in Klausdorf. Out of the depot administrations of the railway regiments the Field Equipment Ersatz Parks 1-4 were formed.

The Commander of the Railway Ersatz Park was based with his Staff in Berlin, the Park itself possessed a procurement and a trials section in Hanau, as well as a motor locomotive park in Cologne. It was the responsibility of the Commander to supply the field equipment for railway and road construction. He had to supply materials and equipment for the railway machine parks and the river detachments. He also had to procure material for the field, for tramways and aerial railways. He had to send repaired material back from the field, to test new constructions and inventions, as well as to train the personnel for field railway and motor locomotives.

---

1 Nos 1 and 4 with the Guard Corps in Berlin-Schöneberg, Nos 2 and 3 with the XVIII A.K. in Hanau.
2 War Ministry of 5.3.1917, No 2228. 2. 17. A. 7. V.
3 On the basis of the War Ministry order of 22.7.1916, No 1904. 6. 16. A. 7. V.

M.

Motorised Vehicle Troops

The Prussian Motorised Vehicle Battalion in the Guard Corps and the Bavarian Aircraft and Motorised Vehicle Battalion were, after mobilisation, each represented by an Ersatz section at home.

But the two home front Ersatz sections were by no means adequate to meet the rising and continuing demand for motor vehicle formations in the Field Army. They were therefore, still in 1914, increased in number to eight, and by 1918 had reached the number of 18. When, in September 1918 a motor vehicle Ersatz section was ordered for every Corps district, there was another increase. In addition to this there had been in existence, since 5 October 1917, a further special Motorised Vehicle Ersatz Section F for the many German formations in Turkey.

The motorised vehicle depots at home, originally eight in number, later were increased to 13, and received in October 1918 the designation Motorised Vehicle Ersatz Parks. For the motorcycle sections, set up in the field, an Ersatz section was formed on 1 November 1914. The same happened, on 21 October 1918, for the fighting vehicle sections that only entered the field in 1918.

The supreme command, of the motorised vehicle service at home, lay in the hands of the Inspectorate of Air and Motorised Vehicle Service. The service had existed since peacetime, but in April 1915 responsibility for the air forces was taken away from it, and they took the name Inspectorate of the Motorised Vehicle Service.[1] It was itself under the command of the Inspector General of the Military Communications Service. This relationship was dissolved in the December 1916 reorganisation of the motorised vehicle service. The Field Motorised Vehicles Chief, at that time, also took the home front Inspectorate of the Motorised Vehicle Service under his direct command. Only the Motorised Vehicle Service Intendance remained under the Military Motorised Vehicle Service Intendance.

From 15 December 1916 service instructions of the Inspector of the Motorised Vehicle Service, it is to be noted that he was to keep in touch with the Artillery and Communications Technical Testing Commission. He was also responsible for supplying fuel and rubber tyres not only for the entire Army but also for industry and agriculture. From July 1917 he bore the service designation Inspector of Motorised Vehicle Troops.[2] To relieve his workload a Commander of Motorised Vehicle Ersatz Sections was appointed.[3] Correspondingly, the Bavarian Inspector took the designation Bavarian Inspector of Motorised Vehicle Troops. On 21 September 1918 Saxony formed an Inspectorate of Motorised Vehicle Troops.

An experimental section of the MV troops with an experimental company came into being on 6 April 1917. But in view of tank construction and the motori-

---

1 War Ministry of 14.4.1915, No 2042. 3. 15. A. 7. V.
2 War Ministry of 31.7.1917, No 1910. 7. 17. A. 7. V.
3 War Ministry of 21.7.1917, No 345. 7. 17. A. 7. V.

sation of the artillery, on 4 November 1918 it left the area of responsibility of the Inspector of MV Troops and came under the Artillery Testing Commission.

In April 1917, the transport difficulties at home caused the Supreme Army Command to hand over, to the Inspectorate of MV Troops, a number of motor vehicles which were no longer suitable for war use. From these the Inspectorate assembled home service MV columns.[4] The number of columns quickly rose, from 13 at the outset, to 131. Therefore, by July 1917 a Captain of MV Troops was assigned as technical adviser to every Deputy General Command.[5] To provide an integrated command for these captains, on 29 July 1918 the Supreme Army Command appointed a Staff Officer of MV Troops for the home front.[6]

4   War Ministry of 16.4.1917, No 195. 4. 17. A. 7. V.
5   War Ministry of 6.7.1917, No 1443. 6. 17. A. 7. V.
6   War Ministry of 29.7.1918, No 250. 7. 18. A. 7. V.

N.

Train

Providing replacements for the train formations in the field was, in each of the 25 home front Corps districts, taken care of by a Train Ersatz Section of 3 squadrons. Only with the III Bavarian Corps did a second Ersatz section appear on 21 April 1915. The supervision of training was the responsibility of the Train Inspectorate.

O.

The General Inspectorate of the Military Communications Service and special technical formations

Before the War, the General Inspectorate of the Military Communications Service was an authority with very wide-ranging responsibilities. Under its command were the Inspectorate of Railway Troops, the Inspectorate of Field Telegraphy, the Inspectorate of the Military Air and Motorised Vehicle Service and the Inspectorate of the Fortress Communications Service. The latter Inspectorate was dissolved on mobilisation and its responsibilities were taken over by the General Inspectorate itself. The other Inspectorates, however, as mentioned in the description of the relevant arm of the service, came directly under the command of its most senior service commanders in the field.

Eventually, therefore, the General Inspectorate only controlled the stationary communications officers in the fortresses, the Communications Technical Testing Commission, the Military Works Directorates, the road-making formations and the Ersatz battalion for the special technical formations, set up on 6 October 1917. In addition, the General Inspectorate since peacetime, had control over the Intendance of the Military Communications Service which remained responsible for railway, signals and MV troops. The air forces received their own special Intendance.

P.

Medical departments and the War Medical Inspectorates

The medical organisations at home continued to exist at mobilisation. The peacetime garrison hospitals from then on were designated as Reserve Hospitals. To these were added the new Reserve, charity and prisoners of war hospitals, nursing homes and sanatoria. All medical organisations were under the control of the Deputy Medical Department in each Corps district.

In February 1915, to relieve the workload of the Corps medical officers directing the medical departments in Prussia, 7 War Medical Inspectorates were set up.[1] No 1 was for the I, XVII and XX Corps, No 2 was for the V and VI Corps, No 3 for the Guard, II and IX Corps, No 4 for the III, IV and X Corps, No 5 for the VII and VIII Corps, No 6 for the XI and XVII Corps and No 7 for the XIV, XV and XVI/XXI Corps. Bavaria, Saxony and Württemberg formed their own War Medical Inspectorates.

In contrast to the medical departments, the War Medical Inspectorates were under the direct control of the War Ministry. The Inspectors were the same rank as the Corps Medical Officers. The responsibilities of the Inspector consisted in visiting, as frequently as possible, all the medical organisations within his area. He had to supervise the correct use of the precautions for special treatment, and other health matters. He also had to ensure that those troops who had been restored to health were brought back at the proper time into military service.

As the war continued, the area of responsibilities of the War Medical Inspectorates grew to such an extent that, in Prussia alone, three new Inspectorates had to be set up in 1915, and two more respectively in 1917 and 1918. Towards the end of the war there was generally one War Medical Inspectorate for each Corps district, with its base in the same place as that of the Deputy General Command. The only exceptions were Inspectorate No 3 in Berlin (for Guard and II), No 7 in Strassburg (for XV and XVI/XXI), No 8 in Altona (for IX and X), and No 11 in Allenstein (for XVII and XX).

1   A.V.Bl. 1915, No 163; War Ministry of 26.2.1915, No 4582. 2. 15. M. A.

Q.

The Inspectorate of Military Penal Institutions

This Inspectorate had been dissolved on mobilisation, since it was thought that it would be a short war that would have a reforming influence. Since these ideas soon proved to be misguided, the Inspectorate had to be set up again as early as June 1915.[1]

---

1   A.V.Bl. 1915, No 519; War Ministry of 24.6.1915, No 3705. 5. 15. C. 3.

Conclusion

Whatever the reasons may have been for concluding the 'shameful' armistice, it is certain that the German Field Army left the enemy countries undefeated, and completed the march back to their homeland in full order. Then, of course, prompted by a 'cowardly' Government, unsure of itself, there followed an over hasty process of discharge, so that only the officers involved in winding-up were left. But in parallel with this process, under the leadership of tried and tested officers, Freiwillige (volunteer) units developed. The Government, on the one hand, accorded to them a lukewarm support, from fear of the Bolshevism that was raging out of Russia, and the anarchy that threatened within Germany. But, on the other hand, the Government met with concealed hostility out of fear of 'reaction'. These units of Freiwillige formed the foundation for the later Reichswehr, into which they developed on 1 October 1919. The relevant order of the Chief of the Reichswehr Command Authority Prussia, set up a worthy memorial to the old Army that may serve as the capping stone to this history of the Army:[2]

On 30 September the units of the 'old' Prussian Army will be dissolved and become the new Reichswehr.

For the present and former members of the Prussian Army, this restructuring means the farewell to many precious memories and to the lofty values of the past. But at the same time it means the beginning of a new development whose bearers have to hold in trust, and turn to good account, as their heritage, the great and good things which past generations have handed on to us.

The Prussian Army Constitution originated, in its founding principles, from the times of the uplifting ideals of the Wars of Liberation. At that time, Prussia's Army became the Volk[3] in arms. They took over the spirit of devotion to dutiful submission, for the good of the State, the firm path of duty, the order of holding in trust as a legacy of the Old Prussian State from the days of the Great Prince, Friedrich Wilhelm I and Friedrich the Great. This spirit had led the soldiers of old, through Fehrbellin and Leuthen, in a hard struggle to retain freedom and homeland. Carried by the enthusiasm of all German races, at Leipzig and Waterloo it was victorious over the tyrannical French domination of Napoleon. After more recent great battles under Prussia's leadership, including Düppel, Königgratz and Sedan, the liberated, but not yet united German Volk

1 Publishers' note: For the sake of completeness we have retained the author's original conclusion, written in 1937. Displaying all the pro-Nazi tendencies one would expect of a German military author writing at this date, it thus gives the reader a clear insight into the opinion of many veterans of the First World War German Army. Inclusion of this conclusion does not indicate in any way that the publishers share the sentiments or opinions of the author.

2 Heeres-Verordnungs-Blatt (Army Order Paper) 1919, No 246, Army Command Authority Prussia 30.9.19 (General Reinhardt).

3 Translator's note: The German word *Volk* means "nation", "race", "people", but at the same time combines and transcends these meanings in a concept which is better left in the original language.

finally reached the goal it had for so long yearned. It was the goal of State unity - the German Reich.

The World War of 1914-1918 brought dreadful burdens for the new Reich. In a manner worthy of their sires, Prussia's sons, in union with their brother races, conducted a heroic struggle for existence against the whole hostile world. Maas and Marne, Somme, Aisne and Yser, the lakes of East Prussia and the rivers of Poland, Galicia and Russia became witnesses to the heroic deeds of German Armies. Indeed, further on through Macedonia, Rumania, Italy, Palestine and beyond, and in all parts of the world's oceans, they laid down their goods and blood, victorious and dying, for the greatness of Germany.

Deeply moving is such a retrospect over the last hour of farewell of the old Army. But we should not be worthy of what has been proudly handed down to us if we were to mourn without deeds. The great German Fatherland needs every man, every force, it needs the spirit of duty and dedication up to the point of self-sacrifice.

In fostering it we see the sacred legacy of the 'old' Prussian Army. We wish to preserve it loyally in our hearts and wish, from this root, to draw forth the power to work for the reconstruction of our beloved Fatherland. Per aspera ad astra!

Afterwards, as at the time of these words of farewell, it dared to harbour the wildest hopes. There arose for the German Volk, in Adolf Hitler, a 'leader of genius', whose boundless energy, on 16 March 1935 in place of the weak Reichswehr, set a new German Volkswehr. The memories, mixed with sadness, of the 'old' Army were dissolved by confidence in the power of the new Reichsheer. Therefore, may this history of the German Army, in the 1914-1918 World War, ring out in the certainty that that unforgettable Army is not dead, but lives on in its virtues, its ability and its power, in the Armed Forces of the Third Reich!

APPENDICES

Appendix I

The Field Army, 17 August 1914

At the disposal of the OHL

General of Foot Artillery A.O.K. No 2, Foot Artillery Brigades 2-5 & 7
The Foot Artillery Regiments and Battalions of the Reserve – excepting II/Res. Foot
    Art. Rgt. 9
Heavy Coastal Mortar Batteries 3 & 4 (30.5cm)
Kurze (Short) Naval Gun Battery 2 (42cm)
Pioneer Experimental Company; Heavy Minenwerfers
7 Army Airships, 3 Siege Telephone Sections, Survey Detachments
11 Hospital and 7 Auxiliary Hospital Sections

Senior Cavalry Commander No 1
(preceding 3rd Army)[1]

Guard Cavalry Division
(24 Sqdns, 3 Batts., 1 MG Det.)
1st Guard Cavalry Brigade (Gardes du Corps, Guard Cuir. Rgt. 2)
2nd Guard Cavalry Brigade (Guard Uhlan Rgts. 1 & 3)
3rd Guard Cavalry Brigade (Guard Dragoon Rgts. 1 & 2)
Divisional troops (Horse Artillery Btn 1 from Guard Field Artillery Rgt, Guard MG
    Det. 1, Pioneer Btn, Signals Det. with Heavy Wireless Station 2 and Light Wire-
    less Stations 1 & 2, Cavalry Motorised Vehicle Column 10)

5th Cavalry Division
(24 Sqdns, 3 Batts., 1 MG Det.)
9th Cavalry Brigade (Dragoon Rgt. 4, Uhlan Rgt. 10)
11th Cavalry Brigade (Leib Cuir. Rgt. 1, Dragoon Rgt 8)
12th Cavalry Brigade (Hussar Rgts. 4 & 6)
Divisional troops (Horse Artillery Btn. from Field Artillery Rgt. 5, MG Det. 1, Pioneer
    Btn., Signals Det. with Heavy Wireless Station 3 and Light Wireless Stations 3 &
    4, Cavalry Motorised Vehicle Column 5)

Senior Cavalry Commander No 2
(preceding 1st and 2nd Armies)[2]

2nd Cavalry Division
(24 Sqdns, 3 Batts., 1 MG Det.)[3]
5th Cavalry Brigade (Dragoon Rgt. 2, Uhlan Rgt. 3)

---

1   Assigned: Jäg. Btns. 11, 12 and 13 (each with 1 Cycle Coy. and a Jäger Motorised
    Vehicle Column).

8th Cavalry Brigade (Cuir. Rgt. 7, Hussar Rgt. 12)
Leib Hussar Brigade (Leib Hussar Rgts. 1 & 2)
Divisional troops (Horse Artillery Btn. from Field Artillery Rgt. 35, MG Det. 4, Pioneer Btn., Signals Det. with Heavy Wireless Station 1 and Light Wireless Stations 5 & 6, Cavalry Motorised Vehicle Column 2)

4th Cavalry Division
(24 Sqdns, 3 Batts., 1 MG Det.)
3rd Cavalry Brigade (Cuir. Rgt. 2, Uhlan Rgt. 9)
17th Cavalry Brigade (Dragoon Rgts. 17 & 18)
18th Cavalry Brigade (Hussar Rgts. 15 & 16)
Divisional troops (Horse Artillery Btn. from Field Artillery Rgt. 3, Guards MG Det. 2, Pioneer Btn., Signals Det. with Heavy Wireless Stations 18 & 19 and Light Wireless Stations 10 & 12, Cavalry Motorised Vehicle Column 4)

9th Cavalry Division
(24 Sqdns, 3 Batts., 1 MG Det.)
13th Cavalry Brigade (Cuir. Rgt. 4, Hussar Rgt. 8)
14th Cavalry Brigade (Hussar Rgt. 11, Uhlan Rgt. 5)
19th Cavalry Brigade (Dragoon Rgt. 19, Uhlan Rgt. 13)
Divisional troops (Horse Artillery Btn. from Field Artillery Rgt. 10, MG Det. 7, Pioneer Btn., Signals Det. with Heavy Wireless Station 21 and Light Wireless Stations 8 & 17, Cavalry Motorised Vehicle Column 9)

Senior Cavalry Commander No 3
(preceding 6th Army)

7th Cavalry Division
(24 Sqdns, 3 Batts., 1 MG Det.)
26th Cavalry Brigade (Dragoon Rgts. 25 & 26)
30th Cavalry Brigade (Dragoon Rgt. 15, Hussar Rgt. 9)
42nd Cavalry Brigade (Uhlan Rgts. 11 & 15)
Divisional troops (Horse Artillery Btn. from Field Artillery Rgt. 15, MG Det. 3, Pioneer Btn., Signals Det. with Heavy Wireless Station 26 and Light Wireless Stations 13 & 15, Cavalry Motorised Vehicle Column 7)

8th Cavalry Division
(24 Sqdns, 3 Batts., 1 MG Det.)
23rd Cavalry Brigade (Guard Reiter Rgt., Uhlan Rgt. 17)
38th Cavalry Brigade (Jäger Rgt. zu Pferede 2 & 6)
40th Cavalry Brigade (Carabinier Rgt., Uhlan Rgt. 21)
Divisional troops (Horse Artillery Btn. from Field Artillery Rgt. 12, MG Det. 8, Pioneer Btn., Signals Det. with Heavy Wireless Station 25 and Light Wireless Stations 16 & 20, Cavalry Motorised Vehicle Column 8)

2   Assigned: Jäg. Btns. 3, 4, 7, 9 and 10 (each with 1 Cycle Coy. and a Jäger Motorised Vehicle Column).
3   Assigned: Guard Jäger Btn. and Guard Schützen Btn. (each with 1 Cycle Coy. and a Jäger Motorised Vehicle Column).

Bavarian Cavalry Division
(24 Sqdns, 3 Batts., 1 MG Det.)[4]
1st Bavarian Cavalry Brigade (Heavy Reiter Rgts. 1 & 2)
4th Bavarian Cavalry Brigade (Uhlan Rgts. 1 & 2)
5th Bavarian Cavalry Brigade (Chevauleger Rgts. 1 & 6)
Divisional troops (Horse Artillery Btn. from Bavarian Field Artillery Rgt. 5, Bavarian MG Det. 1, Pioneer Btn., Signals Det. with Bavarian Heavy Wireless Stations 3 & 4 and Bavarian Light Wireless Stations 1 & 2, Bavarian Cavalry Motorised Vehicle Column 1)

Senior Cavalry Commander No 4
(preceding 4th and 5th Armies)

3rd Cavalry Division
(24 Sqdns, 3 Batts., 1 MG Det.)[5]
16th Cavalry Brigade (Jäger Rgt. zu Pferde 7 & 8)
22nd Cavalry Brigade (Dragoon Rgt. 5, Hussar Rgt. 14)
25th Cavalry Brigade (Guard Dragoon Rgt. 3, Leib Dragoon Rgt. 24)
Divisional troops (Horse Artillery Btn. from Field Artillery Rgt. 11, MG Det. 2, Pioneer Btn., Signals Det. with Heavy Wireless Station 11 and Light Wireless Stations 18 & 19, Cavalry Motorised Vehicle Column 3)

6th Cavalry Division
(24 Sqdns, 3 Batts., 1 MG Det.)[6]
28th Cavalry Brigade (Leib Dragoon Rgt. 20, Dragoon Rgt. 21)
33rd Cavalry Brigade (Dragoon Rgts. 9 & 13)
45th Cavalry Brigade (Hussar Rgt. 13, Jäger zu Pferde Rgt. 13)
Divisional troops (Horse Artillery Btn. from Field Artillery Rgt. 8, MG Det. 6, Pioneer Btn., Signals Det. with Heavy Wireless Stations 4 & 1 and Light Wireless Stations 9 & 11, Cavalry Motorised Vehicle Column 6)

1st Army
(Army HQ Glons, south-east of Tongern)

Lines of Communication Formations
L of C Insp. 1, CO Motorised Vehicle Troop 1, 18 L of C Motorised Vehicle Columns, L of C Motorised Vehicle Park 1, L of C Aircraft Park 1, 8 L of C Munitions Columns, 12 L of C Supply Parks, 4 Magazine Supply Parks furnished by 15 L of C Train Sqdns, L of C Telephone Dept.

---

4   Attached: Bavarian Jäger Btns. 1 & 2 (each with 1 Cycle Coy. and 1 Jäger Motorised Vehicle Column).
5   Attached: Jäger Btn. 6 (with Cycle Coy. and 1 Jäger Motorised Vehicle Column).
6   Attached: Jäger Btn. 5 (with Cycle Coy. and 1 Jäger Motorised Vehicle Column).

Army Troops
Army Telephone Det. 1, Wireless Command 1, Heavy Wireless Stations 5 & 20, Field
    Airship Det. 1, Aviation Det. 12, Staff 1st Guard Foot Artillery Rgt., Pioneer
    General 1, Pioneer Rgt. 18 with Pioneer Siege Train and 2 Park Coys.

Supply Troops
4 Infantry Munitions Sections, 6 Part-motorised Field Artillery Munitions Sections[7], 2
    Motorised Field Artillery Munitions Sections, 3 Foot Artillery Munitions Sec-
    tions, Equipment and Explosive Munitions Supply Unit 1, Gas Supply Unit 1, 2
    Eqpt Supply Units (with L of C Motorised Vehicle Park 1).

II Army Corps
(3rd & 4th Inf. Divs., 4 Heavy Batts., 1 Aviation Det.)
3rd Infantry Division (12 Btns., 4 MGKs, 4 Sqdns., 12 Batts., 1 Pi. Coy.)
    5th Infantry Brigade (Gren. Rgts. 2 & 9)
    6th Infantry Brigade (Füs. Rgt. 34, Inf. Rgt. 42)
    Dragoon Rgt. 3
    3rd Field Artillery Brigade (Field Artillery Rgts. 2 & 38)
    1st Coy. Pioneer Btn. 2, Divisional Pontoon Train 3, Medical Coys. 1 & 3
4th Infantry Division (12 Btns., 4 MGKs, 4 Sqdns., 12 Batts., 2 Pi. Coys.)
    7th Infantry Brigade (Inf. Rgts. 14 & 149)
    8th Infantry Brigade (Inf. Rgt. 49 & 140)
    Dragoon Rgt. 12
    4th Field Artillery Brigade (Field Artillery Rgts. 17 & 53)
    2nd & 3rd Coys. Pioneer Btn. 2, Divisional Pontoon Train 4, Medical
    Coy. 2
Corps Troops
    I Btn. Foot Artillery Rgt. 15 (Hvy. Field Howitzers), Aviation Det. 30,
    Corps Pontoon Train 2, Telephone Det., Pioneer Searchlight Sec. 2, I & II
    Munition Column Sections (4th Inf. & 9th Art. Munition Columns),
    Foot Artillery Munition Section I/15 with 8 Columns, I & II Train Section
    (12 Field Hospitals, 6 Supply Columns, 7 Supply Parks, 2 Horse Depts.), 2
    Field Bakery Columns

III Army Corps
(5th & 6th Inf. Divs., 4 Heavy Batts., 1 Aviation Det.)
5th Infantry Division (13 Btns., 5 MGKs, 3 Sqdns., 12 Batts., 2 Pi. Coys.)
    9th Infantry Brigade (Leib Gren. Rgt. 8, Inf. Rgt. 48)
    10th Infantry Brigade (Gren. Rgt. 12, Inf. Rgt. 52, Jäger Btn. 3)
    ½ Hussar Rgt. 3
    5th Field Artillery Brigade (Field Artillery Rgts. 18 & 54)
    2nd and 3rd Coys. Pioneer Btn. 3, Divisional Pontoon Train 5, Medical
    Coys. 1 & 3
6th Infantry Division (12 Btns., 4 MGKs, 4 Sqdns., 12 Batts., 2 Pi. Coys.)
    11th Infantry Brigade (Inf. Rgt. 20, Füs. Rgt. 35)
    12th Infantry Brigade (Inf. Rgt. 24 & 64)

7   Denoted unit was partly horse-drawn and partly motorised.

½ Hussar Rgt. 3
6th Field Artillery Brigade (Field Artillery Rgts. 3 & 39)
2nd & 3rd Coys. Pioneer Btn. 3, Divisional Pontoon Train 6, Medical
Coy. 2
Corps Troops
I Btn. Guard Artillery Rgt. (Hvy. Field Howitzers), Aviation Det. 7, Corps
Pontoon Train 3, Pioneer Searchlight Sec. 3, Munition Columns and
Train corresponded to II Army Corps.

IV Army Corps
(7th & 8th Inf. Divs., 4 Heavy Batts., 1 Aviation Det.)
7th Infantry Division (12 Btns., 4 MGKs, 3 Sqdns., 12 Batts., 2 Pi. Coys.)
13th Infantry Brigade (Inf. Rgts. 26 & 66)
14th Infantry Brigade (Inf. Rgts. 27 & 165)
Staff & ½ Hussar Rgt. 10
8th Field Artillery Brigade (Field Artillery Rgts. 74 & 75)
2nd and 3rd Coys. Pioneer Btn. 4, Divisional Pontoon Train 8, Medical
Coy. 2
8th Infantry Division (13 Btns., 5 MGKs, 3 Sqdns., 12 Batts., 2 Pi. Coys.)
15th Infantry Brigade (Füs.Rgt. 36, Inf. Rgt. 93, Jäger Btn.4)
16th Infantry Brigade (Inf. Rgt. 72 & 153)
½ Hussar Rgt. 10
8th Field Artillery Brigade (Field Artillery Rgts. 74 & 75)
2nd & 3rd Coys. Pioneer Btn. 4, Divisional Pontoon Train 8, Medical
Coy. 2
Corps Troops
I Btn. Foot Artillery Rgt. 4 (Hvy. Field Howitzers), Aviation Det. 9, Corps
Pontoon Train 4, Pioneer Searchlight Sec. 4, Munition Columns and
Train corresponded to II Army Corps.

IX Army Corps
(17th & 18th Inf. Divs., 4 Heavy Batts., 1 Aviation Det.)
17th Infantry Division (13 Btns., 5 MGKs, 3 Sqdns., 12 Batts., 1 Pi. Coy.)
33rd Infantry Brigade (Inf. Rgts. 75 & 76)
34th Infantry Brigade (Gren. Rgt. 89, Füs.Rgt. 90, Jäger Btn. 9)
Staff & ½ Dragoon Rgt. 16
17th Field Artillery Brigade (Field Artillery Rgts. 24 & 60)
1st Coy. Pioneer Btn. 9, Divisional Pontoon Train 17, Medical Coys. 1 &
3
18th Infantry Division (12 Btns., 4 MGKs, 3 Sqdns., 12 Batts., 2 Pi. Coys.)
35th Infantry Brigade (Inf. Rgt. 84, Füs.Rgt. 86)
36th Infantry Brigade (Inf. Rgt. 31 & 85)
½ Dragoon Rgt. 16
18th Field Artillery Brigade (Field Artillery Rgts. 9 & 45)
2nd & 3rd Coys. Pioneer Btn. 9, Divisional Pontoon Train 18, Medical
Coy. 2

Corps Troops
   I Btn. Foot Artillery Rgt. 20 (Hvy. Field Howitzers), Aviation Det. 11,
   Corps Pontoon Train 9, Telephone Det. 9, Pioneer Searchlight Sec. 9,
   Munition Columns and Train corresponded to II Army Corps.

III Reserve Corps
(5th & 6th Reserve Divs)
5th Reserve Division (13 Btns., 4 MGKs[8], 3 Sqdns., 6 Batts., 1 Pi. Coy.)
   9th Reserve Infantry Brigade (Res. Inf. Rgts. 8 & 48)
   10th Reserve Infantry Brigade (Res. Inf. Rgts. 12 & 52, Reserve Jäger Btn.
   3)
   Reserve Dragoon Rgt. 2
   Reserve Field Artillery Rgt. 5
   4th Coy. Pioneer Btn. 3, Reserve Divisional Pontoon Train 5, Reserve
   Medical Coy. 3
6th Reserve Division (12 Btns., 3 MGKs[9], 3 Sqdns., 6 Batts., 2 Pi. Coys.)
   11th Reserve Infantry Brigade (Res. Inf. Rgts. 20 & 24)
   12th Reserve Infantry Brigade (Res. Inf. Rgts. 26 & 35)
   Reserve Uhlan Rgt. 3
   Reserve Field Artillery Rgt. 6
   1st and 2nd Reserve Coys. Pioneer Btn. 3, Reserve Divisional Pontoon
   Train 6, Reserve Medical Coy. 16
Corps Troops
   Reserve Telephone Det. 3, Reserve Munition Column Sections 5 & 6 (4th
   Reserve Infantry & 5th Reserve Artillery Munition Columns), Reserve
   Train Sections 5 & 6 (4 Reserve Field Hospitals & 7 Reserve Supply Col-
   umns), 2 Reserve Bakery Columns

IV Reserve Corps
(7th & 22nd Reserve Divs)
7th Reserve Division (13 Btns., 2 MGKs[10], 3 Sqdns., 6 Batts., 1 Pi. Coy.)
   13th Reserve Infantry Brigade (Res. Inf. Rgts. 27 & 36)
   14th Reserve Infantry Brigade (Res. Inf. Rgts. 66 & 72, Reserve Jäger Btn.
   4)
   Heavy Reserve Reiter Rgt. 1
   Reserve Field Artillery Rgt. 7
   4th Coy. Pioneer Btn. 4, Reserve Divisional Pontoon Train 7, Reserve
   Medical Coy. 4
22nd Reserve Division (12 Btns.[11], 2 MGKs[12], 3 Sqdns., 6 Batts., 2 Pi. Coys.)
   43rd Reserve Infantry Brigade (Res. Inf. Rgts. 71 & 94, Reserve Jäger Btn.
   11)

8   Res. Jäger Btn. 3 without a MGK.
9   Res. Inf. Rgt. 26 without a MGK.
10 Res. Inf. Rgts. 36 & 66 and Reserve Jäger Btn. 4 without MGKs.
11 Res. Inf. Rgt. 94 only had 2 btns.
12 Res. Inf. Rgts. 32 & 71 and Reserve Jäger Btn. 11 without MGKs.

44th Reserve Infantry Brigade (Res. Inf. Rgts. 32 & 82)
Reserve Jäger zu Pferde Rgt. 1
Reserve Field Artillery Rgt. 22
1st and 2nd Reserve Coys. Pioneer Btn. 4, Reserve Divisional Pontoon
Train 2 Reserve Medical Coy. 11

Corps Troops
Reserve Telephone Det. 4, Munition Trains and Columns corresponded
to III Reserve Corps.

10th Mixed Landwehr Brigade   *(to 15" Ldw D)*
(6 Btns., 1 Sqdn., 1 Batt.)
Landwehr Inf. Rgts. 12 & 52, 1st Landwehr Sqdn. III A.K., 1st Landsturm Batt. III A.K.

11th Mixed Landwehr Brigade   *(to 21ᵃ Ldw D)*
(6 Btns., 1 Sqdn., 1 Batt.)
Landwehr Inf. Rgts. 20 & 35, 1st Landwehr Sqdn. Guard Corps, 2nd Landsturm Batt. III A.K.

27th Mixed Landwehr Brigade   *(to 15ᵗ Ldw D)*
(6 Btns., 1 Sqdn.)
Landwehr Inf. Rgts. 53 & 55, 2nd Landwehr Sqdn. VII A.K.

2nd Army
(Army HQ Lüttich)

Lines of Communication Formations
L of C Insp. 2, CO Motorised Vehicle Troop 2, 18 L of C Motorised Vehicle Columns, L of C Motorised Vehicle Park 2, 11 L of C Munitions Columns, 14 L of C Supply Parks, 5 Magazine Supply Parks furnished by 15 L of C Train Sqdns, L of C Aircraft Park 2, L of C Telephone Dept.

Army Troops
Staff Officer Railways 1, Railway Construction Coys. 2, 4 & 5, 1st-5th Guard Eqpt Units, Armoured Trains 1 & 2, Army Telephone Det. 2, Wireless Command 2, Heavy Wireless Stations 6 & 23, Field Airship Det. 2, Aviation Det. 23, General of Foot Artillery 3, Staff Foot Artillery Rgts. 4, 9 & 20, II & III Btns. Foot Artillery Rgt. 4 (with 4 Minenwerfer Batts.) with 2 I Munition Columns and 2 Munition Column Sections, I & II Btns. Foot Artillery Rgt. 9 (with 4 Minenwerfer Batts.) with 2 I Munition Columns and 2 Munition Column Sections, II Btn. Reserve Foot Artillery Rgt. 9 (10cm) with I Munition Column and Park Coy., 1st and 5th Heavy Coastal Minenwerfer Batts. (30.5cm), Steam Locomotive Park 1, Park Btns. Staff 4 with Park Coys. of the II & III Btns. Reserve Foot Artillery Rgt. 7, Workshop for Siege Artillery Rgt. 4, Requisition Railway Units 26-28, Pioneer General 2, Pioneer Rgt. 24 with Pioneer Siege Train and 2 Park Coys., Pioneer Rgt. 25 with Pioneer Siege Train and 2 Park Coys.

Supply Troops
Corresponding to those of the 1st Army.

Guard Corps

(1st & 2nd Guard Infantry Divs., 4 Heavy Batts., 1 Aviation Det.)

1st Guard Infantry Division (13 Btns., 5 MGKs, 4 Sqdns., 12 Batts., 1 Pi. Coy.)
  1st Guard Infantry Brigade (1st & 3rd Foot Guards Rgts, Guard Jäger Btn.)
  2nd Guard Infantry Brigade (2nd & 4th Foot Guards Rgts.)
  Leib Guard Hussar Rgt. 1
  1st Guard Field Artillery Brigade (1st & 3rd Guard Field Artillery Rgts.)
  1st Coy. Guard Pioneer Btn., Guard Divisional Pontoon Train 1, Medical Coys. 1 & 3

2nd Guard Infantry Division (13 Btns., 5 MGKs, 4 Sqdns., 12 Batts., 2 Pi. Coys.)
  3rd Guard Infantry Brigade (Guard Gren. Rgts. 1 & 3, Guard Schützen Btl.)
  4th Guard Infantry Brigade (Guard Gren. Rgts. 2 & 4)
  2nd Guard Uhlan Rgt.
  2nd Guard Field Artillery Brigade (2nd & 4th Guard Field Artillery Rgts.)
  2nd & 3rd Coys. Guard Pioneer Btn., Guard Divisional Pontoon Train 2, Medical Coy. 2

Corps Troops
  I Btn. 1st Guard Foot Artillery Rgt. (Hvy. Field Howitzers), Aviation Det. 1, Guard Corps Pontoon Train, Guard Telephone Det., Guard Pioneer Searchlight Sec., Munition Columns and Train corresponded to II Army Corps.

Guard Reserve Corps

(3rd Guard Infantry Div., 1st Guard Reserve Division, 4 Heavy Batts.)

3rd Guard Infantry Division (12 Btns., 5 MGKs[13], 3 Sqdns., 12 Batts., 1 Pi. Coy.)
  5th Guard Infantry Brigade (5th Foot Guards Rgt., Guard Gren. Rgt. 5)
  6th Guard Infantry Brigade (Guard Füs. Rgt., Infantry Training Rgt.)
  Guard Reserve Uhlan Rgt.
  3rd Guard Field Artillery Brigade (5th & 6th Guard Field Artillery Rgts.)
  1st Coy. Pioneer Btn. 28, Guard Divisional Pontoon Train 3, Medical Coys. 1 & 3

1st Guard Reserve Division (14 Btns., 4 MGKs[14], 3 Sqdns., 12 Batts., 2 Pi. Coys.)
  1st Guard Reserve Brigade (1st & 2nd Guard Reserve Inf. Rgts., Guard Reserve Jäger Btn.)
  15th Reserve Infantry Brigade (Res. Inf. Rgts. 64 & 93, Guard Reserve Schützen Btn.)
  Guard Reserve Dragoon Rgt.
  Guard Reserve Field Artillery Brigade (1st & 3rd Guard Reserve Field Artillery Rgts.)
  2nd & 3rd Coys. Pioneer Btn. 28, Guard Divisional Pontoon Train 2, Medical Coy. 2

---

13 Infantry Training Rgt. with 2 MGKs.
14 Guard Reserve Jäger Btn. and Guard Reserve Schützen Btn. without MGKs.

Corps Troops
    II Btn. 1st Guard Foot Artillery Rgt. (Hvy. Field Howitzers), Guard Re-
    serve Corps Pontoon Train, Guard Reserve Telephone Det., Pioneer
    Searchlight Sec. 28, Munition Columns and Train corresponded to II
    Army Corps.

VII Army Corps
(13th & 14th Inf. Divs., 4 Heavy Batts., 1 Aviation Det.)
13th Infantry Division (13 Btns., 5 MGKs, 3 Sqdns., 12 Batts., 1 Pi. Coy.)
    25th Infantry Brigade (Inf. Rgts. 13 & 158)
    26th Infantry Brigade (Inf. Rgts. 15 & 55, Jäger Btn. 7)
    Staff & ½ Uhlan Rgt. 16
    13th Field Artillery Brigade (Field Artillery Rgts. 22 & 58)
    1st Coy. Pioneer Btn. 7, Divisional Pontoon Train 13, Medical Coys. 1 &
    3
14th Infantry Division (12 Btns., 4 MGKs, 3 Sqdns., 12 Batts., 2 Pi. Coys.)
    27th Infantry Brigade (Inf. Rgts. 16 & 53)
    79th Infantry Brigade (Inf. Rgts. 56 & 57)
    ½ Uhlan Rgt. 16
    14th Field Artillery Brigade (Field Artillery Rgts. 7 & 43)
    2nd & 3rd Coys. Pioneer Btn. 7, Divisional Pontoon Train 14, Medical
    Coy. 2
Corps Troops
    I Btn. Foot Artillery Rgt. 7 (Hvy. Field Howitzers), Aviation Det. 18,
    Corps Pontoon Train 7, Telephone Det. 7, Pioneer Searchlight Sec. 7,
    Munition Columns and Train corresponded to II Army Corps.

X Army Corps
(19th & 20th Inf. Divs., 4 Heavy Batts., 1 Aviation Det.)
19th Infantry Division (13 Btns., 4 MGKs, 3 Sqdns., 12 Batts., 1 Pi. Coy.)
    37th Infantry Brigade (Inf. Rgts. 78 & 91)
    38th Infantry Brigade (Füs.Rgt. 73 & Inf. Rgt. 74)
    ½ Hussar Rgt. 17
    19th Field Artillery Brigade (Field Artillery Rgts. 26 & 62)
    1st Coy. Pioneer Btn. 10, Divisional Pontoon Train 19, Medical Coys. 1
    & 3
20th Infantry Division (13 Btns., 5 MGKs, 3 Sqdns., 12 Batts., 2 Pi. Coys.)
    39th Infantry Brigade (Inf. Rgts. 79 & 164, Jäger Btn. 10)
    40th Infantry Brigade (Inf. Rgts. 77 & 92)
    Staff and ½ Uhlan Rgt. 17
    20th Field Artillery Brigade (Field Artillery Rgts. 10 & 46)
    2nd & 3rd Coys. Pioneer Btn. 10, Divisional Pontoon Train 20, Medical
    Coy. 2
Corps Troops
    II Btn. Foot Artillery Rgt. 20 (Hvy. Field Howitzers), Aviation Det. 21,
    Corps Pontoon Train 10, Telephone Det. 10, Pioneer Searchlight Sec. 10,
    Munition Columns and Train corresponded to II Army Corps.

VII Reserve Corps

(13th & 14th Reserve Divs.)

13th Reserve Division (12 Btns.[15], 4 MGKs[16], 3 Sqdns., 6 Batts., 1 Pi. Coy.)

 25th Reserve Infantry Brigade (Res. Inf. Rgts. 13 & 56)

 28th Reserve Infantry Brigade (Res. Inf. Rgts. 39 & 57, Reserve Jäger Btn. 7)

 Reserve Hussar Rgt. 5

 Reserve Field Artillery Rgt. 13

 4th Coy. Pioneer Btn. 7, Reserve Divisional Pontoon Train 13, Reserve Medical Coy. 7

14th Reserve Division (12 Btns., 4 MGKs, 3 Sqdns., 6 Batts., 2 Pi. Coys.)

 28th Infantry Brigade (Füs. Rgt. 39 & Inf. Rgt. 159)

 27th Reserve Infantry Brigade (Res. Inf. Rgts. 16 & 53)

 Reserve Hussar Rgt. 8

 Reserve Field Artillery Rgt. 14

 1st and 2nd Reserve Coys. Pioneer Btn. 7, Reserve Medical Coy. 21

Corps Troops

 Reserve Telephone Det. 7, Munition Trains and Columns corresponded to III Reserve Corps.

X Reserve Corps

(2nd Guard Reserve Div. & 19th Reserve Div.)

2nd Guard Reserve Division (12 Btns.[17], 4 MGKs[18], 3 Sqdns., 6 Batts., 1 Pi. Coy.)

 26th Reserve Infantry Brigade (Res. Inf. Rgts. 15 & 55)

 38th Reserve Infantry Brigade (Res. Inf. Rgts. 77 & 91, Reserve Jäger Btn. 10)

 Reserve Uhlan Rgt. 2

 Reserve Field Artillery Rgt. 20

 4th Coy. Pioneer Btn. 10, Guard Reserve Divisional Pontoon Train 2, Guard Reserve Medical Coy. 2

19th Reserve Division (13 Btns., 5 MGKs[19], 3 Sqdns., 6 Batts., 2 Pi. Coys.)

 37th Reserve Infantry Brigade (Res. Inf. Rgts. 73 & 78)

 39th Reserve Infantry Brigade (Res. Inf. Rgts. 74 & 92, III Btn. Res. Inf. Rgt. 79)

 Reserve Dragoon Rgt. 6

 Reserve Field Artillery Rgt. 19

 1st and 2nd Reserve Coys. Pioneer Btn. 10, Reserve Divisional Pontoon Train 19, Reserve Medical Coy. 10

Corps Troops

 Reserve Telephone Det. 10, Munition Trains and Columns corresponded to III Reserve Corps.

---

15 Res. Inf. Rgt. 57 only had 2 btns.

16 Res. Jäger Btn. 7 without a MGK.

17 Res. Inf. Rgt. 55 only had 2 btns.

18 Res. Jäger Btn. 10 without a MGK.

19 III Btn. Res. Inf. Rgt. 79 with a MGK (Remainder of Res. Inf. Rgt. at Borkum).

25th Mixed Landwehr Brigade
(6 Btns., 1 Sqdn., 1 Batt.)
Landwehr Inf. Rgts. 13 & 16, 1st Landwehr Sqdn. VII A.K., 1st Landsturm Batt. VII
A.K.

29th Mixed Landwehr Brigade
(6 Btns., 1 Sqdn., 1 Batt.)
Landwehr Inf. Rgts. 28 & 29, 1st Landwehr Sqdn. VII A.K., 1st Landsturm Batt. VII
A.K.

3rd Army
(Army HQ Clerf)

Lines of Communication Formations
L of C Insp. 3, CO Motorised Vehicle Troop 3, 9 L of C Motorised Vehicle Columns,
L of C Motorised Vehicle Park 3, L of C Aircraft Park 3, 7 L of C Munitions Col-
umns, 12 L of C Supply Parks, 3 Magazine Supply Parks furnished by 9 L of C
Train Sqdns, L of C Telephone Dept.

Army Troops
Army Telephone Det. 3, Wireless Command 3, Heavy Wireless Stations 13 & 22,
Field Airship Det. 7, Aviation Det. 22, Staff Foot Artillery Rgt. 19, III Btn. Foot
Artillery Rgt. 1 (with 2 Minenwerfer Batts.) with I Munition Column and a Mu-
nition Column Section, Pioneer General 3, Pioneer Rgt. 23 with Pioneer Siege
Train and 2 Park Coys.

Supply Troops
Corresponding to those of the 1st Army.

XI Army Corps
(22nd & 38th Inf. Divs., 4 Heavy Batts., 1 Aviation Det.)
22nd Infantry Division (13 Btns., 5 MGKs, 3 Sqdns., 12 Batts., 1 Pi. Coy.)
    43rd Infantry Brigade (Inf. Rgts. 82 & 83)
    44th Infantry Brigade (Inf. Rgts. 32 & 167, Jäger Btn. 11)
    Staff & ½ Cuir. Rgt. 6
    22nd Field Artillery Brigade (Field Artillery Rgts. 11 & 47)
    1st Coy. Pioneer Btn. 11, Divisional Pontoon Train 22, Medical Coys. 1
    & 3
38th Infantry Division (12 Btns., 4 MGKs, 3 Sqdns., 12 Batts., 2 Pi. Coys.)
    76th Infantry Brigade (Inf. Rgts. 71 & 95)
    83rd Infantry Brigade (Inf. Rgts. 94 & 96)
    ½ Cuir. Rgt. 6
    38th Field Artillery Brigade (Field Artillery Rgts. 19 & 55)
    2nd & 3rd Coys. Pioneer Btn. 11, Divisional Pontoon Train 38, Medical
    Coy. 2
Corps Troops
    I Btn. Foot Artillery Rgt. 18 (Hvy. Field Howitzers), Aviation Det. 28,
    Corps Pontoon Train 11, Telephone Det. 11, Pioneer Searchlight Sec. 11,
    Munition Columns and Train corresponded to II Army Corps.

XII Army Corps
(23rd & 32nd Inf. Divs., 4 Heavy Batts., 1 Aviation Det.)
23rd Infantry Division (12 Btns., 4 MGKs, 4 Sqdns., 12 Batts., 1 Pi. Coy.)
    45th Infantry Brigade (Leib Gren. Rgt. 100, Gren. Rgt. 101)
    46th Infantry Brigade (Schützen Rgt. 108 & Inf. Rgt. 182)
    Hussar Rgt. 20
    23rd Field Artillery Brigade (Field Artillery Rgts. 12 & 48)
    1st Coy. Pioneer Btn. 12, Divisional Pontoon Train 23, Medical Coys. 1
    & 3
32nd Infantry Division (13 Btns., 5 MGKs, 4 Sqdns., 12 Batts., 2 Pi. Coys.)
    63rd Infantry Brigade (Inf. Rgts. 102 & 103, Jäger Btn. 12)
    64th Infantry Brigade (Inf. Rgts. 177 & 178)
    Hussar Rgt. 18
    32nd Field Artillery Brigade (Field Artillery Rgts. 28 & 64)
    2nd & 3rd Coys. Pioneer Btn. 12, Divisional Pontoon Train 32, Medical
    Coy. 2
Corps Troops
    I Btn. Foot Artillery Rgt. 1 (Hvy. Field Howitzers), Aviation Det. 29,
    Corps Pontoon Train 12, Telephone Det. 12, Pioneer Searchlight Sec. 12,
    Munition Columns and Train corresponded to II Army Corps.

XIX Army Corps
(24th & 40th Inf. Divs., 4 Heavy Batts., 1 Aviation Det.)
24th Infantry Division (13 Btns., 5 MGKs, 4 Sqdns., 12 Batts., 1 Pi. Coy.)
    47th Infantry Brigade (Inf. Rgts. 139 & 179, Jäger Btn. 13)
    48th Infantry Brigade (Inf. Rgts. 106 & 107)
    Uhlan Rgt. 18
    24th Field Artillery Brigade (Field Artillery Rgts. 77 & 78)
    1st Coy. Pioneer Btn. 22, Divisional Pontoon Train 24, Medical Coys. 1
    & 3
40th Infantry Division (12 Btns., 4 MGKs, 4 Sqdns., 12 Batts., 2 Pi. Coys.)
    88th Infantry Brigade (Inf. Rgts. 104 & 181)
    89th Infantry Brigade (Inf. Rgts. 133 & 134)
    Hussar Rgt. 19
    40th Field Artillery Brigade (Field Artillery Rgts. 32 & 68)
    2nd & 3rd Coys. Pioneer Btn. 22, Divisional Pontoon Train 40, Medical
    Coy. 2
Corps Troops
    II Btn. Foot Artillery Rgt. 19 (Hvy. Field Howitzers), Aviation Det. 24,
    Corps Pontoon Train 19, Telephone Det. 19, Pioneer Searchlight Sec. 22,
    Munition Columns and Train corresponded to II Army Corps.

XII Reserve Corps
(23rd & 24th Reserve Divs.)
23rd Reserve Division (13 Btns., 3 MGKs[20], 3 Sqdns., 9 Batts.[21], 1 Pi. Coy.)

---

20   Res. Inf. Rgt. 102 and Res. Jäg. Btn. 12 without MGKs.
21   Res. Field Art. Rgt. 23 had 3 btns.

45th Reserve Infantry Brigade (Res. Inf. Rgts. 100 & 101, Reserve Jäger Btn. 12)
46th Reserve Infantry Brigade (Res. Inf. Rgts. 102 & 103)
Saxon Reserve Hussar Rgt.
Reserve Field Artillery Rgt. 23
4th Coy. Pioneer Btn. 12, Reserve Divisional Pontoon Train 23, Saxon Reserve Medical Coy. 1
24th Reserve Division (13 Btns., 3 MGKs[22], 3 Sqdns., 9 Batts.[23], 2 Pi. Coys.)
47th Reserve Infantry Brigade (Res. Inf. Rgts. 104 & 106, Reserve Jäger Btn. 13)
48th Reserve Infantry Brigade (Res. Inf. Rgts. 107 & 133)
Saxon Reserve Uhlan Rgt.
Reserve Field Artillery Rgt. 24
1st and 2nd Reserve Coys. Pioneer Btn. 12, Saxon Reserve Medical Coy. 2
Corps Troops
Reserve Telephone Det. 12, Munition Trains and Columns corresponded to III Reserve Corps.

47th Mixed Landwehr Brigade
(6 Btns., 2 Sqdns., 1 Batt.)
Landwehr Inf. Rgts. 104 & 106, 1st and 2nd Landwehr Sqdns. XIX A.K., 1st Landsturm Batt. XIX A.K.

4th Army
(Army HQ Trier)

Lines of Communication Formations
L of C Insp. 4, CO Motorised Vehicle Troop 4, 5 L of C Motorised Vehicle Columns, L of C Motorised Vehicle Park 4, L of C Aircraft Park 4, 6 L of C Munitions Columns, 9 L of C Supply Parks, 4 Magazine Supply Parks furnished by 12 L of C Train Sqdns, Guard L of C Telephone Dept.

Army Troops
Armoured Trains 3 & 4, Army Telephone Det. 4, Wireless Command 4, Heavy Wireless Stations 9 & 14, Field Airship Det. 3, Aviation Det. 6, Aviation Det. 6, Foot Artillery Brigade Command 1, Staff Foot Artillery Rgts. 3 & 7, II & III Btns. Foot Artillery Rgt. 7 (with 4 Minenwerfer Batts.) with 2 I Munition Column and 2 Munition Column Sections, Pioneer General 4, Pioneer Rgt. 30 with Pioneer Siege Train and Park Coy.

Supply Troops
Corresponding to those of the 1st Army.

VI Army Corps
(11th & 12th Inf. Divs., 4 Heavy Batts., 1 Aviation Det.)
11th Infantry Division (13 Btns., 5 MGKs, 4 Sqdns., 12 Batts., 1 Pi. Coy.)

22   Res. Inf. Rgt. 133 and Res. Jäg. Btn. 13 lacked MGKs.
23   Res. Field Art. Rgt. 24 possessed 3 btns.

21st Infantry Brigade (Gren. Rgt. 10, Füs.Rgt. 38)
22nd Infantry Brigade (Gren. Rgt. 11, Inf. Rgt. 51, Jäger Btn. 6)
Jäger zu Pferde Rgt. 11
11th Field Artillery Brigade (Field Artillery Rgts. 6 & 42)
1st Coy. Pioneer Btn. 6, Divisional Pontoon Train 11, Medical Coys. 1 & 3

12th Infantry Division (12 Btns., 4 MGKs, 4 Sqdns., 12 Batts., 2 Pi. Coys.)
24th Infantry Brigade (Inf. Rgts. 23 & 62)
78th Infantry Brigade (Inf. Rgts. 63 & 157)
Uhlan Rgt. 2
12th Field Artillery Brigade (Field Artillery Rgts. 21 & 57)
2nd & 3rd Coys. Pioneer Btn. 6, Divisional Pontoon Train 12, Medical Coy. 2

Corps Troops
II Btn. Foot Artillery Rgt. 6 (Hvy. Field Howitzers), Aviation Det. 13, Corps Pontoon Train 6, Telephone Det. 6, Pioneer Searchlight Sec. 6, Munition Columns and Train corresponded to II Army Corps.

VIII Army Corps

(15th & 16th Inf. Divs., 4 Heavy Batts., 1 Aviation Det.)
15th Infantry Division (12 Btns., 4 MGKs, 4 Sqdns., 12 Batts., 1 Pi. Coy.)
29th Infantry Brigade (Inf. Rgts. 25 & 161)
80th Infantry Brigade (Inf. Rgts. 65 & 160)
Cuir. Rgt. 8
15th Field Artillery Brigade (Field Artillery Rgts. 59 & 83)
1st Coy. Pioneer Btn. 8, Divisional Pontoon Train 15, Medical Coys. 1 & 3

16th Infantry Division (12 Btns., 4 MGKs, 4 Sqdns., 12 Batts., 2 Pi. Coys.)
30th Infantry Brigade (Inf. Rgts. 28 & 68)
31st Infantry Brigade (Inf. Rgts. 29 & 69)
Hussar Rgt. 7
16th Field Artillery Brigade (Field Artillery Rgts. 23 & 44)
2nd & 3rd Coys. Pioneer Btn. 8, Divisional Pontoon Train 16, Medical Coy. 2

Corps Troops
III Btn. Foot Artillery Rgt. 9 (Hvy. Field Howitzers), Aviation Det. 10, Corps Pontoon Train 8, Telephone Det. 8, Pioneer Searchlight Sec. 8, Munition   Columns and Train corresponded to II Army Corps.

XVIII Army Corps

(21st & 25th Inf. Divs., 4 Heavy Batts., 1 Aviation Det.)
21st Infantry Division (12 Btns., 4 MGKs, 4 Sqdns., 12 Batts., 1 Pi. Coy.)
41st Infantry Brigade (Inf. Rgts. 87 & 88)
42nd Infantry Brigade (Füs.Rgt. 80, Inf. Rgt. 81)
Uhlan Rgt. 6
21st Field Artillery Brigade (Field Artillery Rgts. 27 & 63)
1st Coy. Pioneer Btn. 21, Divisional Pontoon Train 21, Medical Coys. 1 & 3

25th Infantry Division (12 Btns., 4 MGKs, 4 Sqdns., 12 Batts., 2 Pi. Coys.)
    49th Infantry Brigade (Leib Guard Inf. Rgt. 115. Inf. Rgt. 116)
    50th Infantry Brigade (Inf. Leib Rgt. 117, Inf. Rgt. 118)
    Dragoon Rgt. 6
    25th Field Artillery Brigade (Field Artillery Rgts. 25 & 61)
    2nd & 3rd Coys. Pioneer Btn. 21, Divisional Pontoon Train 25, Medical
    Coy. 2
Corps Troops
    I Btn. Foot Artillery Rgt. 3 (Hvy. Field Howitzers), Aviation Det. 27,
    Corps Pontoon Train 18, Telephone Det. 18, Pioneer Searchlight Sec. 21,
    Munition Columns and Train corresponded to II Army Corps.

VIII Reserve Corps
(15th & 16th Reserve Divs.)
15th Reserve Division (9 Btns.[24], 2 MGKs[25], 3 Sqdns., 6 Batts., 1 Pi. Coy.)
    30th Reserve Infantry Brigade (Res. Inf. Rgts. 25 & 69)
    32nd Reserve Infantry Brigade (Res. Inf. Rgts. 17 & 30)
    Reserve Uhlan Rgt. 5
    Reserve Field Artillery Rgt. 15
    4th Coy. Pioneer Btn. 8, Reserve Divisional Pontoon Train 15, Reserve
    Medical Coy. 8
16th Reserve Division (12 Btns., 2 MGKs[26], 3 Sqdns., 6 Batts., 2 Pi. Coys.)
    29th Reserve Infantry Brigade (Res. Inf. Rgts. 29 & 65)
    31st Reserve Infantry Brigade (Res. Inf. Rgts. 28 & 68)
    Heavy Reserve Reiter Rgt. 2
    Reserve Field Artillery Rgt. 16
    1st and 2nd Reserve Coys. Pioneer Btn. 8, Reserve Medical Coy. 12
Corps Troops
    Reserve Telephone Det. 8, Munition Trains and Columns corresponded
    to III Reserve Corps.

XVIII Reserve Corps
(21st & 25th Reserve Divs.)
21st Reserve Division (12 Btns., 2 MGKs[27], 3 Sqdns., 6 Batts., 1 Pi. Coy.)
    41st Reserve Infantry Brigade (Res. Inf. Rgts. 80 & 87)
    42nd Reserve Infantry Brigade (Res. Inf. Rgts. 81 & 88)
    Reserve Dragoon Rgt. 7
    Reserve Field Artillery Rgt. 21
    4th Coy. Pioneer Btn. 11, Reserve Divisional Pontoon Train 21, Reserve
    Medical Coy. 17
25th Reserve Division (12 Btns., 3 MGKs[28], 3 Sqdns., 6 Batts., 2 Pi. Coys.)
    49th Reserve Infantry Brigade (Res. Inf. Rgts. 116 & 118)

24   Res. Inf. Rgts. 17, 30 and 69 only had 2 btns. each.
25   Res. Inf. Rgts. 17 and 69 lacked MGKs.
26   Res. Inf. Rgt. 28 and 65 lacked MGKs.
27   Res. Inf. Rgts. 81 and 87 lacked MGKs.
28   Res. Inf. Rgt. 118 lacked a MGK.

50th Reserve Infantry Brigade (Inf. Rgt. 168, Res. Inf. Rgt. 83)
Reserve Dragoon Rgt. 4
Reserve Field Artillery Rgt. 25
1st and 2nd Reserve Coys. Pioneer Btn. 11, Reserve Divisional Pontoon
Train 25, Reserve Medical Coy. 18
Corps Troops
Reserve Telephone Det. 18, Munition Trains and Columns corresponded
to III Reserve Corps.

49th Mixed Landwehr Brigade
(6 Btns., 3 Sqdns., 1 Batt.)
Landwehr Inf. Rgts. 116 & 118, 2nd and 3rd Landwehr Sqdns. XI A.K., 4th Landwehr
Sqdn. XVIII A.K., 2nd Landsturm Batt. XVIII A.K.

5th Army
(Army HQ Diedenhofen)

Lines of Communication Formations
L of C Insp. 5, CO Motorised Vehicle Troop 5, 5 L of C Motorised Vehicle Columns,
L of C Motorised Vehicle Park 5, L of C Aircraft Park 5, 6 L of C Munitions Col-
umns, 8 L of C Supply Parks, 5 Magazine Supply Parks furnished by 15 L of C
Train Sqdns, L of C Telephone Dept. VIII.

Army Troops
Armoured Train 6, Army Telephone Det. 5, Wireless Command 5, Heavy Wireless
Stations 15 & 24, Field Airship Det. 4, Aviation Det. 25, General of Foot Artillery 1, Foot Artillery Brigade Command 6, Staff Foot Artillery Rgts. 5, 6 & 12, I
& II Btns. Foot Artillery Rgt. 6 (with 4 Minenwerfer Batts.) with 2 I Munition
Column and 2 Munition Column Sections, II & III Btns. Foot Artillery Rgt. 12
(with 4 Minenwerfer Batts.) with 2 I Munition Column and 2 Munition Column Sections, Pioneer General 5, Pioneer Rgt. 20 with Pioneer Siege Train and
2 Park Coys., Pioneer Rgt. 29 with Pioneer Siege Train and Park Coy.

Supply Troops
Corresponding to those of the 1st Army.

V Army Corps
(9th & 10th Inf. Divs., 4 Heavy Batts., 1 Aviation Det.)
9th Infantry Division (13 Btns., 5 MGKs, 4 Sqdns., 12 Batts., 1 Pi. Coy.)
17th Infantry Brigade (Inf. Rgts. 19 & 58)
18th Infantry Brigade (Gren.Rgt. 7, Inf. Rgt. 154, Jäger Btn. 5)
Uhlan Rgt. 1
9th Field Artillery Brigade (Field Artillery Rgts. 5 & 41)
1st Coy. Pioneer Btn. 5, Divisional Pontoon Train 9, Medical Coys. 1 & 3
10th Infantry Division (12 Btns., 4 MGKs, 4 Sqdns., 12 Batts., 2 Pi. Coys.)
19th Infantry Brigade (Gren. Rgt. 6. Inf. Rgt. 46)
20th Infantry Brigade (Inf. Rgts. 47 & 50)
Jäger zu Pferde Rgt. 1
10th Field Artillery Brigade (Field Artillery Rgts. 20 & 56)

2nd & 3rd Coys. Pioneer Btn. 5, Divisional Pontoon Train 10, Medical Coy. 2

Corps Troops

I Btn. Foot Artillery Rgt. 5 (Hvy. Field Howitzers), Aviation Det. 19, Corps Pontoon Train 5, Telephone Det. 5, Pioneer Searchlight Sec. 5, Munition Columns and Train corresponded to II Army Corps.

XIII Army Corps

(26th & 27th Inf. Divs., 4 Heavy Batts., 1 Aviation Det.)

26th Infantry Division (12 Btns., 4 MGKs, 4 Sqdns., 12 Batts., 1 Pi. Coy.)

51st Infantry Brigade (Gren. Rgts. 119, Inf. Rgt. 125)

52nd Infantry Brigade (Inf. Rgt. 121, Füs. Rgt. 122)

Uhlan Rgt. 20

26th Field Artillery Brigade (Field Artillery Rgts. 29 & 65)

1st Coy. Pioneer Btn. 13, Divisional Pontoon Train 26, Medical Coys. 1 & 3

27th Infantry Division (12 Btns., 4 MGKs, 4 Sqdns., 12 Batts., 2 Pi. Coys.)

53rd Infantry Brigade (Gren. Rgt. 123, Inf. Rgt. 124)

54th Infantry Brigade (Inf. Rgts. 120 & 127)

Uhlan Rgt. 19

27th Field Artillery Brigade (Field Artillery Rgts. 13 & 49)

2nd & 3rd Coys. Pioneer Btn. 13, Divisional Pontoon Train 27, Medical Coy. 2

Corps Troops

I Btn. Foot Artillery Rgt. 13 (Hvy. Field Howitzers), Aviation Det. 4, Corps Pontoon Train 13, Telephone Det. 13, Pioneer Searchlight Sec. 13, Munition Columns and Train corresponded to II Army Corps.

XVI Army Corps

(33rd & 34th Inf. Divs., 4 Heavy Batts., 1 Aviation Det.)

33rd Infantry Division (12 Btns., 4 MGKs, 4 Sqdns., 12 Batts., 1 Pi. Coy.)

66th Infantry Brigade (Inf. Rgts. 98 & 130)

67th Infantry Brigade (Inf. Rgts. 135 & 144)

Jäger zu Pferde Rgt. 12

33rd Field Artillery Brigade (Field Artillery Rgts. 33 & 34)

1st Coy. Pioneer Btn. 16, Divisional Pontoon Train 33, Medical Coys. 1 & 3

34th Infantry Division (12 Btns., 4 MGKs, 4 Sqdns., 12 Batts., 2 Pi. Coys.)

68th Infantry Brigade (Inf. Rgt. 67, King's Inf. Rgt. 145)

86th Infantry Brigade (Inf. Rgts. 30 & 173)

Uhlan Rgt. 14

34th Field Artillery Brigade (Field Artillery Rgts. 69 & 70)

2nd & 3rd Coys. Pioneer Btn. 16, Divisional Pontoon Train 34, Medical Coy. 2

Corps Troops

I Btn. Foot Artillery Rgt. 10 (Hvy. Field Howitzers), Aviation Det. 2, Corps Pontoon Train 16, Telephone Det. 16, Pioneer Searchlight Sec. 16, Munition Columns and Train corresponded to II Army Corps.

V Reserve Corps

(9th & 10th Reserve Divs.)

9th Reserve Division (10 Btns., 3 MGKs[29], 3 Sqdns., 6 Batts., 1 Pi. Coy.)
  17th Reserve Infantry Brigade (Res. Inf. Rgts. 6 & 7)
  19th Reserve Infantry Brigade (Res. Inf. Rgts. 19, Res. Jäger Btn. 5)
  Reserve Dragoon Rgt. 3
  Reserve Field Artillery Rgt. 9
  4th Coy. Pioneer Btn. 5, Reserve Divisional Pontoon Train 9, Reserve
  Medical Coy. 19

10th Reserve Division (12 Btns., 4 MGKs, 3 Sqdns., 6 Batts., 2 Pi. Coys.)
  77th Infantry Brigade (Füs.Rgt. 37, Inf. Rgt. 155)
  18th Reserve Infantry Brigade (Res. Inf. Rgt. 37 & 46)
  Reserve Uhlan Rgt. 6
  Reserve Field Artillery Rgt. 10
  1st and 2nd Reserve Coys. Pioneer Btn. 5, Reserve Divisional Pontoon
  Train 10, Reserve Medical Coy. 5

Corps Troops
  Reserve Telephone Det. 5, Munition Trains and Columns corresponded
  to III Reserve Corps.

VI Reserve Corps

(11th & 12th Reserve Divs.)

11th Reserve Division (12 Btns., 4 MGKs, 3 Sqdns., 6 Batts., 1 Pi. Coy.)
  23rd Infantry Brigade (Inf. Rgts. 22 & 156)
  21st Reserve Infantry Brigade (Res. Inf. Rgts. 10 & 11)
  Reserve Hussar Rgt. 4
  Reserve Field Artillery Rgt. 11
  4th Coy. Pioneer Btn. 6, Reserve Divisional Pontoon Train 11 Reserve
  Medical Coy. 6

12th Reserve Division (11 Btns.[30], 4 MGKs[31], 3 Sqdns., 6 Batts., 2 Pi. Coys.)
  22nd Reserve Infantry Brigade (Res. Inf. Rgts. 23 & 38, Reserve Jäger Btn.
  6)
  23rd Reserve Infantry Brigade (Res. Inf. Rgt. 22 & 51)
  Reserve Uhlan Rgt. 4
  Reserve Field Artillery Rgt. 12
  1st and 2nd Reserve Coys. Pioneer Btn. 6, Reserve Medical Coy. 20

Corps Troops
  Reserve Telephone Det. 6, Munition Trains and Columns corresponded
  to III Reserve Corps.

13th Mixed Landwehr Brigade

(6 Btns., 1 Sqdn., 2 Batts.)

Landwehr Inf. Rgts. 26 & 27, Landwehr Sqdn. IV A.K., 1st & 2nd Landsturm Batts.
  IV A.K.

---

29 Res. Jäger Btn. 5 lacked a MGK.
30 Res. Inf. Rgts. 23 and 51 each only had 2 btns.
31 Res. Jäger Btn. 6 lacked a MGK.

Senior Landwehr Commander 2
(24 Btns., 4 Sqdns., 5 Batts.)
43rd Mixed Landwehr Brigade
(6 Btns., 1 Sqdn., 2 Batts.)
    Landwehr Inf. Rgts. 32 & 83, 1st Landwehr Sqdn. XI A.K., 1st & 2nd
    Landsturm Batts. XI A.K.
45th Mixed Landwehr Brigade
(6 Btns., 1 Sqdn., 1 Batt.)
    Landwehr Inf. Rgts. 100 & 102, Landwehr Sqdn. XII A.K., Landsturm
    Batt. XII A.K.
53rd Mixed Landwehr Brigade
(6 Btns., 1 Sqdn., 1 Batt.)
    Landwehr Inf. Rgts. 124 & 125, 3rd Landwehr Sqdn. XIII A.K.,
    Landsturm Batts. XIII A.K.
9th Bavarian Mixed Landwehr Brigade
(6 Btns., 1 Sqdn., 1 Batt.)
    Bavarian Landwehr Inf. Rgts. 6 & 7, 1st Landwehr Sqdn. III Bavarian
    A.K., 1st Landsturm Batt. III Bavarian A.K.

6th Army
(Army HQ St Avold)

Lines of Communication Formations
L of C Insp. 6, Bavarian CO of Motor Vehicle Troops 6, 5 Bavarian L of C Motorised
    Vehicle Columns, 3 Bavarian L of C Munition Motorised Vehicle Columns, Ba-
    varian L of C Motorised Vehicle Park 6, Bavarian L of C Aircraft Park 6, 6 Bavar-
    ian L of C Munition Columns, 11 L of C Supply Columns, 4 Magazine Supply
    Parks furnished by 12 L of C Train Sqdns, Bavarian L of C Telephone Dept.

Army Troops
Bavarian Railway Construction Coy. 2, Armoured Train 9, Bavarian Army Telephone
    Det. 6, Bavarian Wireless Command 6, Bavarian Heavy Wireless Stations 1 & 2,
    Bavarian Field Airship Det. 1, Aviation Det. 5, Bavarian Foot Artillery Brigade
    Command 1, Staff Bavarian Reserve Foot Artillery Rgt. 1 & Foot Artillery Rgt.
    18, II & III Btns. Foot Artillery Rgt. 18 (with 4 Minenwerfer Batts.) with 2 I
    Munition Column and 2 Munition Column Sections, II Btn. 3rd Bavarian Foot
    Artillery Rgt. (with 2 Minenwerfer Batts.) with I Munition Column and 1 Muni-
    tion Column Section, Heavy Coastal Mortar Battery 2, Steam Locomotive Park
    2, Short Naval Gun Battery 1 (42cm), Park Company III/Reserve Foot Artillery
    Rgt. 10, Park Coy. II/Reserve Foot Artillery Rgt. 14, Requisition Train Units 12-
    14, Pioneer General 6, Pioneer Rgt. 19 with Pioneer Siege Train and 2 Park
    Coys., Bavarian Pioneer Rgt. with Pioneer Siege Train and 2 Park Coys.

Supply Troops
Corresponding to those of the 1st Army.

XXI Army Corps
(31st & 42nd Inf. Divs., 4 Heavy Batts., 1 Aviation Det.)

31st Infantry Division (15 Btns., 5 MGKs, 4 Sqdns., 12 Batts., 1 Pi. Coy.)
    32nd Infantry Brigade (Inf. Rgts. 70 & 174)
    62nd Infantry Brigade (Inf. Rgts. 60, 137 & 166)
    Uhlan Rgt. 7
    31st Field Artillery Brigade (Field Artillery Rgts. 31 & 67)
    1st Coy. Pioneer Btn. 27, Divisional Pontoon Train 31, Medical Coy. 1
42nd Infantry Division (12 Btns., 4 MGKs, 4 Sqdns., 12 Batts., 2 Pi. Coys.)
    59th Infantry Brigade (Inf. Rgts. 97 & 138)
    65th Infantry Brigade (Inf. Rgts. 17 & 131)
    Dragoon Rgt. 7
    42nd Field Artillery Brigade (Field Artillery Rgts. 8 & 15)
    2nd & 3rd Coys. Pioneer Btn. 27, Divisional Pontoon Train 42, Medical
    Coys. 2   & 3
Corps Troops
    II Btn. Foot Artillery Rgt. 3 (Hvy. Field Howitzers), Aviation Det. 8,
    Corps Pontoon Train 21, Telephone Det. 21, Pioneer Searchlight Sec. 27,
    Munition Columns and Train corresponded to II Army Corps.

I Bavarian Army Corps

(1st & 2nd Bavarian Inf. Divs., 4 Heavy Batts., 1 Aviation Det.)
1st Bavarian Infantry Division (13 Btns., 4 MGKs[32], 4 Sqdns., 12 Batts., 2 Pi. Coys.)
    1st Bavarian Infantry Brigade (Inf. Leib Rgt. & 1st Inf. Rgt.)
    2nd Bavarian Infantry Brigade (2nd & 16th Inf. Rgts., 1st Jäger Btn.)
    8th Chevauleger Regt.
    1st Bavarian Field Artillery Brigade (1st & 7th Field Artillery Rgts.)
    1st & 3rd Coys. 1st Bavarian Pioneer Btn., Bavarian Divisional Pontoon
    Train 1, Bavarian Medical Coys. 1 & 3
2nd Bavarian Infantry Division (12 Btns., 4 MGKs, 4 Sqdns., 12 Batts., 1 Pi. Coy.)
    3rd Bavarian Infantry Brigade (3rd & 20th Inf. Rgts.)
    4th Bavarian Infantry Brigade (12th & 15th Inf. Rgts.)
    4th Chevauleger Rgt.
    2nd Bavarian Field Artillery Brigade (4th & 9th Field Artillery Rgts.)
    2nd Cos. 1st Bavarian Pioneer Btn., Bavarian Divisional Pontoon Train 2,
    Bavarian Medical Coy. 2
Corps Troops
    II Btn. 1st Bavarian Foot Artillery Rgt. (Hvy. Field Howitzers), Bavarian
    Aviation Det. 1, Bavarian Corps Pontoon Train 1, Bavarian Telephone
    Det. 1, Bavarian Pioneer Searchlight Sec. 1, Munition Columns and Train
    corresponded to II Army Corps.

II Bavarian Army Corps

(3rd & 4th Bavarian Inf. Divs., 4 Heavy Batts., 1 Aviation Det.)
3rd Bavarian Infantry Division (12 Btns., 4 MGKs, 4 Sqdns., 12 Batts., 2 Pi. Coys.)
    5th Bavarian Infantry Brigade (22nd & 23rd Inf. Rgts.)
    6th Bavarian Infantry Brigade (17th & 18th Inf. Rgts.)
    3rd Chevauleger Regt.

---

32   Bavarian 1st Jäger Btn. lacked a MGK.

3rd Bavarian Field Artillery Brigade (5th & 12th Field Artillery Rgts.)
1st & 3rd Coys. 2nd Bavarian Pioneer Btn., Bavarian Divisional Pontoon
Train 3, Bavarian Medical Coys. 1 & 3
4th Bavarian Infantry Division (13 Btns., 4 MGKs[33], 4 Sqdns., 12 Batts., 1 Pi. Coy.)
 7th Bavarian Infantry Brigade (5th & 9th Inf. Rgts., 2nd Jäger Btn.)
 5th Bavarian Reserve Infantry Brigade (Res. Inf. Rgts. 5 & 8)
 5th Chevauleger Rgt.
 4th Bavarian Field Artillery Brigade (2nd & 11th Field Artillery Rgts.)
 2nd Coy. 2nd Bavarian Pioneer Btn., Bavarian Divisional Pontoon Train
 4, Bavarian Medical Coy. 2
Corps Troops
 I Btn. 1st Bavarian Foot Artillery Rgt. (Hvy. Field Howitzers), Bavarian
 Aviation Det. 2, Bavarian Corps Pontoon Train 2, Bavarian Telephone
 Det. 2, Bavarian Pioneer Searchlight Sec. 2, Munition Columns and Train
 corresponded to II Army Corps.

III Bavarian Army Corps
(5th & 6th Bavarian Inf. Divs., 4 Heavy Batts., 1 Aviation Det.)
5th Bavarian Infantry Division (13 Btns., 4 MGKs[34], 4 Sqdns., 12 Batts., 2 Pi. Coys.)
 9th Bavarian Infantry Brigade (14th & 21st Inf. Rgts., Reserve Jäger Btn.
 2)
 10th Bavarian Infantry Brigade (7th & 19th Inf. Rgts.)
 7th Chevauleger Regt.
 5th Bavarian Field Artillery Brigade (6th & 10th Field Artillery Rgts.)
 1st & 3rd Coys. 3rd Bavarian Pioneer Btn., Bavarian Divisional Pontoon
 Train 5, Bavarian Medical Coys. 1 & 3
6th Bavarian Infantry Division (12 Btns., 4 MGKs, 4 Sqdns., 12 Batts., 1 Pi. Coy.)
 11th Bavarian Infantry Brigade (10th & 13th Inf. Rgts.)
 12th Bavarian Reserve Infantry Brigade (6th & 11th Inf. Rgts.)
 2nd Chevauleger Rgt.
 6th Bavarian Field Artillery Brigade (3rd & 8th Field Artillery Rgts.)
 2nd Coy. 3rd Bavarian Pioneer Btn., Bavarian Divisional Pontoon Train
 6, Bavarian Medical Coy. 2
Corps Troops
 I Btn. 3rd Bavarian Foot Artillery Rgt. (Hvy. Field Howitzers), Bavarian
 Aviation Det. 3, Bavarian Corps Pontoon Train 3, Bavarian Telephone
 Det. 3, Bavarian Pioneer Searchlight Sec. 3, Munition Columns and Train
 corresponded to II Army Corps.

I Bavarian Reserve Corps
(1st & 5th Bavarian Reserve Divs.)
1st Bavarian Reserve Division (12 Btns., 3 MGKs[35], 3 Sqdns., 6 Batts., 1 Pi. Coy.)
 1st Bavarian Reserve Infantry Brigade (Res. Inf. Rgts. 1 & 2)
 2nd Bavarian Reserve Infantry Brigade (Res. Inf. Rgts. 3 & 12)

33 Bavarian 2nd Jäger Btn. lacked a MGK.
34 Bavarian Reserve Jäger Btn. 2 lacked a MGK.
35 Bavarian Res. Inf. Rgt. 12 lacked a MGK.

Bavarian Reserve Cavalry Rgt. 1
Bavarian Reserve Field Artillery Rgt. 1
1st Reserve Coy. 1st Bavarian Pioneer Btn., Bavarian Reserve Divisional
Pontoon Train 1, Bavarian Reserve Medical Coy. 1
5th Bavarian Reserve Division (13 Btns., 2 MGKs[36], 3 Sqdns., 6 Batts., 2 Pi. Coys.)
    9th Bavarian Reserve Infantry Brigade (Res. Inf. Rgts. 6 & 7)
    11th Bavarian Reserve Infantry Brigade (Res. Inf. Rgt. 10 & 13, Reserve
    Jäger Btn. 1)
    Bavarian Reserve Cavalry Rgt. 5
    Bavarian Reserve Field Artillery Rgt. 5
    4th Coy. and 1st Reserve Cos. 2nd Bavarian Pioneer Btn., Bavarian Re-
    serve Divisional Pontoon Train 5, Bavarian Reserve Medical Coy. 5
Corps Troops
    Bavarian Reserve Telephone Det. 1, Munition Trains and Columns corre-
    sponded to III Reserve Corps.

5th Bavarian Mixed Landwehr Brigade
(6 Btns., 1 Sqdn., 1 Batt.)
Bavarian Landwehr Inf. Rgts. 4 & 5, 1st Landwehr Sqdn. II Bavarian A.K., 1st
Landsturm Batt. II Bavarian A.K.

7th Army
(Army HQ Strassburg i. Elf)

Lines of Communication Formations
L of C Insp. 7, CO Motorised Vehicle Troop 7, 3 L of C Motorised Vehicle Columns,
    L of C Motorised Vehicle Park 7, L of C Aircraft Park 7, 4 L of C Munitions Col-
    umns, 5 L of C Supply Columns, 4 Magazine Supply Parks furnished by 12 L of
    C Train Sqdns, L of C Telephone Dept. XIV.

Army Troops
Armoured Trains 5, 7 & 8, Army Telephone Det. 7, Wireless Command 7, Heavy
    Wireless Stations 10 & 16, Field Airship Det. 6, Aviation Det. 26, Staff Foot Ar-
    tillery Rgt. 14, Pioneer General 7, Heavy Rhine Pontoon Train.

Supply Troops
Corresponding to those of the 1st Army.

XIV Army Corps
(28th & 29th Inf. Divs., 4 Heavy Batts., 1 Aviation Det.)
28th Infantry Division (12 Btns., 4 MGKs, 4 Sqdns., 12 Batts., 2 Pi. Coys.)
    55th Infantry Brigade (Leib Gren. Rgt. 109, Gren. Rgt. 110)
    56th Infantry Brigade (Füs Rgt. 40, Inf. Rgt. 111)
    Jäger zu Pferde Rgt. 5
    28th Field Artillery Brigade (Field Artillery Rgts. 14 & 50)
    2nd & 3rd Coys. Pioneer Btn. 14, Divisional Pontoon Train 28, Medical
    Coy. 2

---

36 Bavarian Res. Inf. Rgts. 7 and 13 as well as Bavarian Jäger Btn. 1 lacked MGKs.

29th Infantry Division (18 Btns., 6 MGKs, 4 Sqdns., 12 Batts., 1 Pi. Coy.)
    57th Infantry Brigade (Inf. Rgts. 113 & 114)
    58th Infantry Brigade (Inf. Rgts. 112 & 142)
    84th Infantry Brigade (Inf. Rgts. 169 & 170)
    Dragoon Rgt. 22
    29th Field Artillery Brigade (Field Artillery Rgts. 30 & 76)
    1st Coy. Pioneer Btn. 14, Divisional Pontoon Train 29, Medical Coys. 1
    & 3
Corps Troops
    II Btn. Foot Artillery Rgt. 14 (Hvy. Field Howitzers), Aviation Det. 20,
    CorpsPontoon Train 14, Telephone Det. 14, Pioneer Searchlight Sec. 14,
    Munition Columns and Train corresponded to II Army Corps.

XV Army Corps
(30th & 39th Inf. Divs., 4 Heavy Batts., 1 Aviation Det.)
30th Infantry Division (12 Btns., 4 MGKs, 4 Sqdns., 12 Batts., 1 Pi. Coy.)
    60th Infantry Brigade (Inf. Rgts. 99 & 143)
    85th Infantry Brigade (Inf. Rgts. 105 & 136)
    Jäger zu Pferde Rgt. 3
    30th Field Artillery Brigade (Field Artillery Rgts. 51 & 84)
    1st Coy. Pioneer Btn. 15, Divisional Pontoon Train 30, Medical Coys. 1
    & 3
39th Infantry Division (14 Btns., 6 MGKs, 4 Sqdns., 12 Batts., 2 Pi. Coys.)
    61st Infantry Brigade (Inf. Rgts. 126 & 132, Jäger Btn. 8)
    82nd Infantry Brigade (Inf. Rgts. 171 & 172, Jäger Btn. 14)
    Dragoon Rgt. 14
    39th Field Artillery Brigade (Field Artillery Rgts. 66 & 80)
    2nd & 3rd Coys. Pioneer Btn. 15, Divisional Pontoon Train 39, Medical
    Coy. 2
Corps Troops
    II Btn. Foot Artillery Rgt. 10 (Hvy. Field Howitzers), Aviation Det. 3,
    Corps Pontoon Train 15, Telephone Det. 15, Pioneer Searchlight Sec. 15,
    Munition Columns and Train corresponded to II Army Corps.

XIV Reserve Corps
(26th & 28th Reserve Divs.)
26th Reserve Division (12 Btns., 4 MGKs, 3 Sqdns., 9 Batts.[37], 1 Pi. Coy.)
    51st Reserve Infantry Brigade (Inf. Rgt. 180, Res. Inf. Rgt. 121)
    52nd Reserve Infantry Brigade (Res. Inf. Rgts. 119 & 120)
    Württ. Reserve Dragoon Rgt.
    Reserve Field Artillery Rgt. 26
    4th Coy. Pioneer Btn. 13, Reserve Divisional Pontoon Train 26, Württ.
    Reserve Medical Coy.
28th Reserve Division (14 Btns., 3 MGKs[38], 3 Sqdns., 6 Batts., 2 Pi. Coys.)

---

37   Res. Field Art. Rgt. 26 possessed 3 btns.
38   Res. Inf. Rgt. 40 and Res. Jäger Btns. 8 and 14 lacked MGKs.

55th Reserve Infantry Brigade (Res. Inf. Rgts. 40 & 109, Reserve Jäger Btn. 8)

56th Reserve Infantry Brigade (Res. Inf. Rgt. 110 & 111, Reserve Jäger Btn. 14)

Reserve Dragoon Rgt. 8

Reserve Field Artillery Rgt. 29

1st and 2nd Reserve Coys. Pioneer Btn. 13, Reserve Divisional Pontoon Train 28, Reserve Medical Coy. 14

Corps Troops

Reserve Telephone Det. 14, Munition Trains and Columns corresponded to III Reserve Corps.

60th Mixed Landwehr Brigade

(5 Btns.[39], 1 Sqdn.)

Landwehr Inf. Rgts. 60 & 99, 1st Landwehr Sqdn. XIV A.K.

Upper Rhine Fortifications

55th Mixed Landwehr Brigade

(6 Btns., 2 Sqdns., 4 Batts.)

Landwehr Inf. Rgts. 40 & 109, 1st and 2nd Landwehr Sqdn. XIII A.K., Landwehr Field Art. Btn. XIV A.K., Reserve Field Art. Btn. 67

Reinforced Landwehr Inf. Rgt. 110

(3 Btns., 1 Sqdn., 3 Batts.)

Landwehr Inf. Rgt. 110, 2nd Landwehr Sqdn. XIV A.K., Landwehr Battery XIII A.K., Reserve Field Art. Btn. 31

1st Bavarian Mixed Landwehr Brigade

(6 Btns., 1 Sqdn., 1 Batt., 1 Pi. Coy.)

Bavarian Landwehr Inf. Rgts. 1 & 2, 1st Landwehr Sqdn. I Bavarian A.K., 1st Landsturm Batt. I Bavarian A.K., 1st Landsturm Pioneer Coy. I Bavarian A.K.

2nd Bavarian Mixed Landwehr Brigade

(6 Btns., 1 Sqdn., 1 Batt., 1 Pi. Coy.)

Bavarian Landwehr Inf. Rgts. 3 & 12, 2nd Landwehr Sqdn. I Bavarian A.K., 2nd Landsturm Batt. I Bavarian A.K., 2nd Landsturm Pioneer Coy. I Bavarian A.K.

1 Batt. I Btn. Foot Art. Rgt. 16 (Hvy. Field Howitzers).

8th Army
(Army HQ Bartenstein)

Lines of Communication Formations

L of C Insp. 8, CO Motorised Vehicle Troop 8, L of C Motorised Vehicle Park 8, L of C Aircraft Park 8, 7 L of C Munitions Columns, 12 L of C Supply Columns, 3 Magazine Supply Parks furnished by 8 L of C Train Sqdns, L of C Telephone Dept. V.

---

39   Ldw. Inf. Rgt. 60 only had 2 btns.

Army Troops
Army Telephone Det. 8, Wireless Command 8, Heavy Wireless Stations 7 & 8, Field Airship Det. 8, Aviation Det. 16, Airships Königsberg, Allenstein & Thorn, Staff Foot Artillery Rgt. 15, Pioneer General 8.

Supply Troops
Corresponding to those of the 1st Army.

I Army Corps
(1st & 2nd Inf. Divs., 4 Heavy Batts., 1 Aviation Det.)
1st Infantry Division (12 Btns., 4 MGKs, 4 Sqdns., 12 Batts., 1 Pi. Coy.)
    1st Infantry Brigade (Gren. Rgt. 1, Inf. Rgt. 41)
    2nd Infantry Brigade (Gren. Rgt. 3, Inf. Rgt. 43)
    Uhlan Rgt. 8
    1st Field Artillery Brigade (Field Artillery Rgts. 16 & 52)
    1st Coy. Pioneer Btn. 1, Divisional Pontoon Train 1, Medical Coys. 1 & 3
2nd Infantry Division (12 Btns., 4 MGKs, 4 Sqdns., 12 Batts., 2 Pi. Coys.)
    3rd Infantry Brigade (Gren. Rgt. 4, Inf. Rgt. 44)
    4th Infantry Brigade (Füs.Rgt. 33, Inf. Rgt. 45)
    Jäger zu Pferde Rgt. 10
    2nd Field Artillery Brigade (Field Artillery Rgts. 1 & 37)
    2nd & 3rd Coys. Pioneer Btn. 1, Divisional Pontoon Train 2, Medical Coy. 2
Corps Troops
    I Btn. Foot Artillery Rgt. 1 (Hvy. Field Howitzers), Aviation Det. 14, Corps Pontoon Train 1, Telephone Det. 1, Pioneer Searchlight Sec. 7, Munition Columns and Train corresponded to II Army Corps.

XVII Army Corps
(35th & 36th Inf. Divs., 4 Heavy Batts., 1 Aviation Det.)
35th Infantry Division (13 Btns., 5 MGKs, 4 Sqdns., 12 Batts., 1 Pi. Coy.)
    70th Infantry Brigade (Inf. Rgts. 21 & 61)
    87th Infantry Brigade (Inf. Rgts. 141 & 176, Jäger Btn. 2)
    Jäger zu Pferde Rgt. 4
    35th Field Artillery Brigade (Field Artillery Rgts. 71 & 81)
    1st Coy. Pioneer Btn. 17, Divisional Pontoon Train 36, Medical Coy. 2
36th Infantry Division (12 Btns., 4 MGKs, 4 Sqdns., 12 Batts., 2 Pi. Coys.)
    69th Infantry Brigade (Inf. Rgts. 129 & 175)
    71st Infantry Brigade (Gren. Rgt. 5, Inf. Rgt. 128)
    Hussar Rgt. 5
    36th Field Artillery Brigade (Field Artillery Rgts. 36 & 72)
    2nd & 3rd Coys. Pioneer Btn. 17, Divisional Pontoon Train 36, Medical Coy. 2
Corps Troops
    I Btn. Foot Artillery Rgt. 11 (Hvy. Field Howitzers), Aviation Det. 17, Corps Pontoon Train 17, Telephone Det. 17, Pioneer Searchlight Sec. 17, Munition Columns and Train corresponded to II Army Corps.

XX Army Corps
(37th & 41st Inf. Divs., 4 Heavy Batts., 1 Aviation Det.)
37th Infantry Division (13 Btns., 5 MGKs, 4 Sqdns., 12 Batts., 1 Pi. Coy.)
    73rd Infantry Brigade (Inf. Rgts. 147 & 151, Jäger Btn. 1)
    75th Infantry Brigade (Inf. Rgts. 146 & 150)
    Dragoon Rgt. 11
    37th Field Artillery Brigade (Field Artillery Rgts. 73 & 82)
    1st Coy. Pioneer Btn. 26, Divisional Pontoon Train 37, Medical Coy. 1
41st Infantry Division (12 Btns., 4 MGKs, 4 Sqdns., 12 Batts., 2 Pi. Coys.)
    72nd Infantry Brigade (Inf. Rgts. 18 & 59)
    74th Infantry Brigade (Inf. Rgts. 148 & 152)
    Dragoon Rgt. 10
    41st Field Artillery Brigade (Field Artillery Rgts. 35 & 79)
    2nd & 3rd Coys. Pioneer Btn. 26, Divisional Pontoon Train 41, Medical Coys. 2 & 3
Corps Troops
    II Btn. Foot Artillery Rgt. 5 (Hvy. Field Howitzers), Aviation Det. 15, Corps Pontoon Train 20, Telephone Det. 20, Pioneer Searchlight Sec. 26, Munition Columns and Train corresponded to II Army Corps.

1st Cavalry Division
(24 Sqdns, 3 Batts., 1 MG Det.)
1st Cavalry Brigade (Cuir. Rgt. 3, Dragoon Rgt. 1)
2nd Cavalry Brigade (Uhlan Rgt 12, Jäger zu Pferde Rgt. 9)
41st Cavalry Brigade (Cuir. Rgts. 5, Uhlan Rgt. 4)
Divisional troops (Horse Artillery Btn. from Field Artillery Rgt. 1, MG Det. 5, Pioneer Btn., Signals Det. with Heavy Wireless Station 17 and Light Wireless Stations 7 & 14, Cavalry Motorised Vehicle Column 1)

I Reserve Corps
(1st & 36th Reserve Divs.)
1st Reserve Division (13 Btns., 7 MGKs[40], 3 Sqdns., 6 Batts., 1 Pi. Coy.)
    1st Reserve Infantry Brigade (Res. Inf. Rgts. 1 & 3)
    72nd Reserve Infantry Brigade (Res. Inf. Rgts. 18 & 59, Res. Jäger Btn. 1)
    Reserve Uhlan Rgt. 1
    Reserve Field Artillery Rgt. 1
    4th Coy. Pioneer Btn. 2, Reserve Divisional Pontoon Train 1, Reserve Medical Coy. 1
36th Reserve Division (13 Btns., 4 MGKs[41], 3 Sqdns., 6 Batts., 1 Pi. Coy.)
    69th Reserve Infantry Brigade (Res. Inf. Rgts. 21 & 61, Reserve Jäger Btn. 2)
    70th Reserve Infantry Brigade (Inf. Rgt. 54, Res. Inf. Rgt. 5)
    Reserve Hussar Rgt. 1
    Reserve Field Artillery Rgt. 36

40 Res. Inf. Rgts. 1, 3 & 18 each with 2 MGKs, Res. Jäger Btn. 1 lacked a MGK.
41 Res. Jäger Btn. 2 lacked a MGK.

1st Reserve Coy. Pioneer Btn. 2, Reserve Divisional Pontoon Train 36, Reserve Medical Coy. 15

Corps Troops

Reserve Telephone Det. 1, Munition Trains and Columns corresponded to III Reserve Corps.

3rd Reserve Division
(12 Btns., 4 MGKs, 3 Sqdns., 6 Batts., 1 Pi. Coy.)

5th Reserve Infantry Brigade (Res. Inf. Rgts. 2 & 9)
6th Reserve Infantry Brigade (Res. Inf. Rgts. 34 & 49)
Reserve Dragoon Rgt. 5
Reserve Field Artillery Rgt. 3
2nd Reserve Coy. Pioneer Btn. 2, Reserve Divisional Pontoon Train 2, ½ Reserve Tel. Det. 2, Reserve Medical Coy. 2, Reserve Munition Column Section 3 (Reserve Inf. Munition Columns 7 & 8, Reserve Art. Munition Columns 10 & 45), Reserve Train Sec. 3 (Reserve Field Hospitals 14-16, Reserve Tel. Columns 2, 4 & 5), Reserve Bakery Column 4

Landwehr Corps (Senior Landwehr Commanders 3 & 4)
Senior Landwehr Commander 3 (12 Btns., 3 Sqdns., 2 Batts., 1 Pi. Coy.)

17th Landwehr Infantry Brigade (Landwehr Inf. Rgts. 6 & 7)
18th Landwehr Infantry Brigade (Landwehr Inf. Rgts. 37 & 46)
Landwehr Cavalry Rgt. Command 1 (1st, 2nd & 3rd Landwehr Sqdns., V A.K.)
1st & 2nd Landwehr Batts. V A.K., Reserve Coy. Pioneer Btn. 5, Landwehr Divisional Pontoon Train 1, Reserve Tel. Sec.

Senior Landwehr Commander 4 (12 Btns., 7 Sqdns., 2 Batts., 1 Pi. Coy.)

22nd Landwehr Infantry Brigade (Landwehr Inf. Rgts. 11 & 51)
23rd Landwehr Infantry Brigade (Landwehr Inf. Rgts. 22 & 23)
Reserve Cavalry Rgt.
Landwehr Cavalry Rgt. Command 2 (1st, 2nd & 3rd Landwehr Sqdns., VI A.K.)
1st & 2nd Landwehr Batts. VI A.K., Reserve Coy. Pioneer Btn. 6, Landwehr Divisional Pontoon Train 2, Reserve Tel. Sec.

Corps Troops

Landwehr Munition Column Section (2 Inf. & 2. Art. Munition Columns), 4 Landwehr Tel. Columns, 2 L of C Motor Vehicle Columns, 2 Landwehr Bakery Columns, 2 Magazine Supply Parks supplied through 4 L of C Train Sqdns.

2nd Mixed Landwehr Brigade
(5 Btns.[42], 2 Sqdns., 2 Batts.)
Landwehr Inf. Rgts. 4 & 33, 2nd & 3rd Landwehr Sqdns. I A.K., Landwehr Field Artillery Btn. I A.K.

6th Mixed Landwehr Brigade
(6 Btns., 3 Sqdns., 2 Batts.)

42 Landwehr Inf. Rgt. 4 possessed only 2 btns.

Landwehr Inf. Rgts. 34 & 49, 1st-3rd Landwehr Sqdns. II A.K., 1st & 2nd Landsturm Field Artillery Batts. I A.K.

70th Mixed Landwehr Brigade
(6 Btns., 5 Sqdns., 2 Batts.)
Landwehr Inf. Rgts. 5 & 18, Insp. of Reserve Sqdns. XVII A.K. (1st-3rd Landwehr Sqdns. XX A.K., 2nd & 3rd Landwehr Sqdns. XVII A.K.), 1st & 2nd Landsturm Batts. XVII A.K.

Army of the North

Lines of Communication Formations
Field Police Sec. 2, Hospital Det. 2, L of C Auxiliary Bakery Column 2, Mobile L of C Cmdts 5-9, 2 Magazine Supply Parks.

Supply Troops
Infantry Munition Section 8, Motorised Field Munition Section 17, Foot Artillery Munition Section 1, Equipment & Explosives Supply Unit 3, Gas Unit 3.

IX Reserve Corps
(17th & 18th Reserve Divs., 4 Heavy Batts., 1 Field Airship Det.)
17th Reserve Division (12 Btns., 3 MGKs[43], 3 Sqdns., 6 Batts., 1 Pi. Coy.)
    81st Infantry Brigade (Inf. Rgts. 162 & 163)
    33rd Reserve Infantry Brigade (Res. Inf. Rgts. 75 & 76)
    Reserve Hussar Rgt. 6
    Reserve Field Artillery Rgt. 17
    4th Coy. Pioneer Btn. 9, Reserve Divisional Pontoon Train 17, Reserve Medical Coy. 9
18th Reserve Division (13 Btns., 2 MGKs[44], 3 Sqdns., 6 Batts., 2 Pi. Coys.)
    34th Reserve Infantry Brigade (Res. Inf. Rgts. 31 & 90)
    35th Reserve Infantry Brigade (Res. Inf. Rgts. 84 & 86, Res. Jäger Btn. 9)
    Reserve Hussar Rgt. 7
    Reserve Field Artillery Rgt. 18
    1st & 2nd Reserve Coy. Pioneer Btn. 9, Reserve Medical Coy. 13
Corps Troops
    II Btn. Guard Foot Artillery Rgt. (10cm guns) with Park Coy., Pioneer Rgt. 31[45], Reserve Telephone Det. 9, Field Airship Det. 5, Munition Trains and Columns corresponded to III Reserve Corps.

Senior Landwehr Commander 1
(24 Btns., 6 Sqdns., 4 Batts.)
33rd Mixed Landwehr Brigade (6 Btns., 2 Sqdns., 1 Batt.)
    Landwehr Inf. Rgts. 75 & 76, 1st Landwehr Sqdn. IX A.K., 2nd Landwehr Sqdn. Guard Corps, 1st Landwehr Batt. IX A.K.

---

43 Res. Inf. Rgt. 76 lacked a MGK.
44 Res. Inf. Rgts. 84 & 90 as well as Res. Jäger Btn. 9 lacked MGKs.
45 Formed from: II Guard Pi. Btl. (1 & 4th Res. Coys.), & II Pi. Btl. 28 (4th Coy. Pi. Btl. 28 & 2nd Res. Coy. Guard Pioneer Btl.).

34th Mixed Landwehr Brigade (6 Btns., 2 Sqdns., 1 Batt.)
  Landwehr Inf. Rgts. 31 & 84, 2nd Landwehr Sqdn. IX A.K., 3rd
  Landwehr Sqdn. Guard Corps, 2nd Landwehr Batt. IX A.K.
37th Mixed Landwehr Brigade (6 Btns., 1 Sqdns., 2 Batts.)
  Landwehr Inf. Rgts. 73 & 74, 2nd Landwehr Sqdn. X A.K., II Landwehr
  Field Artillery Btn. X A.K.
38th Mixed Landwehr Brigade (6 Btns., 1 Sqdn.)
  Landwehr Inf. Rgts. 77 & 78, 3rd Landwehr Sqdn. X A.K.

Coastal Protection
(3 Btns.)
IV Btns. of Landwehr Inf. Rgts. 75 & 76 and V/Landwehr Inf. Rgt. 76

North Sea Islands
(5 Btns., 9 Hvy. Batts., 2 Pi. Coys.)
Borkum: Res. Inf. Rgt. 79[46], II Btn. Foot Art. Rgt. 2 (4 Batts. Heavy Field Howitzers),
  1 Reserve Batt. Foot Art. Rgt. 2, 1st Landwehr Pi. Coy. X A.K.
Sylt: Landwehr Inf. Rgt. 85[47], 1 Batt. from I Btn. Foot Art. Rgt. 2, 2nd Reserve Batt.
  Foot Art. Rgt. 2, 1st Landwehr Pi. Coy. IX A.K.
Pellworm: III/Landwehr Inf. Rgt. 85, 1 Batt. from I Btn. Foot Art. Rgt. 2, 3rd Reserve
  Batt. Foot Art. Rgt. 2.

Central Reserves & Border Fortresses

30th Reserve Division (Strassburg)
(17 Btns.[48], 2 MG Dets., 3 Sqdns., 8 Field Artillery Batts., 1 Pi. Coy.)
3rd Bavarian Reserve Infantry Brigade (Res. Inf. Rgts. 4 & 15)
60th Reserve Infantry Brigade (Res. Inf. Rgts. 60 & 99)
10th Bavarian Reserve Infantry Brigade (Res. Inf. Rgts. 11 & 14)
Fortress MG Det. 2, Reserve MG Det. 3, Reserve Hussar Rgt. 9, Field Artillery Ersatz
  Btns. 15, 51, 80 & 84, 2nd Reserve Coy. of Pi. Btn. 15.

33rd Reserve Division (Metz)
(16 Btns.[49], 2 Sqdns.[50], 8 Field Artillery Batts., 8 Heavy Artillery Batts., 1 Pi. Coy.)
8th Bavarian Infantry Brigade (4th & 8th Inf. Rgts.)
66th Reserve Infantry Brigade (Res. Inf. Rgts. 67 & 130)
Res. Inf. Rgt. Metz., Reserve Hussar Rgt. 2, Field Artillery Ersatz Btns. 33, 34, 69 &
  70, I & II Btns. Bavarian Reserve Foot Artillery Rgt. 2, 4th Coy. of Pi. Btn. 22.

35th Reserve Division (Thorn)
(12 Btns., 5 MGKs, 3 Sqdns., 4 Field Artillery Batts., 4 Heavy Artillery Batts., 1 Pi.
  Coy.)
5th Landwehr Infantry Brigade (Landwehr Inf. Rgts. 2 & 9)

46 Without its III Btn. or MGK.
47 Without its III Btn. (on Pellworm!).
48 Bavarian Res. Inf. Rgt. 11 only had 2 btns.
49 Res. Inf. Rgt. 130 possessed 4 btns.
50 Reserve Hussar Rgt. 2 lacked its 2nd Sqdn.

20th Landwehr Infantry Brigade (Landwehr Inf. Rgts. 19 & 107)
Reserve MG Det. 4, Fortress MG Dets. 1-4, Heavy Reserve Reiter Rgt. 3, Field Artillery Ersatz Btns. 35 & 81, ¾ I Btn. Reserve Foot Art. Rgt. 11, 4th Batt. Reserve Foot Art. Rgt. 15 (10cm guns), 1st Reserve Coy. of Pi. Btn. 17.

Königsberg
(11 Btns.[51], 3 MGKs, 6 Sqdns., 6 Field Art. Batts., 3 Heavy Art. Batts., 1 Pi.Coy.)
Ersatz Infantry Brigade Königsberg (Ersatz Inf. Rgts. 1 & 2)
9th Landwehr Infantry Brigade (Landwehr Inf. Rgts. 24 & 48)
3 Ersatz MGKs. Reserve Dragoon Rgt. 1, Ersatz Cavalry Rgt. I A.K., Ersatz Field Artillery Rgt. (Ersatz Foot Artillery Btns. 1, 37 & 52), ½ II Btn. Reserve Foot Artillery Rgt. 1, 1 Batt. Reserve Foot Art. Rgt. 4 (10cm guns), 4th Coy. Pioneer Btn. 1.

Posen
(9 Btns., 3 MG Dets., 1 Sqdn., 4 Field Art. Batts., 4 Heavy Art. Batts., 2 Pi. Coys.)
19th Landwehr Infantry Brigade (Landwehr Inf. Rgts. 47, 72 & 133)
Reserve MG Det. 5, Fortress MG Dets. 1 & 2, Ersatz Sqdn. Jäger zu Pferde Rgt. 1, Field Artillery Ersatz Btns. 17 & 56, II Btn. Reserve Foot Art. Rgt. 6, 2 Reserve Coys. of Pi. Btn. 1, 2nd Reserve Coys. of Pi. Btn. 26.

Graudenz
(6 Btns., 2 MG Dets., 1 Sqdn., 3 Field Art. Batts., 1 Heavy Art. Batt., 1 Pi. Coy., 1 Fortress Aviation Det.)
Provisional 69th Infantry Brigade (Ersatz Btns. from Gren. Rgt. 5, Füs.Rgt. 34, Inf. Rgts. 59, 129, 141 & 175)
Fortress MG Dets. 3 & 4, Ersatz Sqdn. Cuir. Rgt. 5, Ersatz Btn. Field Art. Btns. 72/73, 1st Batt. Reserve Foot Art. Rgt. 17, 1st Reserve Coy. Pi. Btl. 26, Fortress Aviation Det. 6.

Mobile Ersatz Formations

Guard Ersatz Division
(15 Btns., 6 MG Secs., 3 Cavalry Ersatz Secs., 12 Field Artillery Ersatz Batts., 2 Pioneer Ersatz Coys., 3 Train Ersatz Secs.)
1st Mixed Guard Ersatz Brigade, 5th & 17th Mixed Ersatz Brigades

4th Ersatz Division
(13/5/3/12/3/3)
9th, 13th & 33rd Mixed Ersatz Brigades

8th Ersatz Division
(14/10/3/12/1/3)
20th, 41st & 51st Mixed Ersatz Brigades

10th Ersatz Division
(13/6/3/12/1/3)
25th, 37th & 43rd Mixed Ersatz Brigades

51   Ersatz Inf. Rgt. 2 had only 2 btns.

19th Ersatz Division
(13/6/3/12/2/3)
21st, 45th & 47th Mixed Ersatz Brigades

Bavarian Ersatz Division
(12/6/3/12/2/3)
1st, 5th & 9th Bavarian Mixed Ersatz Brigades

55th Mixed Ersatz Brigade
(6/4/1/4/0/1)

Appendix II

18th Army, 21 March 1918

Army Reserves

1st Guard Infantry Division (OHL Reserve)
7th Reserve Division
10th Reserve Division
23rd Infantry Division

Army Troops

A.

MG School 18, MG Workshop 18
Horse Inspectorate 8 (= Staff, Hussar Regt. 5)

B.

Arko 86 (as CO of the entire artillery within the Army corresponded to an Artillery
    General)
Field Artillery Recruit Depot

C.

Following Foot Artillery Regiment Battalions, each of 3 Batteries:
    IV/Foot Art. Rgt. 1, II/Bavarian Reserve Foot Art. Rgt. I/Foot Art. Rgt. 9,
    IV/Reserve Foot Art. Rgt. 9, III/Reserve Foot Art. Rgt. 10, II/Reserve Foot
    Art. Rgt. 14, II/Reserve Foot Art. Rgt. 17, III/Foot Art. Rgt. 27
Foot Artillery Battalions, each of 3 Batteries:
    Bavarian Foot Art. Btn. 23, Bavarian Foot Art. Btn. 28, Foot Art. Btn. 33,
    Foot Art. Btn. 73, Foot Art. Btn. 101, Foot Art. Btn. 102
Foot Artillery Battalions, each of 6 Batteries:
    Bavarian Foot Art. Btn. 15, Landwehr Foot Art. Btn. 40, Landwehr Foot
    Art. Btn. 61
Foot Artillery Batteries:
    6th Coy./Foot Artillery Rgt. 4, in addition: Nos. 3, 9, 19, 46, 47, 686, 806,
    831, 836, 845, 851, 868, 1016
Heavy Artillery:
    Staff IV Btn. Reserve Foot Art. Rgt. 9, Bavarian Foot Art. Btn. 29 (3
    Batts.), in addition Foot Art. Btns. 4, 40, 551, 629, 717, 797, 1001, 1013,
    1017
Austro-Hungarian Heavy Field Artillery Batteries:
    4 Batts. from Field Art. Rgt. 45, 3 Batts. from each of Field Art. Rgts. 1 &
    72, 2 Batts. from Field Art. Rgt. 10, 1 Batt. from each of Field Art. Rgts. 3,
    4, 6 & 9
Artillery Survey Troops:

Light Survey Troops 7, 35, 71, 104 & 108, Sound Ranging Troop 48, Artillery Correction Troop 35
Army Meteorological Station 207, Carrier Pigeon Unit 207
Naval Special Command 5003

D.
Pioneer General
Staff II Btn. Guard Reserve Pioneer Rgt. (Flamethrowers)
Landsturm Pioneer Park Coy. 25, 2nd Park Coy. Pioneer Siege Train, Electrical Sec. 21, Pioneer Field Recruit Depot 18, Minenwerfer School 18

E.
Aviation Commander 18
Aviation Dets. 23, 39 & 295A
Bomber Groups from OHL: I & IV
Ground Attack Sqdn 8
'R-Plane' Flight 18, 'R-Plane' Training Unit 18
Army Meteorological Station 18, Front Meteorological Station 226
Army Aviation Park 18
Staff Field Airship Det. 23
Flak Commander 18, Flak Group Commander 18
Flak Batts. 567 & 576 (each 4 guns)
MG Flak Secs. 8-10, 16, 56, 64, 72, 103, 171, 172 & 175
Flak Secs. 60 & 139
Motor Vehicle Flak Units 32, 36, 56, 67, 86, 135 & 136
Flak Searchlight Secs. 240, 403, 405 & 729, in addition to 7 independent Flak Searchlights
Flak MGs: 18 from Flak MG Unit 901, 28 from Flak MG Unit 908

F.
Army Signals Commander 15
Army Tel. Dets. 115 & 118
4 Station, 4 Eqpt, 4 Tel. Construction and 6 Motor Vehicle Tel. Construction Secs.
Army Signals Park 15, Army Radio Park 15, Reserve Signals Depot 3, Message Dog Sqdn. 52
Army Radio Det. 15
Survey Det. 26

G.
Munition Columns and Train Commander 8
Munition Columns and Trains as attached to individual units.
H.Staff Officer of Motor Vehicle Troop 51
Army Motor Vehicle Columns 229, 230, 237, 341 & 351
Army Motor Vehicle Sqdn. 51
Army Motor Vehicle Park 51, Army Foot Artillery Motor Vehicle Train Park 6
Medical Motor Vehicle Det. 51, Motorcycle Det. 51

III Army Corps

Divisions:
5th Infantry Division
6th Infantry Division
28th Infantry Division
88th Infantry Division
113th Infantry Division
206th Infantry Division

Attached Troops:

A.
I Btn. & 1st-3rd MGKs, Landwehr Inf. Rgt. 87
¼ Landsturm Inf. Btn. Ludwisgburg XIII A.K./9
¾ Landsturm Inf. Btn. Heidelberg XIV A.K./2
Cycle Coy. 86; 2 Coys. Assault Btn. 12; Mountain MG Sec. 233
Staff Jäger zu Pferde Rgt. 10

B.
Field Art. Rgts. 63, 65, 500, 600
Light Munition Columns 717, 723, 756, 809, 837, 926, 1039, 1115, 1164, 1212,
    1332 & 1334
2 Batts. from Mountain Art. Btn. 7
Inf. Gun Batts. 19 & 26

C.
Foot Artillery Btn. Staffs:
    22, 120, 215, 216 & 223
Btns. from Foot Art. Rgts. each with 3 Batts.:
    II/Foot Art. Rgt. 7, III/Foot Art. Rgt. 7, III/Reserve Foot Art. Rgt. 18, II/
    Foot Art. Rgt. 24, III/Reserve Foot Art. Rgt. 24, I/Foot Art. Rgt. 27
Foot Art. Btns. each with 3 Batts.:
    11th Bavarian Foot Art. Btn., Foot Art. Btn. 56, Foot Art. Btn. 65, Foot
    Art. Btn.82, Foot Art. Rgt. 123
Foot Art. Batt. 14
Light Survey Troop 145, Sound Ranging Troop 128, Artillery Correction Troop 20
Artillery Park Coys. 17 & 45
Artillery Workshops 22 & 32

D.
Pioneer Btn. 25; 9th Coy. Guard Reserve Pioneer Regt. (Flamethrowers); 1st Coy. Pio-
    neer Btn. 22 Minenwerfer Btns. IV & XI (each of 4 Coys.), Minenwerfer Coy. 91
Bavarian Pioneer Park Coy. 3; 1 Sec. Electrical Coy. 111

E.
Aviation Group Commander 17
Aviation Dets. 234A, 245A, 247A & 264A
Ground Attack Sqdns. 2, 5 & 20

Commander, Fighter Sqdn. 1
Fighter Sqdns. 8, 62 & 68
Airship Det. 67 with Balloon Dets. 33, 41, 61 & 125
Front Meteorological Station 125; Carrier Pigeon Unit 125
Group Commander Flak 42
Flak Batt. 566 (4 guns), Heavy Motorised Flak Batt. 127 (2 guns)
MG Flak Secs. 48, 82 & 95
Flak Secs. 18, 105 & 129
Motor Vehicle Flak Units 23, 47 & 69
Flak Searchlight Secs. 207 & 698
8 MGs from Flak MG Unit 908

F.
1 Station, 1 Eqpt, 1 Telephone Construction & 1 Motorised Telephone Construction
    Secs.
3 Signal Lamp Secs., 1 Listening Station, 6 Carrier Pigeon Units
1 Group Mapping Office

G.
Munitions Columns and Trains Commander 18
Group Section Staffs G1 & G2
7 Munition Columns, 12 Rations Columns, 1 Field Bakery Column, 2 Field Butchery
    Secs.
Divisional Pontoon Trains 21, 29, Reserve 44 & 58
Field Hospital 86, Medical Coys. 622, 629 & 643
Equine Hospital 592

H.
Army Motor Vehicle Columns 64, 107, 115, 120, 220, 318, 372, 347 & R.[1]1111.

I.
Equipment Btn. Staffs 114 & 191, Coys.:
    4th/5th Bavarian, 3rd & 4th/17th Bavarian, 5th/31st, 4th/36th, 2nd/
    110th, 2nd & 3rd/114th, 1st/120th, 2nd & 4th/191st.
Road Construction Coy. 11
Administrative Coys. 130 & 131

IX Army Corps

Divisions:
5th Guard Infantry Division
45th Reserve Division
50th Infantry Division
231st Infantry Division

---

1   R. = Raupen, i.e. tractor.

Attached Troops:

A.

II Btn., Landwehr Inf. Rgt. 87, ½ Landsturm Inf. Btn. Rastatt XIV A.K./41
1st Cycle Coy/Guard Jäger Btn.; 1st Cycle Coy./Guard Schützen Btn., Cycle Coy. 202
2 Coys. Assault Btn. 5 (Rohr); 1 Coy. Assault Btn. 12
Mountain MG Sec. 215; Armoured Fighting Vehicle Sec. 11
Staff Cuir. Rgt. 8

B.

Field Art. Rgts. 67, 501, 505
Light Munition Columns 769, 779, 849, 874, 884, 888, 1124, 1313 & 1381
1 Batt. from Mountain Art. Btn. 7
Inf. Gun Batts. 8 & 27

C.

Foot Artillery Btn. Staffs:
        13, 14, Reserve 15 & 115
Btns. from Foot Art. Rgts. each with 3 Batts.:
        IV/3rd Guard Foot Art. Rgt., I/Foot Art. Rgt. 2, I/Foot Art. Rgt. 14, I/
        Foot Art. Rgt. 20
Foot Art. Btns. each with 3 Batts.:
        Foot Art. Btn. 103, Foot Art. Btn. 112, Foot Art. Btn. 129, Foot Art. Rgt.
        158
Foot Art. Batts. 13 & 18
Light Survey Troop 176, Sound Ranging Troop 69, Artillery Correction Troop 28
Artillery Park Command 1, Artillery Park Coys. 32 & 53
Artillery Workshop 33

D.

Pioneer Btn. 29; 11th Coy. Guard Reserve Pioneer Regt. (Flamethrowers); 4th
        Landsturm Pioneer Coy. XIII A.K.
Minenwerfer Btn. VIII (4 Coys.), Minenwerfer Coys. 96, 345 & 347
Landsturm Pioneer Park Coy. 9; 2 Secs. Electrical Coy. 111

E.

Aviation Group Commander 13
Aviation Dets. 237A, 271A & 290A
Ground Attack Sqdn. 6
Commander, Fighter Sqdn. 11
Fighter Sqdns. 17, 22 & 63
Airship Det. 37 with Balloon Dets. 82, 96 & 118
Front Meteorological Station 216; Carrier Pigeon Unit 216
Group Commander Flak 7
Flak Batt. 508 (4 guns), Heavy Motorised Flak Batts. 119 & 162 (2 guns each)
MG Flak Secs. 29, 50 & 176
Flak Secs. 19 & 84
Motor Vehicle Flak Units 80 & 93
Flak Searchlight Sec. 726

24 MGs from Flak MG Unit 912

F.
1 Station, 1 Eqpt, 1 Telephone Construction & 2 Motorised Telephone Construction Secs.
2 Listening Stations, 5 Signal Lamp Secs., 5 Carrier Pigeon Units
1 Group Mapping Office

G.
Munitions Columns and Trains Commander 2
Section Staff 56
3 Munition Columns, 8 Rations Columns, 1 Field Bakery Column, 2 Field Butchery Secs.
Divisional Pontoon Trains 1st Bavarian Reserve, Reserve 9
Field Hospitals 251 & 297, Medical Coys. 630 & 640
Equine Hospital 593

H.
Army Motor Vehicle Columns 92, 126, 127, 231, 247 & 305

I.
Equipment Btn. 179, Equipment Coys. 3rd/136th
Road Construction Coy. 2
Administrative Coys. 2 & 126
Salvage Coy. 3rd Bavarian

XVII Army Corps

Divisions:
1st Bavarian Infantry Division
9th Infantry Division
10th Infantry Division
36th Infantry Division
238th Infantry Division

Attached Troops:

A.
III Btn., Landwehr Inf. Rgt. 87, Reserve Cycle Coy. 75
2 Coys. Assault Btn. 5 (Rohr); 1 Coy. Assault Btn. 12
Armoured Fighting Vehicle Sec. 1
Staff Uhlan Rgt. 16

B.
Field Art. Rgts. 10, 19th Bavarian, 28 & 503
Light Munition Columns 829, 881, 882, 930, 1114, 1165, 1166, 1232, 1335 & Bavarian 110th, 143 & 165
Inf. Gun Batt. 28

C.
Foot Artillery Btn. Staffs:
    Reserve 5, Reserve 18, 117, 122 & Bavarian 125th
Btns. from Foot Art. Rgts. each with 3 Batts.:
    II/Foot Art. Rgt. 3, I/Reserve Foot Art. Rgt. 4, I/Reserve Foot Art. Rgt. 7,
    III/Reserve Foot Art. Rgt. 7, I/Reserve Foot Art. Rgt. 11, I/Foot Art. Rgt.
    13, III/Foot Art. Rgt. 13, III/Foot Art. Rgt. 19
Foot Art. Btns. each with 3 Batts.:
    Foot Art. Btns. 98 & 131
Light Survey Troop 8, Bavarian Sound Ranging Troop 10, Artillery Correction Troop
    24
Artillery Park Command 10, Artillery Park Coys. 3 & 44
Artillery Workshops 7, 15 & 34

D.
Pioneer Btn. 24; 12th Coy. Guard Reserve Pioneer Regt. (Flamethrowers); Pioneer
    Mining Coy. 281
Minenwerfer Btns. V & VII (each of 4 Coys.)
Landsturm Pioneer Park Coy. 10; 2 Secs. Electrical Coy. 112

E.
Aviation Group Commander 8
Aviation Dets. 29, 206A, 212A & 225A
Ground Attack Sqdns. 7, 34 & 37
Commander, Fighter Sqdn. 5
Fighter Sqdns. 48, 53 & 63
Airship Det. 29 with Balloon Dets. 29, 31, 32, 40, 49 & 127
Front Meteorological Station 309; Carrier Pigeon Unit 309
Group Commander Flak 54
Flak Batt. 517 (4 guns), Motorised Flak Batt. 121 (2 guns)
MG Flak Secs. 12, 22, 86, 104 & 180
Flak Secs. 1 & 78
Motor Vehicle Flak Units 35 & 102
Flak Searchlight Secs. 180 & 181
18 MGs from Flak MG Unit 912

F.
1 Station, 1 Eqpt, 1 Telephone Construction & 1 Motorised Telephone Construction
    Sec.
1 Listening Station, 2 Signal Lamp Secs., 8 Carrier Pigeon Units
1 Group Mapping Office

G.
Munitions Columns and Trains Commander 30
3 Munition Columns, 8 Rations Columns, 1 Field Bakery Column, 1 Field Butchery
    Sec.
Divisional Pontoon Train 7
Field Hospitals 45 & 294, Medical Coys. 3rd Bavarian & 28
Equine Hospital 587

H.
Army Motor Vehicle Columns 15, 16, 66, 78, 114, 301, 311 & 330

I.
Equipment Btn. Staffs 44 & 64, Equipment Coys. 1st & 2nd/44th, 4th/64th, 1st & 4th/81st, 1st/84th, 1st & 2nd/116th
Road Construction Coy. 43
Administrative Coys. 132, 134 & 316
L of C Auxiliary Coy. 37

IV Reserve Corps

Divisions:
13th Landwehr Division
33rd Infantry Division
34th Infantry Division
37th Infantry Division
47th Reserve Division
103rd Infantry Division

Attached Troops:

A.
Reserve Jäger Btns. 9 & 15, Jäger Btn. 19
Landsturm Inf. Btn. Gelsenkirchen VII A.K./51 (4 Coys.), 1st Coy. Landsturm Inf. Btn. Ludwigsburg XIII A.K./9
2nd Cycle Coy. Jäger Btn. 11, Mountain MG Sec. 249
Staff Cav. Schützen Rgt. 94

B.
Field Art. Rgts. 49, Reserve 239, 504 & 602
Light Munition Columns 842, 1084, 1090, 1132, 1139, 1153, 1154, 1196, 1214 & 1227
Inf. Gun Batt. 23

C.
Foot Artillery Btn. Staffs:
 1st Bavarian, 9, Reserve 11, 17
Btns. from Foot Art. Rgts. each with 3 Batts.:
 I/Reserve Foot Art. Rgt. 9, III/Reserve Foot Art. Rgt. 11, II/Foot Art. Rgt. 13, I/Reserve Foot Art. Rgt. 17, II/Foot Art. Rgt. 22
Foot Art. Btns. each with 3 Batts.:
 Foot Art. Btns. 39, 43, 60, 100, 136
Light Survey Troop 10, Sound Ranging Troop 129, Artillery Correction Troops 19 & 32
Artillery Park Coys. 5th Bavarian & 57
Artillery Workshop 26

D.

Pioneer Btn. 20

Minenwerfer Btn. VI (4 Coys.), Minenwerfer Coys. 303, 307, 426 & 433

Pioneer Park Coy. Bavarian 15; 1 Sec. Electrical Coy. 112

E.

Aviation Group Commander 9

Aviation Dets. 216A, 226A, 254A, 287A & 297A

Ground Attack Sqdns. 18, 31 & 36

Commander, Fighter Sqdn. 12

Fighter Sqdns. 24, 44 & 79

Airship Dets. 11 & 30 with Balloon Dets. 4, 19, 83, 91, 94, 120 & 126

Front Meteorological Stations 217 & 218; Carrier Pigeon Units 217 & 218

Group Commander Flak 8

Flak Batt. 707 (4 guns), Motorised Flak Batts. 113, 123 & 159 (each of 2 guns)

MG Flak Secs. 81, 177 & 178

Flak Secs. 30, 121 & 170

Motor Vehicle Flak Units 6 & 33

Flak Searchlight Sec. 723

12 MGs from Flak MG Unit 901

F.

1 Station, 1 Eqpt, 2 Telephone Construction & 1 Motorised Telephone Construction Sec.

4 Listening Station, 6 Signal Lamp Secs., 6 Carrier Pigeon Units

1 Group Mapping Office

G.

Section Staffs 57 & 87

3 Munition Columns, 5 Rations Columns, 2 Field Butchery Secs.

Divisional Pontoon Trains: Reserve 15, 23, 28, 36, Reserve 43, Reserve 45, Reserve 46 & 50

Field Hospital 340, Medical Coy. 632

Equine Hospital 591

H.

Army Motor Vehicle Columns 73, 106, 108, 222 & 270

I.

Equipment Btn. Staffs 71, 73 & 136, Equipment Coys. 1st, 3rd & 4th/71st, 4th/73rd, 3rd & 4th/116th, 1st & 2nd/136th

Road Construction Coy. 5

Administrative Coys. 133 & 135

Salvage Coy. 5

Military Prisoner Coys. 1 & 2/18th Army

Line of Communications Inspectorate 18

12 L of C Commandants

6 Landsturm Inf. Btns., 2 Landwehr Sqdns., 2 Field Police Dets.

L of C Munitions & Eqpt. Inspectorate

CO of L of C Munitions Columns and Trains with 10 L of C Supply Columns, 12 Magazine Supply Columns, 1 L of C Munitions Column, 4 L of C Horse Depots, 1 L of C Equine Hospital

L of C Intendant 18, 4 L of C Auxiliary Bakery Columns, 1 Field Butchery Sec.

L of C Doctor with 3 Military Hospital Dets., 5 Hospital Secs. for Minor Illnesses & Wounds, 8 General Hospital Secs., Medical Transport Det. 18, L of C Medical Depot 18

L of C Vet 18, Blood Laboratory 18

Army Postal Director

Construction Direction 9, 4 Administrative Coys., 1 L of C Auxiliary Coy.

Army Clothing Depot 18

Prisoner of War Inspectorate (L of C Cmdt 244) with PoW Labour Btns. and Landsturm Guard Coys.

Siege Artillery Workshop 2, Artillery Workshops 32-34

Additional Units operating within 18th Army's sector

Command of Railway Troops 18

Military Railway Construction Group 35 with Railway Construction Coys. Bavarian Reserve 3, Reserve 18, Reserve 26, 28; Equipment Coys. 5th/37th, 3rd & 4th/ Bavarian 14th

Construction Group 35a with Railway Construction Coys. 13th Fortress, 18, Landwehr 201, Reserve 33, Reserve 37, Equipment Coys. 2nd/Bavarian 17th, 4th/42nd, 4th/181st, Line-laying Construction Column 3, Underwater Det. 6, 1st Coy. Railway Auxiliary Btn. 6

Construction Group 36 with Railway Construction Coys. Landwehr 2, Reserve 22, Reserve 24, Reserve 25, Reserve 36, Equipment Coys. 1st/Bavarian 7th, 3rd/ 29th, 3rd/42nd, 4th/106th, 1st/108th, 4th Coy. Railway Auxiliary Btn. 6, 2nd Coy. Civilian Workers' Btn. 16

Telephone Construction Troop 3, Field Railway Det. 13

Foot Artillery Training Area Mauberge (OHL), Pioneer Training Area Jeumont (OHL), Pioneer School 1

Appendix III

List of Brigade Staffs, Artillery and Pioneer Generals

(a) Infantry Brigades

Brigade	Unit to which attached	Notes
1st Guard	1st Guard Infantry Division	
2nd Guard	1st Guard Infantry Division	26.1.17 > 5th Guard Infantry Division
3rd Guard	2nd Guard Infantry Division	
4th Guard	2nd Guard Infantry Division	15.1.17 > 220th Infantry Division
5th Guard	3rd Guard Infantry Division	8.5.15 > 4th Guard Infantry Division
6th Guard	3rd Guard Infantry Division	
1st Infantry	1st Infantry Division	
2nd Infantry	1st Infantry Division	1.8.16 > renamed Indpt. 2nd Infantry Cycle Brigade
3rd Infantry	2nd Infantry Division	
4th Infantry	2nd Infantry Division	15.5.15 dissolved
5th Infantry	3rd Infantry Division	15.5.15 > Division Beckmann (108th Infantry Division)
6th Infantry	3rd Infantry Division	
7th Infantry	4th Infantry Division	23.9.16 > 222nd Infantry Division; 2.10.18 > 301st Infantry Division
8th Infantry	4th Infantry Division	
9th Infantry	5th Infantry Division	27.3.15 dissolved
10th Infantry	5th Infantry Division	
11th Infantry	6th Infantry Division	7.3.15 renamed 112th Infantry Brigade
12th Infantry	6th Infantry Division	
13th Infantry	7th Infantry Division	6.3.15 dissolved
14th Infantry	7th Infantry Division	
15th Infantry	8th Infantry Division	21.3.15 dissolved
16th Infantry	8th Infantry Division	
17th Infantry	9th Infantry Division	25.3.15 dissolved
18th Infantry	9th Infantry Division	

19th Infantry	10th Infantry Division	25.3.15 renamed 237th Infantry Brigade
20th Infantry	10th Infantry Division	
21st Infantry	11th Infantry Division	
22nd Infantry	11th Infantry Division	8.11.16 became independent
23rd Infantry	11th Infantry Division	
24th Infantry	12th Infantry Division	
25th Infantry	13th Infantry Division	10.3.15 dissolved
26th Infantry	13 Infantry Division	
27th Infantry	14 Infantry Division	1.3.15 renamed 100th Infantry Brigade
28th Infantry	14th Reserve Division	5.3.15 dissolved
29th Infantry	15th Infantry Division	15.8.16 > 185th Infantry Division
30th Infantry	16th Infantry Division	
31st Infantry	16 Infantry Division	10.10.16 > 47th Landwehr Division; 16.1.17 renamed 238th Infantry Brigade
32nd Infantry	31st Infantry Division	
33rd Infantry	17th Infantry Division	27.3.15 dissolved
34th Infantry	17th Infantry Division	
35th Infantry	18th Infantry Division	6.3.15 renamed 108th Infantry Brigade
36th Infantry	18th Infantry Division	
37th Infantry	19th Infantry Division	
38th Infantry	19th Infantry Division	25.3.15 renamed 221st Infantry Brigade
39th Infantry	20th Infantry Division	25.3.15 dissolved
40th Infantry	20th Infantry Division	
41st Infantry	21st Infantry Division	5.3.15 dissolved
42nd Infantry	21st Infantry Division	
43rd Infantry	22nd Infantry Division	
44th Infantry	22nd Infantry Division	15.5.15 renamed 205th Infantry Brigade
45th Infantry	23rd Infantry Division	
46th Infantry	23rd Infantry Division	1.4.15 dissolved
47th Infantry	24th Infantry Division	6.3.15 dissolved
48th Infantry	24th Infantry Division	6.3.15 renamed 116th Infantry Brigade
49th Infantry	25th Infantry Division	
50th Infantry	25th Infantry Division	7.3.15 dissolved
51st Infantry	26th Infantry Division	
52nd Infantry	26th Infantry Division	26.5.15 dissolved
53rd Infantry	27th Infantry Division	
54th Infantry	27th Infantry Division	1.2.17 renamed 242nd Infantry Brigade
55th Infantry	28th Infantry Division	

56th Infantry	28th Infantry Division	30.11.16 > 212th Infantry Division; 4.4.17 > 52nd Infantry Division
57th Infantry	29th Infantry Division	15.9.16 > 212th Infantry Division; 31.1.17 dissolved
58th Infantry	29th Infantry Division	
59th Infantry	42nd Infantry Division	7.11.15 dissolved
60th Infantry	30th Infantry Division	
61st Infantry	39th Infantry Division	
62nd Infantry	31st Infantry Division	23.9.16 > 218th Infantry Division
63rd Infantry	32nd Infantry Division	
64th Infantry	32nd Infantry Division	1.4.15 renamed 245th Infantry Brigade
65th Infantry	42 Infantry Division	
66th Infantry	33rd Infantry Division	
67th Infantry	33rd Infantry Division	7.10.16 > 223rd Infantry Division; 6.10.18 > 44th Landwehr Division
68th Infantry	34th Infantry Division	
69th Infantry	36th Infantry Division	15.5.15 renamed 209th Infantry Brigade
70th Infantry	35th Infantry Division	15.5.15 dissolved
71st Infantry	36th Infantry Division	
72nd Infantry	41st Infantry Division	8.5.15 > 101st Infantry Division
73rd Infantry	37th Infantry Division	
74th Infantry	41st Infantry Division	
75th Infantry	37th Infantry Division	15.5.15 renamed 201st Infantry Brigade
76th Infantry	38th Infantry Division	15.5.15 dissolved
77th Infantry	10th Reserve Division	4.11.14-22.3.16 independent
78th Infantry	12th Infantry Division	15.8.15 dissolved
79th Infantry	14th Infantry Division	
80th Infantry	15th Infantry Division	
81st Infantry	17th Reserve Division	
82nd Infantry	39th Infantry Division	2.4.15 renamed 229th Infantry Brigade
83rd Infantry	38th Infantry Division	
84th Infantry	29th Infantry Division	4.3.15 renamed 104th Infantry Brigade
85th Infantry	30th Infantry Division	3.4.15 dissolved
86th Infantry	34th Infantry Division	3.11.16 dissolved
87th Infantry	35th Infantry Division	
88th Infantry	40th Infantry Division	
89th Infantry	40th Infantry Division	6.3.15 > 24th Infantry Division
100th Infantry	50th Infantry Division	Previously 27th Infantry Brigade
104th Infantry	52nd Infantry Division	10.4.17 > 228th Infantry Division. Previously 84th Infantry Brigade
108th Infantry	54th Infantry Division	Previously 35th Infantry Brigade
112th Infantry	56th Infantry Division	Previously 11th Infantry Brigade

116th Infantry	58th Infantry Division	Previously 48th Infantry Brigade
165th Infantry	83rd Infantry Division	Previously Brigade 1 Posen
166th Infantry	83rd Infantry Division	9.9.17 dissolved. Previously Brigade 2 Posen
167th Infantry	84th Infantry Division	24.11.16 > 35th Reserve Division. Previously 12th Ersatz Brigade
168th Infantry	84th Infantry Division	Previously Brigade 4 Posen
171st Infantry	86th Infantry Division	1.10.16 dissolved. Previously Brigade Grossmann
172nd Infantry	86th Infantry Division	Previously Brigade Windheim
173rd Infantry	87th Infantry Division	13.12.17 > 225th Infantry Division; 13.9.18 > Construction Staff. Previously Brigade Griepenkerl
174th Infantry	109th Infantry Division	10.9.18 > Construction Staff. Previously Brigade Homeyer
176th Infantry	88th Infantry Division	Previously Brigade Buddenbrock
177th Infantry	88th Infantry Division	10.9.16 > 216th Infantry Division; 3.5.17 > 96th Infantry Division. Previously Brigade Zenker
178th Infantry	80th Infantry Division	Previously Brigade Rintelen
179th Infantry	87th Infantry Division	Previously Brigade Normann
180th Infantry	10th Landwehr Division	1.9.18 dissolved. Previously Brigade Königsberg
181st Infantry	10th Landwehr Division	25.11.16 dissolved. Previously Brigade Koppelow
183rd Infantry	183rd Infantry Division	Independent until 5.6.16 > 183rd Infantry Division; 25.10.16 dissolved
185th Infantry	185th Infantry Division	Independent until 5.6.16 > 185th Infantry Division; 8.9.16 > 208th Infantry Division
187th Infantry	187th Infantry Division	Independent until 1.7.16 > 187th Infantry Division
192nd Infantry	192nd Infantry Division	Independent until 12.6.16 > 192nd Infantry Division
201st Infantry	101st Infantry Division	9.11.16 > 302nd Infantry Division; 18.12.17 independent. Previously 75th Infantry Brigade
205th Infantry	103rd Infantry Division	Previously 44th Infantry Brigade
209th Infantry	105th Infantry Division	Previously 69th Infantry Brigade
210th Infantry	197th Infantry Division	Independent until 9.8.16 > 197th Infantry Division; 22.10.18 dissolved
211th Infantry	211th Infantry Division	8.9.18 dissolved
213th Infantry	107th Infantry Division	Previously 98th Reserve Brigade
214th Infantry	Guard Ersatz Division	9.10.17 > 214th Infantry Division

215th Infantry	93rd Infantry Division	14.9.18 > 94th Infantry Division. Previously 4th Landwehr Cavalry Brigade
216th Infantry	224th Infantry Division	Previously 25th Ersatz Infantry Brigade
221st Infantry	111th Infantry Division	Previously 38th Infantry Brigade
225th Infantry	113th Infantry Division	Previously 44th Reserve Infantry Brigade
229th Infantry	115th Infantry Division	Previously 82nd Infantry Brigade
231st Infantry	231st Infantry Division	
232nd Infantry	232nd Infantry Division	
233rd Infantry	117th Infantry Division	Previously 23rd Reserve Infantry Brigade
234th Infantry	234th Infantry Division	
235th Infantry	235th Infantry Division	10.8.18 dissolved
236th Infantry	236th Infantry Division	
237th Infantry	119th Infantry Division	Previously 19th Infantry Brigade
238th Infantry	238th Infantry Division	Previously 31st Infantry Brigade
239th Infantry	239th Infantry Division	
240th Infantry	240th Infantry Division	
241st Infantry	121st Infantry Division	
242nd Infantry	242nd Infantry Division	Previously 54th Infantry Brigade
243rd Infantry	233rd Infantry Division	
244th Infantry	237th Infantry Division	Previously 29th Reserve Infantry Brigade
245th Infantry	123rd Infantry Division	Previously 64th Infantry Brigade
246th Infantry	241st Infantry Division	
247th Infantry	243rd Infantry Division	Previously 51st Ersatz Infantry Brigade
401st Infantry	47th Reserve Division	25.10.16 > Nowogrodek Sector; 1.5.17 dissolved
402nd Infantry	201st Infantry Division	26.10.18 dissolved
403rd Infantry	205th Infantry Division	
405th Infantry	203rd Infantry Division	
406th Infantry	202nd Infantry Division	
407th Infantry	204th Infantry Division	3.9.16 dissolved
407th Infantry	204th Infantry Division	Previously 53rd Landwehr Infantry Brigade
408th Infantry	204th Infantry Division	12.1.17 > 212th Infantry Division
404th, 501st-503rd, 505th 513th Infantry remained unformed		
1st Bavarian	1st Bavarian Infantry Division	9.3.15 renamed 20th Bavarian Infantry Brigade

1st Bavarian	1st Bavarian Infantry Division	Previously 2nd Bavarian Infantry Brigade
2nd Bavarian	1st Bavarian Infantry Division	15.4.15 renamed 1st Bavarian Infantry Brigade
3rd Bavarian	2nd Bavarian Infantry Division	2.4.15 renamed 4th Bavarian Infantry Brigade
4th Bavarian	2nd Bavarian Infantry Division	2.4.15 renamed 21st Bavarian Infantry Brigade
4th Bavarian	2nd Bavarian Infantry Division	Previously 3rd Bavarian Infantry Brigade
5th Bavarian	3rd Bavarian Infantry Division	1.4.15 dissolved
6th Bavarian	3rd Bavarian Infantry Division	
7th Bavarian	4th Bavarian Infantry Division	
8th Bavarian	33rd Reserve Division	3.8.16 > 14th Bavarian Infantry Division; 15.9.18 > 6th Bavarian Reserve Division
9th Bavarian	5th Bavarian Infantry Division	13.1.17 > 16th Bavarian Infantry Division
10th Bavarian	5th Bavarian Infantry Division	
11th Bavarian	6th Bavarian Infantry Division	
12th Bavarian	6th Bavarian Infantry Division	16.1.17 dissolved
20th Bavarian	10th Bavarian Infantry Division	17.8.18 dissolved. Previously 1st Bavarian Infantry Brigade
21st Bavarian	11th Bavarian Infantry Division	Previously 4th Bavarian Infantry Brigade
22nd Bavarian	12th Bavarian Infantry Division	
23rd Bavarian	15th Bavarian Infantry Division	
1st Guard Reserve	1st Guard Reserve Division	
1st Reserve	1st Reserve Division	
5th Reserve	3rd Reserve Division	
6th Reserve	3rd Reserve Division	11.11.15 dissolved
9th Reserve	5th Reserve Division	
10th Reserve	5th Reserve Division	1.6.15 > independent; 25.5.17 > 95th Infantry Division
11th Reserve	6th Reserve Division	14.11.15 dissolved
12th Reserve	6th Reserve Division	16.9.18 dissolved
13th Reserve	7th Reserve Division	4.3.15 dissolved
14th Reserve	7th Reserve Division	

15th Reserve	1st Guard Reserve Division	7.5.15 dissolved
17th Reserve	9th Reserve Division	7.4.16 dissolved
18th Reserve	10th Reserve Division	1.4.16 > 9th Reserve Division
19th Reserve	9th Reserve Division	25.3.15 dissolved
21st Reserve	11th Reserve Division	1.4.15 dissolved
22nd Reserve	12th Reserve Division	
23rd Reserve	12th Reserve Division	1.4.15 renamed 233rd Infantry Brigade
25th Reserve	13th Reserve Division	25.3.15 dissolved
26th Reserve	2nd Guard Reserve Division	10.1.17 dissolved
27th Reserve	14th Reserve Division	
28th Reserve	13th Reserve Division	
29th Reserve	16th Reserve Division	16.1.17 renamed 244th Infantry Brigade
30th Reserve	15th Reserve Division	
31st Reserve	16th Reserve Division	
32nd Reserve	15th Reserve Division	26.9.16 > 25th Landwehr Division
33rd Reserve	17th Reserve Division	27.10.16 > 183rd Infantry Division; 27.9.18 dissolved
34th Reserve	18th Reserve Division	3.3.15 dissolved
35th Reserve	18th Reserve Division	
37th Reserve	19th Reserve Division	8.9.16 > 213th Infantry Division
38th Reserve	2nd Guard Reserve Division	
39th Reserve	19th Reserve Division	
41st Reserve	21st Reserve Division	
42nd Reserve	21st Reserve Division	11.10.16 dissolved
43rd Reserve	22nd Reserve Division	
44th Reserve	22nd Reserve Division	24.3.15 renamed 225th Infantry Brigade
45th Reserve	23rd Reserve Division	29.12.16 dissolved
46th Reserve	23rd Reserve Division	
47th Reserve	24th Reserve Division	29.3.15 dissolved
48th Reserve	24th Reserve Division	
49th Reserve	25th Reserve Division	19.5.15 dissolved
50th Reserve	25th Reserve Division	1.11.18 dissolved
51st Reserve	26th Reserve Division	
52nd Reserve	26th Reserve Division	23.1.17 dissolved
55th Reserve	28th Reserve Division	5.4.15 dissolved
56th Reserve	28th Reserve Division	
60th Reserve	Independent	15.8.14 dissolved
61st Reserve	13th Landwehr Division	Previously independent (until 17.5.15); 15.9.16 > 215th Infantry Division
66th Reserve	33rd Reserve Division	1.9.18 dissolved

69th Reserve	36th Reserve Division	
70th Reserve	36th Reserve Division	8.9.16 dissolved
72nd Reserve	1st Reserve Division	16.6.17 renamed 1st Landsturm Infantry Brigade
75th Reserve	75th Reserve Division	
76th Reserve	76th Reserve Division	
77th Reserve	77th Reserve Division	
78th Reserve	78th Reserve Division	7.9.18 dissolved
79th Reserve	79th Reserve Division	
80th Reserve	80th Reserve Division	
81st Reserve	81st Reserve Division	
82nd Reserve	82nd Reserve Division	
85th Reserve	43rd Reserve Division	13.9.18 > Construction Staff
86th Reserve	43rd Reserve Division	22.4.17 > 216th Infantry Division
87th Reserve	44th Reserve Division	
88th Reserve	44th Reserve Division	10.1.17 dissolved
89th Reserve	45th Reserve Division	27.11.16 > 207th Infantry Division
90th Reserve	45th Reserve Division	
91st Reserve	46th Reserve Division	26.9.16 > 19th Landwehr Division
92nd Reserve	46th Reserve Division	11.8.18 became independent
93rd Reserve	47th Reserve Division	1.5.17 became independent. Previously Reserve Ersatz Brigade 109
94th Reserve	47th Reserve Division	Previously Reserve Ersatz Brigade 110
95th Reserve	48th Reserve Division	14.4.17 became independent; 11.3.18 > 12th Landwehr Division; 2.10.18 dissolved
96th Reserve	48th Reserve Division	
97th Reserve	49th Reserve Division	
98th Reserve	49th Reserve Division	3.6.15 renamed 213th Infantry Brigade
99th Reserve	50th Reserve Division	
100th Reserve	50th Reserve Division	
101st Reserve	51st Reserve Division	2.8.16 > 195th Infantry Brigade
102nd Reserve	51st Reserve Division	
103rd Reserve	52nd Reserve Division	16.8.16 dissolved
104th Reserve	52nd Reserve Division	
105th Reserve	53rd Reserve Division	
106th Reserve	53rd Reserve Division	3.5.17 dissolved
107th Reserve	54th Reserve Division	30.8.18 dissolved
108th Reserve	54th Reserve Division	10.1.17 dissolved
1st Bavarian Reserve	1st Bavarian Reserve Division	5.4.15 dissolved
1st Bavarian Reserve	1st Bavarian Reserve Division	1.8.16 dissolved. Previously 2nd Bavarian Reserve Infantry Brigade

1st Bavarian Reserve	1st Bavarian Reserve Division	Previously Brigade Samhaber
2nd Bavarian Reserve	1st Bavarian Reserve Division	6.4.15 renamed 1st Bavarian Reserve Infantry Brigade
3rd Bavarian Reserve	Independent	17.8.14 dissolved
3rd Bavarian Reserve	Bavarian Ersatz Division	(from 3.10.14)
5th Bavarian Reserve	4th Bavarian Infantry Division	10.3.15 dissolved
9th Bavarian Reserve	5th Bavarian Reserve Division	15.4.15 renamed 11th Bavarian Reserve Infantry Brigade
10th Bavarian Reserve	30th Reserve Division	14.10.16 > 6th Bavarian Landwehr Division
11th Bavarian Reserve	5th Bavarian Reserve Division	4.4.15 renamed Brigade Samhaber
11th Bavarian Reserve	5th Bavarian Reserve Division	Previously 9th Bavarian Reserve Infantry Brigade
12th Bavarian Reserve	6th Bavarian Reserve Division	16.9.18 dissolved
14th Bavarian Reserve	6th Bavarian Reserve Division	23.1.17 dissolved
15th Bavarian Reserve	8th Bavarian Reserve Division	Became independent 21.10.16
16th Bavarian Reserve	8th Bavarian Reserve Division	
17th Bavarian Reserve	9th Bavarian Reserve Division	Previously 13th Bavarian Landwehr Infantry Brigade
Brigade Samhaber	1st Bavarian Reserve	1.8.16 renamed 1st Bavarian Reserve Infantry Brigade. Previously 11th Bavarian Reserve Infantry Brigade
1st Landwehr	Gov. Königsberg	1.7.15 demobilised
2nd Landwehr	16th Landwehr Division	Independent until 5.9.14
5th Landwehr	35th Reserve Division	2.12.16 > 226th Infantry Division; 25.4.18 > Guard Cavalry Schützen Division
6th Landwehr	22nd Landwehr Division	Independent until 20.4.17
9th Landwehr	Independent	From 3.2.15 corresponded to 9th Landwehr Division
10th Landwehr	15th Landwehr Division	Independent until 28.1.15
11th Landwehr	21st Landwehr Division	Independent until 18.2.17
13th Landwehr	23rd Landwehr Division	Independent until 25.4.17
14th Landwehr	5th Landwehr Division	Independent until 23.10.14; 19.4.17 dissolved
17th Landwehr	3rd Landwehr Division	
18th Landwehr	3rd Landwehr Division	8.9.16 > 217th Infantry Division
19th Landwehr	Gov. Posen	4.9.14 > 18th Landwehr Division

20th Landwehr	35th Reserve Division	16.7.15 dissolved
21st Landwehr	87th Infantry Division (Corps Dickhuth)	Independent until 17.2.15; 19.7.15 > 14th Landwehr Division; 17.5.18 > 7th Cavalry Schützen Division
22nd Landwehr	4th Landwehr Division	
23rd Landwehr	4th Landwehr Division	9.9.16 dissolved
25th Landwehr	Independent	13.9.16 dissolved
26th Landwehr	Independent	17.2.15 dissolved
27th Landwehr	15th Landwehr Division	Independent until 13.4.15; 1.5.17 dissolved
28th Landwehr	18th Landwehr Division	30.6.16 > 92nd Infantry Division
29th Landwehr	Independent	
30th Landwehr	Gov. Metz	22.10.14 > 5th Landwehr Division
31st Landwehr	Independent	
33rd Landwehr	1st Landwehr Division	12.10.14 > 11th Landwehr Division; 28.3.18 became independent; 19.10.18 > 93rd Infantry Division
34th Landwehr	1st Landwehr Division	
37th Landwehr	5th Ersatz Division	Independent until 3.6.15
38th Landwehr	38th Landwehr Division	Independent until 25.4.17
41st Landwehr	Independent	16.3.15 dissolved
42nd Landwehr	Independent	3.10.14 dissolved
43rd Landwehr	9th Landwehr Division	Independent until 1.2.15; 4.3.15 renamed 76th Landwehr Infantry Brigade
44th Landwehr	44th Landwehr Division	Independent until 25.4.17
45th Landwehr	Independent	31.12.14 dissolved
45th Landwehr	45th Landwehr Division	From 20.2.17
46th Landwehr	14th Landwehr Division	13.3.17 > 46th Landwehr Division. Previously Brigade Pfeil
47th Landwehr	47th Landwehr Division	Independent until 7.6.16
49th Landwehr	9th Landwehr Division	Independent until 25.1.15; 6.2.17 > 227th Infantry Division
51st Landwehr	Independent	1.4.15 renamed 55th Landwehr Infantry Brigade
51st Landwehr	7th Landwehr Division	18.1.17 > 26th Landwehr Division. Previously 55th Landwehr Infantry Brigade
52nd Landwehr	Independent	28.3.15 renamed 61st Landwehr Infantry Brigade
52nd Landwehr	7th Landwehr Division	Previously 57th Landwehr Infantry Brigade
53rd Landwehr	2nd Landwehr Division	4.1.17 renamed 407th Infantry Brigade
54th Landwehr	2nd Landwehr Division	

55th Landwehr	7th Landwehr Division	Independent until 27.1.15; 1.4.15 renamed 51st Landwehr Infantry Brigade
56th Landwehr	Independent	25.1.15 dissolved
56th Landwehr	8th Landwehr Division	From 13.5.16
57th Landwehr	7th Landwehr Division	1.4.15 renamed 52nd Landwehr Infantry Brigade
59th Landwehr	Bavarian Ersatz Division	15.1.17 > 199th Infantry Division. Previously 59th Ersatz Infantry Brigade
60th Landwehr	1st Bavarian Landwehr Division	Independent until 29.9.14; 17.5.15 > 13th Landwehr Division
61st Landwehr	Independent	Previously 52nd Landwehr Infantry Brigade
62nd Landwehr	Gov. Graudenz	6.10.15 dissolved
70th Landwehr	11th Landwehr Division	Independent until 14.2.15
76th Landwehr	9th Landwehr Division	Previously 43rd Landwehr Infantry Brigade
82nd Landwehr	6th Bavarian Landwehr Division	7.4.15 > 12th Landwehr Division; 25.5.17 > 255th Infantry Division
84th Landwehr	Independent	
169th Landwehr	85th Landwehr Division	
170th Landwehr	85th Landwehr Division	1.3.17 > 94th Landwehr Division; 1.5.18 > 6th Cavalry Schützen Division
175th Landwehr	88th Infantry Division	11.7.16 > 91st Infantry Division. Previously Landwehr Ersatz Brigade 1
182nd Landwehr	17th Landwehr Division	Previously Troop Det. Esebeck
1st Bavarian Landwehr	6th Bavarian Landwehr Division	Independent until 3.4.15; 31.12.16 dissolved
2nd Bavarian Landwehr	6th Bavarian Landwehr Division	Independent until 27.1.15
5th Bavarian Landwehr	1st Bavarian Landwehr Division	Independent until 18.5.15
9th Bavarian Landwehr	2nd Landwehr Division	1.1.16 > 1st Bavarian Landwehr Division; 15.1.17 > 2nd Bavarian Landwehr Division
13th Bavarian Landwehr	1st Bavarian Landwehr Division	25.9.16 renamed 17th Bavarian Reserve Infantry Brigade
14th Bavarian Landwehr	1st Bavarian Landwehr Division	1.1.16 dissolved
1st Guard Ersatz	Guard Ersatz Division	Later dropped the '1' from its designation

5th Ersatz	Guard Ersatz Division	30.11.16 > 225th Infantry Division; 14.10.17 to the German Jäger Division
9th Ersatz	4th Ersatz Division	20.9.16 > 20th Landwehr Division
12th Ersatz	Independent	12.6.15 renamed 167th Infantry Brigade
13th Ersatz	4th Ersatz Division	
17th Ersatz	3rd Landwehr Division	28.9.14 dissolved
21st Ersatz	4th Landwehr Division	14.9.14 dissolved
25th Ersatz	10th Ersatz Division	19.10.16 renamed 216th Infantry Brigade
29th Ersatz	8th Ersatz Division	1.2.17 dissolved
33rd Ersatz	4th Ersatz Division	9.7.15 dissolved
37th Ersatz	10th Ersatz Division	9.7.15 dissolved
41st Ersatz	8th Ersatz Division	9.7.15 dissolved
43rd Ersatz	10th Ersatz Division	
45th Ersatz	19th Ersatz Division	
47th Ersatz	19th Ersatz Division	12.10.16 > 56th Infantry Division; 5.1.17 > 219th Infantry Division
51st Ersatz	8th Ersatz Division	1.4.17 > 243rd Infantry Division
55th Ersatz	Independent	3.1.15 dissolved
59th Ersatz	Bavarian Ersatz Division	22.11.14 renamed 59th Landwehr Infantry Brigade
1st Bavarian Ersatz	Bavarian Ersatz Division	3.10.14 > 39th Reserve Division
5th Bavarian Ersatz	30th Reserve Division	
9th Bavarian Ersatz	Bavarian Ersatz Division	3.10.14 > 39th Reserve Division; 11.12.16 > Construction Training
1st Reserve Ersatz	221st Infantry Division	Independent until 28.9.16
2nd Reserve Ersatz	Division Basedow	Independent until 3.6.15; 5.6.16 > 5th Ersatz Division; 20.8.16 > 206th Infantry Division
109th Reserve Ersatz	47th Reserve Division	12.12.14 renamed 93rd Reserve Infantry Brigade
110th Reserve Ersatz	47th Reserve Division	12.12.14 renamed 94th Reserve Infantry Brigade
1st Landwehr Ersatz	Division Menges (88th Infantry Division)	Independent until 17.11.14; 2.8.15 renamed 175th Landwehr Infantry Brigade
1st Landsturm	L of C Insp 4	25.10.14 dissolved
1st Landsturm	48th Landwehr Division	Independent until 13.9.17. Previously 72nd Reserve Infantry Brigade
1st Bavarian Jäger Brigade	Alpine Corps	

2nd Jäger Brigade	Alpine Corps	6.8.16 > 200th Infantry Division
Naval Infantry Brigade	1st Naval Division	3.6.15 > 2nd Naval Division; 3.6.17 > 3rd Naval Division
1st Naval Brigade	1st Naval Division	
2nd Naval Brigade	1st Naval Division	
3rd Naval Brigade	2nd Naval Division	
4th Naval Brigade	2nd Naval Division	31.10.17 dissolved

(b) Cavalry Brigades

Brigade	Unit to which attached	Notes
Provisional Guard	2nd Cavalry Division	15.1.15 became independent; 12.11.16 dissolved
1st Guard	Guard Cavalry Division	9.4.17 became independent
2nd Guard	Guard Cavalry Division	6.6.16 became independent
3rd Guard	Guard Cavalry Division	18.10.16 became independent
Leib Hussar	2nd Cavalry Division	20.8.16 became independent
1st Cavalry	1st Cavalry Division	3.10.16 became independent (13.10-1.11.16 Staff 3rd Cavalry Division; 2.11.16-31.5.17 as Staff Siebenbürg Cavalry Brigade)
2nd Cavalry	1st Cavalry Division	
3rd Cavalry	4th Cavalry Division	30.11.14 became independent; 17.10.16 > 6th Cavalry Division; 6.5.18 renamed Cavalry Schützen Command 3
5th Cavalry	2nd Cavalry Division	8.8.16 became independent; 19.10.16 > 6th Cavalry Division; 11.5.18 renamed Cavalry Schützen Command 5
8th Cavalry	2nd Cavalry Division	25.7.16 > 1st Cavalry Division; 18.10.16 > 6th Cavalry Division; 6.10.17 became independent
9th Cavalry	5th Cavalry Division	26.12.16 became independent
11th Cavalry	5th Cavalry Division	23.3.18 > Guard Cavalry Division; 8.5.18 renamed Cavalry Schützen Command 11
12th Cavalry	5th Cavalry Division	20.2.18 became independent

13th Cavalry	9th Cavalry Division	8.2.16 renamed Cav. Insp. Gen. Gov. Warsaw; 13.12.16 > Gen.Qmstr.; 21.2.18 renamed Commission of the Gen.Qmstr. for Horses
14th Cavalry	9th Cavalry Division	23.2.18 > Guard Cavalry Division; 8.5.18 renamed Cavalry Schützen Command 14
16th Cavalry	3rd Cavalry Division	1.9.16 became independent
17th Cavalry	4th Cavalry Division	1.2.17 became independent
18th Cavalry	4th Cavalry Division	12.12.16 > 1st Cavalry Division; 15.10.18 > XXXXI Reserve Corps
19th Cavalry	9th Cavalry Division	8.4.17 > Guard Cavalry Division; 12.2.18 became independent
22nd Cavalry	3rd Cavalry Division	13.8.16 > 2nd Cavalry Division
23rd Cavalry	8th Cavalry Division	1.2.17 > 1st Cavalry Division; 22.10.17 became independent
25th Cavalry	3rd Cavalry Division	23.9.16 > 2nd Cavalry Division
26th Cavalry	7th Cavalry Division	6.10.17 became independent
28th Cavalry	6th Cavalry Division	1.2.17 > 4th Cavalry Division; 17.5.18 > 7th Cavalry Schützen Division; 27.5.18 > Cavalry Schützen Command 28
30th Cavalry	7th Cavalry Division	27.5.18 renamed Cavalry Schützen Command 30
33rd Cavalry	6th Cavalry Division	14.9.16 became independent
38th Cavalry	8th Cavalry Division	20.4.18 > Guard Cavalry Division; 8.5.18 renamed Cavalry Schützen Command 38
39th Cavalry	4th Cavalry Division	From 28.9.14; 1.2.17 > 8th Cavalry Division; 6.4.18 > 4th Cavalry Division
40th Cavalry	8th Cavalry Division	10.4.18 dissolved
41st Cavalry	1st Cavalry Division	17.10.16 > 7th Cavalry Division; 27.5.18 renamed Cavalry Schützen Command 41
42nd Cavalry	7th Cavalry Division	14.9.16 became independent
45th Cavalry	6th Cavalry Division	14.10.16 became independent; 1.2.17 > 4th Cavalry Division; 1.5.18 > 6th Cavalry Division; 6.5.18 renamed Cavalry Schützen Command 45
Siebenbürg Cavalry Brigade	Independent	= Staff 1st Cavalry Brigade; 1.6.17 renamed 7th Bavarian Cavalry Brigade
1st Bavarian Cavalry	Bavarian Cavalry Division	

2nd Bavarian Cavalry	Bavarian Cavalry Division	3.7.17 became independent
5th Bavarian Cavalry	Bavarian Cavalry Division	
7th Bavarian Cavalry	2nd Cavalry Division	18.2.18 became independent. Previously Siebenbürg Cavalry Brigade
4th Landwehr Cavalry	4th Landwehr Division	1.10.16 dissolved

(c) Field Artillery Brigades and Artillery Commanders

Brigade	Unit to which attached	Notes
1st Guard	1st Guard Infantry Division	16.2.17 renamed Guard Arko 1
2nd Guard	2nd Guard Infantry Division	16.2.17 renamed Guard Arko 2
3rd Guard	3rd Guard Infantry Division	6.9.15 dissolved
Guard Arko 3	3rd Guard Infantry Division	From 16.2.17
Guard Arko 4	4th Guard Infantry Division	Previously Foot Art. Gen. 26
5th Guard	5th Guard Infantry Division	16.2.17 renamed Guard Arko 5
Guard Arko 6	Guard Ersatz Division	
Guard Arko 7		Previously Guard Reserve Field Art. Brigade
Guard Arko 8	1st Guard Reserve Division	
1st Field Artillery	1st Infantry Division	16.2.17 renamed Arko 1
2nd Field Artillery	2nd Infantry Division	16.2.17 renamed Arko 2
3rd Field Artillery	3rd Infantry Division	16.2.17 renamed Arko 3; 21.12.17 > 87th Infantry Division
4th-6th Field Artillery	4th-6th Infantry Divisions	16.2.17 renamed Arkos 4-6
7th Field Artillery	7th Infantry Division	20.10.16 became independent (Div. Cmd. 302); 16.2.17 > 7th Infantry Division as Arko 7
8th-23rd Field Artillery	8th-23rd Infantry Divisions	16.2.17 renamed Arkos 8-23
24th Field Artillery	24th Infantry Division	16.2.17 renamed Art. Gen. 8
Arko 24	24th Infantry Division	
25th Field Artillery	25th Infantry Division	16.2.17 renamed Arko 25
26th Field Artillery	26th Infantry Division	16.2.17 renamed Arko 26; 8.1.18 > 48th Landwehr Division

27th-28th Field Artillery	27th-28th Infantry Divisions	>From 16.2.17 Arkos 27-28
29th Field Artillery	29th Infantry Division	16.2.17 as Arko 29 > 108th Infantry Division; 16.9.18 Staff only
30th-42nd Field Artillery	30th-42nd Infantry Divisions	>From 16.2.17 as Arkos 30-42
Arko 43	43rd Reserve Division	13.9.18 Staff only
Arko 44	44th Reserve Division	Previously Foot Art. Gen. 30
Arkos 45-46	45th-46th Reserve Divisions	
Arko 47	47th Reserve Division	27.9.18 Staff only. Previously Foot Art. Gen. 19
Arkos 48-49	48th-49th Reserve Divisions	
50th Field Artillery	50th Infantry Division	From 16.2.17 Arko 50
Arko 51	51st Reserve Division	
52nd Field Artillery	52nd Infantry Division	From 16.2.17 Arko 52
54th Field Artillery	54th Infantry Division	>From 16.2.17 Arko 54; 5.1.18 > 84th Infantry Division
Arko 55	54th Infantry Division	
56th Field Artillery	56th Infantry Division	From 16.2.17 Arko 56
Arko 57	58th Infantry Division	
58th Field Artillery	58th Infantry Division	From 16.2.17 Arko 58 with 26th Infantry Division
59th Field Artillery	88th Infantry Division	>From 16.2.17 Arko 59
60th Field Artillery	14th Landwehr Division	From 16.2.17 Arko 60; 1.10.18 > 94th Infantry Division
61st Field Artillery	V Reserve Corps	From 22.6.16; from 16.2.17 Arko 61 > 10th Reserve Division
62nd Field Artillery	200th Infantry Division	From 16.2.17 Arko 62
63rd Field Artillery	199th Infantry Division	From 16.2.17 Arko 63
64th Field Artillery	6th Infantry Division	From 11.9.16; from 16.2.17 Arko 64
65th Field Artillery	X Reserve Corps	From 27.9.16; from 16.2.17 Arko 65; 23.12.17 > 86th Infantry Division
66th Field Artillery	Carpathian Corps	From 27.9.16; from 16.2.17 Arko 66; 1.12.17 > 202nd Infantry Division
67th Field Artillery	29th Infantry Division	From 4.10.16; from 16.2.17 Arko 67
Arko 68	50th Reserve Division	
Arko 69	52nd Reserve Division	
Arko 70	54th Reserve Division	25.8.18 Staff only
Arko 71	1st Reserve Division	Previously Foot Art. Gen. 15

Arko 72	36th Reserve Division	
Arko 73	3rd Reserve Division	Previously Foot Art. Gen. 18
Arko 74	80th Reserve Division	
Arkos 75-82	75th-82nd Reserve Divisions	From 2.4.18 Arko 80 > 83rd Infantry Division. Previously 75th-82nd Reserve Field Artillery Brigades
Arko 85	85th Landwehr Division	
Arko 86	86th Infantry Division	From 17.12.17 with Army High Command
Arko 89	89th Infantry Division	13.6.18 > 301st Infantry Division. Previously Foot Art. Gen. 9
Arko 90	5th Reserve Division	Previously Foot Art. Gen. 23
Arkos 94-95	6th-7th Reserve Divisions	
Arko 96	22nd Reserve Division	
Arko 97	9th Reserve Division	
Arkos 98-100	11th-13th Reserve Divisions	
Arko 102	14th Reserve Division	
Arko 103	103rd Infantry Division	
Arko 104	15th Reserve Division	Previously Foot Art. Gen. 2
Arko 105	105th Infantry Division	Previously Foot Art. Gen. 31
Arko 106		
Arko 109	109th Infantry Division	21.8.18 Staff only. Previously Foot Art. Gen. 32
Arkos 110-112	17th Reserve Division; 111th Infantry Division; 18th Reserve Division	
Arko 113	113th Infantry Division	Previously Foot Art. Gen. 5
Arko 114	19th Reserve Division	Previously Foot Art. Gen. 24
Arko 115	115th Infantry Division	
Arko 116	2nd Guard Reserve Division	
Arko 117	117th Infantry Division	Previously Foot Art. Gen. 27
Arko 118	23rd Reserve Division	Previously 23rd Reserve Field Artillery Brigade
Arko 119	119th Infantry Division	
Arko 120	24th Reserve Division	Previously 24th Reserve Field Artillery Brigade
Arko 121		Previously Foot Art. Gen. 20
Arko 122	26th Reserve Division	Previously 26th Reserve Field Artillery Brigade
123rd Field Artillery	123rd Infantry Division	From 11.9.15; from 16.2.17 Arko 123
Arko 124		Previously 28th Reserve Field Artillery Brigade

Arko 125	33rd Reserve Division	12.10.18 > 3rd Infantry Division. Previously Foot Art. Gen. 7
Arko 126	21st Reserve Division	Previously Foot Art. Gen. 8
Arko 127	25th Reserve Division	22.10.18 dissolved
Arkos 128-129	1st/3rd Landwehr Divisions	
Arko 130	3rd Landwehr Division	Independent until 11.10.18
Arko 131	11th Landwehr Division	16.7.18 > 13th Landwehr Division. Previously Foot Art. Gen. 3
Arkos 132-133	16th/17th Landwehr Divisions	
Arko 134		Previously 4th Reserve Field Artillery Brigade
Arko 135	243rd Infantry Division	
Arko 136	10th Ersatz Division	Previously 10th Ersatz Field Artillery Brigade
Arko 137	19th Ersatz Division	Previously 19th Ersatz Field Artillery Brigade
Arko 138		Previously Foot Art. Gen. 28
Arko 139	4th Ersatz Division	From 28.3.17
Arko 140	46th Landwehr Division	From 29.3.17. 16.4.18 > 96th Infantry Division.
Arko 141	26th Landwehr Division	From 7.4.17
Arko 142	5th Infantry Division	From 13.4.17
Arko 143	12th Landwehr Division	From 17.4.17. 20.3.18 > 7th Cavalry Division.
Arko 144	28th Reserve Division	From 30.4.17
Arko 145	38th Landwehr Division	From 8.5.17
Arko 146	3rd Naval Division	From 31.5.17
Arko 147	8th Landwehr Division	From 6.6.17
Arko 148	2nd Landwehr Division	From 11.6.17
Arko 149	7th Landwehr Division	From 19.6.17
Arko 150	9th Landwehr Division	From 2.7.17
Arko 151	47th Landwehr Division	From 18.7.17. 10.3.18 > 301st Infantry Division
Arko 152	45th Landwehr Division	From 18.7.17
Arko 153	18th Landwehr Division	From 11.8.17. 9.4.18 > 21st Landwehr Division
Arko 154	44th Landwehr Division	From 22.10.17
Arko 155	53rd Reserve Division	From 19.11.17
Arko 156	201st Infantry Division	From 20.11.17
Arko 157	107th Infantry Division	From 20.11.17
Arko 183	183rd Infantry Division	14.9.18 Staff only
Arko 185	185th Infantry Division	
Arko 192	192nd Infantry Division	
Arko 195	195th Infantry Division	Previously Foot Art. Gen. 12

Arko 197	197th Infantry Division	22.10.18 Staff only
Arkos 203, 204, 206, 207, 208, 211, 212 & 213	Correspondingly numbered Infantry Divisions	
Arko 214	214th Infantry Division	Previously Foot Art. Gen. 11
Arko 215	215th Infantry Division	20.7.18 > 5th Landwehr Division. Previously Foot Art. Gen. 14
Arkos 216-217	216th/217th Infantry Divisions	
Arko 218	218th Infantry Division	From 1.4.17. 17.5.18 > 7th Cavalry Schützen Division
Arkos 219-222	Correspondingly numbered Infantry Divisions	
Arko 223	223rd Infantry Division	28.10.18 > 224th Infantry Division
Arko 224	224th Infantry Division	14.3.18 > German Jäger Div. Previously Foot Art. Gen. 10
Arko 225	225th Infantry Division	13.9.18 Staff only
Arko 226	226th Infantry Division	24.10.18 dissolved
Arko 227	227th Infantry Division	Previously 8th Ersatz Field Artillery Brigade
Arkos 228, 231-234	228th, 231st-234th Infantry Divisions	
Arko 235	235th Infantry Division	1.10.18 > 18th Landwehr Division
Arkos 236-242	236th-242nd Infantry Divisions	
Arko 243	2nd Naval Division	Previously Reserve Foot Art. Rgt. 3
Arko 244	25th Landwehr Division	
Arko 245	13th Landwehr Division	1.10.18 > 91st Infantry Division
Arko 255	255th Infantry Division	Previously Arko Sector IV Metz
1st Bavarian Field Artillery	1st Bavarian Infantry Division	From 22.2.17 Bavarian Arko 1
2nd-6th Bavarian Field Artillery	2nd-6th Bavarian Infantry Divisions	From 22.2.17 Bavarian Arkos 2-6
Bavarian Arko 7	Alpine Corps	
Bavarian Arko 8	8th Bavarian Reserve Division	Previously 8th Bavarian Reserve Field Artillery Brigade
Bavarian Arko 9	9th Bavarian Reserve Division	Previously Bavarian Foot Art. Gen. 4

10th Bavarian Field Artillery	10th Bavarian Infantry Division	From 22.2.17 Bavarian Arko 10; 21.10.18 > 2nd Bavarian Landwehr Division
Bavarian Arkos 11-12	11th-12th Bavarian Infantry Divisions	
Bavarian Arko 13	1st Bavarian Reserve Division	Previously 1st Bavarian Reserve Field Artillery Brigade
Bavarian Arko 14	14th Bavarian Infantry Division	Previously Bavarian Foot Art. Gen. 3
Bavarian Arko 15	15th Bavarian Infantry Division	
Bavarian Arko 16	16th Bavarian Infantry Division	Previously Bavarian Foot Art. Gen. 5
Bavarian Arko 17	1st Bavarian Landwehr Division	15.3.17 > 5th Bavarian Reserve Division. Previously 1st Bavarian Landwehr Field Artillery Brigade
Bavarian Arko 18	6th Bavarian Reserve Division	Previously Bavarian Foot Art. Gen. 1
Bavarian Arko 19	Bavarian Ersatz Division	20.10.18 dissolved
Bavarian Arkos 20-23	30th Reserve Division, 39th Reserve Division, 1st & 6th Bavarian Landwehr Divisions	
Guard Reserve Field Artillery	1st Guard Reserve Division	>From 16.2.17 Guard Arko 7
23rd, 24th, 26th, 28th, 75th-82nd Reserve Field Artillery	With the correspondingly numbered Reserve Divisions	>From 16.2.17 renamed Arkos 118, 120, 122, 124, 75-82
1st Bavarian Reserve Field Artillery	I Bavarian Reserve Corps	>From 11.1.15. 22.2.17 renamed Bavarian Arko 13
8th Bavarian Reserve Field Artillery	8th Bavarian Reserve Division	From 22.12.14. From 22.2.17 Bavarian Arko 8
1st Bavarian Landwehr Field Artillery	1st Bavarian Landwehr Division	From 21.4.16. From 22.2.17 Bavarian Arko 17
4th, 8th, 10th & 19th Ersatz Field Artillery	4th, 8th, 10th & 19th Ersatz Divisions	From 9.7.15. From 16.2.17 Arkos 134, 227, 136 & 137
Artillery Brigade Staff z.b.V. 1 (Gas)		>From 1.10.16. Renamed 22.3.17 Artillery Brigade Command z.b.V. 1; 11.8.17 renamed Artillery Staff z.b.V. 3

Artillery Staff z.b.V. 1		From 11.8.1917. Previously Field Rgt. Staff z.b.V. 1 (Gas)
Artillery Staff z.b.V. 2		From 11.8.1917. Previously Foot Art. Rgt. Staff z.b.V. 1 (Gas)

(d) Foot Artillery Generals and Artillery Generals

Brigade	Unit to which attached	Notes
Foot Art. Gen. in Great HQ		From 16.2.17 Artillery Gen. 1; 28.3.17 renamed Gen. Insp. of Artillery Gunnery Schools
Foot Art. Gen. AOK 1	5th Army	From 17.9.15 renamed Foot Art. Gen. 5
Foot Art. Gen. AOK 2 (in Strassburg)		From 14.9.15 renamed Foot Art. Gen. Gen. Govt. Warsaw
Foot Art. Gen. AOK 3	2nd Army	From 17.9.15 Foot Art. Gen. 2
Foot Artillery Brigade Command 1	4th Army	From 17.9.15 Foot Art. Gen. 7
Foot Artillery Brigade Command 2 (in Thorn)		From 17.9.15 Foot Art. Gen. 10
Foot Artillery Brigade Command 3 (in Metz)		From 17.9.15 Foot Art. Gen. 14
Foot Artillery Brigade Command 4 (in Strassburg)		From 17.9.15 Foot Art. Gen. 6
Foot Artillery Brigade Command 5 (in Köln)		From 17.9.15 Foot Art. Gen. 11
Foot Artillery Brigade Command 6	5th Army	From 17.9.15 Foot Art. Gen. 13
Foot Artillery Brigade Command 7 (in Posen)		Foot Artillery Brigade Command 9
Bavarian Foot Artillery Brigade Command 1	6th Army	From 4.10.15 Bavarian Foot Art. Gen. 1
Bavarian Foot Artillery Brigade Command 2		From 22.8.14. >From 4.10.15 Bavarian Foot Art. Gen. 2
Foot Art. Gen. 2		From 17.9.15. From 16.2.17 Art. Gen. 5
Foot Art. Gen. 3		From 16.2.17 Arko 131
Foot Art. Gen. 4		From 16.2.17 Art. Gen. 7
Foot Art. Gen. 5		From 16.2.17 Arko 113. Previously Foot Art. Gen. AOK 1

Foot Art. Gen. 6	From 16.2.17 Art. Gen. 3. Previously Foot Artillery Brigade Command 4
Foot Art. Gen. 7	From 16.2.17 Arko 125. Previously Foot Artillery Brigade Command 1
Foot Art. Gen. 8	From 16.2.17 Arko 126
Foot Art. Gen. 9	From 16.2.17 Arko 89. Previously Foot Artillery Brigade Command 7
Foot Art. Gen. 10	From 16.2.17 Arko 224. Previously Foot Artillery Brigade Command 2
Foot Art. Gen. 11	From 16.2.17 Arko 214. Previously Foot Artillery Brigade Command 5
Foot Art. Gen. 12	From 16.2.17 Arko 195. Previously Foot Art. Rgt. 6
Foot Art. Gen. 13	From 16.2.17 Art. Gen. 4. Previously Foot Artillery Brigade Command 6
Foot Art. Gen. 14	From 16.2.17 Arko 215. Previously Foot Artillery Brigade Command 3
Foot Art. Gen. 15	From 16.2.17 Arko 71. Previously Foot Art. Rgt. 7
Foot Art. Gen. 16	From 16.2.17 Art. Gen. 12. Previously Foot Art. Rgt. 12
Foot Art. Gen. 17	From 16.2.17 Art. Gen. 2. Previously Foot Art. Gen. Gen. Gov. Warsaw
Foot Art. Gen. 18	From 30.6.16. From 16.2.17 Arko 73.
Foot Art. Gen. 19	From 30.6.16. From 16.2.17 Arko 47
Foot Art. Gen. 20	From 30.6.16. From 16.2.17 Arko 121. Previously Reserve Foot Art. Rgt. 17
Foot Art. Gen. 21	From 30.6.16. From 16.2.17 Art. Gen. 11. Previously new Staff Foot Art. Rgt. 7
Foot Art. Gen. 22	From 30.6.16. From 16.2.17 Art. Gen. 9. Previously Reserve Foot Art. Rgt. 11
Foot Art. Gen. 23	From 30.6.16. From 16.2.17 Arko 90. Previously Reserve Foot Art. Rgt. 16

Foot Art. Gen. 24	From 30.6.16. From 16.2.17 Arko 114. Previously Foot Art. Rgt. 18
Foot Art. Gen. 25	From 30.6.16. From 16.2.17 Art. Gen. 6. Previously 1st Guard Foot Art. Rgt.
Foot Art. Gen. 26	From 30.6.16. From 16.2.17 Guard Arko 4. Previously Reserve Foot Art. Rgt. 8
Foot Art. Gen. 27	From 30.6.16. From 16.2.17 Arko 117. Previously Foot Art. Rgt. 8
Foot Art. Gen. 28	From 30.6.16. From 16.2.17 Arko 138. Previously Reserve Foot Art. Rgt. 2
Foot Art. Gen. 29	From 30.6.16. From 16.2.17 Art. Gen. 13
Foot Art. Gen. 30	From 16.9.16. From 16.2.17 Arko 44.
Foot Art. Gen. 31	From 16.9.16. From 16.2.17 Arko 105
Foot Art. Gen. 32	From 16.9.16. From 16.2.17 Arko 109
Foot Art. Gen. in Gen. Gov. Belgium	From 25.11.14. 25.6.17 dissolved
Foot Art. Gen. in Gen. Gov. Warsaw	From 14.9.15. 29.1.16 renamed Foot Art. Gen. 17. Previously Foot Art. Gen. AOK 2
Foot Art. Gen. with AOK Coastal	From 18.5.16. 25.6.17 dissolved.
Bavarian Foot Art. Gen. 1	From 16.2.17 Bavarian Arko 18. Previously Bavarian Foot Artillery Brigade Command 1
Bavarian Foot Art. Gen. 2	From 17.9.15. From 16.2.17 Bavarian Arko 19. Previously Bavarian Foot Artillery Brigade Command 2
Bavarian Foot Art. Gen. 3	From 17.9.15. From 2.3.17 Bavarian Arko 14.
Bavarian Foot Art. Gen. 4	From 30.6.16. From 5.3.17 Bavarian Arko 9.
Bavarian Foot Art. Gen. 5	From 30.6.16. From 21.3.17 Bavarian Arko 16
Art. Gen. 1	From 16.2.17. From 28.3.17 Gen. Insp. of Artillery Gunnery Schools. Previously Foot Art. Gen. in Great HQ

Art. Gen. 2	From 16.2.17. Previously Foot Art. Gen. 17
Art. Gen. 3	From 16.2.17. Previously Foot Art. Gen. 6. 15.4.17 dissolved
Art. Gen. 4	From 16.2.17. Previously Foot Art. Gen. 13
Art. Gen. 5	From 16.2.17. Previously Foot Art. Gen. 1
Art. Gen. 6	From 16.2.17. Previously Foot Art. Gen. 25
Art. Gen. 7	From 16.2.17. Previously Foot Art. Gen. 4. 31.3.17 dissolved
Art. Gen. 8 (Saxon)	From 25.2.17. 18.1.18 dissolved. Previously 24th Field Artillery Brigade
Art. Gen. 8 (Bavarian)	From 18.1.18
Art. Gen. 9	From 16.2.17. Previously Foot Art. Gen. 22. 31.3.17 dissolved
Art. Gen. 10	From 16.2.17. Previously Foot Art. Rgt. 20
Art. Gen. 11	From 16.2.17. Previously Foot Art. Gen. 21
Art. Gen. 12	From 16.2.17. Previously Foot Art. Gen. 16
Art. Gen. 13	From 16.2.17. Previously Foot Art. Gen. 29. 2.3.17 dissolved
Art. Gen. 13	From 16.2.17. Previously Foot Art. Rgt. 4
Art. Gen. 14	From 6.7.17
Art. Gen. 15	>From 14.7.18
Art. Gen. 16	From 14.7.18

(e) Pioneer Generals

2.8.14	Gen. of Engineer & Pioneer Corps in Great Headquarters Pioneer Generals 1-8
1.10.14	Pioneer General 9
1915	Pioneer Generals 10-12
1916	Pioneer Generals 13, 15-19
1917	Pioneer Generals 14, 20 & 31
1.9.18	Gen. of Engineer & Pioneer Corps in Great Headquarters renamed Pioneer General at the Chief of General Staff of the Field Army

(The Bavarian Pioneer General is included in the above).

Appendix IV

List of Mobile Units

(a) Infantry and Jäger

Infantry Regiments:

2.8.1914: 1st-5th Foot Guards, Guard Füsilier Rgt., Guard Gren. Rgts. 1-5, Infantry Training Rgt., Gren. Rgts. 1-7, Leib Gren. Rgt. 8, Gren. Rgts. 9-12, Inf. Rgts. 13-32, Füsilier Rgts. 33-40, Inf. Rgts. 41-72, Füsilier Rgt. 73, Inf. Rgts. 74-79, Füsilier Rgt. 80, Inf. Rgts. 81-85, Füsilier Rgt. 86, Inf. Rgts. 87-88, Gren. Rgt. 89, Füsilier Rgt. 90, Inf. Rgts. 91-99, Leib Gren. Rgt. 100, Gren. Rgt. 101, Inf. Rgts. 102-107, Schützen Rgt. 108, Leib Gren. Rgt. 109, Gren. Rgt. 110, Inf. Rgts. 111-114, Leib Guard Inf. Rgt. 115, Inf. Rgt. 116, Inf. Leib Rgt. 117, Inf. Rgt. 118, Gren. Rgt. 119, Inf. Rgts. 120-121, Füsilier Rgt. 122, Gren. Rgt. 123, Inf. Rgts. 124-182, Bavarian Inf. Leib Rgt., 1st-23rd Bavarian Inf. Rgts.

1915: 6th & 7th Guard Inf. Rgts., Inf. Rgts. 183-190, Inf. Rgts. 192-193, Inf. Rgts. 329-336, Inf. Rgts. 341-347, Inf. Rgts. 351-354, Inf. Rgts. 357-365, Inf. Rgts. 368-378, Inf. Rgts. 380-381, 24th & 25th Bavarian Inf. Rgts.

1916: Inf. Rgts. 389-428, Inf. Rgts. 431-434, Inf. Rgts. 437-439, Inf. Rgts. 442-444, Inf. Rgt. 477, 26th-29th Bavarian Inf. Rgts. (No 29 17th Jäger Rgt. from 11.1.17).

1917: Inf. Rgts. 445-476, Inf. Rgts. 478-479, 30th-32nd Bavarian Inf. Rgts.

Reserve Infantry Regiments:

2.8.1914: 1st & 2nd Guard Reserve Rgts., Res. Inf. Rgts. 1-3, Res. Inf. Rgts. 5-13, Res. Inf. Rgts. 15-32, Res. Inf. Rgts. 34-40, Res. Inf. Rgt. 46, Res. Inf. Rgts. 48-49, Res. Inf. Rgts. 51-53, Res. Inf. Rgts. 55-57, Res. Inf. Rgts. 59-61, Res. Inf. Rgts. 64-84, Res. Inf. Rgts. 86-88, Res. Inf. Rgts. 90-94, Res. Inf. Rgts. 98-99, Gren. Res. Rgt. 100, Res. Inf. Rgts. 101-104, Res. Inf. Rgts. 106-107, Res. Inf. Rgts. 109-111, Res. Inf. Rgt. 116, Res. Inf. Rgts. 118-121, Res. Inf. Rgt. 130, Res. Inf. Rgt. 133, Bavarian Res. Inf. Rgts. 1-8, Bavarian Res. Inf. Rgts. 10-15.

Oct. 1914: Res. Inf. Rgts. 201-248, Bavarian Res. Inf. Rgts. 16-17, Bavarian Res. Inf. Rgts. 20-21.

Dec. 1914: Res. Inf. Rgts. 249-272, Bavarian Res. Inf. Rgts. 18-19, Bavarian Res. Inf. Rgts. 22-23.

1916: Res. Inf. Rgt. 122, Res. Inf. Rgt. 273, Res. Inf. Rgts. 440-441.

Landwehr Infantry Regiments:

Aug. 1914: Landwehr Inf. Rgts. 1-13, Landwehr Inf. Rgts. 15-40, Landwehr Inf. Rgts. 46-49, Landwehr Inf. Rgts. 51-53, Landwehr Inf. Rgts. 55-56, Landwehr Inf. Rgts. 60-61, Landwehr Inf. Rgts. 65-66, Landwehr Inf. Rgt. 68, Landwehr Inf. Rgts. 71-78, Landwehr Inf. Rgts. 80-85, Landwehr Inf. Rgt. 87, Landwehr Inf. Rgts. 93-94, Landwehr Inf. Rgt. 99, Grenadier Landwehr Inf. Rgt. 100, Landwehr Inf. Rgts. 101-102, Landwehr Inf. Rgt. 104, Landwehr Inf. Rgts. 106-

107, Landwehr Inf. Rgts. 109-110, Landwehr Inf. Rgt. 116, Landwehr Inf. Rgts. 118-125, Landwehr Inf. Rgt. 133, Landwehr Inf. Rgt. 350, Bavarian Landwehr Inf. Rgts. 1-8, Bavarian Landwehr Inf. Rgt. 10, Bavarian Landwehr Inf. Rgts. 12-14 (No 14 became No 15 from Dec. 1914). (Staff Landwehr Inf. Rgt. 85 later became Inf. Rgt. 362).

1915: Landwehr Inf. Rgt. 57, Landwehr Inf. Rgt. 103, Landwehr Inf. Rgt. 126, Landwehr Inf. Rgt. 349, Landwehr Inf. Rgt. 379, Landwehr Inf. Rgt. 382.

1916: Landwehr Inf. Rgt. 111, Landwehr Inf. Rgts. 383-388, Landwehr Inf. Rgts. 429-430, Landwehr Inf. Rgts. 435-436.

1917: Landwehr Inf. Rgt. 86, Landwehr Inf. Rgt. 89, Landwehr Inf. Rgt. 105, Landwehr Inf. Rgt. 153, Landwehr Inf. Rgts. 327-328.

Garrison Infantry Regiments:
Aug. 1914: Garrison Inf. Rgts. Posen 1-8 (From June 1915 became Inf. Rgts. 329-336).

Ersatz Infantry Regiments:
1914: 1st & 2nd Guard Ersatz Rgts. (6th & 7th Guard Inf. Rgts. from 1.8.15), Ersatz Inf. Rgts. Königsberg 1-3 (Inf. Rgts. 376-378 from Sept. 1915), 1st-3rd Bavarian Ersatz Inf. Rgts.

1915: Ersatz Inf. Rgts. 23-24, Ersatz Inf. Rgt. 28, Ersatz Inf. Rgt. 32, Ersatz Inf. Rgt. 40, Ersatz Inf. Rgts. 51 & 52 (later became Inf. Rgts. 478 & 479), 4th Bavarian Ersatz Inf. Rgt.

1916: Ersatz Inf. Rgt. 29, 5th Bavarian Ersatz Inf. Rgt.

Reserve Ersatz Infantry Regiments:
Sept. 1914: Reserve Ersatz Inf. Rgts. 1-4.

Landwehr Ersatz Infantry Regiments:
1914: Landwehr Ersatz Inf. Rgts. 1-5 (later became Landwehr Inf. Rgts. 86, 153, 94, 349 & 350).

1915: Landwehr Ersatz Inf. Rgts. 6-9 (late became Landwehr Inf. Rgts. 351-354).

Mobile Landsturm Infantry Regiments:
1914: Landsturm Inf. Rgts. 1 & 2 (= Garrison Inf. Rgts. Posen 1 & 2; from June 1915 became Inf. Rgts. 329 & 330).

1915: Landsturm Inf. Rgts. 3, 7-11, 13, 17, 19, 23, 25, 26, 115 & 109 (this latter became Landwehr Inf. Rgt. 111).

1916: Landsturm Inf. Rgts. 31-36, 38-40 & Bavarian 2nd.

1917: Landsturm Inf. Rgts. 45-48.

Jäger Regiments: (Jäger Btns. in brackets)
21.5.15: Bavarian Jäger Rgt. 1 (Bavarian 1st & 2nd, Bavarian Reserve 2), Jäger Rgt. 2 (10, Reserve 10, Reserve 14), Jäger Rgt. 3 (Ski Btns. 1-4).

July 1916: Jäger Rgt. 4 (11, Reserve 5, Reserve 6), Jäger Rgt. 5 (Reserve 17, Reserve 18, Reserve 23).

Aug. 1916: Jäger Rgt. 6 (5, 6, 14), Jäger Rgt. 7 (13, Reserve 25, Reserve 26), Jäger Rgt. 8 (Reserve 4, Reserve 16, Reserve 24).

Sept. 1916: Jäger Rgt. 9 (8, Reserve 12).

Oct. 1916: Jäger Rgt. 10 (12, Reserve 13).

11.1.1917: Bavarian 29th Jäger Rgt. (Jäger Rgt.) with Bavarian Reserve Jäger Btn. 1, Reserve 7 & Reserve 9.

May 1918: Jäger Rgt. 11 (Staff Dragoon Rgt. 4, Guard Reserve, Guard Reserve Schützen, 1), Jäger Rgt. 12 (Staff Uhlan Rgt. 2, 2, 7, Reserve 1), Jäger Rgt. 13 (Staff Chevauleger Rgt. 8, Reserve 8, Reserve 20, Reserve 21), Jäger Rgt. 14 (Staff Res. Inf. Rgt. 233, Reserve 15, Reserve 19, Reserve 22).

15.8.1918: Bavarian Reserve Jäger Rgt. 15 (Bavarian Reserve Jäger Btn. 1 & Caucasian Railway Protection Btn.).

Mountain Regiments:
3.5.1918: Württemberg Mountain Rgt. (2 Btns.).

Infantry Battalions:
July 1917: Inf. Btns. 701-703 (for Turkey).

Assault Battalions:
1915: Assault Btn. Rohr, later No 5 (Rohr) – Pioneer formation.

1916: Assault Btns. 1-3 (No 3 = Jäger Btn. 3), Assault Btns. 4-12, Assault Btns. 14-16.

Jan. 1917: Assault Btn. 17, Assault Coy. 13 (March 1918 > Assault Btn. 12), Assault Coy. 18 (Aug. 1918 > Assault Btn. 18).

Aug. 1918: Assault Btn. 18.

Ski Battalions:
1914: Bavarian Ski Btn. 1, Ski Btn. 2.

Jan. 1915: Ski Btn. 3.

May 1915: Bavarian Ski Btn. 4.

(These units then became Jäger Rgt. 3 in May 1915).

Mountain Battalions:
1.10.1915: Württemberg Mountain Btn. (3.5.1918 > Württemberg Mountain Rgt.)

Brigade Ersatz Battalions:
Aug. 1914: 1-6 Guard Brigade Ersatz Btns. (1.8.15 > became part of 6th & 7th Guard Inf. Rgts.), Brigade Ersatz Btns. 5-58, 63, 64, 76-84, 86, 88, 89 (from March to July 1915 part of Inf. Rgts. 358-365, 368-371, Landwehr Inf. Rgts. 11, 22-32, 51, Ersatz Inf. Rgts. 23-24, 28-29, 32, 40, 51-52).

Reserve Brigade Ersatz Battalions:
Aug. 1914: Reserve Brigade Ersatz Btns. 1-2, 13-14, 33-39 & 43 (Sept. 1914 > Reserve Ersatz Inf. Rgts. 1-4).

Mobile Landsturm Infantry Battalions:
142 Btns. mobilised up to 31.8.1914. By the end of the year an addition 183 Btns. had come into existence. Additions in the following years – 1915: 93, 1916: 59, 1917: 15 Btns. Of these Battalions 17 (1915), 20 (1916), 1 (1917) were demobilised or dissolved, 30 became part of Inf. Rgts., 7 Landwehr Inf. Rgts., 70 mobile Landsturm Inf. Rgts.

Jäger Battalions:

2.8.1914: Guard Jäger Btn., Guard Schützen Btn., Jäger Btns. 1-14 (No 3 later became Assault Btn. 3), 1st & 2nd Bavarian Jäger Btns.

1.5.1916: Jäger Btn. 27 (dissolved 14.2.18).

Reserve Jäger Battalions:

2.8.1914: Guard Reserve Jäger Btn., Guard Reserve Schützen Btn., Reserve Jäger Btns. 1-14, Bavarian Reserve Jäger Btns. 1 & 2.

10.9.1914: Reserve Jäger Btns. 15-26.

Cycle Battalions:

1916: Cycle Btns. 1-5.

1917: Cycle Btn. 6.

1918: Cycle Btn. 8.

(b) Machine-Gun Formations (does not include the MG sub-units – companies and squadrons – forming parts of Regiments, Battalions and Cavalry Regiments).

MG Detachments:

2.8.1914: Guard MG Dets. 1 & 2, MG Dets. 1-9, Bavarian MG Det. 1.

1915: MG Det. 10.

(Later absorbed into Guard 1, 2 & 3 and Bavarian 1 MG Sqdns.).

AFV MG Detachments:

16.11.1916: AFV MG Det. 1.

Reserve MG Detachments:

2.8.1914: Reserve MG Dets. 1-5 (Nos 3 & 5 later became MGKs/MG Sqdns.).

MG Companies:

1914: MG Coy. 1 Belgium, MG Coys. 7-8 Germersheim.

1915: MG Coys. 2-14 Belgium, MG Coys. 369-370 & 401-405.

1916: MG Coys. 1-5 Army of the South, MG Coys. 601-608 & 701-709, MG Coy. 15 Belgium, MG Coys. 1-4 of 39th Reserve Division.

(These were later absorbed into Inf. Rgts.; MG Coys. 1-5 Army of the South were absorbed into MG Sharpshooter Dets. 63 & 64; those MG Coys. destined to accompany Inf. Btns. 701-703 in 1917 were newly-created and named MG Coys. 701-703).

Field MG Companies:

1915: Field MG Coys. II A.K., 28th & 29th Inf. Divs., 10th, 12th & 24th Inf. Brigades, Nos. 15, 18 & 19.

1916: Field MG Coys. 27, 31, 36 & 46.

(Later absorbed into Inf. Rgts.).

MG Sharpshooter Detachments:
Oct. 1916: MG Sharpshooter Dets. 1-62 & Bavarian 1-4.
May 1917: MG Sharpshooter Dets. 63-79.
(3 companies in each).

Automatic Rifle Battalions:
1915: Automatic Rifle Btns. 1 & 2.

Mountain MG Companies:
1914: Mountain MG Coy. 7 (Strassburg) (later absorbed into a Inf. Rgt.).

Mountain MG Detachments:
1915: Mountain MG Dets. 201-251, Württemberg Mountain MG Dets. 1-3, Bavarian Mountain MG Det. 9, Mountain MG Det. 8 (= MG Coy. 8 Belgium).
(Of the above, 235-238, 241, 243-246, Bavarian 8 & 9 later absorbed into the Infantry; 206, 208, 209, 213, 215, 218, 221, 223, 226, 227, 233, 234, 240 & 247 later became Companies in Mountain MG Dets. 260-265).
1917: Mountain MG Dets. 252-255 and Bavarian 1 & 2.
(Of the above, Nos. 252-255 became Companies in Mountain MG Dets. 260-265).
1918: Mountain MG Dets. 260-265 (each of 3 Companies).

Fortress MG Detachments/Companies:
1914: Königsberg 1st-14th, Posen Dets. 1st-8th and Coys. 1st-5th, Breslau 1st-6th, Wesel, Köln 1st-9th, Borkum, Königstein 1st-2nd, Strassburg 1st-10th, Neubreisach A-C, Metz 1st-7th & 12th-15th, Diedenhofen 1st-2nd & 11th, Graudenz 1st-11th & 14th, Thorn 1st-6th, Marienburg 1st-2nd, Kulm 1st-2nd, Danzig 1st-2nd, Mainz 1st-8th, Lötzen 2nd, Germersheim Bavarian 4th-5th & 7th-8th, Namur, Metz 1st-8th Reserve.
1915: Königsberg 15th-21st, Posen 9th-14th, Neubreisach D, Lötzen 1st, Westerland 4th, Lüttich A-D, Libau 1st-3rd.
(Later became MG Coys. within Inf. units).

AFV MG Sections:
1916: No 1 (soon > AFV MG Det. 1).
1917: Nos. 2-6.
1918: Nos. 7-11.

Field MG Sections:
Nov. 1914: Nos. 1-41.
1915: Nos. 54-530 & Bavarian 1-38.
(Later became MG Coys. within Inf. units).

MG Supplementary Sections:
Aug. 1915: Nos. 331-527 & Bavarian 1-6.
1916: Nos.528-878.
(Later became MG Coys. within Inf. units).

Light MG Troops:
Aug. 1916: Nos. 1-111.

(Later joined Inf. units).

MG Sharpshooter Troops:
April 1916: Nos. 1-200.
(Formed into MG Sharpshooter Detachments in Autumn 1916).

Mountain MG Sections:
1915: Württemberg Nos. 2-6 (later > Württemberg Mountain MG Coys. 1-3).

Fortress MG Troops:
1914: Swinemünde, Spandau, Posen 1st-13th, Ehrenbreitstein, Köln, Coastal 1st-4th, Rendsburg, Neu-Ulm, Freiburg, Mühlheim 2nd-3rd, Strassburg 1st-6th & 12th-13th, Mutzig 1st & 4th-13th, Neubreisach B & 15th, Istein, Neuenburg, Hüningen, Metz 1st-34th & 41st-46th, Diedenhofen 1st-20th, Graudenz 1st-2nd & 12th-13th, Thorn 1st-26th, Mainz 1st-8th, Lötzen 1st-3rd, Sensburg 1st-4th (Sections) & 1st-3rd (Troops), Deutsch-Eylau, Osterode, Antwerp I-II.
(Later absorbed into Inf. units).

(c) Cavalry

Cavalry Regiments:
2.8.1914: Garde du Corps, Guard Cuir., Leib Cuir. 1, Cuir. 2-8, Saxon Guard Reiter, Saxon Carabinier, 1st-2nd Guard Dragoon, Dragoon 1-2, Horse Gren. (Dragoon) 3, Dragoon 4-22, Guard Dragoon 23, Leib Dragoon 24, Dragoon 25-26, Leib Guard Hussar, Leib Hussar 1-2, Hussar 3-20, 1st-3rd Guard Uhlan, Uhlan 1-21, Jäger zu Pferde 1-13, 1st-2nd Bavarian Heavy Reiter, 1st-8th Bavarian Chevauleger, 1st-2nd Bavarian Uhlan.
1915: Cav. Rgts. 84-89, 93 & 94.
Of the above, 27 Rgts. were converted into dismounted/Cavalry Schützen Rgts.

Reserve Cavalry Regiments:
2.8.1914: Heavy Reserve Reiter 1-3, Guard Reserve Dragoon, Reserve Dragoon 1-8, Württemberg Reserve Dragoon, Reserve Hussar 1-2 & 4-9, Saxon Reserve Hussar (later No 18), Guard Reserve Uhlan, Reserve Uhlan 1-6, Saxon Reserve Uhlan (later No 18), Reserve Jäger zu Pferde 1, Bavarian Reserve Cav. 1 & 5.
1914: Bavarian Reserve Cav. 6.
Of the above, 12 Rgts. were converted into dismounted/Cavalry Schützen Rgts.; of these, 10 were later dissolved.

Landwehr Cavalry Regiments:
2.8.1914: Landwehr Cav. 1 & 2 (renamed 10 & 11 at the end of 1916).
Aug. 1915: Landwehr Cav. 90-92.
All later converted into Cavalry Schützen Rgts; dissolved in 1918 except for Nos. 91 & 92.

Ersatz Cavalry Regiments:
1914: Ersatz VI A.K. (dissolved June 1916), 2nd Ersatz VI A.K. (later Cav. Rgt. 88), Ersatz I A.K. (later Cav. Rgt. 89).

Cavalry Squadrons/Detachments:
9.7.1915: Guard, 4, 8, 10 & 19 (those except for No 4 dissolved in Aug. 1916).
Oct. 1916: 201-204 (Dets.), 205-207 (Sqdns.) (those except for No 205 dissolved in Dec. 1918).

Cavalry Sections:
July 1917: 701-703 (for Turkey).

Reserve Cavalry Detachments:
10.9.1914: 43-54.
29.12.1914: 75-82 & Bavarian 8.
(Dissolved in Autumn 1916 with the exception of Nos. 44, 45, 47, 50-53 & Bavarian 8).

Landwehr Cavalry Squadrons:
2.8.1914: 4 Sqdns for each of V, XIII & XVIII A.K.; 3 Sqdns. for each of Guard Corps, I, II, VI, VII, IX, X, XI, XVII & XX A.K.; 2 Sqdns. for each of III, VIII, XIV, XIX & I Bavarian A.K.; 1 Sqdn. in each of IV, XII, XXI as well as II & III Bavarian Reserve A.K.
(All dissolved in October 1916).

Ersatz Squadrons/Detachments:
1914: 1 Sqdn. for each of Cuir. 5, Horse Gren. 3, Dragoon 7 & 11, Leib Hussar 1, Hussar 4 & 6, Uhlan 1-4, 7, 11 & 15, Jäger zu Pferde 1, 4 & 11; 1 Detachment for each A.K.
(Later converted into Cavalry Sqdns. or Dets. or dissolved).

Landsturm Squadrons:
1914: 4 Sqdns. for each of I, IV, V, VII, XVII & I Bavarian A.K.; 3 Sqdns. for each of II, IX, X, XIV, XVIII, II Bavarian & III Bavarian A.K.; 2 Sqdns. for each of III, VI, VIII, XI, XIII & XIX A.K.; 1 Sqdn. in each of XII & XX A.K.
(Dissolved in Autumn 1916).

(d) Field Artillery

Field Artillery Regiments:
2.8.1914: 1st-6th Guard, Nos. 1-84 & 1st-12th Bavarian – each of 2 Btns. except for 1st Guard, 1, 3, 5, 8, 10, 11, 12, 15, 35 & Bavarian 5th, who each had a third Horse Art. Btn.; during 1916/17 eight of these Horse Art. Btns. were converted to IV Btns., leaving only 3 Horse Art. Btns. Field Art. Rgt. 11 had a V Btn.
Sept. 1914: Field Art. Rgt. Belgium (dissolved 31.12.14).
1915: 7th Guard, 85-88, 90-101, 103-104, 107-108, 111-112, 115-116, 201, 205, 209, 213, 217, 219-221, 223, 225, 227, 229, 233, 235, 237, 241, 243, 245-246, Bavarian 19-21 – all of 2 Btns. until 1916/17 when a III Btn. was added to each.
1916: 89, 102, 183, 185, 192, 204, 231, 247-249, 257, 259-261, 263-284, 402-403, 405-406, 408, 500-501, 600, Bavarian 22 & 23, Field Art. Rgt. Staff z.b.V. 1 (Gas) – later renamed Art. Staff z.b.V. 1 – partly each with 3 Btns., those that began with only 2 had 3 Btns. by early 1917.

1917: 238, 287, 301-302, 502-505, 601-602, Field Art. Staff z.b.V. 11.
(Field Art. Rgt. 103 dissolved in May 1918 during creation of Inf. Gun Batts.).

Reserve Field Artillery Regiments:
2.8.1914: 1st & 3rd Guard, 1, 3, 5-7, 9-26, 29, 36, Bavarian 1st, 5th & 6th.
1914: 43-70 (43-54 with III Btns.), Bavarian 8th & 9th.
1915: 32-33, 35, 40, 239 (33 & 35 with III Btns.), Bavarian 10th.
1916: 27-28, Bavarian 11th.
All possessed 3 Btns. from 1916/17.

Landwehr Field Artillery Regiments:
1915: 1-5, 8-9, 15, 19, Bavarian 1st & 6th.
1916: 12-13, 250-252, 254, 256, 258, Bavarian 2nd.
1917: 253 & 255.

Ersatz Field Artillery Regiments:
1915: 45, 47, 65 & Bavarian.
(No 65 became Field Art. Rgt. 238 on 22.3.17; Bavarian unit dissolved Oct. 1918).

Field Artillery Detachments:
1915: 87, 89, 102, 183, 185, 187, 192, 203-204, 231, 247 & Reserve 30.
1916: 262, 285-287, 401, 404, 407, 1001-1003.
1917: 302, 701-703, 1004-1007.
1918: 289, 292-294.
(The above were later assigned to Rgts. with corresponding numbers, or absorbed into
    other Rgts. Only Dets. 270, 286, 701-703, 1002-1007 and Reserve 30 remained
    independent).

Landwehr Field Artillery Detachments:
1915: Bavarian 1-3 (later > Bavarian Landwehr Field Art. Rgts. 1 & 6).

Field Artillery Ersatz Detachments:
2.8.1914: 1st & 2nd Guard, 6, 14, 18, 20, 22-23, 25, 27-29, 31-32, 38-41, 43-48, 53,
    55, 57, 60, 62, 65, 67, 75-77, Bavarian 1st, 2nd, 4th, 8th, 10th & 12th.
1914: 3rd Guard, 1, 9, 13, 15-17, 24, 26, 33-37, 42, 51-52, 54, 59, 63, 69-73, 80-84.
(Later included in Rgts.).

Field Artillery Batteries:
1915: 801-900.
1916: 901-915, 930, 940-942.
1917: 960-965, 971-983.
Later almost all were dissolved.

Mobile Landsturm Batteries:
August 1914: 2 in each of II-VI, XVII & Bavarian I A.K.; 1 in each of VII, VIII, XII,
    XIII, XVIII, XIX, Bavarian II & II A.K. – absorbed into Dets. during 1915.

Mountain Artillery Detachments:
- initially called Mountain Gun Detachments –

1914: 1st.
1915: 2nd-5th.
1916: 6th.
1917: 7th.

Mountain Batteries:
1914: 1st & 2nd.
1915: 3rd-15th.
1916: 16th-18th & Experimental Mountain Howitzer Batt. 941.
1917: 19th-21st.
Apart from 941 absorbed into Mountain Artillery Dets.

Infantry Gun Batteries:
1916: 1-9 (1 dissolved on 2.5.17).
1917: 10-50 (Nos. 29-50 dissolved in Nov. 1917), Inf. Gun Secs. 701-703.
1918: 29-51.

Close-combat Batteries:
Jan. 1917: 201-250.
(In May 1917 dissolved/absorbed into Field Art. Batts., Inf. Gun Batts. 28-50 – of the latter, Nos. 29-50 were dissolved in Nov. 1917).

(e) Foot Artillery & Artillery Survey Units.

Foot Artillery Regiments:
2.8.1914: 1st Guard (III Btn. 15.9.16), 2nd Guard (III & IV Btns. 30.12.16), 1 (IV, 4.8.16), 2 (III, 14.8.16, IV 2.7.17), 3 (III, 15.1.17), 4 (I-III), 5 (III, 1.6.15), 6 (I-III), 7 (IV, 24.9.17), 8 (III, 26.1.16), 9 (I-III), 10 (III, 15.1.17), 11 (III, 15.1.17), 12 (IV, 21.9.16), 13 (III, 22.7.16, IV 28.8.16), 14 (III, 3.11.15, IV, 15.1.17), 15 (III, 30.12.16), 16 (III, 5.9.16), 17 (III, 19.7.18), 18 (IV, 9.11.15), 19 (III, 1.6.15), 20 (III, 15.1.17), 1st Bavarian (III, 3.3.15), 2nd Bavarian (III, 17.9.16), 3rd Bavarian (I & II).
1916: 21 (28.11.16, II & III, 15.1.17), 2nd Bavarian (III, 17.9.16), 3rd Bavarian (I & II), 23 (28.11.16, II & III, 15.1.17), 4th Bavarian (27.12.16, I & II).
1917: 3rd Guard (12.12.17, I-IV), 24 (19.12.17, I & II), 25 (15.1.17, I-III), 26 (15.1.17, I-III), 27 (15.1.17, I-III), 28 (15.1.17, I-III).
11.5.1918: 5th Bavarian (I & II), 6th Bavarian (I & II) – latter formed from 6th Bavarian Reserve Btn.

Reserve Foot Artillery Regiments:
2.8.1914: 1st Guard (III, 4.11.16), 2nd Guard (III, 18.10.16, IV, 21.10.17), 1 (I & II), 2 (III, 4.11.16), 3 (III, 28.8.15), 4 (III, 4.11.16), 5 (I & II), 6 (III, 11.9.15), 7 (I-III, V, 12.3.16)[1], 8 (I & II), 9 (III, 25.8.15, IV, 1.9.16), 10 (IV, 18.10.16), 11 (III, 30.12.15), 13 (III, 22.8.15, IV, 16.6.17), 14 (III, 1.2.15, IV, 4.11.16), 15 (I & II), 16 (I & II), 17 (III, 1.1.16, IV, 4.11.16), 18 (III, 8.9.15), 20 (III, 1.2.15), Bavarian 1 (I & II), Bavarian 2 (I & II), Bavarian 3 (III & IV, 28.1.16).

---

1   IV/Reserve Foot Art. Rgt. 7 only existed for a couple of months from 12.3.16.

31.3.1916: 12 (I-III) – from Reserve Foot Art. Btn. 12.
19.1.1917: 19 (I-III) – from Reserve Foot Art. Btn. 19.

Landwehr Foot Artillery Regiments:
11.7.18 – Landwehr Foot Art. Rgt. Borkum (with Staff IV/2 & Landwehr Foot Art. Btn. 31, Batteries: 13th-15th/2nd & 3rd/Landwehr 31, 1st & 2nd/Landwehr 23, 1st & 2nd/Landwehr 33).

Landwehr Foot Artillery Regimental Staffs:
2.8.1914: 1, 3-5, 7, 8, 10, 11, 14-16, Bavarian 3.
1914: Bavarian 2 (27.10.).
1915: Bavarian 1 (19.2.), 20 (10.6.).
(Later converted into Foot Art. Rgt. Staffs 111-125).

Foot Artillery Regimental Staffs:
22.8.1915: 203.
1916: 101-110, 206-208, 210, 212, 215, 218, 219, 223-225 & Bavarian 1-3 (later Nos. 109, 110, 111 & 218 converted into Staffs of Foot Art. Rgts.).
20.11.1916: Foot Art. Rgt. Staff z.b.V. 1 (later Art. Staff z.b.V. 2) – Gas.
1917: 111th-125th (previously Landwehr Foot Art. Rgt. Staffs).

Foot Artillery Battalions:
1915: 21-24, 26-28, 29-31, 36, 38-40, 50, 52, 54, 56, 58, 84, Bavarian 10.
1916: 25, 32-35, 37, 41-49, 51, 53, 55, 57, 59-83, 85-99, 150-157, 401-404, Bavarian 4, 5, 7-9, 11-17.
1917: 100, 101, 106-118, 124, 158, 159, 405-407, Bavarian 18-27.
1918: 102-105, 119-123, 125-149, 160-164, 167-170, Bavarian 28-29.
(Later Nos. 21-23, 25, 26-28, Bavarian 4 & 5 absorbed into the Foot Art. Rgts. with corresponding numbers; No 24 became IV Btn./3rd Guard Foot Art. Rgt., Bavarian 7 became II Btn./5th Bavarian Foot Art. Rgt.).

Reserve Foot Artillery Battalions:
2.8.1914: 12, 19 & Bavarian 6.
(Absorbed into Foot Art. Rgts. with corresponding numbers on 1.4.16, 19.1.17 & 11.5.18).

Landwehr Foot Artillery Battalions:
2.8.1914: 1st Guard, 2nd Guard, 1-11, 13-20, Bavarian 1-3.
Dec. 1915: 3rd Guard, 4th Guard, 2nd Btn. 1, 2nd Btn. 4, 22, 26, 27, 28.
Spring 1916: 2nd Btn. 6, 21, 23-25.
Autumn 1916: 29-36, 38-45.
1917: 12, 37, 46-71.
Spring 1918: 72-76.
(Many were converted into Foot Art. Btns. The following units remained independent: 4th Guard, 1, 4, 7, 8, 10, 14, 17, 21, 22, 24-26, 29, 30, 32-35, 37, 40-51, 54-57, 59-66, 68-76, Bavarian 2 & 3).

Mobile Landsturm Foot Artillery Battalions:
2.8.1914: I-XV, XVII-XX, Bavarian I & II, 1st & 2nd Bavarian III A.K.

5.2.1915: 2nd VIII A.K.
2.11.1916: 2nd VII A.K.
(Most of the above were dissolved. I, VIII, XI-XIII, XVII & XIX remained, a total of 33
    Batts.).

Mobile Foot Artillery Ersatz Battalions:
1914: 21, 26-28, 2nd & 3rd Bavarian (later absorbed into other formations).
1916: Foot Art. Ersatz Btn. of 1st, 2nd & 5th Armies and Army Group Below (the lat-
    ter of only 2 Batts.).
1917: 1-5 (1, 2 & 5 previously those of 1st, 2nd and 5th Armies).
1918: 6.

Foot Artillery Battalion Staffs:
1915: 201-224.
    201 (Landwehr 3) later Foot Art. Btn. 55.
    202 (Landwehr 9) later Foot Art. Btn. 28.
    203 (Landwehr 16) later Foot Art. Rgt. Staff 203.
    204 later 13th Bavarian Foot Art. Btn.
    205 later Foot Art. Btn. 30.
    206 later Foot Art. Rgt. Staff 206.
    207 later Foot Art. Rgt. Staff 207.
    208 later Foot Art. Rgt. Staff 208.
    209 later Foot Art. Btn. 25.
    210 (Landwehr 18) later Foot Art. Rgt. Staff 210.
    211 (Bavarian Landwehr 1) later 4th Bavarian Foot Art. Btn.
    212 later Foot Art. Rgt. Staff 212.
    213 (Landwehr 13) later Foot Art. Btn. 82.
    214 (Landwehr 20) later Foot Art. Btn. 29.
    215 later Foot Art. Rgt. Staff 215.
    216 later 15th Bavarian Foot Art. Btn.
    217 later 9th Bavarian Foot Art. Btn.
    218 later Foot Art. Rgt. Staff 218.
    219 (Landwehr 8) later Foot Art. Rgt. Staff 219.
    220 later 8th Bavarian Foot Art. Btn.
    221 later 5th Bavarian Foot Art. Btn.
    222 later Foot Art. Btn. 12.
    223 later Foot Art. Rgt. Staff 223.
    224 later Foot Art. Rgt. Staff 224.
1916: 225-235.
    225 later Foot Art. Rgt. Staff 225.
    226 later Foot Art. Btn. 98.
    227 later Foot Art. Btn. 65.
    228 later 16th Bavarian Foot Art. Btn.
    229 later Foot Art. Btn. 83.
    230 later III/1st Guard Foot Art. Btn.
    231 later 24th Bavarian Foot Art. Btn.
    232 later Foot Art. Btn. 85.
    233 later Foot Art. Btn. 53.

234 later Foot Art. Btn. 33.
235 later Foot Art. Btn. 86.

Foot Artillery Batteries:
1914: Reserve Foot Art. Batts. 22-31 (converted to Foot Art. Batts. during 1915).
1915: Foot Art. Batts. 11, 83, 84, 101-138, 199, 201-631.
1916: Foot Art. Batts. 139-149, 632-797.
1917: Foot Art. Batts. 182-198, 1000-1021, 1023-1025.
(Most of the above were absorbed into Btns. The following remained independent: 393, 406-408, 423, 434, 450, 464, 478, 479, 521, 536, 549, 551, 613, 629, 642, 680, 684, 710, 717, 722, 746, 790, 1000-1010, 1012-1019, 1021, 1024-1025. Foot Art. Batts. 1112-1120 were Navy formations, originally named Navy Special Commands 5001-5009).

Short ('Kurze') Navy Gun Batteries (42cm):
2.8.1914: 1st-3rd; the following additional batts. were created in 1914, 4th; 1915, 5th-7th; 1916, 8th-10th; 1917, 7th (new) & 11th.
(Nos. 1, 2, 7, 9 & 11 were absorbed into Foot Art. Btns. Of the seven remaining batteries, one was attached to each of the Landwehr Foot Art. Btn. Guard and 1).

Heavy Coastal Mortar Batteries (30.5cm):
2.8.1914: 1st-5th; the following additional batts. were created in 1914, 6th & 7th; 1915, 8th & 9th; 1916, 10th.
(4th & 10th became 12th & 13th Batts., 2nd Guard Reserve Foot Art. Rgt.; the others remained independent, of which seven were attached to Foot Art. Btns. 32, 43, 44, 48, Landwehr 17, Landwehr 22 & Landwehr 39).

Heavy 15cm Gun Batteries:
1915: 1st-9th; 1916, 10th-31st; 1917, 32nd-41st; March 1918, 42nd-48th.
(2 Batts. (11th & 17th) were dissolved, 12 were absorbed into Foot Art. Btns. and 30 into Landwehr Foot Art. Btns.; only 4 (Nos. 16, 20, 21, 39) remained independent).

Artillery Survey Troops (from 8.11.1917 Light Survey Troops):
20.9.1915: 1-101.
1916: 102-123, 126-129.
19.2.1917: 124, 125, 130-177, Bavarian Mountain Light Survey Troop 1.

Sound Ranging Troops:
25.1.1916: 1-51.
Until Oct. 1916: 52-96.
9.1.1917: 97-129, Bavarian Mountain Sound Ranging Troop 1.

Artillery Correction Troops:
26.8.1917: 1-30 & 107 (No 31 in Sonthofen).
(All dissolved on 28.5.18).

Ground Survey Troops (Experimental):
12.8.1918: 501-505.

Direction Listening Sections:
15.5.1918: 1-3.
(In connection with Light Survey Troops 73, 78 & 100, formed with Sound Ranging
Troops 39, 45, 71, 90 & 106).

Observation Periscope Troops:
1915: 74, 93-97, 99, 101-109, 181.
1916: 1-73, 75-92, 8, 100, 110-180, 182-203, 210, 224.
1917: 204-209, 211-223.
(All dissolved by 31.10.17).

(f) Pioneers and variant units

Pioneer Regimental Staffs:
2.8.1914: Pioneer Rgts. 18-20, 23-25, 29-31, Bavarian Pioneer Rgt.
(All dissolved by 24.1.17, many converting to Stopi (see below). Pioneer Btns. with
Rgt. Nos. were formed containing various companies – see Gas Troops for Pioneer Rgts. 35 & 36).

Staff Officers of Pioneers (Regimental Cos; known as Stopi):
Dec. 1915: Stopi 51-54.
Autumn 1916: Stopi 55, 56 & 73; Bavarian Stopi 1.
1917: 40-42, 57-71, 150-165.
1918: 74-77, 166-168 & 170, Bavarian Stopi 2 & 3.
(Those numbered 150 and above given title 'Stopi bei e. Genkdo.' 11.5.17-4.9.18).

(Old) Pioneer Battalion Staffs:
2.8.1914: 1 Staff from each of the I & II Btns. of Pioneer Btns. – Guard, 1-17, 21, 22,
26-28, Bavarian 1 & 4, as well as I & II Btns. of Pioneer Rgts. 18-20, 23-25, 29,
30 & Bavarian Pioneer Rgt., Staff I Btn. Bavarian Pioneer Btn. 2, Staff I Btn. Bavarian Pioneer Btn. 43.
1915: 1 Staff from each of the III Btns. of Pioneer Btns. – Guard, 16, 24 & 28; Staff I
& II Btns. Pioneer Rgt. 31. (see Gas Troops from Btn. Staffs from Pioneer Rgts.
35 & 36).
1916: Staff IV Btn. Guard Pioneer Btn., Staff III Btn. Bavarian Pioneer Btn. 1, Staff II
Btn. Bavarian Pioneer Btn. 2, Staff II Btn. Bavarian Pioneer Btn. 3.
(Converted into 'new' Pioneer Btn. Staffs from 24.1.17 – II, III & IV Btns. with different numbers).

Reserve Pioneer Battalion Staffs:
1915: Staffs Reserve Pioneer Btns. 22-26, 32-34, 38-41 & Bavarian 2-4.
(Converted into 'new' Pioneer Btn. Staffs from 24.1.17).
1916: I-III Btns. Guard Reserve Pioneer Rgt. (see under Flamethrowers).

Landwehr Pioneer Battalion Staffs:
2.8.1914: Staff Landwehr Pioneer Btn. 6.
(Converted into 'new' Pioneer Btn. Staff 88, 24.1.17).

(New) Pioneer Battalion Staffs:
1916: 42, 402 & 407.

1917: Guard, 1-31, 38 (later 347), 39 (later 43), 40, 41, 50, 83, 84, 86-88, 91, 93, 100, 102-108, 110-130, 132-143, 183, 185, 187, 192, 195, 197, 199, 201, 202, 204-208, 211-214, 217-225, 227, 228, 231-243, 255, 301-303, 305-307, 309-319, 321-324, 326, 328, 333, 335, 343-354, 375, 376, 378-380, 382, 401, 403-405, 408-420, 422, 423, 425, 426, 431, 438, 444, 446, 485, 501, 504, 508 (later 243), 510, 519, Bavarian 1-26.

1918: 43-45, 150-158, 447 (later 44).

(For staffs 35-37, 38 & 39, as well as 94–96, see under Gas Troops).

Companies of Pioneer Battalions:
2.8.1914: 4 Coys. in each of Pioneer Btns. Guard, 1-30 & Bavarian 1-4.; 2 Reserve Coys. in each of Pioneer Btns. Guard, 1-27 & Bavarian 4; 1 Reserve Coy. in Bavarian Pioneer Btns. 1 & 2..

1915: 5 Coys. in Guard Pioneer Btn., 9th-16th Coys. III Btn. Guard Pioneer Btn.; a 5th Coy. added to Pioneer Btns. 1-7, 9, 11, 14-17, 26, 27 & Bavarian 2 & 4; a 5th & 6th Coy. added to Pioneer Btns. 8, 10, 12, 13, 21, 22; a 3rd Reserve Coy. added to Pioneer Btns. 9 & 13; 3rd-5th Reserve Coy. added to Pioneer Btn. 12; 3rd & 4th Reserve Coys. added to Pioneer Btns. 22 & 24; 1st & 2nd Reserve Coys. added to Pioneer Btn. 28; 1st-3rd Reserve Coys. added to Pioneer Btns. 32-34.

1916: 1st & 2nd Coy. IV Btn. to Guard Pioneer Btn.; 6th Reserve Coy. added to Pioneer Btn. 12.

24.1.1917: 4th-6th Coys. tto Pioneer Btn. 31 (= II Btn. Pioneer Rgt. 31).

1918: 1st-5th Coys. to Pioneer Btn. 44.

(The Bavarian Coys. were later converted to Coys. with sequential numbers).

Pioneer Companies with sequential numbers:
1915: Pioneer Coys. 99-108, 111, 112, 115, 116, 183, 185, 187, 192, 201, 205, 209, 213, 221, 225, 229, 233, 237, 241, 245-254, 259-264, 268, 269, 271-274, 275 (Ferry Coy.), Guard 301, 302-308, Bavarian 19-21, Bavarian Mining Coys. 1-3.

1916: Pioneer Coys. 279, 282-287, 310 (Water Fuel Coy.), 334-348, 353, 354, 357-360, 362-372, 377, 378, 402-404, Pioneer Mining Coys. 281, 292-300, 309, 311-314, 318-327, 329, 330, 333 & 352, Bavarian Pioneer Coys. 22-23, Bavarian Mining Coys. 4-8.

1917: Pioneer Coys. 355, 356, 361, 373-376, 379, 382-397 & 401, Pioneer Mining Coys. 398-400, 410-415, Bavarian Pioneer Coys. 1-18, 24-26.

1918: Pioneer Coys. 421 (Drilling), 422 (Liquid Oxygen), 423 (Trench Digging), Bavarian Pioneer Coys. 27-28.

Reserve Pioneer Companies:
1914: Reserve Pioneer Coys. 43-55, 75-86 & Bavarian 20-21.

1915: Reserve Pioneer Coys. 87-91, Bavarian 5-18.

1916: Bavarian Reserve Pioneer Coys. 1-4 & 19 (Nos. 1-4 from Reserve Coys. of Bavarian Pioneer Btn.).

Landwehr Pioneer Companies:

2.8.1914: 2 each from Guard, I-XI, XIII, XVIII, I-III Bavarian A.K., 1 each from XII & XIX A.K.

1915: 3 each from VI & X A.K., 3rd-5th Landwehr Pioneer Coys. from XIII A.K.

1917: Bavarian Landwehr Pioneer Coys. 1-6 (formed by renaming the 1st and 2nd Landwehr Pioneer Coys. from I, II & III Bavarian A.K.).

Mobile Landsturm Pioneer Companies:

1914: 2 each from II, III, V, VII-XI, XIV & Bavarian II & III A.K.; 3 each from Bavarian I A.K.; 1 each from IV, XII, XIII & XI A.K.

1915: 1st & 2nd I, 3rd II, 3rd-6th III, 2nd-4th IV, 2nd & 3rd VI, 3rd-5th VII, 3rd-5th IX, 3rd & 4th X, 1st & 3rd XII, 2nd & 3rd XIII, 1st XVI, 1st & 2nd/XVII, 1st-3rd XVIII, 1st-3rd XIX, 4th Bavarian I, 3rd Bavarian III, Bavarian 11th & 12th.

1916: 1st VI, 3rd XIV.

1917: 4th-6th XIV, Bavarian 1-10 (Nos. 1-9 from 1st-4th I, 1st & 2nd II, 1st-3rd III Bavarian A.K.)

Mobile Landsturm Pioneer Ersatz Companies:

1915: 6th VII, 3rd VIII, 5th IX, 3rd X, 3rd XI, 1st XXI, 5th Bavarian I, 3rd Bavarian II, 4th Bavarian III.

Mobile Pioneer Ersatz Companies:

1914: 1st/Guard, 1st & 3rd/1st, 1st./2nd, 2nd/3rd, 1st/4th, 1st/5th, 2nd/6th, 1st/9th, 1st/10th, 3rd/11th, 1st/12th, 1st & 3rd/14th, 1st/16th, 2nd & 3rd/18th, 1st/21st, 1st/22nd, 1st & 2nd/23rd, 1st-3rd/24th, 3rd/26th, 2nd/Bavarian 1st, 1st/Bavarian 3rd.

1915: 1st/7th, 4th/9th, 1st/11th, 1st/20th, 2nd/26th.

1917: 3rd-5th/13th.

(Of which 9 Coys. were converted into Pioneer Coys. with the same number, one 4th/ Pi.35 – Gas).

Cavalry Pioneer Detachments:

2.8.1914: Guard, 1-9 & Bavarian 1.

Gas Troops:

1.5.1915: Pioneer Rgts. 35 & 36 each with I & II Btns. & Minenwerfer Coy (dissolved 1.9.17).

1.9.1917: Pioneer Btn. 35 (previously I/Pioneer Rgt. 35), Pioneer Btn. 36 (previously I/Pioneer Rgt. 36), Pioneer Btn. 37 (previously II/Pioneer Rgt. 35), Pioneer Btn. 38 (previously II/Pioneer Rgt. 36), each with 1 Minenwerfer Det. (formed from Minenwerfer Dets. from Pioneer Rgts. 35 & 36).

22.9.1917: Gaswerfer Coy. 1.

1.2.1918: Pioneer Btn. 39.

22.6.1918: Pioneer Btns. 94-96.

Flamethrowers:

20.4.1916: Guard Reserve Pioneer Rgt. with Staff I & II Btns. and 1st-10th Coys. (previously III & IV Btns. Guard Pioneer Btn.).

26.9.1916: 11th & 12th Coys.

Minenwerfer Battalions:
1915: Minenwerfer Btns. I-IV.
1916: Minenwerfer Btns. V-VII.
1917: Minenwerfer Btns. VIII-XIII.
1918: Minenwerfer Btns. XIV-XXIII.

Minenwerfer Companies (excepting Minenwerfer Coys within Inf. Rgts.):
1915: 1st-4th Guard, 6th & 7th Guard, 1, 2, 4-7, 10, 11, 13, 15-18, 20, 21, 23, 24, 27-30, 33-35, 37-40, 50, 52, 54, 56, 58, 103, 105 (later 174), 107-109, 111, 113, 117, 119, 121, 161-166, 190-192, 207, 209-211, 213, 216, 217, 221, 222, 224, 226, 230 (later Bavarian 230), 233, 235, 244, 246, 248, 249, 252, 253, 254 (later 160), 281, 302 (later 212), 303, 305, 307-309, 312, 313, 315, 316, Bavarian 1-3, 5, 100, 200, 201, 205, 206, 208, 209, 301, 302, 306.
1916: 5th & 8th Guard, 3, 8, 9, 12, 14, 19, 22, 25, 26, 31, 32, 36, 41, 83, 84, 86-89, 91-93, 115, 123, 167-175, 181-183, 187, 195, 199, 201, 203, 205, 206, 212, 214, 215, 218, 219, 223, 225, 228, 236, 239 (later Bavarian 239), 243, 243, 247, 250, 251, 275-280, 282, 301, 304, 311, 314, 317, 319, 320, 347, 385, 401-413, 415, 416, 421-428, 430-434, Bavarian 4, 6, 10-12, 14 & 15.
1917: 9th Guard, 94-96, 105, 160, 176, 184, 197, 254, 323, 326, 328, 345, 346, 390, 414, 417-420, 429, 435-443, 451-453, 455, 500, Bavarian 16, 230 & 239.
(In August 1918 all transferred to Inf. unit as Minenwerfer Coys.).

Heavy Minenwerfer Detachments & Sections (latter not regulation):
5.2.1915: Heavy Minenwerfer Dets. Guard, 1-52, 54-58, 71-89, Bavarian 1-9 & 25.
3.4.1915: Heavy Minenwerfer Sections Guard, 1-27.
1916: Heavy Minenwerfer Sections 28-100, 701-707, Bavarian 401-404.
(By early Autumn 1915 the above were beginning to be absorbed into Minenwerfer Coys.).

Medium Minenwerfer Detachments & Sections (latter not regulation):
5.2.1915: Medium Minenwerfer Dets. Guard, 1-18 (from April 1915 101-118).
5.4.1915: Medium Minenwerfer Dets. 101-199 (as well as Bavarian 101-107 & 125).
1915: Medium Minenwerfer Sections Guard, 101-135; Medium Supplemental Dets. 1-17, 19-39 & Bavarian 104.
6.1.1916: Medium Minenwerfer Dets. 350-352.
1916: Medium Minenwerfer Secs. 136-200, 801-821 & Bavarian 501-506.
(By early Autumn 1915 the above were beginning to be absorbed into Minenwerfer Coys.).

Light Minenwerfer Detachments & Sections (latter not regulation):
3.4.1915: Light Minenwerfer Dets. Guard, 201-299, 301-305 & Bavarian 201-207 & 210.
1915: Light Minenwerfer Secs. Guard, 201-238, Light Minenwerfer Supplemental Dets. 1-41, Bavarian 203 & 204.

1916: Light Minenwerfer Secs. 239-300, 901-956 & Bavarian 601-605.
(By early Autumn 1915 the above were beginning to be absorbed into Minenwerfer Coys.).

Minenwerfer Troops:
7.7.1917: Minenwerfer Troops 701-703 (for Inf. Btns. 701-703 in Turkey).
Searchlight Sections:
2.8.1914: 1 Searchlight Sec. each with Pioneer Btns. Guard, 1-17, 21, 22, 26-28 & Bavarian 1-4.
1915: Nos. 50-53, 99, 101-103, 107, 111, 115, 183, 185, 187, 192, 201, 205, 209, 213, 221, 225, 229, 233, 237, 241, 245-282, Bavarian 19, 21, 102.
1916: Nos. 283-355, 361-367, 401-404, Bavarian 22.
1917: Nos. 359, 360 & 405.
(7 Secs. transferred to Anti-aircraft defence, 3 received different numbers).

Reserve Searchlight Sections:
1914: Nos. 22-27, 35, 38-41 & Bavarian 1.
1915: Nos. 1, 3, 4, 7-9, 12, 14, 18, 42 & Bavarian 2-4.
1916: Bavarian 5-10.
(4 Secs. transferred to Anti-aircraft defence, 6 received different numbers).

Fortress Searchlight Sections:
1914: Light 1-32 & Bavarian 3, Heavy 1-59 & Bavarian 1, 2, 4, 5.
1915: Light 35, 37-45, Heavy 60-66.
1916: Heavy 67-73.
1917: Heavy 74-77.
(The Light Secs. were later renamed, 39 Heavy Secs. transferred to Anti-aircraft defence).

Heavy Searchlight Sections:
15.9.1915: Nos. 500-503.
1916: Nos. 504-506.

Hand Searchlight Sections:
28.9.1917: Nos. 1-13 & Bavarian 7, 8, 12 & 14.
1918: Nos. 14-149, 180-253, Bavarian 1-6, 9-11, 15, 16, 18-20, 22-24, 26, 30-32.

(g) Airship units

Army Airships (X signifies year craft was destroyed or went out-of-service)
2.8.1914: Hanse (X 1916), Viktoria Luise (X 1915), Sachsen (X 1915), Z. IV (X 1917), Z. V-IX (X 1914), S.L. 2 (X 1916), M. IV (X 1915), P. IV (1916).
1914: Z. X (X 1915).
1915: Z. XI (X 1915), Z. XII (X 1917), LZ. 34, LZ. 35, LZ. 37-LZ. 39 (all X 1915), LZ. 72 (X 1917), LZ. 74 (X 1915), LZ. 77, LZ. 79, LZ. 81, LZ. 85, LZ. 86 (all X 1916), SL. 5 (X 1915), SL. 7 (X 1917).

1916: LZ. 88 (X 1917), LZ. 90 (X 1916), LZ. 93 (X 1917), LZ. 95 (X 1916), LZ. 97,
    LZ. 98, LZ. 101, LZ. 103, LZ. 107 (all X 1917), SL. 10, SL. 11 (both X 1916),
    SL. 13, PL. 25 (both X 1917).
1917: LZ. 111, LZ. 113, LZ. 120, E. 9, E. 10 (all X 1917), F. 2 (X 1918).

Airship Troops:
2.8.1914: 1-17 & Bavarian 1.
1915: 18-24.
(Nos. 1, 2 & 7 dissolved 15.11.14, the remainder demobilised or dissolved in 1917).

Field Airship Detachments:
2.8.1914: 1-8, Bavarian 1 (61 from 2.7.17).
1914: 9-12, Bavarian 2 (62 from 2.7.17).
1915: 13-17 & 47, Bavarian 3-6 (63-66 from 2.7.17).
1916: 38-44, Bavarian 7 & 8 (67 & 68 from 2.7.17).
1917: 45 & 46.
(Dets. 1-45 converted for forming Balloon Sections 1-112 on 3.3.17; Det. Staffs remained; Bavarian Det. remained operational).

Balloon Sections:
3.3.1917: Nos. 1-112, Bavarian 1-23 (later 201-223).
1917: Nos. 113-147, 159-161 & Turkish 2 & 3.
1918: Nos. 148-156.

Fortress Airship Troops:
2.8.1914: Nos. 1, 5, 10, 13-15, 18-24, 26, 29, 30, Metz & Germersheim.
(All converted to Airship Detachments in the field, on 20.9.15).

Balloon Centres:
23.9.1917: Nos. 1-7 & A-C.
1918: Nos. 9, 14, 17-19.

Barrage Balloon Detachments:
20.3.1917: Nos. 1-5.
16.6.1917: Nos. 6 & 7.
14.8.1917: Barrage Balloon Det. 5th Army.
1918: Nos. 8 & 9.

(h) Aviation units

Aviation Group Leaders:
28.12.1916: 2, 3 & 7.
1917: 1, 4-6, 8-16.
1918: 17-24.

Fighter Flight Group Leaders:
28.10.1917: 1-5.
1918: 6-12.

Ground Attack Group Leaders:
6.7.1918: 1-3.

Fortress Aviation Detachments:
2.8.1914: 1st (Metz), 2nd (Strassburg), 3rd (Köln), 4th (Posen), 5th (Königsberg), 6th (Graudenz), 7th (Boyen), Bavarian (Germersheim).
1914: 8th (Breslau), 9th (Glogau), Posen 2, Strassburg 2, Metz 2, Boyen 2, Königsberg 2, Graudenz 2, Lüttich.
(Converted into Field Aviation Detachments at the end of 1914).

Field Aviation Detachments:
2.8.1914: 1-30, Bavarian 1-3.
1914: 31-48, 52, 56, 58, 59, 65 & 71, Bavarian 4-6.
1915: 49-51, 53-55, 57, 60-64, 66-70, 72-74, Bavarian 7-9.
(On 11.1.17 all were converted to Aviation Dets. were Aviation Dets. 'A').

Artillery Aviation Detachments:
6.8.1915: 201-212, Bavarian 101-103.
1916: 213-240.
(All converted to Aviation Dets. 'A', 29.11.16).

Aviation Detachments:
22.1.1916: 300 (Pascha).
11.1.1917: 1 & 2, 3 (Lb.), 4, 5 (Lb.), 6-11, 12 (Lb.), 13-17, 18 (Lb.), 19-22, 23 (Lb.), 24-38, 39 (Lb.), 40 (Lb.), 41-43, 44-46 (Lb.), 47 & 48.
1917: 301-305.
(1-48 were formed from the previously-named Field Aviation Dets.; nos. 4, 11, 15, 21, 24, 25 & 47 were converted into Escort Flts. on 26.1.18).

Aviation Detachments A:
29.11.1916: 201-255.
1917: 256-298.
(These were formed from the Artillery Aviation Dets. and partly from the Field Aviation Dets.; 260, 261, 276 & 289 were converted into Aviation Dets. (Lb.) 10.3.18, 220 became an Escort Flt. 26.1.18).

R-Plane[2] Detachments:
31.1.1916: 500.
3.8.1916: 501.
28.12.1916: 502 & 503.
22.9.1917: 502 & 503 dissolved; 500 & 501 renamed R-Aviation Dets. 500 & 501.
23.10.1918: R-Aviation Dets. 500 & 501 merged to form R-Plane Det. 501.

Combat Groups of the OHL:
1915: Kagohl. 1 & 2 (previously Carrier Pigeon Dets. O & M).
1916: Kagohl 3-7.
(Converted to 'Bogohl' 1.1.17, nos. 5-7 dissolved).

2   'Riesenflugzeuge', heavy bomber aircraft.

Bomber Groups of the OHL:
1.1.1917: Bogohl. 1-4 (previously Kagohl).
17.12.1917: Bogohl. 5-7.
2.3.1918: Bogohl. 8.

Fighter Groups:
23.6.1917: Fighter Group Freiherr von Richtofen No 1.
2.2.1918: Fighter Groups 2 & 3.

Fighter Flights:
1.1.1917: 1, Boelcke No 2, 3-37.
1917: 38-47, 76-78, 81.
1918: 48-75, 79 & 80, Army Group F.
3.10.1918: 82-90 (previously Home Combat Flights on the Home Front).

Combat Flights:
17.8.1915: S. 1 (initially 'Köln', then 'Trier', then 31, then S. 1), S. 2 (initially 'Freiburg', then 32, then S. 2), S. 3 (initially T), Bavarian 36. (On 1.1.17 S. 1-3 became Escort Flts., Bavarian 36 > Bogohl. 6, 17.12.17).
1916: Fokker Combat Flts. 'Falkenhausen', I, II, III, 'Sivry', B, Kofl. 3, Kofl 12, 7th Army (these were either converted into Fighter Flights on 1.1.17, or dissolved), Home Combat Flights 1-6 (renamed Fighter Flts. 90, 82-86 in Autumn 1918).
1917: Home Combat Flights 7-9 (renamed Fighter Flts. 87-89 in Autumn 1918).
(Some Combat Flight pilots were individually attached to Aviation Detachments; many were assigned to Home Combat Flts. during the course of their conversion to Fighter Flts.; these movements are not remarked upon above).

Escort Flights:
1.1.1917: 1-27 (formed from 24 Flts. of Kagohl. 1-7, and Combat Flts. S. 1-S. 3).
1.3.1917: 28-30.
26.1.1918: 31-38 (from Aviation Dets. 4, 11, 15, 21, 24, 25, 47 & Aviation Det. A. 220).
(Renamed Ground Attack Flights 27.3.18).

Ground Attack Flights:
27.3.18: 1-38 (previously Escort Flts.).

(i) Anti-Aircraft units

Staff Officers of Anti-Balloon Guns:
1.7.1915: 1 Stobak per 1st-7th Armies (only until 6.1.17).

Commanders of Anti-Aircraft Guns:
7.1.1917: Koflak 1-7.
25.9.1917: Koflak 14 (Koflak 17 from 1.2.1918).
1.4.1918: Koflak 18 & 19.
25.6.1918: Koflak 9.

Flak Group Commanders:
7.1.1917: Flakgruko 1-54.
1.4.1918: Flakgruko 55.

Flak Batteries:
15.11.1915: Flak Batts. 1-41, Motor Vehicle Flak Batts. 1-4.
1916: Flak Batts. 42-67, 301-340, 501-564, Motor Vehicle Flak Batts. 5-14, 101-103, Emplaced Flak Batts. 1 & 2.
1917: Flak Batts. 68-94, 341, 342, 565-595, 701-732, Motor Vehicle Flak Batts. 15-18, 104-184, Emplaced Flak Batts. 3 & 4, Wagon-mounted Flak Batt. 1.
1918: Flak Batts. 95, 96, 601-611, 733-753, 755-775, Motor Vehicle Flak Batts. 19-40, 185-218, Wagon-mounted Flak Batts. 5-16.

Flak Sections:
1914: Flak Secs. 1-17, 22-26, 56, 60-62, Emplaced Flak Secs. 1, 2, 4-6, Wagon-mounted Flak Secs. 3 & 7.
1915: Flak Secs. 18-21, 27-55, 57-59, 63-174, Emplaced Flak Secs. 9-11, 14-16, 23-26, 31-60, Wagon-mounted Flak Secs. 8, 12, 13, 17-22, 27-30, Automatic Flak Secs. 1-69.
1916: Flak Secs. 175-191, 401-423, Emplaced Flak Secs. 61-89, 91-105, 108-121, Wagon-mounted Flak Secs. 90, 106 & 107, Automatic Flak Secs. 70-83.
1917: Flak Secs. 424-426, Emplaced Flak Secs. 122-154, 161-166, Automatic Flak Secs. 84-101.
1918: Automatic Flak Secs. 102-183.
(The majority of the above were used to create Flak Batts. soon after their creation).

Flak Guns on Motor Vehicles:
2.8.1914: 1-9.
1915: 10-106.
(These individual guns were absorbed into Motor Vehicle Flak Batts. in 1918).

Flak Searchlight Batteries:
27.2.1918: Emplaced Flak Searchlight Batts. 801-838.
1918: Emplaced Flak Searchlight Batts. 839-887, Motor Vehicle Flak Searchlight Batts. 451-468.

Flak Searchlight Sections:
1917: Emplaced Flak Searchlight Secs. 1-200, 601-627, Horse-drawn Flak Searchlight Secs. 201-246, Railway Flak Searchlight Secs. 501-504.
1918: Emplaced Flak Searchlight Secs. 722-795, Railway Flak Searchlight Secs. 505-522, 524-534, Motor Vehicle Flak Searchlight Secs. 401-409.
(To assist in the formation of the Flak Searchlight Batts and Secs. 742-795 261 older Flak Searchlight Secs. were dissolved. Only Flak Searchlight Secs. 742, 745, 754, 755 & 770 remained complete. The formation of Horse-drawn Flak Searchlight Secs. 241-246 entailed the dissolving of twelve older Horse-drawn Flak Searchlight Secs.).

Flak MG Detachments:
1.8.1917: 801-803, 901-921, 925.

Flak MG Sections:
28.8.1917: 1-71.
1918: 72-103.

(j) Signals Troops

Staff Officers of Telegraph Troops:
2.8.1914-14.12.1916: One per Army Command.

Radio Commands:
2.8.1914-14.12.1916: One per Army Command.

Commanders of Telephone Troops with Armies:
14.12.1916-12.9.1917: One per Army Command.

Commanders of Radio Troops:
14.12.1916-12.3.1917: One per Army Command.

Commanders of Radio Troops with Armies:
12.3.-12.9.1917: One per Army Command (title 'Akofunk').

Army Signals Commanders:
12.9.1917: 1-11, 13-26 & 70.

Commanders of Telephone Troops with Corps:
14.12.1916-12.3.1917: One per Corps.

Commanders of Radio Troops with Corps:
14.12.1916-12.3.1917: One per Corps.

Commanders of Telephone Troops with Groups:
12.3-12.9.1917: One per Corps.

Commanders of Radio Troops with Groups:
12.3-12.9.1917: One per Corps.

Group Signals Commanders:
12.9.1917: Guard, 601-621, 623, 625-627, 651-667, Bavarian 601-603, Guard Reserve Corps, 701, 703, 705-710, 712, 714, 715, 718, 722-727, 738-741, Bavarian 701, z.b.V. of OHL 202-204 & 206.
24.6.1918: 669.

Division Signals Commanders:
12.9.1917: Guard 1-5, 1-42, 50, 52, 54, 56, 58, 83, 84, 86-89, 91-96, 101, 103, 105, 107-109, 111, 113, 115, 117, 119, 121, 123, 183, 185, 187, 192, 195, 197, 199-208, 211-228, 231-243, 255, 291-293 (for Naval Divisions), 301-305, Bavarian

1-6, 10-12, 14-16, Guard 401, Guard 402, 403, 405-407, 409-419, 421-426, 428, 433, 435, 436, 443-454, 475-482, Bavarian 401, Bavarian 405, Bavarian 406, Bavarian 408, Bavarian 409, Bavarian 430 & 439, 501-505, 507-523, 525, 526, 538, 544-548, Bavarian 501-502 & 506, Guard 551, 554, 555, 560, 569, 585, 622, 700, 701, Bavarian 551, 901-903, 906.

Army Telegraph Detachments:
2.8.1914: 1-5, 7 & 8, Bavarian 6.
1914: 9
1915: 10, 11, 13-15.
(Converted into Army Telephone Dets., 6.2.1916).

Line of Communication Telegraph Directorates:
2.8.1914-30.8.1916: One per L of C Inspectorate.
(Converted into Army Telephone Dets. with numbers above 100, and deployed as the second such Det. with Armies).

Telephone Detachments z.b.V. with OHL:
24.1.1917: Bavarian 715, 801-805.

Army Group Telephone Detachments:
22.5.1917: 200-202.
1918: 203-204.

Army Telephone Detachments:
6.2.1916: 1-15.
1916: 16-22, 101-119, Supreme Commander East.
1917: 24, 25, 120, 121, 125 & 1701.

Corps Telephone Detachments:
2.8.1914-24.1.1917: One per Corps (later became Group Telephone Dets.).

Group Telephone Detachments:
24.1.1917: Guard, 601, 603-619, 622 (later Mountain Tel. Det. 622), 625-627, Bavarian 601-603.
1917: 623, 628, 651-667, Guard Reserve Corps, 701, 703, 705-710, 712, 714, 717, 718, 722-727, 738-741, Bavarian 701.
1918: Bavarian 669.

Division Telephone Detachments:
24.1.1917: Guard 1-Guard 5, 1-42, 50, 52, 54, 56, 58, 83, 84, 86-89, 91-96, 101, 103, 105, 107-109, 111, 113, 115, 117, 119, 121, 123, 183, 185, 187, 192, 195, 197, 199-208, 211-228, 231-243, 251-255, 291-293, 301, 302, Bavarian 1-6, Bavarian 10-12, Bavarian 14-16, Guard 401, Guard 402, 401, 403, 405-407, 409-419, 421-426, 428, 433, 435, 436, 443-454, 472-482, Bavarian 401, Bavarian 405-406, Bavarian 408-409, Bavarian 430 & 439, 501-505, 507-523, 525, 526, 538, 544-548, 569, Bavarian 501-502 & 506, Guard 551, 554-555, 558, 560, Bavarian 551, 585, 590, 1703.
1918: 901, 904, 907, Bavarian 669, Bavarian 715, Mountain 1704.

Cavalry Telephone Detachments:
2.8.1914 (as Cavalry Signals Dets.): Guard Cav. Div., 1st-9th Cav. Div., Bavarian Cav. Div.
22.12.1917: All above renamed Cav. Tel. Dets.

Army Radio Detachments:
2.8.1914-30.5.1917: 2 Heavy Army Radio Stations per Corps, in addition, from Autumn 1915, 2 Directional Receiver Troops and 1 Radio Receiver Station were added per Corps.

Group Radio Detachments:
23.7.1915-30.5.1917: 1-17, attached to Corps.
30.5-12.9.1917: Group Radio Stations, one per Corps.
12.9.1917: 501-563.

Division Radio Detachments:
28.7-24.11.1916: 1 such Det. created or planned for each Division.
24.11.1916-30.5.1917: 1 such Det. for approx. 100 Divisions.
30.5.1917: 1-107.
1917: 108-110 & 1724.
2.5.1918: 111-192.

Mountain Radio Detachments:
24.10.1916: 1-3.
1917: 4-9, Bavarian 1 (latter formed 3.6.1915 from Bavarian Mountain Radio Troops 1-3).
10.2.1918: 1725 (previously Mountain Radio Det. 8).

'Arendt' (Listening) Stations:
Dec. 1915-26.2.1917: no regulation formations.

'Arendt' (Listening) Detachments:
26.2.1917: 1-17, 19, 21-23 & 25.
(All dissolved 17.3.18 and used to form Listening Stations).

Listening Stations:
17.3.1918: 1-14, 31-45, 61-72, 91-96, 121-139, 151-166, 181-195, 211-226, 241-256, 271-285, 301-315, 331-344, 361-367, 401-416, 431-441, 461-483, 491-501, 521-529, 551-568, 581-593, 611-615, 641-646.

(k) Field Railway Troops

Railway Construction Companies:
2.8.1914: 1-28, Bavarian 1 & 2, Reserve 1-24, Bavarian Reserve 1 & 2, Landwehr 1-6 & Bavarian, Fortress 1-10 & Bavarian.
1914: 29-31, Reserve 25-30, Bavarian Reserve 3 & 4, Fortress 11.
1915: 32-34, Bavarian 3, Reserve 31-40, Bavarian Reserve 5, Fortress 12-14, Bavarian Landsturm 1.

1916: Reserve 41-49, Bavarian Reserve 6-8, Landwehr 7-9 & 200, Special Coy. 5 (previously Railway Constr. Coy. 5).
1917: Landwehr 201-205, Special Coys. 3 & 11.

Railway Companies:
2.8.1914: 1-18, Bavarian 1-3, Fortress 1.
1914: 19-29, Bavarian 4, Naval 1, Fortress 2.
1915: 30-59, Bavarian 5-7, Fortress 3 &4.
1916: 60-86, Bavarian 8 & 9.
1917: 87-100, 201-209, Bavarian 10-13.

Military Railway Detachments:
2.8.1914: 1-5, Bavarian, Borkum, Fortress 1-4.
1914: 6 & 7.
1916: 8, Sylt, Norderney.
1917: 9 & 10.

Field Railway Formations:
2.8.1914: Fortress Dets. 1-4.
1915: Coys. 101-106.
1916: Coys. 107-118.
1917: Coys. 119-128, Dets. 10-53.

Funicular Railway Formations:
1915: Troops 1-13.
1916: Troops 14-27, Bavarian Troops 1-3, Dets. 1-3, Bavarian Dets. 1 & 2.
1917: Troops 28-81, Bavarian Troops 4-11.

Armoured Trains:
2.8.1914: 1 (later I, out-of-service 8.4.17), 2 (out-of-service 8.4.17), 3 (later III), 4 (later IV), 5 (later Ia), 6 (later VI), 7-9 (out-of-service 8.4.17), Mainz 1 (then 10, later II), Mainz 2 (then 11, out-of-service 8.4.17), Thorn 1 (then 12, later V), Thorn 2 (then 13, later VII).

(l) Armoured Fighting Vehicle units

1917: Assault AFV Dets. 1-3.
1918: Assault AFV Dets. 11-15.
22.9.1918: Renamed Heavy AFV Dets. 1-3 & 11-15.

Appendix V

Commanders and their General Staff Chiefs

Supreme Commander East:
Commanders:
1.11.14: Generaloberst (Generalfeldmarschall from 27.11.14) von Hindenburg (previously CO, 9th Army, under the General Staff Chief of the Field Army).
29.8.16: Generalfeldmarschall Prince Leopold of Bavaria (previously CO, Army Group Leopold).
General Staff Chiefs:
1.11.14: Generalmajor (Generalleutnant from 27.11.14) Ludendorff (previously Chief of Staff, 9th Army, under I General Quartermaster).
29.8.16: Colonel (Generalmajor from 29.10.17) Max Hoffmann.

Army Group Archduke Albrecht of Württemberg:
Commander:
7.3.17: Generalfeldmarschall Archduke Albrecht of Württemberg (previously CO, 4th Army).
General Staff Chiefs:
7.3.17: Generalleutnant Krafft von Dellmensingen.
9.9.17: Colonel Heye.
7.9.18: Generalmajor Hell.
31.10.18: Generalmajor von Lossberg (previously Chief of Staff, Army Group Boehn).

Army Group Below (Army Group Scholtz from 22.4.17):
Commanders:
11.10.16: General of Infantry Otto von Below (previously CO, 8th Army, under CO, 6th Army).
22.4.17: General of Artillery von Scholtz (previously CO, 8th Army).
General Staff Chiefs:
11.10.16: Generalleutnant Alfred von Böckmann.
15.7.17: Lieutenant-Colonel (Colonel from 22.3.18) Count Detleft von Schwerin.

Army Group Boehn (dissolved 8.10.18):
Commander:
12.8.18: Generaloberst von Boehn (previously under CO, 7th Army).
General Staff Chief:
12.8.18: Generalmajor von Lossberg (previously CO, 4th Army, under CO, Army Group Archduke Albrecht).

Army Group Crown Prince of Germany:

Commander:

1.8.15: Generalleutnant (General of Infantry from 27.1.17) Crown Prince Wilhelm of Prussia, Crown Prince of Germany (until 29.11.16 also CO, 5th Army).

General Staff Chiefs:

1.8.15: Generalleutnant Konstantin Schmidt von Knobelsdorf.

21.8.16: Generalleutnant Walter Freiherr von Lüttwitz.

30.11.16: Colonel (Generalmajor from 12.6.18) Count Friedrich von d. Schulenberg.

Army Group Command F (Yildirim; passed to the Turkish Commander Mustafa Kemal Pasha, 30.10.18):

Commanders:

20.7.17: General of Infantry von Falkenhayn (previously CO, 9th Army, under CO, 10th Army).

1.3.18: General of Cavalry Liman von Sanders (previously Chief of the German Military Mission in Turkey).

General Staff Chiefs:

20.7.17: Colonel Wilhelm von Dommes.

1.3.18: Turkish Colonel Kiazim Bey.

Army Group Gallwitz – Somme, 28.8.16 expanded to Army Group Crown Prince Rupprecht:

Commanders:

19.7.16: General of Artillery von Gallwitz (previously CO, Attack Group West-Verdun, concurrently under CO, 2nd Army).

28.8.16: Generalfeldmarschall Crown Prince Rupprecht of Bavaria (previously CO, 6th Army).

General Staff Chiefs:

19.7.16: Colonel Bernhard Bronsart von Schellendorf.

28.8.16: Generalleutnant von Kuhl (previously Chief of Staff, 6th Army).

Army Group Gallwitz – Verdun:

Commander:

1.2.18: General of Artillery von Gallwitz (previously and then concurrently – until 27.9.18 – CO, 5th Army).

General Staff Chiefs:

1.2.18: Lieutenant-Colonel von Pawelsz.

18.4.18: Lieutenant-Colonel von Keller.

5.11.18: Generalleutnant von Sauberzweig.

Army Group Hindenburg, from 30.7.16 Army Group Eichhorn – Wilna (dissolved 31.3.18):

Commander:

5.8.15: United with Supreme Commander East.

30.7.16: Generaloberst (Generalfeldmarschall from 18.12.17) von Eichhorn (previously and then concurrently – until 4.3.18 – CO, 10th Army).

General Staff Chiefs:
5.8.15: United with Chief of Staff, Supreme Commander East.
30.7.16: Colonel Freiherr Schmidt von Schmidtseck.
9.7.17: Generalmajor von Sauberzweig.
17.12.17: Generalmajor Freiherr Schmidt von Schmidtseck.
16.2.18: Colonel Frotscher.

Army Group Prince Leopold of Bavaria, from 31.8.16 Army Group Woyrsch (dissolved 15.12.17):

Commanders:
5.8.15: Generalfeldmarschall Prince Leopold of Bavaria (previously and concurrently – until 30.7.16 – CO, 9th Army, under Supreme Commander East).
31.8.16: Generaloberst von Woyrsch (previously and concurrently – until 20.9.16 – CO of the Landwehr Corps and CO, Army Detachment Woyrsch until the dissolving of the Army Group).
General Staff Chiefs:
5.8.15: Generalmajor Grünert.
24.11.15: Colonel Freiherr von d. Wenge, Count von Lambsdorff.
31.8.16: Colonel Heye.
9.9.17: Colonel (Generalmajor from 18.10.17) Freiherr Schmidt von Schmidtseck.

Army Group Mackensen – Galicia and Poland – from 20.9.15, became Army Group Linsingen until 3.4.18, thereafter Army Group Eichhorn – Kiev, until 13.8.18 (authorised 30.4.18), becoming Army Group Eichhorn (from 13.8.18):

Commanders:
27.4.15: Generaloberst (Generalfeldmarschall from 22.6.15) von Mackensen (previously and concurrently CO, 11th Army, under CO Army Group Mackensen against Serbia).
9.9.15: General of Infantry von Linsingen (until 19.9.15 temporarily; previously and concurrently CO, Army of the Bug).
3.4.18: Generalfeldmarschall von Eichhorn (previously CO, Army Group Eichhorn in Wilna, died 30.7.18).
31.7.18: Generaloberst Count von Kirchbach (previously CO, 8th Army).
General Staff Chiefs:
27.4.15: Colonel (Generalmajor from 26.6.15) von Seeckt (previously and concurrently Chief of Staff, 11th Army, under Chief of Staff, Army Group Mackensen against Serbia).
9.9.15: Generalmajor von Stolzmann.
17.7.16: Colonel Hell.
7.12.16: Lieutenant-Colonel Keller.
28.3.18: Generalleutnant Groener.
31.10.18: Generalmajor Hell.
3.12.18: Colonel Rethe.

Army Group Mackensen – Serbia and Macedonia (dissolved 30.7.16):

Commander:

18.9.15: Generalfeldmarschall von Mackensen (previously CO, Army Group Mackensen in Poland, under CO, Army Group Mackensen against Romania).

General Staff Chiefs:

18.9.15: Generalmajor von Seeckt (previously Chief of Staff, Army Group Mackensen in Poland, under Chief of Staff, Austro-Hungarian Army Group Archduke Carl).

14.6.16: Acting Colonel Hentsch.

Army Group Mackensen – Romania. 1.7.-10.11.18 known as Army of Occupation in Romania):

Commander:

29.8.16: Generalfeldmarschall von Mackensen (previously CO, Army Group Mackensen in Macedonia).

General Staff Chiefs:

4.9.16: Generalmajor Tappen.

7.12.16: Colonel (Generalmajor from 20.5.17) Hell.

23.4.18: Colonel Friedrich-Wilhelm von Schwartzkoppen.

1st Army (dissolved 17.9.15):

Commanders:

2.8.14: Generaloberst von Kluck (previously Insp. Gen., 8th Army Inspectorate, wounded 27.3.15).

28.3.15: General of Infantry von Fabeck (previously CO, 11th Army, under CO, 12th Army).

General Staff Chief:

2.8.14: Generalmajor (Generalleutnant from 18.6.15) von Kuhl (under Chief of Staff, 12th Army).

(New) 1st Army:

Commanders:

19.7.16: General of Infantry Fritz von Below (previously CO, 2nd Army, nominally under CO, 9th Army – died from illness).

9.6.18: General of Infantry von Mudra (previously CO, Army Det. A, under CO, 17th Army).

12.10.18: General of Infantry Otto von Below (previously CO, 17th Army, under CO, Homeland Defence West).

8.11.18: General of Infantry Magnus von Eberhardt (previously CO, 7th Army).

General Staff Chiefs:

19.7.16: Colonel von Lossberg (previously Chief of Staff, 2nd Army, under Chief of Staff, 6th Army).

11.4.17: Major (Lieutenant-Colonel from 27.1.18) von Klüber.

22.6.18: Lieutenant-Colonel Faupel.

23.8.18: Lieutenant-Colonel Otto Hasse.

2nd Army:
Commanders:
2.8.14: Generaloberst (Generalfeldmarschall from 27.1.15) von Bülow (previously Insp. Gen., 3rd Army Inspectorate).
4.4.15: General of Infantry Fritz von Below (previously CO, XXI A.K., under CO, 1st Army).
19.7.16: General of Artillery von Gallwitz (previously CO, Attack Group West Verdun, under CO, 5th Army).
17.12.16: General of Cavalry von der Marwitz (previously CO, VI A.K., under CO, 5th Army).
22.9.18: General of Infantry von Carlowitz (previously CO, 9th Army).
General Staff Chiefs:
2.8.14: Generalleutnant von Lauenstein.
24.12.14: Generalmajor von Zieten.
30.6.15: Generalleutnant von Hoeppner (later became Kogenluft).
13.4.16: Generalmajor Grünert.
2.7.16: Colonel von Lossberg (previously Chief of Staff, 3rd Army, under Chief of Staff, 1st Army).
19.7.16: Colonel Bernhard Bronsart von Schellendorf.
25.10.16: Colonel Wild.
17.4.17: Lieutenant-Colonel von Pawelsz.
27.8.17: Major (Lieutenant-Colonel from 18.12.17) Stapff.
27.2.18: Colonel von Tschischwitz.
10.8.18: Lieutenant-Colonel von Klewitz.
21.9.18: Major von Miaskowski.

3rd Army:
Commanders:
2.8.14: Generaloberst Freiherr von Hausen (previously Saxon Minister of War).
12.9.14: General of Cavalry (Generaloberst from 27.1.15) von Einem – von Rothmaler (previously CO, VII A.K.).
General Staff Chiefs:
2.8.14: Generalmajor von Hoeppner.
14.2.15: Generalleutnant Ritter von Höhn.
26.9.15: Colonel von Lossberg (under Chief of Staff, 2nd Army).
2.7.16: Colonel (Generalmajor from 30.11.17) Martin von Oldershausen.
1.2.18: Lieutenant-Colonel von Klewitz.
10.8.18: Major von Miaskowski.
21.9.18: Lieutenant-Colonel von Klewitz.

4th Army:
Commanders:
2.8.14: Generaloberst (Generalfeldmarschall from 1.8.16) Archduke Albrecht von Württemberg) (previously Insp. Gen. of the 6th Army Inspectorate, under CO, Army Group Archduke Albrecht).
25.2.17: General of Infantry Sixt von Arnim (previously CO, IV A.K.).

General Staff Chiefs:

2.8.14: Generalleutnant Freiherr Walter von Luttwitz.

26.9.14: Generalmajor (Generalleutnant from 18.8.15) Ilse.

25.5.17: Major Stapff.

12.6.17: Colonel (Generalmajor from 3.8.17) von Lossberg (previously Chief of Staff, 6th Army, under Chief of Staff, Army Group Boehn).

6.8.18: Major Humser.

5th Army:

Commanders:

2.8.14: Generalmajor (Generalleutnant from 27.1.15) Crown Prince Wilhelm of Prussia, Crown Prince of Germany (under CO, Army Group Crown Prince of Germany).

30.11.16: General of Infantry von Lochow (previously CO, Maas Group East).

17.12.16: General of Artillery von Gallwitz (previously CO, 2nd Army, concurrently from 1.2.18 CO, Army Group Gallwitz).

27.9.18: General of Cavalry von der Marwitz (previously CO, 2nd Army).

General Staff Chiefs:

2.8.14: Generalleutnant Konstantin Schmidt von Knobelsdorf.

21.8.16: Generalleutnant Walter Freiherr von Lüttwitz.

30.11.16: Lieutenant-Colonel Otto Freiherr von Ledebur.

20.12.16: Colonel Bernhard Bronsart von Schellendorf.

27.8.17: Lieutenant-Colonel von Pawelsz.

18.4.18: Lieutenant-Colonel Keller.

25.9.18: Lieutenant-Colonel Wetzell (previously Chief of Operations Dept., General Staff Chief of the Field Army).

6th Army:

Commanders:

2.8.14: Generaloberst (Generalfeldmarschall from 23.7.16) Crown Prince Rupprecht of Bavaria (previously Insp. Gen. of 4th Army Inspectorate, under CO, Army Group Crown Prince Rupprecht).

28.8.16: Generaloberst Freiherr von Falkenhausen (previously CO Coastal Defence, under Gen. Govt. of Belgium).

23.4.17: General of Infantry Otto von Below (previously, CO, Army Group Below, under CO, 14th Army).

9.9.17: General of Infantry von Quast (previously CO, Guard Corps).

General Staff Chiefs:

2.8.14: Generalmajor Krafft von Dellmensingen.

19.5.15: Colonel Freiherr von d. Wenge, Count von Lambsdorff.

24.11.15: Generalleutnant von Kuhl (previously Chief of Staff, 12th Army, under Chief of Staff, Army Group Crown Prince Rupprecht).

28.8.16: Colonel Count Friedrich von d. Schulenburg.

25.11.16: Generalmajor Freiherr von Nagel z. Aichberg.

11.4.17: Colonel von Lossberg (previously Chief of Staff, 1st Army, under Chief of Staff, 4th Army).

12.6.17: Major Stapff.

27.8.17: Lieutenant-Colonel (Ritter von, from 2.3.18) Lenz.

8.8.18: Lieutenant-Colonel Herrgott.

7th Army:

Commanders:

2.8.14: Generaloberst von Heeringen (previously Gen. Insp. of 2nd Army Inspectorate, under CO, Coastal Defence).

28.8.16: General of Artillery (Generaloberst from 27.1.17) Richard von Schubert (previously CO, XXVII Reserve Corps).

11.3.17: General of Infantry (Generaloberst from 22.3.18) von Boehn (previously CO, Army Det. C, under CO, Army Group Boehn).

6.8.18: General of Infantry Magnus von Eberhardt (previously CO, X Reserve Corps, under CO, 1st Army).

15.10.18: Generaloberst von Boehn (previously CO, Army Group Boehn).

General Staff Chiefs:

2.8.14: Generalleutnant von Hänisch.

11.3.15: Acting Colonel Tappen.

28.3.15: Colonel (Generalmajor from 18.8.16) Rudolph von Borries.

15.2.17: Lieutenant-Colonel (Colonel from 18.4.18) Walter Reinhardt.

3.11.18: Lieutenant-Colonel von Pawelsz.

8th Army (dissolved 29.9.15):

Commanders:

2.8.14: Generaloberst von Prittwitz und Gaffron (previously Gen. Insp. of 1st Army Inspectorate).

23.8.14: Generaloberst von Hindenburg (previously CO, 9th Army).

18.9.14: General of Artillery Richard von Schubert (previously CO, XIV Reserve Corps, under CO, XXVII Reserve Corps).

9.10.14: General of Infantry von Francois (previously CO, I A.K., under CO, XXXXI Reserve Corps).

7.11.14: General of Infantry Otto von Below (previously CO, I Reserve Corps, under CO, Army of the Niemen).

26.5.15: Acting General of Artillery von Scholtz (concurrently CO, XX A.K.).

General Staff Chiefs:

2.8.14: Generalmajor Georg Count von Waldersee.

23.8.14: Generalmajor Ludendorff (previously Senior Quartermaster, 2nd A, under Chief of Staff, 9th Army).

16.9.14: Generalmajor Grünert.

3.11.14: Generalmajor Wild von Hohenborn.

10.11.14: Generalmajor Alfred von Böckmann.

26.5.15: Lieutenant-Colonel Detlef Count von Schwerin.

Army of the Niemen (from 30.8.15 'new' 8th Army):

Commanders:

26.5.15: General of Infantry Otto von Below (previously CO, 8th Army, under CO, Army Group Below).

5.10.16: General of Infantry von Fabeck (previously CO, 12th Army, died 16.12.16).

22.10.16: General of Infantry von Mudra (previously CO, XVI A.K., under CO, Army Det. A) – until 19.12.16 provisional.

2.1.17: General of Artillery von Scholtz (previously CO, Army Det. Scholtz, under CO, Army Group Scholtz).

22.4.17: General of Infantry von Hutier (previously CO, Army Det. D, under CO, 18th Army).

12.12.17: General of Infantry (Generaloberst from 27.1.18) Count von Kirchbach (previously CO, Army Det. D, under CO, Army Group Kiev).

31.7.18: General of Infantry von Kathen (previously CO, XXIII Reserve Corps).

General Staff Chiefs:

26.5.15: Generalmajor (Generalleutnant from 6.6.16) Alfred von Böckmann.

5.10.16: Generalmajor von Bergmann.

16.11.16: Generalmajor von Sauberzweig.

15.9.17: Colonel Frotscher.

16.2.18: Major Frantz.

13.12.18: Lieutenant-Colonel Bürkner.

9th Army (dissolved 30.7.16):

Commanders:

18.9.14: Generaloberst von Hindenburg (previously CO, 8th Army, under Supreme Commander East).

2.11.14: General of Cavalry (Generaloberst from 17.12.14) von Mackensen (previously CO, XVII A.K., under CO, 11th Army).

17.4.15: General of Cavalry Prince Leopold of Bavaria (concurrently from 5.8.15 CO, Army Group Leopold).

General Staff Chiefs:

18.9.14: Generalmajor Ludendorff (previously Chief of Staff, 8th Army, under Chief of Staff, Supreme Commander East).

3.11.14: Generalmajor Grünert.

24.11.15: Colonel Freiherr von d. Wenge, Count von Lambsdorff.

'New' 9th Army (dissolved 18.9.18):

Commanders:

6.9.16: General of Infantry von Falkenhayn (previously General Staff Chief, Field Army, under CO, Army Group F).

1.5.17: Acting General of Infantry Kosch (CO, Corps z.b.V. 52).

10.6.17: General of Infantry von Eben (previously CO, I A.K., under CO, Army Det. A) – from 9.6.18 provisional following the death of General of Infantry Fritz von Below).

6.8.18: General of Infantry von Carlowitz (previously CO, XIX A.K., under CO, 2nd Army).

General Staff Chiefs:

6.9.16: Colonel Hans Hesse.

9.4.17: Colonel Wachs.

20.6.17: Lieutenant-Colonel Walter Bronsart von Schellendorf.

18.6.18: Lieutenant-Colonel Freiherr von Esebeck.

4.8.18: Lieutenant-Colonel Otto Hasse.

23.8.18: Lieutenant-Colonel Faupel.

10th Army:

Commanders:

26.1.15: Generaloberst (Generalfeldmarschall from 18.12.17) von Eichhorn (previously Gen. Insp. of 7th Army Inspectorate, concurrently CO from 30.7.16 Army Group Eichhorn).

5.3.18: General of Infantry von Falkenhayn (previously CO, Army Group F).

General Staff Chiefs:

26.1.15: Colonel Hell.

17.7.16: Colonel Freiherr Schmidt von Schmidtseck.

9.9.17: Generalmajor von Sauberzweig.

17.12.17: Generalmajor Freiherr Schmidt von Schmidtseck.

16.2.18: Colonel Frotscher.

4.3.18: Lieutenant-Colonel Stapff.

11th Army (dissolved 8.9.15):

Commanders:

9.3.15: General of Infantry von Fabeck (previously CO, XIII A.K., under CO, 1st Army) – until 27.3.15.

16.4.15: Generaloberst (Generalfeldmarschall from 22.6.15) von Mackensen (previously CO, 9th Army, concurrently from 27.4.15 CO, Army Group Mackensen).

General Staff Chief:

9.3.15: Colonel (Generalmajor from 26.6.15) von Seeckt (previously Chief of Staff, III A.K., concurrently from 27.4.15 Chief of Staff, Army Group Mackensen).

'New' 11th Army:

Commanders:

23.9.15: General of Artillery von Gallwitz (previously CO, 12th Army, under CO, Attack Group West Verdun).

24.3.16: General of Infantry von Winckler (concurrently until 24.7.16 CO, IV Reserve Corps, under CO, I A.K.) – acting until 23.7.16.

5.6.17: General of Infantry von Steuben (previously CO, XVIII Reserve Corps).

General Staff Chiefs:

23.9.15: Colonel Marquard.

24.3.16: Lieutenant-Colonel Völckers (acting until 19.8.16).

22.11.16: Lieutenant-Colonel Walter Reinhardt.

10.2.17: Lieutenant-Colonel Kirch.

17.6.18: Lieutenant-Colonel Lämmerhirt.

30.9.18: Lieutenant-Colonel Kirch.

Army Group Gallwitz, from 7.8.15 - 12th Army (dissolved 9.10.16):

Commanders:

9.2.15: General of Artillery von Gallwitz (previously CO, Guard Reserve Corps, under CO, 11th Army).

22.9.15: General of Infantry von Fabeck (previously CO, 1st Army, under CO, 8th Army).

General Staff Chiefs:

9.2.15: Lieutenant-Colonel Konrad von Redern.

18.3.15: Colonel Marquard.

22.9.15: Generalleutnant von Kuhl (previously Chief of Staff, 1st Army, under Chief of Staff, 6th Army).

24.11.15: Generalmajor von Bergmann.

14th Army (dissolved 22.1.18):
Commander:
9.9.17: General of Infantry Otto von Below (previously CO, 6th Army, under CO, 17th Army).
General Staff Chief:
9.9.17: Generalleutnant Krafft von Dellmensingen.

17th Army:
Commanders:
1.2.18: General of Infantry Otto von Below (previously CO, 14th Army, under CO, 1st Army).
12.10.18: General of Infantry von Mudra (previously CO, 1st Army).
General Staff Chiefs:
1.2.18: Generalleutnant Krafft von Dellmensingen.
18.4.18: Lieutenant-Colonel von Pawelsz.
12.10.18: Lieutenant-Colonel von Klüber.

18th Army:
Commander:
22.12.17: General of Infantry von Hutier (previously CO, 8th Army).
General Staff Chiefs:
22.12.17: Generalmajor von Sauberzweig.
20.6.18: Lieutenant-Colonel Kirch.
7.8.18: Lieutenant-Colonel Bürkner.

19th Army:
Commanders:
4.2.18: General of Infantry (Generaloberst from 9.4.18) von Bothmer (previously CO, Army of the South).
8.11.18: General of Infantry Ritter von Fasbender (previously CO, I Bavarian Reserve Corps).
General Staff Chief:
4.2.18: Colonel Ritter von Hemmer.

Army of the Bug (dissolved 31.3.18):
Commander:
8.7.15: General of Infantry von Linsingen (previously CO, Army of the South, concurrently from 20.9.15 CO, Army Group Linsingen).
General Staff Chiefs:
8.7.15: Generalmajor von Stolzmann.
17.7.16: Colonel Hell.
7.12.16: Lieutenant-Colonel Keller.

Army of the South (dissolved 25.1.18):
Commanders:
11.1.15: General of Infantry von Linsingen (previously CO, II A.K., under CO, Army of the Bug).
8.7.15: General of Infantry Count von Bothmer (previously CO, II Bavarian Reserve Corps, under CO, 19th Army).
General Staff Chiefs:
8.1.15: Generalleutnant Ludendorff (previously Chief of Staff, Supreme Commander East).
20.1.15: Generalmajor von Stolzmann.
8.7.15: Colonel Ritter von Hemmer.

Army Detachment Falkenhausen (Army Detachment A from 15.4.16):
Commanders:
17.9.14: General of Infantry (Generaloberst from 24.12.14) Freiherr von Falkenhausen (previously, CO, Ersatz Corps, under CO, Coastal Defence).
17.4.16: General of Infantry d'Elsa (previously, CO, XII A.K.).
4.1.17: General of Infantry von Mudra (previously CO, 8th Army, under CO, 1st Army).
(9.6.-5.8.18 – whilst von Mudra temporarily took over command of the 1st Army, the newly-appointed CO of Army Det. A, Gen. von Eben, remained with the 9th Army).
6.8.18: General of Infantry von Eben (previously CO, 9th Army).
General Staff Chiefs:
17.9.14: Colonel Weidner.
14.11.16: Colonel von Eulitz.
28.12.16: Major von Klüber.
12.4.17: Major (Lieutenant-Colonel from 27.1.18) Freiherr von Esebeck.
17.6.18: Lieutenant-Colonel Walter Bronsart von Schellendorf.
22.6.18: Lieutenant-Colonel von Klüber.
12.10.18: Lieutenant-Colonel von Pawelsz (until 2.11.18).
9.11.18: Generalmajor Freiherr Martin von Oldershausen.

Army Detachment Gaede (Army Detachment B from 4.9.16):
Commanders:
19.9.14: General of Infantry Gaede (previously CO, temporarily mobile units of XIV A.K.).
3.9.16: General of Infantry von Gündell (previously CO, V Reserve Corps).
General Staff Chiefs:
19.9.14: Lieutenant-Colonel Wilhelm von Wolff.
6.1.15: Lieutenant-Colonel Bernhard Bronsart von Schellendorf.
6.5.15: Lieutenant-Colonel (Colonel from 18.8.15) Hans Hesse.
8.9.16: Colonel Renner.
23.4.17: Lieutenant-Colonel Dreschel.

Army Detachment Strantz (Army Detachment C from 2.2.17):

Commanders:

18.9.14: General of Infantry von Strantz (previously CO, V Reserve Corps).

4.2.17: General of Infantry von Boehn (previously CO, IX Reserve Corps, under CO, 7th Army).

15.3.17: Generalleutnant Fuchs (previously CO, XIV Reserve Corps).

General Staff Chiefs:

18.9.14: Lieutenant-Colonel Erwin Fischer.

7.12.15: Colonel Wild.

27.10.16: Colonel Bernhard Bronsart von Schellendorf.

20.12.16: Lieutenant-Colonel (Colonel from 6.11.17) Otto Freiherr von Ledebur.

22.9.18: Lieutenant-Colonel Faupel.

9.11.18: Colonel Otto Freiherr von Lebedur.

Army Detachment Scholtz (Army Detachment D from 10.1.17, dissolved 2.10.18):

Commanders:

28.10.15: General of Artillery von Scholtz (previously CO, XX A.K., and acting CO, 8th Army, under CO, 8th Army).

2.1.17: Generalleutnant (General of Infantry from 27.1.17) von Hutier (previously CO, XXI A.K., under CO, 8th Army).

22.4.17: General of Infantry Count von Kirchbach (previously CO, Landwehr Corps, under CO, 8th Army).

12.12.17: General of Artillery (Generaloberst from 23.1.18) von Kirchbach (previously CO, XII Reserve Corps).

General Staff Chiefs:

28.10.15: Lieutenant-Colonel Detlef, Count von Schwerin.

8.6.17: Colonel von Kessel.

25.3.18: Colonel Leopold von Kleist.

Army Detachment Woyrsch (dissolved 15.12.17):

Commander:

3.11.14: Generaloberst von Woyrsch (until 20.9.16 concurrently CO, Landwehr Corps, although a deputy replaced him in this capacity from 11.11.14).

General Staff Chiefs:

3.11.14: Lieutenant-Colonel (Colonel from 18.8.16) Heye.

9.9.17: Colonel (Generalmajor from 18.10.17) Freiherr Schmidt von Schmidtseck.

Supreme Commander Coastal Defence (demobilised 1.11.18):

Commanders:

15.4.16: Generaloberst Freiherr von Falkenhausen (previously CO, Army Det. Falkenhausen, under CO, 6th Army).

29.8.16: Generaloberst von Heeringen (previously CO, 7th Army).

Without a commander from 19.9.18.

General Staff Chiefs:

15.4.16: Colonel (Generalmajor from 22.3.18) von Derschau.

10.7.18: Colonel von Zitzewitz.

Appendix VI

Abbreviations and Glossary

A.

A.	Armee	Army
A.Abt.	Armee-Abteilung	Army Detachment
Abschn.	Abschnitt	Sector
Abt.	Abteilung	Detachment[1]
Abw.	Abwehr	Defence
Adj.	Adjutant	Adjutant
Aferna.	Armee-Fernsprech-Abteilung	Army Telephone Detachment
Afernpark.	Armee-Fernsprech-Park	Army Telephone Park
Afunka.	Armee-Funker-Abteilung	Army Radio Detachment
Afunkpark.	Arme-Funker-Park	Army Radio Park
A.Gr.	Armee-Gruppe	Army Group
A.H.Qu.	Armee-Hauptquartier	Army Headquarters
A.K.	Armeekorps	Army Corps
A.K.O.	Allerhöchste Kabinettsordre	Supreme Cabinet Order
Akofern.	Armee-Fernsprech-Kommandeur	Army Telephone Commander
Akofunk.	Armee-Funker-Kommandeur	Army Radio Commander
Akokraft.	Kommandeur der Kraftfahrtruppen einer Armee	Commander of Motor Vehicles of an Army
Akomut.	Kommandeur der Munitions-Kolonnen und Trains einer Armee	Commander of Munitions Columns and Trains of an Army
Akonach.	Armee-Nachrichten-Kommandeur	Army Signals Commander
A.O.K.	Armee-Oberkommando	Army Command
Arko.	Artillerie-Kommandeur	Artillery Commander
Arm.	Armierungs-	Equipment
Art.	Artillerie	Artillery

---

1 Could sometimes also mean Battalion.

Atela. or A.Tel.Abt.	Armee-Telegraphen-Abteilung	Army Telegraph Detachment
Awewa.	Armee-Wetterwarte	Army Meteorological Service

B.

Bäck.	Bäckerei	Bakery
Bag.	Bagage	Baggage
Bak.	Ballonabwehr-Kanone	Anti-Balloon Gun
Battr.	Batterie	Battery
bayer.	bayerisch	Bavarian
Bba.	Bahnbeauftragter des Feldeisenbahn-Chefs	Deputy of the Chief of Field Railways
B.d.G.Pferde	Beauftragter des Generalquartiermeisters in Pferdeangelegenheiten	Deputy of the General Quartermaster responsible for Horses
B.d.G.West.	Beauftragter des Generalquartiermeisters für den westlichen Kriegschauplatz	Deputy of the General Quartermaster responsible for the Western Front
B.d.K.M.	Beauftragter des Kriegsministeriums	Deputy of the War Ministry
Bel.	Belagerungs-	Garrison
Besk.K.	Beskiden-Korps	Beskiden Corps
besp.	bespannt	Horse-drawn
Betr.	Betriebs-	Equipment[2]
Bew.	Bewachungs-	Guard
Bez.	Bezirks-	District
Bhf.	Bahnhofs-	Railway Station
Bi.	Bild	Picture
Bli.	Blinker	Signal Lamp
Bogohl.	Bombengeschwader der Obersten Heeresleitung	Bomber Group of the Supreme Army Command
Brig.	Brigade	Brigade
Br.Tr.	Brückentrain	Pontoon Train
Btl.	Bataillon	Battalion

2 Had a variety of meanings, and could refer to, in the case of railway units for example, rolling stock.

Bvg.	Bevollmächtigter Generalstabsoffizier	General Staff Officer possessing plenipotentiary powers, i.e. control over both military and civilian elements within his sphere of command

C.

Chef Feldeis.	see 'Fech'	
Chefkraft.	Chef des Feldkraftfahrwesens	Chief of Field Motor Vehicle Transport
Chev.R.	Chevauleger-Regiment	Chevauleger Regiment

D.

Dep.	Depot	Department when referring to matters relating to the War Ministry
Det.	Detachement	Detachment
Dir.	Direktion	Directorate
Div.	Division	Division
Div.Br.Tr.	Divisions-Brückentrain	Divisional Pontoon Train
Divkonach.	Divisions-Nachrichten-Kommandeur	Commander, Divisional Signals
Div.St.Qu.	Divisions-Stabs-Quartier	Divisional Headquarters
Drag.R.	Dragoner-Regiment	Dragoon Regiment

E.

E.D.	Ersatz-Division	Ersatz Division
E.Flak.Swf.	Flugabwehrkanonen-Schweinwerfer auf Eisenbahnwagen	Anti-Aircraft Searchlight mounted on a Railway Car
E.I.R.	Ersatz-Infanterie-Regiment	Ersatz Infantry Regiment
Eis.	Eisenbahn	Railway
Ers.	Ersatz	Ersatz
Esk.	Eskadron	Squadron
Et.	Etappen-	Line of Communication

Etkomut.	Kommandeur der Etappen-Munitionskolonnen u. Trains	Commander, Line of Communication Munitions Columns and Trains
Etra.	Eisenbahn-Transportabteilung	Railway Transport Detachment

F.

Fech.	Chef des Feldeisenbahnwesens	Chief of Field Railways
Felda.	Feldartillerie	Field Artillery
Felda.Br.	Feldartillerie-Brigade	Field Artillery Brigade
Felda.Mun. Zug K.	Feldartillerie-Munitionszug für Feldkanonen	Field Artillery Munitions Section for Field Guns
Felda.Mun. Zug K./F.	Feldartillerie-Munitionszug für Feldkanonen und leichte Feldhaubitzen	Field Artillery Munitions Section for Field Guns and Light Field Howitzers
Feldar.R.	Feldartillerie-Regiment	Field Artillery Regiment
Feldbäck.	Feldbäckerei	Field Bakery
Feldbh.	Feldbahn	Military Railway
Feldgend.	Feldgendarm.	Military Police
Feldh.	Feldheer	Field Army
Feldlaz.	Feldlazarett	Field Hospital
Feldluftsch.	Feldluftschiffer	Field/Military Airship[3]
Feldtelchef.	Chef der Feldtelegraphie	Chief of Military Telegraphy
Ferna.	Fernsprechabteilung	Telephone Detachment
Fewewa.	Feldwetterwarte	Military Meteorological Service
Fhaub.	Feldhaubitze	Field Howitzer
Flak.	Flugabwehrkanone	Anti-Aircraft Gun
Flakgruko.	Gruppenkommandeur der Flak.	Flak Group Commander
Flamga.	Flieger-Abwehr-Maschinengewehr-Abteilung	Anti-Aircraft Machine Gun Detachment
Flamwf.	Flammenwerfer	Flamethrower
Fli.	Flieger	Aviation
Fli.Abt.A.	Artillerieflieger-Abteilung	Artillery Observation/Spotter Detachment

---

3   Either meaning could be acceptable dependent upon context.

Fli.Abt.Lb.	Fliegerabteilung mit Luftbildgerät	Aviation Detachment equipped with Air Photography Equipment
Flugz.	Flugzeug	Aircraft
Fluma.	Flugmeldeabteilung	Flight Reporting Detachment
Form.	Formation	Formation
Fp.	Fuhrpark	Supply Park
Frowewa.	Frontwetterwarte	Front Meteorological Service
Fspr.	Fernsprech	Telephone
Fstgs.	Festungs	Fortress
F.T.	Funktelegraphen	Radio Telegraph
Fu.	Funker/Funken	Radio/Radio Operator
Funka.	Funker-Abteilung	Radio Detachment
Fu.Tel.	Funkentelegraphen	Radio Telegraph
Füs.R.	Füsilier-Regiment	Fusilier Regiment
Fußa.R.	Fußartillerie-Regiment	Foot Artillery Regiment

G.

G.	Garde	Guard
Garn.	Garnison	Garrison
Geb.	Gebirgs-	Mountain
Gef.	Gefangenen-	Prisoner
Gekofern.	Fernsprechkommandeur bei einem Generalkommando	Telephone Commander with a Corps
Gekofunk.	Funkerkommandeur bei einem Generalkommando	Radio Commander with a Corps
gem.	gemischte	mixed
Gen.	General	General
	Generalfeldmarschall	Field Marshall
	Generalleutnant	Lieutenant-General
	Generalmajor	Major General
	Generaloberst	General
Gen.Gouv.	Generalgouvernement	General Government
Gen.Int.	Generalintendant	Intendant General
Genkdo.	Generalkommando	Corps
Genstb.	Generalstab	General Staff

Gentel.	General der Telegraphen-Truppen	General of Telegraph Troops
Gen.Qu.M.	Generalquartiermeister	Quartermaster General
Gesch.	Geschütz	Gun
G.K.	Gardekorps	Guard Corps
G.M.G.Abt.	Garde-Maschinengewehr-Abteilung	Guard Machine Gun Detachment
Gouv.	Gouvernement	Government
Gren.R.	Grenadier Regiment	Grenadier Regiment
Gr.H.Qu.	Großeres Hauptquartier	Great Headquarters
G.R.K.	Gardereservekorps	Guard Reserve Corps
G.R.R.	Garde-Reserveregiment	Guard Reserve Regiment
G.R.z.Fß.	Garderegiment zu Fuß	Foot Guards Regiment
Gru.	Gruppe	Group
Grufl.	Gruppenführer der Flieger	Aviation Group Commander
Gruja.	Gruppenführer der Jagdstaffeln	Group Commander of Fighter Flights
Grukdo.	Gruppenkommando	Group Command
Grukofern.	Gruppen-Fernsprechkommandeur	Group Telephone Commander
Grukofunk.	Gruppen-Funkerkommandeur	Group Radio Commander
Grukonach.	Gruppen-Nachrichtenkommandeur	Group Signals Commander

H.

Haub.	Haubitze	Howitzer
H.Gr.	Heeresgruppe	Army Group
H.Gr.Kdo.	Heeresgruppen-Kommando	Army Group Command
H.K.K.	Höherer Kavallerie-Kommandeur	Senior Cavalry Commander
Hptm.	Hauptmann	Captain
Hus.Br.	Husaren-Brigade	Hussar Brigade
Hus.R.	Husaren-Regiment	Hussar Regiment

I.

I.Br.	Infanterie-Brigade	Infantry Brigade

I.D.	Infanterie-Division	Infantry Division
Ideis.	Inspektion der Eisenbahntruppen	Railway Troops Inspectorate
Idflieg.	Inspektion der Fliegertruppen	Aviation Inspectorate
Iflak.	Inspektion der Flugabwehrkanone	Anti-Aircraft Gun Inspectorate
I.G.B.	Infanteriegeschütz-Batterie	Infantry Gun Battery
Ikraft.	Inspektion der Kraftfahrtruppen	Motor Vehicle Troops Inspectorate
Iluft.	Inspektion der Luftschiffertruppen	Airship Troops Inspectorate
Inach.	Inspektion der Nachrichtentruppen	Signals Troops Inspectorate
Inf.	Infanterie	Infantry
Ing.	Ingenieur	Engineer
Insp.	Inspektion	Inspectorate
Inst.Werkst.	Instandsetzungs-Werkstätte	Workshop
Int.	Intendant	Intendant
I.R.	Infanterie-Regiment	Infantry Regiment

J.

Jäg.	Jäger	Jäger
Jäg.R.	Jäger Regiment	Jäger Regiment
Jasta.	Jagdstaffel	Fighter Flight

K.

Kagohl.	Kampfgeschwader der Obersten Heeresleitung	Combat Group of the Supreme Army Command
Kan.	Kanone	Gun
Karab.R.	Karabinier-Regiment	Carabinier Regiment
Karp.K.	Karpathen-Korps	Carpathian Corps
Kav.	Kavallerie	Cavalry
Kav.Br.	Kavallerie-Brigade	Cavalry Brigade
K.Br.Tr.	Korps-Brückentrain	Corps Pontoon Train
K.D.	Kavallerie-Division	Cavalry Division
Kdo.	Kommando	Command

Kdr.	Kommandeur	Commander
Kdt.	Kommandant	Commandant
Kdtr.	Kommandantur	Command/HQ
Kf.	Kraftfahr-	Motor Vehicle
Kftr.	Krafttruppen	Motor Vehicle Troops
Kodeis.	Kommandeur der Eisenbahntruppen	Railway Troops Commander
Kofl.	Kommandeur der Flieger	Aviation Commander
Koflak.	Kommandeur der Flugabwehrkanonen	Anti-Aircraft Artillery Commander
Kogenluft.	Kommandierender General der Luftstreitkräfte	Commanding General, Air Forces
Kojastheim.	Kommandeur der Jagdstaffeln im Heimatgebiet	Commander, Fighter Flights on the Home Front
Kol.	Kolonne	Column
Koluft.	Kommandeur der Luftschiffer	Airships Commander
Komp.	Kompanie	Company
Komut.	Kommandeur der Munitionskolonnen und Trains	Commander of Munitions Columns and Trains
Konach.	Nachrichtenkommandeur	Signals Commander
Kp.	Kompanie	Company
Krgsgl.	Kriegsgliederung	War Organisation
Kr.Min.	Kriegsministerium	War Ministry
K.u.K.	Kaiserlich und Königlich	Imperial and Royal (Austro-Hungarian)
Kür.R.	Kürassier-Regiment	Cuirassier Regiment
Küstmrs.	Küstenmörser	Coastal Mortar
Kw.	Kraftwagen	Motor Vehicle

L.

l.	leichte	Light
Laz.	Lazarett	Hospital
Lb (if prefix)	Leib	Bodyguard/Lifeguard
Lb (if suffix)	mit Lichtbildgerät	Unit supplied with Photographic Equipment
L.D.	Landwehr Division	Landwehr Division

Ldst.	Landsturm	Landsturm[5]
Ldw.	Landwehr	Landwehr[6]
L.I.Br.	Landwehr-Infanterie-Brigade	Landwehr Infantry Brigade
L.I.R.	Landwehr-Infanterie-Regiment	Landwehr Infantry Regiment
L.M.K.	Leichte Munitions-Kolonne	Light Munitions Column
Lok.	Lokomotive	Locomotive
Luftsch.	Luftschiffer	Airship

M.

Mag.	Magazin	Magazine
Mar.	Marine	Navy
Masch.	Maschinen-	Machine
Mannschft.	Mannschaften	Men/Other Ranks
M.E.D.	Militär-Eisenbahn-Direktion	Military Railways Directorate
M.-Flak.	Maschinen-Flugabwehrkanone	Automatic Anti-Aircraft Gun
M.G.	Maschinengewehr	Machine Gun
M.G.Abt.	Maschinengewehr-Abteilung	Machine Gun Detachment
M.G.K.	Maschinengewehr-Kompanie	Machine Gun Company
M.G.Sf.	Maschinengewehr-Scharfschützen	Machine Gun Sharpshooter
Mil.	Militär-	Military
Mrs.	Mörser	Mortar
Msk.	Musketen-	Automatic Rifle
Mun.	Munitions-	Munitions
Mwf.	Minenwerfer	Trench Mortar

N.

Nachr.	Nachrichten	Signals
Nahkpf.	Nahkampf-	Close-combat
Nr.	Nummer	Number

---

5 Consisted of two 'bans' or levies, the first men aged between 17 and 20 awaiting their call-up, the second, men aged 39 to 45 who had previously served in the ranks of the Landwehr.

6 Consisting of two 'bans' or levies, the first of men aged 27 to 32, the second of men aged 33 to 38, who had previously served in the ranks of the Reserve.

O.

O.B.	Oberbefehlshaber	Supreme Commander/CO
O.B.Ost.	Oberbefehlshaber Ost	Supreme Commander East
O.Flak.	Ortsfeste-Flugabwehrkanonen	Emplaced Anti-Aircraft Gun
Offz.	Offizier	Officer
O.H.L.	Oberste Heeresleitung	Supreme Army Command
Ohla.	Auslandsabteilung der O.H.L.	Foreign Dept. of the O.H.L.
Op.	Operations	Operations
O.Qu.	Oberquartiermeister	Senior Quartermaster

P.

Pf.	Pferde	Horse/Equine
Pf.Flak.Swf.	Pferdebespannter Flugabwehrkanonen-Scheinwerfer	Horse-drawn Anti-Aircraft Searchlight
Pi.	Pionier	Pioneer
Pi.Bel.Tr.	Pionier-Belagerungstrain	Pioneer Siege Train
Pi.R.	Pionier-Regiment	Pioneer Regiment

R.

Radf.	Radfahrer	Cyclist
R.D.	Reserve Division	Reserve Division
Regt.	Regiment	Regiment
Reit.Abt.	Reiter Abteilung	Horse Artillery Battalion
Reit.R.	Reiter Regiment	Reiter Regiment
Rekodeis.	Regiments-Kommandeur der Eisenbahntruppen	Regimental Commander of Railway Troops
Rekokraft.	Regiments-Kommandeur der Kraftfahrtruppen	Regimental Commander of Motor Vehicle Troops
Res.	Reserve	Reserve
R.I.Br.	Reserve-Infanterie-Brigade	Reserve Infantry Brigade
R.I.R.	Reserve-Infanterie-Regiment	Reserve Infantry Regiment
R.K.	Reservekorps	Reserve Corps

S.

San.	Sanitäts-	Medical
Sanka.	Sanitäts-Kraftwagen-Abteilung	Motorised Medical Detachment
Schlasta.	Schlachtstaffel	Ground Attack Flight
Schü.	Schützen	Rifles
Schü.R.	Schützen-Regiment	Rifle Regiment
Schusta.	Schutzstaffel	Escort Flight
schw.	schwere(r)	Heavy
selb.	selbständig	Independent
sp.	spännig	Limbered
St. (if prefix)	Stab	Staff/HQ
Sto.	Stabsoffizier	Staff Officer
Stofl.	Stabsoffizier der Flieger	Aviation Staff Officer
Stomag.	Stabsoffizier der Maschinengewehrtruppen	Machine Gun Troops Staff Officer
Swf.	Scheinwerfer	Searchlight

T.

Tel.	Telegraphen	Telegraph
Tr.Üb.Pl.	Truppenübungsplatz	

U.

Ul.R.	Ulanen-Regiment	Uhlan Regiment
Utffz.	Unteroffizier	NCO

V.

Verm.	Vermessungs-	Survey
Verpfl.	Verpflegungs-	Rations
Vet.	Veterinär	Veterinary

W.

W.-Flak.	Flugabwehrkanonen auf Wagen	Anti-Aircraft Gun mounted on a Wagon
Werkst.	Werkstätte	Workshop
Wumba.	Waffen- und Munitions-Beschaffungsamt	Office for the Procurement of Arms and Munitions

Z.

z.b.V.	zur besonderen Verwendung	for Special Purposes
z.Fß.	zu Fuß	Dismounted
z.Pf.	zu Pferde	Mounted

Bibliography

Armeeverordnungsblatt 1914-18.

Arndt, Major a.D.[1] "Die Fliegerwaffe" in *Der Stellungskrieg 1914-1918* (Verlag Mittler).

Arndt, Major a.D. *Die Fliegertruppe im Weltkriege* (Reichsarchiv).

Biermann, Oberstleutnant a.D. "Die Entwicklung der deutschen Minenwerferwaffe" in *Ehrenbuch der Pioniere* (Verlag "Tradition").

Boelcke, Oberstleutnant a.D. "Die Vermessungsabteilungen" in *Ehrenbuch der schweren Artillerie* (Verlag "Tradition").

von Buchholtz, Generalmajor a.D. "Die oberste Pionierwaffenbehörde im Kriege, II Teil" in *Ehrenbuch der Pioniere* (Verlag "Tradition").

Crell, Major a.D. "Das schwerste Flachfeuer" in *Ehrenbuch der schweren Artillerie* (Verlag "Tradition").

Cron, Senior Archivist at the Reichsarchiv *Die Organisation des deutschen Heeres im Weltkriege* (Verlag Mittler).

Cron, Oberstleutnant a.D. "Die höchsten Kommandobehörden des Landheeres" in Band X of Schwarte, *Der große Krieg 1914-1918* (Verlag J.A. Barth).

Cron, Senior Archivist at the Reichsarchiv *Die Kriegseisenwirtschaft* (Reichsarchiv).

Demeter, Dr *Die Kriegsmetall A.G.* (Reichsarchiv).

Eggeling, Oberst a.D. "Die oberste Pionier-Waffenbehörde im Kriege, I Teil" in *Ehrenbuch der Pioniere* (Verlag "Tradition").

Engberding *Luftschiff und Luftfahrt* (Vidiverlag).

von Falkenhayn, General of Infantry *Die oberste Heeresleitung 1914-1918* (Verlah Mittler).

Feeser, Generalmajor a.D. "Infanteriegeschütze, Tankabwehrgeschütze und Begleitbatterien" in *Ehrenbuch der Pioniere* (Verlag "Tradition").

Frahnert, Oberstleutnant a.D. "Die Entwicklung der schweren Artillerie im Weltkriege – die Truppe" in *Ehrenbuch der schweren Artillerie* (Verlag "Tradition").

Großkreutz, Major a.D. "Die Flak" in *Ehrenbuch der Feldartillerie* (Verlag "Tradition").

Heeres-Sanitätsinspektion *Sanitätsbericht über das deutsche Heer im Weltkriege 1914-1918* (Verlag Mittler).

Heeresverordnungsblatt 1919.

Heubes, Oberstleutnant a.D. *Ehrenbuch der Feldeisenbahner* (Verlag "Tradition").

Hoeppner, General of Cavalry *Deutschlands Krieg in der Luft* (Verlag Köhler).

von Hutten-Czapski, Count *60 Jahre Politik und Gesellschaft* (Verlag Mittler).

Krafft von Dellmensingen, General of Artillery "Die Feldartillerie im Gebirgskriege – Gebirgsartillerie" in *Ehrenbuch der Feldartillerie* (Verlag "Tradition").

von Kuhl, General of Infantry *Der Marnefeldzug 1914* (Verlag Mittler).

---

1   Retired.

Ludendorff, General of Infantry *Meine Kriegserinnerungen 1914-1918* (Verlag Mittler).

Muther, Generalleutnant a.D. "Organisation, Bewaffnung, Munition und Munitionsverbrauch der deutschen Feldartillerie im Weltkriege" in *Ehrenbuch der Feldartillerie* (Verlag "Tradition").

Muths, Oberstleutnant a.D. "Munition" in *Ehrenbuch der schweren Artillerie* (Verlag "Tradition").

Peterson, Generalmajor a.D. "Die Pionierwaffe und der Gasangriff" in *Ehrenbuch der Pioniere* ((Verlag "Tradition").

Reddemann, Dr "Der Totenkopfpioniere" [Flamethrowers] in *Ehrenbuch der Pioniere* (Verlag "Tradition").

Reichsarchiv *Der Weltkrieg 1914-1918* Band I-IX (Verlag Mittler).

Reichsarchiv *Kriegsausrüstung und Kriegswirtschaft* Band 1 & 2.

Reichsarchiv *Das deutsche Feldeisenbahnwesen* Band 1.

Reichskriegsministerium *Der Weltkrieg 1914-1918* Band X (Verlag Mittler).

Schacht, Generalmajor a.D. "Organisation der schweren Artillerie 1914, Mobilmachung" in *Ehrenbuch der schweren Artillerie* (Verlag "Tradition").

Schirmer, Generalleutnant a.D. "Geschützinstruktionen" in *Ehrenbuch der schweren Artillerie* (Verlag "Tradition").

Schwab, Major a.D. "Artillerie-Erkendung, Artillerie-Beobachtung: Flieger und Ballone" in *Ehrenbuch der schweren Artillerie* (Verlag "Tradition").

Schwab, Dipl.Ing. "Meßtrupps" in *Ehrenbuch der schweren Artillerie* (Verlag "Tradition").

von Schwerin, Count "Das Sturm-Bataillon Rohr" in *Ehrenbuch der Pioniere* (Verlag "Tradition").

Wiedenfeld, Prof Dr *Rohstoffversorgung* (Kriegspresseamt).

von Winterfeldt, Generalleutnant a.D. "Die deutsche Verwaltung des Generalgouvernements in Belgien 1914-1918" in Band X of Schwarte, *Der große Krieg 1914-1918* (Verlag J.A. Barth).

von Wrisberg, Generalmajor a.D. "Das Kriegsministerium" in Band X of Schwarte, *Der große Krieg 1914-1918* (Verlag J.A. Barth).

Ziethen, Generalleutnant a.D. "Die Artillerieführung" in *Ehrenbuch der schweren Artillerie* (Verlag "Tradition").

Related titles published by Helion & Company

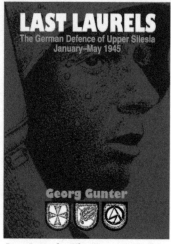

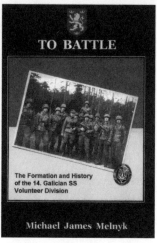

Last Laurels. The German Defence of Upper Silesia, January–May 1945
Georg Gunter
320pp, over 170 b/w photos, 20 maps. Hardback
ISBN 1–874622–65–5

To Battle. The Formation and History of the 14th Waffen-SS Greandier Division
Michael Melnyk
352pp, 300 b/w photos, documents, illustrations, maps. Hardback
ISBN 1–874622–41–8

A selection of forthcoming titles

Adventures in my Youth: A German Soldier on the Eastern Front 1941–45
Armin Scheiderbauer   ISBN 1–874622–06–X

Elite of the Third Reich – The Recipients of the Knight's Cross of the Iron Cross 1939–45: An Illustrated Reference
Walther-Peer Fellgiebel   ISBN 1–874622–46–9

SOME ADDITIONAL SERVICES FROM HELION & COMPANY

BOOKSELLERS
- over 20,000 military books available
- four 100-page catalogues issued every year
- unrivalled stock of foreign language material, particularly German

BOOKSEARCH
- free professional booksearch service; no search fees, no obligation to buy

Want to find out more? Our website is the best place to learn more about Helion & Co. It features online book catalogues, special offers, complete information about our own books (including features on in-print and forthcoming titles, sample extracts and reviews), a shopping cart system and a secure server for credit card transactions, plus much more besides!

HELION & COMPANY

26 Willow Road, Solihull, West Midlands, B91 1UE, England
Tel 0121 705 3393   Fax 0121 711 4075
Website: http://www.helion.co.uk